The Development of Missiological Thinking and Praxis

The Development of Missiological Thinking and Praxis

An Interdisciplinary Exploration of Biblical, Traditional, and Contextual Foundations for Christian Mission

Vinod S. Sailus

Christian World Imprints

First Published in 2025 by

Christian World Imprints
Christian Publishing & Books from India
A-71 Group, Wazirpur Industrial Area
Delhi-110052
cwidelhi2017@gmail.com
www.ChristianWorldImprints.com
Phone: +91 11 41526079

ISBN: 978-93-6065-271-5

Printed in India.

Contents

Foreword

This book stands out as a significant contribution to the ongoing conversations on Christian Mission in India and beyond. What immediately strikes the reader is not merely the breadth of themes engaged but the way they are woven together with theological depth, contextual attentiveness, and pastoral sensitivity. Dr Vinod S. Sailus has managed to hold together and integrate scholarship and spirituality, prophetic critique and pastoral encouragement, doctrinal fidelity and contextual relevance.

The style of writing is both clear and compelling. Dr Vinod demonstrates an ability to engage complex realities without becoming obscure, to handle contested questions without becoming excessively critical, and to bring forward fresh theological insights without losing touch with the lived experiences of communities. There is an evident attentiveness to voices from the margins, yet without neglecting the wider ecclesial and global horizons of Mission. This balance between the local and the global, the biblical and the contextual, the theological and thc practical, makes the book particularly rich and trustworthy.

Different types of readers will find themselves drawn into this work. For theological students and young pastors, it will serve as a guide to think Missiologically in a way that is faithful to Scripture and responsive to present realities. For teachers and scholars, it provides a resource that demonstrates how contextual theology can be articulated with academic rigor while remaining accessible. For church leaders and grassroots ministers, it offers inspiration and practical imagination for living out Mission with courage, humility, and compassion in challenging environments. Even those outside theological circles, readers interested in questions of religion, culture, and society in contemporary India, will find here a thoughtful and respectful engagement that sheds light on some of the most urgent issues of our time.

Above all, the reader is invited into a journey. The author does not simply provide conclusions but models a way of theological reflection that listens, discerns, and responds with faithfulness. The pages do not merely inform; they provoke, encourage, and invite participation in the ongoing task of embodying the gospel in word and deed. That is what makes this book not only worth reading but worth assimilating into self.

I offer my sincerest congratulations to Prof. Rev. Dr Vinod S. Sailus for his commendable work. I wish him that he brings out many more such books. I warmly commend this work to every reader. May it challenge the perspectives, stir your thoughts, and strengthen the hands of all who seek to participate in God's Mission of justice, reconciliation, and renewal in our world today.

Rev. Dr. Lawrence A.
President, St. Peter's Pontifical Institute
Bengaluru

Preface

This book, *The Development of Missiological Thinking and Praxis: An Interdisciplinary Exploration of Biblical, Traditional, and Contextual Foundations for Christian Mission*, is the outcome of many years of teaching, learning, and reflecting on Mission in diverse contexts. The work grew out of my efforts to bring together my lecture notes, classroom experiences, and personal journey as a student and teacher of Missiology.

The initial material for this book comes from my lectures on the subject: "The Development of Missiological Thinking and Praxis" under the Senate of Serampore system at Gurukul Lutheran Theological College and Research Institute, Chennai. These lectures became the framework for engaging students in understanding the historical, biblical, and contextual aspects of Christian Mission. Later, the classroom encounters in different places and with diverse communities deepened these reflections.

One formative experience was teaching Bachelor of Divinity students in Parangipettai, a coastal town where the grassroots realities of Indian villages were evident. My students, mostly from the grassroot backgrounds, brought lived experiences of poverty, marginalization, and resilience. Their insights applied the lived experiences of fisherfolk, Dalit, and outcaste communities reminded and inspired me to comprehend that theology must speak to the struggles of real people and their quest for dignity. Another significant experience was with my students in Ranchi, where the Adivasi community and other marginalized groups shaped our conversations on Mission and Missiology. Their stories of rejection and dispossession and their strong sense of community life opened new ways of thinking about justice, identity, and God's Mission in real life situations.

The classes in Gurukul from 2021 to 2025, both with BD and MTh students, further enriched this journey. The graduate students, full of questions and challenges, pushed me to rethink Mission in fresh ways, while the postgraduate students encouraged deeper engagement with theory and practice. Moreover, my present engagement with postgraduate and doctoral students at St. Peter's Pontifical Institute, Bangalore, along with Fathers and Sisters in formation, has offered a unique ecumenical dimension, showing how Mission can be understood and practiced across different traditions of the Church.

This book also grows out of the struggle I shared with my students in searching for relevant materials on Missiology that address both the academic requirements and the pressing realities of the Indian context. The lack of accessible resources often became an opportunity to create, adapt, and develop new teaching material, much of which is now integrated into this volume.

This book also reflects my own academic journey as a student, beginning with my BD studies (2004-2008), continuing through my MTh (2013-2015), and culminating in my doctoral research (2016-2019), each stage shaping the way I understand and present Missiology in this work. The questions I carried as a student have now become resources for others, and the struggles I faced have become stepping-stones for shaping a Missiology that is biblical, traditional, and contextual.

Finally, this book is written from my own perspective and experience as a Missionary in Andhra Pradesh (now Telangana), where I first encountered the challenges and possibilities of Christian Mission in real life situations. It also reflects my journey as a theological educator, shaped by teaching the subject *The Development of Missiological Thinking and Praxis* and by years of academic engagement with students in Gurukul Lutheran Theological College and Research Institute, Chennai, and St. Peter's Pontifical Institute, Bangalore.

It is my hope that this book will serve both students and teachers, as a resource for understanding the dynamic *Development of Missiological Thinking and Praxis*. More importantly, I pray that it will encourage readers to participate in God's Mission with faithfulness, creativity, and commitment to justice.

Rev. Dr. Vinod S. Sailus
Professor in Missiology
St. Peter's Pontifical Institute, Bengaluru

Acknowledgements

At the very outset, I bow in gratitude to God Almighty, whose grace has sustained me in every step of my life and calling. This book is a testimony to God's guidance, wisdom, and strength, which have carried me through times of struggle and joy. It is to God that all glory and honour belong, for without God's presence and strength this work would have remained incomplete.

I lovingly remember my parents, whose lives and faith shaped my own journey. My late father, Mr. S. Sailus, instilled in me the values of hard work, commitment, and devotion to God. Though he is no longer with us, his example continues to inspire me in my vocation and writing. My mother, Mrs. K. Syamala, has been a constant source of encouragement through her prayers, counsel, and quiet strength.

My heartfelt thanks go to my family, who have shared this journey with me in the most personal way. My wife, Mrs. Vinitha Vinod, has stood beside me with patience and encouragement, often sacrificing her own time and energy so that I could devote myself to teaching, research, and writing. My sons, Aleph V. Vinod, Ankith V. Vinod, and Aadhish V. Vinod have grown up watching me immersed in books and classrooms, and they have lovingly adjusted to the demands of my vocation. Their affection and understanding have been my greatest support and inspiration.

I am especially indebted to my teachers and mentors who guided me in my theological journey. Prof. Sr. Dr. Rani Joseph Mary Shruti, SND, my MTh and Doctoral mentor, walked with me closely through the most demanding years of my academic research. Her scholarly insight, patient guidance, and personal encouragement shaped not only this book but also my way of engaging with Missiological questions. I also recall with deep gratitude Prof. Rev. Dr. K. David Udayakumar, who first stirred in me the passion for Missiology during my BD studies. His teaching opened my eyes to the depth and urgency of Mission in our times, and his influence has been foundational for my work.

I gratefully acknowledge the life-long support of Rev. E. John Victor, the first Missionary from CSI South Kerala Diocese, whose prayers and encouragement have been a steady presence in my life. I also extend my gratitude to my mother Church, CSI Church Nediyakala, which has nurtured me in faith since my early years. The fellowship, teaching, and prayerful support of this congregation laid the spiritual foundation upon which my life and ministry have been built.

This book has also been shaped by my Missionary experiences in Andhra Pradesh (now Telangana), where I served and where my perspective on Mission was first formed. The struggles and hopes of the people in this context offered me lessons in resilience, hospitality, and faith that continue to influence my Missiological thinking. I also owe much to my students, both BD and MTh students at Gurukul Lutheran Theological College and MTh and PhD students at St. Peter's Pontifical Institute, Bangalore. The classroom discussions, their questions, and their eagerness to learn became a living library where new insights were tested and refined.

I also wish to acknowledge the Immanuel Malayalam CSI Church, Anagalapura, where my family and I are now part of the worshiping community. Their prayers, encouragement, and fellowship have been a source of strength and support during the preparation of this book. The warmth of this community has reminded me of the wider body of Christ that accompanies us in our vocation.

I extend my heartfelt gratitude to Prof. Rev. Dr. Lawrence A., President of St. Peter's Pontifical Institute, Bangalore, for his encouragement, guidance, and inspiring leadership throughout the course of this work, and for graciously writing the foreword to this book. I also thank Mr. Praveen W for designing the cover page of this book with creativity and care. I also wish to acknowledge the assistance of Artificial Intelligence tools, which I used mainly for grammar correction, clarity of expression, and coherence in certain parts of this book. The ideas, arguments, and content remain entirely my own, but these tools supported me in presenting them in clear and accessible English for the benefit of readers.

Finally, I sincerely thank Christian World Imprints for their support in publishing this work. Their commitment to making theological scholarship available to students, teachers, and churches has provided me the opportunity to share these reflections with a wider audience.

With gratitude to God and to all who have journeyed with me, I dedicate this book to the service of theological education and the Mission of the Church.

Rev. Dr. Vinod S. Sailus
Professor in Missiology
St. Peter's Pontifical Institute, Bengaluru

Introduction

In today's rapidly changing global context, the need for a biblically rooted, theologically sound, and contextually relevant understanding of Christian Mission is more urgent than ever. Religious pluralism, socio-political polarization, ecological crises, technological shifts, and the resurgence of ethno-religious nationalism, in the Global South, especially in India, present complex challenges for the church's witness. In this milieu, the book titled: ***The Development of Missiological Thinking and Praxis: An Interdisciplinary Exploration of Biblical, Traditional, and Contextual Foundations for Christian Mission*** addresses these realities by offering an, integrated vision of Mission that resists reductionist approaches. By rooting its analysis in Scripture and engaging contemporary social, cultural, and political issues, the book equips readers, especially Christian leaders, theological educators, and Missionaries to discern faithful ways of participating in the *Missio Dei* amid both opportunity and opposition. In such a milieu, reading this volume is not merely an academic exercise but a formative step toward embodying a holistic gospel in complex and contested spaces.

The book covers an impressive range of thirty-one interconnected chapters, each exploring a critical dimension of Missiological thought and practice. These include biblical foundations across the Old and New Testaments, historical trajectories from early church to contemporary traditions, theological paradigms such as the *Missio Dei*, pneumatology, soteriology, and eschatology, as well as thematic areas like Holistic Mission, Mission to the margins, new creation, and multi-faith engagement. Traditions as diverse as Roman Catholic, Orthodox, Evangelical, Pentecostal, and Ecumenical perspectives are represented, alongside interdisciplinary inputs from anthropology, sociology, intercultural theology, and contextual theology. The scope also includes practical concerns such as evangelism, conversion in contested contexts, justice advocacy, ecological responsibility, reconciliation, and interfaith dialogue. This breadth ensures that the book speaks to both the academy and the church, balancing theoretical depth with actionable insights for real-world ministry.

Connecting the urgency of the first paragraph with the thematic breadth of the second, this volume stands as both a theological compass and a practical handbook for Mission today. Its structure moves from foundational principles to tradition-specific insights and then to pressing contextual challenges, creating a coherent learning journey. Each chapter not only contributes to an overarching narrative that Mission is God's work in which the church participates, but also offers distinct lenses for interpreting and engaging diverse realities. Together, these chapters form a composite map for navigating Mission in a pluralistic, postcolonial, and globalized era. The readers of the book are thus able to see the interdependence of biblical fidelity, historical awareness, theological clarity, and contextual responsiveness, with the summaries serving as entry points into deeper reflection and praxis.

One of the special characteristics of this volume is the consistent capitalization of terms such as **Mission, Missionary, Missiology, Missional, and Missiologists**. This is done deliberately to emphasize their theological depth, historical importance, and urgent relevance in today's world. This deliberate choice underscores that Mission is not presented here as a secondary program of the Church, but as the very core of its calling and identity, rooted in the *Missio Dei*, God's own redeeming work in creation. It also means that, in today's context of religious pluralism, cultural fragmentation, social injustice, and environmental crisis, the work of Mission is both urgent and transformative, requiring deep biblical grounding, contextual awareness, and active participation from the whole people of God. Capitalizing these terms draws attention to their central role in shaping theological reflection, guiding ecclesial practice, and inspiring a renewed vision for God's Kingdom on earth. It reminds the reader that Mission is not merely an academic topic but a lived reality that demands faithful engagement, especially in contexts like India where witness and service must guide complex social, political, and religious milieus.

The opening chapter titled: ***God's Sending and Our Proclamation: Defining 'Mission' and 'Evangelism'*** provides a foundational framework for understanding Christian mission by clarifying the distinct yet interconnected concepts of Mission (*Missio Dei*) and Evangelism. Mission is rooted in God's Trinitarian sending, embracing the Church's holistic engagement in spiritual, social, cultural, and ecological transformation, while evangelism is the focused proclamation of the gospel calling individuals to faith and reconciliation with God. Tracing their biblical roots, historical development, and theological articulation from the early Church to the modern era, the study situates both within the *Missio Dei*, warning against separating proclamation from compassionate action. It further presents Missiology as an inherently interdisciplinary field that draws on biblical studies, history, social sciences, linguistics, gender studies, ecology, and interfaith dialogue to ensure contextually sensitive and theologically robust praxis. By integrating these disciplines, the chapter argues for a Mission that is faithful to Scripture, responsive to diverse cultural realities, and committed to holistic transformation in a global and pluralistic world.

The second chapter ***Historical Development of Missiology: From Missiology to Intercultural Theology*** traces the emergence of Missiology from its early roots in figures like Raimon Lull, through the institutional milestones of Gustav Warneck and other key thinkers, to its present transformation into Intercultural Theology. Originally a theological reflection on the Church's Missionary calling, Missiology grew into an interdisciplinary academic field, integrating biblical, historical, cultural, and practical perspectives to engage faithfully with diverse global contexts. The chapter highlights how historical shifts from colonial-era Mission models to postcolonial and pluralistic realities have necessitated a dialogical, inclusive approach that values voices from the Global South, women, indigenous peoples, and marginalized communities. In the Indian context, where "Mission" is often misunderstood as Proselytism or colonial legacy, Intercultural Theology offers a framework for contextual, relational, and holistic witness that unites proclamation with justice, service, and ecological care. This evolution reflects a broader Missional vision rooted in the *Missio Dei*, emphasizing that Mission is participation in God's redemptive work through mutual learning, cultural sensitivity, and transformative engagement.

The third chapter ***Bridging Transcendence and Context: Metaphysical and Empirical Approaches in Missiology*** presents Missiology as an interdisciplinary discipline that unites theological depth with contextual relevance through two complementary methodologies, metaphysics and empiricism. Metaphysics enriches Mission thinking by probing ultimate realities, such as the nature of God, the ontology of humanity, cosmology, and epistemology, grounding Christian Mission in eternal truths and the *Missio Dei*. It frames Mission as participation in God's redemptive plan, shaping the Church's identity and purpose beyond mere social action. Empiricism, by contrast, anchors Mission praxis in lived realities, employing quantitative and qualitative research, and drawing on anthropology, sociology, psychology, history, law, and economics to understand cultural contexts, evaluate Mission effectiveness, and address practical challenges. Together, these approaches ensure that Missiological thinking is both theologically rooted and contextually responsive, equipping the Church to proclaim the gospel with spiritual depth and practical wisdom in a complex, pluralistic world.

The chapter four titled ***Descriptive and Normative Missiology: Shaping Missional Practice for the Church's Witness Today*** presents two complementary pillars of Missiological study. Descriptive Missiology investigates and documents how Christian Mission has been understood and practiced across history and cultures, using empirical methods such as observation, case studies, and surveys to identify patterns, models, and contextual realities. Normative Missiology, by contrast, evaluates Mission in light of Scripture, theology, and ethics to articulate what Mission ought to be, formulating principles, guidelines, and strategies for biblically faithful and contextually relevant practice. Drawing on insights from scholars like David Bosch, Jan A. B. Jongeneel, and William J. Abraham, the chapter argues that effective Mission requires integrating both functions, descriptive analysis grounding normative guidance in real-world realities, and normative vision ensuring descriptive insights are translated into faithful, strategic action. This integration equips the Church to engage in Mission that is historically informed, theologically sound, ethically responsible, and practically effective in diverse cultural contexts.

The fifth chapter ***Integrating Missiology from Above and Missiology from Below: Towards a Contextual Paradigm*** examines two major Mission perspectives such as Mission from Above, which emphasizes God's sovereign initiative, salvation history, and authoritative proclamation, and Mission from Below, which prioritizes incarnational presence, solidarity with the poor, justice, and dialogical engagement. While each has enriched Missional thought, their separation has often led to imbalance, with "from Above" risking cultural insensitivity and "from Below" drifting toward purely social activism. Drawing on models such as S.J. Samartha's Helicopter vs. Bullock-Cart Christology, Jooseop Keum's Mountain-to-Valley imagery, and Vinod S. Sailus's Eagle and Rooster/Hen framework, the chapter proposes integrative approaches that unite theological proclamation with compassionate action. Rooted in the *Missio Dei*, this synthesis affirms Christ's cosmic lordship and incarnational solidarity, applying contextual hermeneutics to adapt Mission faithfully to local cultures while maintaining gospel integrity. The result is a holistic paradigm in which proclamation and service, doctrine and justice, transcendence and immanence work together to embody God's redemptive Mission in diverse contexts.

The sixth chapter ***Power, Practice, and Perspective: Mission History from "Above" and "Below"*** contrasts two complementary historiographical perspectives in Missiology. The "from above" approach records Mission through the lens of Missionaries, colonial authorities, and institutional reports, emphasizing strategic decisions, achievements, and expansion but often reflecting Eurocentric bias, imperial interests, and selective sources that neglect local realities. In contrast, the "from below" approach foregrounds the experiences, agency, and cultural adaptations of ordinary believers, marginalized groups, and indigenous communities, drawing on oral traditions, contextual theology, and liberationist insights to reveal how Christianity was received, reshaped, or resisted at the grassroots level. While each perspective has limitations, "from above" risking triumphalism and cultural misrepresentation, and "from below" facing challenges of scarce records and interpretive complexity, their integration offers a fuller, more truthful account of Mission history. This balanced method not only enriches academic understanding but also equips contemporary Mission practice with greater cultural sensitivity, justice awareness, and respect for diverse voices in the global church.

Chapter seven titled ***Bridging Cultures and Communities: Anthropological and Sociological Foundations for Missiology*** highlights the essential role of social sciences in shaping effective, respectful, and contextually grounded Christian Mission. Cultural anthropology equips Missionaries to engage deeply with local worldviews, values, and customs through ethnographic immersion, participant observation, and cultural relativism, enabling them to communicate the gospel in ways that feel authentic and rooted in indigenous traditions. Sociology complements this by analysing social structures, institutions, leadership patterns, and group dynamics, helping Missionaries identify key influencers, address systemic injustices, and design sustainable, community-led ministries. The integration of these disciplines through mixed-methods research that combining qualitative and quantitative approaches, provides a holistic understanding of how people live, relate, and respond to the gospel. While recognizing challenges such as ethical responsibility, theological alignment, and resource constraints, the chapter affirms that anthropology and sociology, when used in service of the *Missio Dei*, can significantly enhance Missiological praxis, fostering church growth that is biblically faithful, socially relevant, and culturally resonant.

The eighth chapter ***Mission in the Context of Religious Pluralism: Theological Models, Challenges, and Engagement in a Diverse World*** explores how Christian Mission can remain faithful to the gospel while engaging respectfully in a world marked by deep religious diversity. It examines major theological responses to pluralism such as exclusivism, inclusivism, pluralism, pluralistic inclusivism, and pluralistic interculturalism, highlighting their biblical foundations, strengths, and limitations, with particular attention to Indian contextual models by K. P. Aleaz and Vinod S. Sailus. The chapter emphasizes that Mission in such contexts must combine conviction with humility, avoiding both arrogance and relativism, and embracing dialogue, mutual learning, and cooperative action for the common good. Practical expressions include interfaith dialogue, theology of religions, comparative theology, comparative religion, peacebuilding, and public theology, each fostering understanding, justice, and reconciliation. Grounded in the *Missio Dei* and the example of Jesus, the chapter calls for a holistic Mission that is theologically sound, culturally sensitive, and actively engaged in building bridges across religious and ideological divides in today's pluralistic societies.

Chapter nine titled ***Missiological Foundations of the Old Testament: Covenant, Promise, and God's Redemptive Mission to the Nations*** explores the foundational biblical witness that God's redemptive Mission did not begin with the New Testament, but is rooted in creation and unfolds throughout Israel's history. From the covenant with Abraham to the prophetic visions of global worship, the Old Testament consistently reveals a God whose purpose is to bless all nations, using Israel as a servant people to mediate God's presence, justice, and salvation to the world. Historical narratives, wisdom literature, psalms, and prophetic oracles alike affirm that the *Missio Dei* transcends ethnic, cultural, and geographic boundaries, welcoming outsiders, engaging with foreign nations, and envisioning a future where all peoples will acknowledge and worship the one true God. This chapter establishes that the church's Mission today is a continuation of this divine initiative, deeply rooted in the biblical, traditional, and contextual foundations of God's universal plan.

Tenth chapter titled ***Mission Themes in the Hebrew Bible: Election, Covenant, Commandment, Nation, Remnant, Redemption and Hospitality*** traces the theological and practical roots of Mission to the witness of the Hebrew Bible, where God's redemptive purpose for the world unfolds through interwoven themes of election, covenant, commandment, nationhood, remnant, redemption, and hospitality. These themes reveal a coherent Missiological vision in which Israel is chosen not for privilege but for service, called to embody God's holiness, justice, and mercy so that all nations might be blessed. From the Abrahamic covenant's universal promise to the prophetic call for Israel to be a "light to the nations," from the moral witness of the commandments to the inclusive ethic of hospitality toward the stranger, the Hebrew Bible presents a dynamic and outward-facing Mission rooted in God's covenantal love and aimed at the restoration of all creation. By examining these biblical foundations alongside historical and contextual developments, this chapter situates Christian Mission as a continuation of God's universal plan, inaugurated in creation, mediated through Israel, fulfilled in Christ, and entrusted to the global church today.

Chapter eleven titled ***Mission in the Intertestamental Period: The Silent Preparation for the Fulfilment of God's Redemptive Plan*** examines the often-overlooked centuries between the Old and New Testaments as a dynamic era of theological enhancement, cultural engagement, and structural preparation for God's redemptive Mission. Far from being a time of prophetic silence, this period saw Jewish communities, shaped by Persian, Hellenistic, and Roman rule, wrestling with covenant identity, purity, and their role among the nations. Developments such as the translation of the Hebrew Scriptures into Greek (the *Septuagint*), the global spread of diaspora synagogues, and evolving theological currents in covenant, wisdom, and apocalyptic traditions expanded the scope of Mission beyond Israel, fostering both internal renewal and outward witness. Even amidst political upheaval, martyrdom, and contested expressions of outreach, these centuries laid critical biblical, cultural, and institutional foundations for the early Christian Mission, bridging Israel's calling to bless the nations with the universal commission of Christ.

Chapter twelve titled ***From Promise to Fulfilment: The Mission of God in the Ministry of Jesus*** presents Jesus Christ as the climactic fulfilment of God's redemptive plan, symbolizing the *Missio Dei* as the definitive revelation of divine love, justice, and restoration. Rooted in the Old Testament's covenantal promises and prophetic hope, Jesus' incarnation, ministry, crucifixion, and resurrection mark the decisive inbreaking of God's Kingdom into human history. His Mission is Trinitarian in origin, flowing from the sending love of the Father, enacted in the obedience of the Son, and empowered by the Spirit, and it is holistic in scope, transforming individuals, renewing communities, confronting injustice, and anticipating the cosmic restoration of all creation. Through His teaching, miracles, compassion for the marginalized, and self-giving sacrifice, Jesus not only fulfils Israel's vocation to bless the nations but also forms a Missionary community commissioned to carry forward His work to the ends of the earth. This chapter thus situates the church's identity and praxis within the ongoing divine Mission, not as initiators but as participants in God's redemptive movement toward the renewal of all things.

In chapter thirteen titled ***Jesus the Missionary Messiah: An Analysis of Jesus' Mission in the Synoptic Gospels*** provides a unified yet distinct portrayal of Jesus as the Missionary Messiah, whose proclamation, actions, and ultimate sacrifice embody the *Missio Dei* in history. Rooted in Old Testament covenantal promises and prophetic hope, Jesus inaugurates the Kingdom of God through proclamation, parables, healing, table fellowship, and the formation of a Missionary community. His Mission is holistic, confronting physical, spiritual, and social brokenness while redefining messianic expectations through servanthood, suffering, and the cross. The Synoptics reveal that Jesus' life, death, and resurrection are not only the fulfilment of Israel's vocation but also the foundation of the church's identity and calling. By integrating proclamation with compassion, prophetic confrontation, and the empowerment of disciples, this chapter underscores that the Mission of Jesus is inherently participatory, commissioning His followers to extend God's reign to all nations in the power of the Spirit, embodying a Kingdom marked by justice, mercy, humility, and sacrificial love.

Chapter fourteen titled ***Revealed Word, Revealed Mission: The Unique Mission Narrative of Jesus in the Fourth Gospel*** offers a distinctive theological portrait of Jesus' Mission as an outflow of the eternal relationship within the triune God, where the Father sends the Son, the Son reveals the Father, and the Spirit continues the work through the believing community. Unlike the Synoptic Gospels' emphasis on Kingdom proclamation through parables and public preaching, John presents Mission as divine self-revelation, mediated through symbolic "signs," transformative personal dialogues, and explicit "I Am" declarations that unveil Jesus' identity as the eternal Word made flesh. This Mission is relational and participatory, calling disciples to abide in Christ, embody sacrificial love, live in unity, and bear Spirit-empowered witness so that the world may believe. Rooted in servant leadership, invitational encounter, and the promise of the Paraclete, the Johannine vision expands Mission beyond events into an abiding reality where believers reflect God's light in a world marked by darkness, inviting all peoples into the life and love of God.

Chapter fifteen titled ***Mission in the Book of Acts: The Apostolic Mission, Theology, Practice, and Legacy*** explores the dynamic expansion of the early Christian Mission as the apostles, empowered by the Holy Spirit at Pentecost, become witnesses "to the ends of the earth" (Acts 1:8). Rooted in the commissioning of the risen Christ, their Mission integrates proclamation of the gospel, formation of worshipping communities, works of compassion, and prophetic confrontation of social and religious barriers. The apostolic witness reveals a Spirit-led adaptability, engaging Jews and Gentiles alike through contextualized preaching, personal discipleship, public miracles, and the establishment of inclusive fellowship. Through persecution, travel, and cross-cultural encounters, the apostles embody the *Missio Dei*, showing that Mission is not merely geographic expansion but the transformative presence of Christ in diverse contexts. This chapter locates the apostolic era as the crucial bridge between the incarnational Mission of Jesus and the continuing Mission of the church, illustrating how theological conviction, spiritual empowerment, and cultural engagement converge in the advancement of God's redemptive purpose for all nations.

Chapter sixteen titled ***From Damascus to the Nations: Apostle Paul's Role in the Expansion of the Early Church*** presents Paul as both theologian and Missionary, whose ministry is deeply rooted in the revelation of the risen Christ and the commissioning to proclaim the gospel to the Gentiles. Paul's understanding of Mission is shaped by the *Missio Dei*, seeing God as the source, Christ as the content, and the Spirit as the empowering presence. His practice integrates bold proclamation of the gospel, contextual adaptation to diverse cultural settings, the planting and nurturing of local churches, and the formation of disciples who embody the gospel in daily life. Central to Paul's vision is the reconciliation of Jews and Gentiles into one new humanity in Christ, the anticipation of the eschatological fulfilment of God's Kingdom, and the ethical transformation of believers into a Spirit-led community marked by faith, hope, and love. Through his itinerant ministry, pastoral correspondence, and theological depth, Paul models a Mission that is both theologically grounded and strategically adaptive, offering the church a paradigm for cross-cultural engagement, holistic discipleship, and the advancement of God's redemptive purpose among all nations.

Chapter seventeen titled ***Mission in General Epistles and Revelation: Witness, Persecution, Endurance and the Ultimate Triumph of God's Kingdom*** highlights how these New Testament writings articulate a resilient and hope-filled vision of Mission for communities facing persecution, false teaching, and cultural marginalization. The General Epistles ground Mission in steadfast faith, ethical integrity, mutual love, and the active witness of believers whose transformed lives reflect God's truth in hostile environments. Revelation expands this vision to a cosmic scale, portraying the ultimate triumph of the Lamb, the gathering of a redeemed multinational people, and the renewal of creation under God's reign. Together, General Epistles present Mission not merely as expansion but as faithful endurance, prophetic resistance, and eschatological hope, assuring the church that its witness is rooted in Christ's victory and participates in the fulfilment of God's redemptive purpose for all nations and the entire created order.

Chapter eighteen titled ***Missio Dei: A Holistic Perspective on God's Mission*** explores the theological paradigm that frames Mission as originating in the very nature and activity of the triune God, rather than as a human initiative or church activity. Rooted in the eternal love and sending action of the Father, Son, and Holy Spirit, the *Missio Dei* concept redefines Mission as God's comprehensive work of creation, redemption, and restoration, in which the church is graciously invited to participate. This chapter traces the historical development of the term, its biblical foundations, and its implications for a holistic, Kingdom-oriented Mission that comprehends evangelism, social transformation, justice, and care for creation. By emphasizing God's sovereignty, Christ's incarnational example, and the Spirit's empowering presence, the *Missio Dei* framework calls the church to align its identity, priorities, and praxis with God's redemptive purposes for the whole world, making Mission the central vocation of the people of God in every context and generation.

Chapter nineteen titled ***Holistic Mission: A Biblical and Contextual Vision of Mission in a Broken World*** explores the concept of Holistic Mission, which unites evangelism with social action, reflecting both a personal relationship with God and active engagement in justice, peace, and creation's flourishing. Deeply rooted in biblical foundations from Isaiah 61 and Luke 4:18-21, it presents Jesus' ministry as a model of proclaiming good news while healing the sick, freeing the oppressed, and restoring dignity to the marginalized. Drawing from the Old and New Testaments, it affirms that God's Mission (*Missio Dei*) is not limited to saving souls but includes the renewal of individuals, communities, and creation. Theological perspectives from Tulo Raistrick, Samuel Jayakumar, and Deborah Ajulu emphasize that poverty and injustice are rooted in broken relationships, requiring a Mission that addresses both spiritual and social realities. Contextual voices such as Nicta Lubaale and Esther Mombo stress that Mission must be locally shaped, inclusive, and a corrective to colonial models, integrating faith with practical transformation. The chapter also highlights contemporary challenges, including gender, race, class inequalities, and ecological crises, arguing that holistic Mission demands care for creation and the dismantling of unjust structures. Finally, it envisions "shared sacred spaces" where communities experience God's presence through mutual participation, justice, and contextual witness, showing that Mission is not a choice between evangelism and social action, but the living out of the full Gospel in every dimension of life.

Chapter twenty titled ***The Holy Spirit and the Church's Mission: A Pneumatological Foundation for Christian Mission*** examines the essential role of the Holy Spirit in the Church's Mission, showing that Christian Mission is not a human initiative but participation in *Missio Dei*, God's ongoing work of redemption in the world. Rooted in both Old and New Testament witness, it traces the Spirit's activity from creation, prophetic empowerment, and promises of renewal to the anointing of Jesus, the Pentecost outpouring, and the Spirit's continual guidance of the early Church. It identifies key theological themes linking pneumatology and Mission: The Spirit as the divine agent of sending, the giver of boldness and spiritual gifts, and the enabler of cultural translation so the gospel can cross linguistic and social boundaries. Historical perspectives from the early Church's experiences and controversies to the growth of Pentecostal and Charismatic movements and ecumenical affirmations highlight the Spirit's ongoing power to heal, transform, and unite. Practical implications stress that Mission must be Spirit-led through discernment, formation, empowerment, and fostering unity in diversity, as well as intercultural and prophetic engagement with issues of justice and liberation. The chapter concludes that without the Spirit, Mission becomes merely human work, but with the Spirit, the Church embodies God's reconciling love, proclaiming the gospel in both word and deed to the ends of the earth.

Chapter twenty-one titled ***Towards a Transformative Soteriological Missiology: Contextualizing Salvation and Mission in a Pluralistic and Changing World*** explores Soteriological Missiology, the integration of the Christian doctrine of salvation (soteriology) with the study and practice of Mission (Missiology), arguing for a holistic, contextual, and transformative understanding of salvation in today's pluralistic world. Drawing on biblical foundations, it presents the Old Testament vision of salvation as *shalom*, peace, justice, deliverance, and restoration, fulfilled in Jesus' ministry of healing, liberation, and inclusion, and deepened in Paul's theology of justification, reconciliation, new creation, and the "already not yet" hope of cosmic renewal. Historically, the Church's understanding shifted from an exclusive ecclesial model (outside the Church no salvation) to a broader engagement with the world's social, cultural, and ecological realities. Key thinkers such as David Bosch, Stephen Bevans, Alan Tippett, and M. M. Thomas contributed by reframing salvation as God's reconciling work for the whole world, humanization, and contextual transformation. Contemporary themes include contextualization of the gospel, reconciliation, participatory discipleship, justice, ecological renewal, and peace-making, alongside emerging perspectives such as interreligious dialogue, feminist and liberation theologies, postcolonial critique, and digital-age soteriology. The chapter concludes that salvation is not merely about individual destiny after death but about present, active participation in God's Mission to restore relationships, transform societies, and renew creation, calling the Church to proclaim and embody a gospel that is faithful to Christ and relevant to the world's diverse and changing contexts.

Chapter twenty-two titled ***Mission in the Roman Catholic Tradition: From Ecclesial Expansion to Trinitarian Witness*** traces the historical development and theological transformation of Roman Catholic Mission from its early focus on ecclesial expansion to its present Trinitarian, dialogical, and justice-oriented vision. It begins with the pre-Vatican II era, when Mission was closely tied to European colonial expansion, the authority of Rome, and the work of Missionary orders such as the Jesuits and Franciscans. The First Vatican Council (1869-1870) reinforced centralized control through papal primacy and infallibility, resulting in a doctrinally unified but culturally rigid approach, often resistant to dialogue or adaptation. Early 20th century papal documents like *Maximum Illud* (1919), *Rerum Ecclesiae* (1926), *Evangelii Praecones* (1951), and *Fidei Donum* (1957) began to separate Mission from colonialism, emphasize indigenous leadership, and expand lay involvement. The significant shift came with Vatican II's *Ad Gentes* (1965), which grounded Mission in the *Missio Dei* and affirmed inculturation, ecumenical and interfaith dialogue, and the role of all the baptized in witness and service. Subsequent papal writings, from *Evangelii Nuntiandi* (1975) to *Fratelli Tutti* (2020), have expanded Mission to include cultural renewal, ecological responsibility, peacebuilding, and global solidarity. The chapter concludes that Catholic Mission is no longer a one-way act of conversion but a holistic participation in God's reconciling love, expressed through proclamation, justice, mercy, and care for creation in partnership with all people of goodwill.

Chapter twenty-three titled ***Orthodox Perspectives on Christian Mission: Ecclesial, Liturgical, and Trinitarian Foundations for Mission in a Pluralistic World*** presents the Orthodox vision of Christian Mission as an inseparable extension of the Church's life, flowing from its worship, communion, and participation in the love of the Holy Trinity. Unlike some Western approaches shaped by colonialism, activism, or denominational expansion, Orthodox Missiology sees Mission not as a program but as the Church's very identity, rooted in the Eucharist and lived out as "liturgy after the liturgy." Grounded in a Trinitarian, pneumatological, eschatological, and cosmic framework, it emphasizes that Mission is participation in God's own saving work, empowered by the Holy Spirit, pointing toward the Kingdom of God, and encompassing the renewal of all creation. The Orthodox tradition values local and contextual expression through the "Church of Nations," where the gospel takes root in each culture without imposing uniformity. Social justice, ecological care, and compassionate service are viewed as natural fruits of authentic worship, with the Eucharist sending believers to witness and serve in the world. In pluralistic and postcolonial contexts, Orthodox Mission is marked by humility, intercultural dialogue, and mutual respect, offering a witness that is both faithful to apostolic tradition and responsive to contemporary realities. Ultimately, Orthodox Mission embodies the unity of worship and witness, making the Church a living sign of God's reconciling love in every culture and generation.

Chapter twenty-four titled ***Christian Mission in the Ecumenical Tradition: Towards a Unified Witness in a Pluralistic World*** explores the ecumenical tradition in Christian Mission, which seeks unity among diverse churches to strengthen the credibility and impact of the gospel. Rooted in Jesus' prayer "that they may all be one" (John 17:21), ecumenical Mission is grounded in shared faith, theological reflection, ethical commitment to justice, cultural awareness, and practical cooperation. It draws on biblical visions of unity, historical milestones such as the 1910 Edinburgh Missionary Conference, the formation of the Church of South India, the founding of the World Council of Churches, and the reforms of the Second Vatican Council. The chapter outlines a "process model" of unity, emphasizing reception (learning from others), internal reform, and spiral growth through cycles of dialogue and practical collaboration, rather than immediate structural merger. Various Mission models emerge from this tradition, including common witness, inter-church and interfaith dialogue, justice and peace work, unity in diversity, reconciliation, creation care, and mutual learning. By valuing both theological depth and practical service, the ecumenical tradition envisions Mission as a shared journey in which differences are honoured, relationships are deepened, and the Church presents a united voice in proclaiming Christ and addressing global challenges. Ultimately, it affirms that Christian Mission is most faithful when it embodies the unity, humility, and love of the Triune God in the midst of a divided and pluralistic world.

Chapter twenty-five titled ***Mission in the Evangelical Tradition: Theological Foundations, Mission Methodologies, and Holistic Engagement*** outlines the Evangelical approach to Mission, grounded in the deity of Christ, His virgin birth, substitutionary atonement, the authority of Scripture, and the necessity of personal conversion empowered by the Holy Spirit. It traces the development of modern Evangelical Missiology after World War II, shaped by leaders such as Billy Graham and John Stott, and iportant gatherings including the 1966 Berlin Congress and the 1974 Lausanne Congress. These milestones broadened Mission from narrow evangelism to comprehensive evangelization, integrating gospel proclamation with social responsibility. The Lausanne framework identifies three complementary methods such as presence (incarnational living), dialogue (respectful cultural engagement), and proclamation (clear gospel communication) which together reflect the fullness of the gospel. A growing emphasis on Holistic Mission affirms that evangelism and social action are inseparable, addressing both spiritual and material needs following Jesus' example. Influenced by Catharine Padilla's six commitments, this vision calls for Christ-centred service, unity among believers, compassion for the world, shared responsibility in Mission, servant leadership, and cultural adaptability. Methodologically, it follows a cycle of assessment, planning, implementation, and evaluation to ensure contextual relevance and effectiveness. The chapter concludes that Evangelical Mission is participation in the *Missio Dei*, proclaiming Christ with integrity, serving with humility, and embodying the gospel in word and deed for the transformation of individuals, communities, and societies worldwide.

Chapter twenty-six titled ***Pentecostal Missiology in a Pluralistic World: Towards a Holistic Legacy of Mission from Azusa Street to the Ends of the Earth*** presents Pentecostal Missiology as a Spirit-centered, Scripture-rooted, and contextually adaptable approach to Christian Mission, emerging from the Holiness Movement and shaped decisively by the 1906 Azusa Street Revival. Defining Mission as the Spirit's work through evangelism, church planting, social engagement, and interreligious dialogue, it emphasizes lived experience, communal worship, and prophetic guidance over purely institutional strategies. Theologically, Pentecostal Mission rests on three pillars: the Holy Spirit as the primary sender and enabler of the Church's witness, an eschatological urgency arising from the belief in Christ's imminent return, and a holistic vision that integrates evangelism with justice, compassion, and community transformation. Influenced by Wesleyan-Holiness sanctification teaching, African American spirituality, and ecumenical-charismatic encounters, Pentecostalism combines a high view of biblical authority with openness to contemporary prophetic insight. Its Mission ethos such as: experiential, relational, urgent, socially engaged, flexible, and pragmatic adapts to local contexts while maintaining Spirit-led authenticity. Ultimately, Pentecostal Missiology models a vibrant, global witness that proclaims Christ in word and deed, embodying the Kingdom of God now while anticipating its final fulfilment, and offering the wider Church a dynamic, participatory, and transformative way of engaging in God's Mission.

Chapter twenty-seven titled ***Contextual and Methodological Issues in Christian Mission and Evangelism*** presents Christian Mission and evangelism as the Church's participation in God's redemptive work, grounded in Scripture, shaped by theology, and adapted to diverse cultural contexts. Mission is understood broadly as proclaiming and embodying the gospel through word, service, justice, and reconciliation, while evangelism focuses more specifically on sharing the message of salvation and calling people to faith in Christ. Biblically, the Great Commission (Matthew 28:18-20) and the Spirit's empowerment at Pentecost (Acts 1:8) affirm that Mission is God-initiated, Christ-centred, Spirit-led, and church-based. Historically, the chapter traces Mission from the early Church's Spirit-led proclamation and acts of mercy, through medieval monastic outreach, the colonial era's mixture of gospel witness and political entanglement, to modern movements shifting from one-way "sending" to mutual global partnerships. Contemporary Mission faces complex challenges such as religious pluralism, secularism, urbanization, globalization, poverty, injustice, and ecological crises, requiring both cultural sensitivity and biblical faithfulness. Methodologically, effective Mission integrates proclamation with holistic ministry, adapts to local contexts without compromising truth, equips local leadership, engages in discipleship and church planting, and uses technology wisely. The chapter concludes that despite changing contexts and methods, the heart of Mission remains unchanged to witness to Jesus Christ in the power of the Holy Spirit for the transformation of individuals, communities, and creation, trusting in Christ's promise to be with His people until the end of the age.

Chapter twenty-eight titled ***Christian Mission and Conversion in Context: Towards a Culturally Sensitive and Contextually Relevant Gospel Witness*** examines conversion as both a spiritual transformation of turning from sin to new life in Christ through repentance, faith, and the Holy Spirit's work and a socially significant event that reshapes relationships, values, and community belonging. Drawing on biblical models from both Old and New Testaments, it shows that conversion can be sudden or gradual, personal or communal, but always initiated by God and expressed through faith, witness, and changed living. In the Indian context, conversion is deeply contested, often politicized, and associated with cultural identity, historical memory of colonialism, and caste-based power structures. Resistance arises from fears of cultural loss, accusations of coercion, and political agendas such as the *Hindutva*-driven *Ghar Wapsi* movement, which seeks religious reconversion to Hinduism. The chapter proposes several Mission models for navigating this environment, Theological Transformation, Contextual Sensitivity, Freedom of Conscience, Holistic Witness, Prophetic Challenge, Reconciliation and Dialogue, Perseverance under Opposition, and Constitutional Awareness, each integrating biblical faithfulness with cultural respect. It argues that Mission in such a setting must uphold human dignity, avoid coercion, embody justice, and present the gospel as a free invitation, using both word and compassionate action. Ultimately, Christian conversion is not merely a change of religious label but a Spirit-led renewal of persons and communities, and in pluralistic contexts like India, faithful Mission requires wisdom, patience, and a commitment to love, truth, and reconciliation.

Chapter twenty-nine titled ***Mission to the Margins and with the Margins: Reimagining Christian Mission in Solidarity with the Oppressed*** observes how Christian Mission must engage with the marginalized not as passive recipients of charity but as active partners in God's redemptive work. "The margins" include the poor, displaced, Dalits, tribal groups, refugees, women, people with disabilities, and other communities excluded from power and dignity. Biblically, God's Mission begins with the oppressed, from the Exodus to Jesus' ministry of healing, inclusion, and proclamation of good news to the poor, challenging worldly hierarchies and centring those considered "least" by society. Historically, much Mission has been "to" the margins, shaped by top-down or colonial models, but recent theology, including liberation and contextual approaches, has shifted toward Mission "with" the margins, emphasizing solidarity, empowerment, and mutual participation. This requires grassroots leadership development, contextualization of the gospel, advocacy for justice, integration of pastoral care and social transformation, and valuing the lived experiences of the marginalized as theological sources. Global case studies, from Dalit and Black liberation theology to refugee ministry and eco-feminist Mission, illustrate diverse expressions of this vision. The chapter concludes that Mission with the margins is central to discipleship and the *Missio Dei*, calling the Church to repentance from paternalism, courage in confronting injustice, and humility in receiving the margins as places where God's Spirit brings renewal, justice, and hope.

Chapter thirty titled ***New Creation and New Humanity in Christian Mission: Missiological Foundations for Eschatological Hope and Social Transformation*** presents Christian Mission as participation in God's work of renewing all creation and forming a reconciled humanity, rooted in the biblical visions of new creation (II Corinthians 5:17; Revelation 21:5) and new humanity (Ephesians 2:15). It emphasizes that salvation is not limited to individual spiritual change but includes the restoration of relationships, justice, peace, and ecological wholeness. Drawing from Paul's teaching, it shows that in Christ, barriers of ethnicity, caste, class, and gender are dismantled, making the Church a living sign of unity and equality. The chapter integrates Christological and pneumatological perspectives, portraying Jesus as the firstborn of all creation and the beginning of the new humanity, and the Holy Spirit as the one who sanctifies, reconciles, and renews the cosmos. Mission is described as a Spirit-led cooperation with God's ongoing work, engaging in healing, justice, peace-making, environmental stewardship, and bridge-building across divisions. The Church is called to embody the values of the Kingdom as a foretaste of the future new creation, confronting the false divide between evangelism and social action and resisting the temptation to reduce God's eschatological promise to human-made ideals. Ultimately, the chapter envisions Mission as holistic and transformative, anticipating God's final renewal of all things while actively manifesting its reality in the present through communities of reconciliation, justice, and creation care.

The concluding chapter titled ***Mission in Multi-Faith and Multicultural Contexts: A Journey Through Theological Challenges and Practical Witness*** explores how Christian Mission operates within today's multi-faith and multicultural contexts, where diverse religions and cultures exist side by side. Rooted in biblical examples from Abraham's covenant, Jonah's call to Nineveh, Jesus' outreach to Samaritans and Gentiles, and Paul's contextual preaching in Athens, it affirms both the uniqueness of Christ and the dignity of all peoples. Mission in such settings requires holding firm to the gospel while engaging respectfully through dialogue, hospitality, and shared service. Theological foundations emphasize Christ as the only way of salvation, yet call for humility, compassion, and understanding of other faiths' beliefs, values, and customs. Effective Mission involves religious literacy, cross-cultural sensitivity, and contextualization, communicating the gospel in local languages, symbols, and cultural forms without imposing foreign patterns or engaging in cultural imperialism. Practical expressions include relational and incarnational evangelism, community development, healthcare, education, peacebuilding, and storytelling as non-confrontational witness. Interfaith dialogue, seen not as compromise but as a form of authentic witness, builds trust and cooperation for justice and human flourishing. Ultimately, Mission in pluralistic settings is about embodying conviction and compassion together, proclaiming Christ faithfully while serving and loving people across religious and cultural boundaries, with the goal of transforming relationships, communities, and societies through the reconciling love of God.

Thus, for the present-day context of Christian Mission in India, this book offers both prophetic challenge and pastoral encouragement. Theologically, it reaffirms the centrality of Christ and the power of the Holy Spirit while embracing dialogue, justice, and reconciliation as integral to the gospel. Practically, it equips grassroots leaders and theological students to address pressing realities such as caste discrimination, religious nationalism, poverty, ecological degradation, and gender injustice with wisdom, courage, and compassion. By integrating interdisciplinary scholarship with a deep commitment to the *Missio Dei*, the volume serves as a vital resource for renewing theological education in India, ensuring that future leaders are not only doctrinally grounded but also contextually competent. In doing so, it empowers the church at every level to embody a Mission that is faithful to Scripture, relevant to society, and transformative for both communities and creation.

Rev. Dr. Vinod S. Sailus
Professor in Missiology
St. Peter's Pontifical Institute, Bengaluru

1

God's Sending and Our Proclamation Defining 'Mission' and 'Evangelism'

A precise understanding of the definitions, scope, and interrelationships of two foundational Missiological concepts 'Mission' (*Missio Dei*) and 'Evangelism' is more urgent than ever." Although often used interchangeably, "Mission" and "Evangelism" carry diverse theological meanings and practical implications that shape the Church's engagement with society. For over two thousand years, 'Mission' and 'Evangelism' have stood at the heart of Christian identity. Deriving from Latin word *missio* (sending) and Greek *euangelion* (good news), respectively, the concepts 'Mission' and 'Evangelism' articulate 'why the Church exists' and 'how it bears witness to the world.' Though closely related, evangelism may be understood as one aspect of Mission, their distinct emphases have stimulated diverse theological debates, ecclesial Mission models, and academic disciplines. Therefore, it is important to lay the groundwork by defining 'Mission' and 'Evangelism' etymologically and conceptually, tracing their evolution through church history, and surveying key theological frameworks. Thus, it sets the stage for examining how Missiology, as an interdisciplinary field, integrates biblical studies, cultural analysis, social sciences, and more, shaping a coherent praxis that unites word and deed.

Etymology and Early Usage of Mission, Evangelism and Missiology

Mission

The Latin root *mittere* (to send) gave rise to *missio*, which early theologians employed to comprehend the Church's divine commission.[1] In the patristic

[1] Samuel Escobar, *Changing Tides: Latin America and World Mission Today* (London: Fortress Press, 2023), 1-8.

era, *missio* was synonymous with apostleship, reflecting Jesus' mandate: *As the Father has sent me, even so I am sending you* (John 20:21). Church Fathers such as Irenaeus and Augustine understood the Church itself as an extension of Christ's sent nature, but with a more ecclesiological focus than later Missionary movements.[2] It was not until the twentieth century, with Karl Barth's and Küng's articulation of *Missio Dei*, that Mission was reframed not as a human endeavour but as grounded in the 'Trinitarian life of God,' God sending the Son and Spirit into the world, and thus sending the Church in divine solidarity.[3]

Evangelism

Evangelism originates in the Greek noun *euangelion*, (good news), and its verb form *euangelizesthai*, (to bring or announce good news).[4] In classical usage, *euangelion* described civic proclamations of victory or political edicts. Whereas, the New Testament appropriated it for the proclamation of Christ's life, death, and resurrection, emphasizing redemptive transformation.[5] Over succeeding centuries, evangelism developed a more narrowly defined purpose that, the verbal and interpersonal proclamation aimed clearly at conversion, though it always carried an implicit social dimension in the formation of new Christian communities. The Lausanne Covenant (1974) proposes a widely accepted working definition that: "Evangelism is the proclamation of the historical, biblical Christ as Savior and Lord, with a view to persuading people to come to him personally and so be reconciled to God."[6] This definition underscores both content as Christ and goal as reconciliation. D. T. Niles's metaphor of: one beggar telling another where to find bread, emphasizes the humility central to evangelistic witness. Evangelism therefore encompasses *kerugma* (proclamation), *martyria* (testimony), and *koinonia* (community formation), and functions

---

[2] Mark S. M. Scott, "Suffering and Soul-Making: Rethinking John Hick's Theodicy, *The Journal of Religion* 90/3 (2010): 313-314.

[3] Hanna Reichel, "The Sending of the Church and Civil Society: A Test Case for a Comprehensive Missional Paradigm," in *Church and Civil Society* edited by M. Welker, N. Koopman, J. M. Vorster (African Sun Media, 2017), 231-234.

[4] Patrick Hannon, "First, the Good News," *The Furrow* 64/3 (2013): 133-134.

[5] Linford D. Fisher, "Evangelicals and Unevangelicals: The Contested History of a Word, 1500-1950," *Religion and American Culture: A Journal of Interpretation* 26/2 (2016): 184-186.

[6] Al Tizon, *Transformation after Lausanne: Radical Evangelical Mission in Global-Local Perspective* (London: Augsburg Fortress, 2008): 21-36.; Richard V. Peace, "Evangelism," in *Dictionary of Mission Theology: Evangelical Foundations*, edited by John Corrie (Nottingham: InterVarsity Press, 2007), 116.

at the intersection of divine sovereignty, human responsibility to proclaim, and the Holy Spirit's conviction and transforms (I Corinthians 3:6-7).

Missiology

In the light of the understanding of the concepts 'Mission' and 'Evangelism,' Missiologists defines Missiology that captures the breadth, depth and width of Mission. According to A. Scott Moreau, Gary R. Corwin, Gary B. McGee, Francis A. Oborji and Stephen B. Bevans "Missiology is the Theology of Mission, Methodology of Mission and Theory of Mission."[7] A. Scott Moreau describes Missiology as "the conscious, intentional, ongoing reflection on the doing of Mission," highlighting its reflexive dimension. Julian Saldanha sees Missiology as "applied theology," an engagement that moves theological insights from the academy to the public sphere.[8] The Second Vatican Council's Decree *Ad Gentes* (1965) declared that "the pilgrim Church is Missionary by her very nature," showcasing that Mission comprehends all theological disciplines. In the same way Francis Oborji summarizes that Missiology is "the mother of all theologies"[9] setting Mission as the animating principle for doctrinal reflection, ensuring theology remains outwardly focused and socially engaged.

Distinctions and Relationships between Mission and Evangelism

Evangelism focuses primarily on the communication of the gospel and the call to personal faith, whereas Mission encompasses a broader engagement with social, cultural, and ecological spheres. Thus, while every act of evangelism is Missional, not every Missional activity is evangelistic. Mission invites the Church to embody the gospel through justice initiatives, community development, and interfaith dialogue. The concept *Missio Dei* reframes Mission and evangelism as participations in God's own sending. Whereas traditional paradigms emphasized human-driven outreach, the *Missio Dei* emphasizes divine initiative: God sends the Son (John 3:16) and the Spirit (Acts 2), then sends the Church. Within this Trinitarian framework, evangelism serves as the communicative axis of Mission, but

---

[7] A. Scott Moreau, Gary R. Corwin and Gary B. McGee, *Introducing World Missions: A Biblical*..., 74.; Francis Anekwe Oborji, "Contemporary Missiology in Theological Education: Origins and..., 383.; Stephen B. Bevans and Jeffrey Gros, *Evangelization and Religious Freedom*..., 35.

[8] Julian Saldanha, *Mission Today: Themes and Issues* (Bangalore: Claretian Publications, 2006), 7.

[9] Francis Anekwe Oborji, "Contemporary Missiology in Theological Education: Origins and New Perspectives," *Missiology* 34/3 (July, 2006): 385.; Quoted by Hans Kasdorf, "A Personal Journey of Missiological Formation," *Direction* 23/1 (1994): 105.; David Jacobus Bosch, *Transforming Mission: Paradigm Shifts in Theology of Mission* (Maryknol: Orbis Books, 2011), 32 & 413.

Mission itself is rooted in divine love and restorative purpose. But, the concept 'Holistic Mission' integrates proclamation and service, clarifying that evangelism without social engagement risks neglecting Jesus' concern for the poor (Luke 4:18-19), while Mission without proclamation risks reducing Christianity to mere philanthropy. The New Testament model, where Jesus preaches and heals, provides the paradigm for a Mission that proclaims and incarnates the good news.

Historical Development

The story of Christian Mission is the story of how the good news of Jesus Christ spread from a small group of believers in Jerusalem to people all over the world. This did not happen all at once, but step by step through many different times in history. In each period, the Church found new ways to share the gospel, depending on the situation and challenges of the time. From the early days of the apostles preaching after Pentecost, to the work of Missionaries and monks in the Middle Ages, to the powerful changes brought by the Protestant Reformation, and finally to the worldwide Mission movements of the modern era, each stage added something new to the Church's Mission. These changes were shaped by different cultures, leaders, and ideas. As the world changed, Mission work also changed, taking into account local languages, customs, and the importance of respecting people's own cultures. Today, Mission is not just from the West to the rest of the world, but from everywhere to everywhere. By learning about this historical development, we can understand how the Church's Mission has grown, changed, and stayed faithful to the call of Jesus to "go and make disciples of all nations."

Mission and Evangelism in the Early Church

In the days immediately after Pentecost, about three thousand people joined the new faith in a single gathering (Acts 2). This remarkable event gave confidence to the early Christians that God was at work through the Spirit. Encouraged by this outpouring, the apostles set out to share the message of Jesus wherever they went.[10] They focused on major cities like Jerusalem, Antioch, Corinth, and Ephesus using public squares, homes, and marketplaces to preach about Christ's life, death, and resurrection.[11] As the number of believers grew, small groups formed house churches. These gatherings met in homes for worship, teaching, and fellowship, laying a

---

[10] Heather D. Curtis, "Pentecostal Missions and the Global Expansion of Spirit-Filled Christianity," *Fides et Historia* 47/2 (December, 2015): 81-86.

[11] Colin Miller, "The Imperial Cult in the Pauline Cities of Asia Minor and Greece," *The Catholic Biblical Quarterly* 72/2 (2010): 314-332.

strong foundation for community life.[12] Meanwhile, some followers chose to live apart from society in monastic communities. Monks and nuns built simple settlements on the fringes of the Roman Empire, dedicating themselves to prayer, work, and caring for the poor.[13] From Ireland to Germany, these monastic centres became Missionary outposts, drawing people to faith by their example of service and spiritual devotion.

The Medieval Period

During the medieval period, the spread of Christianity often happened through the leadership of kings and rulers who adopted the faith first and then encouraged or even required their people to follow. This 'top-down' approach was seen in the case of King Clovis of the Franks, who converted to Christianity in the late 5th century.[14] After Clovis was baptized around 496 AD, many of his soldiers and subjects followed his example, leading to the Christianization of much of what is now France. His conversion helped strengthen the alliance between the Frankish kingdom and the Roman Church, making Christianity a central part of the political and social structure.[15] In addition to such royal conversions, Missionary Bishops played a major role in expanding the Christian faith into areas that were still pagan. For example, Saint Boniface, an English Missionary, went to the Germanic regions in the 8th century.[16] He preached the gospel, challenged local religions (famously cutting down the sacred Oak of Thor at Geismar), baptized the people who accepted Jesus Christ and organized new churches.[17] Boniface also trained local clergy and worked closely with Christian rulers to protect new believers and promote the faith.[18] This mix of spiritual Mission and royal support helped Christianity spread more securely across Europe.

---

[12] Thomas O'Loughlin, "Sharing Food and Breaking Boundaries: Reading of Acts 10-11:18 as a key to Luke's Ecumenical Agenda in Acts," *Transformation* 32/1 (January, 2015): 27-37.

[13] Jason Byassee, *An Introduction to the Desert Fathers* (Eugene: Cascade Books, 2007), 1-2.

[14] Dane R. Pestano, "Clovis, King of the Franks-Towards a New Chronology," *Dark Age History* (2015): 1-3.

[15] Dane R. Pestano, "Clovis, King of the Franks-Towards a New Chronology…, 4-6.

[16] B. K Kuiper, *The Church in History* (Grand Rapid: Wm Eerdmans Publishing Co.,1995), 48.

[17] F. Hrangkhuma, *Introduction to Church History* (Bangalore: Theological Book Trust, 1996), 124-125.

[18] S. M. Houghton, *Sketches from Church History* (Edinburgh: The Banner of Truth Trust, 1980), 49.

The Reformation Era

The Protestant Reformation in the 16th century brought a major change in how people understood faith and Mission. Leaders like Martin Luther emphasized that salvation is a free gift from God, by grace alone (*sola gratia*) and through faith alone (*sola fide*), and not something earned by good works or church rituals.[19] Luther translated the Bible into German so that ordinary people could read it, understand it, and apply it to their lives. This encouraged personal responsibility in matters of faith.[20] As a result, evangelism during and after the Reformation became more cantered on clear preaching of the Bible and helping individuals come to personal faith in Jesus Christ. Preachers focused on explaining Scripture in the local language, and believers were encouraged to read the Bible for themselves. In places like Geneva under John Calvin, the city became a model of Reformed teaching and sent out Missionaries and pastors to other parts of Europe.[21] Even though the Reformation did not immediately result in large overseas Mission movements, it laid the foundation for later Protestant Missions by emphasizing Scripture, personal faith, and the priesthood of all believers.

Modern Mission Movement

In the nineteenth century, the global Mission movement took shape with organizations like the London Missionary Society and the American Board of Commissioners for Foreign Missions. These Mission organizations professionalized the sending of Missionaries by providing formal training in language, culture, and theology.[22] Missionaries travelled to Asia, Africa, and the Pacific, and started schools, hospitals, and churches to meet both spiritual and practical needs. After colonies gained independence in the twentieth century, Missiology faced a new challenge of addressing the legacy of colonialism.[23] In countries such as India, local church leaders called for an indigenous approach to Mission that honoured native cultures

---

[19] F. Ernest Stoeffler, *The Rise of Evangelical Pietism* (Leiden: E. J. Brill, 1971), 181-182.

[20] Heinz Bluhm, "An 'Unknown' Luther Translation of the Bible" *PMLA* 84/6 (1969): 1537–1544.

[21] M. Thongkhosei Haokip, *A Guide to History of Christianity: From the First to the Eighteenth Centuries* (Secunderabad: Bishop Rt. Rev. Paothang Haokip, 2017), 265-266.

[22] Laurence Kitzan, "The London Missionary Society and the Problem of Authority in India, 1798-1833," *Church History* 40/4 (1971): 457-460.; David W. Kling, "The New Divinity and the Origins of the American Board of Commissioners for Foreign Missions," *Church History* 72/4 (2003): 791-793.

[23] Kenneth Scott Latourette, "Colonialism and Missions: Progressive Separation," *Journal of Church and State* 7/3 (1965): 330-339.

and leadership.[24] Today, Mission flows in every direction, with churches in Africa, Asia, and Latin America supporting work in Western countries, reflecting a global, reciprocal partnership rather than a one-way flow of resources. The nineteenth-century Protestant Mission Movements institutionalized societies like the London Missionary Society and professionalized Missiology, taking insights from anthropology, linguistics, sociology and other social sciences.[25] In postcolonial contexts such as India, Missiology critically engages with colonial legacies, advocating indigenous leadership, contextual theology, and reciprocal Mission between Global South and North.

Interdisciplinary Nature of Missiology

Missiology explains how the message of Jesus is shared with the world. But Mission does not happen in a vacuum. It takes place in real places, among real people, with different histories, cultures, languages, beliefs, and struggles.[26] That enables Missiology to work together with many other fields of study, thus being interdisciplinary. Biblical studies give Missiology its foundation by showing how God's Mission is revealed in Scripture. History helps us learn from past Mission efforts, especially, their successes and failures. Sociology and anthropology teach us about people, cultures, and communities, so that Mission can be respectful and relevant. Linguistics and communication help Missionaries speak clearly and meaningfully in different languages and styles. Gender studies show how men and women can both take part in God's work, while also correcting injustices. Ecology reminds us that caring for the earth is part of God's Mission. And interfaith studies teach us how to relate lovingly and wisely to people of other religions. Thus, the interdisciplinary nature helps Missiology to stay faithful to the Bible while also being sensitive to the world today and becomes effective to all people including creation.

Missiology and Biblical Studies

Biblical studies provide Missiology with its foundational theological and narrative frameworks. Exegesis of Old and New Testament texts uncovers the theological motifs of the covenant, exile, restoration, kingdom of God

---

[24] Andrea Smith, "Decolonization in Unexpected Places: Native Evangelicalism and the Rearticulation of Mission," *American Quarterly* 62/3 (2010): 569-570.

[25] Paul A. Varg, "Motives in Protestant Missions, 1890-1917," *Church History* 23/1 (1954): 68-82.

[26] Jacob Kéhìndé Olúpọ̀nà, "World Christianity: An Agenda for the Twenty-First Century," *Journal of World Christianity* 9/1 (2019): 23–33.

and shapes Missionary impetus.[27] For example, Isaiah's portrayal of the servant's universal and holistic Mission that: *I will also make you a light for the Gentiles, that my salvation may reach to the ends of the earth* (Isaiah 49:6) and the Great Commission (Matthew 28:18-20) frame both the 'why' and 'how' of Christian engagements in the passing times.[28] Methodologies such as narrative criticism and social-scientific exegesis, literary criticism and historical critical analysis enable scholars to locate Mission within the socio-historical realities of the biblical world, making sure that what we do today still stays true to what the Bible teaches.

Missiology and History

Historical studies help us understand how Christian Mission has developed over time and showing not only where and how Missionaries went, but also what worked, what failed, and why. From the days of the apostles in the New Testament to the spread of Christianity through monastic communities in the Middle Ages, and later to modern Mission efforts in the 19th and 20th centuries, history shows how Mission has always been influenced by theology, politics, and culture.[29] For example, the Jesuit Missions in Paraguay during the 17th and 18th centuries tried to protect Indigenous people from colonial exploitation by creating self-governing Christian communities.[30] These Missions taught the gospel in local languages and respected native customs, showing how Mission could work respectfully across cultures.[31] However, when political powers shifted, many of these efforts were dismantled, reminding us how Mission can be vulnerable to outside forces. Another example is the Student Volunteer Movement (SVM) of the late 19th and early 20th centuries. It inspired thousands of young people, mostly from North America and Europe to become Missionaries around the world. While their dedication was strong and they helped build schools, hospitals, and churches, some also carried Western cultural values that clashed with local

---

[27] Michael McGiffert, "From Moses to Adam: The Making of the Covenant of Works," *The Sixteenth Century Journal* 19/2 (1988): 131-155.

[28] Wendel Sun, "New Testament Theology and World Mission," in *World Mission: Theology, Strategy, and Current Issues*, edited by Scott N. Callaham and Will Brooks (London: Lexham Press, 2019), 22-25.

[29] Dwight P. Baker, "The Use of History: Aspects of the Role of History in Missiology," *International Journal of Frontier Missiology* 33/1 (2016): 5.

[30] Robert H. Jackson, "The Population and Vital Rates of the Jesuit Missions of Paraguay, 1700-1767," *The Journal of Interdisciplinary History* 38/3 (2008): 401-403.

[31] Jan A. B. Jongeneel, *Missiological Encyclopedia Part I: The Philosophy and Science of Mission in the 19th and 20th centuries* (Bangalore: Siga Arles, 2006), 249-250.

traditions.[32] This sometimes led to cultural imperialism, where local ways of life were ignored or replaced.

Sociology, Anthropology and Missiology

Sociology and anthropology help Missionaries understand how people live, think, and relate to each other in different cultures.[33] These social sciences provide ways to study how communities are organized, what values they hold, and how they make important life decisions. This is important because sharing the gospel is not just about using the right words, but it is also about understanding the people you are speaking to.[34] For example, participant observation, where Missionaries live among the people and watch how they behave and interact can reveal daily habits, unspoken rules, and community priorities.[35] Ethnographic study involves interviewing and spending time with people to understand their traditions, beliefs, and ways of life in depth.[36] Social network analysis can show how influence and information flow through a community, whether through elders, family heads, or peer groups helping Missionaries know how to connect with key decision-makers.[37]

Anthropology helps Missionaries understand important parts of culture like rites of passage (such as weddings, coming-of-age ceremonies, or funerals), symbols (like flags, clothing, or sacred objects), and kinship systems (how families and clans are structured).[38] These insights help Missionaries present the gospel in a way that makes sense within the culture, without forcing foreign ideas. For example, in many African and Asian societies, respect for ancestors and elders is very strong. Instead of dismissing this practice, Missionaries can explain how honouring parents fits within the biblical command to *Honor your father and your mother, so that you may live long in the land the Lord your God is giving you* (Exodus

---

[32] Archibald Gillies Baker, "The Religious Ideals of the Student Volunteer Movement," *The Journal of Religion* 4/2 (1924): 192-202.

[33] Eugene A. Nida, *Customs and Cultures: Anthropology for Christian Mission* (New York: Harper & Brothers, 1954), 26.

[34] Craig Ott, Stephen J. Strauss and Timothy C. Tennent, *Encountering Theology of Mission: Biblical Foundations, Historical Developments and Contemporary Issues* (Grand Rapids: Baker Academic, 2010), XXII.

[35] Peter Woods, *Inside Schools: Ethnography in Educational Research* (London: Routledge and Regan Paul, 1986), 88.

[36] Paul G. Hiebert, *Anthropological Reflections of Missiological Issues* (Grand Rapids: Baker Books, 1994), 192-196 & 198.

[37] Steven J. Taylor and Robert Bogdan, *Introduction to Qualitative Research Methods: The Search for Meanings* (New York: John Wiley, 1984), 15.

[38] Eugene A. Nida, *Customs and Cultures: Anthropology for Christian Mission* (New York: Harper & Brothers, 1954), 26.

20:12), while clarifying the difference between respect and ancestor worship. This is called contextualization, making the gospel message understandable and relevant without changing its truth.[39] At the same time, these tools help guard against syncretism, which is when Christian beliefs are mixed in the wrong way with non-Christian practices. Thus, Missiology uses sociology and anthropology not to compromise the gospel but to communicate it more clearly and faithfully in each culture.

Linguistics, Communication and Missiology

Mission work is not just about speaking, rather, it is about making people understand the message in their own language and culture. This is why linguistics (the study of language) and communication are so important for Missiology.[40] Every culture has its own way of speaking, listening, and learning. Some people respond well to stories, while others prefer clear explanations or deep discussions. Communication theory helps Missionaries choose the best way to share the gospel, whether through preaching, conversation, drama, radio, or social media. It teaches how people understand messages and what helps them to listen, believe, and respond.[41] Linguistics helps people to understand how words and grammar work in different languages. It also shows us how meaning can change depending on the culture. Bible translation is one of the most important ways Missionaries use linguistics.[42] Missionaries and trained linguists often work with local people to create alphabets for languages that have never been written down before. They also help people learn to read and write, and share the Bible through storytelling, songs, and drama in oral cultures.[43] By using the tools of communication and linguistics, Missionaries can make sure the message of Jesus is clear, meaningful, and faithful to the Bible, so that people in every culture can understand and follow Him.

---

[39] Joel Robbins, "The Anthropology of Christianity: Unity, Diversity, New Directions," *Current Anthropology* 55/10 (December, 2014): 158.

[40] Berdine van den Toren-Lekkerkerker and Benno van den Toren, "From Missionary Incarnate to Incarnational Guest: A Critical Reflection on Incarnation as a Model for Missionary Presence," *Transformation* 32/2 (2015): 81-86.

[41] Brainerd Prince and Benrilo Kikon, "Mission as Translation: A Fusion of Three Horizons," *Transformation* 35/4 (2018): 251-253.

[42] C. Anderson, Review of "Translation as Mission: Bible Translation in the Modern Missionary Movement," by W. A. Smalley *Church History* 64/1 (1995): 149-150.

[43] Brainerd Prince and Benrilo Kikon, "Mission as Translation: A Fusion of Three Horizons…, 251-253.

Missiology and Gender Studies

Historically, women have played a key role in Mission, teaching, nursing, church planting, and serving communities.[44] Yet their voices were often overlooked, their roles are marginalized and their images are distorted.[45] But Missiology takes gender issues seriously because the gospel speaks to all people, both men and women equally. Gender studies help us understand how men and women have been treated differently in both the Church and society, often because of patriarchal systems, ways of thinking and organizing life that give more power to men and less to women.[46] Missiology, when informed by gender studies, challenges these patterns and works to ensure that women are included, respected, and empowered in leadership and Mission. Today, many Mission organizations and churches are rethinking leadership to be more inclusive and in many parts of Africa and Asia, women pastors and evangelists are growing in number and impact, bringing change in places where female leadership was once resisted. Gender justice in Mission also means addressing practices like gender-based violence, child marriage, and educational inequality.[47] Missionaries working in these areas partner with local communities to promote human dignity and the full participation of women and girls in church and society, that aligns with the biblical truth that all people are created in the image of God (Genesis 1:27) and are called to serve and lead according to their gifts.

Missiology and Ecology

Eco-justice is one of the growing concerns in Missiology that looks at the connection between caring for creation and spreading the gospel.[48] The Bible teaches that God created the earth and called it good (Genesis 1), and humans are called to be stewards and caretakers of creation. But nou it is common that the environment is suffering due to pollution, deforestation, climate change, and overuse of resources. This damages the lives of the poor, who often depend most directly on the land and natural rcsources.[49] In this milieu, Missiology recognizes and affirm that caring for the earth

[44] John Mark Terry, *Missiology: An Introduction to the Foundations. History, and Strategies of World Missions* (Nashville: B&H Publishing, 2015), 425-426.

[45] Roger E. Hedlund & Paul Joshua Bhakiaraj ed., *Missiology for the 21st Century* (Delhi: ISPCK, 2004), 585.

[46] Narola Imchen, *Women in the History of Christianity* (Jorhat: Tribal Development and Communication Centre, 2010). 167.

[47] Limatula Longkumer, ed., *Methodological Issues in Theological Research: An Exploration Vol. 4* (West Bengal: SATHRI, 2020), 272.

[48] Stephen B. Bevans & Roger P. Schroeder, *Constants in Context: A Theology of Mission for Today* (Bangalore: Claretian Publications, 2005), 369.

[49] Stephen B. Bevans & Roger P. Schroeder, *Constants in Context: A Theology…*, 369.

is part of Christian Mission and promotes 'Green Mission' initiatives that include planting trees, promoting clean water, reducing waste, using solar energy, and educating communities about sustainable farming.[50] This shows that Mission is not just about saving souls but also about healing the whole world spiritually, socially, and environmentally. When Christians care for creation, they reflect God's love and concern for all of life and bear witness to the Kingdom of God,[51] where peace and justice extend to both people and the planet, thus understand the groaning of the creation (Romans 8:22).

Missiology and Interfaith Studies

In the present-day context, people of different religions live, work, and interact side by side. For Christian Mission to be meaningful in this context, it must engage with religious diversity in ways that are both respectful to other faiths and faithful to the message of Jesus.[52] This is where interfaith studies play an important role in Missiology. Interfaith studies help Missionaries to use different tools to understand other faiths, build relationships, and share the gospel in a spirit of love and truth. One important tool is comparative theology, which looks at similarities and differences between Christianity and other religions.[53] Learning about these similarities and differences helps Missionaries to explain faith clearly and avoid misunderstandings.[54] It also builds trust when conversations are based on understanding rather than stereotypes. There are several other models of interfaith engagement, such as Dialogue Model, promoted by the Second Vatican Council, encourages open, respectful conversations aimed at listening, learning, and peacefully sharing the Christian faith without pressure to convert.[55] Any models in interfaith engagement faces the same challenge that how to remain faithful to Jesus' teachings while being humble and loving toward others.[56] Thus,

---

[50] William Jenkinson, *Trends in Mission: Toward the Third Millennium* (Maryknol: Orbis Books, 1991), 249.

[51] V. J. John, *The Ecological Vision of Jesus: Nature in the Parables of Mark* (Thiruvalla: CSS, 2002), 264.

[52] Harold Kasimow, "Abraham Joshua Heschel and Interreligious Dialogue," *Journal of Ecumenical Studies* 18/3 (1981): 423.

[53] Stanley J. Samartha, "The Progress and Promise of Inter-Religious Dialogues," *Journal of Ecumenical Studies* 9/3 (1972): 473.

[54] Paul Tillich, *Christianity and the Encounter of the World Religions* (New York: Columbia University Press, 1964), 62.

[55] Mark R. Francis, "Another Look at the Constitution on the Sacred Liturgy and the Substantial Unity of the Roman Rite," *Worship* 88/3 (May, 2014): 241.

[56] Øyvind Økland, "Dialogue and Mission in a Globalized World Developments in the World Council of Churches and the Lausanne Movement," in *The Lausanne Movement: A Range of Perspectives*, edited by Lars Dahle, Margunn Serigstad Dahle and Knud Jørgensen (Oxford: Regnum Books International, 2014), 372.

interfaith engagement in Missiology does not mean giving up on the gospel. Instead, it means sharing it in ways that are wise, respectful, and appropriate for today's multi-faith world.

Practical Implications for Contemporary Church

A clear articulation of 'Mission' and 'Evangelism' shapes Mission methods, leadership formation, and resource deployment for the particular time and place. Definitions of Mission and evangelism, while overlapping, serve distinct theological and practical functions. Evangelism focuses on gospel proclamation and conversion and Mission comprehends the broader sending of the church into societal, cultural, and ecological spheres. Framed by the *Missio Dei*, both 'Mission' and 'Evangelism' find their origin in God's Trinitarian movement toward the world. The interdisciplinary nature of Missiology drawing on biblical studies, history, social sciences, communication, gender and ecology, and interfaith engagement ensures that Mission praxis is both theologically strong and contextually sensitive. As the global church faces new frontiers of digital media, religious pluralism, and ecological crisis, a clear and integrated understanding of 'Mission' and 'Evangelism' will remain vital for the Church as an agent of transformative witness.

2

Historical Development of Missiology From Missiology to Intercultural Theology

Missiology, once known as "the study of Mission," has grown into a full academic discipline alongside the global Missionary movements of the 19th century. Often described as "the mother of all theologies," Missiology brings together theological reflection and practical action, asking how Christians are called to share the gospel in different times, places, and cultures. Yet, in present-day India, the term "Mission" is often misunderstood. It is frequently equated with evangelism or even colonialism, resulting in suspicion or resistance. This misunderstanding calls for what some scholars have termed a "reformission,"[1] a renewed and reformed understanding of Mission that responds to present-day realities without abandoning biblical faithfulness. This chapter also proposes that the best way forward is to adopt Intercultural Theology, a more inclusive and context-sensitive framework that integrates various disciplines, voices, and experiences. Intercultural Theology not only addresses contemporary criticisms but also enriches the theory and practice of Mission by drawing from history, culture, language, sociology, gender, ecology, and interfaith dialogue. Therefore, it is important to explore the background and development of Missiology and explain the shift toward Intercultural Theology and to highlight why this shift is particularly relevant and necessary in the Indian context today.

[1] The word 'reformission' is the title of the book, which is written from faith perspective. The researcher found the word as an appropriate expression to use in this research. The whole book highlights the concept 'reformission.' Mark Driscoll, *The Radical Reformission* (Grand Rapids: Zondervan, 2004).

Background and Development of Missiology

Missiology is the theological discipline that studies the Mission of the Church in all its dimensions such as: biblical, historical, theological, cultural, and practical dimensions.[2] While Mission itself has been a core aspect of Christian identity since the earliest days of the Church, the structured and critical study of Mission, Missiology, emerged gradually over time.[3] As a discipline, Missiology seeks to understand and articulate the Church's calling to participate in God's redemptive work in the world. It explores how the gospel is communicated, received, and lived out in various cultural, social, and religious contexts, offering both theological reflection and practical guidance.

The development of Missiology reflects the Church's growing awareness of the need to engage thoughtfully and responsibly with a changing world. As Christianity encountered new cultures, languages, and worldviews, it became necessary to reflect systematically on the methods, motivations, and implications of Missionary activity.[4] This required more than passionate zeal. It demanded theological depth, historical awareness, cultural sensitivity, and ethical responsibility.[5] Missiology thus emerged to serve as a bridge between faith and practice, drawing from multiple disciplines to equip the Church for effective and faithful witness.

Over time, Missiology has expanded from being a subdivision of pastoral or practical theology to becoming a multidisciplinary field in its own right.[6] It incorporates insights from biblical studies, theology, history, anthropology, sociology, linguistics, communication, and even ecology and gender studies. This interdisciplinary nature enables Missiology to address complex global realities while staying rooted in the gospel.[7] In today's world of religious pluralism, cultural diversity, and ecological crisis, Missiology continues to evolve, offering the Church a dynamic framework for engaging in Mission that is both faithful to Scripture and responsive to context.

Raimon Lull, a 13th century Franciscan Missionary, philosopher, and poet from Majorca, is considered one of the earliest thinkers to lay the

---

[2] Ian Hislop, "Missiology," *Blackfriars* 27/320 (November, 1946): 414-421.

[3] Robert J. C. Young, *Post-colonialism: An Historical Introduction* (Oxford: Blackwell, 2001), 2-5.

[4] Ian Hislop, "Missiology..., 416.

[5] Guy W. Sarvis, "Missions, Culture, and Social Change," *The Journal of Religion* 14/3 (1934): 340-341.

[6] David McIlroy, The Mission of Justice, *Transformation* 28/3 (July, 2011), 182-194.

[7] David P. Adams, review of *The Oxford Handbook of Mission Studies*, edited by Kirsteen Kim, Knud Jørgensen and Alison Fithcett-Climenhaga, *Anglican and Episcopal History* 93/2 (June, 2024): 444-447.

intellectual groundwork for Missiology. Unlike many of his contemporaries, Lull believed that Mission required deep respect for and understanding of the cultures and languages of those to whom the gospel was being proclaimed. In 1276, he founded a seminary on the island of Majorca dedicated to teaching Missionaries a variety of languages (*idiomata diversa*), especially Arabic, so they could engage effectively with Muslim communities.[8] Lull's approach marked a significant departure from confrontational models of evangelism and anticipated modern principles of contextualization and intercultural dialogue. His vision influenced the Council of Vienne in 1311 to recommend language training for Missionaries, although the implementation was short-lived. Nevertheless, Lull's holistic and dialogical view of Mission planted a theological and educational seed that would eventually blossom centuries later into the academic discipline of Missiology.[9]

Later, the 17th century witnessed key institutional developments that further shaped the early trajectory of Missiology. In 1622, the East India Trading Company sought to train Protestant pastors for overseas Mission and approached Leiden University's theological faculty in the Netherlands to sketch a Missionary seminary plan for India. Though this initiative was short-lived, ending in 1633, it revealed a growing awareness among Protestants of the need for structured Missionary education. Meanwhile, the Catholic Church made a significant step by founding the *Collegium Urbanum de Propaganda Fide* in Rome in 1627. This institution sought to systematize the training of Missionaries, focusing on theology, languages, and global engagement. Around the same time, German Pietist theologian August Hermann Francke established the *Collegium Orientale Theologicum* in Halle in 1702, aimed at preparing Missionaries through a blend of theological instruction and Enlightenment-era rationalism. Although Francke's efforts had limited long-term influence on Missiology, these developments collectively marked the transition from informal Mission practices to more organized and scholarly reflections on global evangelism.[10]

The 19th century saw the beginnings of formal academic interest in Mission within Protestant theological education. In 1800, J. Flatt, a professor at the University of Tübingen, delivered one of the first university-level lecture series on Mission. Though largely overlooked by the academic

---

[8] Johannes Verkuyl, *Contemporary Missiology: An Introduction*, translated and edited by Dale Cooper (Grand Rapids: William B. Eerdmans Publishing Company, 1978), 11.

[9] Francis Anekwe Oborji, "Contemporary Missiology in Theological Education..., 385.; George Thomas Kurian and James D. Smith III, eds., *The Encyclopedia of Christian Literature*, Volume 1 (Lanham: The Scarecrow Press, 2010), 105.; Johannes Verkuyl, *Contemporary Missiology: An Introduction*..., 12.

[10] Francis Anekwe Oborji, "Contemporary Missiology in Theological Education...," 385.

mainstream, this initiative got an early recognition of the need to study Mission theologically and pedagogically. Later, in 1832, church historian J. T. L. Danz explicitly referenced the "study of Missions," marking one of the earliest uses of that terminology in academic circles. Despite their efforts, Missiology remained marginal within theological faculties, and these early contributions were not institutionally sustained. Nevertheless, the work of Flatt and Danz established an emerging awareness of Mission as a subject worthy of scholarly attention, paving the way for future formalization.[11]

Friedrich Schleiermacher, often regarded as the father of modern theology, significantly influenced the academic structure of theological education and contributed significantly to the development of Missiology. He proposed a fourfold division of theology into Biblical, Systematic, Pastoral, and Church History, situating Practical Theology which included Mission as an integrative component of theological training. Schleiermacher argued that theology must serve the life and witness of the Church, and thus should be inherently Missional in orientation. For him, Practical Theology was the bridge between academic theology and the living practice of faith in society, making it an appropriate home for Mission studies. His vision of a theology that actively engages the world set the stage for Missiology to be taken seriously within academic contexts, even if the term itself was not yet fully developed in his time.[12]

Gustav Warneck is widely recognized as the founding father of modern Missiology as a distinct academic discipline. A German Protestant theologian and former pastor, Warneck was appointed to teach at the University of Halle, where he established the first official university chair in Missiology in 1896.[13] His systematic and scholarly approach helped elevate Missiology from a practical church concern to a legitimate theological science. Warneck's major work, *Evangelische Missionslehre* (Evangelical Mission Theory), published in five volumes between 1892 and 1903, presented a comprehensive analysis of Mission history, theology, and methods.[14] He insisted that Missiology must be deeply rooted in biblical theology while also informed by historical and cultural studies. Warneck also emphasized the importance of documenting

---

[11] Francis Anekwe Oborji, "Contemporary Missiology in Theological Education..., 385.

[12] Klaus Detlev Schulz, "The Development of Missiology in Theological Curricula (historical survey and recent developments)," *Missio Apostolica* 17/2 (November, 2009): 85-86.

[13] K. David Udayakumar, "Methodological Issues in Missiology," in *Methodological Issues in Theological Research: An Exploration*, edited by P. G. George (Serampore: Department of Research/SATHRI, 2016), 219.

[14] K. David Udayakumar, "Methodological Issues in Missiology..., 219.

and analysing the successes and failures of past Missionary movements.[15] His work provided Missiology with both scholarly credibility and theological depth, ensuring its inclusion in university curricula across Europe and shaping the direction of Mission studies well into the 20th century.

Hans-Werner Gensichen (1915-1999) was a German Missiologist and ecumenist who played a vital role in shaping post-war Protestant Missiology.[16] As a professor at the University of Heidelberg, he worked to bridge the gap between theology and Mission by integrating biblical and systematic theology with practical Missional concerns.[17] He strongly emphasized the centrality of Christ in Mission and critiqued any separation between proclamation and social responsibility. He was a key contributor to the ecumenical movement and engaged deeply with the theology of religions, exploring how Christian witness could maintain faithfulness to the gospel while dialoguing with other belief systems. His emphasis on the 'universality of Christ' led him to argue for a Mission approach that was both theologically grounded and culturally sensitive, helping Missiology move beyond colonial assumptions into a more dialogical and relational model.

Walter Freytag (1899-1959) significantly advanced the academic credibility of Missiology in Germany, particularly through his work at the University of Hamburg and within the Evangelical Church in Germany (EKD).[18] Freytag was known for developing a Mission theology that took seriously the challenges of secularism and the growing religious pluralism in post-war Europe.[19] As the director of the Missionary Research Department of the World Council of Churches (WCC), he encouraged empirical research into the life and witness of Christian communities around the world. Freytag's major contribution was his insistence that Missiology be recognized not merely as a church practice but as a theological science worthy of academic inquiry.[20] He promoted interdisciplinary research and engaged with the sociopolitical dynamics shaping Mission, which helped institutionalize Missiology within the broader framework of theological education.

Georg Friedrich Vicedom (1903-1974) was a German Lutheran theologian and Missionary whose influential work, The Mission of God

---

[15] K. David Udayakumar, "Methodological Issues in Missiology…, 220.

[16] Klaus Detlev Schulz, "The Development of Missiology in Theological Curricula…, 90.

[17] Klaus Detlev Schulz, "The Development of Missiology in Theological Curricula…, 90.

[18] John P. Burgess, "Church-State Relations in East Germany: The Church as a 'Religious' and 'Political' Force," *Journal of Church and State* 32/1 (1990): 17–20.

[19] Klaus Detlev Schulz, "The Development of Missiology in Theological Curricula…, 90.

[20] Klaus Detlev Schulz, "The Development of Missiology in Theological Curricula…, 90.

(*Missio Dei*), became foundational for contemporary Missiology.[21] Serving in Neuendettelsau and later as a professor of Missiology, Vicedom's theological insight marked a significant shift in understanding Mission, not primarily as the Church's activity, but as God's own initiative in the world.[22] This "*Missio Dei*" framework placed Mission within the broader Trinitarian action of God, emphasizing that the Church participates in what God is already doing in history and creation. Vicedom also focused on contextualization, arguing that the gospel must be communicated in culturally relevant ways.[23] His work laid the groundwork for Missiology to be understood not just as a sub-discipline of theology but as a unifying framework that draws from and informs all areas of Christian thought and life.

Peter Beyerhaus (1929-2020) was an eminent German theologian who made significant contributions to evangelical Missiology through his teaching at the University of Tübingen and his leadership in global Mission networks.[24] Deeply committed to the authority of Scripture and the uniqueness of Christ, Beyerhaus emphasized the need for a theologically grounded and Christocentric Missiology.[25] He is known for advocating the concept of 'the kingdom of God and the Mission of the Church,' highlighting the integral relationship between salvation, Church, and the kingdom.[26] Beyerhaus was also concerned with guarding Mission from theological liberalism and religious relativism, insisting that Missiology must remain faithful to the biblical gospel.[27] His work helped shape evangelical perspectives on Mission in the context of ecumenical dialogues, defending the need for evangelism even within pluralistic theological environments.

Alexander Duff (1806-1878) was a pioneering Scottish Missionary and educational reformer in India, widely regarded as one of the first to advocate for the integration of education into Mission strategy. As the first official Missionary of the Church of Scotland to India, Duff established schools and colleges that combined Western education with Christian teaching, believing that intellectual and moral transformation would pave the way for spiritual

---

[21] F. Asensio, Review of *Missio Dei: Einführung in eine Theologie der Mission*, by G. F. Vicedom. *Gregorianum*, 40(3), 552-552.

[22] Klaus Detlev Schulz, "The Development of Missiology in Theological Curricula..., 90.

[23] Klaus Detlev Schulz, "The Development of Missiology in Theological Curricula..., 90.

[24] Klaus Detlev Schulz, "The Development of Missiology in Theological Curricula..., 90.

[25] Tony Richie, Najeeba Syeed, and Heidi Hadsell, "An Evangelical/Pentecostal Approach to Interfaith Education for Seminarians and University Students," in *Critical Perspectives on Interreligious Education: Experiments in Empathy*, edited by Najeeba Syeed and Heidi Hadsell (Leiden: Brill, 2020), 183-184.

[26] C. René Padilla, "The Mission of the Church in Light of the Kingdom of God," *Transformation* 1/2 (1984): 16-20.

[27] Klaus Detlev Schulz, "The Development of Missiology in Theological Curricula..., 90.

renewal. Duff briefly held the first academic chair in Missiology at New College, Edinburgh, where he advocated for the inclusion of Missiology in formal theological education. His insistence that Missionaries be intellectually prepared, culturally sensitive, and strategically trained laid an early foundation for Missiology as an academic discipline. Though his chair was later discontinued, Duff's vision of holistic Mission, integrating theology, education, and cultural engagement, remained influential in shaping modern Missionary training.[28]

David J. Bosch (1929-1992) was a South African Missiologist and one of the most influential Mission thinkers of the 20th century. As a professor of Missiology at the University of South Africa and a former Missionary in Transkei, Bosch brought deep pastoral experience, academic rigor, and ecumenical openness to his work.[29] His landmark book *Transforming Mission: Paradigm Shifts in Theology of Mission* (1991) synthesized historical, theological, and contextual perspectives, presenting a dynamic vision of Mission as evolving across cultural and historical paradigms. Bosch proposed that Mission must be both faithful to the gospel and responsive to the complexities of the modern world, including issues like postmodernism, pluralism, and justice. He was a key figure in promoting the *Missio Dei* understanding and is credited with revitalizing Missiology as a critical, interdisciplinary, and global theological discipline. Bosch also helped establish the influential journal *Missionalia*, contributing to Mission in the Global South.[30]

Daniel Johnson Fleming (1877-1969) was a pioneering American Missiologist and educator who significantly advanced Missiology within the theological academy in the United States. Appointed as the first full-time professor of Missions at Union Theological Seminary in New York in 1918, Fleming was instrumental in framing Mission studies as a serious theological discipline. He emphasized the role of culture, interreligious understanding, and social justice in shaping Christian witness, long before these became common themes in Missiological discourse.[31] Fleming's work anticipated many later developments in contextual theology and interfaith dialogue. By integrating biblical, historical, and sociological insights, he laid a foundation for future generations of American Missiologists and helped

---

[28] Klaus Detlev Schulz, "The Development of Missiology in Theological Curricula…, 90.

[29] John Corrie, "The Promise of Intercultural Mission," *Transformation* 31/4 (October, 2014): 291-302.

[30] Klaus Detlev Schulz, "The Development of Missiology in Theological Curricula…, 90.

[31] Paul E. Engle and Gary L. McIntosh, eds., *Evaluating the Church Growth Movement: Five Views* (Grand Rapids: Zondervan, 2004), 15-16.

shape the institutional legitimacy of Mission studies within liberal Protestant seminaries during the 20th century.[32]

Donald Anderson McGavran (1897-1990), a Missionary to India and later a professor at Fuller Theological Seminary, is known as the founder of the modern Church Growth Movement. Deeply concerned with the effectiveness of evangelism, McGavran developed research-based Mission models to understand why some churches grew while others did not.[33] His key insight was that people often come to faith most readily within their own cultural or social groups, a concept he called the "homogeneous unit principle."[34] McGavran's magnum opus, Understanding Church Growth (1970), combined theological conviction with sociological research, marking a new phase in practical Missiology. He argued that Mission should be both faithful to the gospel and focused on measurable results, such as conversions and church planting.[35] Though sometimes criticized for pragmatic tendencies, McGavran's work sparked wide global interest in the use of data, strategy, and cultural analysis in Mission, and his legacy continues to influence evangelical Missiology today.

The Shift from Missiology to Intercultural Theology

While Missiology began within specific church traditions such as: Catholic, Protestant, Orthodox, Evangelical, and Pentecostal, its focus was often shaped by the context of Western Mission to non-Western peoples. Over time, this one-way understanding of Mission proved limiting. With the rise of globalization, migration, and cultural exchange, a new approach was needed to reflect mutual learning, local agency, and cultural diversity in theological reflection and Mission practice.[36]

Intercultural Theology emerged as a response to these new realities. Rather than viewing Mission as a Western project exported to the rest of the world, Intercultural Theology sees Mission as a dialogue between cultures

---

[32] Paul E. Engle and Gary L. McIntosh, eds., *Evaluating the Church Growth Movement…*, 15-16.

[33] David Smith, "The Church Growth Principles of Donald Mcgavran," *Transformation* 2/2 (1985): 25-30.

[34] Mark Pickett, "Caste-Sensitive Church Planting: Revisiting the Homogeneous Unit Principle," *Transformation* 32/3 (July, 2015): 177-187.

[35] Mark Pickett, *Caste-Sensitive Church Planting: Revisiting the Homogeneous…*, 177-187.

[36] Victor Raj, "Missiology of Recontextualization," *Lutheran Mission Matters* 25/1 (2017): 9.

and a shared journey of faith across global Christian communities.[37] It recognizes that all theology is shaped by culture, and that no single tradition has a monopoly on truth. Thus, it values voices from the Global South, women, Indigenous communities, and marginalized groups.[38] This shift from Missiology to Intercultural Theology does not mean abandoning biblical truth. Instead, it means deepening it by seeing how God is at work in diverse contexts. It also means being open to learning from others while remaining faithful to the gospel.[39]

The Indian Context: Why Intercultural Theology is Inevitable

In India, the term "Mission" is often associated with evangelism, conversion, and even colonial power structures. This perception creates mistrust and resistance, especially in multi-religious and pluralistic settings.[40] Evangelism is an essential part of Mission, but it is not the whole. Mission also includes service, dialogue, justice, and care for creation. The current Indian context calls for a renewed understanding of Mission, one that can speak meaningfully to people of different faiths and backgrounds.[41] Intercultural Theology offers such a framework. It allows Indian Christians to reflect theologically from their own cultures, histories, and social realities, while remaining in conversation with the global Church. It encourages contextual theology, where the Bible is interpreted through the lived experiences of Indian communities, especially the poor, Dalits, women, tribals, and religious minorities.[42] Moreover, Intercultural Theology enables Mission to become more inclusive, relational, and holistic. It moves beyond a narrow view of conversion and embraces the full life-giving vision of God's kingdom where justice, peace, reconciliation, and mutual respect guide Christian witness.

---

[37] Pynhunlang N. M. Shullai, "Colonialism, Christianity and Mission Activities in India: A Postcolonial Perspectives," *International Journal of Humanities & Social Science Studies* III/V (March, 2017): 324.

[38] Judith Gruber, "Intercultural Theology as a (Post)colonial project? Reflections from Central Europe," *Intereligious Studies and Intercultural Theology* 1/1 (2017): 1-2.

[39] Ruben C. Mendoza, "Ray of Truth that Enlightens All: *Nostra Aetate* and its Reception by the FABC," *Studies in Interreligious Dialogue* 16 (2006): 149.

[40] Freek L. Bakker, "Editorial: Intercultural Theology and Globalization," *Exchange* 37 (2008): 104.

[41] Stephen B. Bevans, "What has Contextual Theology to offer the Church of the 21st Century," in *Contextual Theology for 21st Century*, edited by Stephen B. Bevans and Katalina Tahaafe-Williams (Eugene: PICKWICK Publication, 2011), 9.

[42] Freek L. Bakker, "Editorial: Intercultural Theology and Globalization…, 104.

Conclusion: A Transformative Journey for Mission Today

Missiology has come a long way from Raimon Lull's visionary emphasis on language and culture in the 13th century, through the establishment of academic Missiology by Gustav Warneck in the 19th century, to today's emerging paradigm of Intercultural Theology. This evolution reflects the Church's ongoing effort to make sense of its global calling in ever-changing contexts. Missiology is no longer seen merely as a Western, church-driven effort to "send" the gospel abroad. Instead, it has grown into a reflective, interdisciplinary, and dialogical field that embraces a diversity of cultures, voices, and experiences. In the 21st century, particularly in contexts like India, where Mission is frequently misunderstood or reduced to either proselytism or colonial legacy, the need for a deeper and more holistic paradigm is urgent. Intercultural Theology offers such a model. It recognizes that Mission today must be rooted in biblical truth, yet open to learning from and engaging with multiple cultural and religious worldviews. It encourages mutual respect, listening, and theological reflection across boundaries of difference. This does not dilute the gospel but clarifies its relevance in a pluralistic and interconnected world. In India's multi-religious and multicultural society, Intercultural Theology enables a faithful and responsible witness that avoids triumphalism and embraces humility, hospitality, and justice. It reimagines Mission as a shared journey, where both the one who proclaims and the one who receives are transformed. It affirms that Mission is not just the Church's activity but a participation in God's redemptive movement in the world. In this way, Intercultural Theology reinvigorates Missiology, making it more inclusive, relevant, and spiritually vibrant for our times.

3

Bridging Transcendence and Context
Metaphysical and Empirical Approaches in Missiology

Missiology is inherently in its very nature interdisciplinary. It draws from theology, philosophy, sociology, anthropology, and the empirical sciences to render Mission work contextually relevant and theologically grounded. This chapter explores two foundational approaches in Missiological methodology such as metaphysics and empiricism, the paradigms represent complementary dimensions as metaphysics providing ontological and transcendental depth, empiricism offering grounded, data-driven insights into Mission contexts. Thus, Missiology stands at the crossroads of various disciplines. While its primary concern remains the fulfilment of the Great Commission, its method involves reflections enriched by philosophy and social sciences. This interdisciplinary orientation ensures a contextual and holistic grasp of Mission praxis and approaches such as metaphysics and empiricism offer distinct yet collaborative contributions to Missiology.

Understanding Metaphysics

Definition and Scope

Metaphysics is a branch of philosophy that explores the most fundamental aspects of reality. It asks deep questions about what truly exists, what it means to be, and whether there are realities beyond what we can see or touch.[1] In the field of Missiology metaphysics helps us think more deeply about spiritual and divine substances and allows us to reflect on questions such as the existence and nature of God, the reality of the human soul, the presence and role of spiritual beings like angels or demons, and the

[1] C. H. Whitley, *An Introduction to Metaphysics* (London: Methuen and CO. LTD., 1964), 26.

ultimate purpose or end of all creation, and that are often described in terms of eschatology.[2] By engaging with metaphysical thought, Missiologists develop a rich understanding of the unseen dimensions of faith, helping to ground Mission work not only in social and historical contexts but also in spiritual and eternal truths.[3] This reflection strengthens the theological basis of Mission, guiding how Christians understand and communicate the message of the Gospel in a world that often focuses only on material or visible realities.

Core Concerns

The metaphysical approach in Missiology aims to explore the deeper reality behind what is seen and experienced, seeking to distinguish what is truly real from what only appears to be real. It is deeply concerned with foundational questions about truth, meaning, and ultimate purpose, questions that are at the heart of the Church's Mission.[4] This approach challenges superficial understandings of reality and invites a more profound reflection on the spiritual dimension of human life and the world. In doing so, it helps the Church understand its Mission not just as social service or cultural engagement, but as participation in a divine purpose that transcends time and space.[5] By grounding Mission in the search for what is ultimately true and meaningful, the metaphysical approach ensures that evangelization and service are rooted in a vision of reality shaped by God's presence, purpose, and plan for creation.

Metaphysical Foundations in Missiology

Missiology is enriched and deepened when informed by metaphysical reflection. Metaphysics, concerned with the ultimate nature of reality, engages foundational questions about existence, truth, purpose, and the unseen dimensions of life.[6] In the context of Christian Mission, metaphysics enables a broader and deeper vision that moves beyond empirical and pragmatic considerations, directing attention to the spiritual and ontological

---

[2] David A. White, *Derrida on Being as Presence: Questions and Quests* (Berlin: De Gruyter, 2017), 269.

[3] C. H. Whitley, *An Introduction to Metaphysics…*, 30.

[4] Jan A.B. Jongeneel, *Missiological Encyclopedia Part 1: The Philosophy and Science of Mission in the 19th and 20th centuries* (Bangalore: Centre for Contemporary Christianity, 2006), 199-200.

[5] P. Iroegbu, *Metaphysics: The Kpim of Philosophy* (Owerri: International Universities Press Ltd, 1995), 7.

[6] Kevin Schilbrack, "Myth and Metaphysics," *International Journal for Philosophy of Religion* 48/2 (October, 2000): 65-80.

realities that shape human life and divine purpose.[7] Three key metaphysical concerns that significantly enlighten the theological and practical dimensions of Missiology are the ontology of being, cosmology, and epistemology.[8] Each of these areas offers critical reflections on the relationship between humanity and God, the divine order of creation, and the means through which knowledge of God and His Mission is apprehended.[9] By engaging with these core concerns, Missiology is better equipped to articulate a vision of Mission that is rooted in eternal truth, aligned with the divine order, and responsive to the complexities of human understanding and spiritual calling.

The Ontology of Being: What Does it Mean to be Human in Relation to the Divine?

In Missiology, the ontology of being refers to understanding the nature of human existence, especially in relation to God. It asks what it truly means to be human and how human beings are connected to the divine. This involves exploring the idea that humans are not just physical bodies but also spiritual beings made in the image of God.[10] From a Christian perspective, humans are created for relationship with God and are called to participate in God's Mission.[11] These understanding shapes the way Mission is approached, emphasizing the dignity of every person, their spiritual purpose, and their need for redemption and communion with God.[12] In this way, ontological questions help clarify why Mission matters and what it aims to restore and thus brings to light the right relationship between humanity and the Creator.

Cosmology: How did the Universe Originate and what is its Divine Order?

Cosmology, in the metaphysical sense, deals with questions about the origin and structure of the universe.[13] In Missiology, the understanding of Cosmology helps to frame the universe not as a random product of chance, but as a purposeful creation of God with a divine order. The Christian Mission is rooted in the belief that God created the world out of love and

---

[7] P. Iroegbu, *Metaphysics: The Kpim of Philosophy…*, 8.

[8] Bouvert Regulas, *Christian Philosophy* (Delhi: ISPCK, 2013), 42.

[9] Bouvert Regulas, *Christian Philosophy…*, 45.

[10] Muhammad U. Faruque, "Heidegger and Mullā Ṣadrā on the Meaning of Metaphysics," Philosophy East and West 67/3 (July, 2017): 629-630.

[11] Bernard Kelly, "Metaphysics Without Ontology," *Blackfriars* 21/243 (June, 1940): 389-394.

[12] Kevin Schilbrack, "Myth and Metaphysics…, 70.

[13] John T. Brinkman, "Cosmology and Consciousness," *Buddhist-Christian Studies* 18 (1998): 135-146.

continues to sustain it.[14] This view shapes how Missionaries understand the world and their role in it. It encourages them to see creation as sacred, meaningful, and awaiting its fulfilment in God's redemptive plan.[15] Such a perspective not only deepens the theological motivation for Mission but also encourages a respectful engagement with the environment, cultures, and societies as part of God's creation.

Epistemology: How is Knowledge of God and Mission Apprehended?

Epistemology is the study of how we know, what we know, and in Missiology, it raises important questions about how people come to know God and understand God's Mission.[16] This includes examining the sources of knowledge such as Scripture, tradition, reason, and experience, and how they guide and follow in their understanding of God's will. Metaphysical epistemology also acknowledges that some knowledge comes through faith, revelation, and spiritual insight, not just through human reasoning.[17] In Mission, such an understanding helps us to clarify how people in different cultures and contexts can truly encounter and respond to the Gospel.[18] It also encourages humility in Mission practice, recognizing that full knowledge of God is always limited and dependent on divine grace. Thus, epistemology supports a Mission approach that is both intellectually grounded and spiritually open.[19]

Metaphysis and its Relevance to Missiology

Metaphysical inquiry helps deepen the understanding of *Missio Dei*, or the Mission of God, by exploring the ultimate nature and purpose of God's actions in the world. Rather than seeing Mission only as something the Church does, metaphysics reveals that Mission begins with God's very being. God is a relational and sending God, Father, Son, and Holy Spirit, whose Mission flows from God's nature as love and truth. This understanding shifts the focus of Mission from human-centred activities to participation in God's divine plan for creation. By reflecting on who God is and why God acts in history, metaphysical thought enriches Missiology

---

[14] "Cosmology," *International Journal of English Language, Literature and Humanities II/VIII* (December 2014): 356.

[15] P. Iroegbu, *Metaphysics: The Kpim of Philosophy…*, 10.

[16] David G. Ritchie, "The Relation of Metaphysics to Epistemology," *The Philosophical Review* 3/1 (January, 1894): 14-15.

[17] Andrew Seth, "Psychology, Epistemology and Metaphysics," *The Philosophical Review* 1/2 (March, 1892): 129-135.

[18] P. Iroegbu, *Metaphysics: The Kpim of Philosophy…*, 11.

[19] M. Chandraiah, "Relation Between Epistemology and Metaphysics - In the Context of Indian Philosophy," *Global Journal for Research Analysis* 11/5 (May, 2022): 63.

by showing that Mission is not optional but flows necessarily from God's essence.

Metaphysical inquiry also helps clarify the Church's ontological status that what the Church is at its core and how that relates to its Mission in the world. From a metaphysical perspective, the Church is not merely a social institution or human organization, but a spiritual body grounded in divine reality. It is the Body of Christ, a visible sign of an invisible grace,[20] called to witness to God's kingdom on earth. This ontological understanding gives the Church a unique identity and purpose, reminding it that its role is not just to serve but to embody the presence of Christ in the world. It also challenges the Church to live out its Mission with authenticity, rooted in its true being as a community shaped by the life and love of the Triune God.

Moreover, a metaphysical approach brings attention to the spiritual dimension of Mission, addressing realities that go beyond the physical and visible. Key theological concepts like sin, salvation, and eternal life are deeply metaphysical in nature, dealing with the human soul, moral responsibility, and the destiny of creation. In a world habitually focused on material concerns, metaphysical reflection reminds Missionaries that the Mission of the Church is ultimately about spiritual transformation and reconciliation with God. It helps explain why Christ's death and resurrection are central to salvation, how sin separates humanity from divine life, and what it means to hope for eternal communion with God. This focus keeps Mission grounded in its ultimate goal, that is 'to lead people into restored and eternal relationship with God.'

Metaphysical inquiry can also offer valuable frameworks for interfaith dialogue by drawing on shared philosophical categories that transcend specific religious doctrines. Concepts such as being, truth, the soul, and the transcendent are explored in many religious and philosophical traditions, including Hinduism, Buddhism, Islam, and indigenous worldviews. By engaging in dialogue at the level of metaphysical questions, Christians can find common ground with people of other faiths and discuss deep issues about existence, the divine, and human purpose. This kind of dialogue does not ignore theological differences but approaches them with respect and openness. In this way, metaphysical reflection supports peaceful and meaningful conversations that foster mutual understanding and deepen the Church's witness in a pluralistic world.

Understanding Empiricism

Empiricism is a philosophical and scientific method that gives importance to knowledge gained through direct experience, observation, and measurable

---

[20] Augustine of Hippo.

evidence. Rather than relying on abstract theories alone, empiricism focuses on what can be seen, heard, and recorded in the real world. In Missiology, empirical approaches involve systematically collecting and analysing data related to Missionary efforts. This may include studying church growth, conversion models, community development, intercultural relationships, or the impact of Mission in a particular context. Methods such as contextualized conversations (interviews), surveys, ethnographic observation, and statistical analysis are commonly used to gather insights from the field. By using empirical tools, Missiologists can better understand how Missions function in various cultural and social settings, identify challenges and opportunities, and evaluate the effectiveness of different Mission models. This practical and evidence-based approach ensures that theological reflections and Mission practices remain connected to the lived realities of people and communities. It also allows Missiology to engage more meaningfully with contemporary global issues and local contexts.

Types of Empirical Methods

Empirical research plays an important role in the study of Christian Mission by helping us to understand how Mission works in real-life situations. Instead of relying only on theological ideas or historical accounts, empirical methods involve gathering information directly from people and communities involved in Mission. This kind of research helps Missiologists explore both the visible results of Mission efforts and the deeper experiences of those affected. To achieve this empirical research uses two primary categories.

Quantitative Research

Quantitative research in Missiology focuses on collecting and analysing numerical data to understand the outcomes and effectiveness of Missionary work. This method uses tools such as surveys, questionnaires, and statistical records to measure specific aspects of Mission activity, like the number of baptisms, church attendance growth, or improvements in literacy and education due to Mission programs.[21] The data collected is then analysed using statistical techniques to identify patterns, trends, and correlations. For example, researchers might compare conversion rates in different regions or assess the impact of Mission schools on literacy rates over time.[22] Quantitative research provides a clear and objective picture of what is happening on the ground and helps Mission organizations make practical

[21] Young-Gi Hong, "Models of the Church Growth Movement," *Transformation* 21/2 (April, 2004): 101-103

[22] Haiying Long, "Research Methodology and Method," *Creativity Research Journal* 26/4 (November, 2014): 430.

decisions about where and how to focus their efforts.[23] It is especially useful for evaluating progress and setting measurable goals for future Mission methods.

Qualitative Research

Qualitative research in Missiology explores the deeper and more personal aspects of Missionary work by focusing on meaning, experience, and context rather than numbers. This approach uses interpretive methods such as contextualized conversations, focus groups, participant observation, and ethnographic fieldwork.[24] Through these methods, researchers listen to the voices of Missionaries, converts, church members, and local communities to understand how people experience and interpret the Christian Mission in their specific cultural and social settings.[25] To achieve this goal, a Missiologist might live within a community for several months to observe how local traditions interact with Christian beliefs, or conduct contextualized conversations to understand how individuals perceive the message of the Gospel.[26] Qualitative research provides rich and detailed insights that help us to grasp the complexities of religious transformation and cultural interaction. It supports a more human-centred understanding of Mission and helps shape Mission methods that are context-sensitive and relational.

Disciplines Involved in Empirical Missiology

Empirical Missiology benefits from the social sciences and provides tools and importantly perspectives that help Missiologists study Mission in real-life situations across cultures, societies, and historical periods. The fields such as anthropology, sociology, psychology, history, law, and economics, provides tools for empirical Missiology to address complex questions about how the Christian Mission is experienced, received, and practiced in diverse contexts. Each discipline contributes to a comprehensive understanding of Mission as both a spiritual and social reality.

Anthropology and Sociology

Anthropology and sociology help Missiologists understand the cultural and social contexts in which Missions take place. Anthropology focuses on the study of human cultures, customs, values, and worldviews, while sociology

---

[23] Wonsuk Ma, '*Life' in Theological Education and Missional Formation: A Reflection for a New Christian Era*, Transformation 33/1 (January, 2016), 1-5.

[24] Haiying Long, "Research Methodology and Method…, 433.

[25] Martina Prosén, "Pentecostal Praise and Worship as a Mode of Theology." In *Faith in African Lived Christianity: Bridging Anthropological and Theological Perspectives*, edited by Karen Lauterbach and Mika Vähäkangas (London: Brill, 2020), 156-159.

[26] Haiying Long, "Research Methodology and Method…, 433.

examines how people interact within social groups and institutions.[27] By focussing on these areas, empirical Missiology explores how local traditions, kinship systems, and community structures influence, and how people respond to the Christian message.[28] Anthropological research also uncovers how indigenous beliefs shape the way a community interprets the Gospel, while sociological analysis could examine how social status or group identity affects conversion and church involvement.[29] Such insights are essential for developing Mission models that are relevant to a context and respect and engage with local realities rather than impose unsuitable models.

Geography and History

Geography and history contribute to empirical Missiology by helping Missiologists to trace the movement and development of Christian Missions across time and space. Geography provides insights to map where Missions have occurred, identify regional patterns, and study how physical location, climate, or access to resources affect Mission work.[30] History provides a timeline of Missionary efforts, showing how Mission practices have evolved and how different eras and political contexts have shaped the church's outreach.[31] Thus, geography and history help Missiologists understand how past events and geographic factors influence present Mission activities.

Psychology and Pedagogy

Psychology and pedagogy are valuable to empirical Missiology because they help assess how individuals and communities receive and process teachings of faith.[32] Psychology studies human behaviour, emotions, and cognitive development, while pedagogy focuses on how people learn and are educated.[33] Together psychology and pedagogy help Missiologists to

---

[27] John M. Hitchen, "Relations Between Missiology and Anthropology Then and Now: Insights from the Contribution to Ethnography and Anthropology by Nineteenth-Century Missionaries in the South Pacific," *Missiology: An International Review* XXX/4 (October, 2002): 470.

[28] Darrell L. Whiteman, "Anthropology and Mission: The Incarnational Connection," *Missiology: An International Review* 31/4 (October, 2003): 397.

[29] Martyn Hammersley, *Reading Ethnographic Research: A Critical Guide* (London: Longman, 1998), 3.

[30] Claire Brickell, "Geographies of Contemporary Christian Mission(aries)" in *Geography Compass 6/12* (December, 2012): 725-739.

[31] Jan A.B. Jongeneel, *Missiological Encyclopedia Part 1…*, 249.

[32] Ronald L. Koteskey, *Psychology for Missionaries* (Maryland: University Press of America, 2014), 29-30.

[33] Jan A.B. Jongeneel, *Missiological Encyclopedia Part 1 …*, 231.

understand how faith is formed, how trauma or personal background affects spiritual openness, and what teaching methods are most effective in different cultural or age groups.[34] Thus, understanding psychological resistance or openness to change can shape how the Gospel is communicated in a sensitive but meaningful way. Pedagogical approaches can be used to train leaders or teach new believers in ways that connect with their experiences and helps them to face the world with openings and courage.

Economics and Law

Economics and law also provide important insights into the ethical and structural dimensions of Mission work. Economics helps Missiologists examine how poverty, wealth distribution, and development affect Mission efforts and the daily lives of the communities they serve.[35] Law provides a framework for understanding human rights, religious freedom, and social justice issues that often arise in Mission contexts. Because, a Mission working in a particular context with economic inequality or legal restrictions on religious practice must face these challenges carefully.[36] Economics and law remind and prepares Missiologists by informing that Mission is not only about spiritual transformation but also about addressing material needs, advocating for justice, and promoting the dignity of every person.[37] Thus, economics and law ensure that Mission practices are holistic, responsible, and contextually appropriate.

Empiricism and its Relevance to Missiology

Empiricism plays a crucial role in identifying the specific needs and opportunities present in diverse Mission contexts. By collecting data through surveys, interviews, and observations, Missiologists can gain a clear understanding of the social, economic, religious, and cultural conditions of a community. This helps to highlight areas where people face spiritual, material, or emotional hardships, and where the Gospel message and practical support can have the greatest impact. Such data-driven insights prevent assumptions and ensure that Mission work is grounded in the real-life situations of people rather than generalized or outdated ideas.

A major strength of empirical research is its ability to uncover how people in different cultural contexts perceive and respond to religious messages. By studying local languages, symbols, values, and traditions,

---

[34] W. L. Gooding, "Psychology and Pedagogy," *The School Review* 3/9 (November, 1895): 556-566.

[35] Jan A. B. Jongeneel, *Missiological Encyclopedia Part 1…*, 231.

[36] Jan A. B. Jongeneel, *Missiological Encyclopedia Part 1…*, 231.

[37] Eugene Allen Gilmore, "The Relation of Law and Economics," *Journal of Political Economy* 25/1 (January, 1917): 69-79.

Missiologists can adapt their methods for the communication of the Gospel in a way that are both respectful and effective. This ensures that the message is not seen as foreign or imposed, but as something meaningful within the local worldview. Empirical insights also help Missionaries avoid cultural insensitivity and build bridges of understanding that enhance receptivity and dialogue.

Empirical analysis also enables the evaluation of Mission activities and models of Mission by providing measurable indicators of their impact. Whether it is church growth, community development, or social transformation, data collection and analysis help the Missionaries to determine what methods are working and which need improvement. This kind of an empirical evaluation supports accountability, encourages learning from both successes and failures, and provides evidence for planning future initiatives. It also ensures that Mission efforts are not just to show passion about, but also practical and results-oriented.

Theological education often remains abstract or theoretical unless it engages with the realities faced in the Mission field. Empirical data provides information, facts and data about the practical challenges Missionaries and the people face such as poverty, migration, religious pluralism, or political conflict. By integrating this information, church, Mission organizations and Mission training centres develop training programs that matches the need in the context and develop the curriculum by including case studies, fieldwork, and contextual theology. This leads to better-prepared Missionaries who can minister effectively in diverse and complex settings.

Metaphysics and Empiricism in Dialogue

Metaphysics, as the philosophical study of being and Ultimate Reality, provides Missiology with a deeper understanding of the spiritual and eternal dimensions of Mission. It explores questions about the nature of God, the purpose of human life, and the meaning of salvation.[38] These metaphysical reflections help Mission work to ground in theological truth and emphasizing that Christian Mission is not just about social service or cultural exchange, but about participating in the divine plan of redemption.[39] When Missiologists reflect on metaphysical themes such as the nature of the Church, the Kingdom of God, or the concept of eternity, they gain a stronger sense of why Mission matters beyond temporal outcomes.[40] This gives Mission work a firm foundation in divine purpose and eternal hope.

---

[38] Kai Nielsen, Christian Empiricism, The Journal of Religion 61/2 (April, 1981): 146-147.

[39] Kevin Schilbrack, "Myth and Metaphysics…

[40] Bouvert Regulas, *Christian Philosophy…*, 45.

While metaphysics gives depth, empiricism ensures that Mission remains grounded in the practical realities of the world. Empiricism emphasizes observation, experience, and data to understand human behaviour and social patterns.[41] In Missiology, this means engaging with real-life contexts such as cultures, communities, and histories to make Mission efforts relevant and effective. By using tools like ethnographic research, demographic surveys, or field interviews, Missionaries can adapt their strategies to specific needs and challenges. Empiricism also promotes accountability by allowing Missions to evaluate their impact and improve their methods. Thus, empirical analysis helps Mission to be both thoughtful and responsible.

To be truly effective, a Missiologist must be able to engage both the spiritual depth of metaphysics and the practical insight of empiricism. These two approaches are not opposed but complementary. The metaphysical vision provides the 'why' of Mission, its divine purpose and eternal significance, while empirical analysis provides the 'how', the concrete ways Mission can be done effectively and meaningfully in a given context. Therefore, a Missiologist is a person who can both reflect theologically and act wisely. They can preach the Gospel with clarity about its eternal meaning while also listening carefully to people's lived experiences. This integration strengthens both Mission theory and practice, allowing for a holistic and faithful witness in today's complex world.

Conclusion

Metaphysics and empiricism, when brought together in Missiology, create a strong and balanced approach to Mission. Metaphysics helps Missiologists understand the deeper spiritual truths of God, creation, and salvation, reminding the Church that Mission begins with God's nature and eternal purpose. Empiricism, on the other hand, focuses on real-life situations, using data and observation to guide Mission work in ways that are practical, effective, and relevant to people's needs. Together, these approaches ensure that Mission is both theologically rooted and contextually appropriate. A Missiologist must therefore well-formed person who can combine theological reflection with practical engagement, allowing Mission to be a faithful witness to God's truth while responding wisely and compassionately to the realities of the world.

[41] Kenneth J. Collins, "The Method of John Wesley's Practical Theology Reconsidered," *Wesley and Methodist Studies* 9/2 (2017): 101-102.

4

Descriptive and Normative Missiology Shaping Missional Practice for the Church's Witness Today

Missiology, the study of Christian Mission, has two main functions, descriptive and normative that together help the Church understand and fulfil its calling in the world. Descriptive Missiology focuses on what has happened and is happening in Mission. It observes, records, and analyses how Mission has been understood and practiced across history and cultures. By looking carefully at patterns, models, and contexts from the Mission of Jesus and the early church to modern and post-modern approaches, it gives us a factual and historical picture of Mission work. Normative Missiology, on the other hand, asks what should be done in Mission today. It evaluates current practices against biblical truth, theological principles, and ethical guidelines. Its aim is to provide clear direction so that the Church's witness remains faithful to the gospel and relevant to the world. Normative Missiology shapes principles, methods, and standards for engaging in Mission in ways that honour God's Mission in creation, redemption, and sanctification. Descriptive Missiology provides the foundation by showing what Mission has looked like and what lessons can be learned from past and present experiences. Normative Missiology builds on this by offering a theological and practical vision for the future. Together, they help the Church develop a Missional practice that is historically informative, biblically faithful, and contextually sensitive.

The Dual Functions of Missiology

Missiology performs two closely related but distinct functions, descriptive and normative. Both are necessary for a complete understanding of the

Church's Mission. The descriptive function of Missiology involves the systematic documentation and analysis of Mission history and practice. It examines how Mission has been carried out in different times and places, recording events, identifying patterns, and interpreting contexts. This function is primarily concerned with "what is," "what actually happened" or "is happening" in the work of Mission.[1] By carefully studying historical records, Mission reports, cultural contexts, and statistical data, descriptive Missiology helps us recognise trends, understand various Mission models, and see how the gospel has engaged different societies over time. Its goal is to provide a clear, accurate picture of Mission realities so that the Church can learn from the past and present.

The normative function of Missiology moves beyond description to prescription. It asks "what ought to be" in the life and work of Mission. This function evaluates Mission activities in the light of Scripture, theological principles, and ethical standards. Its purpose is to articulate comprehensive principles, guidelines, and methods that will help the Church carry out its Mission faithfully and effectively. Normative Missiology focuses on defining the theological essence of Mission, clarifying its message, and setting priorities that align with God's redemptive purposes. While distinct, the descriptive and normative functions are not separate compartments; they inform and support each other. Without description, prescription may lack real-world grounding. Without prescription, description may fail to provide meaningful direction. Thus, descriptive and normative functions together ensure that Mission is both contextually aware and theologically sound, enabling the Church to witness to Christ with truth, relevance, and integrity.

Descriptive Missiology

Descriptive Missiology is the branch of Mission studies that critically examines how the Christian Mission has been understood, expressed, and carried out throughout history. It investigates the theological concepts, cultural adaptations, and practical strategies that have shaped Mission work in different contexts.[2] This includes the study of significant historical Mission models such as the Mission of Jesus, the Mission of the Early Church, and the approaches developed by the Eastern Orthodox tradition, the

---

[1] Olive Zhimómi, "Methodological Intersections in Missiology: An Analysis of Descriptive and Normative Methodologies," in *Methodological Issues and Research Design in Missiology*, edited by Vinod S. Sailus (Delhi: Christian World Imprints, 2024), 119.

[2] Jan A. B. Jongeneel, *Missiological Encyclopedia Part 1: The Philosophy and Science of Mission in the 19th and 20th Centuries* (Bangalore: Centre for Contemporary Christianity, 2006), 72-73.

Roman Catholic Church, and various Protestant movements.[3] It also engages with the Mission perspectives that emerged during the Enlightenment, the modern and post-modern eras, as well as ecumenical movements that seek unity and holistic Mission practice.

The primary purpose of Descriptive Missiology is to provide an accurate and objective account of Mission realities.[4] By documenting events, Mission methods, and contexts without imposing immediate judgment, it preserves a factual record that can be used for deeper analysis. This historical and empirical understanding serves as a vital foundation for theological reflection and future planning. It enables the Church to learn from both the successes and failures of past Mission efforts and to appreciate the diversity of Mission expressions across cultures and time periods.[5]

Descriptive Missiology has two main areas of application. First, it facilitates internal comparisons within the Christian tradition.[6] For example, it can compare ancient Mission methods with modern approaches, or examine the differences and similarities between Roman Catholic and Protestant Missionary efforts.[7] Second, it enables external comparisons between Christian Missions and the Missionary activities of other religious or ideological movements. By engaging in these comparative studies, descriptive Missiology not only enriches the Church's self-understanding but also sharpens its awareness of the wider religious and cultural landscape in which it operates.

Research Methods in Descriptive Missiology

Descriptive Missiology relies on a variety of research methods to gather, organise, and interpret information about Mission history and practice with accuracy, clarity, and objectivity, to build a reliable picture of Mission realities. Among the most widely used approaches are observational methods, case studies, and survey research.[8] Observation plays a central role in descriptive research, enabling the direct study of Mission contexts and activities. There are two main types of observational approaches.

---

[3] Paul Kollman, "At the Origins of Mission and Missiology: A Study in the Dynamics of Religious Language," *Journal of the American Academy of Religion* 79/2 (June, 2011): 425-426.

[4] Kate Yanina DeConinck, "The Successfulness of a Descriptive Approach: A Response to Jones and Meyer," *The Journal of Interreligious Studies* 36 (December, 2022): 59-63.

[5] Sonia Sikka, "Descriptive vs. Theological Pluralism," *Journal of the American Academy of Religion* 89/2 (December, 2021): 705-712.

[6] David Bosch, *Transforming Mission- Paradigm Shift in Theology of Mission* (New York: Orbis Books, 1991), 1.

[7] David Bosch, *Transforming Mission- Paradigm Shift in Theology of Mission…*

[8] Olive Zhimomi, "Methodological Intersections in Missiology…, 119-120.

Quantitative observation focuses on measurable, statistical data such as the number of Mission workers in a given area, church attendance rates, the distribution of Bible translations, or the reach of media-based evangelism.[9] This type of observation produces data that can be analysed statistically to reveal trends and patterns. Qualitative observation, on the other hand, concentrates on non-measured characteristics such as cultural practices, worship styles, leadership dynamics, and interpersonal relationships in Mission settings.[10] This method often involves the researcher observing naturally occurring situations without interference, allowing for an authentic portrayal of the context.

The case study method involves an in-depth examination of a particular individual, community, organisation, or event within the Mission field. It allows for an authentic, detailed exploration of specific contexts and can reveal insights into unique challenges or effective practices with caution.[11] Because they focus on a limited sample, there is a risk of researcher bias, the inclusion of atypical cases, and the temptation to make generalisations that may not apply to other contexts.[12] As such, while case studies are valuable for deep understanding, they should be complemented with broader research to ensure accuracy and balance.

Survey research is a key tool for gathering information from a large number of respondents. It employs structured questionnaires or polls to collect data on attitudes, experiences, or perceptions related to Mission work.[13] Effective surveys often combine open-ended questions, which encourage detailed, personal responses, with close-ended questions, which provide fixed response options for easier statistical analysis.[14] Surveys will be conducted in person, or any flexible methods, making them highly adaptable to different contexts.[15] In large-scale Mission studies, survey research is particularly useful for identifying broad trends, evaluating

---

[9] Jeremy Spoon, "Quantitative, Qualitative, and Collaborative Methods: Approaching Indigenous Ecological Knowledge Heterogeneity," *Ecology and Society* 19/3 (September, 2014): 7.

[10] Robert A. Witter, William A. Stock, Morris A. Okun and Marilyn J. Haring, "Religion and Subjective Well-Being in Adulthood: A Quantitative Synthesis," *Review of Religious Research* 26/4 (June, 1985): 332-333.

[11] Olive Zhimomi, "Methodological Intersections in Missiology…, 120.

[12] Katharine Jocher, "The Case Method in Social Research," *Social Forces* 7/2 (December, 1928): 203-211.

[13] Olive Zhimomi, "Methodological Intersections in Missiology…, 120.

[14] Frances Henry, "The Survey Research Design Some Practical Problems," *Anthropologica* 9/1 (1967): 51-57.

[15] Michael R. Welch, "Surveying Denominations and Congregations: An Introduction," *Review of Religious Research* 31/2 (December, 1989): 113-114.

program effectiveness, and capturing the perspectives of diverse participant groups.

Normative Missiology

Normative Missiology is the branch of Mission studies that engages in critical theological reflection on the rationale, purpose, and methodology of Mission.[16] While descriptive Missiology focuses on what has happened, normative Missiology addresses what should happen in light of the gospel and God's revealed purposes. It examines the theological foundations of Mission, clarifying the essence of the gospel message and its implications for practice.[17] Central to its scope is an understanding of God's Mission in creation, redemption, and sanctification, recognising that Mission originates in God's own nature and work.[18] Normative Missiology therefore provides the principles and guidelines that shape how the Church carries out its Mission in ways that remain faithful to biblical truth and responsive to contemporary challenges.

Normative Missiology operates in two main dimensions. First, the internal normative Missiology, grounded in the authority of the Church and its doctrinal tradition. It draws from Scripture, theology, and ecclesial teaching to define Mission priorities, strategies, and ethical boundaries. This ensures that Mission activities remain aligned with the Church's confession of faith and theological identity.[19] Second, the external normative Missiology, by contrast, is informed by the wider social and legal context. It takes into account civil laws, international human rights frameworks, and cultural norms, ensuring that Mission practice not only upholds biblical principles but also respects lawful and ethical boundaries in different contexts.[20] Together, these dimensions help the Church engage Missionally with integrity, credibility, and cultural sensitivity.

In the context of theological education, normative Missiology plays a vital role in equipping future church leaders and Missionaries to think critically and act faithfully.[21] It calls for maintaining a creative tension between the Missional dimensions, the outward, evangelistic and service-oriented focus of the Church and the Missional intention, the theological

---

[16] Olive Zhimomi, "Methodological Intersections in Missiology…, 120-121.

[17] Johannes Aagaard, "Trends in Missiological Thinking During the Sixties," *International Review of Mission* 62/245 (January, 1973): 8.

[18] Olive Zhimomi, "Methodological Intersections in Missiology…, 121.

[19] Rian Venter, "Thinking God in a Global Multi-religious Context: Trends, Challenges and Possibilities," *Journal for the Study of Religion* 31/1 (2018): 81.

[20] Rian Venter, "Thinking God in a Global Multi-religious Context…, 74, 79.

[21] Olive Zhimomi, "Methodological Intersections in Missiology…, 120-121.

and spiritual purposes that undergird Mission.[22] This tension ensures that Mission is neither reduced to mere activism nor confined to theological abstraction. Normative Missiology also safeguards theological integrity, ensuring that Mission practices are firmly rooted in the gospel while engaging meaningfully with different cultural and social contexts.[23] In this way, it prepares the Church to bear witness in ways that are both contextually relevant and theologically sound.

Research Methods in Normative Missiology

Normative Missiology employs research methods that not only analyse the current state of Mission but also propose ways to strengthen and improve its practice. Unlike descriptive approaches, which focus on documenting what is, normative research is concerned with identifying what ought to be and designing strategies to achieve it. Its methods combine theological reflection with strategic planning, ensuring that Mission work remains faithful to the gospel while addressing real-world challenges.[24]

General normative research seeks to develop "theories of practice" for Mission by articulating clear principles, guidelines, and standards. This approach is primarily conceptual, focusing on the formulation of frameworks that can guide Missional activity without necessarily implementing them directly. It may involve constructing theological models for cross-cultural engagement, ethical guidelines for evangelism, or methodological priorities for holistic Mission.[25] While these outcomes may remain at the theoretical level, they serve as essential reference points for churches, Mission agencies, and academics.

The normative case study method moves beyond theory into practical application. It identifies specific areas of weakness or opportunity within Mission work and designs interventions to address them.[26] This approach often progresses toward research and development for Mission methods, in which proposed solutions (Mission fields) are tested and refined in real contexts.[27] For instance, a normative case study might examine a Mission training program, identify gaps in cultural preparation, and implement a

[22] Thinandavha D. Mashau, "A Reformed Perspective on taking Mission and Missiology to the Heart of Theological Training," *die Skriflig* 46/2 (December, 2012): 5.

[23] Olive Zhimomi, "Methodological Intersections in Missiology…, 121-122.

[24] Olive Zhimomi, "Methodological Intersections in Missiology…, 122.

[25] Yahia Mahmoud, Anne Jerneck, Annica Kronsell and Karin Steen, "At the Nexus of Problem-Solving and Critical Research," *Ecology and Society* 23/4 (December, 2018): 3.

[26] Olive Zhimomi, "Methodological Intersections in Missiology…, 122-123.

[27] Michael Cox, "A Basic Guide for Empirical Environmental Social Science," *Ecology and Society* 20/1 (March, 2015): 8.

revised curriculum to improve cross-cultural effectiveness. Such case studies bridge the gap between Missiological understandings and Mission realities.

The research process in normative Missiology typically follows three key steps. First, problem identification involves diagnosing challenges or deficiencies in current Mission practices, whether theological, functional, or contextual. Second, formulation of improvement strategies entails developing biblically grounded and contextually appropriate solutions. Finally, testing solutions against Mission principles to ensure that any proposed changes remain consistent with the gospel and with the Church's Missiological convictions.[28] This evaluative cycle fosters continual refinement of Mission practice, helping the Church to remain both faithful and effective in its witness.

Comparative Analysis of Descriptive and Normative Missiology

Descriptive and normative Missiology represent two distinct yet complementary approaches to the study and practice of Christian Mission. Each has its own focus, methodology, and strengths, as well as limitations. A balanced understanding of both is essential for a holistic Missiological framework.

Descriptive Missiology is primarily empirical in nature, relying on observation, documentation, and analysis of Mission history and current practice. It is often inductive, moving from specific data to broader insights, and frequently ecumenical, encompassing diverse traditions and perspectives within global Christianity. Its chief strength lies in its ability to present an accurate, objective portrayal of Mission realities, revealing patterns, trends, and cultural influences without prematurely judging them. However, its limitation is that it stops short of prescribing change. Without a normative dimension, descriptive findings may remain purely academic, offering insight but not direction for improving Mission practice.

Normative Missiology, by contrast, is primarily theological and often deductive, starting from biblical principles, doctrinal convictions, and theological frameworks to determine what Mission ought to be. In different contexts, it is associated with evangelical traditions that emphasise faithfulness to Scripture and intentional gospel proclamation. Its main strength is that it provides clear guidance for Mission practice, shaping strategies, ethics, and priorities that align with God's purposes. However, if not grounded in accurate data and contextual understanding, normative Missiology risks overlooking the factual realities of Mission contexts, which can lead to impractical or culturally insensitive approaches.

[28] Olive Zhimomi, "Methodological Intersections in Missiology…, 123.

Thus, descriptive and normative Missiology should not operate in isolation. Descriptive research offers the factual foundation upon which normative principles can be applied, while normative reflection ensures that descriptive insights are translated into faithful and effective action. The integration of both approaches creates a healthy Missiological framework that is historically informed, contextually aware, biblically faithful, and practically relevant. Such a balanced methodology enables the Church to engage in Mission with both clarity of vision and sensitivity to the realities of the world it seeks to reach.

Case Study: Paul and the Athenians at the Areopagus

The encounter between Paul and the Athenians at the Areopagus (Acts 17:16-34) provides a rich biblical case study for applying both descriptive and normative Missiology. On the descriptive level, Luke records Paul's careful observation of the Athenian context such as their religious practices, philosophical interests, and cultural symbols before delivering his message. Paul notes their altar to the "unknown god" (v. 23) and engages with Epicurean and Stoic philosophers (v. 18), demonstrating attentiveness to their worldview and intellectual climate. On the normative level, Paul interprets these observations through a theological lens, affirming God's role as Creator and Sustainer of all (vv. 24-28) and confronting idolatry with the truth of God's self-revelation in Christ and the certainty of future judgment (vv. 29-31). This integration of cultural sensitivity with theological clarity produces enduring principles for cross-cultural gospel engagement: beginning with shared points of contact, affirming truths already recognized in the culture, yet faithfully proclaiming the uniqueness and demands of the gospel. The Areopagus episode thus models how Missionaries can move from cultural description to theological prescription in ways that respect the hearers while remaining faithful to the biblical message.

Descriptive Application

From a descriptive perspective, Luke's account offers detailed observations of Paul's actions, emotional state, and audience responses. Paul is recorded as waiting in Athens, becoming "provoked in spirit" upon seeing the city full of idols (v. 16). His ministry describes in multiple venues, the synagogue with Jews and God-fearing Gentiles, the marketplace with daily public discourse, and finally, the Areopagus before an elite audience of philosophers. The cultural mapping in this passage reveals a context of deep religious pluralism, with altars to numerous deities, including one "to an unknown god" (v. 23), and a rich intellectual climate shaped by Epicurean and Stoic traditions. Audience reactions vary: some mock, others express curiosity for further dialogue, and a few such as Dionysius and Damaris believe (vv. 32-34). The Mission method identified here is one of contextual engagement, where Paul skilfully uses local references, quoting Greek poets and referring to familiar cultural symbols to build a bridge toward the gospel.

Outcome of the Descriptive Application

The descriptive application of Acts 17:16-34 provides a detailed understanding of the Athenian Mission context and Paul's adaptive approach. It identifies Athens as a city steeped in religious pluralism and philosophical sophistication, with audiences ranging from devout worshipers to critical thinkers. By tracing Paul's movements, cultural observations, and audience reactions, descriptive Missiology captures the complexity of a pluralistic urban environment. It also highlights Paul's method of contextual engagement, using familiar cultural references such as the altar to the "unknown god" and quoting local poets, thereby building a bridge between the Athenians' worldview and the gospel message. This outcome equips contemporary Mission practitioners with an empirical model of how to navigate culturally diverse and intellectually engaged contexts.

Normative Application

On the other hand, the normative analysis evaluates Paul's approach in light of the gospel's theological core. Paul proclaims the Creator God as the sovereign Lord of heaven and earth (vv. 24-25), rejecting idolatry and affirming God's transcendence and providence. His contextualization is intentional and respectful as he begins where the people are, using the altar to the "unknown god" as a point of connection, yet without compromising theological truth. From this encounter, several practical Mission principles emerge. The principle of contextualization urges Missionaries to begin with the audience's own worldview and cultural symbols, using them as entry points for gospel proclamation. The principle of incarnational engagement models a readiness to enter public spaces, engage in reasoned dialogue, and participate in local discourse rather than remaining isolated from the community. The principle of theological integrity safeguards against syncretism by affirming the uniqueness of God and the exclusivity of Christ while engaging with diverse cultural settings.

Outcome of the Normative Application

The normative application produces a set of theological and strategic principles for Mission engagement in similar contexts. It affirms that Mission must begin with cultural entry points (principle of contextualization), proceed through respectful and participatory dialogue (principle of incarnational engagement), and remain grounded in the exclusive truth of the gospel (principle of theological integrity). These principles safeguard the Mission from both cultural irrelevance and theological compromise. Normative Missiology thus provides a prescriptive framework for shaping Mission strategies that are biblically faithful while being sensitive to local cultural dynamics.

Integrated Outcome

When combined, the descriptive and normative applications of Acts 17:16-34 brings out a holistic model for Mission that is both informed by context and guided by theological conviction. The descriptive approach supplies the factual and cultural insights necessary to understand a complex Mission field, while the normative approach translates these insights into actionable principles rooted in the gospel. Together, they demonstrate that effective Mission requires both an accurate reading of the cultural landscape and a steadfast commitment to theological truth. This integrated outcome equips the Church to engage in cross-cultural Mission with credibility, relevance, and faithfulness.

Perspectives on Integrating Descriptive and Normative Missiology

The relationship between descriptive and normative Missiology has been a significant topic of discussion among leading Missiologists. While the two functions serve different purposes, many scholars argue that they are most effective when used together in a complementary manner. The perspectives of David J. Bosch, Jan A. B. Jongeneel, and William J. Abraham illustrate both the necessity and the practical implications of integrating these approaches.

David J. Bosch

David J. Bosch strongly emphasised the importance of holding descriptive and normative Missiology in dynamic tension.[29] For Bosch, descriptive Missiology provides the factual grounding necessary for meaningful theological reflection, while normative Missiology offers the theological and ethical direction required for Mission practice. He warned against treating the descriptive function as a secondary task or a mere academic exercise, noting that without careful historical and contextual analysis, normative proposals risk becoming detached from reality.[30] Bosch's integration model reflects his broader vision of Mission as a holistic and contextually engaged enterprise, where the Church's understanding of "what is" must always inform its vision for "what ought to be."

[29] Olive Zhimomi, "Methodological Intersections in Missiology…, 123.

[30] Jan A. B. Jongeneel, *Philosophy, Science, and Theology of Mission in the 19th and 20th Centuries*, Part 1 (Berlin: Peter Lang, 2002), 179.

Jan A. B. Jongeneel

Jan A. B. Jongeneel critiqued approaches that reduce normative Missiology to matters of organisational structure or ecclesiastical law.[31] Drawing on Seumois' narrow definition of normative Missiology as the study of the legal framework of Missionary organisations, Jongeneel argued for a broader and more holistic understanding. He insisted that normative Missiology should encompass the entire spectrum of theological principles, ethical norms, and practical strategies that shape Mission. By widening the scope beyond institutional governance, Jongeneel affirmed that normative Missiology must remain deeply theological while still being attentive to organisational and practical realities.[32] His perspective reinforces the need for integration, since normative insights can only be fully effective when they are grounded in the descriptive study of actual Mission contexts.

William J. Abraham

William J. Abraham advocated for what he called "double vision" in Missiological reflection, keeping one eye firmly fixed on descriptive analysis and the other on normative evaluation.[33] For Abraham, the descriptive lens ensures that the Church's reflection on Mission remains rooted in accurate observation and empirical data, while the normative lens guarantees that such reflection leads to theological clarity and practical guidance. He argued that separating the two results in an incomplete and unbalanced approach: descriptive studies without normative guidance risk irrelevance, while normative prescriptions without descriptive grounding risk impracticality or cultural insensitivity.[34] Abraham's call for "double vision" aligns closely with Bosch's holistic perspective, highlighting the mutual dependence of the two functions.

The insights of David J. Bosch, Jan A. B. Jongeneel, and William J. Abraham converge on a shared conviction: descriptive and normative Missiology are most fruitful when integrated. Descriptive work ensures that normative recommendations are grounded in real-world contexts, while normative frameworks ensure that descriptive findings are translated into biblically faithful and strategically relevant action. Thus, both descriptive and normative Missiology together form a balanced approach that strengthens the Church's capacity to engage in Mission with both accuracy and theological depth.

---

[31] Olive Zhimomi, "Methodological Intersections in Missiology..., 123-124.

[32] Jan A. B. Jongeneel, *Philosophy, Science, and Theology of Mission...*, 203.

[33] Olive Zhimomi, "Methodological Intersections in Missiology..., 124.

[34] Jan A. B. Jongeneel, *Philosophy, Science, and Theology of Mission...*, 203.

Conclusion

Descriptive and normative Missiology together form the two essential pillars of Mission studies. Descriptive Missiology provides the factual foundation by carefully documenting and analysing how Mission has been understood and practiced throughout history and across cultures. It offers the Church a clear picture of Mission realities such as its contexts, patterns, successes, and challenges. Normative Missiology, in turn, provides theological and ethical direction. It evaluates Mission practice in light of Scripture, core doctrines, and moral principles, ensuring that the Church's witness remains faithful to the gospel while speaking meaningfully into contemporary contexts. When used together, these two approaches create a balanced and holistic framework for Mission studies. Descriptive analysis grounds normative prescriptions in real-world realities, while normative guidance ensures that descriptive findings lead to practical strategies that honour God's Mission. This integration enriches both academic scholarship by fostering rigorous, evidence-based theological reflection and field practice by equipping Missionaries with contextually relevant, biblically faithful strategies. Ultimately, descriptive and normative Missiology together enable the Church to be both attentive to the world it serves and obedient to the God who sends it. This balance ensures that the Church's Mission is historically informed, theologically sound, ethically responsible, and practically effective.

5

Integrating "Missiology from Above" and "Missiology from Below" Towards a Contextual Paradigm

Missiology has long wrestled with the tension between a transcendent, God-centred proclamation and an incarnational, context-sensitive engagement. 'Missiology from Above' emphasizes divine sovereignty and salvation history, situating Mission as a top-down pouring out of grace. In contrast, 'Missiology from Below' focuses on solidarity with the marginalized, community-building, and the "preferential option for the poor." Historically, both 'Missiology from Above' and 'Missiology from Below' have enriched Mission thought, yet their division has led to imbalances. Therefore, it is important to trace their origins, delineates their characteristics, and offers integrative models for the global church to face the challenges of the time such as religious pluralism and social dehumanization.

Historical and Theological Background

History plays two vital roles in the study and practice of Christian Mission. First, it records what has happened, the triumphs and the mistakes of those who have gone before. By looking back, we see how Mission efforts have succeeded when people relied on God's guidance, and how they have failed when human agendas took over. Second, history teaches us. It corrects our ideas and methods by showing where we went wrong and challenges us to learn better ways of sharing the gospel. In this way, history becomes both a mirror and a map and reflects our actions honestly and points us toward a faithful practice of Mission that depends on God rather than on our own strength or institutions. Moreover, understanding historical movements reminds the church that, even when human leaders stumble, God's purposes continue to move forward. Missionary stories whether marked by victories or setbacks reveal that divine initiative does not fail. Thus, history should inspire both gratitude for how far God has carried the Mission and humility about our ongoing need for divine direction.

The theological background begins with the term *Missio Dei*, Latin for "the sending of God," roots Mission firmly in the life of the Trinity. In classical Christian thought, God the Father sends the Son into the world, and the risen Christ sends the Holy Spirit to empower the church. From this perspective, Mission is not first a program of the church but the activity of God in restoring all creation. When describe Mission, it is unfolding what God is already doing in the world, calling people to new life in Christ and renewing communities by the Spirit's power. Thus, even though *Missio Dei* often linked with a "top-down" or "from Above" approach that emphasizing God's sovereign actions, it also supports "from Below" emphases. Theologians such as Lalsangkima Pachuau highlight that, because Mission comes from God's own heart, it necessarily includes solidarity with the poor, justice for the oppressed, and respect for every culture.[1] In other words, while God sends the gospel from on high, that sending always takes shape in local, human forms. Thus, *Missio Dei* unites divine initiative ("Above") with human participation ("Below"), showing that true Mission must hold both together.

Mission from Above

In simple terms, Missiology "from Above" describes Mission as originating with God and flowing downward into the world. This approach highlights the sovereignty of the triune God, Father, Son, and Holy Spirit, as the primary actor in sending the church out, rather than placing human effort at the centre.[2] By focusing on divine initiative, it stresses that every step of Mission depends upon God's power, purpose, and promise. At its heart, Missiology "from Above" roots itself in the great story of salvation history.[3] It begins with God's eternal purpose revealed in the Father's sending of the Son, continues through Christ's life, death, and resurrection, and reveals in the pouring-out of the Spirit at Pentecost. In this view, Mission is simply the ongoing movement of that same Trinitarian sending into new places and

---

[1] Lalsangkima Pachuau, ed., *Ecumenical Missiology: Contemporary Trends, Issues and Themes* (Bangalore: UTC Publications, 2002), 30.

[2] Jan A. B. Jongeneel, Missiological Encyclopedia, Part One: The Philosophy and Science of Mission in the 19th and 20th Centuries (Zoetermeer: Peter Lang AG, 2002), 199.

[3] Charles Van Engen, *Mission on the Way: Issues in Mission Theology* (Michigan: Baker Books, 1996), 37.

among new peoples. The church's task is not to invent Mission but to join in what the triune God is already doing in the world.

Because the initiative belongs to God, "from Above" paradigm gives priority to clear and faithful proclamation of the gospel. It upholds the necessity of personal conversion, calling people to repentance and faith in Christ.[4] Alongside preaching, it values the sacraments as visible signs of God's grace at work.[5] By keeping gospel proclamation at the central, it seeks to guard against reducing Mission to social programs or purely cultural engagement, reminding the church that spiritual renewal is its deepest concern.[6] In the "from Above" model, the church itself is the principal steward of God's sending. Local congregations and global networks are seen as the primary instruments through which the gospel is carried to every nation. Leaders, Missionaries, and laypeople alike participate under ecclesial authority, confirming that Mission remains connected to the teaching, fellowship, and discipline of the body of Christ.[7] This emphasizes accountability, shared vision, and the sacramental life of the church as the context in which Mission is both sent and received.

Critiques in Plural Contexts

In settings where many faiths and cultures meet, a Mission method that feels imposed from above can do more harm than good. Critics describe this approach as "helicopter Christology," because it swoops in with powerful assertions but creates a cloud of dust that blinds local people to its message. When proclamation comes only from a distant centre, it can seem insensitive to the real questions and values of a community, shutting down genuine conversation and mutual learning. This top-down approach also tends to highlight Jesus' divine majesty at the expense of his human life among ordinary people, making it harder for those who have never heard the gospel to see how it speaks to their daily struggles. Moreover, by overlooking the gifts and agency of local believers, it risks reducing Mission to a one-way transmission instead of a shared journey of discovery. To engage faithfully in plural contexts, Mission must therefore balance authoritative proclamation

---

[4] Joy Ann McDougall, "The Return of Trinitarian Praxis? Moltmann on the Trinity and the Christian Life," *The Journal of Religion* 83/2 (April, 2003): 177-203.

[5] William E. Sanger, "God's Means of Grace: Symbols - Sacraments," *Brethren Life and Thought* 3/1 (December, 1958): 53-59.

[6] Paul Sciberras, "Shaped by His Upbringing: Jesus' Mission in Luke 4:16-22 Aligned with Luke 2:51-52 as a Paradigm for Youth Formation, Empowerment, and Social Engagement Today," *Religions* 15/12 (January, 2024): 1-10.

[7] Davidson Razafiarivony, "A Biblical Assessment of Luther's View on Priesthood of All Believers and the Office of Ministry," *Journal of Biblical Theology* 4/3 (January, 2021): 71-90.

with deep respect for local voices and experiences that can be expressed as 'Missiology from Below.'

Missiology "from Below"

While Missiology "from Above" describes Mission as originating with God and flowing downward into the world, Missiology "from Below" begins by closely observing the daily lives of people who face hardship. Instead of bringing abstract ideas, Missiology "from Below" seeks to understand how poverty, injustice, and religious diversity shape a community's hopes and struggles.[8] In Missiology "from Below" Missionaries live within the context and share the struggles, helping with practical needs, and thus joining in community life.[9] Such an involvement not only meets material needs but also builds trust and shows that the gospel truly cares about people and their real problems. Thus, Missiology "from Below" exemplifies I Corinthians 1:22-25, that the cross becomes more than a symbol. It becomes a demonstration that God stands with those whom society has pushed aside, giving them a message of both present comfort and future hope.[10]

A key conviction in Missiology "from Below" model is the 'Preferential Option for the Poor' that Jesus consistently reached out to society's most vulnerable.[11] Taking seriously Matthew 25:42-46, Mission "from Below" insists that feeding the hungry, visiting prisoners, comforting the sick, and sheltering the homeless are not optional but central to living out the gospel. Such a focus does not mean neglecting other ministries; rather, it places justice and compassion at the heart of Mission. By prioritizing those in greatest need, the church echoes Jesus' own ministry and demonstrates in practical ways that God's Kingdom breaks down barriers between rich and poor, powerful and powerless.

Building on its solidarity with the poor, Missiology "from Below" paradigm often adopts both liberationist and dialogical methods. Liberationist theology sees Christ as one who frees people from political and economic chains, urging Christians to work toward political change and systemic justice.[12] Dialogical Mission, on the other hand, emphasizes respectful

---

[8] David J. Bosch, *Transforming Mission Paradigm Shifts in Theology of Mission* (New York. Orbis Books, 2011), 390.

[9] Kennedy Dhanabalan, *Biblical Perspectives on Mission, Mission Mandate - 2018* (Chennai: Mission Educational Books, 2018), 172.

[10] Jooseop Keum, "Together Towards Life: An Introduction to the New WCC Mission Statement," *Swedish Missiological Themes* 101/3-4 (2013): 295.

[11] Julia Fleming, "The Right to Reputation and the Preferential Option for the Poor," *Journal of the Society of Christian Ethics* 24/1 (Spring/Summer, 2004): 73-87.

[12] Roger Haight, "Liberation and Spirituality," *Buddhist-Christian Studies* 34 (2014): 135.

conversation with people of other faiths and listening deeply to their beliefs and experiences.[13] Thus, liberationist and dialogical approaches in Missiology "from Below" perspective remind the church that Mission is not just about speaking but also about hearing, learning, and acting together for the common good.[14] Moreover, by advocating earth-conscious stewardship, Missiology "from Below" extend God's care to all creation, affirming that justice for people includes care for the planet.

Contributions and Limitations

The "from Below" approach powerfully recovers the church's prophetic role, calling attention to social injustice and urging active solidarity with the poor and oppressed. It brings fresh energy to Mission by showing that faith must engage real human suffering and work for systemic change. However, if released from a clear sense of divine calling, this model can drift toward becoming merely a charitable or political movement. Without grounding in the *Missio Dei*, that Mission is ultimately God's own sending, there is a danger that human effort overshadows God's grace. Thus, a balanced Missiology must therefore weave together both divine initiative and human solidarity, ensuring that acts of compassion flow from, and point back to, the source of all life and hope.

Models of 'Missiology from Above' and 'Missiology from Below'

To bring together "from Above" and "from Below" Missions, scholars have offered several images or models. Each model highlights a different way that Christ's life and the church's work can balance the heavenly and the human, combining lofty vision with humble presence. Important models are the 'Helicopter vs. Bullock-Cart Christology' of S. J. Samartha, which contrasts rapid top-down proclamation with slow, community-grounded growth, the 'Mountain to Valley' image of Jooseop Keum, which calls for descent from transcendent proclamation into grassroots engagement, and the 'Eagle and Rooster/Hen Model,' of Vinod S. Sailus, which pairs wide-ranging vision with close-in caretaking. Each of these helps us see how Mission can hold together doctrine and practice, authority and empathy, transcendence and immanence.

Helicopter vs. Bullock-Cart Christology of S. J. Samartha

S. J. Samartha contrasts two styles of Mission outreach. The 'Helicopter Model' represents a quick, top-down delivery of Christian teaching. Like

---

[13] S. Wesley Ariajah, "Interfaith Dialogue," in *Dictionary of the Ecumenical Movement* (Geneva: WCC Publications), 285.

[14] William Cenkner, "Mission and/or Dialogue: A Roman Catholic Perspective," *Buddhist-Christian Studies* 17 (1997): 130-139.

a helicopter dropping supplies, it arrives with much power but can leave a cloud of dust, making it hard for locals to see clearly and feel welcomed. Such an approach often ignores local cultures and wisdom, creating distance rather than genuine relationship. In contrast, the 'Bullock-Cart Model' moves slowly and steadily along local paths. It travels with the rhythms of village life, allowing deep listening, mutual learning, and respectful adaptation of the gospel to cultural forms. By staying grounded, the bullock-cart style builds trust and shows that Christian faith can live within local stories and practices.[15]

Mountain to Valley Model of Jooseop Keum

Jooseop Keum offers the 'Mountain to Valley' image to describe how Mission must both proclaim and participate. From the mountain, the church enjoys a high view of God's nature, salvation history, and the universal scope of Christ's lordship. From here, it sees the big picture and hears the call to global Mission. But true obedience means descending into the valley and stepping into concrete human needs, daily struggles, and diverse cultures. The valley is where real people live, with their joys and pains. By journeying from mountain to valley, Missionaries keep their vision of God's greatness while also embracing the gritty details of life among those they serve.[16]

Beyond-the-Wilderness Model of Mission by Vinod S. Sailus

The "Beyond-the-Wilderness Model" draws from Moses' daring act of leading his flock past the familiar grazing lands into the uncharted territory of God's Mountain (Exodus 3:1). In ancient shepherding, such a move was unheard of, sheep were kept within safe limits, but Moses chose a path of risk, vision, and encounter. This journey reflects a Mission approach that refuses to be confined by tradition or fear, pressing instead into spaces where God's glory can be revealed not only to the leader but to the whole community. In the present-day Indian context, going "beyond the wilderness" means confronting deep social wounds: caste discrimination, religious intolerance, poverty, ecological crisis, gender injustice, fundamentalism, corporate exploitation, media distortion, and the politicization of religion. Like Moses with his sheep, the church is called to guide people into God's liberating presence, not avoiding the difficult terrain but walking through it together.

---

[15] S. J Samartha, *One Christ-Many Religions. Toward a Revised Christology* (New York: Orbis Books, 1992), 132.

[16] Jooseop Keum, "Mission as an Invitation to the Feast of Life: Re-visioning the Ecumenical Understanding and Practice of Mission in the 21st Century," in *Contextual Theology for the 21st Century*, edited by Stephen B. Bevans and Katalina Tahaafe-Williams (Eugene: PICKWICK Publication, 2011), 120-123.

This model combines prophetic courage with pastoral care, insisting that Mission must engage the hardest realities of society while keeping its eyes fixed on the mountain of God.[17]

Eagle and Rooster/Hen Model of Vinod S. Sailus

Eagle and Rooster/Hen Model is a newer approach that pairs two birds to capture the dual nature of Mission. The Eagle Model soars high above, using sharp vision to spot new Mission fields and moving swiftly to proclaim the gospel. It represents the "from Above" perspective: strong, far-seeing, and quick to act. Yet, from that height, the eagle may miss the needs and voices of ordinary people below. The Rooster/Hen Model, by contrast, lives at ground level among the flock. It nests in the soil, pecks through what others discard, and turns scraps into nourishment. The rooster warns of danger with its crow, while the hen gathers her chicks close. This image symbolizes "from Below" Mission, close presence, care for the weak, and transformation that begins in everyday life. Thus, the eagle and the hen remind us that Mission needs both wide vision and rooted engagement, blending transcendence with compassionate immanence.[18]

Toward Integration in the *Missio Dei*

To hold together the "from Above" and "from Below" approaches, the church must root its Mission in the *Missio Dei*, God's own sending. In this unity, divine initiative and human response work in harmony. Because, firstly, healthy Mission begins when each paradigm learns from the other. The "from Above" approach can challenge "from Below" methods to avoid reducing faith to social programs, while "from Below" can remind "from Above" to stay sensitive to local cultures and suffering. This ongoing dialogue prevents either model from becoming rigid or one-sided, fostering a balanced Mission that listens as well as proclaims.

Secondly, a balanced Mission depends on understanding Christ in both heavenly and human dimensions. Holistic Christology affirms Christ's cosmic lordship, his authority over all creation, and also his deep solidarity with humanity through the Incarnation. In practice, this means preaching the gospel with confidence in its power to save, while also living out Christ's

---

[17] Vinod S. Sailus, "The Hermeneutical Spiral and Intercultural Theology Convergences for Reimagining Theological Education in India," *NCC Review* CXXXVIII/8 (September, 2018), 25.; Suneesh S. S., "Bridging Theory and Contextual Realities Exploring Mission from Below," in *Methodological Issues and Research Design in Missiology*, edited by Vinod S. Sailus (Delhi: Christian World Imprints, 2024), 146.

[18] Vinod S, Sailus, "The Hermeneutical Spiral and Intercultural Theology..., 32.; Suneesh S. S., "Bridging Theory and Contextual Realities Exploring Mission from Below..., 146-147.

compassion among people in need. Mission thus should integrate theological reflection on both aspects, so that we articulate the full gospel, one that declares Christ as King, yet serves him by serving the least.

Third, to apply above-and-below insights in diverse settings, Mission must use contextual hermeneutics, interpreting Scripture and theology through the lens of local cultures. Models such as Mountain-to-Valley and Eagle-and-Rooster provide practical frameworks that enables Missionaries to start with a clear overview of biblical truth (the mountain or the eagle's height) before descending to live out that truth in specific communities (the valley or the hen's ground level).

Finally, sustainable integration requires training the church, its leaders and members to live out both proclamation and service. Ecclesial formation programs should include courses on theology and evangelism alongside hands-on community development and justice work. Small groups and congregational ministries can practice joint worship and outreach events, combining teaching with acts of compassion. Through mentoring, peer accountability, and reflective study of Mission history, the church develops habits that weave doctrine and justice into everyday life, symbolizing the *Missio Dei* in word and deed.

Conclusion

In combining "Missiology from Above" and "Missiology from Below," the church learns to honour both God's sovereign plan and Christ's close presence among people and makes clear that the balanced Mission does not choose only proclamation or only service, rather it holds both together in every context. When we speak of Jesus as King and also serve him by feeding the hungry, we show the fullness of the gospel. By adapting our message with respect for local cultures, we prove that Christianity is neither foreign nor forceful but life-giving and deeply human. This integrated approach calls us to move freely between high vision and humble action that helps us to both look upward for strength in God's eternal purposes and stoop downward to embrace the struggles of those on society's margins. By doing both, we become a church that not only tells the story of God's saving work but also lives it out in practical love. Such a Missional stance transforms both the church and the world and transforms the churches into the communities of learning and service, where doctrine inspires justice and compassion deepens faith. Ultimately, the integration of "Missiology from Above" and "Missiology from Below," reflects the very nature of the *Missio Dei*: a God who reigns in glory and yet draws near to redeem every person and every place.

6

Power, Practice, and Perspective
Mission History from "Above" and "Below"

Mission history has long been written in two main ways. The first way is "from above" that tells the story of Missionaries and colonial leaders, focusing on official reports, big events, and the decisions made in distant Mission offices. This top-down view often highlights grand achievements, such as new schools, hospitals, or churches, but it can overlook how people on the ground actually responded. The second way is "from below" that looks at ordinary people, local voices, and grassroots experiences, paying attention to the daily lives of converts, the ways communities adapted Christian practices, and even the quiet acts of resistance. By studying both approaches side by side, we gain a fuller, more honest picture that integrates not only the plans and strategies but also the hope, struggle, and creativity of the men, women, and children who lived through these changes. Together, both 'Mission History from Above' and 'Mission History from Below' help us understand how Christianity truly spread and how it was shaped by the people it touched.

Mission History "From Above"

From "above" histories are often written by European colonizers or by the Missionary societies they supported. In this "top-down" view, Missionaries are presented as civilizing heroes who brought faith, schools, and hospitals to distant lands.[1] Writers of Mission history from above depend deeply on letters the Missionaries sent to home, detailed journals, and official reports,

[1] Renison Muchiri Githige, "The Mission State Relationship in Colonial Kenya: A Summary," *Journal of Religion in Africa* 13/2 (1982): 110-111.

documents that celebrate every new church built or language translated.[2] These sources proudly record statistics of conversions, stories of Mission expansion, and awards given to Missionaries. But because the focus stays on the big picture, plans drawn up in Mission offices, successes celebrated at annual meetings, everyday realities on the ground get little attention. In such a "top-down" approach, writers rarely included about the farmers who struggled to tend Mission activities, the children who adapted lessons in a foreign tongue, or the elders who quietly questioned foreign customs.[3] In short, "from above" accounts can leave out local dreams, doubts, and hardships, offering a one-sided story of triumph without the fuller context of human experience.

Features of "above" Histories

Mission history has often been written from the perspective of those in power, especially European Missionaries and colonial officials. Such narratives tend to reflect the values, interests, and assumptions of Western cultures, especially during the colonial era. As a result, they often reinforce ideas of European superiority, support imperial agendas, and rely heavily on official written records while dismissing local perspectives.

Eurocentric Bias

"Above" histories often show a strong Eurocentric bias, meaning they are written from a Western point of view and treat European culture as more advanced or civilized than others.[4] This bias leads to the portrayal of European Missionaries as heroes who brought progress, education, and religion to the 'uncivilized' lands. Non-European cultures are often described in negative or simplistic ways, ignoring their rich traditions and complex societies. For example, many early Mission records in Africa described African religious practices as 'pagan' or 'superstitious' without trying to understand their deeper meanings.[5] This kind of writing reinforced the idea that European ways were the only right or rational ones, while local cultures were seen as needing correction or replacement.

---

[2] Samuel Escobar, "Mission from the Margins to the Margins: Two Case Studies from Latin America," *Missiology: An International Review,* 26/1 (August, 1998): 88.

[3] Felix Wilfred, "Mission, Christian Witness and Theological Education Today," *Bangalore Theological Forum* 40/1 (September, 2008): 145.

[4] Renison Muchiri Githige, "The Mission State Relationship in Colonial Kenya..., 110-111.

[5] David Maxwell, "Writing the History of African Christianity: Reflections of an Editor," *Journal of Religion in Africa* 36/3-4 (2006): 379.

Imperial Interests

Missionary reports during colonial times often aligned with imperial interests, helping justify and support foreign rule. These reports portrayed Mission work as part of a larger 'civilizing Mission, suggesting that colonialism was not only about political control but also about helping native people improve their lives.[6] Missionaries were often seen as bringing moral and spiritual improvement, which made colonial governments appear more humane. For example, in British-ruled India, Missionaries reported that converting Indians to Christianity helped them become more disciplined and moral citizens.[7] Such narratives helped defend British control as beneficial and necessary, even when it involved exploitation or violence. These connections between Mission work and empire reveal how religious efforts were sometimes used to support colonial agendas.

Authority of Sources

"Above" histories usually rely on written documents from church archives, colonial administrators, or Missionary societies, treating them as the most reliable sources. This approach overlooks other types of evidence, especially oral traditions, local languages, or writings from indigenous perspectives. As a result, the voices of local people are either absent or filtered through a Western lens. For example, in the Solomon Islands, much of the early Mission history was written by Missionaries who kept detailed journals, but these journals rarely included native viewpoints.[8] Local stories, songs, and oral histories that reflected how islanders understood or responded to the Missionaries were ignored. This selective use of sources limits the full picture of what really happened and silences the experiences of those being Missionized.

Methodological Issues in Writing Mission History "From Above"

Writing Mission history "from above" involves several important methodological problems that affect the accuracy, fairness, and depth of historical understanding. These issues arise because this approach mainly

---

[6] A. M. Mundadan, "Changing Approaches to Mission Historiography: A Study with Special Reference to India," in *Ecumenical Missiology: Contemporary Trends, Issues and Themes*, edited by Lalsangkima Pachuau (Bangalore: The United Theological College, 2002), 3.

[7] Ravinder Salooja, "Mission Justifying Colonial Violence," in *Climbing High Mountains: Colonial Entanglement & Postcolonial Reflections*, edited by Ravinder Salooja (Malawi: Luviri Press, 2024), 103-117.

[8] David Hilliard, "Colonialism and Christianity: The Melanesian Mission in the Solomon Islands," *The Journal of Pacific History* 9 (1974): 93-116.; Moore Clive, *Making Mala: Malaita in Solomon Islands, 1870s-1930s* (Canberra: ANU Press, 2017), 230.

relies on the voices, views, and records of powerful such as European Missionaries, church leaders, or colonial administrators. As a result, it often presents a one-sided picture that overlooks the experiences of local communities.

Over-reliance on Official Records

Mission history "from above" depends heavily on written records such as church reports, Missionary journals, and colonial documents. These sources are often seen as objective or authoritative, but in reality, they reflect the views and goals of those who produced them. Missionaries and church leaders often wrote to impress donors or gain support, so their accounts may exaggerate successes and hide failures.[9] These documents rarely show how local people actually experienced Mission work. Because this approach gives so much importance to official texts, it risks ignoring alternative forms of evidence like oral history, local art, or non-written cultural practices that could offer a holistic picture.

Heroic Narratives and Success Bias

Another common issue is the way "from above" history tends to glorify Missionaries and present them as heroes who brought light, truth, and 'civilization' to the uncivilized world. This creates what is called a "success bias," where the focus is on positive outcomes like conversions, church growth, or new schools, while problems and resistance are left out.[10] Such narratives can oversimplify complex situations, making it seem like Mission work was always welcome or effective. In reality, there were many difficulties, including rejection by local communities, cultural misunderstandings, and even conflict. Ignoring these aspects creates a false impression of smooth progress and hides the struggles involved.

Lack of Local Perspectives

Histories written "from above" often fail to include the voices of the people who were most affected by Missionary work such as local converts, non-converts, and communities in Mission areas. Their beliefs, feelings, and actions are usually described through the eyes of outsiders rather than through their own words.[11] This leads to an imbalanced narrative where local agency is minimized or distorted. Without including local perspectives, Mission history becomes incomplete and risks reinforcing colonial or racial

---

[9] Ravinder Salooja, "Mission Justifying Colonial Violence…

[10] David R. Syiemlieh, "Colonial Encounter and Christian Missions in North East India," *Proceedings of the Indian History Congress* 73 (2012): 509-527.

[11] Bhangya Bhukya, "The Mapping of the Adivasi Social: Colonial Anthropology and Adivasis," *Economic and Political Weekly* 43/39 (September-October, 2008): 103, 105-109.

stereotypes. It also prevents us from understanding how local people shaped Christianity in their own ways, which is essential to grasp the full story of Mission encounters.

Cultural Misrepresentation

Missionary writers often misunderstood or misrepresented local cultures because they viewed them through a Western or colonial lens. They sometimes described local customs as "primitive," "pagan," or "evil," without trying to understand their deeper meanings. As a result, "from above" histories may carry cultural prejudices that distort the truth.[12] These misrepresentations influence how entire societies are remembered and judged in history. If historians repeat these accounts without question, they continue to spread stereotypes and inaccurate information. A careful and critical approach is needed to avoid repeating these cultural biases.

Ignoring Power Dynamics

Finally, Mission history "from above" often overlooks the power dynamics at play between Missionaries and local communities. It tends to present the Mission encounter as a spiritual or religious exchange, without acknowledging the political, economic, and social power that Missionaries often held especially in colonial contexts.[13] This creates a partial view of Mission work as neutral or purely religious, when in fact it was often tied to larger systems of colonial control.[14] Ignoring these power structures limits our ability to see how Mission efforts were shaped by, and sometimes helped to maintain, inequality and domination. Thus, by relying mainly on elite voices, ignoring local perspectives, and failing to question cultural and political bias, Mission history "from above" presents a narrow and often distorted version of events.

Mission History "From Below"

"From below" history takes a different approach by focusing on the lives and experiences of ordinary people rather than those in positions of power, such as Missionaries, colonial officials, or church leaders.[15] This

---

[12] Karen Chancey, "The Star in the East: The Controversy over Christian Missions to India, 1805-1813," *The Historian* 60/3 (Spring, 1998): 507-522.

[13] James P. Alter, "American Presbyterians in North India: Missionary Motives and Social Attitudes under British Colonialism," *Journal of Presbyterian History (1962-1985)* 53/4 (Winter, 1975): 291-312.

[14] V. Subramaniam, "Consequencies of Christian Missionary Education," *Third World Quarterly* 1/3 (July, 1979): 129-131.

[15] Andrea Sterk, ""Representing" Mission from Below: Historians as Interpreters and Agents of Christianization," *Church History* 79/2 (June, 2010): 271-304.

method gives attention to voices that have long been ignored or silenced in traditional Mission histories, especially indigenous converts, women, lower-caste groups, enslaved peoples, and others who were marginalized by both colonial and religious systems.[16] Rather than celebrating grand Missionary achievements or focusing only on church growth, "from below" history looks at how Christianity was received, questioned, resisted, and reshaped by local communities.[17] It highlights the importance of everyday life, how people merged Christian teachings with local beliefs, how women created new spaces for faith and leadership, or how converts used religion to challenge social injustices.

This perspective values oral histories, folk traditions, local writings, and community memories, the sources that are often dismissed by "above" histories.[18] It recognizes that Mission work was not just a one-way act of giving but involved complex, two-way relationships between Missionaries and local people. Influenced by postcolonial and subaltern studies, "above" histories try to decolonize how we write history.[19] It challenges the assumption that Europeans were always in control and shows that indigenous people had agency, they made choices, shaped their faith, and sometimes resisted colonial structures through subtle or open forms of protest. By doing so, "from below" history offers a balanced, inclusive, and truthful account of the Mission experience.

Important Characteristics of "Below" Histories

"Below" histories emphasize local experiences and perspectives by highlighting key themes such as contextual Mission, liberation theology, marginalized voices, and oral traditions. Contextual Mission means sharing and living out the gospel in a way that connects deeply with the local culture and people. Instead of bringing a ready-made, foreign version of Christianity and forcing it onto others, Missionaries and believers work together to understand how the gospel speaks within their own cultural setting. This approach respects local customs, values, and spiritual insights, and avoids treating European or Western Christianity as the only correct form.[20] For example, in Africa, some churches have developed worship styles that

---

[16] A. M. Mundadan, "Changing Approaches to Mission Historiography..., 7.

[17] Andrea Sterk, ""Representing" Mission from Below: Historians as Interpreters..., 7.

[18] A. M. Mundadan, "Changing Approaches to Mission Historiography..., 7.

[19] Rollin G. Grams, "Transformation Mission Theology: Its History, Theology and Hermeneutics," *Transformation* 24/3-4 (July & October 2007), 193-212.

[20] Sam Nesamony, Missionaries, "Literacy and Intellectual Consciousness in South Travancore," *Proceedings of the Indian History Congress* 77 (2016): 651-664.

include traditional music, dance, and local languages.[21] These churches still follow Christian teachings, but they express their faith in ways that are familiar and meaningful to their own people. Contextual Mission allows Christianity to take root in diverse cultures without erasing their identities.

Liberation theology views Christian faith not only as a spiritual journey but also as a powerful tool for confronting and overcoming injustice. It emphasizes God's concern for the poor and oppressed and calls believers to take action against systems that cause suffering.[22] This approach often arises in contexts of poverty, violence, or discrimination, where people are struggling to survive and be heard. For example, in Latin America, liberation theology became influential during the 20th century when church leaders and theologians began working with poor communities to resist political oppression and economic inequality.[23] They read the Bible as a story of God siding with the oppressed, from the Exodus to Jesus, and used their faith to organize for social change. Thus, liberation theology gives hope and purpose to those fighting for dignity and justice.

As fresher approaches to Mission history, the voices of marginalized communities are brought to the centre. These include Dalits, tribal peoples, and women groups that were often overlooked or silenced in earlier records. Listening to their stories allows us to understand how they experienced the gospel in their own words and contexts. Instead of being passive recipients of Mission work, many of them were active participants who reshaped Christian faith according to their needs and struggles.[24] For example, many Dalit Christians in India have interpreted the message of Jesus as a call for equality and liberation from caste oppression. Their testimonies and songs reflect deep faith, resistance, and a desire for social change.[25] By paying attention to these voices, Mission history becomes more inclusive and truthful, showing how the gospel interacted with real lives at the margins of society.

Oral traditions are also important as part of "from below" history because they preserve the memories, values, and beliefs of communities through spoken stories, songs, and rituals. In many cultures, especially

---

[21] Robert Strayer, "Mission History in Africa: New Perspectives on an Encounter *African Studies Review* 19/1 (April, 1976): 1-15.

[22] William Cosgrave, "The Theology of Liberation," *The Furrow* 37/8 (August, 1986): 506-516.

[23] Daniel H. Levine, "Assessing the Impacts of Liberation Theology in Latin America," *The Review of Politics* 50/2 (Spring, 1988): 241-263.

[24] Dana L. Robert, "Voices of the Poor in Missions History," *Missiology: An International Review* 28/3 (2000): 321-34.

[25] Prakash Louis, "Dalit Christians: Betrayed by State and Church," *Economic and Political Weekly* 42/16 (April, 2007): 1410-1414.

those with limited written records, oral history is the main way knowledge is passed from one generation to the next.[26] These stories often contain rich spiritual insights and reveal how people understood and lived out their faith in everyday life. Elders have passed down stories about how their ancestors first encountered Christian Missionaries, accepted or resisted their teachings, and blended new beliefs with traditional practices.[27] Such oral narratives offer a valuable counterpoint to official Mission reports, which often ignored or misrepresented local experiences. By valuing oral traditions alongside written sources, we gain a fuller, more respectful view of how Christianity spread and took shape in different places.

Methodological Issues in Writing Mission History "from Below"

Writing Mission history "from below" is an important effort to uncover the experiences of marginalized communities who were often ignored in traditional accounts. However, this approach brings its own set of methodological challenges. Unlike "from above" histories that rely on abundant official records, "from below" histories must seek out hidden or alternative sources such as oral traditions, community memory, and local knowledge. This challenges historians to tackle with issues such as limited written records, biased documents, cultural translation, and complex personal identities. These challenges make the task more difficult, but also more rewarding, as it leads to a dynamic and more accurate understanding of how Mission work was lived and shaped by people at the grassroots level.

Source Scarcity

One of the biggest problems in writing Mission history "from below" is that there are very few written records from the perspective of ordinary people. The voices of Dalits, tribal communities, women, and other marginalized groups are often missing because they did not have the same access to writing or education as Missionaries or upper-caste converts. Their stories were usually passed down through spoken word, such as through songs, stories, or community memories, rather than written down in books or church archives. These oral sources are harder to find and are sometimes forgotten over time.[28] As a result, historians have to work harder to recover these voices, using interviews, local traditions, and cultural clues. This takes

---

[26] Robert Harms, "Oral Tradition and Ethnicity," *The Journal of Interdisciplinary History* 10/1 (Summer, 1979): 61-85.

[27] Sitakant Mahapatra, "Oral Tradition: Words, Signs and Gestures," *Indian Literature* 37/5 (September-October, 1994): 69-78.

[28] P. M. Mercer, "Oral Tradition in the Pacific: Problems of Interpretation," *The Journal of Pacific History* 14/3 (1979): 130-153.

time and care, but without it, our understanding of Mission history would remain incomplete and one-sided, focusing only on those in power.

Bias in Records

Most of the Mission records that have survived were written by European Missionaries, colonial officers, or elite Indian Christians. Because of this, these documents often reflect the views and interests of those in authority. They tend to present Mission work as successful and helpful, and often ignore the struggles, doubts, or resistance of the local people.[29] These records may include numbers and statistics, but not the real-life stories or feelings behind them. Historians have to be very careful when using such sources, they need to read between the lines and ask what is missing or left unsaid. This means looking beyond what is written, questioning who wrote the record and why, and trying to piece together a fuller story that includes the voices of those left out.

Translation Problems

Another challenge is the difficulty of translation, not just of language, but of ideas. Western scholars often use Christian theological terms and categories that make sense in their own culture but do not always fit local beliefs or practices.[30] When historians try to explain indigenous Christian faith using these outside terms, they might misunderstand or misrepresent what people actually believe.[31] Local communities may combine Christian ideas with traditional beliefs in ways that are meaningful to them but are hard to explain using Western theology. This creates confusion and leads to unfair judgments. To avoid this, historians need to be aware of local worldviews and willing to learn from them, instead of forcing everything into foreign frameworks.

Complex Identity

People who became Christians during the Mission period did not have simple identities. They were often handled many roles at once as Christians, as members of local castes or tribes, and as subjects of colonial rule. These different identities could sometimes be in conflict or change depending on

---

[29] G. M. Trevelyan, "Bias in History," *History New Series* 32/115 (March, 1947), pp. 1-15

[30] Saurabh Dube, "Colonial Registers of a Vernacular Christianity: Conversion to Translation," *Economic and Political Weekly* 39/2 (January, 2004): 161-171.

[31] Gerald A. Larue, "Another Chapter in the History of Bible Translation," *Journal of Bible and Religion* 31/4 (October, 1963): 301-310.

the situation.[32] For example, people might follow Christian beliefs at home, but still take part in local customs for social reasons (Multiple Religious Belongings).[33] These overlapping roles make it difficult to write a single, clear story about their lives. Historians must avoid putting people into fixed boxes like "Christian" or "tribal," and instead show how individuals moved between identities. This makes the history more honest and shows the complex realities of how people lived during Mission encounters.

Significance for Mission Studies

Studying Mission history by combining both "from above" and "from below" approaches bring great value to the field of Mission studies. When we only focus on the writings of Missionaries, Mission boards, or colonial records, we get only part of the story, usually the part told by those in positions of power. These sources help us understand the larger picture of Mission plans, strategies, and how institutions worked. However, they often miss the experiences of the people who were most affected by Mission activity such as ordinary converts, local leaders, women, lower-caste groups, and tribal communities.

By including "from below" perspectives, we learn how people received, adapted, or resisted Christian teachings in their own cultural settings. It helps historians and Missiologists to see how power, culture, and faith came together in complex ways, not just through official actions, but also through everyday choices and experiences. This balanced approach helps modern Mission to avoid repeating mistakes from the past, such as ignoring local voices or promoting foreign values. It teaches that real Mission work must involve listening carefully, respecting culture, and empowering local communities to shape their own expressions of faith. In this way, historical study becomes not just an academic exercise but a guide for doing Mission today with greater sensitivity and justice.

Conclusion

Mission history becomes more accurate, inclusive, and meaningful when we bring together both the "from above" and "from below" viewpoints. The "from above" approach provides valuable insights into the policies, goals, and achievements of Missionary societies and colonial powers. It helps us understand how Missions were planned, funded, and expanded globally. On the other hand, the "from below" approach brings out the voices of those on the ground, how individuals and communities experienced Mission

---

[32] Susan VanZanten, "Introduction: African Narrative and the Christian Tradition: Storytelling and Identity," *Christianity and Literature* 61/3 (Spring, 2012): 368-376.

[33] Michelle Voss Roberts, "Religious Belonging and the Multiple," *Journal of Feminist Studies in Religion* 26/1 (Spring, 2010): 43-62.

efforts, how they responded with faith or resistance, and how they shaped Christianity in their own unique ways. By combining these two methods, we get a clear understanding of how Christianity spread across different cultures and places. Thus, we move beyond just praising Missionary efforts or highlighting church growth, and instead, we see the Mission story as a shared journey involving many voices, some powerful, others silenced. This inclusive way of studying Mission history encourages honesty about the past and respect for diverse contributions to the Christian faith. It challenges us to write history with humility and to approach Mission work today with open ears, open hearts, and a willingness to learn from all people, not just those at the top.

7

Bridging Cultures and Communities Anthropological and Sociological Foundations for Missiology

Missiology as the study of Christian Mission, focusing on how the church can share the good news of Jesus in different parts of the world. In doing so, Missionaries learn about the people they want to reach, their customs, beliefs, family structures, and social networks. In the past, the most successful Missionaries acted like cultural anthropologists, they lived alongside local people, listened carefully, and took time to understand how that society worked. This helped them speak in ways that made sense to the people, rather than using foreign words or ideas that cut people off at once. At the same time, sociology offers tools for seeing how communities are organized and how they change over time. By studying institutions such as families, schools, markets, and religious groups, Missionaries can discover who the key decision-makers are, where people gather, and what social pressures influence daily life. This knowledge helps Mission to choose the right places to work, build genuine relationships of trust, and design programs that meet real needs, not just spiritual ones. Bringing together anthropology and sociology makes Missiology more effective and respectful.

Defining Terms

Missiology seeks to understand not just the message of the Gospel but the people and societies to whom it is shared. To do this well, Missionaries draw on cultural anthropology and sociology, two branches of the social sciences that offer complementary insights. Cultural anthropology teaches us how to observe and participate in a community's daily life, uncovering the beliefs, values, and rituals that shape its worldview. Sociology, in turn, reveals how individuals are connected through families, schools, religious bodies, and other institutions, and how those networks influence change.

Anthropology

Anthropology is the scientific study of human beings and their cultures, coming from the Greek words *anthropos* (human) and *logos* (study). As a behavioural science, it asks questions such as "How do people make a living?" "What do they believe about the world?" and "How do they pass customs to their children?"[1] Anthropology splits into subfields like biological anthropology looks at human evolution and physical differences, while cultural anthropology studies learned behaviours and social systems.[2] In Missiology, anthropological skills like careful listening, unbiased observation, and open-minded inquiry help Missionaries enter a new community without judgment, so they can accurately learn local language usages, family roles, and daily routines before sharing the Gospel.

Culture

Culture is the collection of learned behaviours, beliefs, values, and material objects that a group of people share and pass down from one generation to the next. It includes the language they speak, the ways they celebrate and mourn, the foods they eat, the tools they use, and the rules they follow in daily life.[3] Culture shapes how people understand the world, how they make decisions, and how they relate to one another. In Missiology, recognizing and respecting a community's culture allows Missionaries to communicate the Gospel in ways that feel familiar and meaningful, rather than foreign or confusing.[4] Culture is everything a group of people learns and passes along. Thus, culture acts like a shared insights that tells people how to act, what to value, and how to interpret events.[5] When Missionaries understand a community's culture, they can choose stories, examples, and worship styles that fit local customs, avoiding misunderstandings and making the message of Jesus both clear and meaningful.

---

[1] Ursula Rao, "Debates in Anthropology: Introduction," *Current Debates in Anthropology* 139/1 (2014): 1-5.

[2] Ellen Messer, "Anthropology and Human Rights," *Annual Review of Anthropology* 22 (1993): 221-222.

[3] Letty M. Russell, "Cultural Hermeneutics: A Postcolonial Look at Mission," *Journal of Feminist Studies in Religion* 20/1 (Spring, 2004): 23-40.

[4] Travis Dumsday, "Counter-Cultural Religious Experiences," *Religious Studies* 47/3 (September, 2011): 317-320.

[5] Jorge Presmanes, "Inculturation as Evangelization: The Dialogue of Faith and Culture in the Work of Marcello Azevedo," *U.S. Catholic Historian* 30/1 (Winter, 2012): 59-60.

Cultural Anthropology

Cultural Anthropology is the branch of anthropology that studies how people in different societies create, share, and use meaning.[6] It focuses on the everyday lives of communities, examining their beliefs, rituals, languages, art, economic activities, and social roles to understand why people behave the way they do. Cultural anthropology helps us to understand how beliefs, rituals, and daily practices shape a society's way of life.[7] It uses the main tool, ethnography, means living side by side with community members, watching what they do, asking questions, and even taking part in festivals or work routines.[8] Anthropologists record myths, songs, food customs, and greetings to understand underlying values like honour, respect, or solidarity.[9] In Mission, Cultural Anthropology prevents assumptions and instead of guessing what people need, it helps to discover hopes and fears firsthand. Thus, cultural anthropology shows us that, for many communities, a ceremony is just as much about bringing people together as it is about physical healing. Such insight helps Missionaries introduce prayer or any form of ministries in ways that fit naturally with local traditions.

Sociology

Sociology is the scientific study of how people organize themselves into groups and institutions, and how those structures shape individual behaviour and society as a whole. It examines how individuals fit into larger social structures such as families, clans, religious bodies, markets, and governments, and how those structures influence behaviour and change. Sociologists use tools like surveys to measure attitudes, social network maps to see who talks to whom, and case studies to trace how a new idea spreads. For Missionaries, sociological insight reveals who the natural leaders are (village elders, teachers, or shopkeepers), how decisions get made in the community, and which institutions hold the most influence.[10] Equipped with such knowledge, Missionaries act wisely, working with trusted local groups, designing training that empowers future church leaders, and introduce programs that meet both spiritual and social needs in ways local people value and sustain.

---

[6] Ruth Marshall, "Christianity, Anthropology, Politics," *Current Anthropology* 55/S10 (December, 2014): S344-S346.

[7] W. B. Bizzell, "Cultural Anthropology," *Bios* 14/4 (December, 1943): 180-181.

[8] Oscar Lewis, "Comparisons in Cultural Anthropology," *Yearbook of Anthropology* (1955): 259-292.

[9] Melford E. Spiro, "Cultural Relativism and the Future of Anthropology," *Cultural Anthropology* 1/3 (August, 1986): 259-286.

[10] Anton Quack, "Anthropology and Missionaries: A Review Essay," *Anthropos* 103/2 (2008): 560-567.

Contributions of Cultural Anthropology to Missiology

Cultural anthropology gives Missionaries practical tools and perspectives for engaging deeply with the people they serve.[11] By using anthropology, Missionaries can move beyond surface-level impressions to form lasting relationships, communicate meaningfully, and help local churches grow in ways that fit each community's own patterns of life.

Understanding Another Culture

To share the Gospel effectively, Missionaries first need to grasp how a community structures its world. Ethnographic research, living alongside local people for weeks, months, or even years allows Missionaries to observe daily work routines, social rituals, and patterns of interaction. Participant observation, a core anthropological method, means that Missionaries actively join in local activities such as farming, festivals, or storytelling circles. This involvement reveals unspoken rules, for example, who leads a ceremony, how disputes are settled, or what taboos exist around food. Scholars like Clifford Geertz have shown that culture is a system of shared meanings, and only by decoding these meanings can Missionaries frame the Gospel in ways that echo with local priorities and avoid unintended offense.

Entering Another Culture

Cross-cultural entry involves more than learning a few phrases, it requires developing cultural empathy and gaining trust through respectful behaviour. Anthropologists emphasize the importance of "cultural relativism," the idea that one's own cultural standards should not be used to judge another society.[12] Missionaries trained in this mindset work to understand local proverbs, honorific titles, and nonverbal signals such as gestures or seating arrangements. For instance, using the correct term of respect for an elder or standing at the proper distance during conversation can communicate genuine respect.[13] When Missionaries learn these linguistic distinctions and social codes, they demonstrate humility, openness and respect. This respectful posture often defuses suspicion, opens doors for deeper dialogue, and lays the groundwork for a two-way relationship rather than a one-sided message.

---

[11] Annette Rosenstiel, "Anthropology and the Missionary," *The Journal of the Royal Anthropological Institute of Great Britain and Ireland* 89/1 (January-June, 1959): 107-115.

[12] Craig Ott, Stephen J. Strauss and Timothy C. Tennent, *Encountering Theology of Mission: Biblical Foundations, Historical Developments and Contemporary Issues* (Grand Rapids: Baker Academic, 2010), XXII.

[13] Eugene A. Nida, *Customs and Cultures: Anthropology for Christian Mission* (New York: Harper & Brothers, 1954), 26.

Communicating the Gospel

Once inside the cultural framework, Missionaries must translate Gospel truths into local symbols and narratives. Anthropologist H. Russell Bernard notes that every culture has its own "semantic domains" clusters of related meanings attached to words, stories, and symbols. By identifying and employing these spheres, Missionaries can present Christian concepts in familiar terms.[14] For instance, a community that values ancestor wisdom might find the story of Jesus honouring his parents particularly compelling. Contextualization models, such as those developed by James Kraft and Stephen Bevans, encourage Missionaries to use local art forms, music styles, and storytelling techniques so that the Gospel is not seen as a foreign import but as speaking within the community's own voice.[15] This approach helps ensure that believers can articulate their faith in a way that feels natural and rooted in their own cultural heritage.

Planting the Church

Sustainable church growth depends on structures and leadership styles that align with existing social patterns. Cultural anthropologists study kinship systems, age-grade associations, and traditional authority figures to map out how decisions and responsibilities flow within a community. For example, if leadership typically resides in a council of elders, new congregation governance can mirror that structure, ensuring local believers see it as legitimate.[16] Anthropologist Paul Hiebert's concept of "conversion systems" reminds Missionaries to look at how people adopt new ideas socially, cognitively, and institutionally and to build church models that fit those patterns.[17] Training local leaders in culturally appropriate forms of ministry rather than imposing a foreign model, promotes self-reliance and avoids dependency on external support. In this way, churches can become truly indigenous, owned, led, and sustained by the people themselves.

---

[14] Ruth Marshall, "Christianity, Anthropology, Politics," *Current Anthropology* 55/10 (December, 2014): 344.

[15] Charles H. Kraft, *Anthropology for Christian Witness* (New York: Orbis Books, 2001), 2.; Paul Duane Matheny, Contextual Theology: The Drama of Our Times (Cambridge: The Lutterworth Press, 2011), 59-82.

[16] Joel Robbins, "The Anthropology of Christianity: Unity, Diversity, New Directions," *Current Anthropology* 55/10 (December, 2014): 158.

[17] Jan A. B. Jongeneel, *Missiological Encyclopedia Part One, The Philosophy and Science of Mission in the 19th and 20th Century* (Bangalore: Centre for Contemporary Christianity, 2006), 331.

Contributions of Sociology to Missiology

Sociology offers Missionaries a set of tools and theories for understanding how people form groups, how those groups interact, and how social change happens. Such insights help Missionaries to design Mission models that fit community structures, address systemic issues, and build strong, locally led institutions.

Analysis of Social Institutions

Social institutions such as families, kinship ties, economic systems, political councils, and religious bodies, structure daily life and shape collective values. Émile Durkheim taught us that institutions act as "social facts," influencing behaviour even when individuals are unaware of their power.[18] Talcott Parsons later described how institutions function together to maintain social solidarity and stability.[19] In Christian Mission, mapping these institutions shows who holds authority and how resources flow. When Missionaries see a patron-client system, where a few households hold the keys to land, credit, or social influence, they follow the biblical example of Paul, who engaged local leaders like Sergius Paulus in Pisidian Antioch (Acts 13:7-12), and Jesus, who started His ministry by teaching in the synagogue where He was welcomed (Luke 4:16-30). In a similar way, Mission might invite respected patrons to open their homes for Scripture teaching and practical training. By equipping these local patrons with both the Word and skills in community health or literacy, Missionaries practice incarnational ministry, entering the culture as Paul did, "becoming all things to all people" (I Corinthians 9:22). This approach honours existing authority structures, builds trust through shared service, and ensures that new church communities grow with local endorsement, just as the early church spread when key influencers like Lydia in Philippi believed and hosted fellowship in their homes (Acts 16:14-15).

Group Dynamics and Change

Understanding how communities bond and evolve is essential for guiding lasting transformation. Ferdinand Tönnies distinguished *Gemeinschaft* (communities bound by personal ties) from *Gesellschaft* (impersonal, contractual relationships), reminding us that rural and urban contexts demand different approaches.[20] Mark Granovetter's theory of "the strength of weak ties" shows that casual acquaintances often spread new ideas more

[18] Grace M. Barnes, "Emile Durkheim's Contribution to the Sociology of Education," *The Journal of Educational Thought* 11/3 (December, 1977): 213-223.

[19] N. A. "Talcott Parsons, 1902-1979," *Theory and Society* 8/2 (1979): 299–301.

[20] Niall Bond, ""*Gemeinschaft und Gesellschaft*": The Reception of a Conceptual Dichotomy," *Contributions to the History of Concepts* 5/2 (2009): 162-186.

effectively than close friends.[21] Missionaries follow the apostolic pattern by first cultivating deep trust within tight-knit family or household networks, much as Jesus began with His own relatives (John 2:12) and Paul found a home church in Lydia's household (Acts 16:14-15) and then reaching out through connections, such as market vendors, craftsmen, or gatherings in public squares (Acts 17:17). In this two-fold approach, the close bonds of family and friendship provide a firm foundation for discipleship and mutual support, while the "weak ties" of marketplaces and social events echoing Philip's evangelism in Samaria (Acts 8:5-8) allow the good news to spread quickly into new circles. By building first on the intimacy of household faith and then on the broader networks of daily life, Missionaries see both lasting community transformation and rapid Gospel diffusion.[22]

Social Stratification and Justice

All societies sort people into layers like class, caste, ethnicity, or status which affects access to power and resources. Karl Marx emphasized how economic class drives conflict,[23] while Max Weber added that "status groups" (based on honour or lifestyle) and "party" affiliations (power in politics) also matter.[24] Pierre Bourdieu introduced the idea of "habitus," the ingrained habits shaped by one's social position.[25] In many Mission fields, caste or ethnic divisions limit social mobility and fellowship. In such a milieu, sociological analysis helps Missionaries to expertise holistic ministries to mirror Jesus' holistic care, as He reached out to Samaritan women (John 4:4-30) and healed the man at the pool (John 5:1-9) by integrating marginalized groups like lower-caste women into worship and service. A sociological reading of Paul's teaching that "there is neither Jew nor Greek, slave nor free, male nor female, for you are all one in Christ Jesus" (Galatians 3:28) promote unity in Christ. Through these combined spiritual and social interventions, sociology helps the Missionaries to demonstrate that the Gospel restores relationships and justice, showing God's care for every aspect of human life.

---

[21] Herbert J. Gans, "Gans on Granovetter's "Strength of Weak Ties"," *American Journal of Sociology* 80/2 (September, 1974): 524-527.

[22] Rian Venter, "Thinking God in a Global Multi-religious Context: Trends, Challenges and Possibilities," *Journal for the Study of Religion* 31/1 (2018): 70-85.

[23] Thomas Munro, "The Marxist Theory of Art History: Socio-Economic Determinism and the Dialectical Process," *The Journal of Aesthetics and Art Criticism* 18/4 (June, 1960): 430-445.

[24] Seymour Martin Lipset, "Party Systems and the Representation of Social Groups," *European Journal of Sociology* 1/1 (1960): 50-85.

[25] Anthony King, "Thinking with Bourdieu against Bourdieu: A 'Practical' Critique of the *Habitus*," *Sociological Theory* 18/3 (November, 2000): 417-433.

Organizational Development

Mission agencies and emerging churches are organizations that need clear roles, accountability, and adaptability. Max Weber's model of bureaucracy highlights how defined rules and hierarchical structure can ensure fairness and continuity.[26] At the same time, scholars of organizational networks like Harrison White remind us that informal ties and flexible collaboration foster innovation.[27] Kurt Lewin's change model (unfreeze-change-refreeze) offers a simple roadmap for implementing new practices, first creating awareness, then introducing change, and finally solidifying it into routine.[28] By following the biblical pattern of clear leadership roles and open, Spirit-led participation, Mission leaders build both order and flexibility into their work. Paul instructed Titus to appoint elders in every town with specific qualifications and responsibilities (Titus 1:5-9), and he taught Timothy to select faithful deacons to serve practical needs in the church (I Timothy 3:8-13). These "job descriptions" and "reporting lines" give Mission stability and accountability. At the same time, the early church valued grassroots input as it is recorded in Acts 15, leaders gathered from all the churches to discuss Gentile inclusion, and ordinary believers spoke up, guided by the Spirit. This approach ensures that churches and agencies remain faithful to Scripture, organized in service, and sensitive to the Spirit's leading and the real needs of their communities.

Methodological Integration

To understand people more deeply and serve them more effectively, Missionaries often combine tools from both anthropology and sociology. This approach is called mixed-methods research, because it brings together both qualitative methods (like observation and interviews) and quantitative methods (like surveys and data analysis). By using multiple ways to study a community, Missionaries can get a clear picture of how people live, think, relate, and respond to the Gospel.

Ethnographic fieldwork is a core method from cultural anthropology. It involves living in the community for an extended period, participating in daily life, and learning through experience. Missionaries may join in local farming, cooking, worship, or storytelling, and they often keep journals of what they observe. Through life histories, long interviews where people share

[26] Helen Constas, "Max Weber's Two Conceptions of Bureaucracy," *American Journal of Sociology* 63/4 (January, 1958): 400-409.

[27] J. Lotus Seeley, "Harrison White as (Not Quite) Poststructuralist," *Sociological Theory* 32/1 (March, 2014): 27-42.

[28] Dale E. Zand and Richard E. Sorensen, "Theory of Change and the Effective Use of Management Science," *Administrative Science Quarterly* 20/4 (December, 1975): 532-545.

their personal journeys, Missionaries learn how culture shapes individual experiences. Key-informant interviews, where trusted local leaders or elders explain cultural practices, also provide deep insights. This hands-on, immersive method helps Missionaries to understand the "why" behind people's behaviour, values, and beliefs, which is essential for contextualizing the Gospel in ways that feel authentic and respectful.

Survey research is a sociological tool that uses questionnaires or interviews to gather data from the context. Such surveys help Missionaries to understand general attitudes, religious beliefs, education levels, income patterns, and other important social trends in a community. A survey also reveals how many people identify with a particular religion, what they believe about God, or what social issues concern them most such as unemployment, addiction, or discrimination. These information helps Missionaries to develop programs that are not only biblically faithful but also socially relevant, addressing real concerns alongside spiritual needs.

Social network analysis looks at how people are connected to one another, who talks to whom, who influences decisions, and who holds leadership or trust. This method helps Missionaries to see beyond formal titles to understand informal leadership. For example, in some villages, the person with no official position may still be the one everyone consults. By identifying such key influencers, Missionaries can form effective discipleship relationships and train emerging leaders who already have the trust of the community. This approach builds on natural networks, making the spread of the Gospel more organic and sustainable.

Linguistic analysis is used to study the local language, not just the words people speak, but how they use those words in prayers, songs, greetings, and storytelling. Understanding tone, metaphor, and local expressions helps Missionaries to develop Scripture translations, sermons, and liturgies that speak directly to people's hearts. For example, if a language uses different words for "love" depending on family, friendship, or marriage, choosing the right word for God's love becomes vital for clear communication. By working closely with native speakers and local translators, Missionaries can create worship materials and Bible translations that sound natural and respectful, not foreign or confusing.

Challenges

Integrating social science into Mission work brings many benefits, but it also comes with challenges that Missionaries must carefully consider. One major concern is ethics. Missionaries must learn to respect the people they serve, especially when dealing with sensitive issues or communities with a history of being marginalized. This means being aware of power differences and always gaining informed consent before collecting information.

Another important issue is theological alignment. While anthropology and sociology offer helpful tools, they must never replace or contradict the authority of Scripture or the leading of the Holy Spirit, rather, these disciplines should serve the Mission of God, not redefine it. There are also contextual limitations. Terms like 'family,' 'church,' or 'leadership' may mean very different things in different cultures, so Missionaries must stay flexible and avoid forcing Western ideas into every setting. Finally, there are practical constraints as well. Doing good research takes time, money, and training. Many Missions may struggle to find the resources needed for in-depth study, especially in remote or under-resourced areas. Therefore, while social science can enrich Missiology, it must be used wisely, humbly, and in service of the Gospel.

Conclusion

Cultural anthropology and sociology give Missiology strong tools and methods to better understand people and the societies they live in. These social sciences help Missionaries develop approaches that are more effective, culturally appropriate, and holistic addressing both spiritual and social needs. By studying how communities think, relate, and organize themselves, Missionaries can share the Gospel in ways that truly connect with local people. Such contextual research should focus on long-term studies that measure how social-scientific methods affect church growth over time, and compare different cultural settings to improve models of contextualization. Moreover, using participatory research, where local believers help shape the Mission methods, can lead to stronger ownership and lasting impact. As Missiology continues to collaborate with anthropology and sociology, it will deepen its understanding of culture and community, making the church's witness more faithful, relevant, and globally effective.

8

Mission in the Context of Religious Pluralism Theological Models, Challenges, and Engagement in a Diverse World

In today's globalized and interconnected world, Christians live and interact daily with people from a wide range of religious traditions, spiritual beliefs, and secular ideologies. Communities are becoming increasingly diverse, where followers of Christianity, Islam, Hinduism, Buddhism, indigenous religions, and also atheists share common spaces. This reality of religious pluralism is no longer distant, rather, it is local, visible, and unavoidable and become new normal. In this new context, the Church cannot continue its Mission as though it exists in isolation. The Mission of the Church must now respond thoughtfully to the rich diversity of faiths that shape human culture and understanding. This pluralistic setting poses both challenges and opportunities for Christian Mission. Therefore, the Mission of the Church today must be marked by clarity, humility, and compassion. It must be rooted in the gospel message, yet open to listening and learning. It must also avoid both arrogance and relativism, choosing instead the path of faithful presence and loving witness.

Understanding Religious Pluralism

Religious pluralism means that many different religions exist and are practiced in the same society. It is more than just the presence of many religions, rather, it is the belief that people of different faiths can live together peacefully and with mutual respect.[1] Some also believe that all religions are different paths to the same truth or salvation. Others accept the presence of

[1] William L. Rowe, "Religious Pluralism," *Religious Studies* 35/2 (June, 1999): 139-150.

multiple religions but still believe that only one is fully true. In Christian theology, this leads to five main views: exclusivism (only Christianity saves), inclusivism (Christ saves, but people may be saved without knowing Him), pluralism (all religions are valid paths to God), pluralistic inclusivism (the truth of the Christian Gospel can be enriched and fulfilled through the insights and contributions of other living faiths across different times and cultures) and pluralistic interculturalism (the respectful integration of one's own faith and culture within a diverse society, promoting harmony without diluting identity or disturbing others, and fostering shared spiritual space beyond ownership or conversion). Understanding these definitions helps Christians know how to engage others without confusion or disrespect.

Exclusivism (Only Christianity Saves)

Exclusivism, originally, we see in the understanding of Karl Barth, is the belief that only the Christian faith leads to salvation, and all other religions are ultimately false or insufficient,[2] later, the threefold typology of exclusivism-inclusivism-pluralism in Christian theology of religions was most famously popularized by Alan Race in his 1983 book *Christians and Religious Pluralism: Patterns in the Christian Theology of Religions*.[3] This view is based on clear biblical teachings, such as John 14:6 where Jesus says, *I am the way, the truth, and the life. No one comes to the Father except through me*, and Acts 4:12, which states that salvation is found in no one else but Jesus. Many Church traditions, especially during the medieval period, held this view strictly, as seen in the statement *extra ecclesiam nulla salus* (outside the Church there is no salvation).[4] The implication of this view is that Mission and evangelism are urgent and necessary because those who have not heard or accepted the gospel are considered lost. However, this view is often criticized for being intolerant or dismissive of the spiritual value in other religions.

Inclusivism (Christ Saves, Even Without Knowing Him)

Inclusivism, classically represented by Karl Rahner, is the belief that while salvation is only through Christ, God's grace can operate in followers of other religions, making them "anonymous Christians" within the scope of

---

[2] Hendrik M. Vroom, "Do All Religious Traditions Worship the Same God?," *Religious Studies* 26/1 (March, 1990), 76.

[3] Gavin D'Costa, "The Impossibility of a Pluralist View of Religions," *Religious Studies* 32/2 (June, 1996): 223.

[4] Gavin D'Costa, "Traditions and Reception: Interpreting Vatican II's Declaration on the Church's Relation to Non-Christian Religions, *New Blackfriars* 92/1040 (July, 2011): 484.

salvation.[5] Inclusivism is a middle position that affirms Jesus Christ as the only Savior, but believes that people can be saved through Him even if they don't know Him directly or have never heard the gospel.[6] This view sees truth and grace present in other religions to some extent. For example, Acts 10:35 speaks of people in every nation who fear God and do what is right as being accepted by Him. The best-known supporter of this view is Karl Rahner, who introduced the idea of the "anonymous Christian", someone who, though not identifying as a Christian, responds to God's grace and is unknowingly included in Christ's salvation.[7] This view was reflected in the Catholic Church's Vatican II documents, such as *Lumen Gentium*, which acknowledged the work of the Spirit in other faiths.[8] Inclusivism offers a more hopeful view of salvation for non-Christians, promoting humility and openness in Mission, but it still sees Christianity as the final and complete truth, which may seem condescending to other faiths.

Pluralism (Many Valid Paths to God)

Pluralism, most notably articulated by John Hick, is the belief that all major world religions are valid and equally effective paths to the same ultimate reality, each offering genuine salvation and truth.[9] Pluralism holds that all major religions are valid and equally true ways to reach God or the ultimate reality. It denies that any one religion has the full truth or exclusive claim to salvation. Prominent pluralist John Hick argued that different religions are different responses to the same divine reality, shaped by culture and history.[10] The idea is supported by sayings like Jesus' words in John 14:2 *In my Father's house there are many rooms* which theologian Harvey Cox, interpret as suggesting that heaven can include people of various faiths. Pluralism encourages deep interfaith dialogue and mutual respect, aiming for peaceful coexistence.[11] However, it challenges core Christian beliefs about the uniqueness of Christ and may lead to relativism, where no religious truth is seen as absolute. Critics also argue that by flattening

---

[5] Paul Lakeland, "*Lumen Gentium*: The Unfinished Business," *New Blackfriars* 90/1026 (March, 2009): 146.

[6] Kevin Meeker, "Pluralism, Exclusivism, and the Theoretical Virtues," *Religious Studies* 42/2 (June, 2006): 193-206

[7] Gavin D'Costa, "The Impossibility of a Pluralist View of Religions…, 223.

[8] Paul Lakeland, "*Lumen Gentium*: The Unfinished Business…, 146.

[9] Paul R. Eddy, "Religious Pluralism and the Divine: Another Look at John Hick's Neo-Kantian Proposal," *Religious Studies* 30/4 (December, 1994): 467-478.

[10] Bernard J. Verkamp, "Hick's Interpretation of Religious Pluralism," *International Journal for Philosophy of Religion* 30/2 (October, 1991): 103-124.

[11] Kevin Meeker, "Pluralism, Exclusivism, and the Theoretical Virtues…

all differences, pluralism can ignore what makes each religion unique and deeply meaningful.

Pluralistic Inclusivism: A Contextual Indian Christian Theology

Pluralistic Inclusivism, as developed by Indian Christian theologian K. P. Aleaz, is a unique theological model that seeks to open Christian faith to the religious and spiritual insights of other traditions, particularly in the Indian context.[12] Unlike exclusivism, which claims that only Christianity is true, or inclusivism, which sees other religions as partially true but still subordinate to Christ, and pluralism, which treats all religions as equally valid, pluralistic inclusivism blends inclusivity with openness to plural contributions.[13] Aleaz proposes that the revelation of God in Jesus Christ can become truly pluralistic when it is enriched by the contributions of other living faiths across time and place. This model does not merely tolerate other religions, rather, it encourages each faith to be transformed and fulfilled through mutual interaction.[14] Aleaz, influenced by *Advaita Vedānta* and his engagement with traditions like the Ramakrishna Mission, envisioned pluralistic inclusivism as both a theology of religions and a way of life. He argued that in a pluralistic society like India, Christians are called not to dominate others through Mission, but to witness to Christ by living in mutual respect and shared spirituality.[15] For him, people of other faiths are not to be converted or rejected, but embraced as fellow pilgrims whose religious experiences can deepen one's own.[16] Thus, pluralistic inclusivism becomes a viable Indian Christian theology, one that affirms Christ without negating the value and truth present in other traditions, and one that celebrates life and faith in a deeply pluralistic world.

---

[12] K. P. Aleaz, "Pluralistic Inclusivism: A Suggested Perspective in Theology of Religions," *Asian Journal of Theology* 12/2 (October, 1998): 268.

[13] D. Isaac Devadoss, "Life and Evolution of K. P. Aleaz's Thought," in *Many Ways of Pluralism, Essays in Honour of Kalarikkal Poulose Aleaz*, edited by Vempanolil John John (Kolkata: Bishop's College & ISPCK, 2010), 16.

[14] Anderson Jeremiah, "Inculturation: A Subaltern Critique of K. P. Aleaz' Indian Christian Vedanta," *Asian Journal of Theology* 21/2 (2007): 400.

[15] K. P. Aleaz, *Theology of Religions: Birmingham Papers and Other Essays* (Calcutta: Moumita Publishers & Distributors, 1998), 172.

[16] S. Robertson, "Toward a Theology of the Convergence of Religion: A Critique of Rev. Dr. K. P. Aleaz's Theological Contributions," *Asian Journal of Theology* 22/1 (2008): 177.

Pluralistic Interculturalism (Viable Model for Celebrating Life Together)

Pluralistic Interculturalism proposed by Vinod S. Sailus is an emerging model that promotes harmonious living in a religiously and culturally diverse society without requiring individuals to compromise their own identity or impose it on others.[17] It moves beyond the frameworks of Pluralistic Inclusivism, as proposed by K. P. Aleaz, and the concept of Multiple Religious Belongings, by offering a more grounded and respectful approach to interreligious engagement.[18] While pluralistic inclusivism views religious truth as shared and open to enrichment from other faiths, and multiple religious belonging allows individuals to draw from more than one tradition, pluralistic interculturalism emphasizes rootedness in one's own tradition while engaging others in shared spaces. This model resists the idea that the world is a common property owned by all, acknowledging instead that the world is plural and diverse, and that people can share from their unique cultural and spiritual locations. It encourages believers to offer their "own world" generously to others, fostering mutual hospitality and spiritual exchange, thus, it enables people to experience unity without uniformity, affirming diverse religious expressions while cultivating a common spiritual life.[19] Unlike multiple religious belonging, which may unintentionally lead to the loss of distinct religious identity or result in syncretism, pluralistic interculturalism allows individuals to remain faithful to their own beliefs while respecting and learning from others. It is, therefore, a viable and inclusive model for the celebration of life in a pluralistic society, where difference is not a threat but a gift.

Biblical Basis for Mission in Pluralism

The Bible provides a strong foundation for engaging in Mission within a pluralistic context that is, among people of different religions and beliefs. In the Old Testament, we see God's concern for all nations, not just Israel. In Genesis 12:3, God promises Abraham that *all the families of the earth will be blessed* through him, showing that God's plan was always for the whole world.[20] In the book of Jonah, God sends the prophet to the city of Nineveh, a non-Israelite people. Jonah resists, but God's mercy on the repentant

---

[17] Vinod S. Sailus, *Borderless Spirituality: An Intercultural Inquiry into the Appropriation of Faiths in South Indian Religious Context* (Bangalore: Omega Book World, 2023), 295.

[18] Vinod S. Sailus, *Borderless Spirituality: An Intercultural Inquiry…*, 309.

[19] Vinod S. Sailus, *Borderless Spirituality: An Intercultural Inquiry…*, 324.

[20] J. A. Emerton, "The Origin of the Promises to the Patriarchs in the Older Sources of the Book of Genesis," *Vetus Testamentum* 32/1 (January, 1982): 14-32.

city reveals that His compassion extends beyond Israel.[21] Isaiah 49:6 also affirms this when God says His servant will be *a light to the nations*, so that salvation may reach the ends of the earth.[22]

In the New Testament, this vision continues and becomes even more clear through the life and teaching of Jesus and the early Church. In Matthew 28:19-20, Jesus commands His followers to make disciples of all nations, showing that the gospel is for everyone, not just the Jews.[23] In John 4, Jesus speaks with the Samaritan woman, someone from a religious group despised by Jews. Jesus respects her, speaks truthfully, and offers her living water, showing how Mission can begin with honest and respectful conversation.[24] Acts 10, describes how Peter learns that God does not show favouritism but accepts those from every nation who fear Him and do what is right.[25] In Acts 17:22-31, Paul addresses the people of Athens by referring to their own religious practices and quoting their poets. He uses what they already believe to introduce the message of Christ.[26] Finally, in Romans 2:14-16, Paul explains that even those who do not know the law can act according to their conscience, suggesting that God is at work even among those outside the formal boundaries of the Church.[27]

Challenges and Criticisms of Engaging Religious Pluralism

While engaging in religious pluralism offers many opportunities for peaceful coexistence and mutual understanding, it also brings several challenges and criticisms, both theological and practical. One of the main theological concerns is the fear of compromising the uniqueness of Christ. Critics argue that affirming the value of other religions might lead to a weakening of core Christian beliefs, such as the divinity of Jesus or the necessity of His death and resurrection for salvation. This concern is especially strong among those who hold exclusivist views, who worry that pluralism may lead to

---

[21] Hyun Chul Paul Kim, "Jonah Read Intertextually," *Journal of Biblical Literature* 126/3 (Fall, 2007): 497-528.

[22] D. W. Van Winkle, "The Relationship of the Nations to *Yahweh* and to Israel in Isaiah XL-LV," *Vetus Testamentum* 35/4 (October, 1985): 446-458.

[23] Timothy Radcliffe, "Go and Make Disciples of All Nations: Preaching the Kingdom or Religious Imperialism?", *New Blackfriars* 84/989-990 (July, 2003): 323-334.

[24] James D. Purvis, "The Fourth Gospel and the Samaritans," *Novum Testamentum* 17/3 (July, 1975): 161-198.

[25] Darrell L. Whiteman, "The Conversion of a Missionary: A Missiological Study of Acts 10," *Missiology: An International Review* 51/1 (2023): 19-30.

[26] Joshua W. Jipp, "Paul's Areopagus Speech of Acts 17:16-34 as Both Critique and Propaganda," *Journal of Biblical Literature* 131/3 (2012): 567-588.

[27] Jane Heath, "The Righteous Gentile Interjects (James 2:18-19 and Romans 2:14-15)," *Novum Testamentum* 55/3 (2013): 272-295.

relativism, where all truth claims are seen as equally valid and no single truth is affirmed. Another challenge is the danger of syncretism, where elements from different religions are mixed in ways that distort or dilute the Christian faith. In efforts to be inclusive, some may unintentionally adopt beliefs or practices that conflict with biblical teachings. This can develop confusion among people and weaken the Church's theological clarity. There is also the risk of passive witness, where Christians, out of respect or fear of offending others, may avoid sharing their faith altogether, thus neglecting the call to evangelism and Mission.

Another practical struggle is that, engaging in pluralism requires deep understanding and sensitivity, which not all Christians are prepared for. It involves careful listening, cultural awareness, and the ability to have honest yet respectful conversations, skills that are not always taught or emphasized in churches. Moreover, pluralism may not be welcomed by everyone. Some may respond with suspicion, hostility, or resistance, especially if they feel their traditions are being challenged or misrepresented. Thus, while religious pluralism offers a way to live peacefully and meaningfully in diverse societies, it also presents real tensions. Because engaging in pluralism must guide through the fine line between respecting others and remaining faithful to the gospel, ensuring their approach is both truthful and loving.

Mission in the Context of Religious Pluralism

We live in a world where people follow many different religions and belief systems. This religious diversity, known as pluralism, is now a normal part of life. In this context, the Christian Mission of sharing the good news of Jesus Christ must be done with both faithfulness and respect. Christians are called to be clear about their beliefs while also listening to and learning from others. Mission today is not just about preaching, rather, it involves dialogue, understanding, peacebuilding, and public engagement. It means living out the gospel in a way that shows love, builds bridges, and seeks the good of all people. This approach helps the Church remain a strong witness to Christ while also contributing to unity and peace in a diverse world. In response to this pluralistic reality, the Christian Mission today must take on multiple forms, which include the academic study and practical implication of interfaith dialogue, theology of religions, comparative religion, comparative theology, peacebuilding, and public theology.

Interfaith Dialogue

Interfaith dialogue is a vital part of Christian Mission in a religiously plural world. It involves building respectful and honest relationships with people from other religions, not for the purpose of debate or conversion, but to foster mutual understanding.[28] Through dialogue, Christians can listen to the beliefs, practices, and values of others while also sharing their own faith in Christ with integrity.[29] This kind of engagement promotes peace, cooperation, and shared concern for justice, the environment, and human dignity.[30] It does not mean compromising the gospel message, but rather communicating it in a spirit of love and humility. Thus, interfaith dialogue helps break down stereotypes, reduces fear, and opens doors to collaborate on common goals in diverse societies.

Theology of Religions

Theology of religions is the study of how Christian faith understands and relates to other world religions. It provides different frameworks that help Christians answer important questions like: Can people from other religions be saved? What truth or value might exist in non-Christian faiths?[31] The main models often discussed are exclusivism (only Christianity saves), inclusivism (Christ saves, but others may be saved unknowingly), and pluralism (many religions are valid paths to God). The two perspectives from the Indian context such as 'pluralistic inclusivism' is the belief that the truth of the Christian gospel can be enriched and fulfilled through the insights and contributions of other living faiths across different times and cultures. It sees other religions not as threats but as partners in discovering God's truth.[32] The second model, 'pluralistic interculturalism' is about respectfully living out one's own faith and culture in a diverse society, without losing identity or forcing beliefs on others. It encourages people to share spiritual spaces and grow in understanding, without needing to convert or dominate.[33] Each view has its strengths and challenges, and they shape how Christians approach Mission. A clear theology of religions helps believers stay faithful to Christ while avoiding arrogance, offering a thoughtful way to engage respectfully with people of other faiths in a pluralistic context.

---

[28] Yong Huang, "Religious Pluralism and Interfaith Dialogue: Beyond Universalism and Particularism," *International Journal for Philosophy of Religion* 37/3 (June, 1995): 127-144.

[29] Masatoshi Doi, "On Interfaith Dialogue: Some Important Aspects," *Buddhist-Christian Studies* 4 (1984): 17-28.

[30] David B. Burrell, "Some Requisites for Interfaith Dialogue," *New Blackfriars* 89/1021 (May, 2008): 300-310.

[31] Glyn Richards, "Towards a Theology of Religions," *The Journal of Theological Studies* 31/1 (April, 1980): 44-66.

[32] Reid B. Locklin and Hugh Nicholson, "The Return of Comparative Theology," *Journal of the American Academy of Religion* 78/2 (June, 2010): 477-514.

[33] Rian Venter, "Thinking God in a Global Multi-religious Context: Trends, Challenges and Possibilities," *Journal for the Study of Religion* 31/1 (2018): 70-85.

Comparative Theology

Comparative theology involves studying the sacred texts, teachings, and spiritual practices of other religions deeply and respectfully. It is not done to argue or to convert, but to better understand both the other religion and one's own.[34] Through this process, Christians can gain renewed insights into their own theology by encountering how other faiths deal with questions about God, humanity, suffering, or salvation.[35] This type of learning encourages humility and openness, as well as a more thoughtful and knowledgeable Christian witness.[36] Thus, comparative theology can strengthen Mission by showing respect for others' beliefs while offering the good news of Jesus in a way that connects meaningfully with people's lived experiences.

Comparative Religion

Comparative religion is the academic study that compares the beliefs, practices, and sacred texts of different world religions.[37] Unlike comparative theology, which often comes from within a particular faith (like Christianity), comparative religion is usually more neutral and descriptive. It looks at similarities and differences across religions to understand how they address questions about God, life, death, morality, and meaning. For example, it might compare how Christianity, Islam, and Hinduism view salvation, prayer, or the nature of the divine.[38] This study helps people appreciate the richness of global religious traditions and challenges stereotypes or misunderstandings.[39] For Christians involved in Mission, learning about other religions through comparative religion can lead to deeper respect, better communication, and a meaningful engagement in a pluralistic world.

Peacebuilding in the Context of Religious Violence

Religion has the power to unite or divide. In many parts of the globe, religious difference has led to violence, persecution, and mistrust. In such

---

[34] Michelle Voss, "Hindu-Christian Comparative Theology in a Decolonial Key," *Modern Theology* 40/2 (December, 2024): 285-306.

[35] Catherine Cornille, "Epistemology in Comparative Theology," *Perspectiva Teológica* 56/3 (December, 2024): 451-468.

[36] Hugh Nicholson, "The Reunification of Theology and Comparison in the New Comparative Theology," *Journal of the American Academy of Religion* 77/3 (September, 2009): 609-646.

[37] Merwin-Marie Snell, "The Nature and Scope of the Science of Comparative Religion," *The Biblical World* 8/3 (September, 1896): 203-210.

[38] Robert Segal, "What Does Comparative Religion Compare?", *Method & Theory in the Study of Religion* 1/1 (SPRING, 1989): 65-70.

[39] Frank N. Riale, "The Value and Danger of the Study of Comparative Religion," *The Biblical World* 4/1 (July, 1894): 14-19.

a milieu, the Church is called to be a peacemaker, promoting healing and reconciliation. Mission in such contexts involves responding to hate and extremism with the message of peace found in Jesus Christ. It also means supporting victims, engaging in forgiveness, and building bridges across religious lines. Jesus' teaching in the Beatitudes *Blessed are the peacemakers* (Matthew 5:9) calls Christians to be agents of peace in divided communities. The Church's Mission in times of conflict must go beyond preaching to include action, creating safe spaces, promoting justice, and standing with the marginalized.[40]

Public Theology and Ideologies

Mission today also involves addressing secular ideologies such as nationalism, consumerism, atheism, and individualism, the belief systems that shape society but often stand in opposition to the gospel.[41] Public theology brings Christian values into public spaces like education, politics, media, and economics, presenting a vision of human life based on dignity, community, and care for creation.[42] In a pluralistic world, the Christian voice must contribute to conversations about what is good, true, and just.[43] Rather than withdrawing from society, Christians are called to engage public life with wisdom and compassion, challenging harmful systems and offering hope rooted in the gospel.[44] This dimension of Mission seeks not just personal salvation, but the transformation of culture and society for the common good.

Conclusion

In today's world of many religions, cultures, and ideologies, the Christian Mission faces both great challenges and great opportunities. Christians are called to remain faithful to Jesus Christ while also showing deep respect for the beliefs of others. Engaging with religious pluralism does not mean weakening or changing the gospel. Instead, it means living out the message of Christ with humility, wisdom, and love. The Church must no longer approach others with superiority or fear, but with a desire to understand,

---

[40] Johan Strijdom and Joram Tarusarira, "The Role of Religion in Violence and Peacebuilding," *Journal for the Study of Religion* 30/1 (2017): 1-4.

[41] Felix Wilfred, "Public Theology in Service of Liberation," *Vidyajyoti Journal of Theological Reflection* 83/7 (December, 2019): 485-504.

[42] Linell E. Cady, "A Model for a Public Theology," *The Harvard Theological Review* 80/2 (April, 1987): 193-212.

[43] Felix Wilfred, "*Fratelli Tutti* as an Exercise in Subaltern Public Theology," *Vidyajyoti Journal of Theological Reflection* 85/4 (December, 2021): 246-268.

[44] Owen C. Thomas, "Public Theology and Counter-Public Spheres," *The Harvard Theological Review* 85/4 (October, 1992): 453-466.

build relationships, and witness through words and actions. Mission today must include interfaith dialogue, theological reflection, peaceful engagement, and public presence, all shaped by the example of Jesus. In a complex and diverse world, the Church's role is to be a light of truth, compassion, and reconciliation, showing that the gospel is GOOD NEWS for all people, everywhere.

9

Missiological Foundations of the Old Testament Covenant, Promise, and God's Redemptive Mission to the Nations

The Bible is not just a book about religion or laws, rather, it is a story of God's Mission to redeem the world. The word "Missiology" means the study of such a Mission, that how God works to save people and how God invites God's people to join in this work. While many people think that Mission begins only in the New Testament with Jesus and the apostles, the truth is that the Mission of God starts much earlier. The Old Testament, from the first pages of Genesis, reveals that God's plan was never only for Israel. Instead, God always wanted to bless all nations, all peoples, and all cultures through God's chosen people. From creation and the call of Abraham, to the laws, the prophets, the poetry, and the wisdom books, the Old Testament lays a strong foundation for understanding God's global purpose. The goal is to help us recognize that Mission is not a new idea in the Bible, it is part of God's plan from the very beginning.

Genesis: The Beginning of God's Mission

In Genesis 1:1, God's Mission begins by bringing order and life out of chaos. Since then, the book of Genesis provides the foundational framework for understanding the Mission of God in the Old Testament. It begins by showing that God is the Creator of the entire world and of all human beings. In Genesis 1:26-27, God says, *Let us make human being in God's image.* This statement highlights the universal dignity and value of every person. All people regardless of ethnicity, language, or culture are made in the image of God. In Genesis 1:28, God blesses humanity and commands them to *be fruitful and multiply, fill the earth and subdue it*, shows that from the beginning, God's purpose was for God's image to be spread throughout the whole earth. Therefore, the Mission of God begins with creation itself. It is not just a spiritual idea but part of the original design for humanity to reflect God's glory across the world.[1]

However, the harmony of creation is quickly broken by sin. Genesis 3 describes the disobedience of Adam and Eve, which results in a curse not only upon them but upon all of creation.[2] The effects of sin are seen in the chapters that follow when Cain kills Abel (Genesis 4), human wickedness grows to such a degree that God sends a flood (Genesis 6-9), and people once again rebel against God at the Tower of Babel (Genesis 11). In each of these stories, the damage caused by sin becomes deeper and more widespread.[3] Genesis 11:4 shows that the people tried to build a tower to "make a name" for themselves, rejecting God's authority. In response, God confuses their language and scatters them over the face of the earth (Genesis 11:8-9).[4] Although this scattering was a punishment, it also leads to the formation of different nations, setting the stage for God's Mission to reach all of them.

In Genesis 12:1-3, God calls Abram and makes a covenant with him, one of the most important turning points in the Bible. God says to Abram, *I will bless you... and all the peoples on earth will be blessed through you.* This covenant reveals that God's plan of salvation will now move forward through one family and its descendants. However, the goal is not just to bless Abram's family, but to bless "all the peoples on earth."[5] This is a clear statement of God's Mission to reach the nations. The covenant with Abram is not only about forming Israel, but about using Israel as a channel of blessing to the world. Through this promise, God shows that God has not given up on the nations scattered at Babel, instead, God chooses to begin God's redemptive Mission through one family, with the goal of bringing salvation to all families of the earth.

---

[1] Julian Morgenstern, "The Sources of the Creation Story-Genesis 1:1-2:4," *The American Journal of Semitic Languages and Literatures* 36/3 (April, 1920): 169-212.

[2] Alexandra Pârvan, "Genesis 1-3: Augustine and Origen on the 'Coats of Skins'," *Vigiliae Christianae* 66/1 (2012): 56-92.

[3] John H. Walton, "Babel's Invitation: The Tower of Babel Story May Be about Pride, but Not in the Way We Think," *Christianity Today* 67/2 (December, 2023): 73–77.

[4] John H. Walton, "Babel's Invitation: The Tower of Babel Story May Be about Pride…

[5] Silviu Tatu, "Interpreting the Call of Abram: Between Scylla and Carybdis," *Transformation* 30/3 (July, 2013): 208-216.

Exodus to Deuteronomy: Israel as a Missional People

The books of Exodus through Deuteronomy make it clear that Israel was chosen by God not just for privilege, but for a purpose, to serve as a witness to the nations. After God rescued Israel from slavery in Egypt, God brought them to Mount Sinai and made a special covenant with them.[6] In Exodus 19:5-6, God make it clear to the Israelites that: *If you obey my voice and keep my covenant, you shall be my treasured possession out of all the peoples. Indeed, the whole earth is mine, but you shall be for me a priestly kingdom and a holy nation*. This suggests Israel had a special role among all the nations of the world. As a "kingdom of priests," they were called to act as mediators between God and the rest of humanity.[7] Just as priests in Israel helped connect the people to God, Israel as a nation was meant to connect other nations to the one true God. Their identity as a "holy nation" meant they were to live differently, set apart by their values, worship, and way of life so that others could see God's greatness through them.

This calling is emphasized again in Deuteronomy 4:6-8, where Moses teaches the people that obedience to God's laws will make other nations take notice. When people from other countries would see the justice, fairness, and wisdom in Israel's laws, they would recognize that Israel had a close relationship with a powerful and righteous God.[8] Thus, the laws given by God were not meant to keep Israel separated from the world, but rather to display God's character to the world. Through their way of life, Israel was meant to attract the attention of other nations and point them toward God.

Moreover, the Old Testament shows that God's concern extended beyond Israel's borders. Foreigners, strangers, and outsiders were not to be mistreated or excluded. Instead, God commanded the Israelites to love and care for them. In Deuteronomy 10:18-19, it commands the Israelites to *executes justice for the orphan and the widow, and who loves the strangers, providing them food and clothing. You shall also love the stranger, for you were strangers in the land of Egypt*. This reveals the heart of God for all people, including those who were not born into the nation of Israel. Israel was to remember their past and treat outsiders with kindness and compassion, just as God had shown mercy to them when they were enslaved in Egypt.[9] It

---

[6] Louis H. Feldman, "Josephus' Portrait of Moses," *The Jewish Quarterly Review* 82/3-4 (January-April, 1992): 285-328.

[7] Herbert McCabe, "A Kingdom of Priests?," *New Blackfriars* 71/844 (December, 1990): 524-526.

[8] E. W. Nicholson, "The Decalogue as the Direct Address of God," *Vetus Testamentum* 27/4 (October, 1977): 422-433.

[9] Kenneth P. Cecil, "The Origin and Uniqueness of the גר in Deuteronomy 10:18-19," *Presbyterion* 44/2 (December, 2018): 162-163.

makes clear that the Israel's calling was to reflect God's light to the world, showing that God's love, justice, and mercy were not just for one people group, but for all nations.

Joshua to II Chronicles: God's Mission History

The historical books from Joshua to II Chronicles continue to reveal God's Mission through the life and actions of God's people. These books do not only tell the story of Israel's battles, kings, and temple, but also show how God's heart for the nations was active throughout Israel's history. Even during times of war, national growth, and political struggle, God's desire to include people from outside of Israel in His plan of salvation remains clear. Several key stories show how non-Israelites were welcomed into God's people or experienced God's power and mercy, demonstrating that God's Mission was always larger than Israel alone.

One of the clearest examples is the life of Rahab, found in Joshua 2. Rahab was a Canaanite woman living in Jericho, a city that was about to be destroyed as part of Israel's entry into the Promised Land. However, Rahab chose to trust in the God of Israel.[10] She protected the Israelite spies and confessed her faith, saying, *The Lord your God is God in heaven above and on the earth below* (Joshua 2:11). Because of her faith, Rahab and her family were saved, and she became part of the people of Israel.[11] Remarkably, she is later listed in the genealogy of Jesus (Matthew 1:5), showing how even outsiders could play a vital role in God's redemptive plan.

Another important personality worth mentioning is Ruth, a woman from Moab. In the book of Ruth chapters 1-4, we learn how she chose to stay with her Israelite mother-in-law Naomi and follow the God of Israel.[12] Ruth's famous words in Ruth 1:16 express her commitment: *Your people will be my people, and your God my God.* She eventually marries Boaz, a relative of Naomi, and becomes the great-grandmother of King David. Like Rahab, Ruth is also included in the family line of the Messiah (Matthew 1:5), showing that God welcomes those from every nation who turn to Him in faith.[13]

---

[10] K. M. Campbell, "Rahab's Covenant: A Short Note on Joshua II 9-21," *Vetus Testamentum* 22/2 (April, 1972): 243-244.

[11] K. M. Campbell, "Rahab's Covenant: A Short Note on Joshua II 9-21…

[12] Athalya Brenner, "Naomi and Ruth," *Vetus Testamentum* 33/4 (October, 1983): 385-397.

[13] Andrew D. Heffern, "The Four Women in St. Matthew's Genealogy of Christ," *Journal of Biblical Literature* 31/2 (1912): 69-81.

The story of Naaman, found in II Kings 5, also shows God's Mission of reaching beyond Israel's borders. Naaman, a commander of the Syrian army and suffered from leprosy.[14] When he came to the prophet Elisha in Israel, he was healed after following God's instructions. After his healing, Naaman declares: *Now I know that there is no God in all the world except in Israel* (II Kings 5:15). Although he came as a foreigner and outsider, he left as a worshiper of the true God.[15] This event shows that God's power and grace were not limited to the people of Israel, they could touch the lives of anyone, even 'military leaders from enemy nations.'

Another most powerful expressions of God's Mission to the nations appears in Solomon's prayer at the dedication of the temple, recorded in I Kings 8:41-43 and II Chronicles 6:32-33. Solomon prays that when foreigners come from distant lands because they have heard of God's name, God would hear their prayers and answer them. He asks that all peoples of the earth may know God's name and fear Him. This is a clear recognition that the temple was not just for Israel, but for people from all nations who would seek Him. It reflects the idea that worship of the true God should extend far beyond Israel's borders.

Job: A Universal Perspective of Mission on Humanity

The book of Job stands out in the Old Testament as a deeply philosophical and theological reflection on human suffering, divine justice, and the relationship between God and people. Although the exact background of Job is not fully explained, it is widely believed by many scholars that Job was not an Israelite. He lived in the land of Uz, a place located outside of Israel's territory, and the book contains few direct references to the covenant, the law, or Israel's history.[16] Despite this, Job is described as: *blameless and upright, a man who feared God and shunned evil* (Job 1:1). This introduction shows that a sincere relationship with the one true God was possible even outside of Israel, signifying a universal dimension to faith and righteousness.

---

[14] Thomas L. Brodie, "Towards Unraveling the Rhetorical Imitation of Sources in Acts: 2 Kgs 5 as One Component of Acts 8:9-40," *Biblica* 67/1 (1986): 41-67.

[15] Robert L. Cohn, "Form and Perspective in 2 Kings V," *Vetus Testamentum* 33/2 (April, 1983): 171-184.

[16] Andrew E. Steinmann, "The Structure and Message of the Book of Job," *Vetus Testamentum* 46/1 (January, 1996): 85-100.

Job's life demonstrates that God is not only the God of Israel, but the God of all creation, concerned with justice, morality, and personal integrity wherever they are found. Job is tested through extreme suffering in the ways he loses his wealth, his children, and his health, even though he had lived a righteous life.[17] His struggle raises deep questions about why good people suffer, why evil sometimes seems to go unpunished, and how humans can make sense of pain and loss in a world governed by a holy God. These are questions that concern all human beings, not just the people of Israel.[18] In this way, the book of Job addresses universal human experiences and reveals that God's relationship with humanity is broader than national or ethnic boundaries.

The dialogues between Job and his friends explore the nature of divine justice, often challenging the assumption that suffering is always a punishment for sin.[19] At the end, when God speaks, God does not give Job a direct answer to his suffering but instead reminds him of the greatness of God's wisdom and power (Job 38-41).[20] Job responds with humility and respect, saying: *My ears had heard of you but now my eyes have seen you* (Job 42:5). This shows a deepened understanding of who God is not just a God of rules and rewards, but a personal, sovereign, and wise Creator who is worthy of trust even when life is difficult to understand.

From a Missiological perspective, the book of Job teaches that the fear of God is not limited to Israelite religion. It affirms that people from other backgrounds can know, worship, and be in right relationship with God. It also shows that the challenges of faith, suffering, and human limitations are shared across cultures and nations. The life and witness of Job reminds us that God's Mission is universal and God engages with all people, invites them into a personal relationship with God, and is present in their struggles. This reinforces the message that the Old Testament, even in its wisdom literature, points to a God who is active in the whole world, not just within the borders of Israel.

---

[17] Michael V. Fox, "The Meanings of the Book of Job," *Journal of Biblical Literature* 137/1 (Spring, 2018): 7-18.

[18] Naphtali Meshel, "Whose Job Is This?: Dramatic Irony and double entendre in the Book of Job," in *The Book of Job: Aesthetics, Ethics, Hermeneutics*, edited by Leora Batnitzky and Ilana Pardes (Berlin: De Gruyter, 2015), 47-76.

[19] Carol Ann Newsom, "Job and His Friends: A Conflict of Moral Imaginations," *Interpretation* 53/3 (December, 1999): 239-253.

[20] John J. Collins, "Job and His Friends; God as a Pastoral Problem," *Chicago Studies* 14/1 (December, 1974): 97-109.

Psalms: Mission as Global Worship and God's Rule Over the Nations

The book of Psalms plays a powerful role in the Old Testament's Missional vision by showing that God is worthy of worship from all people everywhere, not just from the nation of Israel. While many of the psalms reflect personal prayers, national struggles, or Israel's worship traditions, a number of them express a clear global focus, calling on all nations and peoples to recognize and praise the one true God. Through these songs and prayers, we see that Mission is expressed through worship, not only in sharing God's message with others, but in inviting the world to join in glorifying God.

One such example is Psalm 67, which begins and ends with a vision of global praise:[21] *May God be gracious to us and bless us... so that Your ways may be known on earth, Your salvation among all nations... Let all the peoples praise You* (Psalm 67:1-3). This connects God's blessing on people with a desire for the nations to know God.[22] The goal of God's favour is not only Israel's good, but the spreading of God's salvation and praise throughout the earth.[23] Similarly, Psalm 96 provides a bold declaration of God's greatness that is meant to be shared globally:[24] *Declare His glory among the nations, His marvellous works among all the peoples* (Psalm 96:3). The psalm calls on the whole earth to sing to the Lord, worship, and recognize that God alone is God.[25] It also looks forward to a time when God will judge the world with justice and righteousness, showing that God's rule is not limited to Israel, but includes all creation.[26] Psalm 117, though very short, carries a powerful message: *Praise the Lord, all you nations. Extol Him, all you peoples.* Despite being only two verses long, this psalm clearly shows that the invitation to worship is universal. It does not speak only to Israel, but to all nations and all peoples, calling them to praise God because of God's love and faithfulness.[27]

---

[21] Gérard Nissim Amzallag, "Psalm 67 and the Cosmopolite Musical Worship of *YHWH*," *Bulletin for Biblical Research* 25/2 (December, 2015): 171-187.

[22] Gérard Nissim Amzallag, "Psalm 67 and the Cosmopolite Musical Worship of *YHWH*...

[23] Eep Talstra and Carl J. Bosma, "Psalm 67: Blessing, Harvest, and History: A Proposal for Exegetical Methodology," *Calvin Theological Journal* 36/2 (December, 2001): 290-313.

[24] W. Dennis Tucker, Jr., "Hortatory Discourse and Psalm 96," *Vetus Testamentum* 61/1 (December, 2011); 119-132.

[25] Robert L. Foster, "A Plea for New Songs: A Missional/Theological Reflection on Psalm 96," *Currents in Theology and Mission* 33/4 (August, 2006): 285-290.

[26] Raymond C. Van Leeuwen, "Why Do the Trees of the Forest Sing a New Song? (Psalms 96 and 98)," The Covenant Quarterly 62/3 (December, 2004): 22-34.

[27] Fanie Snyman, "Reading Psalm 117 against and Exilic Context," *Vetus Testamentum* 61/1 (December, 2011): 109-118.

Thus, Psalms as a whole reveal that the heart of Old Testament worship was not inward or exclusive, it was outward and inclusive, pointing toward a time when people from every nation would know and honour God. Through these songs, the Psalms encourage believers not only to worship God themselves but also to proclaim God's glory so that others might join in. In this way, the Psalms support the idea that Mission is not separate from worship, rather, it flows from it.

Proverbs and Ecclesiastes: Missional Perspective of Wisdom for All People

The books of Proverbs and Ecclesiastes, part of the Old Testament's wisdom literature, also contribute to the Missional vision of the Bible. Unlike the historical or prophetic books that focus directly on Israel's covenant relationship with God, Proverbs and Ecclesiastes offer wisdom for all people, dealing with universal themes such as justice, morality, work, suffering, and the search for meaning in life. Their teachings are not limited to one nation or culture but are grounded in God's moral order for all humanity. In this way, they reflect the idea that God's truth is relevant and accessible to every nation, pointing toward God's Missional vision of desire for all people to live wisely.

The book of Proverbs proposes practical instruction for daily life and emphasizes that true wisdom begins with the fear of the Lord (Proverbs 1:7). It teaches principles such as honesty, hard work, humility, kindness, and justice, the values that are important in every culture. These are often expressed in short, memorable sayings that communicate eternal truths about human behaviour and the consequences of choices.[28] Proverbs 14:31 says, *Those who oppress the poor insult their Maker, but those who are kind to the needy honour him.* This shows that how we treat others reflects our understanding of God's character, and this message applies across all social and cultural boundaries. Because Proverbs speaks to basic human concerns, it can guide not only Israelites, but people from every background who desire to live a life that honours God.

Ecclesiastes, written from the perspective of someone seeking purpose and meaning in life, explores questions that are deeply human but global in nature. The writer looks at wealth, work, pleasure, knowledge, and time, and finds that many things in life are "meaningless" or "temporary" when viewed apart from God.[29] In Ecclesiastes 1:2, the author famously says,

[28] Faith Ochenia Opade and Victor Umaru, "The Epistemological Significance of the Pursuit of Wisdom in Proverbs 1:7 and 9:10 in the Context of Belief in the Existence of God," *Journal of Biblical Theology* 8/1 (January, 2025): 50-73.

[29] Jaco W. Gericke, "ה כל הבל in Ecclesiastes 1:2 and 12:8 - Descriptive Metaphysics of Properties as Comparative-Philosophical Supplement," HTS Theological Studies 77/1 (January, 2021): 1-7.

Meaningless! Meaningless! Everything is meaningless! This cry reflects a deep sense of frustration with life's emptiness when it is lived only for earthly gain.[30] However, the book does not leave the reader in despair, but the conclusion points to the ultimate answer: *Fear God, and keep His commandments, for that is the whole duty of everyone* (Ecclesiastes 12:13). This closing statement is not directed only at Israel but at all of humanity, showing that the fear of God is the true foundation for a meaningful life.[31]

Isaiah to Daniel: Major Prophets and Mission to the Nations

The books of the Major Prophets Isaiah, Jeremiah, Ezekiel, and Daniel offer an authoritative and clear expression of God's Mission to the nations. While the Major Prophets often focus on calling Israel back to faithfulness and warning of judgment, they also consistently speak about God's global Mission. Their messages show that God is not only concerned with God's covenant people, Israel, but also with the surrounding nations. These prophetic texts reveal that God desires all peoples to know, worship, and live under God's rule. Through warnings, promises, visions, and calls to repentance, the Major Prophets communicate a universal Mission, where the God of Israel is shown to be the God of all the earth.

The book of Isaiah contains some of the most striking and beautiful visions of God's global plan. In Isaiah 2:2-4, the prophet describes a future time when "all nations" will come to the mountain of the Lord to be taught God's ways and to walk in God's paths. The vision includes people from every land turning away from war and violence, choosing peace and justice instead.[32] This shows that the God of Israel will one day be recognized and worshipped by the entire world. God declares that it is "too small a thing" for Israel to be God's servant only to restore the tribes of Jacob; instead, God says, *I will give you as a light to the nations, that my salvation may reach to the end of the earth* (Isaiah 49:6). This shows that Israel's calling was always meant to be Missional, they were chosen not just to receive God's light, but to share it with others. Later, in Isaiah 56:6-8, the prophet speaks of foreigners who bind themselves to the Lord and are welcomed into His house of prayer.[33] God says, "My house will be called a house of prayer for

---

[30] Jaco W. Gericke, "ה כל הבל in Ecclesiastes 1:2 and 12:8..., 1-7.

[31] Claude Cox, "When Torah Embraced Wisdom and Song: Job 28:8, Ecclesiastes 12:13, and Psalm 1:2," *Restoration Quarterly* 49/2 (December, 2007): 65-74.

[32] Rick W. Byargeon, "The Relationship of Micah 4:1-3 and Isaiah 2:2-4: Implications for Understanding the Prophetic Message," *Southwestern Journal of Theology* 46/1 (December, 2003): 6-26.

[33] Raymond de Hoop, "The Interpretation of Isaiah 56:1-9: Comfort or Criticism?," *Journal of Biblical Literature* 127/4 (Winter, 2008): 671-695.

all nations." This passage reflects God's inclusive heart, inviting all people regardless of their background to worship God.

The book of Jeremiah also reveals God's concern for the nations. In Jeremiah 12:14-17, God speaks about the possibility of restoration even for enemy nations, if they learn the ways of the Lord and turn to Him. God says that if these nations truly honour God, they will be built up among His people.[34] This demonstrates a radical openness in God's Mission, even those who once opposed Israel are not beyond the reach of God's mercy. Thus, prophet declares that God's ultimate goal is not destruction but redemption, and the door remains open for any nation willing to repent and follow God's ways.

Ezekiel continues this theme by showing how God's actions toward Israel are also meant to reveal God's holiness and glory to the nations. In Ezekiel 36:22-23, God tells Israel that God is not acting for their sake alone, but to uphold God's holy name among the nations.[35] God says, *the nations shall know that I am the Lord* (Ezekiel 36:23). This shows that God's judgment and restoration of Israel are Missional acts that they are meant to demonstrate God's power, justice, and mercy to the world. God's purpose is to use Israel as a visible sign to the nations of who God is and what God requires.

The book of Daniel, though set in exile, also provides a powerful witness to God's Mission among the nations. In Daniel 4, King Nebuchadnezzar of Babylon, a Gentile ruler, is humbled by God and eventually acknowledges that God's kingdom is eternal and that God rules over all (Daniel 4:34-37).[36] In Daniel 6, King Darius of Persia witnesses God's miraculous protection of Daniel in the lion's den and then issues a decree that all people in his kingdom should fear and reverence the God of Daniel (Daniel 6:25-27). These show that even the most powerful rulers of the world are subject to the authority of the one true God. Through the faithful witness of individuals like Daniel, Gentile kings come to know and proclaim God's greatness.[37]

---

[34] Carolyn J. Sharp, "The Call of Jeremiah and Diaspora Politics," *Journal of Biblical Literature* 119/3 (Autumn, 2000): 421-438.

[35] John W. Herbst, "Recreation in Ezekiel 36," *The Living Pulpit* 25/1 (December, 2016): 4-6.

[36] David S. Vanderhooft, "'Nebuchadnezzar, King of Babylon, My Servant': Contrasting Prophetic Images of the Great King," *Hebrew Bible and Ancient Israel* 7/1 (December, 2018): 93-111.

[37] Kristin Joachimsen, "Yehudite Imaginations of King Darius and His Officials: Views from the Province beyond the River," *Religions* 13/3 (January, 2022): 1-18.

Hosea to Malachi: Minor Prophets and Mission as God's Heart for the Nations

The Minor Prophets, from Hosea to Malachi, even though often focused on Israel's sin and judgment, also present a strong and clear picture of God's global Mission. These shorter prophetic books reveal that God's heart is not limited to Israel, rather God is deeply concerned with the destiny of the nations. Even while calling God's people to repentance, the minor prophets consistently point to a future in which Gentiles will come to know and worship the one true God.[38] Through their messages, we see that God's justice, mercy, and salvation are meant for all peoples, not just one chosen nation.

The book of Jonah provides one of the most direct examples of God's Missionary concern for the nations. God commands Jonah to go to Nineveh, the capital of Assyria, a Gentile city and an enemy of Israel and call the people to repent (Jonah 1:1-2).[39] Jonah resists this Mission, not because he fears failure, but because he knows God is merciful and might forgive them (Jonah 4:2). When the people of Nineveh repent, God shows them mercy. This reveals that God's compassion extends even to Israel's enemies, and God's desire is not to destroy nations but to lead them to repentance.[40] Thus, Jonah becomes a powerful reminder that God's Mission is never meant to stay within national or ethnic boundaries, rather, God's grace reaches even those whom consider unworthy.

In Amos, the prophet speaks of a future time when God will restore *booth of David that is fallen* and *all the nations who are called by my name* (Amos 9:11-12). This prophecy points to a restored kingdom where people from other nations are welcomed into God's family.[41] It is significant that this passage was later quoted in the New Testament (Acts 15:16-17) to support the inclusion of Gentiles in the early church. This shows that the Minor Prophets laid the groundwork for a global understanding of God's kingdom, where Gentiles are not outsiders but full participants.

---

[38] Alice L. Camille, "Minor Prophets: For God, There Is No Such Thing as Being Too Young," *U.S. Catholic* 77/6 (December, 2012): 44-46.

[39] Arthur W. Ackerman, "The Purpose of Jonah's Mission to Nineveh," *The Biblical World* 12/3 (September, 1898): 190-195.

[40] Hyun Chul Paul Kim, "Jonah Read Intertextually," *Journal of Biblical Literature* 126/3 (Fall, 2007): 497-528.

[41] H. Neil Richardson, "Skt (Amos 9:11): 'Booth' or 'Succoth'?," *Journal of Biblical Literature* 92/3 (September, 1973): 375-381.

Micah resembles the themes from Isaiah, describing a time when many nations will come to the mountain of the Lord, seeking to learn God's ways and walk in God's paths (Micah 4:1-3). This vision sees the nations no longer in rebellion, but in humility, coming to God for wisdom and guidance.[42] It portrays the Lord's house as a place of teaching and peace for all peoples, showing that God intends for God's truth to be shared and embraced globally.

Zephaniah adds another dimension by declaring that God will purify the speech of the nations, so that they may all call on God's name and serve God together (Zephaniah 3:8-10). This highlights God's desire to unite people of all languages and cultures in worship, reversing the confusion of languages at Babel (Genesis 11).[43] Zephaniah even mentions worshipers coming *from beyond the rivers of Cush my suppliants, my scattered ones, shall bring my offering* (Zephaniah 3:10) pointing to distant lands in Africa. This shows that God's Mission is not only for nearby nations but extends to the farthest corners of the earth.

Zechariah provides a beautiful picture of Gentiles actively seeking God (Zechariah 8:20-23). It says that many peoples and strong nations will come to Jerusalem to pray and seek the Lord. Zechariah clearly describes that people from many nations grabbing hold of a Jew and saying: *Let us go with you, for we have heard that God is with you* (Zechariah 8:23).[44] This shows the magnetic effect of God's presence among God's people, the nations are drawn not by force, but by the witness of God's people and the reality of God's presence.

Finally, the book of Malachi, the last of the Minor Prophets, ends with a powerful global vision saying: *For from the rising of the sun to its setting my name is great among the nations…for my name is great among the nations, says the Lord of hosts* (Malachi 1:11). This all-encompassing statement makes it clear that God's desire is for God's name to be known and worshiped across the entire earth.[45] It reminds us that God's ultimate purpose is global worship, and that God's Mission reaches to every place and every people.

---

[42] Jack Y. Sara, "Teach Us Your Ways, Lord (Micah 4:1-3)," *Ex Auditu* 35 (December, 2019): 208-213.

[43] Adrian Schenker, "Israelite or Universal Horizon: Zephaniah 3.8-10 in the Hebrew and Greek Bibles," *The Bible Translator* 64/2 (January, 2013): 151-158.

[44] Yo-han Im and P. M. Venter, "The Function of Zechariah 7-8 within the Book of Zechariah," *HTS Theological Studies* 69/1 (January, 2013): 1-10.

[45] Joyce G. Baldwin, "Malachi 1:11 and the Worship of the Nations in the Old Testament," *Tyndale Bulletin* 23 (December, 1972): 117-124.

Conclusion

The Old Testament presents a clear and consistent vision of God's Mission, a Mission that begins in Genesis and continues through every book until the final words of Malachi. From the very beginning, God reveals God's desire to bless all nations, not just one people group. Israel was chosen not as an exclusive or superior nation, but as a servant and witness to the rest of the world. Through covenants, laws, worship, wisdom, and prophetic voices, the Old Testament tells the history of a God whose heart is for all people, regardless of race, culture, or geography. This vision appears in many forms: God's promise to Abraham to bless all nations through his family (Genesis 12:3), the call for Israel to be a kingdom of priests (Exodus 19:6), the welcoming of foreigners into the covenant community, the inclusion of Gentiles in key biblical stories, and the prophetic promises that one day all nations will come to worship the Lord. This makes clear that, from being narrow or nationalistic, the Old Testament consistently points to a future where people from every language and land will turn to God in faith, justice, and worship.

10

Mission Themes in the Hebrew Bible
Election, Covenant, Commandment, Nation, Remnant, Redemption and Hospitality

The Hebrew Bible is not merely a collection of ancient religious texts for Israel, rather, it is also a theological narrative shaped by God's unfolding Mission to redeem the world. Throughout the Old Testament, we find the inclusion of themes that speak to this divine purpose such as: election, covenant, commandment, nation, remnant, redemption, and hospitality, that are central to understanding how Israel's story fits into the broader narrative of God's Mission. Because, these concepts are not isolated theological ideas but are deeply interconnected and reveal how God chooses, forms, instructs, disciplines, and sends His people to be a blessing to others. Together, these Mission themes show that the Hebrew Bible is not inward-looking but deeply concerned with God's plan for all nations. Exploring these concepts reveals the theological depth and Missional coherence of the Old Testament, laying essential foundation for understanding both Israel's identity and the global Mission that continues in the New Testament.

Election: Israel's Missional Calling for the Sake of the Nations

The theme of election in the Hebrew Bible is central to understanding God's Mission in the world. Election refers to God's choice of individuals or nations for a specific purpose, not for privilege, but for service. From the very beginning, God chooses people to play a part in God's redemptive plan for all humanity.[1] Abraham as the first major example, God calls him

[1] Nathan MacDonald, "The *Imago Dei* and Election: Reading Genesis 1:26-28 and Old Testament Scholarship with Karl Barth," *International Journal of Systematic Theology* 10/3 (January, 2008): 303-327.

and promises to bless him so that *in you all the families of the earth shall be blessed* (Genesis 12:1-3). This reveals that election is deeply Missional and Abraham is not chosen for his own benefit, but to become a channel of blessing to all nations.[2] Similarly, Moses is chosen in Exodus 3 to lead Israel out of slavery, showing that God's calling involves delivering others and participating in God's justice.

Another significant example of election is God's choice of Israel as God's covenant people. Deuteronomy explains that God chose Israel not because they were great in number or power, but because of His love and faithfulness: *For you are a people holy to the Lord your God; the Lord your God has chosen you out of all the peoples on earth to be his people, his treasured possession* (Deuteronomy 7:6-8). In Exodus, God calls Israel to be a kingdom of priests and a holy nation: *but you shall be for me a priestly kingdom and a holy nation* (Exodus 19:5-6) clearly states that their election comes with responsibility. As priests represent God to others, Israel is meant to reflect God's character to the nations.[3] Because their obedience to God's commandments serves as a testimony. Moses clears this by saying in Deuteronomy that: *Surely this great nation is a wise and discerning people* (Deuteronomy 4:6-8), and declares that when Israel obeys God's laws, other nations will see their wisdom and be drawn to God.[4] In this way, election is a direct Mission theme, that Israel is chosen to display God's justice, mercy, and holiness so the world may know Him.

The prophets often reminded Israel that their election was for the sake of the nations. For example, in Isaiah God declares that: *It is too light a thing that you should be my servant to raise up the tribes of Jacob and to restore the survivors of Israel... I will give you as a light to the nations, that my salvation may reach to the end of the earth* (Isaiah 49:6). This reinforces the idea that Israel's election is not an end in itself but a means through which God's universal Mission is fulfilled.

Covenant: Israel's Role in God's Redemptive Mission

In the Hebrew Bible, a covenant is a sacred agreement or binding relationship between God and humans, established by God, in which God makes promises and requires a faithful response by the people. It is more

---

[2] J. Richard Middleton, "The Blessing of Abraham and the *Missio Dei*: Reframing the Purpose of Israel's Election in Genesis 12:1-3," in *Orthodoxy and Orthopraxis: Essays in Tribute to Paul Livermore*, edited by Douglas R. Cullum and J. Richard Middleton (Eugene: Pickwick Publications, 2020), 44-64.

[3] Prescott H. Williams, "'And Now, If...55': A Study of Exodus 19:1-6," *Austin Seminary Bulletin* 78/6 (December, 1963): 39-51.

[4] Yitzhaq Feder, "The Aniconic Tradition, Deuteronomy 4, and the Politics of Israelite Identity," *Journal of Biblical Literature* 132/2 (2013): 251-274.

than just a contract, it is a relational commitment based on God's initiative, rooted in God's grace, and often sealed with signs, laws, or rituals. In the Old Testament, the theme of covenant is a key part and plays a major role in understanding God's Mission to the world. In the Bible, God makes covenants not only to bless individuals or nations, but to fulfil His greater purpose of restoring and blessing all creation. These covenants reveal God's desire to work through people to carry out God's Mission to bring justice, healing, and salvation to the world. Thus, in simple terms, the covenant is how God connects with humanity and invites them to join in God's Mission.

The Noahic Covenant

One of the first important covenants is made with Noah is recorded in Genesis 9. After the flood, God promises that God will never again destroy the earth in this way, and God places a rainbow in the sky as a sign of this promise.[5] This covenant is not just for Noah, but for all people and all living creatures (Genesis 9:8-17). It shows that through the covenant God cares for the entire world and has a plan to preserve and bless it. This covenant sets the stage for God's ongoing relationship with humanity. Thus, the Noahic Covenant is a universal and unconditional covenant in which God promises to preserve the world and never again destroy it by flood.[6] It reveals God's gracious initiative toward all creation and establishes God's commitment to the stability and continuity of life.[7] This covenant forms a theological foundation for God's ongoing Mission, setting the stage for future covenants through which God will redeem and bless all nations.

The Abrahamic Covenant

A second major covenant is made with Abraham in Genesis 12, 15, and 17. God promises to bless Abraham, give him many descendants, and make him into a great nation.[8] But the purpose is clear: *I will bless those who bless you, and the one who curses you I will curse, and in you all the families of the earth shall be blessed* (Genesis 12:3). This covenant shows that Abraham

---

[5] Peter Benjamin Boeckel, "Exploring Narrative Forms and Trajectories: Form Criticism and the Noahic Covenant," in *Partners with God: Theological and Critical Readings of the Bible in Honor of Marvin A. Sweeney*, edited by Shelley L. Birdsong and Serge Frolov (London: Claremont Press, 2017), 27-40.

[6] David VanDrunen, "Natural Law in Noahic Accent: A Covenantal Conception of Natural Law Drawn from Genesis 9," *Journal of the Society of Christian Ethics* 30/2 (Fall/ Winter, 2010): 131-149.

[7] Jeong Koo Jeon, "The Noahic Covenants and the Kingdom of God," *Mid-America Journal of Theology* 24 (December, 2013): 179-209.

[8] David Andrew Dean, "Covenant, Conditionality, and Consequence: New Terminology and a Case Study in the Abrahamic Covenant," *Journal of the Evangelical Theological Society* 57/2 (December, 2014): 281-308.

and his descendants (Israel) are chosen not just for themselves, but to be a blessing to all nations. The Missiology of the Abrahamic Covenant is that it is a particular covenant in which God elects Abraham and his descendants not for privilege, but for participation in God's redemptive plan for all nations.[9] This covenant combines divine election with a universal purpose, revealing that God's blessing to Israel is intended to overflow to *all the families of the earth* (Genesis 12:3). It establishes the foundation of biblical Mission theology, showing that from the beginning, God's covenantal relationship with God's people is meant to be a means of global blessing and inclusion.

The Sinai Covenant

The Sinai covenant with Israel, given through Moses in Exodus 19-24, provides extended element to how God's people should live. God gives Israel the "Ten Commandments" and other laws, calling them to be *a priestly kingdom and a holy nation* (Exodus 19:6). This means Israel is supposed to show God's character to the world. Just as priests represent God to the people, Israel is to represent God to the nations.[10] When Israel obeys God's law, they display God's justice, mercy, and holiness. According to Deuteronomy 4:6-8, the surrounding nations will see Israel's wisdom and understand that their God is near and righteous. The Sinai Covenant is Missional because Israel is called to reflect God's holiness and justice to the surrounding nations by living according to God's laws, they serve as a visible witness to God's character and purposes in the world (Deuteronomy 4:6-8).[11] This covenant underscores Israel's vocation to represent God among the nations and participate in God's redemptive Mission through faithful living.

The Davidic Covenant

The Davidic covenant, found in II Samuel 7, is God's promise to King David that one of his descendants will rule forever. This covenant looks forward to a future king who will bring peace, justice, and salvation, not only for Israel but for all people.[12] The prophets later explain that this king (the Messiah) will bring God's justice to the nations (Isaiah 9:6-7; Isaiah 11:1-10). The covenant with David points forward to Jesus Christ, who fulfils the promise

---

[9] Robert I. Vasholz, "The Character of Israel's Future in Light of the Abrahamic and Mosaic Covenants," *Trinity Journal* 25/1 (December, 2004): 39-59.

[10] Allan Macdonald Harman, "The Exodus and the Sinai Covenant in the Book of Psalms," *The Reformed Theological Review* 73/1 (December, 2014): 3-27.

[11] J. Duane Beals, "The Covenant of Sinai," *Reflections* 1617 (January, 2015), 21-25.

[12] Hayyim Angel, "The Eternal Davidic Covenant in II Samuel Chapter 7 and Its Later Manifestations in the Bible," *Jewish Bible Quarterly* 44/2 (December, 2016): 83-90.

of a global, eternal kingdom. The Missiology of the Davidic Covenant is that it is an unconditional, royal, and messianic covenant in which God promises to establish the eternal reign of a descendant of David (II Samuel 7:12-16).[13] This covenant not only safeguards God's commitment to the Davidic line but also points forward to the Messiah, a future king who will bring peace, justice, and salvation to Israel and all nations (Isaiah 9:6-7; 11:1-10). The Davidic Covenant reveals God's plan to establish a universal and everlasting kingdom, ultimately fulfilled in Jesus Christ, whose reign extends beyond national boundaries and embodies God's global Mission of redemption.[14]

The New Covenant

Even when Israel breaks the covenant, God promises to make a new covenant. In Jeremiah 31:31-34, God says, God will write God's law on people's hearts and forgive their sins.[15] This new covenant is fulfilled in Jesus, who offers salvation not just to Israel but to all who believe in Jesus (Luke 22:20; Hebrews 8). The new covenant continues God's Mission by making it possible for people from all nations to become part of God's people.[16] Missiologically, the New Covenant broadens the scope of God's Mission. No longer limited to ethnic Israel, this covenant opens the door for people from every nation to become part of the covenant community through faith in Christ.[17] It symbolizes the universal promise to bless all nations (Genesis 12:3) and enables the formation of a new people of God, the Church, called to proclaim the good news of salvation to the ends of the earth.[18] Thus, the New Covenant reveals God's ultimate goal: a redeemed, Spirit-transformed, global community living in faithful relationship with God and participating in God's Mission to restore the world.

The Missiological Role of Commandments in the Hebrew Bible

The theme of commandment in the Hebrew Bible is deeply connected to God's Mission for God's people and the world. Commandments are not

---

[13] Hayyim Angel, "The Eternal Davidic Covenant in II Samuel Chapter 7…

[14] Mario M. C. Melendez, "The Davidic Covenant as an Interpretational Key," *Journal for Baptist Theology & Ministry* 18/1 (January, 2021): 41-61.

[15] Phillip Michael Lasater, "Psalm 40 and the 'New Covenant' of Jeremiah 31?: Contextualizing the Legal Anthropology of a Liturgical Text," *Vetus Testamentum* 74/4-5 (December, 2024): 645-668.

[16] Phillip Michael Lasater, "Psalm 40 and the 'New Covenant' of Jeremiah 31…

[17] Gary L. Shultz Jr., "The Spirit in Elisha's Life: A Preview of Jesus Christ and the New Covenant," *Themelios* 47/1 (December, 2022): 36-48.

[18] Gregory Ross Goswell, "Forgiveness and the New Covenant of Jeremiah 31," *Zeitschrift Für Die Alttestamentliche Wissenschaft* 134/3 (December, 2022): 370-377.

merely religious rules or legal duties, rather, they are the revealed will of God, given to form a community that reflects God's character and purpose. In the context of Mission, the commandments shape Israel's identity as a witnessing nation, a people through whom God's justice, holiness, and compassion are displayed to the surrounding nations. Obedience to God's commandments was never meant to be an internal or isolated practice. Rather, it was intended to demonstrate to the world who God is and how life under God's rule brings blessing, justice, and peace.

A key example of this Missional perspective is found in Deuteronomy 4:6-8, where Moses tells Israel to observe the laws carefully, because other nations will see their wisdom and say, "Surely this great nation is a wise and understanding people." This passage shows that God gave the commandments not just for Israel's internal order, but also as a testimony to the nations. Through their way of life, Israel was to display a different kind of society, one built on justice, mercy, and faithfulness to God. In this way, the commandments had a Missional function, serving as a visible witness of God's goodness and righteousness.

The Ten Commandments (Exodus 20 and Deuteronomy 5) form the heart of the covenantal law and express foundational values such as honouring God, respecting life, protecting marriage and family, and living truthfully. These are not just moral standards for personal behaviour, but, reflect God's order for human life. When Israel lived according to these commandments, they created a community where people flourished. This was to be a light to the nations (Isaiah 42:6), showing that God's ways bring life, not bondage. The structure of the commandments beginning with love for God and continuing with love for neighbour and also reflects the relational and ethical core of God's Mission.

Moreover, many laws in the Torah deal with how to treat foreigners, the poor, widows, and orphans, subaltern groups that were always marginalized. Deuteronomy 10:18-19 is the commandment that declares that God loves the foreigner and provides for them, and commands Israel to do the same because they themselves were once foreigners in Egypt. This shows that the commandments were meant to form a compassionate and inclusive society, one that reflects God's heart for justice and hospitality. These laws were Missional in the sense that they are universal and revealed God's concern for all people, not just Israelites.

In the *Sabbath* laws, there is also a strong Mission element. The *Sabbath* was a day of rest not only for Israelites but also for foreigners living among them, servants, and even animals: *But the seventh day is a Sabbath to the Lord your God; you shall not do any work, you, your son or your daughter, your male or female slave, your livestock, or the alien resident in your towns* (Exodus 20:10). This inclusive rest reflects God's desire for universal peace and restoration, a sign of the future kingdom where all creation is renewed. Through such practices, the commandments offered a foretaste of God's redemptive plan, showing that God's care extended beyond national or ethnic boundaries.

When Israel disobeyed God's commandments, the prophets reminded them of their failure not only to live rightly, but also to fulfil their role as God's witness to the nations. The exile, as described in books like Jeremiah and Ezekiel, was not just a punishment but a way for God to correct God's people so that God's name would be honoured among the nations (Ezekiel 36:22-23). This reinforces the idea that keeping the commandments was never just optional or for personal holiness, rather, it was essential to God's global Mission. Thus, the commandments in the Hebrew Bible were much more than religious obligations. They were instruments of Mission, shaping Israel into a community that could reflect God's character and attract the nations to Him. By living according to God's instructions, Israel was meant to be a visible sign of God's kingdom, a people whose justice, mercy, and worship pointed others toward the one true God.

The Nations in God's Story: The Missional Purpose of Nationhood in the Hebrew Bible

The theme of "nation" plays an important role in the Hebrew Bible and in the understanding of God's Mission. In the biblical context, the word "nation" (Hebrew: *goyim*) often refers to non-Israelite peoples, while *am* refers to a people group, including Israel. From the beginning, the Bible presents God as the 'Creator' and 'Ruler' of all nations, not just of Israel. Thus, the history of redemption is not only about individuals but about how entire nations are invited into relationship with God. This makes clear that, God's plan involves calling one nation, Israel, not to remain exclusive, but to be a blessing to other nations and God is working through history to reach and redeem all nations of the earth.

Israel as a Missional Nation

The Israel as a Missional nation emphasizes that God's election of Israel was vocational and representative, not exclusive or self-serving. In Exodus 19:5-6, Israel is called to be "a kingdom of priests and a holy nation," indicating a unique role among the nations, to serve as mediators of God's presence, truth, and blessing to the wider world. Just as priests serve on behalf of others, Israel was chosen to serve the nations by revealing God's character through their way of life. This calling is not rooted in superiority, but in God's purpose to reach all nations through the witness of one nation.[19]

[19] Ronald Errol Bartholomew, "The Gathering of Scattered Israel: The Missional Enterprise of The Church of Jesus Christ of Latter-Day Saints," *International Bulletin of*

In Deuteronomy 4:6-8, Israel's obedience to God's just and wise laws is presented as a witness to the nations, showing that God's ways are good and worthy of imitation. Therefore, Israel's identity is Mission-shaped identity. Their holiness, justice, and communal life are designed to reflect God's glory and draw other nations toward Him. This affirms that election is for Mission, and that the people of God are called to embody God's purposes in the world.[20] Israel was not merely to enjoy God's blessings, but to become a living sign of God's kingdom, showing what it means to live under God's rule. This Missional vocation sets a foundation for the Church's identity in the New Testament, which continues the call to be a holy people and a light to the nations: *But you are a chosen people, a royal priesthood, a holy nation, God's own people, in order that you may proclaim the excellence of Him who called you out of darkness into His marvellous light* (I Peter 2:9).

The Nations in the Abrahamic Covenant

The Missional role of nations is rooted in God's covenant with Abraham. The Abrahamic Covenant (Genesis 12:1-3 & 17:4-5) reveals that God's act of election, choosing Abraham and his descendants, was never meant to be an exclusive privilege but a means of extending God's blessing to all nations.[21] In Genesis 12:1-3, God calls Abraham with a threefold promise such as: land, descendants, and blessing. But the ultimate purpose of that blessing is made clear that *in you all the families of the earth shall be blessed* (Genesis 12:3). This Missiological foundation shows that Israel's identity, from its beginning, is tied to God's Mission for the world. The repetition and expansion of this promise in Genesis, where Abraham is promised that: *You shall be the ancestor of a multitude of nations* (Genesis 17:4) further emphasizes that God's redemptive plan is not limited to one ethnic group but through Abraham God is aimed at bringing all nations into relationship with Him: *I have made you the ancestor of a multitude of nations* (Genesis 17:5). This underscores that election is for service, not superiority. Abraham is chosen to become the channel through which God's global Mission reveals, a Mission of reconciliation, blessing, and renewal for all peoples. Thus, the Abrahamic Covenant sets the trajectory for the rest of the biblical narrative, revealing that God's plan has always included the nations, and Israel was called to play a central role in fulfilling that purpose.

Mission Research 46/4 (December, 2022): 540-554.

[20] Kim, Jin-Hak. "A Missional Challenge to Pre-Exilic Faith Community for the Practice of Idolatry." *Gospel and Mission* 28 (January, 2014): 377-399.

[21] Louis E. Newman, "Covenant and Contract: A Framework for the Analysis of Jewish Ethics," *Journal of Law and Religion* 9/1 (1991): 89-112.

Nations in the Psalms and Prophets

The nations in Psalms and Prophets reflect the universal scope of God's redemptive Mission and the inclusion of all nations in worship and knowledge of God. It reflects a Missiology in which God's purpose extends beyond Israel to embrace the whole world, inviting every nation into relationship with Him. In the Psalms, nations are repeatedly called to worship the Lord (e.g., Psalms 67, 96, 117), revealing that worship is not restricted to Israel but is the intended response of all peoples to God's glory and salvation.[22] This shows that God's presence and rule are not confined to a single people group, but are meant to be proclaimed globally. The Prophets expand this vision, particularly in texts like Isaiah 2:2-4 and Micah 4:1-3, where the nations are depicted as streaming to God's Mountain to receive instruction and live in peace under God's reign. This imagery reflects hope and restoration, where all nations participate in God's future kingdom of justice, peace, and truth.[23] In Isaiah 49:6, the calling of Israel as a "light to the nations" reveals that Israel's election is Missional in purpose, to not only proclaim God's truth but also to embody it through holy living. Thus, Psalms and Prophets reveals that God's desire is not merely to form a chosen people, but to reach all people through them, forestalling the global Mission fulfilled in the New Testament: *I will give you as a light to the nations, that my salvation may reach to the end of the earth* (Isaiah 49:6) *Go therefore and make disciples of all nations* (Matthew 28:19). *But you will receive power when the Holy Spirit has come upon you, and you will be my witnesses in Jerusalem, in all Judea and Samaria, and to the ends of the earth* (Acts 1:8)

God's Judgment and Restoration of the Nations

'God's Judgment and Restoration of the Nations' reflects a balanced vision of divine justice and mercy in the Hebrew Bible. The prophetic literature consistently affirms that God is the sovereign ruler of all nations, not just Israel, and therefore holds all peoples accountable for their moral and spiritual failures. Prophets such as Amos, Isaiah, and Jeremiah pronounce judgment on foreign nations for sins like oppression, violence, idolatry, and pride, affirming that God's justice is universal.[24] Yet, this is not limited to

---

[22] Theodore Mascarenhas, *The Missionary Function of Israel in Psalms 67, 96, and 117* (London: University Press of America, 2005).

[23] Rick W. yargeon, "The Relationship of Micah 4:1-3 and Isaiah 2:2-4: Implications for Understanding the Prophetic Message," *Southwestern Journal of Theology* 46/1 (December, 2003): 6-26.

[24] Benjamin L. Merkle, "Old Testament Restoration Prophecies Regarding the Nation of Israel: Literal or Symbolic?," *The Southern Baptist Journal of Theology* 14/1 (December, 2010): 14-25.

condemnation. The Hebrew Bible also offers a redemptive perspective that God's judgment is not an end in itself, but a means toward repentance and renewal. In Jeremiah 12:14-17, even Israel's enemies are offered restoration if they turn to God and learn God's ways. Similarly, Zephaniah 3:9 envisions a day when God will "purify the speech of the nations," so that all may call upon God's name in unity.[25] These examples reveal that God's ultimate desire is not the destruction of the nations, but their inclusion in God's covenantal purposes. From a Missiological perspective, this affirms that God's Mission includes both correction and invitation. Thus, 'God's Judgment and Restoration of the Nations' reveals a Missional theology of global restoration, a world where all nations, having been disciplined and renewed, come together to worship and serve the one true God.

The Missional Significance of Nationhood

'The Missional Significance of Nationhood' affirms that God's redemptive plan is global in scope and that the nations are not merely recipients of divine blessing but active participants in God's Mission. In the Hebrew Bible, God calls Israel to model life under God's rule, acting as a visible sign of God's justice, holiness, and mercy. The nation of Israel was never intended to exist in isolation but to function as a witness among the nations, showing what it means to live in covenant relationship with God (Deuteronomy 4:6-8). This vision expands throughout the prophetic writings, where the nations are not only judged for their wickedness but also invited into God's redemptive purposes.[26] Prophets like Isaiah envision a time when nations will come to God's Mountain to learn God's ways and live in peace (Isaiah 2:2-4). Thus, nationhood in the Hebrew Bible presents a Missional path from one nation chosen to reflect God, to all nations gathered to worship and serve God.[27] This thread culminates in the New Testament, where Jesus, echoing the prophetic vision, commissions His disciples to "make disciples of all nations" (Matthew 28:19). Therefore, nationhood in the Hebrew Bible is not a static identity but a dynamic calling within God's unfolding global Mission.

---

[25] Adrian Schenker, "Israelite or Universal Horizon: Zephaniah 3.8-10 in the Hebrew and Greek Bibles." *The Bible Translator* 64/2 (January, 2013): 151-158.

[26] A. D. H. Mayes, "Deuteronomy 4 and the Literary Criticism of Deuteronomy," *Journal of Biblical Literature* 100/1 (March, 1981): 23-51.

[27] Tikva Simone Frymer-Kensky, "A Jewish Look at Isaiah 2:2-4," *Criterion* 41/3 (December, 2002): 20-25.

The "Remnant" in the Hebrew Bible: Survivors of Judgment and Agents of God's Mission

In the Hebrew Bible, the term "remnant" refers to a small group of people who survive or are preserved after a time of judgment or crisis. The Hebrew word often used is *she'ar*, which means "survivor" or "remainder." This concept appears frequently throughout the Old Testament and carries both theological and Missional meaning.[28] From a Missiological perspective, the remnant represents God's faithfulness to God's covenant, even when the majority of God's people fall into disobedience. God does not abandon God's promises, but instead preserves a faithful group through whom God continues God's redemptive work.[29] This remnant is not only saved from destruction but also plays a key role in God's Mission. They are chosen not only to survive but to serve, to carry forward God's purpose, reflect God's character, and point others to God. The idea of the remnant appears in historical contexts, such as the survivors of the Babylonian exile, as well as in prophetic literature, where prophets like Isaiah, Micah, and Zephaniah speak of a future faithful remnant.[30] This theme "remnant" also holds Missional significance, as the remnant becomes a channel of hope and restoration for both Israel and the nations. In this way, the remnant functions as a bridge between judgment and renewal, showing that God's plan continues even through a small and faithful people.

Remnant as Recipients of God's Mercy

'Remnant as Recipients of God's Mercy' highlights God's unwavering commitment to preserve a faithful people, even when the majority fall into sin and rebellion. Thus, the theme 'remnant' reveals that God's mercy is selective not in favouritism, but in faithfulness, God chooses to preserve those who trust in God and remain loyal to God's covenant, often in the midst of overwhelming unfaithfulness. The remnant does not survive because of their strength, but because of God's grace and divine initiative.[31] Biblical examples make this clear. In Genesis 6-9, God saves Noah and his family from the flood, not only to rescue them from destruction, but to reestablish His purpose for humanity through them. In I Kings 19:18, during a time of widespread idolatry, God assures Elijah that 7,000 in Israel

---

[28] Kenneth D. Mulzac, "*Ytr* as a Remnant Term in the Book of Jeremiah," *Journal of the Adventist Theological Society* 19/1-2 (December, 2008): 3-17.

[29] C. A. Strine, "The Role of Repentance in the Book of Ezekiel: A Second Chance for the Second Generation," *The Journal of Theological Studies* 63/2 (October, 2012): 467-491.

[30] Jeremiah W. Cataldo, "Embracing Nehemiah: Restoration as a Performance of Social Cohesion," *Reflections* 1617 (January, 2015): 57-71.

[31] Kenneth D. Mulzac, "*Ytr* as a Remnant Term in the Book of Jeremiah…

have not bowed to Baal, showing that even in spiritual darkness, a faithful remnant remains by God's doing.[32] In Isaiah 7-8, the prophet's own children serve as living signs of God's promise to preserve a remnant, those who will trust in God despite judgment. This shows that mercy and Mission are deeply connected. The remnant is preserved not just to survive, but to carry forward God's redemptive work. Their existence is a sign of hope, proving that God's purposes will not be defeated by human failure.[33] In this way, the remnant becomes a living testimony to God's mercy, and a reminder that God's Mission continues through a faithful few who embody God's grace.

The Prophets and the Missional Role of the Remnant

'The Prophets and the Missional Role of the Remnant' emphasizes that the remnant is not only a group of survivors, but also the instrument of God's ongoing Mission and renewal. The prophetic books portray the remnant as God's means of restoring God's people and extending God's purposes beyond Israel. Rather than ending with judgment, the prophetic vision moves toward hope, restoration, and global impact through a faithful and purified community. In Isaiah 10:20-23, the remnant is described as a purified group who return to the Lord in truth and dependence. They are seen as a 'holy seed,' a small, faithful beginning through which God will bring about renewal.[34] This theme is extended in Isaiah 11:11-12, where the remnant is gathered from the nations, pointing toward an inclusive and global dimension of God's redemptive plan.[35] Similarly, in Micah 5:7-8, the remnant is portrayed as a source of blessing and strength among the nations, like dew from the Lord, quietly influential and life-giving. Zephaniah 3:12-13 presents the remnant as humble, righteous, and dependent on God, forming the true people through whom God will dwell and act. This remnant reflects the values of the kingdom such as: truth, humility, and trust and becomes the foundation for a restored and just society. Thus, the remnant in the prophets functions as a Missional community, that they are preserved not only for themselves but to be a renewed people who embody and extend

---

[32] Gina Hens-Piazza, "Dreams Can Delude, Visions Can Deceive: Elijah's Sojourn in the Wilderness of Horeb (I Kings 19:1-21)," *Biblical Theology Bulletin* 48/1 (January, 2018): 10-17.

[33] Warren Carter, "Evoking Isaiah: Matthean Soteriology and an Intertextual Reading of Isaiah 7-9 and Matthew 1:23 and 4:15-16," *Journal of Biblical Literature* 119/3 (December, 2000): 503-520.

[34] Fabrizio Marcello, "'The Yoke Before the Oil' (Isa 10:27d) in the Light of Neo-Assyrian Covenant-Making Rituals," *Vetus Testamentum* 74/3 (December, 2024): 352-368.

[35] Matthew L. Bowen, "'We Are a Remnant of the Seed of Joseph': Moroni's Interpretive Use of Joseph's Coat and the Martial Nēs-Imagery of Isaiah 11:11-12," *Interpreter* 41 (December, 2020): 169-191.

God's character and calling, because, God's Mission does not end with the failure of the many but continues through the faithfulness of the few. In this way, the remnant bridges judgment and hope, exile and restoration, and becomes a prophetic sign of God's mercy and Mission to the world.

The Remnant and the Nations

The theology of "The Remnant and the Nations" emphasizes that the biblical concept of the remnant is not just about surviving judgment, but about becoming a community with an outward, Missional purpose. In the Hebrew Bible, the remnant is preserved and restored by God, not only for the sake of Israel, but also to serve as a witness to the nations. Their renewed relationship with God is intended to attract others and draw them into God's redemptive plan. One of the key passages, Isaiah 11:10-12, presents the vision of the remnant's global impact. It describes a time when the nations will seek the root of Jesse (a messianic figure), and God will gather God's scattered people from all over the earth.[36] This shows that the restored remnant will become a signpost for the nations, pointing them toward God's salvation and justice. The remnant's existence becomes a visible testimony to God's power to save, heal, and renew. Rather than retreating into isolation, the faithful remnant is meant to embody God's holiness and hope in such a way that it invites others into the covenant. In this sense, the remnant plays a crucial role in advancing God's universal Mission, foreshadowing the New Testament vision of the Church as a community of witness among the nations.

Divine Redemption and Mission in the Old Testament

Redemption is one of the central themes in the Hebrew Bible and plays a vital role in understanding God's relationship with God's people. The word "redemption" refers to the act of saving, rescuing, or buying back something that is lost, enslaved, or broken. Throughout the Old Testament, God is portrayed as a Redeemer who actively intervenes in history to deliver individuals, communities, and even creation from sin, oppression, and exile. These redemptive acts are not only personal or national in scope, rather, they also reveal God's wider purpose for the world. The Hebrew Bible shows that God's work of redemption flows from God's own character as God is loving, just, and faithful, and God desires to make Godself known among the nations through God's saving actions.[37] Redemption, therefore, is

---

[36] Jacob Stromberg, "The 'Root of Jesse' in Isaiah 11:10: Postexilic Judah, or Postexilic Davidic King?," *Journal of Biblical Literature* 127/4 (Winter, 2008): 655-669.

[37] Joel R. Beeke and Devon Rossman, "The Mission of God and the Old Testament: Tracing God's Redemptive Plan of Salvation," *Puritan Reformed Journal* 15/1 (December, 2023): 153-167.

deeply connected to Mission. God redeems God's people not only for their own sake, but so they may become a light to others and a means through which God's blessings can reach all nations. In this way, redemption is both a gracious gift and a call to participate in God's ongoing Mission to restore the world. This redemptive Mission is visible throughout the Hebrew Bible in a series of key events and people that reveal how God's saving purposes are both particular to Israel and directed toward the blessing of all nations.

Redemption Through the Covenant with Abraham

The life of Abraham marks the beginning of God's redemptive plan for the world through a chosen people. God calls Abraham out of his homeland and makes a covenant with him, promising not only to bless him and make him into a great nation, but also to bless "all the families of the earth" through him (Genesis 12:3). This covenant reveals that God's plan of redemption is Missional from the beginning and it is not limited to Israel but is intended for all nations.[38] By choosing Abraham, God sets in motion a redemptive purpose that reaches far beyond his descendants. Election, therefore, for Abraham was not about privilege but about purpose that Abraham's family is called to redeem and bless the whole world.[39] Redemption, in this sense, begins with God's initiative and has a global goal.

Redemption Through Joseph and His Family

The life of Joseph and his family demonstrates how God can use human suffering and broken relationships to fulfil His redemptive purposes. Although Joseph is betrayed by his brothers and sold into slavery, he eventually rises to a position of great authority in Egypt. During a severe famine, he is able to provide for both Egypt and his own family, thus preserving many lives.[40] Joseph's statement *You meant evil against me, but God meant it for good* (Genesis 50:20) highlights a key truth of redemption that God can transform human wrongdoing into a means of blessing and deliverance. This narrative also reflects the wider scope of God's redemptive Mission.[41] Joseph's actions not only restore his family but also bring benefit to the surrounding nations, showing that God's purposes are not limited to

---

[38] Rolf Rendtorff, "'Covenant' as a Structuring Concept in Genesis and Exodus," *Journal of Biblical Literature* 108/3 (Autumn, 1989): 385-393.

[39] John Thomas Bunn, "The Covenant with Abraham," *Old Testament Abstracts* 11/2 (December, 1988): 149.

[40] Frederick J. Gaiser, "'You Meant Evil against Me; but God Meant It for Good': Thinking Genesis 50:20," *Word & World* 4 (December, 2000): 33-47.

[41] Chaya Greenberger, "Joseph and His Brothers: The Unexpected Encounter," *Jewish Bible Quarterly* 49/3 (December, 2021): 158-164.

Israel. His life becomes a testimony to God's providence and a reminder that redemption often emerges through unexpected and painful circumstances.

Exodus from Egypt and Redemption

The Exodus is the foundational redemption event in the Old Testament. God delivers the Israelites from slavery in Egypt through miraculous signs and wonders, showing Godself as the Redeemer (*go'el*) who hears the cry of the oppressed (Exodus 6:6). This act of redemption is not only about freedom from slavery, but also about forming a people who will serve and represent God among the nations.[42] The Exodus shows that redemption involves both liberation and vocation. At Mount Sinai, God declares that Israel is to be a "kingdom of priests and a holy nation" (Exodus 19:5-6), a people set apart to reflect God's character and Mission.[43] The power of God's redemptive work in Egypt becomes a testimony to the nations, revealing God's justice, faithfulness, and authority over all earthly powers.

The Year of Jubilee and the Kinsman-Redeemer

The laws of Israel, particularly those concerning the Year of Jubilee and the role of the kinsman-redeemer, reflect God's desire for justice and restoration. In the Year of Jubilee, debts were forgiven, land was returned, and slaves were set free that showing that redemption involved social and economic renewal.[44] The story of Boaz and Ruth illustrates this on a personal level: Boaz, as a kinsman-redeemer, restores Naomi's family line by marrying Ruth and redeeming her late husband's land (Ruth 4). This act of redemption preserves both inheritance and dignity, pointing forward to the Messiah, who will redeem humanity fully.[45] These practices show that God's redemptive Mission touches every area of life such as: economic, social, and familial and that God's people are called to be agents of that justice and mercy.

Redemption from Idolatry and Sin

The prophetic books of Hosea and Isaiah reveal God's commitment to redeem God's people even when they fall into sin and idolatry. Hosea's marriage to Gomer, an unfaithful woman, becomes a living parable of Israel's unfaithfulness to God. Yet Hosea is called to redeem her, symbolizing God's

---

[42] Benjamin Bixler, "Trauma, Revenge, and Cycles of Violence in the Exodus Story," *The Conrad Grebel Review* 40/1 (December, 2022): 59-77.

[43] Prescott H. Williams, "'And Now, If…55': A Study of Exodus 19:1-6…, 39-51.

[44] John Sietze Bergsma, "The Year of Jubilee and the Ancient Israelite Economy," *Southwestern Journal of Theology* 59/2 (December, 2017): 155-164.

[45] Thomas Wingate Mann, "Ruth 4," *Interpretation* 64/2 (December, 2010): 178-180.

steadfast love and mercy toward God's wayward people (Hosea 3:1).[46] In the same way, in Isaiah, God promises to purify and restore God's people despite their rebellion (Isaiah 1:18). Redemption here includes forgiveness, moral cleansing, and spiritual renewal. Thus, the prophets emphasize that God's love is not conditional on Israel's faithfulness, rather, it is covenantal and redemptive in nature.[47] God's redemptive actions serve as a witness to the nations, showing that God is a God who forgives, restores, and calls all people to repentance through redemption.

Psalms of Redemption

The Psalms are filled with personal and communal expressions of gratitude for God's redemptive acts. In Psalm 103, the psalmist praises God who "redeems your life from the pit" and forgives all iniquity. Psalm 107 recounts various situations of distress such as hunger, captivity, and storm and celebrates how God redeems those who cry out to Him.[48] Psalm 130 speaks of waiting on the Lord because "with God is plentiful redemption." These songs show that redemption is not only a national event like the Exodus but also a deeply personal experience. The psalms also include a Missional element that they often call the nations to join in praise (e.g., Psalm 67:1-2).[49] Thus, the redeemed are not only restored, but they are also witnesses who invite others to experience God's mercy.

The Return from Exile

After Israel's exile in Babylon, God's promise to redeem and restore God's people remains central. In Isaiah 40-55, God declares that God has not forgotten God's people and will bring them back with comfort and hope. This redemption includes the forgiveness of sin, the rebuilding of Jerusalem, and the renewal of national identity.[50] In Ezra and Nehemiah, these promises begin to describe as the exiles return, rebuild the temple, and renew their covenant with God. This redemption is more than political, rather, it is

---

[46] Felipe Fruto Ll Ramirez, "Hosea 3:1-5: Afterwards the Israelites Shall Repent and Seek the Lord Their God," *Landas* 32/2 (December, 2018): 17-32.

[47] J. Christopher Samuel Devanesan, "Sin and Colour: A Critical Evaluation of the Western Scholarly Exegesis of Isaiah 1:18," *Black Theology* 2/2 (December, 2004): 188-194.

[48] Colin J. Smothers, "Miraculous Redemption: Psalm 107 and the Markan Miracle Catenae," *Presbyterion* 47/1 (December, 2021): 16-29.

[49] Gérard Nissim Amzallag, "Psalm 67 and the Cosmopolite Musical Worship of *YHWH*," *Bulletin for Biblical Research* 25/2 (December, 2015): 171-187.

[50] Rikki E. Watts, "Echoes from the Past: Israel's Ancient Traditions and the Destiny of the Nations in Isaiah 40-55," *Journal for the Study of the Old Testament* 28/4 (December, 2004): 481-508.

spiritual and communal.[51] Isaiah 49:6 makes clear that Israel's restoration has a global Mission as they are called to be "a light to the nations." God's redemptive work in the post-exilic period reveals God's faithfulness and reaffirms God's desire to glorify God's name among all peoples.

Redemption and the Suffering Servant

The Suffering Servant passage in Isaiah is one of the most profound expressions of redemption in the Old Testament. This servant figure bears the sins of others, suffers in their place, and brings healing and peace through his affliction.[52] Isaiah 53:5 declares, "by his wounds we are healed," showing that redemption involves substitution, sacrifice, and deep compassion. While the identity of the servant is debated in Jewish tradition, Christian Mission see this as a prophetic anticipation of Christ's redemptive work. The servant's suffering leads not only to Israel's restoration but also impacts "many nations" (Isaiah 52:15). This points to the universal scope of God's Mission, the redemption through the servant is meant to reach the ends of the earth.[53] The suffering servant thus becomes the clearest sign in the Old Testament that redemption is both costly and Missional.

Hospitality as a Missional Practice in the Hebrew Bible

Hospitality is a significant theological and ethical theme in the Hebrew Bible, deeply connected to the Mission of God. More than a social custom, biblical hospitality reflects the character of God and God's purposes for the world. It involves welcoming the stranger, caring for the vulnerable, and creating space for divine encounter and redemptive transformation. From the patriarchal narratives to the prophetic literature and wisdom writings, hospitality consistently appears as a vehicle through which God's presence is made known and God's covenant purposes are extended. Importantly, such a form of of hospitality often serve as a Mission model as they attract outsiders into the community of faith, revealing God's justice and mercy, and point forward to God's global redemptive plan.

Abraham Welcomes the Three Visitors (Genesis 18:1-8)

Abraham's encounter with three visitors at Mamre is a foundational example of hospitality in the Hebrew Bible. Without knowing their full identity, Abraham welcomes the strangers with honour, provides water for their feet,

---

[51] Lisa J. Cleath, "Rebuilding Jerusalem: Ezra-Nehemiah as Narrative Resilience," *Jewish Studies Quarterly* 30/1 (December, 2023): 1-27.

[52] Allen S. Maller, "Isaiah's Suffering Servant: A New View," *Jewish Bible Quarterly* 37/4 (December, 2009): 243-249.

[53] Clarence Tucker Craig, "The Identification of Jesus with the Suffering Servant," *The Journal of Religion* 24/4 (October, 1944): 240-245.

prepares a meal, and personally serves them. This act is later revealed to be a divine visitation, as one of the visitors is the Lord Godself.[54] From a Missiological point of view, this passage shows that hospitality opens space for divine encounter and blessing. It also has Missional implications, as Abraham's hospitality anticipates his role in God's redemptive plan to bless all nations (Genesis 12:3).[55] Thus, hospitality becomes a channel through which God's Mission unfolds, showing that welcoming others can be an act of faith that brings about God's purposes.

Lot Welcomes the Angels in Sodom (Genesis 19:1-11)

Lot's hospitality in Sodom contrasts sharply with the violent inhospitality of the city's inhabitants. He offers lodging, protection, and food to two strangers, risking his own safety in doing so.[56] From a Missiological point of view, this hospitality highlights a form of righteousness, especially when practiced in the midst of moral decline. In the context of Mission, Lot's actions highlight how receiving the stranger reflects God's justice and mercy, while the city's hostility leads to judgment.[57] This narrative emphasizes that how one treats outsiders is a spiritual matter with communal consequences, and faithful hospitality can bear witness to God's values in a corrupt society.

Rebekah's Hospitality at the Well (Genesis 24:10-20)

Rebekah's generous hospitality toward Abraham's servant and his camels goes beyond cultural expectations. Without hesitation, she offers water not only to the Abraham's servant but also to his ten camels, an act requiring significant effort.[58] Thus, Rebekah's hospitality highlights the virtue of selfless generosity, a mark of true hospitality. Importantly, Rebekah's initiative and agency in offering hospitality without being prompted challenges passive stereotypes of women in patriarchal narratives, portraying her as an active participant in God's Mission and a model of empowered faithfulness.[59] Thus, from a Missiological perspective, Rebekah's kindness

---

[54] Peter Ochs, "Three Visitors and Scriptural Hermeneutics," *Journal of Scriptural Reasoning* 2/3 (December, 2002).

[55] Jeffrey Kirby, "How to Nurture Hospitality: Lessons from Abraham," *The Priest* 80/9 (December, 2024): 12.

[56] Herman A. Peterson, "Abraham and Lot: A Librarian's Reflections on Hospitality," *Catholic Library World* 69/3 (December, 1999): 20-22.

[57] T. Desmond Alexander, "Lot's Hospitality: A Clue to His Righteousness," *Journal of Biblical Literature* 104/2 (December, 1985): 289-291.

[58] Yael Shemesh, "The Sacrifice of Jephthah's Daughter (Judges 11) as a Reflection Story of Rebecca's Betrothal and Marriage (Genesis 24)," *Jewish Studies* 15 (December, 2019): 1-10.

[59] Yael Shemesh, "The Sacrifice of Jephthah's Daughter (Judges 11)..., 1-10.

leads to her inclusion in the covenant family, becoming the wife of Isaac and mother of Jacob. Her generous attitude demonstrates how hospitality can open doors to participation in God's redemptive plan. It shows that even ordinary acts of kindness can align with divine purposes and further the Mission of God.

The Israelites Commanded to Love the Stranger (Leviticus 19:33-34; Deuteronomy 10:18-19)

God commands Israel to love the foreigner and treat them as one of their own, reminding them of their own experience as strangers in Egypt (Leviticus 19:35). This command is rooted in the character of God, who defends the cause of the vulnerable and acts with justice and mercy. This shows that hospitality is not merely a social duty but a reflection of divine compassion.[60] From the perspective of Israel's community rule, hospitality toward the foreigner was a covenantal obligation rooted in their legal and social structures. *When an alien resides with you in your land, you shall not oppress the alien* (Leviticus 19:34) reveal that Israel's identity as God's covenant people was inseparable from practicing justice and extending hospitality as a lived testimony of God's character. Thus, Israel's treatment of the stranger was meant to display God's inclusive love and righteousness to the nations.[61] The ethical practice of hospitality thus becomes a key component of Israel's Mission as witness to the world.

Rahab Welcomes the Spies (Joshua 2:1-21)

Rahab, a Canaanite woman, welcomes and protects the Israelite spies in Jericho. Her hospitality is not only brave but also an expression of faith in the God of Israel, whom she acknowledges as the true God of heaven and earth. Thus, her act demonstrates that hospitality can be a way for salvation and covenant inclusion.[62] Rahab's decisive action challenges traditional power dynamics, portraying her not as a passive recipient of grace but as a courageous and strategic woman whose faith-driven hospitality actively contributes to God's redemptive history.[63] From a Missiological perspective,

---

[60] Alfred Marx, "The Relationship between the Sacrificial Laws and the Other Laws in Leviticus 19," *The Journal of Hebrew Scriptures* 8 (December, 2008).

[61] Hans-Georg Wünch, "The Stranger in God's Land--Foreigner, Stranger, Guest: What Can We Learn from Israel's Attitude towards Strangers?," *Old Testament Essays* 27/3 (January, 2014): 1129-1154.

[62] Rose Nyirimana Mukansengimana and Jonathan A. Draper, "The Role of Women in Creating Safe Space for 'Strangers': Reading of Joshua 2:1-21 and John 18:15-17 from the Context of Rwandan Conflict," *Journal of Theology for Southern Africa* 152 (December, 2015): 96-113.

[63] Rose Mary Sheldon, "Spy Tales," *BR Washington D.C.* 19/5 (December, 2003): 12.

Rahab's inclusion in the people of Israel and eventually in the genealogy of Jesus (Matthew 1:5) shows that God's redemptive Mission extends to those outside of Israel.[64] This also reveals that simple acts of hospitality, motivated by faith, can play a critical role in God's global purposes.

The Widow of Zarephath Hosts Elijah (I Kings 17:8-16)

During a severe famine, a Gentile widow in Zarephath offers Elijah her last portion of food, despite having very little for herself and her son. In response to her hospitality and faith, God miraculously provides food for her household throughout the drought. This narrative affirms that hospitality, even from those in poverty, invites divine provision.[65] Thus, the widow of Zarephath emerges as a powerful figure of resilience and agency, whose courageous decision to care for another in the midst of her own vulnerability highlights the strength and theological significance of marginalized women in God's Mission.[66] From a Missiological perspective, her life is remarkable because it takes place outside Israel, showing that God's concern and power reach beyond national borders. The widow's generous response becomes a sign that faith and hospitality among the nations are part of God's redemptive plan.

Elisha and the Shunammite Woman (II Kings 4:8-37)

A wealthy woman in Shunem offers Elisha a place to stay and provides for him regularly. In return for her generosity, God blesses her with a son and later raises the child from the dead. This narrative emphasizes that hospitality makes room for the presence and power of God.[67] It is through the woman's initiative and care that a relationship with the prophet is formed, leading to miraculous encounters.[68] Thus, the Shunammite woman exemplifics spiritual authority and initiative, as she not only provides for the prophet but shapes the space where divine activity discloses and demonstrating that women play a vital, often underrecognized role in evolving God's Mission.

---

[64] John C. Hutchison, "Women, Gentiles, and the Messianic Mission in Matthew's Genealogy," *Bibliotheca Sacra* 158/630 (December, 2001): 152-164.

[65] Chloe Breyer, "The Widows Might," *Journal of Religion and Health* 43/2 (Summer, 2004): 123-126.

[66] John Peter Lewis, "Salvation, Pseudo-Modernism, Suffering and Hope: A Study of I Kings 17," *Evangelical Review of Theology* 35/4 (January, 2011): 360-364.

[67] Jose Varickasseril, "The Shunammite Woman Converts Prophet Elisha: Kindness Generates Kindness," *Vidyajyoti Journal of Theological Reflection* 85/6 (December, 2021): 433-441.

[68] Melissa Eitenmiller, "Elisha and the Shunammite: Woman of Hope and Mediatrix: A Narrative Analysis of 2 Kings 4:8-37," *The Josephinum Journal of Theology* 23/1-2 (December, 2016): 56-75.

From a Missiological perspective, the Shunammite woman illustrates how welcoming God's messengers enables households to participate in God's work and receive God's blessing. Thus, it affirms that hospitality is a sacred act with redemptive outcomes.

Job's Righteousness Includes Hospitality (Job 31:32)

In defending his integrity, Job declares that he never let a stranger spend the night in the street and always opened his doors to travellers. This simple statement reveals that hospitality was an essential aspect of righteous living.[69] From the perspective of communal ethics, Job's practice of hospitality underscores that justice and righteousness are not confined to worship or ritual, but are personified in everyday actions toward others.[70] His open-door ethic reflects a vision of godliness that integrates compassion, dignity, and social responsibility, making hospitality a vital expression of faithful witness.[71] Thus, Job's righteousness reflects God's own concern for the outsider and the vulnerable. In the frame of Missiology, Job's life shows that personal piety includes a public ethic of inclusion and care and models how God's people are to reflect God's character in everyday life, especially in how they treat those in need.

The Book of Ruth (Ruth 1-4)

The life and witness of Ruth is one of profound hospitality and covenant inclusion. Ruth, a Moabite widow, is welcomed by Boaz, who protects and provides for her according to God's law. Boaz's generous treatment of Ruth leads to their marriage, and Ruth becomes part of the lineage of David and ultimately of Jesus.[72] Ruth embodies courageous loyalty and agency as she demonstrates social and economic vulnerability with resilience and determination.[73] Likewise, Boaz's recognition of Ruth's worth challenges patriarchal norms by honouring a foreign woman not as a burden, but as a

---

[69] Randy Klassen, "Job's Thirst for Righteousness: A Parable of Post Modernism," *Direction* 25/2 (December, 1996): 44-53.

[70] Daniel E. Fleming, "Job: The Tale of Patient Faith and the Book of God's Dilemma," *Vetus Testamentum* 44/4 (October, 1994): 468-482.

[71] Morris Stockhammer, "Righteousness of Job," *Judaism* 7/1 (December, 1958): 64-71.

[72] Beth E. Elness-Hanson, "'If You Bless the Women...': An Intercultural Analysis of Blessings in the Book of Ruth," *Journal of Theology for Southern Africa* 170 (December, 2021): 109-126.

[73] Jonathan A. Thambyrajah, "Israelite or Moabite?: Ethnicity in the Book of Ruth," *Journal for the Study of the Old Testament* 46/1 (December, 2021): 44-63.

partner in God's redemptive history.[74] Thus, the Book if Ruth shows how hospitality creates space for redemptive transformation. Missiologically, the inclusion of a foreign woman in the messianic line reveals that God's Mission is open to all nations and peoples.

Conclusion

The Hebrew Bible presents a coherent and unfolding vision of God's Mission, rooted in God's sovereign initiative and gracious purposes for the world. God elects a people, beginning with Abraham, not as an exclusive group but as instruments through whom all nations may be blessed. The covenant establishes a relationship of mutual commitment, shaping Israel's identity and vocation. The commandments provide a moral and spiritual framework, guiding Israel to live in a way that reflects God's holiness and justice. As a nation, Israel is called to be a light to the Gentiles, symbolizing God's reign on earth. Even in times of failure and judgment, the theme of the remnant assures the continuity of God's Mission and God's faithfulness to God's promises. Redemption, whether personal, communal, or cosmic, reveals God's intent to restore what is broken and to invite all peoples into God's saving grace. Hospitality, as both a virtue and a Missional practice, demonstrates God's welcoming heart and opens space for divine encounter and inclusion. Together, these themes form a Missiological perspective highlights God's unwavering commitment to bless the nations through God's people. The Hebrew Bible thus sets the foundation for a Mission that is both deeply rooted in God's covenantal love and oriented toward the redemption of the whole world.

[74] Timothy Paul Erdel, "The Book of Ruth and Hope in Hard Times," *Priscilla Papers* 25/1 (December, 2011): 5-8.

11

Mission in the Intertestamental Period The Silent Preparation for the Fulfilment of God's Redemptive Plan

The Intertestamental Period (ca. 400 BCE to 4 BCE) represents a critical interval in Jewish religious and cultural history, marked by shifting political powers, theological developments, and emerging concepts of Mission. Though traditionally portrayed as a time of prophetic silence (generally known as 400 years of silence), this era witnessed powerful responses to exile, Hellenistic influence, and diaspora dispersion that shaped early Jewish understanding of God's redemptive purposes and hospitality toward the nations. While this period saw shifting empires and cultural influences that reshaped how Jews understood themselves, it also witnessed new ideas of God's calling and community hospitality. The period witnessed developments in the areas such as translating Scripture, adapting worship in the diaspora, and forming distinct religious groups, that not only addressed immediate challenges but also became Mission foundations used in later Missionary movements.

Historical Context

The period following Malachi's prophecy and preceding the advent of Jesus has often been categorized as the "400 years of silence" since it witnessed a dynamic milieu of religious movements. Political confusions under Persian, Hellenistic, and Roman rule forced Jewish communities to confront deep questions about their identity, religious purity, and the extent of God's covenant promises.[1] Under Persian rule, the return from Babylonian exile

[1] Robert George Raymer, "Tendencies and Development of Judaism of the Intertestamental Period," *The Methodist Review Quarterly* 70/4 (December, 1921): 727-739.

led to efforts to rebuild the Temple and reestablish Jewish life in Jerusalem.[2] Leaders like Ezra and Nehemiah emphasized strict obedience to the Law, rejected intermarriage with foreigners, and defined the covenant community in exclusive terms, aiming to preserve purity and restore national identity.[3] During the Hellenistic period, especially under Seleucid rule, the spread of Greek language and culture challenged Jewish traditions.

This tension reached a breaking point during the Maccabean revolt (167-160 BCE), when Jewish resistance against forced Hellenization led to a violent struggle for religious and political independence.[4] The Maccabees' defence of the Temple and the Law highlighted the ongoing concern with purity and covenant faithfulness.[5] Later, under Roman rule, many Jews continued to wrestle with foreign control and spiritual compromise. Groups like the Qumran community, associated with the Dead Sea Scrolls, withdrew from mainstream society, viewing the Temple leadership in Jerusalem as corrupt and awaiting God's final judgment.[6] They emphasized strict purity laws and a renewed covenant for the faithful remnant, reflecting a belief that God's Mission would be fulfilled through a purified, obedient community.[7] In each period, these historical responses show how Jewish communities actively redefined their identity, upheld purity, and reconsidered the scope of God's covenant in light of new political realities.

Persian Restoration (537-332 BCE)

Cyrus the Great's decree (Ezra 1:1-4) allowed Jewish exiles to return to Jerusalem and rebuild the Temple, which was completed in 515 BCE. This marked a major turning point in Jewish self-understanding. Although the Davidic monarchy was no longer functioning, spiritual leadership shifted to priests and scribes, known as Sopherim, who began to define community

---

[2] George A. Barton, "Influence of the Babylonian Exile on the Religion of Israel," *The Biblical World* 37/6 (June, 1911): 369-378.

[3] Peter R. Bedford, "Diaspora: Homeland Relations in Ezra-Nehemiah," *Vetus Testamentum* 52/2 (April, 2002): 147-165.

[4] W. G. Jordan, "The Significance of the Maccabean Period," *The Biblical World* 38/5 (November, 1911): 294-305.

[5] Katell Berthelot, "Reclaiming the Land (1 Maccabees 15:28-36): Hasmonean Discourse between Biblical Tradition and Seleucid Rhetoric," *Journal of Biblical Literature* 133/3 (Fall, 2014): 539-559.

[6] Alex P. Jassen, "Prophets and Prophecy in the Qumran Community," *AJS Review* 32/2 (November, 2008): 299-334.

[7] Magen Broshi, Hanan Eshel, and Claude Grenache, "Daily Life at Qumran," *Near Eastern Archaeology* 63/3 (September, 2000): 136-137.

life around the Law rather than a king.[8] Theological reflections during this time emphasized God as sovereign over all nations, as seen in Isaiah's portrayal of Cyrus as God's "anointed" (Isaiah 45:1), suggesting that God's purposes could be fulfilled even through Gentile rulers, that broadened the idea of God's Mission beyond ethnic Israel.[9]

Religiously, this period saw the rise of local synagogues and a renewed focus on *Torah* reading and interpretation. With the Temple accessible only to those in Judea, dispersed Jews increasingly gathered in synagogues for worship and instruction.[10] The role of the *Torah* became central, not only for personal piety but also for communal identity. The scribes and early rabbis developed teaching traditions that laid the foundation for later Jewish Missionary activity through texts and ethical witness (Zechariah 8:20-23).[11]

Missiologically, the exile and return fostered an understanding of dispersion and witness. While the Temple was being restored in Jerusalem, Jews remained scattered across the Persian Empire. This diaspora reality led to new questions such as: Could God be worshipped outside the land? Was *Torah* observance possible in foreign settings? The answer, gradually, was yes. This shift prepared Jewish communities to be a light to the nations through their way of life, scriptural teaching, and moral distinctiveness, even while living under foreign rule. In this way, the Persian period quietly set the stage for a text-based and globally-aware expression of Jewish Mission.

Hellenistic Era (332-164 BCE)

The conquests of Alexander the Great, beginning in 332 BCE, spread Greek language, philosophy, and culture, known as Hellenism across the ancient Near East. Jewish communities, especially those living outside Judea, were deeply affected by this cultural shift. In cities like Alexandria, where a large and influential Jewish population lived, Greek became the primary language.[12] To preserve access to Scripture and religious identity in a Greek-speaking world, Jewish scholars translated the Hebrew Bible into Greek, producing the Septuagint (LXX). According to the Letter of Aristeas,

---

[8] John W. Betlyon, "A People Transformed Palestine in the Persian Period," *Near Eastern Archaeology* 68/1-2 (March-June, 2005): 4-58.

[9] Lisbeth S. Fried, "Cyrus the Messiah?: The Historical Background to Isaiah 45:1," *Harvard Theological Review* 95/4 (December, 2002): 373-393.

[10] Jacob Rodriguez, "'All That Yahweh Has Commanded We Will Obey': The Public Reading of Torah as Covenant Praxis in Early Judaism," *Journal of the Jesus Movement in Its Jewish Setting* 4 (December, 2017): 91-117.

[11] Walter Wink, "Standing on the Rock of the Impossible: From Zechariah 8 through History to Recent Events--and Hope," *Church & Society* 85/5 (December, 1995): 3-9.

[12] Cecilia M. Peek, "Alexander the Great Comes to Jerusalem: The Jewish Response to Hellenism," *Brigham Young University Studies* 36/3 (1996-97): 99-112.

this was not only for diaspora Jews but also aimed at making God's Word accessible to Gentiles.[13] This translation marked a major Missionary step that Scripture was now available in the language of the empire, that provided broader engagement with both Jews and non-Jews.

At the same time, tensions grew within Jewish society over how much Greek culture should be accepted. Some Jews embraced Hellenism, adopting Greek names, customs, and even altering religious practices. Others resisted, viewing these changes as threats to covenantal faithfulness. This conflict gave rise to major religious groups.[14] The Pharisees emphasized strict Torah observance and oral traditions to maintain purity.[15] The Sadducees, often associated with the priestly elite, were more open to Hellenistic influences and limited their authority to the written *Torah*.[16] The Essenes, a separatist group, possibly linked to Qumran, withdrew from society entirely, believing that the Temple and its leaders were corrupt.[17]

Biblically, this period reflects themes of faithful witness under cultural pressure, such as in the book of Daniel, though set earlier, was widely read during this time for its message of perseverance amid foreign domination. Thus, the Hellenistic period was a time of deep theological reflection for the Jewish people.[18] Challenged with foreign rule and cultural pressure, Jews were forced to ask important questions about God's presence, faithfulness, and the meaning of holiness in a changing world. Without political power or full control of the Temple, many began to see the study of the Torah, prayer, and moral living as ways to remain faithful to God.[19]

This shift moved the focus of worship from sacrifice alone to personal and communal obedience. The idea of God as sovereign over all nations became more prominent, especially as Jewish communities lived among Gentiles and engaged with new philosophies. The belief that God's wisdom

---

[13] George Holley Gilbert, "The Hellenization of the Jews between 334 B. C. and 70 A. D.," *The American Journal of Theology* 13/4 (October, 1909): 520-540.

[14] Gregg Gardner, "Jewish Leadership and Hellenistic Civic Benefaction in the Second Century BCE," *Journal of Biblical Literature* 126/2 (December, 2007): 327-343.

[15] Jacob Neusner, "Pharisaic-Rabbinic Judaism: A Clarification," *History of Religions* 12/3 (February, 1973): 250-270.

[16] Pieter J. J. Botha, "History and Point of View: Understanding the Sadducees," *Neotestamentica* 30/2 (1996): 235-280.

[17] Mihail Teodorescu, "Early Christianity and Essenes-Convergence or Hostility?," *International Journal of Orthodox Theology* 13/3 (December, 2022): 97-126.

[18] Patrick Pouchelle, Patrick. "The Septuagintal Paideia and the Construction of a Jewish Identity during the Late Hellenistic and Early Roman Period," *The Catholic Biblical Quarterly* 81/1 (December, 2019): 33-45.

[19] Gregg Gardner, "Jewish Leadership and Hellenistic Civic Benefaction in the Second Century B.C.E.," *Journal of Biblical Literature* 126/2 (Summer, 2007): 327-343.

could be shared beyond Israel grew stronger, preparing the way for future Mission. Books written during this period, like Wisdom of Solomon and Sirach, emphasized God's justice, wisdom, and care for all humanity.[20] This laid a foundation for later Jewish and Christian teaching about God's universal purposes and the role of God's people as witnesses among the nations.

Thus, Missiologically, the Hellenistic period posed new challenges and opportunities. While some Jews feared assimilation, others saw the dispersion and the availability of Scripture in Greek as a means for spreading knowledge of the one true God. The Jewish presence in multiple cities, combined with the shared Greek language and growing Scripture access, developed an appropriate ground for later Missionary movements, including the early Christian Mission.

Hasmonean Independence and Roman Overlordship (164-4 BCE)

The Maccabean Revolt (167-160 BCE) was a direct response to the radical Hellenization policies of Antiochus IV Epiphanes, who sought to suppress Jewish religious identity and unify his empire under Greek customs and religion.[21] According to I and II Maccabees, as well as Josephus, Antiochus outlawed several core Jewish practices that were foundational to covenant life. Observance of the *Sabbath* was forbidden, circumcision, the key sign of the Abrahamic covenant, was banned under penalty of death.[22] Dietary laws were nullified, and Jews were compelled to eat unclean foods such as pork, in violation of the Torah. Possession and reading of the Law of Moses were criminalized, with sacred scrolls burned and *Torah* teachers executed.[23] Temple worship was defiled by the erection of a pagan altar to Zeus within the sanctuary, upon which pigs were sacrificed, an act described in I Maccabees 1:54 as the "abomination of desolation."[24] Moreover, major Jewish festivals were outlawed, and Jews were forced to participate in pagan rituals. These actions were not merely political but theological attacks, aiming to dismantle Israel's covenantal distinctiveness.

---

[20] John J. Collins, "Cosmos and Salvation: Jewish Wisdom and Apocalyptic in the Hellenistic Age," *History of Religions* 17/2 (November, 1977): 121-142.

[21] Erich S. Gruen, "Hellenism and Persecution: Antiochus IV and the Jews," in *The Construct of Identity in Hellenistic Judaism: Essays on Early Jewish Literature and History*, edited by De Gruyter (Boston: De Gruyter, 2016) 333-358.

[22] Shailer Mathews, "Antiochus Epiphanes and the Jewish State," *The Biblical World* 14/1 (July, 1899): 13-26.

[23] Jonathan A. Goldstein, *Semites, Iranians, Greeks, and Romans: Studies in Their Interactions* (Michigan: Scholars Press, 2020), 27.

[24] Erich S. Gruen, "Hellenism and Persecution: Antiochus IV and the Jews…, 333-358.

Led by Judas Maccabeus and his brothers, the revolt successfully drove out Seleucid forces and reclaimed the Temple, an event still remembered during Hanukkah.[25] This victory led to the establishment of the Hasmonean dynasty, a line of Jewish priest-kings who ruled with a degree of independence.[26] During their rule, the Hasmoneans expanded Jewish territory and sometimes imposed Jewish customs and laws on conquered neighbouring groups, including the forced circumcision and conversion of the Idumeans (as noted by Josephus, Antiquities 13.257-259).[27] This marked a shift in Jewish political power, where national strength was used to define and protect religious identity.

However, internal divisions and external pressures eventually weakened the Hasmonean rule. In 63 BCE, the Roman general Pompey intervened in a dispute between rival Hasmonean claimants to the throne and brought Judea under Roman control.[28] From then on, Jewish leaders ruled only with Roman permission. Rome installed client kings like Herod the Great (ruled 37-4 BCE), who was ethnically Idumean but politically loyal to Rome. Herod rebuilt the Temple in grand fashion but was seen by many Jews as a foreign usurper, more interested in Roman approval than in God's law.[29]

This created a politically and religiously tense environment. On one hand, there was a strong desire among Jews to maintain their identity, purity, and faithfulness to God's covenant. On the other hand, they had to lead life under Roman imperial rule, which brought new cultural influences, heavy taxation, and a constant threat to their autonomy. It was in this complex setting, marked by national pride, foreign rule, and messianic longing that different Jewish groups emerged, each offering a vision of how to remain faithful to God while living under empire.

Biblically, this period is not directly recorded in the Hebrew canon, but it is comprehended in the books of I and II Maccabees, stress themes of faithfulness to God, martyrdom, and hope in resurrection. Theologically, the idea of zeal for the Law became central, with martyrdom seen as a witness to covenant loyalty (e.g., the mother and her seven sons in II Maccabees 7). This emphasis on purity, national election, and divine justice shaped Jewish expectations for deliverance and messianic hope.

---

[25] Jonathan A. Goldstein, *Semites, Iranians, Greeks, and Romans…*, 25.

[26] Shuai Zhang, "The Early Interaction between the Hasmonean Dynasty and the Roman Republic: A Comparative Study of Maccabees and Jewish Antiquities," *Biblical Literature Studies* 28 (December, 2024): 131-160.

[27] Neil Joseph McEleny, "The Maccabean Revolt: A Struggle to Remain Faithful," *The Bible Today* 25 (December, 1987): 73-80.

[28] Lester L. Grabbe, *An Introduction to First Century Judaism: Jewish Religion and History in the Second Temple Period* (London: T&T Clark, 1996), 27-29.

[29] Lester L. Grabbe, *An Introduction to First Century Judaism…*, 34-37.

Thus, the Hasmonean period is complex. On the one hand, the expansionist policies and forced conversions show an aggressive, territorial view of God's people, far from the prophetic vision of being a light to the nations through justice and mercy. On the other hand, the diaspora continued to grow, and synagogues outside Judea remained key centres for engaging both Jews and Gentiles. This tension between national restoration and global witness set the stage for the varied Jewish responses to Roman rule and later, to the Mission of Jesus. When Rome took control in 63 BCE, installing client kings like Herod the Great, Jewish hopes for deliverance were again challenged. Yet amid political oppression, many Jews continued to seek God's kingdom, deepening their expectation of a Messiah who would restore Israel and extend God's reign to all nations.

Theological Foundations of Mission

The period between the Hebrew Bible and the New Testament was not only marked by political upheaval and social transformation, but also by significant theological development. In the face of exile, foreign domination, and ongoing hopes for restoration, Jewish thinkers and communities reflected deeply on their identity, purpose, and the role of Israel in God's plan for the world. This reflection gave rise to renewed interpretations of key biblical themes such as covenant, election, wisdom, and divine judgment. These theological currents helped to shape a broader understanding of Mission, not as proselytism, but as a dynamic witness to God's justice, holiness, and universal reign. Particularly through prophetic, wisdom, and apocalyptic texts, Jewish theology in this era began to articulate a vision in which Israel's faithfulness served not only its own restoration but also the moral and spiritual renewal of the nations.

Covenant and Election

In the post-exilic period, Jewish wisdom placed new emphasis on Israel's covenantal identity as God's chosen people through election and began to reflect more deeply on the global implications of *Yahweh's* sovereignty. This was not a retreat into exclusivism but rather a reframing of Israel's role in the light of exile, restoration, and the persistence of foreign rule. The prophetic literature like Second Isaiah (Isaiah 40-55) provides a meaningful vision of this broader Mission. Here, Israel is not only the recipient of divine mercy but is also called to be a "light to the nations" (Isaiah 42:6 & 49:6), suggesting that election carries responsibility, not privilege alone. This text envisions Israel as God's servant, tasked with bearing witness to God's justice, salvation, and covenant faithfulness before the whole world.

This universal concern is echoed and developed in intertestamental literature. For example, the Wisdom of Solomon presents a vision of divine justice and righteousness that extends to all humanity, while affirming Israel's unique relationship with God.[30] It upholds monotheism and ethical instruction as part of a universal divine order that comprehends Gentiles as potential recipients of truth and life.[31] Similarly, I Enoch, particularly in the "Book of the Watchers" and the "Parables," introduces the idea of eschatological judgment that includes both Israel and the nations.[32] These texts depict a future where God's rule will be fully recognized on a cosmic scale, and the righteous, Jew and Gentile alike will be vindicated. Therefore, covenant and election in this period were not limited to Israel alone, but increasingly carried theological weight for how God would ultimately restore justice, bless the nations, and fulfil the promises made to Abraham (Genesis 12:3).

Wisdom and Apocalyptic Traditions

The intertestamental period also saw the flourishing of wisdom and apocalyptic traditions, both of which shaped Jewish understanding of Mission in unique ways.[33] Wisdom literature, such as Sirach (Ecclesiasticus) and the Wisdom of Solomon, emphasizes the importance of moral instruction, ethical living, and the pursuit of divine truth. These writings describe Israel's calling as a teacher of nations through the embodiment and communication of wisdom.[34] In Sirach, the *Torah* is equated with wisdom (Sirach 24:23), and the wise are called to instruct others, indicating a social Mission rooted in everyday righteousness and teaching.[35] The Wisdom of Solomon goes further, portraying Wisdom as a divine agent that permeates all creation and leads both rulers and common people toward justice and truth.[36] Here, the Jewish community's role in proclaiming and living by

---

[30] Michael Kolarcik, "The Wisdom of Solomon: Justice and Creation," *The Bible Today* 40/6 (December, 2002): 341-347.

[31] Larry W. Hurtado, "'Ancient Jewish Monotheism' in the Hellenistic and Roman Periods," *Journal of Ancient Judaism* 4/3 (January, 2013): 379-400.

[32] Elena L. Dugan, "Enochic Biography and the Manuscript History of 1 Enoch: The *Codex Panopolitanus* Book of the Watchers," *Journal of Biblical Literature* 140/1 (December, 2021): 113-138.

[33] Cornelis Bennema, "The Strands of Wisdom Tradition in Intertestamental Judaism: Origins, Developments and Characteristics," *Tyndale Bulletin* 52/1 (December, 2001): 61-82.

[34] Oswald Hugh Ewart Khs-Burmester, "The Bohairic Pericopae of Wisdom and Sirach [1] (Text)," *Biblica* 16/1 (December, 1935): 25-57.

[35] Kivatsi Jonathan Kavusa, "The Torah Likened with Nurturing Water of Rivers in Sirach 24:23-34: Eco-Theological Significance," *Pharos Journal of Theology* 99 (December, 2018): 1-12.

[36] Shannon Burkes, "Wisdom and Apocalypticism in the Wisdom of Solomon," *Harvard Theological Review* 95/1 (December, 2002): 21-44.

divine wisdom becomes a form of quiet but powerful witness to the Gentile world.

In contrast, apocalyptic texts like I Enoch, IV Ezra, and II Baruch reflect a different kind of Mission, that rooted in cosmic struggle, divine judgment, and ultimate vindication.[37] These writings emerged in times of suffering and political oppression, offering hope that God would soon intervene to restore justice. In this literature, Israel's suffering is not seen as random, but as representative of a broader human and cosmic brokenness. Israel's faithfulness amid persecution becomes a sign to the nations of God's coming judgment and salvation.[38] For example, in IV Ezra, the lament over Jerusalem's destruction becomes a platform for affirming God's justice and the future restoration not only of Israel but of creation itself.[39] This cosmic vision expands the scope of Mission beyond national restoration to a universal hope, where God's final purposes will be revealed to all peoples.

Thus, the wisdom and apocalyptic traditions shaped a twofold vision of Mission: a present calling to instruct and live wisely among the nations, and a future hope in which God's justice would transform the world. This laid the foundation for New Testament themes, where both wisdom (e.g., Jesus as the *Logos*) and apocalyptic expectation (e.g., kingdom of God, final judgment) merge in the early Christian proclamation.

Expressions of Mission

While the Missionary activity in the modern sense was not a central feature of Second Temple Judaism, the intertestamental period saw several key developments that functioned as expressions of Mission. These were not always deliberate efforts to convert Gentiles, but they nevertheless extended the reach of Jewish faith, values, and Scripture beyond ethnic and geographic boundaries. Through the translation of sacred texts, the formation of diaspora communities, and even through political expansion, Jewish engagement with the wider world grew. These expressions of Mission laid foundations for the Missional shape of early Christianity.

Scriptural Translation and Dispersal

One of the most significant Missional developments of the intertestamental period was the translation of the Hebrew Scriptures into Greek, known as

---

[37] Shannon Burkes, "'Life' Redefined: Wisdom and Law in Fourth Ezra and Second Baruch," *The Catholic Biblical Quarterly* 63/1 (December, 2001): 55-71.

[38] Philip F. Esler, "Political Oppression in Jewish Apocalyptic Literature: A Social-Scientific Approach," *Listening* 28 (December, 1993): 181-191.

[39] Gregory K. Beale, "The Problem of the Man from the Sea in IV Ezra 13 and Its Relation to the Messianic Concept in John's Apocalypse," *Novum Testamentum* 25/2 (April, 1983): 182-188.

the Septuagint (LXX). This project, traditionally linked to Jewish scholars in Alexandria during the 3rd century BCE, rendered the *Torah* and eventually other writings accessible to a much broader audience. While initially intended to serve the needs of Hellenistic Jews who no longer spoke Hebrew fluently, the Septuagint also exposed non-Jews to Jewish theology, ethics, and worldview.[40] This marked a major shift that the word of God was now available in the language of the Mediterranean world. From a Missiological perspective, the Septuagint became a powerful expression of Mission, that it helped cross-cultural communication of divine truth without requiring relocation or assimilation.[41] It became the primary version of Scripture used by the early Church, cited frequently in the New Testament, and serve as a foundational tool for Christian evangelism among Gentiles. The translation thus functioned both as a preservation of Jewish identity and Mission.

Diaspora Synagogues

In the absence of the Temple, especially for Jews living outside Judea, synagogues emerged as vital centres of religious life, community identity, and scriptural instruction. Found throughout the Mediterranean and Near Eastern cities, diaspora synagogues enabled Jewish communities to maintain worship practices, uphold the *Torah*, and foster a strong sense of belonging. Yet their role extended beyond internal cohesion.[42] These synagogues also practiced hospitality, welcoming not only traveling Jews but also Gentile sympathizers known as "*phoboumenoi*" (God-fearers). These Gentiles, while not full converts, were drawn to the ethical monotheism, Scripture, and moral order of Judaism.[43] The presence of *phoboumenoi* created a natural setting for dialogue and shared religious inquiry.[44] In the New Testament, synagogues play a central role in early Christian Mission, especially in the ministry of Paul, who often began his evangelism in synagogues (Acts 13:16-47). Thus, the synagogue structure provided both a platform for preserving Jewish faith and an opening for Missional engagement across cultural lines.

---

[40] James Keltie Aitken, and Marieke Dhont, "The Septuagint within the History of Greek: An Introduction," *Journal for the Study of Judaism in the Persian* 54/4-5 (December, 2023): 432-449.

[41] William W. Combs, "The Transmission-History of the Septuagint," *Bibliotheca Sacra* 146/583 (December, 1989): 255-269.

[42] Helen Rosenau, "The Synagogue and the Diaspora," *Palestine Exploration Quarterly* 69 (December, 1937): 196-202.

[43] Thomas M. Finn, "The God-Fearers Reconsidered," *The Catholic Biblical Quarterly* 47/1 (December, 1985): 75-84.

[44] J. M. Lieu, "The Race of the God-Fearers," *The Journal of Theological Studies* 46/2 (october, 1995): 483-501.

Forced Conversions and Political Policy

A more controversial expression of Mission in this period emerged during the rule of the Hasmonean dynasty, particularly under leaders like John Hyrcanus I and Aristobulus I. As the Hasmoneans expanded their territory, they implemented policies of forced conversion on conquered peoples such as the Idumeans. Circumcision and observance of Jewish law were imposed as conditions for inclusion in the Jewish nation.[45] These actions reflected a politicized understanding of Mission aimed more at strengthening national unity and religious purity than at freely sharing the faith. While such policies expanded the Jewish population and reinforced identity, they also raised theological tensions.[46] Rabbinic tradition would later critique forced conversions as undermining the voluntary nature of covenant allegiance. This complex intersection of power, religion, and identity demonstrates a hesitant approach for Mission, in way that zeal for covenantal boundaries coexisted with aggressive expansion. It shows that not all expressions of religious outreach in this era were purely spiritual or benevolent, yet they significantly impacted the broader Jewish-Gentile relationship.

The Intertestamental Foundations of New Testament Mission

The intertestamental period, though often considered as a time of prophetic silence, in fact served as fertile ground for the emergence of New Testament Mission.[47] Far from beginning of the 400 years of silence, the early Christian movement inherited and reinterpreted theological motifs, scriptural tools, and institutional structures and thus can be called as the formative era of the early Christian movement.[48] The translation of the Hebrew Scriptures into Greek through the Septuagint made God's word accessible to both Jews and Gentiles across the Hellenistic world, becoming the primary textual foundation for Jesus' teachings and apostolic preaching.[49] Likewise, the widespread presence of diaspora synagogues offered ready-made spaces for instruction, debate, and worship, which apostles like Paul utilized as key starting points for proclaiming the gospel (Acts 13-18).[50] *Phoboumenoi* who

[45] Steven Weitzman, "Forced Circumcision and the Shifting Role of Gentiles in Hasmonean Ideology," *The Harvard Theological Review* 92/1 (January, 1999): 37-59.

[46] Steven Weitzman, "Forced Circumcision and the Shifting Role of Gentiles…

[47] J. Julius Scott, "On the Value of Intertestamental Jewish Literature for New Testament Theology," *Journal of the Evangelical Theological Society* 23/4 (December, 1980): 315-323.

[48] Samuel Dickey, Christianity and the Hope of Social Redemption, *The Biblical World* 40/3 (September, 1912): 153.

[49] Jan Joosten, "Pillars of the Sacred: Septuagint Words Between Biblical Theology and Hellenistic Culture," *Svensk Exegetisk Årsbok* 83 (December, 2018): 1-15.

[50] Helen Rosenau, "The Synagogue and the Diaspora…, 196-202.

had previously associated with Jewish communities now became some of the earliest supporters of the Christian faith.[51]

Moreover, apocalyptic and prophetic expectations rooted in texts like Isaiah, I Enoch, and IV Ezra cultivated a hope for God's universal reign, justice, and final restoration.[52] These longings were fulfilled and reinterpreted in Jesus' proclamation of the Kingdom of God, Jesus' self-understanding as the one sent by God (John 20:21), and the commissioning of Jesus' disciples to make disciples of all nations (Matthew 28:19-20). These developments reflect continuity with Jewish beliefs about divine election and eschatological Mission, now expressed through the life, death, and resurrection of Christ and the global outpouring of the Spirit. Thus, the intertestamental period stands as a bridge, linking the covenantal calling of Israel to the universal Mission of the early Church.

Conclusion

Far from being a period of silence, the intertestamental era was a dynamic time of theological reflection, cultural adaptation, and preparation for Mission. Political challenges under Persian, Hellenistic, and Roman rule forced Jewish communities to reexamine their identity, purity, and purpose. These challenges gave rise to deep theological currents, renewed visions of covenant and election, wisdom and apocalyptic hope that broadened the scope of God's redemptive intentions beyond Israel. Mission took many forms. Through the translation of Scripture, the presence of diaspora synagogues, and even the complexities of political expansion, these diverse expressions laid the groundwork for the early Christian movement, which inherited and reinterpreted them in light of the life and Mission of Jesus. Thus, the intertestamental period stands not as a theological vacuum but as a vital connection, where Jewish faith, shaped by exile and empire, began to turn outward, preparing the way for the gospel to go to all nations.

---

[51] J. M. Lieu, "The Race of the God-Fearers…, 483-501.

[52] Shannon Burkes, "'Life' Redefined: Wisdom and Law in Fourth Ezra…, 55-71.

12

From Promise to Fulfilment
The Mission of God in the Ministry of Jesus

The concept of the "Mission of God in Jesus" lies at the heart of Christian theology and biblical revelation. It is primarily rooted in the idea of *Missio Dei*, that Mission originates in the nature and initiative of God, it becomes clear that Jesus Christ is the definitive expression of God's redemptive purpose for the world. Jesus is not merely a messenger but the embodiment of God's self-giving love. Jesus' life, death, and resurrection are central acts in God's ongoing Mission to redeem humanity and restore creation. Understanding Jesus in light of God's Mission provides a holistic perspective on salvation history and provides the Church's identity and purpose within that divine plan (John 20:21). The "Mission of God" thus refers to the belief that Mission flows from the nature of the Triune God' movement aimed at the redemption of all creation (Ephesians 1:9-10) and Jesus Christ is represented as the climax of God's redemptive plan. In his incarnation, ministry, crucifixion, and resurrection, the eternal purposes of God are fully revealed and enacted. It emphasises that, in this Mission, Jesus does not operate independently but functions in obedience to the Father's will, carrying out the divine Mission (John 4:34). This reveals the character of God as one who seeks the lost, restores the broken, and inaugurates the kingdom (Luke 19:10; Mark 1:15). Thus, through Jesus, the Mission of God becomes visible, personal, and accessible.

Biblical Foundations of God's Mission in Jesus

The Mission of Jesus is deeply rooted in the biblical narrative as the fulfilment of God's redemptive plan revealed throughout Scripture. Central to this view is the understanding that God is a sending God, one who calls, blesses, and redeems for the sake of the world.[1] From the call of Abraham in Genesis 12:1-3 to the prophetic visions of Isaiah (Isaiah 49:6), the Old Testament reveals a God whose covenant with Israel was always intended to bless the nations. Jesus enters this ongoing redemptive story not as a break from the past but as its fulfilment and continuation. As Jesus declares in Matthew 5:17, Jesus did not come to abolish the Law or the Prophets, but to fulfil them. This reflection is seen as the continuity between the Old and New Testaments, centred in Christ. Jesus represents Israel's true vocation, bringing to completion the promises of God while extending them universally. Missiologically, this is grounded in the concept of *Missio Dei*, the Mission of God, where the Triune God sends the Jesus (John 3:16-17), and through Jesus, the blessings promised to Israel are made available to all nations. Thus, the Mission of Jesus reveals the heart of God's redemptive purposes and anchors it within the unified story of Scripture.

Old Testament Background: The Expectation of a Redeemer

The Old Testament lays a strong foundation for the expectation of a Redeemer by revealing God's Missionary intention through God's covenant with Abraham and the election of Israel.[2] In Genesis 12:1-3, God promises Abraham that he will be the source of blessing for "all the families of the earth," that point to a redemptive purpose that extends far beyond Israel. This covenantal promise is not merely nationalistic but anticipates a global Mission in which Israel serves as a channel for God's blessing to the nations.[3] Likewise, in Exodus 19:5-6, Israel is designated as a "kingdom of priests and a holy nation," emphasizing its mediating role in making God known to the world. This priestly identity is Missional in nature, it implies that Israel was called not only to be holy but to represent God to the nations.[4] The Psalms contain a rich tapestry of Messianic expectation, with scholars identifying thirty-six psalms bearing direct Messianic content and fifty-two others with less explicit but significant allusions to the hope of the coming Anointed One, indicating that such expectation permeates the Psalter more extensively than is often assumed (Psalms 2; 22; 72; 110).[5] The prophetic

---

[1] William R. Burrows, "Jesus and Christology: Mission and the Paradox of God's Reign," *International Bulletin of Missionary Research* 39/4 (December, 2015): 232-235.

[2] Nicholas King, "Expectation: Jesus in the Old Testament," *The Way* 21/1 (December, 1981): 14-21.

[3] Shailer Mathews, "The Jewish Messianic Expectation in the Time of Jesus," *The Biblical World* 12/6 (December, 1898): 437-443.

[4] Simeon Chavel, "A Kingdom of Priests and its Earthen Altars in Exodus 19-24," *Vetus Testamentum* 65/2 (2015): 169-222.

[5] George Dahl, "The Messianic Expectation in the Psalter," *Journal of Biblical Literature* 57/1 (March, 1938): 1-12.

writings, especially in Isaiah, further develop this vision by introducing the figure of the Servant of the Lord, who will bring justice, healing, and light to the Gentiles (Isaiah 42:1-6; 49:6; 61:1-3).[6] These cultivate a deep hope for a coming Redeemer, one who would fulfil Israel's calling and extend salvation universally. Therefore, the Old Testament shapes a theological expectation of a Messiah who would embody Israel's vocation and inaugurate God's Mission to redeem all peoples.

New Testament Fulfilment in Jesus

In the New Testament, Jesus is portrayed as the fulfilment of the Old Testament hope and the embodiment of God's redemptive Mission. Jesus' coming marks the significant moment in salvation history, where promise becomes fulfilment and anticipation gives way to realization. As John 1:14 declares *the Word became flesh and dwelled among us*, pointing the incarnation as the turning point of God's engagement with the world. In Jesus, God enters human history personally, not only to reveal Godself but to redeem.[7] Jesus' baptism (Matthew 3:16-17), accompanied by the descent of the Spirit and the voice of God, confirms Jesus' identity as the beloved Son and the Spirit-anointed Servant anticipated redeemer in Isaiah.[8] This is followed by Jesus' inaugural sermon in Nazareth (Luke 4:18-19), where Jesus publicly claims to fulfil Isaiah's vision of liberation, healing, and good news for the poor.[9] Throughout the ministry, Jesus establishes the value of God's kingdom through signs, wonders, and miracles that are not ends in themselves but concrete expressions of restoration, justice, and divine compassion (Matthew 11:4-6). His deliberate association with tax collectors, sinners, women, and Gentiles further reveals the inclusive scope of God's Mission. By reaching the marginalized and outcast, Jesus reveals a kingdom that welcomes all and fulfils Israel's calling to be a light to the nations (Luke 5:32; 19:10).[10] Thus, the New Testament presents Jesus not only as the long-

---

[6] Robert A. Falconer, "Jesus as the Prophetic Servant of the Lord. (Matthew 12:18-21.)," *The Biblical World* 24/1 (July, 1904): 22-25.

[7] Edmondo Lupieri, "'The Law and the Prophets Were until John': John the Baptist between Jewish *Halakhot* and Christian History of Salvation," *Neotestamentica* 35/1-2 (December, 2001): 49-56.

[8] Markus N. A. Bockmuehl, "The Baptism of Jesus as 'Super-Sacrament' of Redemption," *Theology* 115/2 (December, 2012): 83-91.

[9] Elfriede Janz de. Verón, "The Mission of Jesus Christ: According to Luke 4:18-19," *Direction* 41/2 (December, 2012): 293-297.

[10] Michaelis Christoffel Dippenaar, "Table Fellowship and Lukan Christology I Jesus as Guest of Tax Collectors and Pharisees," *Taiwan Journal of Theology* 35 (December, 2012): 2-43.

expected Redeemer but as the inaugurator of God's Kingdom, bringing to completion the redemptive trajectory begun in the Old Testament.

Missiological Dimensions of Jesus' Life and Ministry

The Mission of Jesus cannot be fully grasped apart from its theological foundations, particularly its Trinitarian and incarnational dimensions. Jesus is not merely a historical figure enacting a noble cause, rather Jesus is the eternal Son, sent by God and empowered by the Holy Spirit to accomplish the redemptive purposes of God (John 3:16; 6:38; Luke 4:18). This divine sending (*Missio Dei*) reveals the inner life of the Trinity as one of self-giving love and unity directed toward the world. The incarnation itself is the most radical expression of this love, as God entering human history, taking on flesh, and identifying fully with human suffering (John 1:14; Hebrews 2:14-18). Jesus' obedient life, vicarious suffering, sacrificial death, and victorious resurrection are not isolated events, but integral to God's Mission to redeem and restore creation. Jesus' suffering on the cross reveals the cost of divine justice and mercy (Mark 10:45; II Corinthians 5:18-19), while Jesus' resurrection signifies the inauguration of new creation and the ultimate triumph of life over death (I Corinthians 15:20-28). Through Jesus' Mission, the triune God is revealed as relational, redemptive, and purposeful, drawing humanity into communion with Godself and extending that communion toward the renewal of all things, thus reveals the core of the Trinitarian Missiology. Thus, the Mission of Jesus is not only historical but Missiological, a living reflection of the character and activity of the Triune God in the world.

Trinitarian Foundation of Jesus' Mission

The Mission of Jesus is fundamentally rooted in the life and love of the Triune God. It is not an isolated initiative of Christ, but a divine movement that flows from the eternal communion of the God, Jesus, and Holy Spirit.[11] God sends Jesus into the world as an expression of divine love and purpose (John 3:16; 20:21-22), and Jesus willingly obeys the God's will, declaring, "I have come down from heaven not to do my own will but the will of him who sent me" (John 6:38). This dynamic of sending and obedience reveals the internal unity and harmony of the Trinity in the redemptive Mission. At Jesus' baptism, the Spirit descends upon Jesus (Luke 3:22) and publicly affirming his identity and Mission, and subsequently empowers Jesus' ministry (Luke 4:18) as the Spirit-anointed Servant foretold by Isaiah.[12]

[11] David Thang Moe, "The Word to the World: Johannine Trinitarian Missiology (John 20:21-22)," Journal of Pentecostal Theology 26/1 (December, 2017): 68-85.

[12] Santosh Kumar, "A Missiological Exploration of Luke 4:18 and the Challenge of Caste Discrimination in Seventh-Day Adventist Churches of India," *International Review of*

This Trinitarian cooperation underscores that Mission is not a secondary function or divine response to human sin, but an essential expression of God's being.[13] The mutual self-giving of God, Jesus, and Spirit reveals that God is inherently relational and outward-moving.[14] Therefore, Christian Mission arises from the very nature of God, it is the overflow of divine love reaching toward a broken world. Understanding Mission as a Trinitarian act reorients the Church's calling, not as initiating Mission on God's behalf, but as participating in the ongoing work of the Triune God who sends in love and power.[15]

Missionary Nature of the Incarnation

The incarnation represents the most meaningful and radical act of Mission in salvation history. In the person of Jesus Christ, God does not remain transcendent or detached, but enters fully into the human condition with all its weakness, vulnerability, and suffering.[16] This movement of God toward humanity is not merely to accomplish salvation, but relational and participatory.[17] As Hebrews 2:14-18 explains, Jesus took on flesh and blood to share in humanity's struggles, becoming a merciful and faithful high priest who can intercede on behalf of those he came to redeem.[18] In doing so, the incarnation reveals a God who not only acts to save but who chooses to suffer with and for the world. This Missional self-emptying (*kenosis*) is expressed in Philippians 2:6-8, where Christ, though equal with God, humbled himself by taking on the form of a servant and becoming obedient to death.[19] Missiologically, the incarnation embodies divine solidarity with the poor, the oppressed, and the broken, demonstrating that Mission is not about domination but about identification. God in Christ crosses every

---

Mission 113/2 (December, 2024): 436-450.

[13] Henry Pietersma, "Church and Kingdom: A Trinitarian View," *Reformed Journal* 27/5 (December, 1977): 22-24.

[14] Titus M Ingaboh, Caroline G Seed, A le R Du Plooy and Amanda Linda Du Plessis "Reconsidering the Place of Christ in Trinitarian Mission in the African Divine Church of Kenya," *In Die Skriflig* 56/1 (January, 2022): 1-10.

[15] Pablo T. Gadenz, "The Mission of Jesus: To Proclaim Liberty," *The Bible Today* 60/3 (December, 2022): 141-146.

[16] Darrell L. Guder, "Incarnation and the Church's Evangelistic Mission," *International Review of Mission* 83/330 (December, 1994): 417-428.

[17] Gareth Robinson, "Three Keys to Mission: Kingdom, Incarnation and Discipleship," *Theology* 118/2 (December, 2015): 107-114.

[18] Emma Ford, "Our Suffering, Sympathetic High Priest: Accomplishments and Implications of Christ's Incarnation in Hebrews 2:14-18 and 4:14-16," *Presbyterion* 47/1 (December, 2021): 127-133.

[19] Peter Forrest, "The Incarnation: A Philosophical Case for *Kenosis*," *Religious Studies* 36/2 (June, 2000): 127-140.

boundary such as spiritual, social, and existential to reconcile humanity to Godself. Thus, the incarnation is not only the means of redemption but also the model of Mission engagement, a movement of love that goes to the margins, enters the pain of the world, and offers healing through presence, humility, and sacrificial love.

Cross and Resurrection as the Heart of the Mission

The cross and resurrection of Jesus Christ stand as the climax and turning point of his earthly Mission, not as a tragic end, but as the decisive fulfilment of God's redemptive purpose.[20] On the cross, Jesus willingly bears the burden of human sin, offering Jesus' life as a ransom for many (Mark 10:45).[21] This sacrificial death is not merely a legal transaction but a deep expression of divine love and justice, where God deals with the reality of sin while opening the way to forgiveness and reconciliation.[22] Paul affirms that "God was in Christ reconciling the world to Godself" (II Corinthians 5:18-19), emphasizing the Missional nature of the crucifixion as a cosmic act of peace-making. The resurrection, far from being an isolated miracle, is the mystery of Jesus' Mission and the inauguration of a new creation.[23] As the "first fruits" of those who have died (I Corinthians 15:20-23), Christ's resurrection announces the defeat of death and the beginning of the eschatological renewal of all things.[24] In these events, the Kingdom of God is decisively established in power, not through political conquest but through suffering love and divine triumph. Thus, the cross and resurrection are not peripheral to Jesus' Mission but its very heart, where God's purposes for redemption, justice, and restoration converge and are accomplished.

The Scope of Jesus' Mission

The Mission of Jesus is marked by a powerful and comprehensive scope, addressing the personal, social, and cosmic dimensions of human existence. It begins with the transformation of individuals, as seen in Jesu's call to repentance, faith, and discipleship (Mark 1:15; John 3:3), where people like the Samaritan woman and Zacchaeus are restored to dignity, purpose, and

---

[20] Darío López Rodriguez, "The Liberating Mission of Jesus: A Reading of the Gospel of Luke in a Missiological Key," *Transformation* 14/3 (July/September, 1997): 23-30.

[21] Andrew Reid, "The Significance of the 'Ransom Saying' in Mark 10:45," *The Catholic Biblical Quarterly* 84/3 (December, 2022): 424-441.

[22] C. A. Joachim Pillai, "The Way of the Cross: Resurrection," *Worship* 37/4 (December, 1963): 250-253.

[23] Jeffrey Kaster, "The Main Mystery: Cross and Resurrection," *Youth Update* (December, 2003): 1-4.

[24] José Granados, "The First Fruits of the Flesh and the First Fruits of the Spirit: The Mystery of the Ascension," *Communio* 38/1 (December, 2011): 6-38.

community. Yet Jesus' Mission does not stop at individual renewal. It is extended to the healing of broken social relationships and the confrontation of unjust structures. Jesus' outreach to the marginalized groups like women, lepers, tax collectors, and Gentiles demonstrates an ethic of inclusion and affirms the value of every human life (Luke 4:18-19; Matthew 5-7). Through acts of compassion and teachings that promote justice, mercy, and humility, Jesus redefines community life around the values of the Kingdom of God. Moreover, the scope of Jesus' Mission embraces the entire created order. As Paul affirms in Colossians 1:20, God, through Christ, is reconciling "all things…whether on earth or in heaven," pointing to a cosmic restoration that reaches beyond human society.[25] Jesus' resurrection as "first fruits" (I Corinthians 15:20-23) and the eschatological vision of a new heaven and new earth (Revelation 21:1-5) confirm that Jesus' Mission ultimately anticipates the renewal of all creation. Thus, Jesus' Mission is not narrowly spiritual or private, but it is holistic, redemptive, and universal, embodying God's desire to renew people, communities, and the cosmos itself.

Personal Transformation

At the core of Jesus' Mission is the transformation of individual lives through the call to repentance, faith, and discipleship. Jesus' message begins with the urgent invitation: "Repent and believe the good news" (Mark 1:15), emphasizing that entry into the Kingdom of God requires a radical reorientation of the heart.[26] This inner transformation is not merely moral improvement but spiritual rebirth, as Jesus teaches Nicodemus[27] that *Very truly, I tell you, no one can see the kingdom of God without being born from above* (John 3:3). The Gospels also offer rich portraits of such personal encounters with Jesus that lead to meaningful change. The Samaritan woman (John 4), once isolated and burdened by shame, becomes a witness to her community after meeting Christ.[28] Zacchaeus, a wealthy tax collector (Luke 19), responds to Jesus' initiative with repentance and restitution, demonstrating a heart transformed by grace.[29] Nicodemus, though initially

---

[25] James M. Robinson, "A Formal Analysis of Colossians 1:15-20," *Journal of Biblical Literature* 76/4 (December, 1957): 270-287.

[26] Poulose Mangai, "'Repent and Believe in the Gospel,'" *Vidyajyoti Journal of Theological Reflection* 86/2 (December, 2022): 155-157.

[27] Athanasios Despotis, "Drawing and Transcending Boundaries in the Dialogue between Jesus and Nicodemus: Fresh Perspectives from John's Hellenistic Background and Chrysostomic Reception," *Journal of Early Christian History* 8/1 (January, 2018): 68-87.

[28] Hanna-Maria Mehring, "The Samaritan Woman as a Quick-Witted Border Crosser in John 4," *Religions* 15/8 (January, 2024): 1-13.

[29] John T. Carroll, "Young Child, Wealthy Elite, Despised Tax Collector: Status Reversals on the Approach to Jerusalem (Luke 18:15-19:10)," *Currents in Theology and*

cautious, is drawn into deeper understanding and ultimately appears as a disciple (John 3:1-21; 7:50-51 and 19:39-40).[30] These narratives highlight that the Mission of Jesus begins at the personal level, bringing forgiveness, healing, and new identity. Such transformation is not an end in itself but serves as the foundation for wider participation in God's redemptive Mission. Changed individuals become bearers of the Kingdom, demonstrating that the gospel reshapes not only human hearts but the world through those hearts made new.

Social and Ethical Transformation

The Mission of Jesus extends beyond individual salvation to encompass social and ethical transformation, challenging unjust systems and affirming the dignity of every human being. Rooted in the prophetic vision of Isaiah, Jesus announces Jesus' Mission in Luke 4:18-19 as one of liberation for the oppressed, healing for the broken, and good news for the poor. Jesus' actions consistently reflect this proclamation as he touches lepers (Mark 1:40-42), restores the demon-possessed (Mark 5:1-20), and defends the marginalized, including women caught in sin (John 8:1-11) and beggars rejected by society (Mark 10:46-52). Through such acts, Jesus confronts societal exclusion and reveals the Kingdom of God as a realm of justice, compassion, and inclusion.[31] Jesus' ethical teachings, especially in the Sermon on the Mount (Matthew 5-7), introduce a radical way of life shaped by humility, mercy, forgiveness, and non-retaliation.[32] These teachings do not simply reform behaviour but redefine relationships based on the values of God's reign.[33] Furthermore, Jesus' inclusion of women, children, Samaritans, and Gentiles disrupts prevailing social norms and anticipates the gospel's global reach.[34] Paul later captures this inclusivc vision in Galatians 3:28, where in Christ, "there is neither Jew nor Greek, slave nor free, male nor female."[35] Jesus'

Mission 51/4 (December, 2024): 4-7.

[30] J. N. Suggit, "Nicodemus: The True Jew," *Neotestamentica* 14 (1980): 90-110.

[31] Theo J. W. Kunst, "The Kingdom of God and Social Justice," *Bibliotheca Sacra* 140/558 (December, 1983): 108-116.

[32] Ernest Findlay Scott, "The Originality of Jesus' Ethical Teaching," *Journal of Biblical Literature* 48/1-2 (December, 1929): 109-115.

[33] Samuel Rayan, "The Kingdom of God, Religious Pluralism and Communalism: The Kingdom of Justice and Peace," *The Bulletin of the Henry Martyn Institute of Islamic Studies* 10/4 (December, 1991): 6-16.

[34] Joy Jones-Carmack, "Relational Demography in John 4: Jesus Crossing Cultural Boundaries as Praxis for Christian Leadership," *Feminist Theology* 25/1 (January, 2016): 41-52.

[35] Lung-kwong Lo, "'Neither Jew nor Greek': Galatians 3,28 Revisited," *Annali Di Storia Dell'Esegesi* 27/2 (December, 2010): 25-33.

Mission thus confronts both personal sin and structural injustice, inviting a transformed community shaped by love, equity, and the ethics of the Kingdom.

Cosmic and Eschatological Renewal

The Mission of Jesus reaches beyond the personal and social to incorporate the entire created order, pointing to the ultimate renewal of all things. Far from being limited to human souls or spiritual realities, Jesus' redemptive work is cosmic in scope.[36] Paul affirms this in Colossians 1:20, declaring that through Christ, God is reconciling "all things…whether on earth or in heaven," thus indicating that the effects of sin and brokenness extend to creation itself, and that redemption must likewise be comprehensive. The resurrection of Jesus is not only the proof of his person and Mission but also the beginning of new creation.[37] As Paul writes in I Corinthians 15:20-23, Christ is "the first fruits" of those who have died, signifying that his resurrection inaugurates a future where death and decay are no more.[38] The eschatological vision of Revelation 21:1-5 further affirms this cosmic scope as a renewed heaven and earth, the dwelling of God with humanity, and the complete removal of suffering and death.[39] This final vision is not escapist but restorative, depicting the fulfilment of God's original intention for creation. Therefore, the Mission of Jesus is not merely redemptive in a spiritual or human-centred sense but also restorative on a cosmic level, anticipating a future in which all creation is liberated, healed, and brought into perfect harmony under the reign of God.

Jesus and the Formation of a Missionary Community

Jesus did not carry out Jesus' Mission in isolation but intentionally formed a community to embody and extend the purposes of God in the world. From the beginning of Jesus' ministry, Jesus called individuals to follow not merely as learners but as participants in his redemptive work (Matthew 4:19). Through consistent teaching, shared experiences, and personal mentorship, Jesus shaped a group of disciples into a relational and Missionary community, to

---

[36] David Stuart Yeago, "Jesus of Nazareth and Cosmic Redemption: The Relevance of St Maximus the Confessor," *Modern Theology* 12/2 (December, 1996): 163-193.

[37] Maurice Lee, "Colossians, Resurrection, and New Creation," *Word & World* 41/4 (December, 2021): 325-333.

[38] Jacob Thiessen, "Firstfruits and the Day of Christ's Resurrection: An Examination of the Relationship between the 'Third Day' in 1 Cor 15:4 and the 'Firstfruit' in 1 Cor 15:20," *Neotestamentica* 46/2 (December, 2012): 379-393.

[39] G. Daan Cloete, and Dirk Jacobus Smit. "'And I Saw a New Heaven and a New Earth, for the First…Were Passed Away' (Revelation 21:1-8)," *Journal of Theology for Southern Africa* 81 (December, 1992): 55-65.

manifest mutual service, humility, and dependence on God. This formation was not accidental but deliberate by sending out the Twelve (Matthew 10) and the Seventy-Two (Luke 10), Jesus both tested and trained followers in practical Mission, preparing them for a life of witness and service. Following Jesus' resurrection, this community was given a formal commission to make disciples of all nations (Matthew 28:18-20), demonstrating that they were now entrusted with the continuation of Jesus' own Mission. In John 20:21, Jesus declares the divine pattern of sending, saying, "As the Father has sent me, I am sending you." This strengthens the truth that the Church is not simply a gathered people, but a sent people and a community shaped by, and participating in, the *Missio Dei*. Through the formation of this Missionary body, Jesus ensured that God's redemptive purposes would advance beyond his earthly ministry, continuing through the life, witness, and sacrificial love of his followers.

Calling and Training the Disciples

A vital aspect of Jesus' Mission was the intentional formation of a community who would not only follow him but also participate in Jesus' redemptive work. From the outset, Jesus' call to the disciples was Missional in nature: "Follow me, and I will make you fishers of people" (Matthew 4:19). This invitation was not merely to observe his teachings but to be transformed into active participants in the proclamation and embodiment of the Kingdom.[40] As Mark 3:13-15 records, Jesus appointed the Twelve "that they might be with him and that he might send them out to preach and to have authority to drive out demons." Their training, therefore, involved both presence and practice, being with Jesus and being sent by Jesus.[41] Jesus' pedagogy was deeply relational and experiential as Jesus taught them through parables, personal interactions, acts of compassion, and shared moments of prayer and suffering.[42] The goal was not only intellectual understanding but the internalization of Kingdom values and the development of character and courage. Through this formation, the disciples were shaped into witnesses who could carry forward Jesus' Mission in a world that would often reject them, just as it had rejected their Master. In calling and training his disciples, Jesus established a pattern of Missionary discipleship, an integrated life of

---

[40] Chip Anderson, "'You Will Appear as Fishers' (Mark 1:17): Disciples as Agents of Judgment," *Africanus Journal* 5/1 (January, 2013): 21-36.

[41] Scot McKnight, "Jesus and the Twelve," *Bulletin for Biblical Research* 11/2 (December, 2001): 203-231.

[42] Jairo Alfredo Roa Barreto, "The Pedagogy of Jesus as a Transforming Practice," *Ministerial Formation* 111 (December, 2008): 13-17.

learning, service, proclamation, and self-giving love that would define the community of the Church.[43]

Sending of the Twelve and the Seventy

During the earthly ministry, Jesus intentionally involved Jesus' followers in the extension of Jesus' Mission, indicating that participation in God's redemptive work is central to discipleship. In Matthew 10, Jesus sends out the Twelve with authority to proclaim the Kingdom, heal the sick, raise the dead, and cast out demons, acts that reflect Jesus' own ministry and extend Jesus' presence through them.[44] Similarly, in Luke 10, Jesus commissions seventy-two others, sending them "two by two" into towns where he himself would later go. This act of delegation marks a significant turning point in Jesus' approach, as it affirms that the Mission is not to be carried out by Jesus alone but shared by those he has called and formed.[45] These commissioning episodes are not merely training exercises but a foretaste of the Church's broader post-resurrection Mission. By entrusting others with the message and power of the Kingdom, Jesus models a participatory and multiplying vision of Mission. The disciples' involvement in preaching, healing, and spiritual fighting emphasizes that Mission is not a peripheral activity but a defining characteristic of what it means to follow Jesus. Their experiences, including rejection and opposition, prepare them for the cost and responsibility of future witness. Thus, the sending of the Twelve and the Seventy reveals that Mission is not optional for the disciple, rather, it is the path by which they grow in faith, obedience, and identity as agents of God's Kingdom.

The Great Commission

Following the resurrection, Jesus entrusted the continuation of Jesus' Mission to disciples through what is known as the Great Commission. In Matthew 28:18-20, the risen Christ declares that all authority in heaven and on earth has been given to him, and on that basis, Jesus commands his followers to "go and make disciples of all nations." This directive is not a new initiative but the continuation and expansion of Jesus' own Mission, now to be carried out by his followers in every corner of the world.[46] The

[43] Terrelle B. Sales, "Culture: A Critical Pillar in the Pedagogy of Jesus," *Christian Education Journal* 20/2 (December, 2023): 176-191.

[44] Francis Wright Beare, "Mission of the Disciples and the Mission Charge: Matthew 10 and Parallels," *Journal of Biblical Literature* 89/1 (December, 1970): 1-13.

[45] Isak J du Plessis, "The Church before the Church: Focussing on Luke 10:1-24," *Neotestamentica* 32/2 (1998): 343-366.

[46] Scott Geminn, "Staying within the Story: Understanding the Great Commission According to Matthew's Gospel," *Lutheran Mission Matters* 32/1 (December, 2024): 89-97.

scope of the Mission is clearly universal, embracing all peoples, languages, and cultures and involves not only evangelism but teaching, baptism, and ongoing discipleship.[47] In John 20:21, Jesus setting this commission in Trinitarian terms: "As the Father has sent me, I am sending you."[48] This statement places the Church within the very flow of divine sending, the *Missio Dei*, where the Son, having been sent by the Father, now sends his followers in the power of the Spirit (Acts 1:8).[49] The Church, therefore, does not possess a Mission of its own, rather, it participates in the Mission of God, serving as the visible and active agent of Christ's redemptive presence in the world.[50] This participation is both a privilege and a responsibility, calling the Church to embody the gospel in word, deed, and communal life until the Mission reaches its eschatological fulfilment.

Conclusion

Understanding and living out the Mission of Jesus is vital for the Church to remain faithful to its calling and relevant in today's world. The Mission of God, fully revealed in Jesus Christ, is not just a part of Scripture, rather, it is the central message that shapes the entire biblical story. From creation to new creation, God's purpose has always been to redeem and restore all things. Through Jesus' life, death, and resurrection, God has reconciled humanity and creation to Godself. This Mission continues through the Church, which is called not merely to observe but to actively participate in God's work. Therefore, the Church must bear faithful witness to the good news of the Kingdom in every part of life, embodying the love, justice, and hope that flow from the Mission of Jesus.

---

[47] D. J. Konz, "The Even Greater Commission: Relating the Great Commission to the *Missio Dei*, and Human Agency to Divine Activity, in Mission," *Missiology* 46/4 (December, 2018): 333-349.

[48] John. Füllenbach, "Called to Mission: As The Father Has Sent Me, So I Am Sending You," *SEDOS Bulletin* 28 (December, 1996): 74-78.

[49] Thomas S. Moore, "'To the End of the Earth': The Geographic and Ethnic Universalism of Acts 1:8 in Light of Isaianic Influence on Luke," *Journal of the Evangelical Theological Society* 40/3 (December, 1997): 389-399.

[50] Robert Newton, "The Divine Service and *Missio Dei*," *Lutheran Mission Matters* 32/1 (December, 2024): 20-30.

13

Jesus the Missionary Messiah
An Analysis of Jesus' Mission in the Synoptic Gospels

The Mission of Jesus, as presented in the Synoptic Gospels, Matthew, Mark, and Luke, is foundational for understanding the nature of God's redemptive work in history. Recognizing that the Synoptics offer both unique and shared perspectives, this includes coherence concerning Jesus' proclamation of the Kingdom of God, Jesus' role as the suffering Messiah, and the Missiological implications of Jesus' life, death, and resurrection. Understanding Jesus' Mission is crucial not only for biblical theology but also for the Church's contemporary witness and identity since the Synoptic writers trace in a systematic way how to frame Jesus' ministry in continuity with the Old Testament and in anticipation of the Church's ongoing participation in that Mission.

Authorship, Context, and Composition

The Synoptic Gospels emerged within the historical context of the first-century Greco-Roman world and reflect the early Christian community's response to the life, death, and resurrection of Jesus.[1] While the precise authorship of these Gospels remains a matter of scholarly debate, early church tradition attributes them respectively to the apostle Matthew,[2] John Mark (a companion of Peter),[3] and Luke (the physician and associate

---

1 James W. Barker, "Ancient Compositional Practices and the Gospels: A Reassessment," *Journal of Biblical Literature* 135/1 (Spring, 2016): 109-121.

2 Shirley Jackson Case, "The Origin and Purpose of the Gospel of Matthew," *The Biblical World* 34/6 (December, 1909): 390-402.

3 Pierson Parker, "John and John Mark," *Journal of Biblical Literature* 79/2 (June, 1960): 97-110.

of Paul).[4] Modern scholarship, drawing on literary and textual analysis, supports the theory of Markan priority, holding that Mark was the earliest Gospel, likely composed around AD 65, possibly in Rome during a time of persecution. Matthew and Luke, written between AD 70 to 90,[5] are believed to have used Mark as a primary source, along with other oral and written traditions, most notably the hypothetical Q source.[6] Each Gospel reflects distinct theological aims shaped by the needs of different audiences as well. Matthew writes to a predominantly Jewish-Christian community, emphasizing Jesus as the fulfilment of Old Testament prophecy. Luke addresses a broader Gentile audience, highlighting themes of inclusion and salvation. And Mark presents a vivid, action-oriented account of Jesus as the suffering Son of God. In common the Synoptic Gospels shares on common sources, yet theologically dynamic perspectives making them foundational for understanding the historical Jesus and the early Church's proclamation of Jesus' Mission.

The Structural Unity of the Synoptic Gospels

The Synoptic Gospels share a remarkably consistent narrative structure that distinguishes them as a unified literary and theological tradition within the New Testament. This common framework typically includes a shared chronology: beginning with Jesus' baptism and temptation, progressing through Jesus' Galilean ministry, followed by a journey toward Jerusalem, and culminating in the passion, death, and resurrection narratives. Mark is widely regarded as the earliest Gospel and serves as a narrative pattern for both Matthew and Luke, who adapt and expand its content with unique theological emphases and additional material such as birth narratives (in Matthew and Luke) and resurrection appearances. Central to this shared structure is the theme of Mission, Jesus' announcement of the Kingdom of God, teaching in parables, healing ministry, the formation and sending of disciples, and eventual suffering and death as the climax of God's redemptive plan. The Synoptics thus provide not merely biographical accounts but carefully arranged theological portraits that present Jesus as the embodiment of God's Kingdom Mission. Such a structural unity allows the scholarship for a comparative study and reinforces a coherent vision of Jesus' identity and purpose across three distinct yet harmonized voices.

---

[4] Henry J. Cadbury, "Luke: Translator or Author?," *The American Journal of Theology* 24/3 (July, 1920): 436-455.

[5] Warren J. Moulton, "The Dating of the Synoptic Gospels," *Journal of Biblical Literature* 37/1-2 (1918): 1-19.

[6] John S. Kloppenborg, "The Sayings Gospel Q and the Quest of the Historical Jesus," *The Harvard Theological Review* 89/4 (October, 1996): 307-344.

The Background of Jesus' Mission

The Mission of Jesus is deeply rooted in the Jewish expectations of the Messiah and the Kingdom of God.[7] In first-century Judaism, there was widespread hope for a divinely anointed deliverer who would liberate Israel from foreign oppression and restore the Davidic kingdom. This expectation often carried political and nationalistic overtones.[8] However, Jesus redefined messianic identity and Mission in ways that both fulfilled and subverted popular hopes. Jesus' Mission, while continuous with Israel's story, redirected attention from political restoration to spiritual transformation and universal reconciliation (Luke 17:20-21).

The roots of Jesus' Mission lie in the Old Testament vision of redemption and restoration.[9] The Hebrew Scriptures consistently portray God as a Missionary God who seeks to bless all nations through Israel (Genesis 12:1-3; Isaiah 49:6). Prophetic texts like Isaiah and Jeremiah forestall a time of renewed covenant, justice, and peace, a hope that Jesus fulfils through Jesus' ministry.[10] In this way, Jesus' Mission emerges not as a break from Israel's story but as its climactic fulfilment (Luke 4:16-21).

John the Baptist serves as the pivotal prophetic figure who prepares the way for Jesus.[11] His call to repentance (Matthew 3:2) and his identification of Jesus as the one who baptizes with the Holy Spirit and fire (Luke 3:16) indicate a transition from prophetic anticipation to eschatological fulfilment. John the Baptist represents the culmination of the Old Covenant prophetic tradition, while Jesus inaugurates the Kingdom in both word and deed.[12] The Synoptics present this handing over as a decisive moment in redemptive history (Mark 1:2-11), marking the beginning of Jesus' public Mission.

---

[7] Jacob Neusner, "Messianic Themes in Formative Judaism," *Journal of the American Academy of Religion* 52/2 (June, 1984): 357-374.

[8] Jacob Neusner, "Messianic Themes in Formative Judaism...

[9] Douglas D. Scott. *Is Jesus of Nazareth the Predicted Messiah?: A Historical-Evidential Approach to Specific Old Testament Messianic Prophecies and Their New Testament Fulfilments* (London: Wipf and Stock, 2018).

[10] David E. Aune, "The Problem of the Messianic Secret," *Novum Testamentum* 11/1-2 (January-April, 1969): 1-31.

[11] David H. Wenkel, "The Hidden Prophet Bursting Forth: John the Baptist's Appearing According to Luke," *The Expository Times* 134/5 (December, 2023): 201-210.

[12] John H. Hughes, "John the Baptist: The Forerunner of God Himself," *Novum Testamentum* 14/3 (July, 1972): 191-218.

The Proclamation of the Kingdom of God

At the heart of Jesus' Mission in the Synoptic Gospels is the proclamation of the Kingdom of God.[13] This message is inaugurated with Jesus' first public words: *The time is fulfilled, and the kingdom of God has come near; repent, and believe in the good news* (Mark 1:15). The Kingdom signifies God's dynamic reign over creation, which brings liberation, healing, and restoration.[14] Jesus' preaching does not merely announce a future reality but declares that God's rule is breaking into the present through Jesus' own person and ministry. The Kingdom Jesus proclaims is both present and future, manifesting the "already but not yet" tension.[15] While God's reign is inaugurated through Jesus' words and deeds, its full consummation awaits the *eschaton*. This tension is seen in Jesus' miracles and exorcisms, which are signs of the Kingdom's arrival (Luke 11:20), and in Jesus' teaching on watchfulness and perseverance, which point toward its future fulfilment (Matthew 24-025). Jesus' Mission thus initiates a new era, while pointing forward to its ultimate completion. Jesus frequently employs parables to reveal the nature of the Kingdom.[16] The Synoptics present these parables such as the sower, the mustard seed, and the leaven (Matthew 13; Mark 4; Luke 8) as veiled disclosures of divine truth. Parables serve a dual purpose: they reveal the mysteries of the Kingdom to those who are receptive and conceal them from the unrepentant (Mark 4:11-12). Through these, Jesus invites his hearers into a transformative encounter with God's reign, marked by humility, faith, and fruitfulness.

The Suffering Messiah: Passion and the Cross

A significant feature of Jesus' Mission in the Synoptic Gospels is his voluntary embrace of suffering. Contrary to popular messianic expectations, Jesus teaches that suffering is necessary for the fulfilment of his Mission.[17] Three passion predictions in each Gospel, Mark 8:31; Luke 9:22 and Matthew 16:21 emphasize that the Son of Man must suffer, be rejected, killed, and raised. Jesus' journey to the cross is not a tragic diversion but

---

[13] Paul Schubert, "The Synoptic Gospels and Eschatology," *Journal of Bible and Religion* 14/3 (August, 1946): 151-157.

[14] James Orr, "The Value of the Idea of the Kingdom of God," *The Biblical World* 25/3 (March, 1905): 196-200.

[15] Graham Cray, "A Theology of the Kingdom," *Transformation* 5/4 (1988): 24-31.

[16] George Eldon Ladd, "The Life-Setting of the Parables of the Kingdom," *Journal of Bible and Religion* 31/3 (July, 1963): 193-199.

[17] Clarence Tucker Craig, "The Identification of Jesus with the Suffering Servant," *The Journal of Religion* 24/4 (October, 1944): 240-245.

the very path ordained by God for the redemption of humanity.[18] Thus, the cross stands as the climax of Jesus' redemptive work.[19] Because, in the Synoptics, the crucifixion is not merely a political execution but a Missiological event in which Jesus bears the weight of sin and fulfils the divine plan of salvation (Mark 10:45; Matthew 26:28). Jesus' death is the ultimate expression of obedience and love, representing that the Kingdom advances not through domination but through self-giving sacrifice.[20] The cross, therefore, reveals both the depth of human rebellion and the breadth of divine mercy. Thus, the resurrection supports Jesus' Mission and affirms the truth of Jesus' identity and message. It is not only the reversal of death but the confirmation that Jesus' suffering was redemptive. The risen Christ commissions the disciples to proclaim repentance and forgiveness of sins to all nations (Luke 24:46-49), suggesting that the Mission continues in the power of the resurrection. Thus, Jesus' death and resurrection together form the foundation of the Church's gospel and Missional calling.

Missiological Themes Emerging from the Synoptics

The Synoptic Gospels present Jesus as the agent of God's redemption, sent to seek and save the lost (Luke 19:10). Jesus' Mission is both divine in origin and holistic in scope, addressing physical, social, and spiritual brokenness.[21] Jesus heals the sick, feeds the hungry, forgives sins, and restores the marginalized, thereby enacting God's redemptive purposes in concrete ways. Through Jesus, God's salvation breaks into history, fulfilling the prophetic hope of a renewed creation and reconciled humanity.[22] The Kingdom of God emerges as the central message of Jesus' Mission. It is not a static concept but a dynamic reality that transforms individuals and communities. The Synoptics depict the Kingdom as advancing wherever God's will be done, especially among the poor, the meek, and the repentant. Mission, in this context, is the invitation to participate in God's reign and align one's life with its values of justice, mercy, and humility (Matthew 5-7).

---

[18] Ardel B. Caneday, "Revealed Forward: Figural Revelation of the Messiah's Suffering and Glory in Israel's Scripture According to Luke 24:13-35," *The Southern Baptist Journal of Theology* 26/3 (December, 2022): 30-48.

[19] Lois Malcolm, "The Crucified Messiah and Divine Suffering in the Old Testament," *Word & World* 5/2 (December, 2006): 136-144.

[20] Lois Malcolm, "The Crucified Messiah and Divine Suffering… 136-144.

[21] Jeffrey W. Barbeau, "Coleridge, Christology, and the Language of Redemption," *Anglican Theological Review* 93/2 (December, 2011): 263-282.

[22] Willem Leendertz, "God and Man Reconciled," *Mennonite Life* 10/2 (December, 1955): 51.

Discipleship in the Synoptic Gospels is not merely an invitation to follow Jesus but a call to share in Jesus' Mission.[23] Jesus forms a community of disciples who are trained, sent, and empowered to proclaim the Kingdom (Luke 9-10; Matthew 10). Thus, the disciples are presented not as spectators but as active participants who embody the message they proclaim. The cost of discipleship, taking up the cross and denying oneself (Mark 8:34), reflects the pattern of Jesus' own Mission and demands total commitment.[24] Finally, the cross and resurrection function as the foundation for reconciliation.[25] Through the cross, Jesus overcomes the powers of sin and death, and through the resurrection, Jesus inaugurates new creation. This redemptive act is not limited to individuals but incorporates all of creation (Luke 24; Romans 8:19-23). The Synoptics thus present a vision of Mission that is both personal and cosmic, grounded in Jesus' self-giving love and extended through the witness of the Church.

The Mission Methods of Jesus in the Synoptic Gospel

The Synoptic Gospels reveal not only the message of Jesus but also the diverse and intentional methods through which Jesus carried out God's Mission. These methods were theologically rich, spiritually grounded, and contextually responsive, reflecting a Missiology rooted in God's redemptive purposes. Each method demonstrates how Jesus both proclaimed and enacted the Kingdom of God, providing the Church with a paradigm for holistic and incarnational Mission.

Mission as Proclamation of the Kingdom of God

One of the primary methods Jesus employed was the public proclamation of the Kingdom of God.[26] From the outset of Jesus' ministry, it is the declaration that: *The time is fulfilled, and the kingdom of God has come near; repent, and believe in the good news* (Mark 1:15). Matthew presents it as: *From that time Jesus began to proclaim, "Repent, for the kingdom of heaven has come near"* (Matthew 4:17). This proclamation, that waves throughout the Synoptics, was not merely an announcement but an eschatological declaration that God's reign was breaking into history through God's

---

[23] Deblois, Marjolein. "Kingdom Discipleship to the End: The Synoptic Gospels on Perseverance," *Puritan Reformed Journal* 12/1 (December, 2020): 17-31.

[24] Matthew L. Skinner, "Denying Self, Bearing a Cross, and Following Jesus: Unpacking the Imperatives of Mark 8:34," *Word & World* 23/3 (December, 2003): 321-331.

[25] Jeffrey Kaster, "The Main Mystery: Cross and Resurrection," *Youth Update* (December, 2003): 1-4.

[26] Mark Saucy, "Miracles and Jesus' Proclamation of the Kingdom of God," Bibliotheca Sacra 153/611 (December, 1996): 281-307.

person and work.[27] Jesus preached in diverse settings like synagogues (Luke 4:16), open fields (Mark 6:34), villages, and cities, that provided broad accessibility to the message. Jesus' method combined urgency and invitation, challenging the hearers to a radical change of mind (*metanoia*) and faith in the good news.[28] Missiologically, Jesus' proclamation fulfilled Old Testament hopes of divine intervention and inaugurated a new era in salvation history. Mission, then, is not merely ethical or social in nature; it begins with the heralding of divine rule.

Mission as Teaching through Parables

In addition to proclamation of the Kingdom of God, Jesus taught extensively through parables, a method that communicated the mysteries of the Kingdom in narrative form.[29] The Synoptic Gospels record over thirty parables, many of which explains on the nature, growth, and value of the Kingdom of God (Matthew 13; Mark 4; Luke 8). This story telling method is drawn from everyday life of farming, family dynamics and economics functioned both as a revelatory and concealing methods (Mark 4:11-12). For those open to Jesus' message, parables invited reflection, faith, and transformation.[30] For others, they veiled truth as a form of divine judgment. Beyond Matthew 13, Mark 4, and Luke 8, Jesus told parables like the Good Samaritan (Luke 10:25-37), the Lost Sheep, Coin, and Son (Luke 15:1-32), and the Workers in the Vineyard (Matthew 20:1-16) to confront self-righteousness, highlight God's grace, and call for radical love and inclusion. In parables such as the Wicked Tenants (Mark 12:1-12) and the Rich Fool (Luke 12:13-21), Jesus exposed the dangers of rejecting God's messengers and trusting in wealth, showing that parables were central to Jesus' redemptive Mission.[31] This pedagogical method was relational and participatory, requiring engagement from the listener. From a Mission perspective, parables served as expectations about God's reign, that are emphasizing its hiddenness, unexpected growth, and reversal of human values. Thus, Jesus' teaching method was deeply Missiological that fostered both reasoning, understanding and existential response to the Kingdom of God.

---

[27] David Foster Estes, "Christ's First Proclamation of the Kingdom," *Review & Expositor* 16/1 (December, 1919): 33-52.

[28] C. A. Nwaosu, "Jesus' Kingdom Proclamation in the Gospel of Matthew: A Review," *BTSK Insight* 6/2 (December, 2009): 64-71.

[29] Eugene A. LaVerdiere, "Teaching in Parables," *Emmanuel* 94 (December, 1988): 438.

[30] Stephen J. Wellum, "Preaching and Teaching the Parables of Jesus," *The Southern Baptist Journal of Theology* 13/3 (December, 2009): 2-3.

[31] Edward Ferdinand Siegman, "Teaching in Parables: (Mk 4:10-12; Lk 8:9-10; Mt 13:10-15)," *The Catholic Biblical Quarterly* 23/2 (December, 1961): 161-181.

Mission as Healing and Exorcism

Jesus also advanced Mission through healing the sick and casting out demons, acts which visibly demonstrated the arrival of God's Kingdom.[32] Throughout the Synoptic narratives (Matthew 8-9; Mark 1:29-34; Luke 7:22), Jesus' healing ministry addresses both physical suffering and spiritual bondage. These miracles were not performed for public acceptance, but as signs that the Kingdom was present in power. Healing restored individuals to community life and worship, while exorcism revealed Jesus' authority over demonic forces (Luke 11:20). Besides these, Jesus' healing and exorcism ministry is seen throughout the Synoptic Gospels as a core method of Mission.[33] Jesus healed a paralytic to show both physical and spiritual authority (Mark 2:1-12; Luke 5:17-26), restored a demon-possessed man in the region of the Gerasenes (Matthew 8:28-34; Mark 5:1-20; Luke 8:26-39), and healed a bleeding woman alongside raising Jairus' daughter (Mark 5:21-43). These miracles demonstrated the power of God's Kingdom, showing compassion, restoring dignity, and revealing divine authority over sin, sickness, and demonic powers.[34] This method also embodied a holistic Mission, addressing body, mind, and spirit, and reflected God's compassion and justice. From the Missiological perspective, Jesus' miracles fulfilled prophetic expectations of messianic restoration (Isaiah 35:5-6) and anticipated the full healing of creation. Jesus' healing acts validated Jesus' message and provided a foretaste of the Kingdom's comprehensive renewal.

Mission as Table Fellowship with Sinners and Subaltern Community

A particularly radical method Jesus used was table fellowship with tax collectors, sinners, and the marginalized.[35] In contexts such as Matthew 9:10-13, Mark 2:15-17, and Luke 19:1-10, Jesus eats with tax collectors and sinners, those considered unclean or socially deviant by religious standards. In a culture where meals signified social boundaries and status, Jesus' practice redefined Mission as inclusion and righteousness. Jesus' meals became acts of Missional hospitality, offering grace, dignity, and

---

[32] Christoffer H. Grundmann, "Inviting the Spirit to Fight the Spirits?: Pneumatological Challenges for Missions in Healing and Exorcism," *International Review of Mission* 94/372 (December, 2005): 51-73.

[33] Paul W. Hollenbach, "Jesus, Demoniacs, and Public Authorities: A Socio-Historical Study," *Journal of the American Academy of Religion* 49/4 (December, 1981): 567-588.

[34] George Saxenmeyer, "Approaching the Ministries of Healing and Exorcism (Methodologies for Approach)," *The Journal of Pastoral Counseling* 11 (December, 1977): 32-36.

[35] Cecilia Wassén, "Jesus' Table Fellowship with 'Toll Collectors and Sinners': Questioning the Alleged Purity Implications," *Journal for the Study of the Historical Jesus* 14/2 (January, 2016): 137-157.

belonging.[36] This method though offended the religious elites, but presented as an open invitation of the Kingdom (Luke 14:15-24). Missiologically, table fellowship functioned as a visible sign of God's inclusive and reconciling Mission. Through shared meals, Jesus enacted the coming banquet of the Kingdom (Luke 13:29), where the last are welcomed first. Such a Mission practice highlighted the role of relationship and hospitality in extending God's grace.

Mission as Discipleship and Mentorship

Another characteristic of Jesus' Mission was the formation of a community of disciples through intentional mentorship and training.[37] Jesus did not simply attract crowds, rather, called specific individuals to follow (Mark 3:13-19; Luke 6:12-16), investing in their growth through relational proximity, teaching, demonstrating, and correction. This method included both instruction such as Sermon on the Mount (Matthew 5-7), and active participation in ministry (Luke 9:1-6). Discipleship in the Synoptic Gospels is costly and transformative, demanding a call to deny oneself, take up the cross, and follow (Mark 8:34). Jesus' relational pedagogy aimed not only to inform but to form the followers into participants in the dynamic Kingdom Mission.[38] Missiologically, discipleship is an extension of the Mission itself, Jesus multiplies His presence and work through those He mentors. This method established a framework for Mission rooted in community, reflection of the life of Jesus, and faithful obedience.

Sending Out Others as Mission and Mission Delegations

A further dimension of Jesus' Mission method was sending His disciples to carry forward His ministry.[39] In Matthew 10, Mark 6:7-13, Luke 9:1-6, and 10:1-20, Jesus sends the Twelve, and later the Seventy-two on a Mission to preach, heal, and confront evil. This delegation was not merely pragmatic. It was Missiological, expressing the shared nature of Mission between Jesus and the followers. Jesus' instructions emphasized simplicity, urgency, and dependence on God and local hospitality. This method trained disciples

---

[36] Dennis Hamm, "Zacchaeus Revisited Once More: A Story of Vindication or Conversion?," *Biblica* 72/2 (1991): 249-252.

[37] Semuel Tulak, "Discipleship in Contemporary Mission: Case Examples of Discipleship by Followers of Jesus in Non-Christian Communities in Indonesia," *International Review of Mission* 113/1 (December, 2024): 115-127.

[38] Richard Hicks, "Markan Discipleship according to Malachi: The Significance of μὴ ἀποστερήσῃς in the Story of the Rich Man (Mark 10:17-22)," *Journal of Biblical Literature* 132/1 (2013): 179-199.

[39] Kenneth Nehrbass and Jane Rhoades, "Jesus' Use of Experiential Learning in the Sending of the Seventy: Implications for Ministry Practicums," *Christian Education Journal* 18/1 (December, 2021): 74-88.

to rely on divine provision and to expect both reception and rejection.[40] Missiologically, it reflects the participatory and expanding nature of God's Mission, extending beyond the person of Jesus to a commissioned community. This practice also prefigures the Church's post-resurrection Missionary calling, rooted in Christ's authority and sustained by His presence.

Mission as Constant Prayer and Active Communion with God

Prayer was a consistent and foundational method by which Jesus sustained His Mission through communion with God.[41] The Synoptic Gospels frequently depict Jesus withdrawing to pray (Mark 1:35; Luke 5:16; Matthew 14:23), especially before significant events such as choosing disciples or facing temptation and suffering. He prayed all night before choosing the Twelve (Luke 6:12), sought solitude on the Mount of Transfiguration (Luke 9:28-29), and agonized in prayer at Gethsemane before the arrest (Matthew 26:36-46; Mark 14:32-42; Luke 22:39-46). These moments of solitude and intercession reveal that Jesus' Mission was not self-directed, but rooted in divine initiative and empowerment. Prayer served as a means of discernment, spiritual nourishment, and alignment with the God's will.[42] Missiologically, Jesus' dependence on the Father underscores the Trinitarian nature of Mission, a work initiated by God, embodied by Jesus, and empowered by the Holy Spirit. Jesus' examples of prayers demonstrate the necessity of spiritual discipline for any authentic and effective participation in God's Mission.

Mission as Prophetic Confrontation

Another essential method Jesus employed in Mission was prophetic confrontation of religious corruption and social injustice. Passages such as Matthew 23, Mark 11:15-18, and Luke 11:37-52, Jesus condemns hypocrisy, pride, and the misuse of religious power. Jesus' cleansing of the temple (Mark 11) dramatizes this critique, confronting a system that exploited the poor and distorted true worship.[43] Jesus' prophetic confrontation is also evident when jesus rebuke of the Pharisees for prioritizing human traditions

---

[40] Anto Karokaran, "Discipleship: A Participation in Jesus' Sending," *Review for Religious* 58 (January, 1999): 609-620.

[41] Peter Vryzas, "On the Jesus Prayer," *Theologia Orthodoxă* 67/2 (December, 2022): 337-351.

[42] Edmund Neufeld, "Revisiting Penal Substitution and Recovering the Passion Prayers of Jesus: Which 'Cup,' and How 'Forsaken' (Matt 26:39; 27:46)?," *Didaskalia* 30 (December, 2021): 18-36.

[43] Craig A. Evans, "Jesus' Action in the Temple: Cleansing or Portent of Destruction,?" *The Catholic Biblical Quarterly* 51/2 (December, 1989): 237-270.

over God's commands (Mark 7:1-13; Matthew 15:1-9) and in lament over Jerusalem's rejection of prophets (Luke 13:34-35). Jesus also directly challenged religious hypocrisy when healing on the *Sabbath* (Luke 13:10-17; 14:1-6) and when questioning the religious leaders' authority (Mark 11:27-33). These confrontations reveal Jesus' Mission to call out injustice, expose false religiosity, and call people back to authentic righteousness in relation with God's Kingdom.[44] This confrontational method aligns Jesus with the Old Testament prophets who spoke truth to power and called Israel back to covenant faithfulness. Jesus' confrontations were not simply reactive but Missiological, intended to reform people and the systems in light of God's holiness. Thus, the method of Prophetic Confrontation affirms that Mission includes support for justice and integrity, challenging systems and leaders that obstruct the Kingdom values.

Non-Hierarchical Mission

One of the distinctive features in Luke's Gospel is the Mission of the seventy (Luke 10:1-12), which expands the scope of Mission beyond the exclusive circle of the Twelve. While Matthew and Mark focus primarily on the commissioning of the Twelve (Matthew 10; Mark 6), Luke introduces a broader Missionary team, emphasizing that the authority and responsibility of Mission are not limited to the apostolic elite. Jesus' sending of the seventy-two in Luke 10:1-20 exemplifies the non-hierarchical approach to Mission, showing that Kingdom work was not limited to a select elite but entrusted to a broader group of disciples. Jesus' inclusive teaching in Luke 9:49-50, where Jesus affirms someone casting out demons in Jesus' name despite not being part of the Twelve, further reveals that Mission authority is shared among all faithful followers, not confined to a hierarchical structure. Thus, the Non-Hierarchical Mission of Jesus affirms the legitimacy of lay participation and anticipates the Mission identity of the entire Church. In doing so, Luke reinforces a Missiology of empowerment, where all followers of Jesus are co-labourers in the Kingdom, regardless of status or position.

Mission in the Midst of Hostility

Jesus' sending of the seventy by saying: *Go on your way; I am sending you out like lambs into the midst of wolves* (Luke 10:3) underlines the vulnerability and risk inherent in Kingdom Mission. This metaphor refers to Old Testament images of unjust leadership and predatory elites (Ezekiel 34:5, 10), and finds further expression in intertestamental and Greco-Roman literature, where 'wolves' symbolize corrupt political and religious

[44] Babu Immanuel, "Jesus' Cross, Conflicts and the New Testament," *Transformation* 23/1 (January, 2006): 24-29.

figures.[45] Jesus personally carried out Mission in the midst of hostility, facing rejection in His own hometown (Luke 4:16-30), opposition from religious leaders for healing on the *Sabbath* (Mark 3:1-6), and accusations of operating by demonic power (Matthew 12:24; Luke 11:15). Jesus also warned His disciples that they too would face persecution, arrests, and betrayal for the sake of the gospel (Matthew 10:16-22; Luke 21:12-17), showing that hostility is a defining feature of faithful participation in God's Mission. Jesus' Missionaries, therefore, stand in direct contrast to worldly power structures and they embody the suffering and humility of their Lord. This model reflects a Missiology shaped by nonviolence, prophetic witness, and suffering. Rather than retreating from danger, disciples are sent into the heart of opposition, participating in Jesus' own path of sacrificial love and confrontation with oppressive systems.

Counter-Cultural Mission

Luke 9:52-62 presents a radical vision of discipleship where cultural, familial, and traditional expectations are subordinated to the urgent demands of the Kingdom of God. Jesus' call to follow Him requires a break from convention, whether it be foregoing family obligations, relinquishing social security, or embracing rejection.[46] Another example of Jesus' counter-cultural Mission is found in Matthew 5-7 (the Sermon on the Mount), where Jesus overturns conventional values by blessing the poor, commanding love for enemies, and rejecting outward religiosity in favour of inward righteousness, challenging both societal norms and religious expectations.[47] Jesus' counter-cultural Mission is also evident in deliberate actions that challenged societal, religious, and cultural norms such as touching a leper (Matthew 8:1-4), dining with tax collectors and sinners (Matthew 9:9-13; Mark 2:13-17; Luke 5:27-32), welcoming children (Mark 10:13-16), and redefining greatness through servanthood (Matthew 20:25-28; Mark 10:42-45), commending a poor widow's offering (Mark 12:41-44), receiving a sinful woman's anointing (Luke 7:36-50), and teaching to invite the marginalized (Luke 14:12-14). Through these counter-cultural Mission Jesus reveals that the values of God's Kingdom radically oppose the prevailing standards of purity, status, and power. This demonstrate that, Mission is not merely an activity but a radical reorientation of identity and commitment.

---

[45] William D. Watley, "Lambs and Wolves: A Vision of Hope," *Mid-Stream* 24/2 (December, 1985): 150-154.

[46] James C. Wayne, "Mission and Counter-Mission or 'Learning to Live Outside!': Mark 3:20-30," *Review & Expositor* 89/4 (December, 1992): 535-539.

[47] Troy M. Troftgruben, "Prayer and Ethics in the Sermon on the Mount," *Word & World* 40/3 (December, 2020): 227-235.

Interdependent Mission

Jesus envisioned Mission as a communal endeavour, not a solitary pursuit.[48] In Luke 10, Jesus instructs disciples to depend on the hospitality of others (Luke 10:4-7), revealing that the needs of the Missionaries are to be met within the mutuality of the believing community. Such an interdependent Mission can be seen also in Jesus' instructions for disciples to rely on others for hospitality and provision (Matthew 10:9-11; Luke 9:3-4; 10:4-8), in financial support from followers like the women mentioned in Luke 8:1-3. Jesus delegated Mission in pairs (Luke 10:1-20), relied on others to prepare for significant events like the Passover (Luke 22:7-13), and even sought companionship in suffering (Matthew 26:36-41), signifying that God's Mission is carried out in community, not in isolation. This pattern reflects the interdependence at the heart of the early Church's life and Mission.[49] Rather than promoting self-sufficiency, Jesus encourages vulnerability, trust, and shared provision. The Mission of God, therefore, is not a private enterprise but a collective calling. It highlights the Church's role not only in sending but in sustaining Mission through prayer, support, and active partnership.

Mission as Interpersonal Relationships

The Mission of Jesus, as portrayed in the Synoptic Gospels, was not only theological and cosmic in scope but also profoundly relational in character.[50] While Jesus frequently preached to large crowds, the Gospels consistently emphasize that some of the most transformative and revelatory moments occurred in personal, one-on-one encounters. These relational engagements reveal a central methodological feature of Jesus' Mission, the intentional affirmation of individual dignity and the pastoral care of the marginalized. For instance, Jesus' calling of Matthew, a tax collector (Matthew 9:9-13), proves Jesus' readiness to initiate relationship with those viewed as socially and religiously unclean. Similarly, Jesus' interaction with Zacchaeus (Luke 19:1-10) display Jesus' capacity to transform lives through presence and personal attention. The healing of the woman with the issue of blood (Mark 5:25-34) in the midst of a pressing crowd underlines Jesus' sensitivity to individual suffering, while Jesus' response to the sinful woman in the house of Simon the Pharisee (Luke 7:36-50) reveals commitment to restorative

---

[48] Walter T. Wilson, "Finding the Sectarian Self: Strategies of Communal Legitimation in the Matthean Mission Discourse," *Religion & Theology* 22/3-4 (December, 2015): 275-300.

[49] Rollin G. Grams, "Narrative Dynamics in Isaiah's and Matthew's Mission Theology," *Transformation* 21/4 (October, 2004): 238-255.

[50] Maria L. Boccia, "Human Interpersonal Relationships and the Love of the Trinity," *Priscilla Papers* 25/4 (December, 2011): 22-26.

grace in the context of rejection and judgment. These examples from the Synoptic tradition affirm that Jesus did not perceive people merely as objects of ministry but as persons bearing the image of God, worthy of engagement, understanding, and transformation. Jesus' approach redefied the impersonal nature of much religious activity of the time and demonstrated a Mission rooted in compassion, mutual encounter, and pastoral attentiveness. Thus, Jesus embodied a relational model of Mission that invites the Church to move beyond proclamation alone, toward personal presence, active listening, and restorative action in the lives of others.

Mission as Symbolic Actions

Jesus' Mission in the Synoptic Gospels was not limited to verbal proclamation. It also included powerful symbolic and prophetic actions that visibly embodied the realities of God's Kingdom. These gestures were deeply Mission oriented, often disruptive, and intentionally confrontational, designed to provoke reflection, challenge existing systems, and reveal the character of God's redemptive rule. One of the most striking examples is the cleansing of the temple (Matthew 21:12-13; Mark 11:15-18; Luke 19:45-46), where Jesus overturned tables and drove out merchants in a dramatic protest against the commercialization of worship and the marginalization of Gentile seekers.[51] This act was not merely an expression of moral outrage but a prophetic sign of judgment and a call for the restoration of true worship. Other examples include Jesus' triumphal entry into Jerusalem riding on a donkey (Matthew 21:1-11; Mark 11:1-10; Luke 19:28-40), which fulfilled messianic prophecy (Zechariah 9:9) and symbolized a Kingdom founded not on military conquest but on humility and peace.[52] Similarly, Jesus' act of welcoming and blessing children (Matthew 19:13-15; Mark 10:13-16; Luke 18:15-17) served as a prophetic critique of societal norms that devalued the vulnerable and excluded them from religious significance.[53] Jesus' practice of touching lepers (Mark 1:40-45; Matthew 8:1-4; Luke 5:12-16), despite their ritual impurity, also constituted a powerful symbolic act of inclusion, healing, and restoration, showing that the Kingdom breaks through boundaries of purity and exclusion. Thus, the Symbolic Actions confronted injustice, subverted oppressive religious and cultural systems, and enacted the vision of a new world order under God's reign.

---

[51] Hans Dieter Betz, "Jesus and the Purity of the Temple (Mark 11:15-18): A Comparative Religion Approach," *Journal of Biblical Literature* 116/3 (Autumn, 1997): 455-472.

[52] Brent Kinman, Parousia, "Jesus' "A-Triumphal" Entry, and the Fate of Jerusalem (Luke 19:28-44)," *Journal of Biblical Literature* 118/2 (Summer, 1999): 279-294.

[53] J. Duncan M. Derrett, "Why Jesus Blessed the Children (Mk 10:13-16 par.)," *Novum Testamentum* 25/1 (January, 1983): 1-18.

Mission as Embodied Witness (Leading by Example)

Jesus did not only speak about God's Kingdom, but lived it. In the Synoptic Gospels, Jesus' Mission is shown not just through words, but through actions that reflect the very heart of God. He demonstrated humility, compassion, justice, and obedience in every part of His life. Jesus touched the untouchable, like lepers (Mark 1:40-45), welcomed children (Mark 10:13-16), and ate with sinners and outcasts (Matthew 9:10-13; Luke 5:29-32), showing that everyone mattered in God's Kingdom. Jesus forgave His enemies, even on the cross (Luke 23:34), and refused to respond to violence with violence (Matthew 26:52-54). Jesus also endured suffering and death not with resentment, but with love and surrender to God's will (Mark 14:36; Luke 23:46). Jesus' actions were not separate from the message; they were the message in visible form. Thus, Jesus' life was a living sermon, and the death was the clearest expression of God's love and forgiveness. Even in the final moments, Jeus remained faithful to the Mission, offering grace and hope to a thief beside Jesus (Luke 23:39-43). In all these ways, Jesus led by example, showing that true Mission is not only about preaching but about living in a way that reflects God's character.

Mission as Suffering and the Cross

Perhaps the most paradoxical method of Jesus' Mission is His embrace of suffering and crucifixion.[54] The Synoptic Gospels repeatedly record Jesus' foretelling of suffering (Mark 8:31-33; Matthew 16:21-28; Luke 9:22-27) and willingness to endure the cross for the redemption of the world. Jesus presents suffering not as failure but as fidelity to God's redemptive plan. Jesus' path of self-emptying love becomes the model for authentic discipleship and Mission (Mark 10:45). Missiologically, the cross reveals the cost of reconciliation and the nature of divine love. Jesus' suffering is not incidental but essential, through it, Jesus defeats sin and inaugurates the new covenant. His method teaches that Mission requires sacrifice, endurance, and a willingness to lose for the sake of God's purposes.

Post-Resurrection Commission as Mission

Finally, Jesus concluded the earthly Mission with a commissioning of the disciples to continue the Mission.[55] In Matthew 28:18-20 and Luke 24:46-49, the risen Christ authorizes and sends the followers to make disciples of all nations, teaching and baptizing them in the power of the Spirit. This commission is grounded in Jesus' universal authority and accompanied

---

[54] Lisa Sowle Cahill, "Kingdom and Cross: Christian Moral Community and the Problem of Suffering," *Interpretation* 50/2 (December, 1996): 156-168.

[55] John Munsey Turner, "The Great Commission," *The Expository Times* 106/7 (December, 1995): 209-210.

by His abiding presence. The method of post-resurrection commissioning establishes the Church's vocation as a Missionary community called to continue Jesus' words and works.[56] Thus, it affirms the Church's identity as the Body of Christ, empowered by Holy Spirit and sent into the world to exemplify the good news. This final method summarizes the totality of Jesus' Mission, proclamation, presence, and empowerment and offers a durable framework for the Church's ongoing engagement with the world.

Conclusion

The Synoptic Gospels present a unified yet richly diverse representation of Jesus as the Missionary Messiah, whose life and ministry embody the very heart of God's redemptive Mission. From the announcement of the Kingdom of God to the call for repentance, healing of the broken, confrontation with injustice, and ultimately the death and resurrection, Jesus demonstrated a Mission that is both theological and practical, rooted in divine purpose and directed toward the restoration of humanity and creation. The common structure, historical background, and literary strategies of Matthew, Mark, and Luke reveal not only the coherence of their witness but also the multifaceted nature of Jesus' Mission. The methods such as preaching, parables, table fellowship, healing, disciple-making, and sacrificial suffering and validate a holistic approach that integrates proclamation, compassion, and confrontation. Moreover, the post-resurrection commission reaffirms that the Mission of Jesus is ongoing, now entrusted to His followers. Thus, understanding Jesus' Mission in the Synoptic Gospels provides the Church with a foundational paradigm for faithful witness and Mission engagement in every age, challenging the believers not merely to admire Jesus but to actively participate in the Kingdom as Jesus proclaimed and embodied.

---

[56] John H. Strong, "The Great Commission: Does It Merit the Name?," *The Biblical World* 29/5 (May, 1907): 352-356.

14

Revealed Word, Revealed Mission The Unique Mission Narrative of Jesus in the Fourth Gospel

John's Gospel stands apart from the Synoptic narratives by offering a richly symbolic and deeply theological account of Jesus' Mission. Rather than presenting a chronology of deeds and sayings, John explains a cosmic performance in which Jesus is the pre-existent Word who enters time to bring life and light. The Fourth Gospel invites readers into a contemplative journey through metaphors of light and darkness, water and Spirit, vine and branches, it reveals that Jesus' Mission is as much about transforming hearts and relationships as it is about teaching or healing. In John's vision, Mission flows from the very being of God, Jesus, and the Holy Spirit, and into the life of the community. Every encounter in the Gospel is designed to draw the Johannine audience into an intimate relationship with Christ, believing leads to seeing, and abiding leads to bearing fruit. Unlike the more action-focused accounts, John emphasizes the ongoing experience of God's presence through mutual love and inner transformation. Thus, the Gospel according to St. John does not simply recount events, rather, it offers a theological meditation on who Jesus is, why Jesus came, and how Jesus' followers are invited to live in the reality of eternal life here and now.

Authorship, Context, and Composition

Scholars generally agree that the Fourth Gospel was written toward the end of the first century CE, most likely between 90 and 100 CE, within a community of believers in Asia Minor, probably around Ephesus.[1]

[1] Andreas J. Köstenberger, "The Destruction of the Second Temple and the Composition of the Fourth Gospel," *Trinity Journal* 26/2 (December, 2005): 205-242.

Although the Gospel never names its author outright, early church writers uniformly identify him with "the beloved disciple," traditionally understood to be John the son of Zebedee.[2] This disciple's close personal experience with Jesus provides the foundation for the vivid eyewitness details found throughout the text. At the same time, the author shows a deep awareness of both Jewish worship practices and Greek philosophical ideas, especially in the famous Prologue where Jesus is introduced as the eternal *Logos*, or divine Word.[3] The community for whom the Gospel was written appears to have been grappling with internal and external challenges. Internally, they were seeking to strengthen faith and community identity by reflecting on who Jesus really is, the pre-existent Son sent by the Father. Externally, they faced growing tension with local synagogue leaders, which shaped the Gospel's frequent use of dualistic symbols like light and darkness or above and below. Modern scholars also see evidence of a multi-stage composition process. First, the community preserved and collected the beloved disciple's firsthand memories of Jesus' signs and teachings. Later, editors wove these traditions into a unified narrative, adding theological reflections and structured sections, often called the "Book of Signs" and the "Book of Glory" to help readers move from simple belief to a deeper, abiding trust in Christ. In this way, the Fourth Gospel emerges as both a historical testimony and a carefully crafted Mission work, designed to nurture faith and define the community's place in a complex religious world.

The Structural Unity of the Fourth Gospel

The Fourth Gospel presents a remarkably clear and balanced design that guides readers from Jesus' first appearance all the way through his resurrection and beyond. It opens with a concise Prologue (John 1:1-18), which presents Jesus as the eternal Word who becomes flesh. Such an introduction sets the stage for what follows and points forward to the themes of life, light, and belief. After the Prologue, the Gospel divides into two main sections.[4] The first half, often called the "Book of Signs" (chapters 1-12), is built around seven key miracles, "signs", that include turning water into wine, feeding the five thousand, and raising Lazarus from the dead. Each sign is chosen to reveal a different aspect of who Jesus is and to encourage the reader to trust in him. Among these signs, there are important

---

[2] Tom Thatcher, "The Beloved Disciple, the Fourth Evangelist, and the Authorship of the Fourth Gospel," *The Oxford Handbook of Johannine Studies* (2018): 83-100.

[3] John Ashley Nixon, "Who Wrote the Fourth Gospel?: The Authorship and Occasion of the Fourth Gospel According to Patristic Evidence Form the First Three Centuries," *Faith and Mission* 20/3 (January, 2003): 81-98.

[4] Edward Allison McDowell, "The Structural Integrity of the Fourth Gospel," *Review & Expositor* 34/4 (December, 1937): 397-416.

conversations like those with Nicodemus and the Samaritan woman and "I Am" declarations that deepen our understanding of Jesus' identity.[5]

The second half, known as the "Book of Glory" (chapters 13-20), shifts focus to Jesus' final hours, his farewell teachings to the disciples, arrest and trial, death on the cross, and his resurrection. Central to this section are themes of glory and "the hour" when Jesus is lifted up, which link the passion narrative directly to the divine Mission. Finally, the Gospel concludes with an Epilogue (John 21) in which the risen Christ appears by the Sea of Galilee, reaffirms Peter's calling, and invites the community to continue His work.[6] Altogether, this two-part structure, framed by Prologue and Epilogue, creates a perfectly connected narrative. Every miracle, dialogue, and symbolic statement points back to the Prologue's opening claims and forward to the Epilogue's commission, making the Gospel a unified and purposeful account of Jesus' life, death, resurrection, altogether, the Mission.[7]

Missiological Themes in the Fourth Gospel

The Gospel of John provides a distinct vision of Mission that flows directly from the identity and activity of the triune God. Unlike the Synoptic accounts, which emphasize the proclamation of the Kingdom through parables and preaching, John presents Mission as an outflow of the Father-Son-Spirit relationship, revealed through symbolic "signs," deep dialogues, and the promise of indwelling life. In this Johannine framework, Mission is both divine initiative and human response: God sends, Christ reveals, the Spirit empowers, and disciples bear witness.

Divine Sending (Missio Dei)

The heart of Johannine Missiology is the repeated motif of sending. From the Prologue's assertion that "the Word became flesh" to Jesus' own declarations that "the Father sent me" (John 3:17; 5:24), John makes clear that Mission is God's activity before it ever becomes human work. This divine sending does not simply hand out tasks, rather it establishes an eternal relationship in which Jesus participates fully in God's purpose. In turn, Jesus commissions the Spirit to continue that sending, and the Spirit commissions the community of believers.[8] By framing Mission as *Missio Dei*, John shifts

[5] Edward Allison McDowell, "The Structural Integrity of the Fourth Gospel..., 397-416.

[6] Edward Allison McDowell, "The Structural Integrity of the Fourth Gospel..., 397-416.

[7] Elizabeth Liebert, "That You May Believe: The Fourth Gospel and Structural Developmental Theory," *Biblical Theology Bulletin* 14/2 (January, 1984): 67-73.

[8] James Swetnam, "Bestowal of the Spirit in the Fourth Gospel," *Biblica* 74/4 (1993): 556-576.

the focus from human ambition or strategy to faithful orientation with God's own movement into the world, reminding readers that true Mission flows from a prior, divine initiative.

Revelatory Signs as Evangelistic Acts

In the "Book of Signs" (John 1-12), each miracle is more than a display of power, but it is a purposeful act that reveals the character and glory of the Sent One. Turning water into wine at Cana introduces Jesus as the agent of a new creation, feeding the five thousand points to him as the 'Bread of Life.'[9] Even the raising of Lazarus demonstrate Jesus' ultimate conquest over death. These signs function as evangelistic compositions, drawing both characters in the story and Gospel readers into a journey from amazement to faith. John shows that authentic evangelism does not end with a miraculous demonstration but always directs attention beyond the event to the person of Jesus, calling witnesses to trust in the one whose glory the signs reveal.[10]

Abiding in Christ and Fruitfulness

John 15 presents the vine and branches metaphor to explain how disciples participate in Christ's life. John presents abiding as an ongoing, intimate connection with Jesus, and described as the essential condition for bearing spiritual fruit.[11] Without this connection, disciples cannot love deeply, endure hardship, or bear witness effectively. With it, love, joy, peace, and witness naturally flow. Thus, in Johannine thought, Mission is not an external program or a series of tasks but a lived reality of communion with Christ. When followers remain in Jesus, they do not simply act, but they live out Jesus' life in the world, and their transformed character becomes the most powerful form of Missionary witness.[12]

Covenantal Love as Missional Witness

Unique among the Gospels, John's narrative elevates mutual love as the chief symbol of true discipleship and Mission. Jesus' command, *I give you a new commandment, that you love one another. Just as I have loved you, you also should love one another* (John 13:34), is presented not just as good

---

[9] Shyam K. Humagain, "Dialogue in the Book of Signs: A Polyvalent Analysis of John 1:19-12:50," *Bangalore Theological Forum* 56/2 (January, 2024): 299-301.

[10] Stephen S. Kim, "The Relationship of John 1:19-51 to the Book of Signs in John 2-12," *Bibliotheca Sacra* 165/659 (December 2008): 323-337.

[11] Davi Miguel Manço, "The Vine and the Branches: An Exegetical Study of John 15:1-8 and the Implications of 'Abiding in Christ' (Unio Mystica) for Christian Formation Ministries," *Christian Education Journal* 21/2 (December, 2024): 155-168.

[12] Davi Miguel Manço, "The Vine and the Branches…

advice but as the defining mark of his followers.[13] In his high priestly prayer, Jesus prays for the unity of believers so that "the world may know" the God's love through their oneness (John 17:21). In this framework, sacrificial love within the community becomes the primary evangelistic testimony, when outsiders see believers caring deeply for one another, they glimpse the reconciling love of God.[14] Thus, John teaches that genuine Mission is measured less by numbers or strategies and more by the depth of love that binds the community together.

The Paraclete and Spirit-Empowered Mission

In chapters 14-16, John devotes extended teaching to the Holy Spirit, or *Paraclete*, whom Jesus sends to guide, comfort, and empower the disciples. Rather than relying on human wisdom, *charisma*, or persuasive methods, Johannine Mission depends on the Spirit's presence to bear witness to truth, recall Jesus' words, and convict the world of sin and righteousness.[15] The Spirit enables the community to speak and act in ways that align with God's will, ensuring that Mission is a divine rather than merely human enterprise. This pneumatological emphasis underscores that effective Mission and faithful witness come not from human approaches alone but from participation in the life and power of God through the Spirit.[16]

Witness/Testimony and Eyewitness Authority

John's Gospel claims to record the testimony of an eyewitness, the "beloved disciple" (John 21:24) and repeatedly calls both Jesus and his followers to bear witness (John 15:27). In this context, testimony is more than a recounting of events; it is a relational presentation of the one who is Life and Light, inviting others into the same encounter.[17] Johannine Mission therefore involves the careful handing on of reliable, personal testimony about what the disciples have seen, heard, and touched. As this testimony spreads, new believers join the community not merely because of doctrinal

---

[13] Seung-In Song, "Seeing the Johannine Last Meal as a Covenant Meal (John 13 and Exodus 24)," *Biblica* 100/2 (December, 2019): 282-292.

[14] Kim, Ju-Heon. "The Meaning of Johannine Footwashing in the Light of Jewish Purification Law: Analysis of the Purification Factors in the Footwashing Pericope in John 13," *Canon & Culture* 17/1 (December, 2023: 191-227.

[15] V. George Shillington, "The Spirit-Paraclete as Jesus' Alter Ego in the Fourth Gospel (John 14-16)," *Vision* 13/1 (December, 2012): 31-39.

[16] David Yoon, "The Church as Revealed in John 14-16: The Incorporation of the Triune God and the Believers as the Issue of Christ's Glorification," *Affirmation & Critique* 26/2 (December, 2021): 29-42.

[17] Andrew T. Lincoln, "The Beloved Disciple as Eyewitness and the Fourth Gospel as Witness," *Journal for the Study of the New Testament* 24/3 (December, 2002): 3-26.

statements but because they too have encountered the risen Christ through the word and Spirit-empowered witness of others.[18]

Universal Scope of Mission

Although John focuses also on personal encounters, with Nicodemus, the Samaritan woman, and individual disciples, the Gospel consistently affirms the cosmic reach of Jesus' work. John clearly declares that Christ's light and life are meant "for the world" (John 3:16; 12:32), embracing both Jews and Gentiles.[19] The Samaritan dialogue, in particular, suggests the breaking down of ethnic barriers as Jesus offers "living water" beyond traditional bounds. John's narrative thus balances intimate, one-on-one dialogues with a universal horizon, reminding the community that Mission extends not only to local neighbours but to all peoples across cultural and religious divides.[20]

Eschatological Dimension

In Johannine thought, believing is already passing from death into life (John 5:24), and Mission is the invitation for others to enter this present experience of eternal life. At the same time, the Gospel looks ahead to a future completion, as Jesus promises that He is going to prepare a place for His followers and that Jesus will return to take them along with (John 14:2-3).[21] This tension between the "already" of the new birth and the "not yet" of final glory shapes the community's Mission, giving it a confident hope that transcends present suffering. Disciples are called to live in the light of this eschatological promise, presenting others a foretaste of the life that awaits and thus energizing their witness with both urgency and joy.[22]

Light and Darkness as Missional Metaphors

Throughout John, the sharp contrast between light and darkness (John 1:5; 3:19-21; 8:12) frames the Gospel's Mission. Jesus, as the true Light, enters a world shrouded in darkness, revealing truth and exposing falsehood. Disciples are invited to reflect that light by living in honesty, integrity, and truthfulness, both in word and deed. Missional engagement for John,

---

[18] Dennis Eric Nineham, "Eyewitness Testimony and the Gospel Tradition," *The Journal of Theological Studies* 9/2 (December, 1958): 243-252.

[19] Johnson Thomaskutty, "Reading John's Gospel from a Glocal-Mission Perspective" *Bangalore Theological Forum* 54/2 (January, 2022): 86-104.

[20] Carmel Posa, "The Name Sufficiently Indicates the Scope: Good Samaritan Mission and the Benedictine Vows," *Tjurunga* 84 (December, 2014): 20-31.

[21] Jeffrey A. Gibbs, "Already Dwelling in the Father's House: Reading John 14:2-3 in Context," *Concordia Journal* 49/1 (December, 2023): 13-34.

[22] Robert M. Johnston, "The Eschatological Sabbath in John's Apocalypse: A Reconsideration," *Andrews University Seminary Studies* 25/1 (January, 1987): 39-50.

therefore, involves not only proclaiming the light in speech but embodying it in daily life so that darkness is driven back and the glory of God shines more brightly.[23] By living transparently in the light, the community becomes a visible sign of God's transforming presence in a broken world.

The Unique Mission Methods of Jesus in the Gospel of John

The Gospel of John presents a distinct picture of Jesus' Mission that differs in both form and emphasis from the Synoptic Gospels. While Matthew, Mark, and Luke often describe Jesus as a traveling preacher proclaiming the Kingdom of God through parables and public sermons, John's Gospel focuses more on revelation through relationship, symbolic acts, and intimate encounters. Jesus' Mission in John is not only about proclaiming a message but about revealing God, drawing individuals into deeper communion, and establishing a community marked by love, truth, and the Spirit. Moreover, Jesus' methods are theological in nature, aimed at unveiling divine identity and inviting transformative belief.

Revealing through Signs (Symbolic Miracles)

One of the most distinct Mission methods in John's Gospel is the use of miraculous signs to reveal Jesus' identity and invite belief.[24] Unlike the Synoptic Gospels, where miracles often demonstrate compassion or power, John selects seven specific signs such as turning water into wine (John 2) or raising Lazarus from the dead (John 11) to communicate theological truths. Each sign is symbolic, pointing beyond the event itself to a deeper spiritual reality. The Gospel of John also includes other symbolic signs such as healing the official's son (John 4), healing the lame man at Bethesda (John 5), feeding the five thousand (John 6), walking on water (John 6), healing the man born blind (John 9), and the miraculous catch of fish (John 21). Each of these signs reveals who Jesus is, points to deeper spiritual truths, and invites belief in him as the giver of life, light, and salvation. These signs are not performed to impress or attract the gathering, but to lead individuals into faith by revealing Jesus as the Christ, the Son of God.[25] John himself states this purpose clearly that: *these are written so that you may continue to believe that Jesus is the Messiah, the Son of God, and that through believing you may have life in his name* (John 20:31). In this way,

---

[23] Alexander James Reedrow, "From Darkness to Light: Nicodemus, 'the Jews,' and John's Gospel," *Journal of Theological Interpretation* 18/1 (December, 2024): 77-96.

[24] Ardel B. Caneday, "The Word Made Flesh as Mystery Incarnate: Revealing and Concealing Dramatized by Jesus as Portrayed in John's Gospel," *Journal of the Evangelical Theological Society* 60/4 (December, 2017): 751-765.

[25] Ardel B. Caneday, "The Word Made Flesh as Mystery Incarnate…

Jesus' miracles are central to Mission they are intentional acts of revelation that disclose who Jesus is and what Jesus has come to offer.

Engaging in Personal and Theological Dialogues

Another unique method in John's Gospel is Jesus' use of extended, personal conversations to lead individuals toward faith.[26] Rather than preaching to large crowds, Jesus often engages people individually in deeply discussions. Jesus' conversations with Nicodemus (John 3), the Samaritan woman at the well (John 4), and Mary and Martha (John 11) show a Mission method that is relational, patient, and adapted to the person's spiritual condition. In addition to these, the Fourth Gospel presents Jesus engaging in several other personal and theological conversations such as with Nathanael (John 1), the invalid at Bethesda (John 5), the man born blind (John 9), and Pontius Pilate (John 18-19) where Jesus reveals his identity, invites faith, and challenges superficial understandings of truth, healing, and salvation. These interactions reflect the Johannine emphasis on transformative encounters that intertwine personal revelation with deep theological meaning.[27] Through these dialogues, Jesus gently challenges assumptions, reveals spiritual truths, and invites transformation. This method emphasizes that Mission is not only about public teaching but about personal encounter. Jesus meets people where they are, across boundaries of gender, ethnicity, and religious status and leads them to deeper understanding through dialogue.

Use of "I Am" Sayings

A key feature of John's Gospel is Jesus' repeated use of "I Am" sayings, which serve as theological declarations of his divine identity.[28] Phrases such as "I am the bread of life" (John 6:35), "I am the light of the world" (8:12), and "I am the resurrection and the life" (11:25) are not found in the same form in the Synoptic Gospels. Jesus also uses other "I Am" sayings such as "I am the door" (10:9), "the good shepherd" (10:11), "the way, the truth, and the life" (14:6), and "the true vine" (15:1). These sayings resemble the divine name revealed to Moses in Exodus 3:14 ("I Am who I Am"), linking Jesus directly with God. In John, these self-revelations are a central part of Jesus' Mission method. Rather than hiding the identity or revealing it gradually, Jesus openly declares who Jesus is and invites people to respond in faith. Moreover, the "I Am" sayings combine metaphor with revelation, helping people understand Jesus' role in salvation through images from

---

[26] G. A. Van Den Heever, "Theological Metaphorics and the Metaphors of John's Gospel," *Neotestamentica* 26/1 (1992): 89-100.

[27] G. A. Van Den Heever, "Theological Metaphorics…

[28] Andrew Mbama Okorie, "The Self-Revelation of Jesus in the 'I Am' Sayings of John's Gospel," *Currents in Theology and Mission* 28/5 (December, 2001): 486-490.

daily life.[29] Thus, the method establishes that Mission involves clear, bold self-disclosure rooted in divine authority, helping listeners encounter not just a teacher or prophet, but God.

Demonstrating Servant Leadership

In John 13, Jesus provides a powerful example of servant leadership by washing the feet of his disciples. Unlike the Synoptic Gospels, which highlight the institution of the Lord's Supper, John focuses on this symbolic act of humility. By taking the role of a servant, Jesus redefines leadership and Mission, not as power or position, but as love in action.[30] He tells his disciples, "I have set you an example that you should do as I have done for you" (John 13:15). John records such a servant leadership throughout the Fourth Gospel. For example, by feeding the hungry (John 6), healing the sick (John 5; 9), and laying down his life for others as the Good Shepherd (John 10:11). These servant leadership models show that true leadership means humble service, sacrificial love, and caring for the needs of others. This method of Mission teaches that followers of Jesus are called not to dominate, but to serve.[31] In this way, John presents Mission as embodied love, showing that true witness flows from actions that reflect the character of Christ.

Relational Discipleship and Abiding

In John 15, Jesus uses the metaphor of the vine and branches to describe discipleship as a living relationship rather than a set of religious duties. Jesus invites his followers to "abide" in him, meaning to remain, dwell, or stay connected.[32] This abiding is the foundation for fruitfulness that apart from him, they can do nothing (John 15:5). Beyond the image of the vine and branches in John 15:5, the Fourth Gospel emphasizes relational discipleship and abiding through Jesus' call to remain in his word (John 8:31), Jesus' prayer for unity and love among believers (John 17), and Jesus' personal care for his disciples, such as calling them friends (John 15:15) and restoring Peter after failure (John 21). These examples highlight that discipleship in John is deeply relational, marked by trust, love, obedience, and ongoing connection with Jesus. This method shows that Mission begins not with activity but with spiritual intimacy. Disciples are not simply sent

[29] Billy E. Simmons, "A Christology of the 'I Am' Sayings in the Gospel of John," *The Theological Educator* 38 (December, 1988): 94-103.

[30] Jan van der Watt, "The Meaning of Jesus Washing the Feet of His Disciples (John 13)," *Neotestamentica* 51/1 (2017): 25-40

[31] Jan van der Watt, "The Meaning of Jesus Washing the Feet of His Disciples…

[32] Réka Valentin, "Abiding in Life: The Functionality of the Relationship with God in the Gospel of John," *Theologia Catholica Latina* 61/1 (December, 2016): 43-56.

out to work for Jesus, rather, they are called to stay close to Jesus and draw life from the presence of Jesus. Only then will their witness bear lasting fruit. In contrast to performance-driven Mission models, John's approach emphasizes inner transformation, personal connection, and dependence on Christ as the source of all effective Mission.

Missional Prayer and Intercession

In John 17, often called the High Priestly Prayer, Jesus uses a Mission method that is grounded in prayerful intercession. Jesus prays for his disciples and for all future believers, asking for their protection, unity, sanctification, and effectiveness in the world. This shows that prayer is not simply preparation for Mission, rather, it is part of the Mission itself. Jesus' prayer reveals a deep concern for the success and faithfulness of the church's witness. He prays "that the world may believe" (John 17:21), connecting the Mission of the disciples with their unity and holiness. In addition to praying for unity in John 17:21, Jesus uses Missional prayer and intercession throughout the Fourth Gospel. For example, by praying for his followers' protection and sanctification (John 17:11, 17), interceding for their future witness (John 17:20), and giving thanks before feeding the crowds (John 6:11) and raising Lazarus (John 11:41-42). These prayers show Jesus' deep concern for his disciples' Mission, spiritual growth, and the glory of God through their faithful witness.[33] In this way, John teaches that Mission must be immersed in prayer, and that praying for the world and for the church is a central part of participating in God's redemptive work.

Gradual Self-Revelation ("Come and See" Approach)

John's Gospel highlights a Mission method that is invitational and exploratory, rather than confrontational or forced. In John 1, when Jesus meets the first disciples, Jesus does not give them a list of doctrines to believe or actions to perform. Instead, Jesus invites them with the simple words, "Come and see" (John 1:39). This approach is repeated when Philip invites Nathanael, using the same phrase (John 1:46). Jesus' method is one of gentle invitation, allowing people to experience, observe, and gradually come to faith through relationship. In the same way, the Fourth Gospel shows Jesus gradually revealing himself through other personal encounters such as with the Samaritan woman (John 4), the man born blind (John 9), and Martha (John 11:21-27), they were understanding Jesus step by step. This "come and see" approach allows people to discover who Jesus is through relationship, experience, and growing faith. This patient, non-forcible model respects the seeker's journey and encourages Mission that

---

[33] Réka Valentin, "Abiding in Life: The Functionality…43-56.

welcomes people into discovery rather than pressuring them into decision.[34] Thus, John highlights that Jesus emphasizes openness, hospitality, and personal encounter as central elements of Mission.

Witness through Love and Unity

One of the most powerful Mission methods in John's Gospel is Jesus' teaching that love and unity among believers will be the clearest sign to the world of his divine Mission. In John 13:35, Jesus teaches his disciples, "By this everyone will know that you are my disciples, if you love one another." Yet again, in John 17, Jesus prays that they may be one "so that the world may believe that you sent me." Apart from John 13:35 and Jesus' prayer in John 17, the Fourth Gospel highlights witness through love and unity in passages like Jesus laying down his life for his friends (John 15:13), calling his disciples to remain in his love and obey his commands (John 15:9-12), and welcoming them as part of one flock under one shepherd (John 10:16). These examples show that love, obedience, and unity among believers are central to their witness in the world. Unlike other Mission methods focused only on external outreach, John emphasizes the internal life of the community as a powerful testimony.[35] When believers love each other with Christ-like love and live in unity, the watching world sees a visible sign of God's transforming power. Mission, therefore, is not just about words or actions directed outward, it is also about how the church lives together as a reflection of the gospel.

Empowering through the Holy Spirit

Finally, Jesus prepares his disciples for Mission by promising the coming of the *Paraclete*, the Holy Spirit. In John 14-16, Jesus teaches that the Spirit will remind them of all he has said, guide them into all truth, and empower them to bear witness.[36] The Fourth Gospel also shows the Spirit's empowering role when Jesus breathes on the disciples and says, "Receive the Holy Spirit" (John 20:22). This marks the beginning of their Spirit-enabled Mission, showing that Jesus equips his followers with divine power and presence to continue his work in the world. This emphasizes that Mission is not driven by human strength or cleverness but by divine presence and power. The Spirit will not only comfort the disciples but also equip them

---

[34] Daniel Kearney, "Come and See: Faith and Vision in John's Gospel," *The Pastoral Review* 13/5 (December, 2017): 61-64.

[35] Dorothy A. Lee, "Witness in the Fourth Gospel: John the Baptist and the Beloved Disciple as Counterparts," *Australian Biblical Review* 61 (January, 2013): 1-17.

[36] Steve H. Mathews, "The Holy Spirit in the Gospel of John," *Journal of Biblical Theology* 7/3 (January, 2024): 199-212.

for faithful witness in a hostile world.[37] This Spirit-led Mission is deeply relational; the Spirit continues the work of Jesus and enables the community to participate in the ongoing Mission of God. John's Gospel thus presents a Trinitarian model of Mission, where God sends Jesus, Jesus sends the Holy Spirit, and the Holy Spirit empowers the church.

Conclusion

The Gospel of John presents a distinctive and deeply theological vision of Jesus' Mission, one that flows directly from the heart of the triune God. Unlike the Synoptic Gospels, which emphasize the proclamation of the Kingdom through parables, healings, and exorcisms, John portrays Mission as an act of divine self-revelation: God sends Jesus, Jesus reveals God, and the Spirit continues the work through the believing community. Jesus' Mission in John is not only about declaring truth but about embodying it, through signs that reveal his glory, conversations that lead individuals into personal transformation, and a life of humble service that redefines leadership and discipleship. At the centre of this Mission is relationship. Jesus invites people to abide in him, to love one another, and to live in unity so that the world may believe. Jesus' method is not mass-oriented but personal and intimate, focused on revealing divine love through tangible acts, symbolic language, and Spirit-empowered witness. The promise of the *Paraclete* ensures that Mission will continue beyond Jesus' earthly ministry, not through human strength but through divine guidance and presence. In John's Gospel, Mission is a participation in the eternal sending of God. It is rooted in love, expressed through unity, revealed through signs, and sustained by the Spirit. The Johannine vision thus highlights a Mission shaped not merely by strategy but by spiritual depth, relational witness, and faithful abiding in the One who was sent into the world to give life.

---

[37] Ronald D. Witherup, "The Spirit of God: The Holy Spirit According to John's Gospel," *The Priest* 70/7 (December, 2014): 40-42.

15

Mission in the Book of Acts The Apostolic Mission, Theology, Practice, and Legacy

The apostolic Mission refers to the task given by the risen Christ to his chosen disciples, the apostles, to continue His work of proclaiming the Kingdom of God and making disciples of all nations. This Mission is rooted in the historical and theological context that follows the resurrection of Jesus and the outpouring of the Holy Spirit at Pentecost. After Jesus' resurrection, Jesus commissioned disciples to go into the world as Jesus' representatives, and this commissioning was empowered by the Holy Spirit (Acts 1:8). In John 20:21, Jesus clearly states that the apostolic Mission as Jesus' own responsibility, saying, "As the Father has sent me, I am sending you." Similarly, Acts 1:1-2 describes the apostles' Mission as a direct continuation of all that Jesus began to do and teach. The apostles are not merely successors but foundational witnesses who carry forward the Mission of Jesus with divine authority. According to Ephesians 2:20, the church is "built on the foundation of the apostles and prophets," highlighting their central role in the life and expansion of the early Christian community. As Missionary leaders, they bore witness to the resurrection, preached the gospel, established churches, and guided the spiritual formation of new believers, as the shape of the church's ongoing Mission in the world.

Foundations of Apostolic Mission

The Mission of the apostles in the book of Acts is not just a historical record of early church activity; it is deeply grounded in *Missi Dei*. At its core, this Mission flows from the very nature and purpose of God. The apostles did not act on their own but were part of God's greater plan to bring salvation to the world. There are three major foundations of the apostolic Mission: its Trinitarian origin, its focus on witnessing to the resurrection of Jesus Christ, and its eschatological vision. These foundations show that the Mission is a divine initiative, carried out by the power of the Holy Spirit, centred on the risen Christ, and directed toward the fulfilment of God's Kingdom. By understanding these theological themes, we can see that the apostolic Mission is not only a task for a specific time but a continuing call for the church today.

The Trinitarian Origin of Mission

The foundation of the apostolic Mission is deeply rooted in the Trinitarian nature of God. Mission begins with God, who sent Jesus into the world out of love to bring salvation to humanity (John 3:16-17). This divine act of sending reflects the heart of God's redemptive purpose. Jesus, thus, continues this Mission by sending His apostles into the world.[1] In John 20:21, he says, "As the Father has sent me, I am sending you," showing that the apostolic Mission flows directly from the Mission of Jesus. Yet, the apostles are not sent in their own strength. The Holy Spirit plays a vital role by empowering them for this Mission. Before Jesus' ascension, Jesus promised that the apostles would receive power when the Holy Spirit comes upon them (Acts 1:8), and this promise was fulfilled on the day of Pentecost (Acts 2:1-4).[2] Thus, the Mission of the apostles is not merely a human effort but a divine initiative that reflects the unity and purpose of the Triune God, working together to bring the message of salvation to the world.

Apostolic Witness to the Resurrection

Another foundation of the apostolic Mission is the witness to the resurrection of Jesus Christ. The resurrection is not just one part of the message; it is the core of the apostles' preaching. In their early sermons, the apostles consistently declared that God raised Jesus from the dead, confirming Jesus as the promised Messiah (Acts 2:32; 3:15; 10:40).[3] This event was the turning point that gave the apostles boldness and clarity in their Mission. Their role as eyewitnesses of the risen Lord gave authority to their message and formed the basis of their call to others to believe and repent. Moreover, the resurrection is closely linked to the exaltation of Christ. According to Acts 2:36, God has made Jesus both "Lord and Messiah," and Philippians

---

[1] Paul J. Palma, "Baptized in Jesus' Name: Oneness and Trinitarian Pentecostal Readings of Acts 2:38," *Cyberjournal for Pentecostal-Charismatic Research* 25 (December, 2018): 1-20.

[2] Paul J. Palma, "Baptized in Jesus' Name: Oneness and Trinitarian…

[3] L. Russ Bush, "Apostolic Hermeneutics: 'Proof Texts' and the Resurrection," *Criswell Theological Review* 2 (December, 1988): 291-307.

2:9-11 confirms that, because of Jesus' obedience unto death, God exalted him and gave Jesus the name above every name. This exalted status of Christ strengthened the apostolic Mission, as the apostles are driven by the truth that Jesus is Lord over "all" and deserves the worship of every nation.[4] Therefore, their Mission is not only to proclaim a risen Savior but also to call the world to recognize Jesus' lordship and submit to Jesus' reign.

Eschatological Vision and Mission

Another key foundation of the apostolic Mission is its strong eschatological vision, the belief that the coming of Jesus has inaugurated the "last days." This vision is clearly stated in Peter's sermon at Pentecost, where he quotes the prophet Joel, saying, "In the last days, God says, I will pour out my Spirit on all people" (Acts 2:17). Thus, the outpouring of the Holy Spirit marks the beginning of a new era in God's redemptive plan, highlighting that the kingdom of God has entered into human history.[5] In this context, the apostolic Mission becomes urgent and universal. The apostles preach not only because Christ has risen but also because the world is moving toward a final day of judgment. As Paul proclaims in Acts 17:30-31, God now commands all people everywhere to repent, because the day is set when God will judge the world through Jesus Christ.[6] This eschatological awareness gives the Mission a sense of urgency and global scope. The apostles understand that the time for salvation is now, and their task is to call all people to repentance and faith before the coming Day of the Lord.

Apostolic Commissioning and Authority

The apostolic Mission is a central theme in the life and growth of the early church. After the resurrection and ascension of Jesus, the apostles were chosen and commissioned to continue this Mission in the world. Their work was not based on personal ambition but on the authority of the risen Christ and the empowerment of the Holy Spirit. Thus, the apostolic Mission is rooted in the Mission of the Triune God. The apostles were called to bear witness to the resurrection of Jesus, proclaim His lordship, and call all people to repentance and faith. Their role involved not only preaching and teaching but also leading the church with spiritual authority and performing signs and wonders that confirmed their divine calling.

---

[4] August H. Konkel, "The Apostolic Preaching of the Resurrection," *Didaskalia* 2/1 (December, 1990): 12-22.

[5] Arco den Heijer, "Worshipping God in the Eschatological Age: The Contest over Jewish Sacred Space and Time in the Book of Acts," *European Journal of Theology* 27/1 (December, 2018): 18-30.

[6] David P. Moessner, "Paul in Acts: Preacher of Eschatological Repentance to Israel," *New Testament Studies* 34/1 (January, 1988): 96-104.

The Great Commission and Apostolic Sending (Matthew 28:18-20; Acts 1:8)

The apostolic Mission begins with the clear commissioning of Jesus, often called the Great Commission. In Matthew 28:18-20, Jesus announces that all authority in heaven and on earth has been given to Jesus, and on this basis, Jesus sends His apostles to make disciples of all nations. This command includes teaching, baptizing, and obeying everything Jesus has taught. It highlights that apostolic authority is not self-given but flows from the authority of the risen Christ. In the same way, in Acts 1:8 Jesus promises the power of the Holy Spirit to enable this Mission, starting in Jerusalem and extending to the ends of the earth.[7] Thus, the apostles are sent not just with a message, but with divine authority and spiritual power to carry out their Mission. This global and Spirit-empowered sending forms the foundation of Christian Mission and shows that apostolic work is part of God's larger redemptive plan for the world.

Selection and Qualifications of Apostles (Acts 1:21-22)

After the resurrection and ascension of Jesus, the early church recognized the importance of replacing Judas Iscariot to maintain the integrity of the apostolic witness. In Acts 1:21-22, Peter outlines the key qualifications for someone to be chosen as an apostle as: the person must have been with Jesus throughout His ministry and be a witness to Jesus' resurrection. This shows that the apostolic role was not open to anyone but required a deep, firsthand relationship with Jesus and personal experience of Jesus' resurrection. Thus, the apostles were not merely leaders or teachers, rather, they were unique witnesses to the historical reality of Christ's life, death, and resurrection.[8] This qualification ensured that their preaching and authority were grounded in the actual events of Jesus' ministry, giving credibility and theological weight to their message.

Signs and Wonders as Apostolic Credentials (Acts 5:12; II Corinthians 12:12)

Apostolic authority was further confirmed through signs and wonders performed by the apostles. These miracles served not only to demonstrate the power of God but also to validate the apostles as true messengers of Christ. Acts 5:12 records that "many signs and wonders were done among the people by the hands of the apostles," which provide respect and led to a steady growth in the early church. Paul also refers to this in II Corinthians 12:12, calling such miracles as the "marks of a true apostle." These supernatural

---

[7] Charles E. Lawless, "'To All the Nations': The Great Commission Passages in the Gospels and Acts," *The Southern Baptist Journal of Theology* 15/2 (December, 2011), 16-27.

[8] Alastair Campbell, "The Elders of the Jerusalem Church," *The Journal of Theological Studies* 44/2 (October, 1993): 511-528.

acts were not performed for personal gain but were signs pointing to the truth of the gospel and the presence of the Kingdom of God.[9] They affirmed that the apostles were uniquely empowered and commissioned by God to establish the early church and extend Christ's Mission in the world.

Apostolic Unity and Leadership in the Early Church (Acts 15:6; Galatians 2:9)

The apostles played a key role in maintaining unity and providing leadership in the early church. Their authority was not authoritarian but collaborative and rooted in shared commitment to the gospel. In Acts 15:6, during the Jerusalem Council, the apostles and elders met to resolve a major theological issue concerning Gentile believers. This shows the apostles' role in guiding the church with wisdom and spiritual clarity. Similarly, Galatians 2:9 highlights the unity among the apostles, as Paul mentions the recognition and fellowship extended to him by key leaders like James, Peter, and John.[10] This unity strengthened the church's Mission and prevented divisions. The apostles functioned as spiritual shepherds and theological anchors, ensuring that the message of Christ remained faithful and that the church grew in both truth and love.

Geographical Expansion of Apostolic Mission

The apostolic Mission did not remain limited to a small group or a single region but expanded geographically and ethnically, based on Jesus' instruction in Acts 1:8 disciples are to be witnesses in Jerusalem, Judea, Samaria, and to the ends of the earth. This expansion reflects God's redemptive purpose to reach all nations through the gospel. The early chapters of Acts show how the apostles first preached to the Jewish people in Jerusalem, fulfilling God's promises to Israel. As persecution scattered believers, the message spread to Judea and Samaria, breaking through long-standing ethnic and religious barriers. A major turning point came when the gospel was preached to Gentiles, beginning with the conversion of Cornelius, showing that salvation was for all people, not just Jews. The four Missionary journeys of Paul (Acts 13-14; 15:36-18:22; 8:23-21:17 and 27-28) then carried the gospel into the wider Roman world, as Paul established churches in diverse cities and cultures. This expansion of the apostolic Mission demonstrates the universal scope of God's salvation and the church's calling to be a global, multi-ethnic community rooted in the message of Christ.

---

[9] Robert Lee Hamblin, "Miracles in the Book of Acts," *Southwestern Journal of Theology* 17/1 (December, 1974): 19-34.

[10] Frederick Fyvie Bruce, "True Apostolic Succession: Recent Study of the Book of Acts," *Interpretation* 13/2 (December, 1959): 131-143.

Mission in Jerusalem: To the Jews First (Acts 2-7)

The apostolic Mission began in Jerusalem, the centre place of Jewish religious life, in obedience to Jesus' command to start there (Acts 1:8). This initial phase focused on reaching the Jewish people with the message that Jesus is the promised Messiah. On the day of Pentecost, Peter preached boldly, declaring that Jesus had risen from the dead and now reigns as Lord and Christ (Acts 2:36). Thousands of Jews responded in repentance and faith, and the early Christian community grew rapidly (Acts 2:41; 4:4).[11] This Mission to the Jews fulfilled God's covenant promises to Israel and showed that the gospel was not a rejection of Judaism but its true fulfilment. The apostles' ministry in Jerusalem also involved public teaching, healing, and defending the gospel before religious authorities (Acts 5:17-42), which emphasized the central role of Jesus in God's plan for salvation.[12]

Mission in Judea and Samaria: Overcoming Ethnic and Religious Barriers (Acts 8-9)

After persecution broke out in Jerusalem, the gospel began to spread to the surrounding regions of Judea and Samaria (Acts 8:1). This marked a turning point in the apostolic Mission, as it crossed ethnic and religious boundaries. Philip's ministry in Samaria was especially significant, because the Samaritans were viewed by Jews as religious outsiders. Yet, they received the gospel with joy and were baptized, showing that the message of Jesus was for more than just the Jewish people (Acts 8:5-12). The apostles confirmed this expansion when Peter and John visited Samaria and witnessed the Holy Spirit being given to the new believers (Acts 8:14-17).[13] The conversion of Saul and his transformation into Paul as a Missionary in Acts 9 further prepared and strengthened the church for broader Mission, as he was chosen to carry the gospel to Gentiles and kings as well as the people of Israel. This phase exemplifies how the apostolic Mission began to break down long-standing divisions, extending the reach of the gospel across cultural lines.

Mission to the Gentiles: Peter and Cornelius (Acts 10-11)

The Mission to the Gentiles began clearly and decisively with Peter's encounter with Cornelius, a Roman centurion and "*phoboumenoi*" (God-

---

[11] Ky-Chun So, "Jewish Mission and Gentile Mission in the New Testament," *Mission and Theology* 12 (December, 2003): 350-365.

[12] Rudolph D. González, "To the Jew First and Also the Gentile: Capturing the Fullness of Matthew's Commission 2," *Mishkan* 63 (December, 2010): 20-29.

[13] Patrick L. Dickerson, The Sources of the Account of the Mission to Samaria in Acts 8:5-2, *Novum Testamentum* 39/3 (July, 1997): 210-234.

fearers) Gentiles.[14] In Acts 10, God revealed to Peter through a vision that he should no longer call any person "unclean." This prepared him to preach the gospel to Cornelius and his household, who received the Holy Spirit even before baptism (Acts 10:44-48). This event was groundbreaking, as it affirmed that Gentiles could become full members of God's people without first becoming Jews.[15] When Peter reported this to the church in Jerusalem, they acknowledged that "God has granted even the Gentiles repentance unto life" (Acts 11:18). This confirmed that the Mission of Jesus was truly for all nations, fulfilling Old Testament promises that the Gentiles would one day worship the God of Israel.[16] It also marked a major shift in the identity of the church as a multi-ethnic and global community of believers.

Beyond: Mission to the Ends of the Earth (Acts 13-28; Romans 15:18-24)

The final stage of the apostolic Mission is its expansion to the ends of the earth, led primarily by the apostle Paul. Beginning in Acts 13, Paul and his companions decided on Missionary journeys that took the gospel across Asia Minor and into Europe. They preached in cities such as Antioch, Ephesus, Corinth, and eventually Rome, establishing churches and appointing leaders. Paul's vision was global, as seen in his desire to preach where Christ was not yet known (Romans 15:20), even expressing a longing to reach Spain (Romans 15:24). This phase of the Mission shows the universal scope of the gospel, rooted in the belief that Jesus is Lord of all and that all nations are called to faith in him.[17] It highlights that the fulfilment of Jesus' command in Acts 1:8 and reflects the church's growing understanding of its role in God's plan to bless all peoples through the message of salvation in Christ.

Models of Apostolic Mission in Acts

The book of Acts presents a diverse model of apostolic Mission, presenting how different individuals, empowered by the Holy Spirit, carried out the Mission in diverse contexts. Each individual models contribute exceptionally to the early church's understanding and practice of Mission. Peter's leadership reflects the transition from Jewish-centred Mission to the inclusion of Gentiles, showing the expanding scope of God's salvation.

---

[14] Max Wilcox, "The 'God-Fearers' in Acts-A Reconsideration," *Journal for the Study of the New Testament* 4/13 (December, 1981): 102-122.

[15] Timothy W. Reardon, "Cleansing through Almsgiving in Luke-Acts: Purity, Cornelius, and the Translation of Acts 15:9," *The Catholic Biblical Quarterly* 78/3 (December, 2016): 463-482.

[16] William S. Kurz, "Effects of Variant Narrators in Acts 10-11," *New Testament Studies* 43/4 (January, 1997): 570-586.

[17] Andreas J. Köstenberger, "Reconceiving a Biblical Theology of Mission: Salvation to the Ends of the Earth Revisited," *Themelios* 45/3 (December, 2020): 528-536.

Philip establishes the church's movement beyond Jerusalem, engaging in cross-cultural evangelism in Samaria and beyond. Stephen, through his courageous preaching and martyrdom, shows that faithful witness can lead to suffering but also serve as a model for wider Mission. Paul, as the apostle to the Gentiles, represents the careful expansion of the gospel to the Roman world, especially through urban church planting and Missionary journeys. These examples show that apostolic Mission was not limited to one person or method but involved a variety of Spirit-led approaches to fulfil Christ's commission to make disciples of all nations.

Peter's Role as Missionary

Peter plays a central role in Acts as a leading figure in the apostolic Mission. As one of Jesus' closest disciples and a witness to the resurrection, Peter takes the initiative in preaching, healing, and opening the gospel to new heights. His ministry reflects the broader pattern of apostolic Mission exemplified in proclaiming Christ with boldness, performing signs and wonders, and expanding the boundaries of the early church. Peter's actions demonstrate his obedience to Christ's commission and his dependence on the Holy Spirit. Through his leadership, the Mission of the church begins to move outward from Jerusalem, touching both Jews and Gentiles with the transforming power of the gospel.

Peter's sermon at Pentecost marks the formal beginning of the church's public Mission. After the Holy Spirit is poured out on the disciples, Peter stands and boldly proclaims that Jesus, who was crucified, has been raised and exalted by God as both Lord and Messiah (Acts 2:36). He connects the coming of the Spirit with the fulfilment of Joel's prophecy, showing that the "last days" have begun (Acts 2:17). His message focuses on repentance, baptism, and forgiveness of sins through Jesus. About three thousand people respond in faith, showing the powerful impact of Spirit-filled preaching.[18] Missiologically, this episode established preaching as a central tool of Mission and reveals that salvation is now open to all who responds to the message and call on the name of the Lord.

Acts 3 and 4, records Peter continues Mission by combining acts of healing with the proclamation of the gospel. When Peter and John heal a lame man at the temple gate, it was noticed by the gathering and provided a platform for Peter to preach about Jesus' resurrection and power (Acts 3:6-16). He urges the people to repent so that their sins may be wiped away (Acts 3:19). This healing is not just a miracle; it is a sign that the risen

---

[18] John D. Griffiths, "Upon All Flesh: An Ecological Reading of Acts 2.17-21," *Journal for the Study of the New Testament* 47/3 (December, 2025): 437-453.

Christ continues His work through the apostles.[19] When Peter and John are arrested and questioned by the religious leaders, Peter boldly declares that salvation is found in no one else but Jesus (Acts 4:12). These chapters highlight that apostolic Mission includes both compassionate action and courageous proclamation, demonstrating that Jesus is alive and active in the world through his followers.

Peter's visit to Cornelius in Acts 10 represents a major shift in the direction of the apostolic Mission. Cornelius, a Roman centurion and Gentile, receives a vision from God, and Peter is likewise led by a vision to overcome Jewish purity laws and visit him. Peter preaches the gospel to Cornelius and his household, and while he is still speaking, the Holy Spirit falls on them, just as it did on the Jewish believers at Pentecost (Acts 10:44-45).[20] This incident confirms that the gospel is for Gentiles as well, without requiring them to become Jews first. Peter later explains that he could not oppose God, who had clearly accepted the Gentiles (Acts 11:17). Missiologically, this foreshadows the universal scope of God's salvation and reveals the church's calling to include all people, regardless of ethnicity or background, in the body of Christ.

Philip's Evangelistic Mission

Philip, one of the seven appointed servants in Acts 6, plays a significant role in the early church's Mission as an evangelist. His ministry reflects the expanding vision of the gospel beyond Jerusalem and shows how the Holy Spirit guided the church into new cultural and geographical territories. Philip's work reveals that Mission is not limited to the apostles alone, but is the calling of all Spirit-filled believers. His efforts reveal two major developments in early Christian mission: the breaking of ethnic barriers in Samaria and the beginning of cross-cultural engagement with non-Jewish individuals, such as the Ethiopian eunuch. These examples highlight that the gospel is for all people and must be taken to every corner of the earth.

Philip's Mission in Samaria marks a major step in the church's movement beyond Jewish boundaries. In Acts 8:5-12, he proclaims Christ to the Samaritans, a group traditionally despised by Jews due to historical and religious tensions. The Samaritans, however, respond with joy, and many are healed and delivered from evil spirits, showing the power of the gospel

---

[19] Dennis Hamm, "Acts 3:12-26: Peter's Speech and the Healing of the Man Born Lame," *Perspectives in Religious Studies* 11/3 (December, 1984): 199-217.

[20] Elfrieda Fleischmann, Ignatius W Ferreira and Francois Muller, "Protestant Revivals (Awakenings) and Transformational Impact: A Comparative Evaluation Framework Applied on the Revival among the Zulus (South Africa)," *Transformation* 38/4 (October, 2021): 296-315.

to bring healing and transformation.[21] This model of Mission reflects the fulfilment of Jesus' words in Acts 1:8, where he promised that the gospel would go to Samaria. When Peter and John arrive and see the Spirit poured out on the Samaritan believers, it confirms their full inclusion in the people of God. This event proves that the Mission of the church must overcome cultural prejudices and include those once seen as outsiders.

Philip's encounter with the Ethiopian eunuch is one of the clearest examples of cross-cultural Mission in Acts. Directed by the Holy Spirit, Philip meets this high-ranking official on the road from Jerusalem to Gaza and finds him reading from the prophet Isaiah. Philip explains that the passage points to Jesus and shares the gospel with him. The eunuch responds in faith and is immediately baptized (Acts 8:36-38). This account shows that the gospel is not limited by race, status, or nationality. Rather, it reveals that God's plan comprises the inclusion of Gentiles and those marginalized in Jewish society.[22] The story also emphasizes the role of the Holy Spirit in guiding Mission and opening hearts to receive the good news. Through Philip's obedience and the eunuch's faith, the gospel begins to reach the wider world, fulfilling the church's global Mission.

Stephen's Witness through Martyrdom

Stephen, one of the seven chosen to serve in the early church (Acts 6:5), became the first Christian martyr and an important model of faithful witness.[23] His life and death demonstrate that Mission is not only about going to new places but also about standing boldly for the truth of the gospel, even in the face of opposition. Stephen's role in the early church highlights how courageous proclamation and suffering can serve God's purposes. His life shows that Mission often involves both preaching and bearing witness through personal sacrifice. Stephen's example thus reminds the church that suffering for Christ is not a failure but a powerful testimony that can advance the gospel in unexpected ways.

Stephen's speech before the Jewish council in Acts 7 is one of the longest in the book of Acts and provides a deep Missiological reflection on Israel's history. He boldly accuses the Jewish leaders of resisting the Holy Spirit and rejecting God's messengers, just as their ancestors did. His message climaxes with the charge that they have betrayed and murdered

---

[21] Patrick L. Dickerson, The Sources of the Account of the Mission to Samaria in Acts 8:5-25, *Novum Testamentum* 39/3 (July, 1997): 210-234.

[22] Robert F. O'Toole, "Philip and the Ethiopian Eunuch (Acts 8:25-40)," *Journal for the Study of the New Testament* 5/17 (December, 1983): 25-34.

[23] P. Doble, "The Son of Man Saying in Stephen's Witnessing: Acts 6:8-8:2," *New Testament Studies* 31/1 (January, 1985): 68-84.

the Righteous One, referring to Jesus (Acts 7:52).[24] Stephen's speech is not just historical, rather, it was prophetic, calling the people to repentance and exposing the hardness of their hearts. This bold proclamation demonstrates that Mission from time to time involves confronting injustice and religious hypocrisy. Even though it led to his death, Stephen's witness is faithful and Christ-centred, reflecting Jesus' own courage before His opponents.

Stephen's martyrdom had a powerful and far-reaching effect on the Mission of the church. After his death, a great persecution broke out in Jerusalem, and many believers were scattered throughout Judea and Samaria (Acts 8:1). While this scattering might seem like a setback, it actually served God's purpose in spreading the gospel beyond the city.[25] Acts 8:4 notes that "those who had been scattered preached the word wherever they went." Stephen's death, though tragic, became a turning point in the expansion of the church's Mission. Missiologically, this shows that God can use suffering and opposition to advance God's kingdom. The blood of the martyrs, as seen in Stephen's case, becomes the seed of the church's growth, reminding believers that faithful witness, even unto death, has eternal value in God's Mission.

Paul's Apostolic Expansion

(See Chapter 16 for a comprehensive discussion of Paul's Mission)

Methods and Strategies of Apostolic Mission

The success of the apostolic Mission in the book of Acts was not accidental but the result of clear methods and Spirit-led approaches. The apostles, guided by Jesus' instructions and empowered by the Holy Spirit, used various approaches to proclaim the gospel, form communities, and expand the church across cultures and regions. Their methods were grounded in deep Missiological conviction with practical wisdom. They preached the core gospel message on Christ's death and resurrection and called people to repentance and faith. They used the Scriptures to show how Jesus fulfilled God's promises and engaged in thoughtful dialogue with both Jews and Gentiles. The apostles also contextualized their message, adapting it to different cultural settings while remaining faithful to the truth of the gospel. Small gatherings in homes became important places for worship and

---

[24] Michal Beth Dinkler, "The Politics of Stephen's Storytelling: Narrative Rhetoric and Reflexivity in Acts 7:2-5," *Journal for New Testament Studies and the Knowledge of the Early Church* 111/1 (December, 2020): 33-64.

[25] Allan Chapple, "'Except the Apostles' (Acts 8:1b)." *The Reformed Theological Review* 70/2 (December, 2011): 107-134.

Mission, and signs, wonders, and spiritual gifts confirmed their message with divine power.

Kerygma: Proclamation of the Gospel Message

The heart of apostolic Mission was the proclamation of the gospel, known in Greek as *kerygma*. This proclamation was centred on the person and work of Jesus Christ. The apostles preached not abstract ideas but the historical reality of Jesus' death and resurrection, which fulfilled God's redemptive plan.[26] Their message was simple yet powerful: Jesus, who was crucified, is now risen and exalted as Lord and Savior. This message formed the foundation of faith and the basis of the church's Mission. The apostles consistently preached that Jesus died for our sins and was raised by God as proof of his victory over death (Acts 2:23-24; 3:15). This was not only a historical claim but a Missiological act, that Jesus' death fulfilled the Scriptures, and His resurrection confirmed His identity as the Messiah.[27] The resurrection was central to their preaching because it validated everything Jesus said and did. Without the resurrection, there would be no gospel to proclaim (I Corinthians 15:14). The apostolic message always demanded a response. In Acts 2:38, Peter calls his listeners to "repent and be baptized... in the name of Jesus Christ for the forgiveness of your sins." This shows that gospel proclamation was not just informative, rather, it was transformative.[28] It called people to turn from sin and believe in Christ. Repentance and faith were the necessary responses that led to salvation and entrance into the Christian community, empowered by the Holy Spirit.

Use of Scripture in Mission

The apostles grounded their preaching in the Hebrew Scriptures. They did not invent a new religion but showed how Jesus fulfilled the promises made by God in the Old Testament. Scripture served both to validate the gospel message and to connect with Jewish and Gentile audiences in ways they could understand. Peter and Paul often explained that what happened to Jesus was in direct fulfilment of Scripture.[29] For example, in Acts 2, Peter quotes the prophet Joel and Psalms to show that Jesus' resurrection and exaltation were foretold. Likewise, Paul in Acts 13 shows how the

---

[26] Carl R. Holladay, "Acts as Kerygma: Λαλεῖν Τὸν Λόγον," *New Testament Studies* 63/2 (January, 2017): 153-182.

[27] Clarence Tucker Craig, "The Apostolic Kerygma in the Christian Message," *Journal of Bible and Religion* 20/3 (July, 1952): 182-186.

[28] John J. Kilgallen, "'With Many Other Words' (Acts 2,40): Theological Assumptions in Peter's Pentecost Speech," *Biblica* 83/1 (2002): 71-87.

[29] Joseph A. Fitzmyer, "The Use of the Old Testament in Luke-Acts," *Society of Biblical Literature Seminar Papers* 31 (December, 1992): 524-538.

resurrection fulfilled promises made to the patriarchs. This use of Scripture affirmed the continuity between the old covenant and the new, showing that Jesus is the fulfilment of God's redemptive plan.[30] The apostles also used Scripture to reason with both Jews and Gentiles. In Jewish contexts, Paul would explain and prove from the Scriptures that the Messiah had to suffer and rise from the dead (Acts 17:2-3). In Gentile settings like Athens, Paul appealed to natural revelation and local beliefs while still pointing to the one true God (Acts 17:22-31). This shows that, defending the faith was part of the Mission method that was matching to the audience's background but always leading to Christ.

Contextualization of the Message

The apostles practiced contextualization, adapted their message to different cultural settings without changing the truth of the gospel. They used familiar language, symbols, and examples to communicate effectively with their audiences while guarding against compromise or syncretism. In Lystra, Paul and Barnabas addressed a pagan audience by speaking of the living God as the Creator who gives rain and harvest (Acts 14:15-17).[31] In Athens, Paul connected with Greek philosophy by referring to their altar to an "unknown god" and quoting Greek poets (Acts 17:22-28).[32] These show the apostles' ability to meet people where they were, using familiar ideas to lead them toward the truth of Christ. While the apostles adapted their approach, they never compromised the gospel. They did not mix Christian truth with pagan practices but clearly called people to turn away from idols and false beliefs (Acts 14:15; 17:30). Missiologically, this shows the importance of holding firmly to the core message of salvation in Christ while expressing it in culturally meaningful ways, since, true contextualization respects both the audience and the integrity of the gospel.

House Churches and Community Formation

A key method of the apostolic Mission was the formation of small, local gatherings of believers, commonly known as house churches, which became the primary setting for worship, teaching, fellowship, and Mission. These communities were both spiritual families and Missionary bases. The apostles

[30] Darrell L. Bock, "The Use of the Old Testament in Luke-Acts: Christology and Mission," *Society of Biblical Literature Seminar Papers* 29 (December, 1990): 494-511.

[31] Philip T. Laryea, "Reading Acts 14:8-17 & 17:22-31 in Ga: A Critical Examination of the Issues, Meanings and Interpretations Arising from Exegesis in the Mother Tongue," *Journal of African Christian Thought* 6/1 (December, 2003): 35-43.

[32] P. A. Godwin, "Tarsus and Jerusalem: The Interplay of Knowledge and Spirituality Reading Acts 17:22-28 as a Theological Response to the Quest for Gospel," *Journal of Biblical Theology* 3/1 (January, 2020): 42-69.

often started churches in homes, such as in the house of Lydia in Philippi (Acts 16:15, 40). These households later became centres of Christian life and witness in the local community. House churches provided flexibility, intimacy, and a strong sense of belonging, and became essential for the spread of the gospel, especially in places where public Christian worship was not yet accepted.[33] The early church devoted itself to the apostles' teaching, fellowship, the breaking of bread, and prayer (Acts 2:42), that only built up the believers but also served as a witness to outsiders, as the church grew in favour with the people (Acts 2:47). Missiologically, such gatherings exemplified the life of the Kingdom of God marked by love, generosity, and worship, providing a powerful model for Mission through community.

Empowerment through Signs, Wonders, and the Holy Spirit

The apostolic Mission was not carried out by human strength alone but by the power of the Holy Spirit. Signs and wonders confirmed the truth of the gospel and confirmed the presence of the risen Christ in the church's Mission. Miracles such as healing the lame man at the temple gate (Acts 3:1-10) and many others performed through the apostles (Acts 5:12-16) served to draw attention to the gospel and authenticate the message. These miracles were not merely acts of compassion but signs pointing to the Kingdom of God and the authority of Jesus.[34] They demonstrated that the gospel had both spiritual and physical power to restore what was broken. The Holy Spirit also empowered the apostles with boldness to speak and spiritual discernment in difficult situations. After praying, the early believers were filled with the Spirit and spoke the word of God boldly (Acts 4:31).[35] In Acts 13:9-11, Paul, filled with the Spirit, confronts and rebukes a false prophet, showing that Mission involves not only proclamation but also spiritual authority. Missiologically, signs and wonders affirm that Mission is ultimately God's work, carried out by human servants who rely fully on the guidance and power of the Holy Spirit.

Challenges Confronted by the Apostoles in Mission

The apostolic Mission, while marked by boldness and growth, was also shaped by many difficulties. The apostles and early believers faced persecution, internal tensions, and even death for the sake of the gospel. These challenges were not signs of failure but one of the faces

[33] Gregory John Lockwood, "The House Church: From Acts to Constantine," *Lutheran Theological Journal* 43/2 (December, 2009): 97-100.

[34] Kennedy Poumai, "Use of Miracles in the Acts of the Apostles," *The Indian Journal of Theology* 53/1-2 (December, 2011): 135-174.

[35] Scott MacDonald, "Does Acts 4:23–31 Support the Practice of Simultaneous Prayer?," *Themelios* 47/1 (December, 2022): 60-69.

of participating in the Mission of Christ. Missiologically, suffering was understood not as a hindrance to Mission but as a testimony to the truth and cost of discipleship. In the book of Acts and throughout the New Testament, suffering is closely linked to faithfulness, perseverance, and the spread of the gospel. The apostles accepted these hardships with joy and conviction, seeing them as part of God's purpose in extending God's Kingdom.

Persecution and Imprisonment (Acts 4:3; 5:18; 12:1-5)

From the early days of the church, the apostles faced direct opposition from religious and political authorities. In Acts 4:3, Peter and John were arrested for preaching about the resurrection. In Acts 5:18, all the apostles were imprisoned for performing signs and proclaiming Jesus. Later, in Acts 12:1-5, Herod arrested and killed James and imprisoned Peter, seeking to silence the church's influence.[36] In Acts 16, the imprisonment of Paul and Silas becomes a turning point that shows God's power and moves the gospel forward.[37] These acts of persecution were meant to stop the Mission, but instead, they often resulted in greater boldness and the spread of the gospel. Missiologically, this shows that God's Mission does not depend on favourable conditions but can advance even through opposition. Thus, in many cases, persecution served to strengthen Christian faith, and publicly display the power of God at work.

Internal Conflict and Cultural Tensions (Acts 6:1-6; 15:1-29)

During the early Christianity, not all challenges came from outside the church, but also arose from within. In Acts 6:1-6, a dispute occurred between Greek-speaking and Hebrew-speaking Jewish believers over food distribution threatened the unity of the church. The apostles responded by appointing spiritually mature leaders to oversee this to preserve peace and allowing the Mission to continue.[38] Acts 15 records a major debate developed over whether Gentile believers needed to follow Jewish laws, such as circumcision. The Jerusalem Council resolved this conflict with wisdom and unity, affirming that salvation is by grace through faith alone.[39]

[36] Frederick Fyvie Bruce, "The Church of Jerusalem in the Acts of the Apostles," *Bulletin of the John Rylands University Library of Manchester* 67/2 (December, 1985): 641-661.

[37] Abraham Smith, "Incarceration on Trial: The Imprisonment of Paul and Silas in Acts 16," *Journal of Biblical Literature* 140/4 (December, 2021): 797-817.

[38] B. Y. Quarshie, "Peace Building and Conflict Transformation in a Multilingual Congregation: Insights from a Mother-Tongue (Ga) Reading of Acts 6:1-7," *Journal of African Christian Thought* 27/1 (December, 2024): 34-45.

[39] Deborah L. Welch, "Acts 15: The Jerusalem Council as a Model for Unity, Diversity, and Discipleship," *Journal of Biblical Perspectives in Leadership* 12/1 (December, 2022): 43-54.

These internal challenges show that cultural diversity within the church requires wise leadership, humility, and theological clarity. Addressing such tensions was essential to maintaining the integrity and unity of the gospel Mission.

Martyrdom and Missional Endurance (Acts 7; 12:2)

Some apostles and early believers paid the ultimate price for their faith. Stephen, in Acts 7, became the first Christian martyr after boldly confronting the Jewish leaders with the truth about Jesus.[40] His death sparked a wave of persecution, but it also became a turning point for Mission as believers were scattered and preached the word (Acts 8:4).[41] As it is recorded in Acts 12:2, James the brother of John was killed by Herod, showing that apostles were not safe from suffering.[42] These deaths were not seen as defeat but as testimonies of faith. Missiologically, martyrdom became a witness to the worth of Christ and the seriousness of the gospel. It demonstrated that the Mission of the church was more important than personal safety, and that God could bring growth even through loss.

Ecclesial Structures and Missional Leadership

The apostolic Mission was not only about preaching and converting individuals but also about forming and strengthening churches with lasting leadership. As the gospel spread across regions, the apostles recognized the need for structure and guidance within the growing Christian communities. Ecclesial structures such as elders, deacons, and leadership teams were put in place to ensure the healthy growth and sustainability of the Mission. Missiologically, these structures reflected both spiritual maturity and practical wisdom. They helped to maintain unity, doctrinal purity, and Missional focus. The apostles, while having a unique foundational role, worked closely with other leaders to equip and send out new ministers, showing that leadership in the church is both relational and accountable to the Mission of Christ.

Appointment of Elders and Deacons (Acts 6:1-6; 14:23)

One of the earliest signs of Missional leadership development appears in Acts 6, where the apostles appoint seven deacons to oversee the fair distribution of food among widows. This appointment of leaders was necessary to address practical needs while allowing the apostles to continue

---

[40] Michal Beth Dinkler, "The Politics of Stephen's Storytelling...

[41] Christoph W. Stenschke, "'Now Those Who Were Scattered Went about Preaching the Word' (Acts 8:4): Migration, Poverty and Mission in the Book of Acts," *Asian Horizons* 8/4 (December, 2014): 692-705.

[42] Frederick Fyvie Bruce, "The Church of Jerusalem in the Acts of the Apostles...

focusing on prayer and the ministry of the Word. Acts 14:23 shares that Paul and Barnabas appoint elders in every church they had planted, showing that leadership was not centralized but extended locally. These appointments were made with prayer and fasting, recognizing that church leaders must be spiritually mature and called by God.[43] Missiologically, this reflects the belief that leadership is a gift of the Spirit for the building up of the body of Christ (Ephesians 4:11-12), and that proper church governance supports both pastoral care and ongoing Mission.

Discipleship and Leadership Training (II Timothy 2:2)

The development of leaders was not limited to appointment alone but involved intentional discipleship and training. Paul's instruction to Timothy *what you have heard from me...entrust to faithful people who will be able to teach others also* in II Timothy 2:2 reflects this model. This shows a multi-generational vision for leadership development, where teaching and mentoring are key to sustaining the Mission. Paul's relationship with Timothy, Titus, and others demonstrates how leadership in the early church was shaped through personal guidance, practical ministry experience, and deep theological teaching.[44] Missiologically, this kind of training reflects the model of Jesus Himself, who contributed deeply in His disciples. Thus, equipping new leaders was not just a strategy, rather, it was part of God's plan to multiply gospel workers across time and place.

Council of Jerusalem: Defining the Missional Identity of the Church (Acts 15)

The Council of Jerusalem in Acts 15 was a defining moment in the life of the early church. Faced with the growing number of Gentile converts, the church had to decide whether non-Jews needed to follow the law of Moses, especially circumcision, to be saved. After careful discussion, prayer, and discernment, the apostles and elders agreed that salvation is by grace and declared that: *we believe that we will be saved through the grace of the Lord Jesus* (Acts 15:11), and Gentile believers should not be burdened with the full weight of Jewish law. This decision preserved the unity of the church and clarified its gospel-centred identity.[45] Missiologically, the Jerusalem council affirmed that the church is a diverse, grace-based community, not defined by ethnic or legal boundaries but by faith in Christ. It also shows

---

[43] George William Knight, "Two Offices (Elders or Bishops and Deacons) and Two Orders of Elders (Preaching or Teaching Elders and Ruling Elders): A New Testament Study," *Presbyterion* 11/1 (December, 1985): 1-12.

[44] Suzana Dobric Veiss, "Follower Development: Paul's Charge to Timothy," *Journal of Biblical Perspectives in Leadership* 8/1 (December, 2018): 150-167.

[45] Deborah L. Welch, "Acts 15: The Jerusalem Council as a Model for Unity..., 43-54.

that major Missional questions must be addressed with spiritual discernment and communal wisdom.

Team-Based and Collaborative Mission (Acts 13:2-3; 15:36-40)

A striking feature of apostolic Mission in Acts is its team-based nature. When the Holy Spirit called Paul and Barnabas in Acts 13:2-3, the church in Antioch fasted, prayed, and sent them out together. This shows that Mission was not an individual effort but a collaborative endeavour, rooted in the life of the church.[46] Even when disagreements arose, as recorded in Acts 15:36-40, where Paul and Barnabas parted ways, Mission continued through new teams, such as Paul and Silas.[47] Missiologically, this highlights the value of diversity in ministry gifts and personalities and shows that even conflict, when handled with integrity, can serve the broader purposes of God. Working in teams allowed for mutual support, accountability, and greater impact in spreading the gospel.

Thus, the early church's structures and leadership practices were not rigid systems but Spirit-led responses to the needs of a growing, global Mission. Apostolic leadership was both foundational and flexible, balancing authority with service and vision with accountability. By appointing leaders, training disciples, resolving doctrinal issues, and working in collaborative teams, the apostles laid a pattern for faithful and effective Mission that continues to guide the church today. These practices remind us that Mission flourishes when supported by strong, Spirit-filled leadership and a clear gospel-centred identity.

Missiology in Apostolic Preaching

The apostolic Mission was not only about spreading the message of Jesus but also about presenting a clear theological vision grounded in God's purposes. The sermons and teachings in Acts show the foundational understanding of who God is, what God has done through Christ, and what God desires for all people. Apostolic preaching was rooted in the conviction that Mission begins with God's initiative, *Missio Dei*, and is carried forward through a sovereign plan. The apostles proclaimed the gospel as the fulfilment of God's promises, centred on Christ's death and resurrection, and aimed at the salvation of all people.

---

[46] Erwin Ochsenmeier, "Antioch as a Church Planting Community: Revisiting Barnabas and Paul's Departure in Acts 13:1-4," *Neotestamentica* 56/2 (December, 2022): 317-336.

[47] Clyde Weber Votaw, "Inductive Studies in the Acts. The Primitive Era of Christianity. VII," *The Biblical World* 10/2 (August, 1897): 133-142.

God's Sovereignty and Redemptive Plan (Acts 2:23; 17:26-27)

One of the core themes in apostolic preaching is the sovereignty of God in history. In Peter's sermon at Pentecost, he declares that: *Jesus was handed over to you according to the definite plan and foreknowledge of God* (Acts 2:23), showing that the crucifixion was not an accident but part of God's redemptive purpose.[48] Similarly, Paul in Athens teaches that God: *made all peoples to inhabit the whole earth, and he allotted the times of their existence and the boundaries of the places where they would live*, so that they might seek God (Acts 17:26-27).[49] These examples show that Mission is not human invention but the unfolding of God's eternal plan. Missiologically, this reminds the church that God is always in control and is actively working in history to bring people to God through Jesus Christ.

The Kingdom of God and Apostolic Witness (Acts 1:3; 28:31)

Another major theme in apostolic preaching is the Kingdom of God. Acts begins with Jesus' teaching about the Kingdom for forty days after His resurrection (Acts 1:3) and ends with Paul proclaiming the Kingdom while under house arrest in Rome (Acts 28:31). This shows that the Kingdom is central to the apostolic Mission.[50] Thus, the Kingdom represents God's reign through Christ, which brings justice, peace, and salvation. The apostles did not only preach about individual salvation but also about the arrival of God's rule in the world. Missiologically, this means that Mission involves calling people into a new way of life under the lordship of Christ, marked by obedience, transformation, and hope for the final fulfilment of God's reign.

Salvation in Christ (Acts 4:12)

The apostles boldly proclaimed that salvation is found in Jesus Christ. Peter declares that: *There is salvation in no one else, for there is no other name under heaven given among mortals by which we must be saved* (Acts 4:12). This exclusive claim was central to apostolic preaching. It affirmed that Jesus' death and resurrection are the only sufficient means for forgiveness and reconciliation with God.[51] Missiologically, this teaching is essential to the Christian faith. It means that the Mission of the church is not merely to offer one religious option among many but to bear witness to the only

---

[48] Charles Frederick William Dallmann, "God in History: Acts 2:23," *Concordia Historical Institute Quarterly* 15/4 (January, 1943): 102-111.

[49] Wallace N. Stearns, "The Apostle Paul in Athens," *The Biblical World* 37/6 (June, 1911): 411-419.

[50] Alex Evans, "Between Text and Sermon: Acts 28:11-31," *Interpretation* 66/3 (December, 2012): 312-315.

[51] Allan Aubrey Boesak, "In the Name of Jesus: Acts 4:12," *Journal of Theology for Southern Africa* 52 (December, 1985): 49-55.

true way to eternal life. This truth gave urgency and clarity to the apostles' preaching and should do the same for the church today.

Universal Scope of Salvation (Acts 10:34-35; 13:47)

While salvation is found only in Christ, the apostles also emphasized that it is offered to all people without distinction. When Peter witnessed the conversion of Cornelius, he declares that: *I truly understand that God shows no partiality, but in every people anyone who fears Him and practices righteousness is acceptable to Him* (Acts 10:34-35).[52] Paul and Barnabas resounded this saying that the Lord commanded them to be a light for the Gentiles *For so the Lord has commanded us, saying, 'I have set you to be a light for the gentiles, so that you may bring salvation to the ends of the earth'* (Acts 13:47).[53] Missiologically, this reveals the universal scope of God's Mission, that the gospel is not limited by race, culture, or geography, rather, it is for all nations. This global vision drove the apostles to cross boundaries and preach to both Jews and Gentiles, and it continues to inspire the church to carry the gospel to the ends of the earth.

Legacy and Continuation of Apostolic Mission

The Mission of the apostles did not end with their lives but continues through the church's ongoing witness to the world. The book of Acts and the rest of the New Testament make clear that the apostles laid a strong foundation for Christian Mission through their teachings, their writings, and their example. Their Mission was not simply a historical event but a lasting pattern for the church to follow. Missiologically, the apostolic legacy includes the preservation of truth through Scripture, the formation of the church through sound teaching, the training of new leaders, and the call for every generation to participate in God's Mission. This enduring Mission remains vital for the identity and purpose of the global church today.

Apostolic Tradition and the Authority of Scripture (II Peter 3:15-16)

One key aspect of the apostolic legacy is the written Word of God. The apostles did not only preach and plant churches, they also wrote letters and recorded teachings that became part of the New Testament. Peter refers to Paul's letters as Scripture: *So also, our beloved brother Paul wrote to you according to the wisdom given him...as they do the other scriptures* (II Peter 3:15-16), placing apostolic writings on the same level of authority as the

---

[52] Timothy W. Reardon, "Cleansing through Almsgiving in Luke-Acts..., 463-482.

[53] Herbert Hoefer, "Principles of Cross-Cultural/Ethnic Ministry: The Stories of Barnabas and Paul and the Jerusalem Council," *Missio Apostolica* 13/2 (December, 2005): 139-153.

Old Testament.[54] This affirms that the apostles, guided by the Holy Spirit, conveyed God's truth in a reliable and lasting form. Missiologically, this means the church's Mission must be grounded in Scripture. The Bible preserves the apostolic message and continues to guide the church in faith and practice. Upholding the authority of Scripture is essential for staying faithful to the Mission God has entrusted the apostles.

Apostolic Teaching as Missional Foundation (Acts 2:42)

Acts tells us that the early believers *devoted themselves to the apostles' teaching and fellowship, to the breaking of bread and the prayers* (Acts 2:42), which formed the basis of their life together. This teaching included the message of the gospel, ethical instructions, and guidance for church life. The apostles taught what they had received from Jesus and passed it on faithfully to the early communities.[55] Missiologically, this shows that Mission is not only about outreach but also about forming communities grounded in truth. The church grows and remains healthy when it remains rooted in sound apostolic doctrine.

Succession through Disciples and Missionaries

Another way the apostolic Mission continues is through the training and sending of new leaders. The apostles mentored younger coworkers such as Timothy, Titus, and Silas, who carried the gospel into new regions and helped lead the churches. Paul, in particular, saw this as part of his Mission strategy, urging Timothy to teach others who could teach as well (II Timothy 2:2). This multiplication model ensured that the Mission would continue beyond the first generation.[56] Missiologically, this reflects the importance of discipleship and leadership development in the life of the church. Every generation of believers is called not only to follow Jesus but also to raise up others who will do the same. This is how the apostolic Mission continues to move forward.

Conclusion

The apostolic Mission reveals the essential characteristics of Christian witness as designed and empowered by God. At its core, this Mission was Christ-centred, Spirit-empowered, Scripture-based, and globally oriented.

---

[54] Hunter Brown, "The Early Reception of 2 Peter 3:15-16," *Journal for New Testament Studies and the Knowledge of the Early Church* 115/2 (December, 2024): 249-264.

[55] Kelebogile Thomas Resane, "Pentecostal Missional Ecclesiology Based on Acts 2:42-47 Contributes towards Sustainable Development in Communities," *Missionalia* 52 (December, 2024): 172-184.

[56] Suzana Dobric Veiss, "Follower Development: Paul's Charge to Timothy..., 150-167.

The apostles preached the death and resurrection of Jesus, called people to repentance and faith, demonstrated the power of the Holy Spirit through signs and wonders, and crossed cultural and ethnic boundaries to reach the nations. Their Mission was marked by bold proclamation, suffering, community formation, and deep dependence on God's guidance. These elements defined the nature of apostolic Mission and continue to shape the church's identity and purpose today. Missiologically, the apostolic Mission laid the foundation for the expansion of the Christian faith across the world. Through their teachings, church planting, leadership development, and written Scriptures, the apostles provided a framework for how the gospel is to be preserved, taught, and lived. Their obedience to Jesus' commission (Matthew 28:18-20; Acts 1:8) established the pattern for Christian Mission: empowered by the Holy Spirit, rooted in God's Word, and aimed at the transformation of individuals and communities. Their legacy is not simply historical but foundational for all generations of Christian witness.

16

From Damascus to the Nations
Apostle Paul's Role in the Expansion of the Early Church

The apostle Paul is one of the most influential persons in New Testament and Mission. His life and writings shaped the early Church's understanding of Mission, particularly regarding the expansion of the gospel beyond the Jewish community. Paul's Missional role is central to the development of Christian theology and practice because he both taught and personified the Church's calling to bring the gospel to all nations. Through his Missionary journeys, theological reflections, and church-planting efforts, Paul became a key instrument in God's redemptive plan. Paul's apostleship was also unique in both its origin and its focus. Unlike the Twelve Apostles who were primarily called to the Jews, Paul was divinely set apart as the apostle to the Gentiles (Romans 11:13; Galatians 2:8). His calling was not based on his association with Jesus during Jesus' earthly ministry but came through a direct revelation from the risen Christ (Galatians 1:15-16). This distinct calling gave Paul a special place in God's Mission, as he became the bridge between Jewish and Gentile worlds. Paul's Mission broke cultural and religious boundaries and reflected the universal scope of God's salvation. The primary sources for understanding Paul's Mission are the Pauline Epistles and the Book of Acts. They reveal his deep commitment to the gospel, his thinking about Mission, and his convictions about the inclusion of the Gentiles. This study approaches Paul's Missional role through a blend of theological, historical, and Missional analysis.

Paul's Early Life and Pre-Christian Background

Paul's early life was deeply shaped by his Jewish heritage and Pharisaic training. Born into a Jewish family from the tribe of Benjamin, Paul identified himself as a "Hebrew of Hebrews" and a strict observer of the Law (Philippians 3:4-6).[1] He studied under the respected teacher Gamaliel in Jerusalem (Acts 22:3), which placed him within the Pharisaic tradition that valued Scripture, oral law, and religious purity. This rigorous training made Paul a scholar of the Hebrew Scriptures and gave him a deep understanding of the covenantal relationship between God and Israel.[2] His Jewish background later enabled him to argue persuasively from the Scriptures that Jesus was the Messiah, especially when preaching in synagogues.

In addition to his Jewish identity, Paul was also a Roman citizen, which brought significant privileges and access within the Roman Empire (Acts 22:25-29). He was born in Tarsus, a city known for its Greek culture and intellectual activity, suggesting that Paul was familiar with Hellenistic thought and ways of life.[3] This dual identity, being both Jewish and Roman, placed Paul at the crossroads of two major cultures. It helped him to communicate effectively in diverse settings and relate to both Jewish and Gentile audiences and his Roman citizenship later provided legal protections and opportunities during his Missionary travels, including his right to appeal to Caesar.[4]

Before becoming a follower of Christ, Paul was a fierce persecutor of the early Church. His zeal for Judaism led him to actively oppose the Christian movement, which he viewed as a threat to Jewish tradition and law (Acts 8:1-3; Galatians 1:13-14). Paul participated in the imprisonment and execution of Christians, believing he was defending the true faith. This intense opposition underscores the radical nature of his later conversion and Mission. His former hostility toward the Church became a key part of his testimony, demonstrating the transforming power of God's grace.[5] Paul's experience as a persecutor also gave him a unique empathy for those who misunderstood or resisted the gospel.

---

[1] Andrew S. Jacobs, "A Jew's Jew: Paul and the Early Christian Problem of Jewish Origins," *The Journal of Religion* 86/2 (April, 2006): 258-286.

[2] Quency E. Wallace, "The Early Life and Background of Paul the Apostle," *Journal of Biblical Theology* 2/2 (January, 2019): 137-153.

[3] Peter van Minnen, "Paul the Roman Citizen," *Journal for the Study of the New Testament* 17/56 (December, 1995): 43-52.

[4] Boyd Reese, "Apostle Paul's Exercise of His Rights as a Roman Citizen as Recorded in the Book of Acts," *The Evangelical Quarterly* 47 (January, 1975): 138-145.

[5] Ronald D. Witherup, "St. Paul: Fierce Persecutor Becomes Fervent Evangelist," *Saint Anthony Messenger* 116/8 (December, 2009): 22-26.

Thus, Paul's backgrounds such as, rich in religious tradition, cultural diversity, and personal intensity had deep implications for his future Mission. His knowledge of the Hebrew Scriptures enabled him to explain the gospel as the fulfilment of God's promises to Israel. His Roman citizenship and familiarity with Greek culture allowed him to cross cultural barriers and preach Christ in cities across the empire. His dramatic conversion from persecutor to apostle became a powerful witness to the gospel's ability to change lives. These aspects of his background were not accidental but providentially used by God to shape Paul into a Missionary who could reach both Jews and Gentiles. In short, Paul's early life was not simply a prelude to his conversion but a significant foundation for his Mission.

Paul's Encounter with the Risen Christ and Call to Mission

Paul's encounter with the risen Christ on the road to Damascus was the turning point of his life and the foundation of his Mission (Acts 9:1-19; 22:6-21; 26:12-18). As he travelled with the intent to persecute Christians, he was suddenly confronted by a divine light and the voice of Jesus asking, "Saul, Saul, why are you persecuting me?" (Acts 9:4). This encounter revealed to Paul that Jesus was truly the risen Lord and that persecuting His followers was equivalent to persecuting Jesus. Blinded and humbled, Paul was led into Damascus, where Ananias was sent to restore his sight and confirm his calling.[6] This moment marked both his conversion and commissioning, making it clear that his life would now be devoted to serving the very gospel he once tried to destroy.

Paul's apostleship was rooted in a direct revelation from Christ, not from human instruction or authority (Galatians 1:11-16). He emphasized that the gospel he preached was not man-made but received through a divine encounter with Jesus Himself. This revelation gave Paul the authority to speak as an apostle, even though he was not among the original Twelve. It also formed the foundation of his Mission to the Gentiles, as he was called and sent by the risen Christ.[7] Paul's apostleship was not based on tradition but on God's initiative and grace. This direct calling gave him both the confidence and the responsibility to proclaim the gospel boldly and faithfully.

In his commissioning, Paul was given a specific task: to be a "light to the Gentiles" and to bring salvation to the ends of the earth (Acts 26:16-18; cf. Isaiah 49:6). This language echoes the servant Mission described in Isaiah, where God's chosen servant would extend God's salvation beyond

[6] Brian Schmisek, "Paul's Vision of the Risen Lord," *Biblical Theology Bulletin* 41/2 (January, 2011): 76-83.

[7] J. Andrew Cowan, "The Legal Significance of Christ's Risen Life: Union with Christ and Justification in Galatians 2.17-20," *Journal for the Study of the New Testament* 40/4 (December, 2018): 453-472.

Israel to all nations. Paul understood that his Mission was part of God's larger redemptive plan, now fulfilled in Christ and extended to all people. He was called to open the eyes of the nations, turn them from darkness to light, and proclaim forgiveness of sins through faith in Jesus.[8] This universal Mission became the driving force of Paul's life and ministry.

Paul's encounter with Christ also brought about a deep theological reorientation. Formerly grounded in the Law and the traditions of Israel, Paul now centred his faith on the grace of God revealed in Christ. Salvation was no longer about strict obedience to the Law but about receiving righteousness through faith. This shift also meant that God's Mission was no longer Israel-centric but global in scope. Paul came to see the Church as the new people of God, made up of Jews and Gentiles united in Christ.[9] His theology moved from exclusivity to inclusion, from legalism to grace, and from ethnic boundaries to the universality of the gospel.

Thus, Paul's encounter with the risen Christ was not only a personal transformation but a divine commissioning into a new kind of Mission. His call was based on a direct revelation, shaped by Old Testament prophecy, and marked by a radical shift in the understanding of Mission. This encounter set the stage for a lifelong Mission to proclaim Christ to the nations. Paul's experience teaches that Mission begins with a personal encounter with Christ, and that such encounters often lead to new understandings, new communities, and a new purpose rooted in God's global plan of redemption.[10]

Paul's Missiology

Paul's Missiology is one of the most influential understandings of Mission in the New Testament. As a chosen apostle to the Gentiles, Paul saw his entire life and ministry as part of God's great plan to bring salvation to all people through Jesus Christ. His Mission was not based on human ideas or personal ambition, but strongly founded on the gospel, the good news of Jesus' death and resurrection. For Paul, the gospel was at the centre of everything. It shaped his message, his calling, Mission methods and the way he built churches. Paul believed that salvation was not limited to one group of people. He taught that through faith in Christ, both Jews and Gentiles could become part of God's family. This made his Mission truly universal, reaching across barriers of race, culture, and class. He also believed that the gospel had the power to change not only individuals, but entire communities,

---

[8] Dennis Hamm, "Paul's Blindness and Its Healing: Clues to Symbolic Intent (Acts 9; 22 and 26)," *Biblica* 71/1 (December, 1990): 63-72.

[9] Herbert Mccabe, "What is the Church?-II: The People of God," *Life of the Spirit (1946-1964)* 15/180 (June, 1961): 529-540.

[10] Albert L. A. Hogeterp, "Prophecy and the Prophetic as Aspects of Paul's Theology," *Stellenbosch Theological Journal* 4/2 (January, 2018): 169-196.

and even the whole creation. Thus, Paul's vision of Mission was both personal and cosmic, it brought peace between people and God, and looked forward to the renewal of all things. At the same time, Paul understood his Mission as a participation in the *Missio Dei*.

Gospel-Centred Missiology

At the heart of Paul's Mission was the gospel, the good news of Jesus Christ. Paul's Missiology was not driven by human wisdom, political agendas, or cultural programs, but by the proclamation of the gospel. This message centred on the person and work of Christ, particularly the death and resurrection of Jesus that he explains as: *Now I want you to understand, brothers and sisters, the good news that I proclaimed to you...that Christ died for our sins in accordance with the scriptures and that He was buried and that He was raised on the third day in accordance with the scriptures* (I Corinthians 15:1-4). For Paul, the gospel was not just one message among many, it was the essential truth that gave life to the Church and guided its Mission to the world.[11]

A central theme in Paul's gospel message was justification by faith. Paul emphasized that people are made right with God not by works of the law, but by faith in Jesus Christ. In Romans he explains this as: *But now, apart from the law, the righteousness of God has been disclosed...the righteousness of God through the faith of Jesus Christ for all who believe* (Romans 3:21-26). Similarly, in Galatians, Paul writes: *yet we know that a person is justified not by the works of the law but through the faith of Jesus Christ* (Galatians 2:16). This doctrine had significant Missional significance. It meant that salvation was available to all, Jews and Gentiles alike, through faith, not through adherence to Jewish customs.[12] Paul's teaching on justification opened the door for a truly universal Mission that invited all people into right relationship with God.

Another key aspect of Paul's Missional theology was the idea of the "new creation." Paul believed that the gospel not only brings forgiveness but also transforms lives. In II Corinthians he states: *So, if anyone is in Christ, there is a new creation: everything old has passed away; look, new things have come into being* (II Corinthians 5:17). This transformation was both individual and communal. It created new people with new identities, and it formed new communities, the Church, as signs of God's renewing

---

[11] Michael J. Gorman, "Cross, Participation, and Mission: 'In Christ' in Paul Means Being on the Move," *Bangalore Theological Forum* 56/2 (January, 2024): 9-34.

[12] David Lertis Matson, "Divine Forgiveness in Paul?: Justification by Faith and the Logic of Pauline Soteriology," *Stone-Campbell Journal* 19/1 (December, 2016): 59-83.

work in the world.[13] Paul's Mission, therefore, was not just about converting individuals, but about building communities that reflected the character of the Kingdom of God.

Closely related to this theme of new creation was Paul's understanding of reconciliation. The gospel, according to Paul, reconciles humanity to God and people to one another. In II Corinthians, he writes: *All this is from God, who reconciled us to himself through Christ and has given us the ministry of reconciliation; that is, in Christ God was reconciling the world to Himself, not counting their trespasses against them, and entrusting the message of reconciliation to us.* For Paul, Mission was a ministry of reconciliation (II Corinthians 5:18-19). As God had reconciled believers to Himself, they were now entrusted with the task of bringing this message of peace and restoration to others.[14] This shaped Paul's vision of the Church as a reconciling community across lines of race, class, and culture.

Thus, Paul's theology of Mission was deeply rooted in the gospel of Jesus Christ. The death and resurrection of Christ were the foundation of his message. Justification by faith ensured that salvation was open to all, not based on works but on God's grace. The vision of new creation and reconciliation gave the Mission a transformational and relational goal. These convictions not only shaped how Paul preached the gospel but also how he formed churches and encouraged believers to live out their faith.

Universal Scope of Salvation

One of the most important aspects of Paul's Mission was the universal scope of salvation. Paul believed that the gospel was not limited to the Jewish people but was intended for all nations. This belief was rooted in God's original promise to Abraham, which Paul refers to in Galatians: *And the scripture, foreseeing that God would reckon as righteous the gentiles by faith, declared the gospel beforehand to Abraham, saying, "All the gentiles shall be blessed in you"* (Galatians 3:8). Paul emphasized that this promise is fulfilled in Christ, and through faith in Him, Gentiles are fully included in the people of God.[15] This he powerfully establishes by saying that: *There is no longer Jew or Greek; there is no longer slave or free; there is no longer male and female, for all of you are one in Christ Jesus. And if you belong to Christ, then you are Abraham's offspring, heirs according to the promise*

---

[13] Paul Sciberras, "New Man - New Creation in the Theology of Paul," *The Person and the Challenges* 9/1 (December, 2019), 225-238.

[14] Robert J. Schreiter, "St Paul's Vision of Reconciliation," *Origins* 38/46 (December, 2009), 725-732.

[15] Michael William Holmes, "Paul's Soteriological Pas: Universal or Limited?: An Examination of Three Pauline Texts," *Trinity Journal* 6/2 (December, 1977): 153-161.

(Galatians 3:28-29). This radical inclusion was a foundational part of Paul's Missional vision.

In Paul's letter to the Ephesians, he further explains how the gospel abolishes the dividing walls between Jews and Gentiles. Ephesians 2:11-22 provides a powerful picture of reconciliation through Christ. Paul writes: *For he is our peace; in his flesh he has made both into one and has broken down the dividing wall, that is, the hostility between us* (Ephesians 2:14). Through the cross, Jesus created one new humanity, uniting all believers into one body. This truth had deep Mission implications: it meant that the Church was to be a new kind of community, multiethnic, unified, and reconciled.[16] Thus, Paul's Mission was to build such communities, where former enemies lived together as brothers and sisters in Christ.

Paul's understanding of the Mission also extended beyond human reconciliation to include the entire creation. In Romans he describes that the creation is "groaning" and waiting for liberation: *For the creation waits with eager longing for the revealing of the children of God, for the creation was subjected to futility, not of its own will, but by the will of the one who subjected it, in hope that the creation itself will be set free from its enslavement to decay and will obtain the freedom of the glory of the children of God* (Romans 8:19-21). Paul saw salvation as cosmic in scope, not only saving individuals but also restoring the entire created order.[17] This broader vision gave his Mission a cosmic dimension, rooted in the belief that Christ's redemptive work would one day renew all things.

Paul also expressed this cosmic vision in Colossians, where he writes about Christ's work as: *and through him God was pleased to reconcile to himself all things, whether on earth or in heaven, by making peace through the blood of his cross* (Colossians 1:20). The gospel, therefore, for Paul, is not only about personal forgiveness or community reconciliation; it is about the renewal of the universe. Thus, in Paul's Missiology, Christ's death and resurrection have universal significance, pointing toward a future in which everything will be restored under God's reign.[18] This cosmic perspective gave Paul's Mission urgency and hope, as he preached a gospel that touched every part of life and creation.

---

[16] Richard D. Crane, "At Cross Purposes with the Cross?: Real and Rhetorical Dividing Walls of Hostility, Christian Formation, Ecclesial Witness and Political Engagement," *American Baptist Quarterly* 40/2 (December, 2021): 74-109.

[17] James W. Thompson, "The Groaning and Redemption of Creation: Does Paul Speak to the Environmental Crisis?'," *Restoration Quarterly* 66/3 (December, 2024): 170-183.

[18] Norman Wirzba, "Reconciliation with the Land," in *Making Peace with the Land: God's Call to Reconcile with Creation*, edited by Fred Bahnson and Norman Wirzba (Downers Grove: InterVarsity Press, 2012), 18.

Thus, Paul's theology of salvation was deeply universal. It embraced the inclusion of the Gentiles, broke down social and ethnic barriers, and pointed toward the reconciliation of all creation. This expansive vision of salvation shaped the way Paul preached, planted churches, and instructed believers to live. For Paul, the Church was a sign of the coming Kingdom, a diverse, unified, and renewed people living under Christ's lordship.[19]

Missio Dei and Paul's Participation

Paul understood his Mission as a participation in the *Missio Dei*, the Mission of God. He saw his work not as something self-initiated, but as a response to God's eternal purpose revealed in Christ.[20] In Ephesians Paul writes: *he has made known to us the mystery of his will, according to his good pleasure that he set forth in Christ, as a plan for the fullness of time, to gather up all things in him, things in heaven and things on earth* (Ephesians 1:9-10,). This grand purpose was not new but hidden in God from eternity and now revealed in Christ. In Ephesians 3:1-13, Paul explains that he was made *a prisoner for Christ Jesus for the sake of you Gentiles*, and that *the mystery was made known to me by revelation* (Ephesians 3:1, 3). He affirms that this mystery is that: *the gentiles have become fellow heirs, members of the same body, and sharers in the promise in Christ Jesus through the gospel* (Ephesians 3:6). Paul saw his Mission as a continuation of God's plan to unite all things under Christ.

This sense of divine calling shaped Paul's identity as a servant and steward. He was not simply a preacher or church planter, but someone entrusted with God's mystery. In Colossians Paul writes: *I became its minister according to God's commission that was given to me for you, to make the word of God fully known, the mystery that has been hidden throughout the ages and generations but has now been revealed to his saints. To them God chose to make known how great among the gentiles are the riches of the glory of this mystery, which is Christ in you, the hope of glory* (Colossians 1:25-27). Paul understood that he was called to reveal the mystery of Christ dwelling among the Gentiles, a deep truth that expressed God's desire to dwell with all people through faith.

In this way, Paul's Mission was a direct participation in the *Missio Dei*. His work was not about personal ambition but about fulfilling God's purpose in history. He aligned himself with God's redemptive plan to reconcile and renew all things through Christ. Paul's understanding of Mission, therefore,

---

[19] Herman C. Waetjen, "A Postmodern Reading of Paul's Letter to the Romans and Its Disclosure of a New Image of God and a New Understanding of Salvation," *Theology Today* 69/2 (December, 2012): 197-212.

[20] Richard Last, "What Purpose did Paul Understand His Mission to Serve?," *The Harvard Theological Review* 104/3 (July, 2011): 299-324.

was deeply Missiological. It began with God, was centred in Christ, and extended to the nations. This view shaped his life, his message, and his suffering for the sake of the gospel.

Eschatological Motivation for Mission

Paul's Mission was driven by a strong eschatological vision, the belief that history was moving toward a definite end under God's sovereign plan. He proclaimed the gospel with urgency because he believed that the final judgment was coming. In Acts he expresses this while speaking to the philosophers in Athens.[21] Paul states that: *While God has overlooked the times of human ignorance, now He commands all people everywhere to repent, because He has fixed a day on which he will have the world judged in righteousness by a man whom He has appointed, and of this He has given assurance to all by raising Him from the dead* (Acts 17:30-31). Thus, for Paul, the resurrection of Jesus was not only the foundation of salvation but also the guarantee of future judgment.[22] This coming judgment gave Paul's Mission a sense of urgency and he called people everywhere to repentance and faith before it was too late.

At the same time, Paul was motivated by the future hope promised in the gospel. He believed that the sufferings of the present time were temporary and would one day be replaced by eternal glory.[23] This he makes it clear while writing to Romans. Paul writes: *I consider that the sufferings of this present time are not worth comparing with the glory about to be revealed to us* (Romans 8:18) and he further states the intensity of it by saying: *and not only the creation, but we ourselves, who have the first fruits of the Spirit, groan inwardly while we wait for adoption, the redemption of our bodies* (Romans 8:23). This hope sustained Paul through persecution, hardship, and rejection. His endurance was not rooted in human strength but in the confident expectation of God's final victory.[24] The future glory promised to believers gave meaning to the Mission and inspired perseverance in the face of trials.

Thus, for Paul, the coming judgment and the hope of glory formed a powerful eschatological framework for his Mission understanding and

---

[21] Michael Parsons, "Time and Location: Aspects of Eschatological Motivation in Paul," *The Reformed Theological Review* 60/3 (December, 2001): 109-122.

[22] Joshua W. Jipp, "Paul's Areopagus Speech of Acts 17:16-34 as Both Critique and Propaganda," *Journal of Biblical Literature* 131/3 (2012): 567-588.

[23] Jason S. DeRouchie, "'Him We Proclaim!': Paul's Motivation, Means, and Mandate for Missions in Colossians 1:24-29," *The Master's Seminary Journal* 36/1 (December, 2025): 65-87.

[24] Matthew T. Warnez, "On Romans 8 and the Integrity of Creation," *The Catholic Biblical Quarterly* 86/2 (December, 2024): 326-347.

practice. The urgency of salvation compelled him to preach boldly, while the assurance of future redemption gave him strength to suffer joyfully. Paul's eschatological vision reminds the Church today that Mission is not just about improving the present world but preparing for the fulfilment of God's kingdom. The Church is called to proclaim repentance in light of judgment and to embody hope in a world still marked by suffering.[25] In this way, Paul's eschatological motivation gives depth and direction to Christian Mission, rooted in the conviction that Christ will come again to judge and to save.

Paul's Missionary Practices: Methods and Designs

Paul's Missionary practice was a crucial part of his contribution to the early Church and to the development of Christian Mission. More than a theologian or letter-writer, Paul was a Missionary planner who travelled across vast regions to preach the gospel, establish churches, and strengthen new believers. His methods were shaped by Missiological convictions, guided by the Holy Spirit, and adapted to different cultural and social contexts.[26] Through his journeys, Paul demonstrated a deep understanding of how to reach both Jews and Gentiles with the message of Christ. His practice combined bold proclamation, pastoral care, community building, and intercultural exchanges.

Chronology, Geography and Theology of Paul's Missionary Journeys

Paul's Missionary activity extended in a series of journeys that reflect both deliberate planning and sensitivity to the leading of the Holy Spirit. These journeys formed the backbone of his Missionary method, as he moved across geographical regions with a clear gospel purpose: to preach Christ, establish churches, and strengthen believers. The Book of Acts provides a narrative framework for these journeys, while Paul's own letters offer theological reflections on his experiences. Each journey reflects different aspects of Paul's Mission approach, proclamation, church planting, leadership training, and perseverance through suffering.[27]

Paul's First Missionary Journey, recorded in Acts 13-14, began with the commissioning of Paul and Barnabas by the church in Antioch. Led by the Holy Spirit, they travelled to Cyprus and then into Southern Galatia, preaching the gospel in cities such as Pisidian Antioch, Iconium, Lystra, and Derbe. This journey established Paul's basic Missionary pattern: preaching

---

[25] Walter Cardinal Kasper, "Hope in the Final Coming of Jesus Christ in Glory," *Communio* 12 (December, 1985): 368-384.

[26] Theodore Gerald Soares, "Paul's Missionary Methods," *The Biblical World* 34/5 (November, 1909): 326-336.

[27] Thomas H. Campbell, "Paul's 'Missionary Journeys' as Reflected in His Letters," *Journal of Biblical Literature* 74/2 (June, 1955): 80-87.

in synagogues where possible, facing opposition, turning to Gentiles, and forming communities of believers.[28] This he summarizes in Acts 13 saying: *for so the Lord has commanded us, saying, 'I have set you to be a light for the gentiles, so that you may bring salvation to the ends of the earth'* (Acts 13:47). This Mission laid the foundation for a Church that would transcend ethnic and cultural boundaries.

During the Second Missionary Journey (Acts 15:36-18:22), Paul expanded his reach into Macedonia and Greece, responding to a vision of a man from Macedonia calling for help (Acts 16:9-10). He travelled to key cities such as Philippi, Thessalonica, Berea, Athens, and Corinth. In these places, Paul adapted his message to different audiences.[29] In Philippi, he encountered Lydia and a Roman jailer (Acts 16), while in Athens, he engaged with Greek philosophers at the Areopagus (Acts 17:22-31), proclaiming the one true God and the resurrection of Christ. This journey showed Paul's ability to contextualize the gospel and confirmed his Mission to the Gentiles, strengthening churches along the way.[30]

Paul's Third Missionary Journey (Acts 18:23-21:17) focused more on strengthening existing churches than on pioneering new ones. He revisited churches in Galatia and Phrygia and then spent an extended period in Ephesus, a major urban centre.[31] His satisfaction in the Missionary journeys he mentioned as: *all the residents of Asia, both Jews and Greeks, heard the word of the Lord* (Acts 19:10). In Ephesus, Paul taught daily, performed miracles, and addressed false teachings. His letters from this period, such as I Corinthians and Romans, reveal his deep concern for doctrinal clarity and church unity.[32] This journey reflects Paul's commitment not only to evangelism but also to long-term discipleship and church development.

Paul's Fourth Journey, also called his journey to Rome, was different from the previous ones, in that Paul was undertaken as a prisoner. Acts 27-28 describes the adventurous sea voyage, including shipwreck and survival, which ultimately brought Paul to Rome. In this situation, Paul did not stop

---

[28] Muthuphei A. Mutavhatsindi, "The Preliminary Urban Missionary Outreach of the Apostle Paul as Referred to in Acts 13-14," *Verbum et Ecclesia* 38/1 (January, 2017): 1-10.

[29] Glen L. Thompson and Mark Wilson. "The Route of Paul's Second Journey in Asia Minor: In the Steps of Robert Jewett and Beyond," *Tyndale Bulletin* 67/2 (December, 2016): 217-246.

[30] William A. McDonald, "Archaeology and St. Paul's Journeys in Greek Lands," *The Biblical Archaeologist* 3/2 (May, 1940): 18-24.

[31] Mark W. Wilson, "The 'Upper Regions' and the Route of Paul's Third Journey from Apamea to Ephesus," *Scriptura* 117/1 (January, 2018): 1-21.

[32] Warren P. Behan, "Paul's Third Missionary Journey," *The Biblical World* 34/2 (August, 1909): 120-130.

preaching. He shared the gospel with soldiers, sailors, and Roman officials.[33] In Philippians Paul reflects on this period as: *I want you to know, brothers and sisters, that what has happened to me has actually resulted in the progress of the gospel...and to everyone else that my imprisonment is for Christ, and most of the brothers and sisters, having been made confident in the Lord by my imprisonment, dare to speak the word with greater boldness and without fear* (Philippians 1:12-14). This makes clear that, even in chains, Paul saw his life as part of God's Mission.

Paul's journeys reveal a consistent Missional design. He followed major roads and urban centres, choosing cities that had both Jewish and Gentile populations. His methods involved preaching, forming churches, appointing leaders, writing letters, and revisiting communities. Yet he remained open to divine redirection, such as the Macedonian call in Acts 16. His methods were flexible but always gospel-centred. He faced persecution, hardship, and resistance, but he continued with boldness, depending on God's grace and the power of the Holy Spirit. Each journey had a theological focus, spreading the gospel of Christ, forming diverse communities of believers, and nurturing mature churches. Whether free or imprisoned, Paul saw himself as an ambassador of Christ, sent to proclaim salvation to all nations.

Urban and Strategic Focus

Paul's Missionary efforts were not only guided by theological conviction but also marked by clear and deliberate planning. One of the most notable aspects of his Mission practice was his intentional focus on cities, major urban centres that held cultural, economic, and political influence in the ancient world. Rather than targeting isolated villages or rural areas, Paul chose to begin his ministry in strategic urban centres such as Corinth (Acts 18:1-11), Ephesus (Acts 19:1-10), Thessalonica (Acts 17:1-4), and Philippi (Acts 16:11-15), knowing that what happened in these cities could impact entire regions. His approach reflects a keen awareness of how the gospel could spread quickly and effectively through networks of commerce, communication, and community life.[34] In addition to preaching and church planting, Paul aimed to establish regional hubs. Paul established regional hubs such as Antioch (Acts 13:1-3), Ephesus (Acts 19:8-10), Corinth (Acts 18:1-11), Thessalonica (I Thessalonians 1:6-8), and Rome (Acts 28:30-31) as centres of Mission, equipping local believers to spread the gospel to surrounding regions. These key cities became bases for evangelism,

[33] Sin-pan Daniel Ho, "Changes in the Centurion on Paul's Last Journey to Rome in Acts 27," *Biblical Theology Bulletin* 52/2 (January, 2022): 99-110.

[34] Jey J. Kanagarai, "The Strategies of Paul the Missionary," in *Integral Mission the Way Forward: Essay in Honour of Dr. Saphir P. Athyal,* edited by C. V. Mathew (Kottayam: Christava Sathiya Samithi, 2006), 160.

leadership development, and church growth across the Roman world. This urban and strategic focus reveals not only Paul's Missionary wisdom but also his deep trust in the power of the gospel to transform cities and influence the world.

A key feature of Paul's Missionary method was his deliberate focus on urban centres. He targeted major commercial and cultural cities such as Corinth, Ephesus, Thessalonica, and Philippi, recognizing that these urban locations had great influence over surrounding regions. These cities were not only densely populated but also hubs of trade, politics, and religious activity, making them ideal starting points for spreading the gospel.[35] For example, Corinth was a major port city known for its diversity and immorality, yet Paul spent 18 months there preaching and forming a strong church (Acts 18:1-11). Similarly, Ephesus was a centre of pagan worship and learning, but it became a base for Paul's extended teaching and outreach. By planting churches in such cities, Paul ensured that the gospel could reach many people and spread outward through natural networks of communication and commerce.

This urban focus reflects Paul's Missiological conviction that the gospel is meant to reach all nations and transform all spheres of life. By beginning in cities, Paul tapped into the cultural and economic arteries of the ancient world, trusting that the gospel's influence would ripple outward. In these cities, Paul's Mission methods combined bold evangelism, community formation, and leadership development in places where ideas, people, and trade were constantly moving. In doing so, Paul aligned his Mission with the broader purposes of God, to reach all peoples through faithful witness and Spirit-led expansion.[36] His example continues to guide the Church in recognizing cities as key arenas for Mission and gospel transformation today.

Church Planting and Nurture

A central part of Paul's Missionary method was the planting and nurturing of churches. His work followed a clear and purposeful design: evangelism, followed by discipleship, the appointment of elders, and finally, entrustment to local leadership. Paul did not merely preach and move on, rather. he worked to establish stable, growing communities of believers.[37] This reflects in the words of Paul saying: *After they had proclaimed the good news to that city and had made many disciples, they returned to Lystra, then on to Iconium and Antioch. There they strengthened the souls of the disciples and*

---

[35] Craig Ott, Stephen J. Strauss and Timothy C. Tennet, *Encountering Theology of Mission: Biblical Foundations, Historical Developments and Contemporary Issues* (Grand Rapids: Baker Academic, 2010), 47-48.

[36] Jey J. Kanagarai, "The Strategies of Paul the Missionary…, 160.

[37] L. Mhonthung Humtsoe, *Life of Paul and his Missionary Strategy: Exploring a Contextual Mission-Naga Context* (Dimapur: L. Mhonthung Humtsoe, 2016), 10-11.

encouraged them...and after they had appointed elders for them in each church (Acts 14:21-23). This model shows that Paul's Mission aimed not just at conversions but at forming mature, structured churches with capable leadership for long-term gospel witness.

Paul also used his letters as Missional tools to nurture the churches he had planted. These letters addressed theological issues, moral concerns, leadership challenges, and practical questions within the Christian communities. For example, I Thessalonians Paul writes, *As you know, we dealt with each one of you like a father with his children, urging and encouraging you and pleading that you lead a life worthy of God* (I Thessalonians 2:11-12). In his letters to the Corinthians, he corrected errors and called for unity (I Corinthians 1:10), while in Philippians he offered encouragement and thanksgiving (Philippians 1:3-6). These epistles were not only personal correspondences but instruments of teaching, correction, encouragement, and instruction.[38] They formed an essential part of Paul's method to sustain the faith and Mission of the churches in his absence.

A key component of Paul's nurturing approach was delegation to local leaders, trustworthy men who would continue the work in his place. He mentored individuals like Timothy and Titus, entrusting them with responsibility for churches. To Timothy Paul writes, *and what you have heard from me through many witnesses entrust to faithful people who will be able to teach others as well* (Timothy 2:2). Titus was left in Crete and Paul exhorts his expectation as: *I left you behind in Crete for this reason, so that you should put in order what remained to be done and should appoint elders in every town, as I directed you* (Titus 1:5). Paul also commended Epaphroditus in Philippians 2:25, calling him and sharing the purpose as: *my brother and coworker and fellow soldier, your messenger and minister to my need.* These partnerships show that Paul did not rely solely on his own efforts, rather, he built teams and raised leaders, ensuring the continuity and expansion of the Mission.[39]

This way of church planting and nurture reflects Paul's Missiological understanding of the Church as the body of Christ and the dwelling place of God's Spirit. The formation of local congregations was not a secondary part of Paul's Mission, rather, it was the visible expression of the gospel taking root in real communities. These churches were to grow in faith, love, and hope, and serve as centres of witness in their cities. Paul's methods highlight the importance of 'Holistic Mission,' proclaiming the gospel, forming

---

[38] W. B. Hunter, "Prayer," in *Dictionary of Paul and His Letters*, edited by Gerald F. Hawthorne and Ralph P. Martin (Illinois: InterVarsity Press, 1993), 523.

[39] Michael Robertson, "Neophyte Pastors: Can Titus 1 Be Used to Justify Placing New Converts in the Office of Pastor?," *Southwestern Journal of Theology* 57/1 (December, 2014): 77-86.

disciples, establishing leadership, and empowering local believers to carry on the work. Through this model, Paul demonstrated that Mission is not only about starting something new, but about nurturing what God has begun to maturity and fruitfulness.

Use of Synagogues and Gentile Forums

Paul's Missionary methods included a consistent pattern of preaching first to the Jews and then to the Gentiles. This approach was rooted in his theological conviction that the gospel was for all people but came "to the Jew first." In Romans 1:16, Paul writes: *For I am not ashamed of the gospel; it is God's saving power for everyone who believes, for the Jew first and also for the Greek.* Following this conviction, Paul regularly began his ministry in a new city by preaching in the local synagogue. This gave him the opportunity to connect with people who already had some knowledge of the Scriptures and the expectation of the Messiah. However, when the message was rejected, Paul turned to the Gentiles.[40] This he expresses during his ministry in Pisidian Antioch, Paul and Barnabas said: *It was necessary that the word of God should be spoken first to you. Since you reject it and judge yourselves to be unworthy of eternal life, we are now turning to the gentiles* (Acts 13:46). This pattern highlights both the inclusive scope of the gospel and the tragic reality of its rejection by many in Israel.

In addition to synagogues, Paul actively used Gentile forums and public spaces to engage non-Jewish audiences. One of the most striking examples is found in Acts 17:17-34, where Paul reasons with people in the marketplace of Athens and later addresses the Areopagus, a council of philosophers and thinkers.[41] In Acts 17:17, it says: *So, he argued in the synagogue with the Jews and the devout persons and also in the marketplace every day with those who happened to be there.* Paul observed the religious life of the city and used it as a starting point for dialogue. In Acts 17:22-23, he begins his address by saying: *Athenians, I see how extremely spiritual you are in every way. For as I went through the city and looked carefully at the objects of your worship, I found among them an altar with the inscription, 'To an unknown god.'* Paul then skilfully presents the truth of the one Creator God and calls all people to repentance in light of the resurrection of Jesus (Acts 17:30-31). His engagement was respectful, contextual, and theological.[42]

[40] Anthony J. Saldarini, "Synagogue," in *The HarperCollins Bible Dictionary*, edited by Paul J. Achtemeier (New York: HarperCollins Publishers, 1996), 1079-1081.

[41] Eric M. Meyers, 'Synagogue,' in *The Anchor Bible Dictionary*, Vol. 6, edited by David Noel Freedman, Gary A. Herian, et al (New York: Doubleday, 1992), 251-252.

[42] Karl Olav Sandnes, "Prophet-Like Apostle: A Note on the 'Radical New Perspective' in Pauline Studies," *Biblica* 96/4 (2015): 550-564.

Contextualization and Cultural Adaptation

Paul's Mission was also marked by a strong commitment to contextualization. He adapted his approach to fit the cultural, religious, and social contexts of his audience without changing the gospel itself.[43] Paul clearly expresses this principle as: *For though I am free with respect to all, I have made myself a slave to all, so that I might gain all the more. To the Jews I became as a Jew, in order to gain Jews. To those under the law I became as one under the law...To those outside the law I became as one outside the law...so that I might gain those outside the law. To the weak I became weak, so that I might gain the weak. I have become all things to all people, that I might by all means save some* (I Corinthians 9:19-23). Paul's goal was to remove unnecessary barriers so that people could hear and receive the message of Christ. This did not mean compromising the truth, but humbly entering into the lives of others to communicate the gospel in ways they could understand and accept.

Paul also showed deep sensitivity to both Jewish and Gentile practices. He was careful not to offend unnecessarily, especially in areas related to food, festivals, and conscience. In Romans 14-15, he urges the strong not to look down on the weak, and the weak not to judge the strong, especially regarding dietary practices and special days. He says in Romans: *Let us then pursue what makes for peace and for mutual upbuilding* (Romans 14:19). Paul's concern was to maintain unity in the body of Christ without forcing everyone to conform to one cultural expression. In Acts 21:20-26, Paul himself agreed to participate in Jewish purification rites in Jerusalem to show that he was not opposed to the law, even though he no longer saw it as necessary for salvation.[44] These actions demonstrate his pastoral wisdom in navigating complex cultural dynamics.

Paul also used elements of language, philosophy, and local custom to connect with his audiences. In Acts 17:28, while speaking to the philosophers in Athens, he quotes their own poets: *For 'In Him we live and move and have our being'; as even some of your own poets have said, 'For we, too, are His offspring.'* By using familiar references, Paul created a bridge between the culture of his listeners and the truth of the gospel.[45] He also addressed questions of food offered to idols in I Corinthians 8, acknowledging as: *we*

---

[43] Arminta Fox, "Decentering Paul, Contextualizing Crimes: Reading in Light of the Imprisoned," *Journal of Feminist Studies in Religion* 33/2 (Fall, 2017): 37-54.

[44] Berdine van den Toren-Lekkerkerker, "From Missionary Incarnate to Incarnational Guest: A Critical Reflection on Incarnation as a Model for Missionary Presence," *Transformation* 32/2 (April, 2015): 81-96.

[45] Wallace N. Stearns, "The Apostle Paul in Athens," *The Biblical World* 37/6 (June, 1911): 411-419.

know that "no idol in the world really exists" and that "there is no God but one" (I Corinthians 8:4), yet advising believers to consider the consciences of others. This shows how Paul balanced use of doctrinal truth in Mission with practical wisdom, helping new believers navigate their cultural environments in light of their faith in Christ.

Miracles as a Mission Method in Paul's Ministry

Miracles were a vital part of Paul's Mission method, not merely as displays of power, but as signs of God's kingdom breaking into the world through the gospel. In various cultural and religious contexts, miracles authenticated Paul's message, opened doors for evangelism, and demonstrated the authority of Christ over sickness, evil, and death. Paul's miracles associated with the larger theological theme of God's redemptive presence working through his chosen servants to restore creation and invite people into new life.[46] Each miracle carried contextual and theological meaning, revealing the transformative nature of the gospel in action.

In Lystra (Acts 14:8-10), Paul encountered a man crippled from birth who had never walked. Seeing that the man had faith to be healed, Paul said loudly, *"Stand up on your feet!"* The man leaped up and began walking (Acts 14:10). This miracle took place in a Gentile setting where pagan worship was dominant. The healing amazed the crowds, who mistakenly identified Paul and Barnabas as gods (Acts 14:11-13). Paul used this opportunity to redirect their attention to the living God, the Creator of all things (Acts 14:15). Missiologically, this miracle reflected the gospel's power to restore what was broken, pointing beyond human ability to divine grace and inviting people into worship of the true God. It also demonstrated Paul's sensitivity to cultural misunderstanding and his boldness to proclaim monotheism in a polytheistic society.

In Philippi (Acts 16:16-18), Paul met a slave girl possessed by a spirit that enabled her to tell fortunes, bringing profit to her owners. For days she followed Paul, shouting, *"These men are slaves of the Most High God, who proclaim to you the way of salvation."* (Acts 16:17). Though her words were true, Paul discerned the spiritual disturbance and cast out the spirit in the name of Jesus Christ (Acts 16:18). This miracle highlighted Paul's authority over demonic forces and affirmed the power of Christ's name. In a Roman colony where spiritual power was highly respected, this act demonstrated that Christ's lordship extends over all spiritual realms.[47] It also had social

---

[46] Jaap Doedens, "The Things That Mark an Apostle: Paul's Signs, Wonders, and Miracles," *The Biblical Annals* 11/1 (December, 2021): 99-119.

[47] Gary W. Derickson, "The Cessation of Healing Miracles in Paul's Ministry," *Bibliotheca Sacra* 155/619 (December, 1998): 299-315.

consequences, Paul's action disrupted economic exploitation and led to his imprisonment, showing that gospel Mission often confronts unjust systems.

During Paul's extended ministry in Ephesus, God performed extraordinary miracles through him (Acts 19:11-12), such that even handkerchiefs and aprons that had touched Paul's body were taken to the sick, and they were healed, and evil spirits left them (Acts 19:11-12). Ephesus was a city known for its magic, idol worship, and occult practices. These miracles demonstrated that the power of Christ was far superior to magic or sorcery.[48] These signs affirmed that God's healing presence was active in the Mission, and that faith in Christ, not magical rituals, brings true deliverance. This led many to renounce magic and publicly burn their scrolls (Acts 19:19), showing the miracle's power to transform not only individuals but entire communities.

While preaching in Troas, Paul spoke until midnight. A young man named Eutychus, sitting on a windowsill, fell asleep and plunged from the third floor (Acts 20:9-12). He was picked up dead, but Paul went down, embraced him, and said: *Do not be alarmed, for his life is in him* (Acts 20:10). Eutychus was restored to life, and the believers were greatly comforted (Acts 20:12). This miracle underscored the power of the gospel over death, affirming Paul's apostolic authority and offering a tangible sign of hope in the resurrection.[49] In the context of a small, vulnerable house church, this act of restoration was a source of encouragement and strengthened the believers' faith in God's life-giving power.

Acts 28:3-6 records that, after surviving a shipwreck, Paul gathered firewood on the island of Malta. A viper fastened onto his hand, and the locals expected him to die. But Paul shook off the snake and suffered no harm (Acts 28:5). The islanders changed their minds and said he was a god. This incident recalled Jesus' promise in Mark 16:18 that his followers would survive deadly things without harm.[50] This miracle demonstrated God's sovereign protection over Paul's life and Mission. It also served to elevate Paul's credibility among the islanders, preparing the way for gospel witness.

Acts 28:7-9 share another miracle performed by Paul, following the snakebite.[51] Paul was welcomed by Publius, the chief official of the island.

---

[48] Graham H. Twelftree, "Paul's Experience of the Miraculous," *The Evangelical Quarterly* 87/3 (January, 2015): 195-206.

[49] David H. Wenkel, "The Primacy of Preaching in the Resurrection of Eutychus in Acts 20,7-12," *Biblische Notizen* 197 (January, 2023): 95-110.

[50] Horatio Balch Hackett, "The Voyage and Shipwreck of Paul as Related by Luke: A Commentary on Acts 27:1-44; 28:16," *Bibliotheca Sacra and Theological Review* 7/28 (December, 1850): 743-771.

[51] M. David Litwa, "Paul the "god" in Acts 28: A Comparison with Philoctetes," *Journal of Biblical Literature* 136/3 (Fall, 2017): 707-726.

Paul healed his father, who was sick with fever and dysentery (Acts 28:8), and afterward many others who were ill on the island came and were cured (Acts 28:9).[52] This series of healings showed that even in unexpected and remote locations, the Mission of God continued through acts of compassion and healing. These miracles led to hospitality, favour, and the spreading of the gospel in a place Paul never planned to visit, illustrating that Mission includes both planned strategy and divine interruptions.

Mission Ecclesiology in Paul

Paul's understanding of the Church was deeply Missional. He saw the Church not only as a gathering of believers but as the living Body of Christ, formed and sent into the world for the work of God's Mission. In I Corinthians 12, Paul describes how believers are united by one Spirit into one body, each member being essential for the health and functioning of the whole: *Now you are the body of Christ and individually members of it* (I Corinthians 12:27). Similarly, in Ephesians 4:11-16, Paul explains that Christ gave various gifts as apostles, prophets, evangelists, pastors, and teachers to equip the saints for ministry and build up the body. The goal is that the Church may grow into maturity, united in faith and love, reflecting Christ to the world.[53] This vision of the Church highlights its role as a Missional community, shaped by Christ and called to serve His purposes.

To fulfil this Mission, Paul emphasized the role of spiritual gifts, which were given not for personal pride but for building up the Church and extending its witness. In Romans 12:4-8, Paul encourages believers to use their different gifts such as prophecy, service, teaching, encouragement, giving, leading, and showing mercy with diligence and humility. He writes: *We have gifts that differ according to the grace given to us* (Romans 12:6). In I Corinthians 12:7, he declares: *To each is given the manifestation of the Spirit for the common good.* These gifts are the Spirit's provision to empower the Church for both internal growth and outward Mission.[54] The proper use of these gifts demonstrates the unity and diversity of the Church and strengthens its capacity to carry out God's work in the world.

Paul also taught that the Church's witness must be visible in holiness and love. In Philippians 2:14-16, he urges believers to: *Do all things without murmuring and arguing, so that you may be blameless and innocent, children of God without blemish in the midst of a crooked and perverse generation, in*

---

[52] Joshua W. Jipp, "Hospitable Barbarians: Luke's Ethnic Reasoning in Acts 28:1-10," *The Journal of Theological Studies* 68/1 (December, 2017): 23-45.

[53] Michael Plekon, "*Creator Spiritus*: Paul Hinlicky on Pneumatology, Ecclesiology, and the Life of Holiness," *Pro Ecclesia* 26/2 (December, 2017): 159-62.

[54] Susann Liubinskas, "The Body of Christ in Mission: Paul's Ecclesiology and the Role of the Church in Mission," *Missiology* 41/4 (December, 2013): 402-15.

which you shine like stars in the world. Thus, for Paul, the Church bears public testimony to the transforming power of Christ. Likewise, in I Thessalonians 4:11-12, Paul instructs the Church to: *to aspire to live quietly, to mind your own affairs, and to work with your hands, as we directed you, so that you may behave properly toward outsiders.* Holiness in conduct and love in relationships are essential aspects of the Church's Missional identity.[55] The world is to see in the Church a reflection of God's character and a foretaste of God's coming Kingdom.

In addition to its witness, Paul saw the Church as playing an active role in supporting and participating in Mission. He thanked the Philippians for their *partnership in the gospel from the first day until now* (Philippians 1:5), acknowledging their partnership in his ministry. This support was both spiritual and material. In Romans 15:24-28, Paul writes of his plan to visit Rome on his way to Spain and of the financial collection he was taking from Gentile churches to help the believers in Jerusalem.[56] These examples show that local churches were not isolated but interconnected in a shared global Mission. Every congregation, regardless of size or location, had a part to play in advancing the gospel through prayer, giving, sending, and going.

Co-workers and Apostolic Teams

Paul's Mission was never an individual effort. From the beginning of his ministry, he worked within a collaborative Mission model, forming apostolic teams that helped plant and nurture churches across the Roman Empire.[57] Paul's co-workers included men and women from different backgrounds were all united by the call of God. Among his closest companions were Timothy, Titus, Silas, Barnabas, Luke, and the husband-wife team of Priscilla and Aquila. They were not simply assistants but trusted partners in the work of the gospel. In Acts 16, Timothy joins Paul's Mission in Lystra and becomes one of his most faithful co-workers (Acts 16:1-3). Titus is mentioned in several letters as a reliable leader and Missionary, particularly in Crete (Titus 1:4-5). Silas accompanied Paul during his second Missionary journey (Acts 15:40), while Barnabas was his early companion, especially on the first journey (Acts 13:1-3). Luke, the author of Acts, was also a part of Paul's team, as suggested by the "we" sections in Acts (e.g., Acts 16:10-17). Priscilla and Aquila played a key role in instructing Apollos and supporting the church in Corinth and Ephesus (Acts 18:18-26; Romans

[55] Jason B. Hood, "The Temple and the Thorn: 2 Corinthians 12 and Paul's Heavenly Ecclesiology," *Bulletin for Biblical Research* 21/3 (December, 2011): 357-370.

[56] Richard E. Oster, "'Congregations of the Gentiles' (Rom 16:4): A Culture-Based Ecclesiology in the Letters of Paul," *Restoration Quarterly* 40/1 (December, 1998): 39-52.

[57] David J. Bosch, *Transforming Mission: Paradigm Shifts in Theology of Mission Twentieth Anniversary Edition* (New York: Orbis Books, 2011), 126.

16:3-4). Paul's team approach shows his belief in shared ministry and the power of community in Mission.[58]

Notably, Paul also affirmed the role of women in Mission, highlighting their importance in the early Church. In Romans 16, Paul greets numerous women who laboured with him in the gospel.[59] Phoebe is introduced as "a deacon of the church at Cenchreae" and "a benefactor of many and of myself as well" (Romans 16:1-2). Junia is described, along with Andronicus, as "prominent among the apostles" (Romans 16:7), suggesting a significant Missionary role. Lydia, a businesswoman in Philippi, welcomed Paul into her home and helped establish the first Christian community in that city (Acts 16:14-15, 40).[60] These examples show that Paul did not limit gospel ministry to men alone but welcomed the Spirit's work through all believers. The inclusion of women in important roles challenges narrow views of ministry and reflects the inclusive nature of the gospel Paul preached.[61]

Paul's Mission teams were not only diverse but also built on mutual support, mentorship, and delegation. Paul trained and mentored younger leaders, entrusting them with significant responsibilities. For example, he left Titus in Crete "to put in order what remained to be done and to appoint elders in every town" (Titus 1:5). He urged Timothy to "guard the good treasure entrusted to you, with the help of the Holy Spirit" (II Timothy 1:14). Paul also wrote of sending co-workers to encourage and teach the churches, showing a model of Mission that was decentralized but unified in purpose. In Philippians 2:19-22, Paul commends Timothy for having "genuine concern" for the Philippians, saying, "I have no one like him." This relational investment reveals Paul's heart not only as a Missionary but also as a spiritual father, raising leaders for ongoing Mission.

Paul's approach to apostolic Mission highlights the importance of teamwork, diversity, mentorship, and pastoral care. His willingness to collaborate, empower others, and share ministry responsibilities reflects his belief that the Mission of God is too great for any one person to carry alone. Through his co-workers and apostolic teams, Paul established a model of Missional leadership that became a model rooted in relationship, shared vision, and the power of the Spirit at work in every believer.

---

[58] A. Behera, *Paul, The Tentmaking Missionary* (Kashmere Gate: ISPCK, 2002), 93-94.

[59] C. S. Keener, "Man and Woman," in *Dictionary of Paul and His Letters*, edited by Gerald F. Hawthorne and Ralph P. Martin (Illinois: InterVarsity Press, 1993), 431-432.

[60] C. C. Kroeger, "Women in the Early Church," in *The Dictionary of the Later New Testament and its Development*, edited by Ralph P. Martin and Peter H. David (Leicester: InterVarsity Press, 1995), 99-101.

[61] C. S. Keener, "Man and Woman," in *Dictionary of Paul and His Letters*...

Challenges in Paul's Mission

Paul's Mission was marked not only by remarkable growth and expansion but also by intense persecution and suffering. His ministry constantly involved hardship, which he saw not as a hindrance but as a sign of his participation in Christ's suffering. When writes to Corinthians, Paul lists the many trials he endured: *far more imprisonments, with countless floggings, and often near death. Five times I have received from the Jews the forty lashes minus one. Three times I was beaten with rods. Once I received a stoning. Three times I was shipwrecked; for a night and a day I was adrift at sea; on frequent journeys, in danger from rivers, danger from bandits, danger from my own people, danger from gentiles, danger in the city, danger in the wilderness, danger at sea, danger from false brothers and sisters; in toil and hardship, through many a sleepless night, hungry and thirsty, often without food, cold and naked* (II Corinthians 11:23-27). These hardships were not occasional but a regular part of Paul's life. He also faced life thread as it is mentioned in Acts as: *they stoned Paul and dragged him out of the city, supposing that he was dead* (Acts 14:19), but Paul re-entered the city and later told believers that: *It is through many persecutions that we must enter the kingdom of God* (Acts 14:22). Thus, for Paul, suffering was not accidental, it was part of the cost of faithfulness to Christ and a way to show the power of the gospel in weakness.

Another significant challenge came from opposition by both Jews and pagans. Paul's message that Jesus was the crucified and risen Messiah offended Jewish leaders and disrupted pagan society. In Acts 13:50, Jews in Pisidian Antioch stirred up persecution against Paul and Barnabas and drove them out of the region.[62] Similarly, in Acts 19:23-41, Paul's preaching in Ephesus threatened the business of idol-makers, leading to a public riot led by Demetrius the silversmith. These reactions reflect the disruptive nature of the gospel in cultures shaped by religious traditions and economic interests. Paul's Mission also challenged the status quo, calling Jews to believe in Jesus as the Messiah and calling Gentiles to turn away from idols.[63] The resulting conflict showed the spiritual battle behind his ministry and the radical call of the gospel to all peoples.

In addition to external hostility, Paul also faced serious internal conflicts within the Church, including theological crises and divisions. A major conflict occurred in Galatians 2 when Paul publicly opposed Peter for withdrawing

---

[62] Clare K. Rothschild, "Pisidian Antioch in Acts 13: The Denouement of the South Galatian Hypothesis," *Novum Testamentum* 54/4 (December, 2012): 334-353.

[63] C. L. Brinks, "'Great Is Artemis of the Ephesians': Acts 19:23-41 in Light of Goddess Worship in Ephesus," *The Catholic Biblical Quarterly* 71/4 (December, 2009): 776-794.

from Gentile believers under pressure from Jewish Christians. Paul writes: *But when Cephas came to Antioch, I opposed him to his face because he stood self-condemned* (Galatians 2:11). This controversy centred on whether Gentiles needed to follow the Jewish law to be full members of God's people. Paul defended the gospel of justification by faith, apart from works of the law.[64] Similarly, in I Corinthians 1-4, he addressed divisions in the church where members were aligning with different leaders, Paul, Apollos, Cephas, or Christ, undermining unity. Paul responded by pointing them back to the central message of the cross and the foolishness of worldly wisdom.[65] These conflicts tested Paul's leadership and revealed the importance of theological clarity and Christ-centred unity in the Church's Mission.

Paul also struggled with personal physical weakness, which he understood in light of the cross. In II Corinthians 12, he espouses that: *a thorn was given me in the flesh* (II Corinthians 12:7), but shares that it was *to keep me from being too elated* (II Corinthians 12:7). Despite pleading with the Lord to take it away, he heard the response: *My grace is sufficient for you, for power is made perfect in weakness* (II Corinthians 12:9). About this, Paul concludes as: *So I will boast all the more gladly of my weaknesses, so that the power of Christ may dwell in me* (II Corinthians 12:9). This deep insight shaped Paul's theology of Mission as God works through weakness, not strength. The cross, not human wisdom or power, is the centre of Paul's message and model. His own vulnerability became a testimony to the sufficiency of Christ's grace and the power of God to use fragile vessels for great purposes.

These various challenges, external persecution, cultural opposition, internal church conflicts, and personal weakness, did not defeat Paul. Rather, they helped him to perfect his Mission and deepened his dependence on Christ. His perfect conviction about the suffering is expressed when he writes: *We are afflicted in every way but not crushed, perplexed but not driven to despair, persecuted but not forsaken, struck down but not destroyed, always carrying around in the body the death of Jesus, so that the life of Jesus may also be made visible in our bodies* (II Corinthians 4:8-10). Thus, Paul's perseverance in the face of suffering demonstrates a Missiology rooted in the cross and sustained by the resurrection. His life and ministry reveal that Mission is not about ease or success by worldly standards, but about faithfulness to God's call, whatever the cost.

---

[64] Melancthon W. Jacobus, "Paul and His Teaching in Galatians 2:11-21," *The Biblical World* 24/5 (November, 1904): 351-358.

[65] Walter Ogle Fitch, "Paul, Apollos, Cephas, Christ," *Theology* 74/607 (December. 1971): 18-24.

Funding and Support of Paul's Mission

Paul's approach to funding his Mission reflects a balance of self-reliance, partnership, and theological integrity. One of the primary ways Paul supported himself was through tentmaking (Acts 18:1-3), a form of manual labour he engaged in during his Missionary travels.[66] In Acts 18:3, we read that Paul stayed and worked with Aquila and Priscilla in Corinth, "because he was of the same trade, he stayed with them, and they worked together, by trade they were tentmakers. Similarly, Paul reminds the church of his labour: *You remember our labor and toil, brothers and sisters; we worked night and day so that we might not burden any of you while we proclaimed to you the gospel of God* (I Thessalonians 2:9). Paul's tentmaking was not merely practical, it was Missiological.[67] It demonstrated his desire not to be a financial burden to new believers and to model a gospel that was not tied to personal gain.

At the same time, Paul welcomed and affirmed financial support from established churches that willingly partnered with him in the gospel. In Philippians 4:15-19, he praises the Philippian church for their unique generosity. This mutual giving and receiving formed a spiritual partnership grounded in love and Mission.[68] In II Corinthians 8-9, Paul also organized a collection among Gentile churches to support the poor in Jerusalem. He urged the Corinthians to give generously, reminding them in II Corinthians 9:7, *Each of you must give as you have made up your mind, not regretfully or under compulsion, for God loves a cheerful giver*. These passages reveal how financial giving was not transactional but an act of worship and solidarity in the Mission of God.[69]

Paul's writings show that his financial practices were governed by deep principles of generosity, integrity, and stewardship. Paul explains that he took great care in handling the offering: *We are making this arrangement lest anyone blame us about this generous gift that we are administering, for we are setting our minds on what is right not only before the Lord but also before the people* (II Corinthians 8:20-21). Paul believed that how money was handled in Mission mattered just as much as the money itself. He viewed all resources as belonging to God and to be managed with accountability. Generosity was a

---

[66] A. Behera, *Paul, The Tentmaking Missionary*..., 93-94.

[67] Samson Uytanlet, "Tentmaking: Paul's Missionary Strategy?," *Evangelical Missions Quarterly* 59/1 (January, 2023): 53-55.

[68] Woo Min Lee, "A Hybrid Christian Identity in Philippians 1:15-18," *HTS Theological Studies* 77/4 (January, 2021): 1-9.

[69] Alvaro Michelin Salomon, "Service, Stewardship, and Christian Communities in 2 Corinthians 8-9," *Journal of Latin American Theology* 13/2 (December, 2018): 51-65.

reflection of God's grace, not merely a financial transaction.[70] He taught that believers are stewards of God's blessings and that giving is an expression of their love, faith, and participation in the work of the gospel.

Final Vision and Legacy of Paul's Mission

Paul's passion for reaching unreached regions was a defining characteristic of his apostolic Mission. He never settled for ministering only in places where the gospel was already known. He writes: *Thus, I make it my ambition to proclaim the gospel, not where Christ has already been named, so that I do not build on someone else's foundation...But now, with no further place for me in these regions, I desire, as I have for many years, to come to you when I go to Spain* (Romans 15:20-24). This desire shows that Paul's Mission was not only pastoral but also pioneering. His heart was burdened for those who had never heard of Christ. The mention of Spain represents his vision of taking the gospel to the western edge of the Roman Empire. Paul saw Mission as an ever-expanding work, always moving outward to include new peoples and places.[71] His example challenges the Church to continually pursue the unreached and to think globally about God's saving purpose.

Another essential element of Paul's final vision was his hope for the full inclusion of Israel in the plan of salvation. In Romans 11:11-26, Paul explains that Israel's rejection of the gospel was not final but served a purpose in God's plan, to bring the Gentiles into the covenant. In this regard he writes: *I want you to understand this mystery...so that you may not claim to be wiser than you are: a hardening has come upon part of Israel until the full number of the gentiles has come in. And in this way all Israel will be saved* (Romans 11:25-26). Paul longed for a future restoration where Jews and Gentiles together would worship the Messiah. His understanding was not content with partial inclusion, rather, it pointed to a future where God's covenant promises to Israel would be fulfilled in Christ. This longing reflects Paul's deep love for his people (Romans 9:1-5) and his vision of a unified Church made up of all nations, including Israel.[72]

Paul's legacy through his letters became one of the most significant contributions to the Mission of the Church. There are thirteen letters of Paul in the New Testament. Nine were written to churches or groups of churches

---

[70] Cullen I. K. Story, "Nature of Paul's Stewardship with Special Reference to I and II Corinthians," *The Evangelical Quarterly* 48 (January, 1976): 212-229.

[71] Kelly Malone, "Broadening the Tent: Expanding the Strategic Use of Tent-Making in Cross-Cultural Mission," *Missiology* 42/2 (December, 2014): 195-206.

[72] Caroline Schleier Cutler, "New Creation and Inheritance: Inclusion and Full Participation in Paul's Letters to the Galatians and Romans," *Priscilla Papers* 30/2 (December, 2016): 21-29.

(Romans, I and II Corinthians, Galatians, Ephesians, Philippians, Colossians, I and II Thessalonians) and four to individuals (I and II Timothy, Titus, Philemon).[73] These epistles provide the theological foundation and practical guidance for Christian life and ministry. Through letters such as Romans, Galatians, Ephesians, and Corinthians, Paul articulated key doctrines such as justification by faith, the unity of the Church, and the nature of spiritual gifts.[74] These writings not only addressed immediate concerns but were also inspired by the Holy Spirit to serve future generations. His letters have equipped the Church with a practical framework for Mission, emphasizing grace, faith, reconciliation, and the role of the Church as a witness to the world. As II Timothy 3:16 affirms, *All scripture is inspired by God and is useful for teaching, for reproof, for correction, and for training in righteousness.*

Paul's martyrdom sealed his Missional life with ultimate faithfulness. When he writes to Timothy, written near the end of his life, Paul reflects on his journey with powerful words: *As for me, I am already being poured out as a libation, and the time of my departure has come. I have fought the good fight; I have finished the race; I have kept the faith. From now on there is reserved for me the crown of righteousness, which the Lord, the righteous judge, will give me on that day, and not only to me but also to all who have longed for his appearing* (II Timothy 4:6-8). Despite imprisonment, suffering, and loneliness, Paul remained faithful to his calling until death.[75] He died as a witness to Christ, believing that a crown of righteousness awaited him. His endurance in suffering and unwavering commitment to the gospel serve as a model for all Christians. His death was not a defeat but a testimony that the Mission of God is worth every cost.

Conclusion

The Mission of the Apostle Paul represents a powerful integration of theology and practice, deeply rooted in the gospel of Jesus Christ and guided by the leading of the Holy Spirit. Paul's Missiology shaped every aspect of his Mission methods, from his message of justification by faith (Romans 3:21-26) to his vision of the Church as the Body of Christ actively participating in God's redemptive plan (I Corinthians 12:12-27; Ephesians 4:11-16). His Missionary efforts were not abstract theological exercises but the living out of his deep convictions about the death and resurrection

---

[73] Tremple Longman III edits., *The Baker Illustrated Dictionary* (Grand Rapids: Baker Publishing Group, 2013), 1713.

[74] P. T. O' Brien, "Letters, Letter Forms," *The Dictionary of the Later New Testament and its Development*, edited by Ralph P. Martin and Peter H. David (Leicester: InterVarsity Press, 1995), 404.

[75] Frederick John Foakes-Jackson, "Evidence for the Martyrdom of Peter and Paul in Rome," *Journal of Biblical Literature* 46/1-2 (December, 1927): 74-78.

of Christ (I Corinthians 15:1-4), the inclusion of all nations in God's family (Galatians 3:28-29), and the urgent need to proclaim the gospel to all people (Romans 10:14-15). Paul's life and writings reveal a unified vision where doctrine and Mission work together in the service of God's eternal purpose in Christ (Ephesians 1:9-10). Paul also stands as a model of Christ-centred, Spirit-empowered, and contextually sensitive Mission. His identity and message were fully anchored in the person of Jesus Christ, whom he proclaimed as the crucified and risen Lord (Galatians 2:20; Philippians 3:8-10). Empowered by the Holy Spirit (Romans 15:18-19), Paul demonstrated spiritual discernment, boldness, and endurance in the face of suffering. At the same time, he adapted his methods to different cultural and religious settings without compromising the gospel. He became "all things to all people" for the sake of the gospel (I Corinthians 9:19-23), showing sensitivity to both Jewish and Gentile contexts (Romans 14:1-6; Acts 21:20-26). His use of local customs, language, and philosophical ideas such as quoting Greek poets in Athens (Acts 17:28) reveals a Missional posture that is both faithful and flexible.

17

Mission in General Epistles and Revelation
Witness, Persecution, Endurance and the Ultimate Triumph of God's Kingdom

The General Epistles and the Book of Revelation play a central role in shaping a comprehensive understanding of biblical Missiology. While much attention has been given to Mission in the Gospels, Acts, and Pauline letters, the General Epistles (Hebrews, James, I and II Peter, I, II and III John and Jude) and Revelation provide rich insights that are often overlooked. These Books reflect the Church's experience in the post-apostolic period, shaped by persecution, dispersion, doctrinal challenges, and the need for spiritual endurance.[1] In these challenging contexts, the *Missio Dei* is not abandoned, rather, it is reaffirmed and deepened through exhortations to faithful witness, hospitality, holiness, and hope in God's ultimate victory. Canonically, these writings serve the Church at a critical historical juncture since they were written to communities scattered across the Roman Empire, many of whom were enduring trials and social marginalization. Missiologically, the General Epistles and Revelation contribute to the broader narrative of the Mission of God by emphasizing key themes such as perseverance in suffering (Hebrews 12:1-3), love and hospitality (Hebrews 13:1-2; 3 John 1:5-8), truth and discernment (I John 4:1-6; Jude 1:3), and eschatological hope (James 5:7-8; Revelation 21:1-4). Thus, the General Epistles and Revelation highlights key elements such as witness, endurance, holiness, love, and hope that are the foundations of Christian Mission.

[1] Harry Gamble, The Redaction of the Pauline Letters and the Formation of the Pauline Corpus, *Journal of Biblical Literature* 94/3 (September, 1975): 403-418.

Authorship, Date, and Context of the General Epistles and Revelation

The General Epistles, also known as the Catholic Epistles, are addressed to a broader Christian audience rather than to specific individuals or churches, and they are considered non-Pauline letters. Their diverse backgrounds and purposes offer valued vision into the life and Mission of the early Church. Likewise, the Book of Revelation, though apocalyptic in nature, shares theological concerns that overlap with those of the General Epistles. Understanding their authorship, date, and historical context is essential for interpreting their Missional theology.

The Letter to the Hebrews is traditionally anonymous, though early suggestions of authorship included Paul, Barnabas, Luke, or Apollos. Modern scholarship generally agrees that the precise author remains unknown. It was likely written before AD 70, since the destruction of the Jerusalem temple is not mentioned, though some place it slightly later. The letter is addressed to Jewish Christians who were tempted to abandon their faith under pressure and return to Judaism. Its main purpose is to show the superiority of Christ, greater than angels, Moses, and the Levitical priesthood and to present Him as the perfect high priest who offered a once-for-all sacrifice. Hebrews encourages believers to persevere in faith, holding firmly to Christ as the fulfilment of God's promises and the mediator of a new covenant.[2]

James is traditionally attributed to James, the brother of Jesus and a leading personality in the Jerusalem church (Acts 15:13). While some question the authorship based on its polished Greek style, early Church tradition strongly supports James as the author. It was likely written between AD 45-62, before James's martyrdom. The letter addresses Jewish Christians facing trials and encourages a practical, living faith that reflects the values of the Kingdom of God in daily life.[3]

I Peter claims to be written by the apostle Peter and is addressed to believers scattered across Asia Minor. Many scholars accept Petrine authorship, though some suggest a later composition by a disciple or secretary of Peter. It was probably written in the early 60s AD, possibly from Rome, because of the reference to as Babylon in 5:13.[4] The epistle encourages perseverance in suffering, emphasizing the identity of Christians as a holy people with a Mission to declare God's praises (I Peter 2:9).

---

[2] David Lewis Allen, "The Authorship of Hebrews: Historical Survey of the Lukan Theory," *Criswell Theological Review* 8/2 (December, 2011): 3-18.

[3] Charles Keogh, "James Wrote You a Letter!: A Service on the Book of James," *Reformed Worship* 155 (December, 2025): 26-28.

[4] Fika Van Rensburg, "Constructing the Economic-Historic Context of 1 Peter: Exploring a Methodology," *HTS Theological Studies* 67/1 (January, 2011): 1-11.

II Peter, though also attributed to Peter, has faced greater scholarly scepticism due to its literary style, references to other New Testament texts, and its concern with combating false teaching. It may have been written in the late 60s AD if by Peter, or later in the early second century if by a follower.[5] The letter aims to reaffirm apostolic teaching and warn against distortions of the gospel, especially concerning the second coming of Christ.[6]

I John is anonymous but closely linked to the apostle John, traditionally understood as the author due to its thematic and linguistic similarity to the Gospel of John. It likely originated from the Johannine community in Ephesus around AD 85-95. The letter addresses internal divisions within the church, emphasizing love, truth, and adherence to the apostolic message as marks of authentic Christian identity. II John and III John are the shortest New Testament writings and are also attributed to the "elder," widely identified as the apostle John or a leader within the Johannine tradition. They were likely written around the same time as I John (AD 85-95). II John warns against deceivers who deny the incarnation, while III John encourages hospitality toward true gospel workers, contrasting them with those who reject apostolic authority.[7]

Jude, who identifies himself as the brother of James, is traditionally considered a relative of Jesus. The letter, written possibly between AD 60-80, addresses urgent concerns about false teachers who have infiltrated the Christian community. Jude draws on Jewish apocalyptic imagery to call believers to contend for the faith and remain faithful to God's Mission amid deception and moral decline.[8]

The Book of Revelation is attributed to John, who identifies himself as a servant of Jesus exiled on the island of Patmos (Revelation 1:9). While many early Church fathers viewed this John as the apostle, others suggested a different prophetic figure known as "John the Seer." Revelation was likely written during the reign of Emperor Domitian, around AD 95-96, a time of increasing persecution.[9] The book uses vivid apocalyptic imagery to reveal

---

[5] Terrance Callan, "Reading the Earliest Copies of 2 Pete," *Biblica* 93/3 (2012): 427-450.

[6] Sam, Whittaker, "Inaugurated Eschatology and the Petrine Imagination: An Argument for the Unity of 1 and 2 Peter," *Midwestern Journal of Theology* 23/2 (January, 2024): 139-162.

[7] James C. Pakala, "A Librarian's Comments on Commentaries 23 1 John, 2 John, 3 John," *Presbyterion* 33/1 (December, 2007): 44-48.

[8] C. I. David Joy, "Anatomy of the Socio-Cultural Context of the Epistle of Jude," *Bangalore Theological Forum* 52/1 (January, 2020): 43-59.

[9] Vern S. Poythress, "Johannine Authorship and the Use of Intersentence Conjunctions in the Book of Revelation," *The Westminster Theological Journal* 47/2 (December, 1985): 329-336.

the spiritual conflict between the Kingdom of God and the forces of evil, encouraging the Church to remain faithful and hopeful in its witness, even in the face of suffering and martyrdom.

The Canonization of the General Epistles and Revelation

The process of canonization refers to the recognition and collection of certain writings as inspired Scripture, forming what we now call the New Testament. The General Epistles and the Book of Revelation had a unique and yet complex journey toward full acceptance in the canon. Unlike the Pauline letters, which were widely circulated and recognized early in church history, the General Epistles and Revelation were accepted gradually due to various historical, geographical, and theological reasons.[10]

One reason for the delayed recognition of the General Epistles was their limited early circulation. These letters were often addressed to specific communities or individuals and did not spread as widely or quickly as the letters of Paul. II and III John are very brief and personal, and Jude closely resembles II Peter, leading to questions about originality and authorship. James and II Peter were also slow to be accepted in some churches because of uncertainties about who wrote them. Likewise, Hebrews did not name its author, and its theological content, especially its emphasis on the high priesthood of Christ, raised questions among early readers.[11] However, over time, the theological depth and consistency of these writings with apostolic teaching contributed to their acceptance.

The Book of Revelation also faced difficulties in the canonization process. While it was accepted early in the churches of Asia Minor, it was viewed with caution in other regions, especially because of its symbolic and apocalyptic style. Some early Christians were uncomfortable with its vivid imagery and strong judgments. Others feared that its content could be misused by radical groups.[12] However, Revelation's strong testimony to the victory of Christ, its encouragement to persevere under persecution, and its final vision of God's Kingdom aligned clearly with the broader message of the New Testament. Church fathers such as Irenaeus (late 2nd century)

---

[10] Robert D. Heaton, "Toward the New Testament Canon as Fourth-Century Invention: The Scriptural List of Athanasius and Its Reverberations," *Religion & Theology* 30/1-2 (December, 2023): 30-54.

[11] Donald W. Riddle, "Factors in the Formation of the New Testament Canon," *The Journal of Religion* 19/4 (October, 1939): 330-345.

[12] Andrew R. Koperski, "Eusebius, Revelation, and Its Place in the New Testament Canon," *Journal of Early Christian History* 11/3 (January, 2021): 79-94.

strongly supported Revelation's apostolic authority, affirming that it was written by the Apostle John.[13]

By the fourth century, church councils such as the Synod of Hippo (393 AD) and the Council of Carthage (397 AD) affirmed the twenty-seven books of the New Testament, including the General Epistles and Revelation.[14] This process did not grant these books authority but rather recognized the authority they already had in the life of the Church.[15] The criteria for inclusion in the canon included apostolic authorship or connection, theological consistency with the gospel, widespread use in worship, and spiritual fruitfulness in the life of the Christian community.[16] Thus, the canonization of the General Epistles and Revelation was a gradual process shaped by historical use, theological evaluation, and communal discernment.

Mission in the General Epistles

The General Epistles, James, I and II Peter, I, II, and III John, and Jude, provides a diverse yet coherent contribution to Missiology in the New Testament. These letters, written to scattered and often persecuted Christian communities, reflect a deeply practical and ecclesial approach to Missional life. Unlike the Pauline epistles, which often address specific congregational issues or doctrinal concerns, the General Epistles emphasize how the Church is to live out its faith in public and communal settings manifested by suffering, marginalization, and moral challenge. In this way, they articulate a form of Mission that is both embodied and ethical one that witnesses to the gospel not only through proclamation but through love, holiness, endurance, and communal faithfulness. Each epistle contributes uniquely to the understanding of Mission by highlighting key themes such as faith expressed through works, care for the poor, speech that builds community, the vision of the Church as a chosen people called to declare God's praises even while suffering as exiles in a hostile world, and the emphasis on truth and love as central to the Church's identity and its Missional calling to discern, protect, and support the gospel. Together, the General Epistles expand the scope of New Testament Missiology by integrating theological

---

[13] Charles A. Gieschen, "The Relevance of the Homologoumena and Antilegomena Distinction for the New Testament Canon Today: Revelation as a Test Case," *Concordia Theological Quarterly* 79/3-4 (December, 2015): 279-300.

[14] Bruce M. Metzger, *The Canon of the New Testament: Its Origin, Development, and Significance* (Oxford: Clarendon Press, 1987), 211-218.

[15] F. F. Bruce, *The Canon of Scripture* (Downers Grove: InterVarsity Press, 1988), 230-236.

[16] Philip Schaff, *History of the Christian Church, vol. 3: Nicene and Post-Nicene Christianity* (Grand Rapids: Eerdmans, 1910), 607-610.

reflection with ethical practice, showing that the Church's witness is most powerful when it is rooted in Christlike living and sustained communal love.

Mission in Hebrews

The Mission of the Church in the Book of Hebrews begins with its Christological focus. The letter reveals that God's Mission in the world is centred on Jesus Christ, who brings humanity into right relationship with God through his unique role and redemptive work. Rather than presenting Mission as a human effort alone, Hebrews roots it in God's initiative, God sends Jesus into the world to accomplish salvation.[17] This divine sending reflects the broader biblical theme of the *Missio Dei*. Through Jesus, God reveals divine purposes and invites believers to participate in His redemptive work. In this way, the Mission of the Church is inseparable from who Christ is and what He has done.

Secondly, the Book of Hebrews identifies Jesus in a dual role that has direct implications for Mission: *Therefore, brothers and sisters, holy partners in a heavenly calling, consider that Jesus, the apostle and high priest of our confession* (Hebrews 3:1). The word apostle means "one who is sent," emphasizing that Jesus is sent by the Father with a divine Mission to bring salvation to the world.[18] As high priest, Jesus mediates between God and humanity, offering Himself as the perfect sacrifice and enabling access to God.[19] These two roles together provide a model for Christian Mission: like Jesus, the Church is sent into the world (apostolic), and like Jesus, it serves as a priestly community, interceding, witnessing, and embodying God's holiness. Therefore, the Mission of the Church is patterned after Christ's own Mission.

Third, the Book of Hebrews presents suffering not as contrary to God's Mission but as central to its fulfilment. Jesus' redemptive suffering is portrayed as the means through which salvation is made possible for all. The writer declares: *But we do see Jesus, who for a little while was made lower than the angels, now crowned with glory and honour because of the suffering of death, so that by the grace of God he might taste death for everyone. It was fitting that God, for whom and through whom all things exist, in bringing*

[17] David Stephen Schrock, "Resurrection and Priesthood: Christological Soundings from the Book of Hebrews," *The Southern Baptist Journal of Theology* 18/4 (December, 2014): 89-114.

[18] Joey McCollum, "Textual Criticism in the Gaps: The Likelihood of P46's Readings in Galatians 3:1 and 4:17, Hebrews 11:4, and Philippians 1," *Novum Testamentum* 66/2 (December, 2024): 257-278.

[19] David M. Moffitt, "Jesus as Interceding High Priest and Sacrifice in Hebrews: A Response to Nicholas Moore," *Journal for the Study of the New Testament* 42/4 (December, 2020): 542-552.

many children to glory, should make the pioneer of their salvation perfect through sufferings (Hebrews 2:9-10). Through suffering, Jesus identifies fully with humanity and becomes the "pioneer" of salvation. This sets a Missional paradigm for the Church that Mission involves identification with the broken, and suffering becomes a means of witness and transformation, not something to be avoided at all costs.

Fourth, the Mission in Hebrews is portrayed as a journey of faith, likened to a pilgrimage toward God's eternal city. Believers are not static citizens of this world but pilgrims moving toward a heavenly homeland. This image strengthens the Church's Missional identity as a people living in hope, pressing forward through trials. The journey motif emphasizes endurance and faithfulness in the face of hardship.[20] Mission is not only about sending others out but about remaining faithful as we travel together toward God's promised future. The pilgrim Church witnesses by how it lives, by faith, not by sight and by its confident hope in God's eternal purposes. The theme of pilgrimage is clearly expressed in Hebrews 11 and 13. The saints of old are commended for living as strangers in a land not their own: *All of these died in faith without having received the promises...They confessed that they were strangers and foreigners on the earth... But as it is, they desire a better country, that is, a heavenly one. Therefore, God is not ashamed to be called their God; indeed, he has prepared a city for them* (Hebrews 11:13, 16). This theme is echoed in the concluding chapter as: *For here we have no lasting city, but we are looking for the city that is to come* (Hebrews 13:14). The Church's identity as sojourners calls it to live in distinction from the world, witnessing to a greater reality yet to come.[21] This Missional identity invites the Church to hold loosely to earthly attachments and to live in faithful expectation, pointing others toward the heavenly city.

Fifth, one of the most direct Missional exhortations in Hebrews is the call to endurance and corporate faithfulness, particularly in the face of suffering (Hebrews 2:14-18; 4:14-16; 10:23-25; 12:1-3).[22] *Let us hold fast to the confession of our hope without wavering, for he who has promised is faithful. And let us consider how to provoke one another to love and good deeds, not neglecting to meet together, as is the habit of some, but encouraging one another, and all the more as you see the Day approaching* (Hebrews 10:23-25). This call is grounded in a shared confession and a

[20] Sean Winter, "Journey and Rest: Hebrews, Pilgrimage, and the Work of Theological Education," *Pacifica* 28/2 (January, 2015): 192-207.

[21] Paul B. Decock, Migration as a Basic Image for the Life of Faith: The Letter to the Hebrews, Philo and Origen, *Neotestamentica* 51/1 (2017): 129-150.

[22] Emma Ford, "Our Suffering, Sympathetic High Priest: Accomplishments and Implications of Christ's Incarnation in Hebrews 2:14-18 and 4:14-16," *Presbyterion* 47/1 (December, 2021): 127-133.

communal Mission.[23] The author also reminds readers of their past struggles: *But recall those earlier days when, after you had been enlightened, you endured a hard struggle with sufferings...Do not, therefore, abandon that confidence of yours; it brings a great reward* (Hebrews 10:32, 35).[24] Mission here is expressed not only through bold proclamation but through enduring faith and mutual encouragement, which testify to God's sustaining power.

Sixth, love and hospitality are essential aspects of Mission in Hebrews, reflecting the communal and outward-facing nature of the Church's witness (Hebrews 13:1-2). The Christian community is encouraged to practice mutual care and openness, especially toward strangers. These acts reflect God's character and create space for divine encounter. Mission is not always public or dramatic; it often takes the form of small, faithful acts that embody God's love in everyday life. Sacrificial love demonstrates the gospel in tangible ways and invites others into the community of grace.[25] In Hebrews, love and hospitality are presented not as optional virtues but as integral to Christian witness in the world.

Seventh, the Missional life according to Hebrews also involves a willingness to suffer disgrace for the sake of Christ, following his example outside the camp and bearing his reproach (Hebrews 13:12-13).[26] The author writes: *Therefore, Jesus also suffered outside the city gate in order to sanctify the people by his own blood. Let us then go to him outside the camp and bear the abuse he endured* (Hebrews 13:12-13). The image of going "outside the camp" recalls Old Testament sacrificial rituals and the marginalization of the unclean.[27] By applying this image to Jesus and to Christian discipleship, Hebrews calls believers to a radical form of Mission, one that embraces suffering and shame for the sake of witness.[28] Thus, to follow Jesus in Mission means being willing to step outside of cultural acceptance and religious comfort in order to be where Christ is, among the rejected and hurting.

---

[23] D. A. Hayes, "The Practical Outcome of the Epistle to the Hebrews. (Heb. 10:19-25.)," *The Biblical World* 24/6 (December, 1904): 443-447.

[24] Justus A. Freeman, "'Those in Prison': The 'Least of These' in Hebrews 10:32-35 and 13:1-3," *The Journal of Biblical Pentecostalism* 2/2 (December, 2021): 5-15.

[25] Paul Hartog, "Abraham and the Rhetoric of Hospitality and Foreignness in Hebrews and 1 Clement," *Science et Esprit* 72/3 (December, 2020): 281-296.

[26] Ched E. Spellman, "When Hope Screams: Learning How to Suffer as Sons from the Book of Hebrews," *Southwestern Journal of Theology* 53/2 (December, 2011): 112-134.

[27] Edwin A. Schick, "Priestly Pilgrims: Mission Outside the Camp in Hebrews," *Currents in Theology and Mission* 16/5 (December, 1989): 372-376.

[28] Mi Sun Kim, "What Is the Meaning of the Book of Hebrews' Call to 'Suffer Outside the Camp' Both Then and Now?," *Journal of Korean Christian Theology* 97 (January, 2015): 127-145.

Finally, Hebrews ties together worship and Mission through the practice of praise, hospitality, and good deeds.[29] The author expresses by saying: *Let mutual love continue. Do not neglect to show hospitality to strangers, for by doing that some have entertained angels without knowing it* (Hebrews 13:1-2). Later, the author adds: *Through him, then, let us continually offer a sacrifice of praise to God, that is, the fruit of lips that confess his name. Do not neglect to do good and to share what you have, for such sacrifices are pleasing to God* (Hebrews 13:15-16). Mission is thus both doxological and ethical, it involves both worshiping God and serving others.[30] The Church's praise must be matched by practical expressions of love and generosity. Such actions are seen as "sacrifices" pleasing to God, demonstrating that Mission is not only about going out but also about how the Church lives out the gospel through ordinary acts of kindness and communal life.[31]

Mission in James

The central concern of James is that 'faith must be demonstrated through action.' In James 2:14-26, he strongly argues that faith without works is incomplete and ineffective: *What good is it, my brothers and sisters, if you say you have faith but do not have works? Can faith save you?* (James 2:14). James illustrates this through the practical example of responding to someone in need: *If a brother or sister is naked and lacks daily food... and yet you do not supply their bodily needs, what is the good of that?* (James 2:15-16). *He concludes that: faith by itself, if it has no works, is dead* (James 2:17). Drawing on examples from Abraham and Rahab, James demonstrates that true faith is always active and embodied. This view of Mission challenges any separation between belief and practice.[32] Mission is not merely the proclamation of truth but the living out of that truth in acts of mercy, justice, and service to others.

Secondly, James emphasizes that authentic faith must be visibly expressed in the life of the believer. Faith is not only a matter of correct belief but of faithful living: *You believe that God is one; you do well. Even the demons believe and shudder* (James 2:19). This penetrating statement reveals that intellectual belief is not enough, but what God desires is faith that

---

[29] James W. Thompson, "Drawing Near: Corporate Worship in the Epistle to the Hebrews," *Restoration Quarterly* 63/1 (December, 2021): 1-9.

[30] Barry Clyde Joslin, "Theology Unto Doxology: New Covenant Worship in Hebrews," *The Southern Baptist Journal of Theology* 24/1 (December, 2020): 69-82.

[31] Joshua Caleb Hutchens, "Christian Worship in Hebrews 12:28 as Ethical and Exclusive," *Journal of the Evangelical Theological Society* 59/3 (December, 2016): 507-522.

[32] Thorwald Lorenzen, "Faith without Works Does Not Count before God: James 2:14-26," *The Expository Times* 89/8 (December, 1978): 231-235.

expresses itself in love (cf. Galatians 5:6).[33] By using Abraham's willingness to offer Isaac and Rahab's courageous protection of the spies as examples, James affirms that faith expresses itself in obedient and courageous acts: *For just as the body without the spirit is dead, so faith without works is also dead* (James 2:26). Mission, then, is not fulfilled by belief alone but by the Church's active, loving response to God's call in everyday life.[34] The Church's service becomes a visible sign of God's presence in the world.

Third, James calls the Church to a Mission of justice, with particular concern for the poor and the oppressed (James 1:27; 2:1-7). *Religion that is pure and undefiled before God, the Father, is this: to care for orphans and widows in their distress, and to keep oneself unstained by the world* (James 1:27). This reveals that authentic religion is not defined by ritual but by justice, compassion, and moral purity.[35] James also condemns the unjust practices of the rich who exploit workers: *Listen! The wages of the labourers who mowed your fields, which you kept back by fraud, cry out...You have condemned and murdered the righteous one, who does not resist you* (James 5:4, 6). The Church is thus called to stand in solidarity with the marginalized, to confront exploitation, and to model economic and social justice as a witness to the kingdom of God.[36] Mission includes both proclaiming good news and practicing justice that reflects God's righteous character.

Fourth, James presents Mission as a way of life shaped by God's wisdom, marked by purity, peace, and humility (James 1:5-8 and 3:13-18). Mission is not merely about outward actions but also about the inner qualities that shape the life of the community.[37] The Church is called to embody divine wisdom that leads to peace, purity, and humility. This wisdom stands in contrast to worldly ambition and conflict. Mission, therefore, involves living with integrity, humility, and peace as a witness to God's presence and truth.[38] A wise community becomes a Missional community by showing the world a different way to live, one rooted in God's character rather than human pride.

---

[33] Michael L. Sweeney, "James 2:18-26: Diatribe or Dishonor," *The Catholic Biblical Quarterly* 85/3 (December, 2023): 524-539.

[34] Vasiliki Limberis, "The Provenance of the Caliphate Church: James 2:17-26 and Galatians Reconsidered," *The Greek Orthodox Theological Review* 64/1-2 (December, 2019): 143-172.

[35] Mariam J. Kamell, "The Implications of Grace for The Ethics of James," *Biblica* 92/2 (2011): 274-287.

[36] Joseph Daniel Peters and Bradley Wayne Ellison, "James' Warning Against Inauthentic Faith: Confronting the Actions of the Wealthy (James 5:1-6)," *Eleutheria* 8/2 (December, 2025): 135-150.

[37] David W. Perkins, "The Wisdom We Need: James 1:5-8, 3:13-18," *The Theological Educator* 34 (December, 1986): 17-25.

[38] David W. Perkins, "The Wisdom We Need: James 1:5-8, 3:13-18..., 17-25.

Fifth, James describes the kind of wisdom that aligns with God's Mission as being pure, peace-loving, gentle, open to reason, full of mercy and good fruits, impartial, and sincere: *But the wisdom from above is first pure, then peaceable, gentle, willing to yield, full of mercy and good fruits, without a trace of partiality or hypocrisy* (James 3:17). This wisdom produces a *harvest of righteousness" and is "sown in peace for those who make peace* (James 3:18). Unlike worldly wisdom marked by envy and selfish ambition, God's wisdom fosters reconciliation, humility, and mercy. This passage calls the Church to be a peace-making and peace-loving community.[39] Mission in this context is not aggressive or manipulative but gentle and fruitful. When Christians embody this wisdom, they reflect the character of Christ and become a witness to God's reconciling Mission in a divided world.

Sixth, James strongly emphasizes the importance of speech in the life of faith and Mission, warning that the tongue, though small, holds great power to build or destroy (James 3:1-12). He instructs believers by saying that: *Let everyone be quick to listen, slow to speak, slow to anger; for your anger does not produce God's righteousness* (James 1:19-20). Speech has power, and the community must be careful in how words are used. In James 3:1-12, the tongue is described as a small but powerful member: *The tongue is a fire... With it we bless the Lord and Father, and with it we curse those who are made in the likeness of God* (James 3:6, 9). This contradiction reveals a major challenge to Christian witness. Words can either build up or destroy. Therefore, responsible and gracious speech is essential for communal harmony and for the Church's credibility in Mission.[40] A community that uses words to encourage, teach, and reconcile offers a powerful witness to the transforming grace of God.

Seventh, a key dimension of Mission in James is the call to repentance and restoration, urging believers to turn from sin and to help bring back those who wander from the truth (James 4:7-10; 5:19-20). James does not ignore sin within the believing community but urges believers to deal with it in love. This internal concern is part of the Church's wider witness. A community that repents and restores reflects the mercy and justice of God. Mission involves not only reaching the world but also caring for the spiritual health of the Church. Holiness and humility are part of the Church's Missional calling.[41] The call to repentance becomes a sign that God's grace is active and available to all who return.

---

[39] Rudy Taylor, "True Faith and Wisdom: James 3:13-4:10," *Brethren Life and Thought* 65/1 (December, 2020); 75-90.

[40] Andrea L. Robinson, "Reflecting the Image of God through Speech: Genesis 1-3 in James 3:1-12," *Evangelical Review of Theology* 44/4 (January, 2020): 313-323.

[41] William L. Blevins, "A Call to Repent, Love Others, and Remember God: James 4," *Review & Expositor* 83/3 (December, 1986): 419-426.

Eighth, James closes his letter with a deeply pastoral and Missional appeal, calling the community to pray, care for the suffering, and restore those who have strayed, thus participating in God's redemptive work (James 5:13-20): *My brothers and sisters, if anyone among you wanders from the truth and is brought back by another, you should know that whoever brings back a sinner from wandering will save the sinner's soul from death and will cover a multitude of sins* (James 5:19-20). Mission is thus, not only directed outward to the world but also inward toward the community itself. Bringing back someone who has strayed is a redemptive act that aligns with God's Mission to seek and save the lost. This verse emphasizes that every believer shares a responsibility in the spiritual care of others. Such restorative action embodies grace, mercy, and truth. It is a form of Mission that demonstrates God's heart for reconciliation.

Finally, James affirms that Mission includes the ongoing spiritual restoration of the Church, as believers are called to mutual confession, intercessory prayer, and the pursuit of communal wholeness (James 5:16-20). Spiritual drift is a reality, and believers are called to engage one another in love, prayer, and truth. The community must not ignore sin or disengage from those who are struggling. Instead, it must reflect God's compassion by actively seeking to restore. Restoration is not about judgment but about salvation and healing. When the Church prioritizes spiritual restoration, it becomes a sign of God's renewing work in the world. This inward focus is deeply connected to outward Mission. A spiritually restored Church becomes a credible and powerful witness to the world.

Mission in I and II Peter

The First Letter of Peter addresses Christians who are dispersed across various regions in Asia Minor, calling them "exiles" (I Peter 1:1). This term conveys both geographical and spiritual meaning, highlighting the Church's marginal status in society and its distinct identity as citizens of God's Kingdom. The sense of being exiles does not imply aimless wandering but a purposeful calling. These believers live under social pressure and persecution, yet Peter affirms that their scattered condition is part of God's providential plan. Their identity as exiles is foundational to their Mission: they are not of the world, yet they are sent into the world to reflect God's glory.[42] As such, their distinctiveness becomes their witness, especially in times of suffering and misunderstanding.

Secondly, Peter grounds the Church's Mission in its covenantal identity, drawing on Old Testament language to describe believers as a chosen

[42] Brett M. McDonald, "Exile, Suffering, and Holiness: The Use of Psalm 34 in 1 Peter," *Presbyterion* 48/2 (December, 2022): 67-84.

race, a royal priesthood, and a holy nation called to declare God's praises (I Peter 2:9-10; II Peter 1:4).[43] He writes: *But you are a chosen race, a royal priesthood, a holy nation, God's own people, in order that you may proclaim the mighty acts of him who called you out of darkness into his marvellous light* (I Peter 2:9). The Church is not merely a gathered community for worship or fellowship but a people set apart to declare God's redemptive work. Peter continues: *Once you were not a people, but now you are God's people; once you had not received mercy, but now you have received mercy* (I Peter 2:10). This divine transformation commissions the Church to be a Missionary community, testifying to God's grace not only in word but through a transformed communal life.[44] Mission, then, begins with being and flows into proclaiming.

Third, Peter exhorts believers to embrace their identity as spiritual exiles and sojourners in this world, called to live honourably among the nations while abstaining from sinful desires (I Peter 2:11-12). He addresses them as "exiles of the Dispersion" (I Peter 1:1) and later urges that: *Beloved, I urge you as aliens and exiles to abstain from the desires of the flesh that wage war against the soul* (I Peter 2:11). These titles remind the Church that it does not belong to the prevailing cultural or political systems but to a heavenly kingdom. The call to live as sojourners emphasizes the temporary nature of earthly life and the importance of living with eternal purpose. Such a mindset cultivates a Missional posture of humility, holiness, and detachment from worldly corruption.[45] The Christian life becomes a visible signpost of God's Kingdom, pointing others toward a higher reality.

Fourth, a central theme in I Peter is the call to bear witness through both holy living and faithful endurance in suffering, reflecting Christ's own example (I Peter 3:15-17; 4:12-16). Peter reframes suffering not as a sign of divine abandonment but as a vital aspect of Christian discipleship and Mission. He urges the believers not to retaliate when insulted or mistreated but instead to endure suffering for doing good.[46] This form of patient endurance becomes a powerful testimony to the world. Peter writes: *But even if you do suffer for doing what is right, you are blessed. Do not fear what they fear, and do not be intimidated, but in your hearts sanctify Christ as Lord* (I Peter 3:14-15a). Believers are instructed to: *always be ready to make your defence to anyone who demands from you an accounting for the hope that is in you,*

---

[43] Wolters, Albert M. "'Partners of the Deity': A Covenantal Reading of 2 Peter 1:4," *Calvin Theological Journal* 25/1 (December, 1990): 28-44.

[44] Wolters, Albert M. "'Partners of the Deity': A Covenantal Reading…

[45] Brett M. McDonald, "Exile, Suffering, and Holiness…

[46] Gordon E. Kirk, "Endurance in Suffering in 1 Peter," *Bibliotheca Sacra* 138/549 (December, 1981): 46-56.

yet do it with gentleness and reverence (I Peter 3:15b-16). Here, suffering becomes an occasion for gospel proclamation, not through argument alone but through a life that reflects Christ's humility and strength. Peter draws a close parallel between Christ's sufferings and the Christian experience: *For it is better to suffer for doing good, if suffering should be God's will, than to suffer for doing evil. For Christ also suffered for sins once for all, the righteous for the unrighteous, in order to bring you to God* (I Peter 3:17-18). Furthermore, suffering is not only expected but welcomed as participation in the life of Christ: *Beloved, do not be surprised at the fiery ordeal that is taking place among you...but rejoice insofar as you are sharing Christ's sufferings* (I Peter 4:12-13).[47] Such suffering strengthens the Church and deepens its credibility before the watching world.[48] By responding to hostility with holiness, the Church embodies the cross-shaped nature of Mission, where weakness becomes a witness and injustice is answered with grace.

Fifth, Peter emphasizes that Christian character is itself a form of Mission: *Conduct yourselves honourably among the Gentiles, so that, though they malign you as evildoers, they may see your honourable deeds and glorify God when he comes to judge* (I Peter 2:12). In a context where the Church was misunderstood or slandered, good behaviour served as a living defence of the gospel. He also encourages Christian wives to witness through conduct: *so that, even if some of them do not obey the word, they may be won over without a word by their wives' conduct, when they see the purity and reverence of your lives* (I Peter 3:1-2). The witness of holiness and quiet strength demonstrates the transforming power of grace.[49] Mission here is not only verbal proclamation but a lifestyle that points others to God. Sixth, Peter's letters place strong emphasis on hope and the return of Christ, shaping the Church's Mission with an eschatological perspective that calls believers to live in holiness and expectation (I Peter 1:3-5, 13; II Peter 3:11-14). For Peter, Christian Mission is not just a response to current needs but a forward-looking participation in God's future kingdom. The hope of salvation is not abstract optimism but a living reality grounded in the resurrection of Jesus Christ. As Peter declares: *Blessed be the God and Father of our Lord Jesus Christ! By his great mercy he has given us a new birth into a living hope through the resurrection of Jesus Christ from the dead* (I Peter 1:3). This living hope is not only personal but communal and cosmic in scope. It orients the Church toward *an inheritance that is imperishable, undefiled, and unfading, kept in heaven for you* (I Peter 1:4),

---

[47] J. L. de Villiers, "Joy in Suffering in 1 Peter," *Neotestamentica* 9 (1975): 64-86.

[48] Gordon E. Kirk, "Endurance in Suffering in 1 Peter..., 46-56.

[49] Earl J. Richard, "Honorable Conduct among the Gentiles: A Study of the Social Thought of 1 Peter," *Word & World* 24/4 (December, 2004): 412-420.

thereby shaping its life and witness in the present. This eschatological hope is not passive waiting but active preparation. The Mission of the Church is energized by the reality that time is moving toward the full revelation of God's kingdom.[50] In II Peter, this hope is clarified with theological urgency: *The Lord is not slow about his promise... but is patient with you, not wanting any to perish, but all to come to repentance* (II Peter 3:9). The apparent delay of Christ's return is actually a divine opportunity for Mission. In this context, the Church is to live with holy expectation and Missional urgency: *Since all these things are to be dissolved in this way, what sort of persons ought you to be in leading lives of holiness and godliness...while you are waiting for these things, strive to be found by him at peace, without spot or blemish* (II Peter 3:11, 14). The eschatological vision in Peter calls the Church to live in light of eternity, engaging the world with boldness, integrity, and the hope of the gospel.[51]

Seventh, Peter begins with a doxology that sets the tone for Christian hope, praising God for the new birth into a living hope through the resurrection of Jesus Christ from the dead: *Blessed be the God and Father of our Lord Jesus Christ! By his great mercy he has given us a new birth into a living hope through the resurrection of Jesus Christ from the dead* (I Peter 1:3). This hope points toward *an inheritance that is imperishable, undefiled, and unfading, kept in heaven for you* (I Peter 1:4). This future inheritance motivates believers to remain steadfast and to carry out their Mission with confidence. As they endure trials, they do so with the assurance that they are *being protected by the power of God through faith for a salvation ready to be revealed in the last time* (I Peter 1:5).[52] This forward-looking faith sustains a resilient, Missional Church.

Finally, in II Peter, the delay of Christ's return is not portrayed as a failure but as an expression of divine patience, allowing more people the opportunity to repent and be saved (II Peter 3:8-9). *But do not ignore this one fact, beloved, that with the Lord one day is like a thousand years, and a thousand years are like one day* (II Peter 3:8). Peter explains that *The Lord is not slow about his promise...but is patient with you, not wanting any to perish, but all to come to repentance* (II Peter 3:9). This waiting period has a Missional purpose: it allows more time for people to hear the gospel

---

[50] D. Edmond Hiebert, "Selected Studies from 1 Peter: Pt 3, Living in the Light of Christ's Return: An Exposition of 1 Peter 4:7-11," *Bibliotheca Sacra* 139/555 (December, 1982): 243-254.

[51] Adetola Ipadeola, "Eschatological Tension between Romans 8:19-22 and 2 Peter 3:10-12: A Reorientation of the Church toward Responsive Sustainable Development," *Ogbomoso Journal of Theology* 21/1 (December, 2016): 43-56.

[52] Ronaldo Silveira Motta, "Blessed Be God-The Doxology and Orthopraxy Presented in 1 Peter 1 and 2," *Artistic Theologian* 8 (December, 2020); 117-118.

and repent.[53] Therefore, believers are urged: *While you are waiting for these things, strive to be found by him at peace, without spot or blemish* (II Peter 3:14). The Church is called to live in light of eternity, actively engaging in God's Mission while anticipating the new heavens and new earth.[54] Eschatological hope and urgency energize the Church to be faithful in word, deed, and holy expectation.

Mission in Johannine Epistles

The Johannine epistles begin with a strong emphasis on the Mission of proclamation that leads to fellowship. The writer of I John anchors Christian Mission in the witness of the apostolic community to the incarnate Word of life. He writes: *We declare to you what was from the beginning, what we have heard, what we have seen with our eyes...and touched with our hands, concerning the word of life...so that you also may have fellowship with us; and truly our fellowship is with the Father and with his Son Jesus Christ* (I John 1:1-3). This shows that proclamation is not only about transmitting information but about inviting others into a relational community grounded in divine fellowship. The joy of Christian Mission, according to verse 4, *We are writing these things so that our joy may be complete* (I John 1:4), flows from sharing in the life of God.[55] Thus, Christian Mission in the Johannine perspective is deeply relational, aiming to expand the community of those who live in communion with God and one another.

Second, in this foundational text, the proclamation of the gospel is intrinsically connected to the theological truth of the incarnation and to the communal life of the Church.[56] The writer insists that the message proclaimed is rooted in personal experience of the historical Jesus, *what we have heard, seen, and touched* underscoring the reality of the incarnation (I John 1:1). The goal of this proclamation is clear: *so that you also may have fellowship with us* (I John 1:3). This invitation into fellowship reveals the inherently Missional nature of the Christian message. Mission is not only outward-reaching but also inward-building, forming a new community of those united in Christ.[57] The Church becomes the space where divine fellowship is lived and extended through faithful witness and spiritual intimacy.

---

[53] Charles H. Talbert, "2 Peter and the Delay of the Parousia," *Vigiliae Christianae* 20/3 (December, 1966): 137-145.

[54] Charles H. Talbert, "2 Peter and the Delay of the Parousia..., 137-145.

[55] Susangeline Y. Patrick, "Johannine Theology of Mission: Major Themes and Approaches," *Asian American Theological Forum* 5/2 (December, 2018): 22-26.

[56] David Rensberger, "Conflict and Community in the Johannine Letters," *Interpretation* 60/3 (December, 2006): 278-291.

[57] Russell B. Sisson, "Unity in Faith and Fullness of Knowledge in the Johannine Epistles," *Biblical Research* 61 (December, 2016): 77-95.

Third, the Church's Mission is further grounded in the divine nature of love, which both originates from God and shapes every aspect of communal witness. In I John 4:7-21, the author links the act of loving one another directly to God's Missional work in the world: *Beloved, let us love one another, because love is from God; everyone who loves is born of God and knows God* (I John 4:7). The clearest expression of God's love is seen in the sending of the Son: *God's love was revealed among us in this way: God sent his only Son into the world so that we might live through him* (I John 4:9). The Church, having received this love, is now sent to embody and share it. Love becomes a sign of authentic discipleship and a public witness to the world. As verse 12 declares: *No one has ever seen God; if we love one another, God lives in us, and his love is perfected in us* (I John 4:12).[58] The community's love is therefore not merely internal encouragement but a visible reflection of God's presence, fulfilling a Missional role in revealing God to others.

Fourth, love is not merely a command but the essential symbol of Christian identity and Mission. The author of I John writes: *We know that we have passed from death to life because we love one another. Whoever does not love abides in death* (I John 3:14). This love is not abstract or sentimental, rather, it is practical and sacrificial. The author writes: *Little children, let us love, not in word or speech, but in truth and action* (I John 3:18). Mission, in this view, is not first about preaching but about embodying the life of Christ through acts of love and service. The authenticity of the Church's message is tested by its communal ethics. A community that loves in deed becomes a credible witness to the transforming power of the gospel.[59] This relational and ethical witness stands at the heart of Johannine Missiology.

Fifth, continuing the ethical dimension of Mission, I John 3:14-18 presents love as the evidence of spiritual life and divine indwelling. The contrast between Cain, who murdered his brother, and the love commanded of believers illustrates that the Christian life is marked by non-violence, sacrifice, and care for others: *How does God's love abide in anyone who has the world's goods and sees a brother or sister in need and yet refuses help?* (I John 3:17). This rhetorical question exposes the gap between profession and practice. Love is the channel through which God's invisible presence becomes visible in the Church.[60] Therefore, love is not only a moral duty but a Missionary symbol, pointing others to the God who is love.

---

[58] Pheme Perkins, "Continuity and Conflict in the Johannine Tradition: Closing Love's Circle," *The Bible Today* 56/5 (December, 2018): 279-284.

[59] D. Edmond Hiebert, "An Expositional Study of 1 John Pt 6 An Exposition of 1 John 3:13-24," *Bibliotheca Sacra* 146/583 (December, 1989): 301-319.

[60] Mavis M. Leung, "Ethics and Imitatio Christi in 1 John: A Jewish Perspective," *Tyndale Bulletin* 69/1 (December, 2018): 111-131.

Sixth, the incarnation is the theological foundation of Johannine love and Mission. We read: *God's love was revealed among us in this way: God sent his only Son into the world so that we might live through him* (I John 4:9). This sending reveal both God's initiative and the self-giving nature of divine love. The Mission of Jesus becomes the model for the Mission of the Church. The passage continues to explain as: *In this is love, not that we loved God but that he loved us and sent his Son to be the atoning sacrifice for our sins* (I John 4:10). The Church's love is thus a response to God's prior action. When believers extend love to others, especially outsiders, they participate in the very movement of God's redemptive Mission.[61] The incarnation not only makes love possible but defines what true love looks like: sacrificial, initiating, and redemptive.

Seventh, in a context of competing claims and false teachings, the Johannine letters emphasize the need for truth and discernment as part of the Church's Mission. Truth is not merely doctrinal precision but relational faithfulness to Jesus as the Christ come in the flesh. II John warns that: *Many deceivers have gone out into the world, those who do not confess that Jesus Christ has come in the flesh...Be on your guard, so that you do not lose what we have worked for* (II John 7-8). The Church is called to be a discerning community, one that guards its message without compromising love. The epistle urges believers by saying: *Do not receive into the house or welcome anyone who comes to you and does not bring this teaching* (II John 10). This instruction is not about exclusion for its own sake but about maintaining the integrity of the gospel.[62] Mission, in this light, includes protecting the truth of Christ's identity and resisting distortions that undermine the incarnation.

Eighth, the warning against false teachers is not merely a doctrinal concern but a dynamic Mission imperative. In II John, truth is described as something believers *walk in* (II John 4), not only believe intellectually. The community must recognize that welcoming teachers who deny Christ compromises its witness. It explains that: *Everyone who does not abide in the teaching of Christ, but goes beyond it, does not have God* (II John 9). The command not to offer hospitality to such individuals (II John 10-11) is intended to preserve the community's faithfulness to the gospel and to prevent confusion among believers and seekers alike.[63] In a world filled with competing spiritual voices, the Church's Mission includes a responsibility

[61] D. Edmond Hiebert, "An Expositional Study of 1 John Pt 8 An Exposition of 1 John 4:7-21," *Bibliotheca Sacra* 147/585 (December, 1990): 69-88.

[62] Dirk J. Van der Merwe, "Understanding 'Sin' in the Johannine Epistles," *Verbum et Ecclesia* 26/2 (January, 2005): 543-570.

[63] E. R. Wendland, "What is Truth? Semantic Density and the Language of the Johannine Epistles (with special reference to 2 John)," *Neotestamentica* 24/2 (1990): 301-333.

to speak the truth in love and to maintain fidelity to the revelation of Jesus Christ.

Finally, III John introduces a practical dimension of Mission by urging the community to support those who are actively proclaiming the gospel (III John 1:8). The elder commends Gaius for his faithful hospitality: *Beloved, you do faithfully whatever you do for the friends, even though they are strangers to you; they have testified to your love before the church* (III John 5-6).[64] These "friends" are likely itinerant Missionaries or evangelists sent out for the sake of Christ. The writer exhorts Gaius: *You will do well to send them on in a manner worthy of God; for they began their journey for the sake of Christ, accepting no support from non-believers. Therefore, we ought to support such people, so that we may become co-workers with the truth* (III John 6-8). This passage highlights that Mission is a shared task. Even those who remain in the local church have a vital role in God's Mission by providing resources, encouragement, and hospitality.[65] Thus, Support for Mission workers are itself a Missional act, reflecting the collaborative nature of the gospel movement.

Mission in Jude

Jude opens his letter with an urgent summons to *contend for the faith that was once and for all handed on to the saints* (Jude 1:3). Here Mission is cast not as a passive reception of doctrine but as an active defence of the apostolic gospel against distortion. The verb "contend" (ἐρίζω) evokes the image of a courtroom advocate or athlete striving in competition, underscoring that the community's task is to guard carefully what has been entrusted to them.[66] By framing gospel-keeping in this way, Jude insists that every believer share responsibility for preserving doctrinal integrity. Thus, the Church's Mission begins with vigilance: each member must know the apostolic deposit well enough to recognize and repel any teaching that would undermine the truth of Christ's saving work.

Second, immediately after his call to contend, Jude identifies the chief adversaries, those *who pervert the grace of our God into debauchery and deny our only Master and Lord, Jesus Christ* (Jude 1:4). This stark warning clarifies that Mission includes exposing and resisting those who pervert

---

[64] Bruce John Malina, "The Received View and What It Cannot Do: III John and Hospitality," *Semeia* 35 (December, 1986): 171-194.

[65] David Shaw, "The Eagle Has Landed: 3 John and Its Theological Vision for Pastoral Ministry," *Themelios* 48/1 (December, 2023): 106-113.

[66] Nicholas J. Moore, "'Contend for the Faith': The Structure of Jude and the Scope of 'Contending,'" *The Westminster Theological Journal* 85/2 (December, 2023): 207-221.

God's mercy into moral license.[67] By naming the threat plainly, Jude helps the community sharpen its witness: true faith bears visible fruit in holiness, whereas heretical teaching always leads to ethical collapse. In Missionary praxis, then, the Church must both proclaim God's grace and uphold the moral vision implicit in the gospel, ensuring that no one abuses divine forgiveness as a license to sin.

Third, to motivate steady Mission and faithful living, Jude recalls Israel's rebellion in the wilderness and the angels who abandoned their station (Jude 1:5-6). These Old Testament and intertestamental examples serve as sober reminders that God judges corruption without fail.[68] Yet Jude balances this with assurance of divine keeping: *Now to him who is able to keep you from falling and to make you stand without blemish in the presence of his glory with rejoicing, to the only God our Savior, through Jesus Christ our Lord* (Jude 1:24-25). From a Mission perspective, this dual emphasis fosters both reverent fear of divine judgment and confident hope in God's sustaining mercy. As a result, the Church's outreach is shaped by a healthy tension, warning the wayward of coming judgment while comforting the faithful with promises of preservation.

Fourth, beyond doctrinal defence, Jude exhorts believers to positive communal practices: *But you, beloved, build yourselves up on your most holy faith; pray in the Holy Spirit; keep yourselves in the love of God* (Jude 1:20-21). Here Mission comprehends the inward work of spiritual formation. Prayer in the Spirit fosters dependence on God's guidance, while mutual encouragement rooted in love sustains the community amid trials. This inward edification is not self-serving; strengthened and unified, the Church is better equipped to proclaim Christ to outsiders.[69] Thus, the task of Mission includes deliberate investment in one another's spiritual health, ensuring that the witness of the body of Christ remains vibrant and authentic.

Fifth, the vision of Jude's Mission is not purely defensive, rather, it also extends compassionate outreach: *And have mercy on some who are wavering; save others by snatching them out of the fire; and have mercy on still others with fear, hating even the tunic defiled by their bodies* (Jude 1:22-23). This mandate calls the Church to identify those wavering in faith and to intervene

---

[67] Charles H. Landon, "The Text of Jude 4," *HTS Theological Studies* 49 (January, 1993): 823-843.

[68] Simon J. Joseph, "'Seventh from Adam' (Jude 1:14-15): Re-Examining Enochic Traditions and the Christology of Jude," *The Journal of Theological Studies* 64/2 (December, 2013): 463-481.

[69] William J. Hassold, "'Keep Yourselves in the Love of God': An Interpretation of Jude 20, 21," *Concordia Theological Monthly* 23/12 (December, 1952): 884-894.

with patient care rather than harsh judgment.[70] The image of "snatching… out of the fire" evokes rescue from imminent peril. In practical terms, this means offering forgiveness, guidance, and repentance opportunities to those led astray by false teaching or moral failure.[71] By combining firmness in truth with gentleness in restoration, the community embodies the gospel's redemptive power and fulfils its calling to bring sinners safely back into God's fold.

Jude concludes with a majestic doxology that frames all Mission activity as grounded in God's sovereign grace: *Now to him who is able to keep you from falling and to make you stand without blemish in the presence of his glory with rejoicing, to the only God our Savior, through Jesus Christ our Lord, be glory, majesty, power, and authority, before all time and now and forever. Amen.* (Jude 1:24-25). This hymn of praise reminds the Church that its Mission does not rest on human strength but on divine power. By ascribing ultimate glory to God, believers find the courage and humility needed for both bold proclamation and gentle care. In worshipful confidence, the community is sent into the world, not relying on its own resources but on the One whose mercy compels and sustains every Mission effort.

Mission in the Book of Revelation

The Book of Revelation, though often highlighted for its apocalyptic imagery and eschatological visions, is a Mission text. It presents a cosmic vision of God's redemptive purpose for all nations and calls the Church to faithful witness in the midst of spiritual conflict, persecution, and empire. First, at its heart, Revelation reveals Jesus Christ as the victorious Lamb and sovereign King, who has ransomed people from every tribe and language to form a kingdom of priests who serve and proclaim God's reign. This Christocentric focus drives the Missional theology of the book: the Lamb's sacrifice becomes the pattern for the Church's witness, and His victory assures the ultimate fulfilment of God's global Mission. Revelation also portrays the Church not only as a recipient of God's promises but as an active agent in His Mission. It is called to prophesy, to persevere through tribulation, and to remain faithful even unto death.

At the heart of the Missiology in the book of Revelation is a strong Christology that portrays Jesus Christ as the central agent and goal of God's redemptive Mission. The vision of Revelation begins with a declaration of Christ's identity: *Jesus Christ, the faithful witness, the firstborn of the dead, and the ruler of the kings of the earth* (Revelation 1:5). As the "faithful

---

[70] Darian Lockett, "Objects of Mercy in Jude: The Prophetic Background of Jude 22-23," *The Catholic Biblical Quarterly* 77/2 (December, 2015): 322-336.

[71] Olagoke Bolaji, "Guarding the Christian Faith in Jude 17-23: Implications for Spiritual Awakening," *Ogbomoso Journal of Theology* 27/3 (December, 2022): 37-51.

witness," Jesus embodies the Mission of truth, testifying to the nature and will of God even unto death. His designation as "firstborn of the dead" signifies his resurrection and victory over death, establishing Jesus as the beginning of the new creation.[72] This foundational statement places Jesus not only at the centre of salvation history but also as the one through whom God's Mission to the nations is revealed and fulfilled.

The theme of Christ as the Lamb is the central to Revelation's vision of Mission.[73] In the heavenly throne room scene of Revelation 5, the Lamb is worshiped as the one who has accomplished God's redeeming Mission: *You are worthy to take the scroll and to open its seals, for you were slaughtered and by your blood you ransomed for God saints from every tribe and language and people and nation; you have made them to be a kingdom and priests serving our God, and they will reign on earth* (Revelation 5:9-10). This connects Christ's atoning death directly to the global Mission of God. The Lamb's sacrifice is not limited to one group but extends to all peoples, highlighting the universal scope of divine redemption. The Church, formed through this ransom, is called to a priestly and kingly role, mediating God's presence and participating in His reign on earth. This vision propels the Church outward in witness and service, grounded in the cross of Christ.

Moreover, in Revelation, Christ is portrayed not only as Redeemer but also as the reigning King who wields universal authority (Revelation 19:16). In Revelation 11:15, the announcement is made as: *The kingdom of the world has become the kingdom of our Lord and of his Messiah, and he will reign forever and ever*. This eschatological declaration affirms the ultimate triumph of Christ's Mission over the kingdoms of the world. The portrayal is intensified in Revelation 19, where Christ is depicted as a victorious rider on a white horse: *He is clothed in a robe dipped in blood, and his name is called The Word of God... On his robe and on his thigh, he has a name inscribed, 'King of kings and Lord of lords'* (Revelation 19:13, 16). His rule is not merely symbolic; it signifies the final establishment of God's justice, truth, and peace across the nations.[74] This kingly imagery affirms that Mission is not only about present proclamation but also about aligning with the cosmic reign of Christ that will be fully revealed in the end.

Second, in the Book of Revelation, the Church is portrayed not merely as a recipient of salvation but as an active participant in God's Mission

---

[72] S. Joseph Kidder, "The Faithful and True Witness of Revelation 1:5 and 3:14," *Journal of the Adventist Theological Society* 28/1 (December, 2017): 114-131.

[73] David Yoon, "The Revelation of Jesus Christ as the Lamb," *Affirmation & Critique* 22/1 (December, 2017): 45-60.

[74] David Yoon, "The Revelation of Jesus Christ as the Lamb...

through a dual vocation such as: prophetic witness and priestly service.[75] This identity is introduced early in the vision with the affirmation that Christ *made us to be a kingdom, priests serving his God and Father* (Revelation 1:6). This priestly calling reflects Israel's vocation in Exodus 19:6 and is now applied to the multinational Church, which mediates God's presence in the world through worship, intercession, and faithful obedience. Simultaneously, the Church shares in Christ's prophetic office, bearing witness to the truth of the gospel in a hostile world.[76] This prophetic Mission is emphasized when John is recommissioned: *You must prophesy again about many peoples and nations and languages and kings* (Revelation 10:11), indicating that the Church's message transcends cultural and political boundaries.

The priestly and prophetic nature of the Church is expressed in the symbolic imagery of the two witnesses. Revelation 11:3 states: *And I will grant my two witnesses authority to prophesy for one thousand two hundred sixty days, wearing sackcloth.* These figures, while echoing Moses and Elijah, are widely interpreted as a symbol of the witnessing Church, marked by suffering, perseverance, and spiritual authority. The witnesses are empowered by God but are also vulnerable to persecution, reflecting the Church's calling to speak truth even at the cost of martyrdom.[77] Their death and resurrection symbolize the Church's participation in the death and vindication of Christ. After their apparent defeat, *a breath of life from God entered them, and they stood on their feet* (Revelation 11:11), portraying divine validation of their Mission and the ultimate triumph of faithful witness.

This witness takes place in the context of great tribulation and opposition. Jesus commends the Church in Smyrna that: *Do not fear what you are about to suffer... Be faithful until death, and I will give you the crown of life* (Revelation 2:10). The Church's suffering is not meaningless but is intrinsically connected to its Mission. In Revelation 6:9-11, the souls of the martyrs cry out for justice, symbolizing the Church's role in confronting evil through sacrificial witness. *They were each given a white robe and told to rest a little longer* (Revelation 6:11), indicating that their faithfulness will be honoured in God's time.[78] Thus, the Church is called not only to declare the

---

[75] Robert Clark, "The Imperial Priesthood of the Believer: (Revelation 1:6; 1 Peter 2:5,9)," *Bibliotheca Sacra* 92/368 (December, 1935): 442-449.

[76] Robert Clark, "The Imperial Priesthood of the Believer: (Revelation 1:6...

[77] Chee-Chiew Lee, "'Fire from Their Mouths': The Power of Witnessing in the Face of Hostility and Suffering (Rev 11:3-13)," *Journal of Asian Evangelical Theology* 17/1 (January, 2013): 85-103.

[78] Bohdan Kuryliak and Ihor Kuryliak. "The Intermediate State: Revelation 6:9-11 and 20:4-6, 13 in the Light of Daniel 12:2, 13," *The Biblical Annals* 15/1 (December, 2025): 145-164.

Word of God but also to embody it through endurance, holiness, and hope amid suffering.

Third, a central theme in the Book of Revelation is the universal scope of God's redemptive Mission. The vision is not limited to a particular ethnicity or nation but covers all of humanity. This inclusive dimension of the *Missio Dei* is clearly expressed in the heavenly worship scene where the Lamb is praised: *You are worthy to take the scroll and to open its seals, for you were slaughtered and by your blood you ransomed for God saints from every tribe and language and people and nation* (Revelation 5:9). This doxology highlights that Christ's atoning work is global in intent and reach. The Church is thus not a narrow or ethnocentric community but a transnational body formed by the redeeming blood of the Lamb.[79] The Mission of the Church reflects this divine vision: to proclaim Christ's salvation to all peoples without distinction.

The universality of God's Mission is reaffirmed in Revelation 7:9, where John sees a great multitude *that no one could count, from every nation, from all tribes and peoples and languages, standing before the throne and before the Lamb, robed in white, with palm branches in their hands*. This eschatological picture reflects the outcome of faithful witness and divine grace, a global community worshiping God in unity. It also serves as a Mission mandate, urging the Church to bear witness to the gospel across cultural and linguistic boundaries.[80] The scene reminds believers that Mission is not simply local or occasional; it is a global calling that anticipates the ultimate gathering of all peoples in worship and fellowship.

This global outreach is explicitly affirmed in Revelation 14:6-7, where an angel proclaims the "eternal gospel" to the whole world: *Then I saw another angel flying in midheaven, with an eternal gospel to proclaim to those who live on the earth, to every nation and tribe and language and people*. The use of the phrase "eternal gospel" signifies a message that is unchanging and universally relevant. Its proclamation to "those who live on the earth," a phrase often used in Revelation to denote the entire human race, demonstrates God's desire for all to hear and respond.[81] The angel's call to *fear God and give him glory* (Revelation 14:7) points to a Mission command to repentance and worship, echoing the Church's task in the present age.

---

[79] Craig R. Koester, "Revelation's Vision of New Jerusalem: God's Life-Giving Reign for the World," *Word & World* 40/2 (December, 2020): 112-119.

[80] Timote Naulivou, "A Vision of Cultural Flourishing: Revelation 7:9 as an Aspirational Vision for Superdiverse Aotearoa and a Critique of Whiteness," *The Pacific Journal of Theological Research* 18/1 (January, 2023): 11-19.

[81] Willem Altink, "Theological Motives for the Use of 1 Chronicles 16:8-36 as Background for Revelation 14:6-7," *Andrews University Seminary Studies* 24/3 (January, 1986): 211-221.

Revelation concludes with a powerful vision of the nations restored in the new creation.[82] In the New Jerusalem, the nations are not abolished but healed and integrated into God's eternal kingdom. *The nations will walk by its light, and the kings of the earth will bring their glory into it... People will bring into it the glory and the honour of the nations* (Revelation 21:24, 26). Furthermore, *the leaves of the tree are for the healing of the nations* (Revelation 22:2). These images depict not only the fulfilment of the Missionary hope but also the dignity of cultural diversity redeemed by Christ. The nations, once opposed to God, are now participants in God's reign, bringing their gifts and uniqueness into His eternal presence.

Fourth, the Book of Revelation portrays Christian Mission within the framework of an intense spiritual conflict. The Church's witness to Christ does not occur in neutral territory but in a world where forces of evil resist the advance of the gospel.[83] This conflict is dramatized through apocalyptic symbols, particularly the figures of the dragon and the beast, who represent satanic opposition to God's purposes and the persecution of God's people. Revelation 12-13 presents a cosmic struggle where the dragon is cast down from heaven and wages war against the Church.[84] *Then the dragon was angry with the woman, and went off to make war on the rest of her children, those who keep the commandments of God and hold the testimony of Jesus* (Revelation 12:17). The beast, empowered by the dragon, demands worship and persecutes those who remain faithful to Christ (Revelation 13:7-8). These images highlight that Missional faithfulness often involves suffering and conflict in the face of demonic and imperial powers.

Despite the ferocity of this opposition, Revelation affirms that the Church's victory lies not in violence or political power but in sacrificial witness.[85] Revelation 12:11 declares the source of triumph as: *But they have conquered him by the blood of the Lamb and by the word of their testimony, for they did not cling to life even in the face of death.* The reference to the Lamb's blood points to Christ's atoning death as the foundation of all victory, while the "word of their testimony" emphasizes the Church's bold proclamation of the gospel even unto death. This embodies a central theme in Revelation that: martyrdom is not defeat but victory, as it mirrors the

[82] Ruth Padilla DeBorst, "A New Heaven and a New Earth: Community Restored," *Journal of Latin American Theology* 5/1 (December, 2010): 43-55.

[83] Alan Le Grys, "Conflict and Vengeance in the Book of Revelation," *The Expository Times* 104/3 (December, 1992): 76-80.

[84] Andreas Hoeck, "A New Measure: From Nomadic Tent to Cosmic City (Revelation 21:15-17)," *Estudios Bíblicos* 71/1 (January, 2013): 57-75.

[85] Allan Aubrey Boesak, "The Woman and the Dragon: Struggle and Victory in Revelation 12," *Sojourners* 16/4 (December, 1987): 27-31.

Lamb's own path and fulfils the Church's calling to bear witness regardless of the cost.[86]

This doctrine of martyrdom is further developed in Revelation 6:9-11, where the souls of the slain cry out from under the altar: *I saw under the altar the souls of those who had been slaughtered for the word of God and for the testimony they had given* (Revelation 6:9). These martyrs are assured that their blood has not been shed in vain and are given white robes as a symbol of purity and vindication, while they wait for the fullness of God's justice.[87] In Revelation 20:4, those who were beheaded for their witness to Jesus are said to reign with Christ: *They also had not worshiped the beast or its image and had not received its mark...They came to life and reigned with Christ a thousand years.* Here, martyrdom leads not to loss but to participation in the reign of Christ, underscoring its Missional power and eschatological reward.[88]

Fifth, the Book of Revelation presents eschatology not as a distant theological abstraction but as the climactic fulfilment of God's redemptive Mission. Throughout the text, Mission is portrayed as the Church's active participation in God's unfolding plan of salvation, which moves history toward its ultimate goal, the restoration of creation and the complete realization of God's presence among His people.[89] Revelation thus locates Christian Mission within a cosmic drama, where the faithful witness of the Church contributes to God's final purposes.[90] This eschatological vision includes the final judgment and the salvation of the nations. In Revelation 20:11-15, John describes the scene of the great white throne, where all the dead stand before God for judgment: *And I saw the dead, great and small, standing before the throne, and books were opened. Also another book was opened, the book of life. And the dead were judged according to their works, as recorded in the books* (Revelation 20:12).[91] This passage affirms that history is accountable before God, and while justice is assured, the presence of the "book of life"

---

[86] Cornish R. Rogers, "Images of Christian Victory: Notes for Preaching from the Book of Revelation," *Quarterly Review* 10/3 (December, 1990): 69-78.

[87] Charles A. Gieschen, "Which Happened from the Foundation of the World According to the Book of Revelation: The Lamb Was Slain or Some Names Were Not Written in the Book of Life?," *Concordia Theological Quarterly* 88/2-3 (December, 2024): 240-245.

[88] David M. May, "Interpreting Revelation with Roman Coins: A Test Case, Revelation 6:9-11," *Review & Expositor* 106/3 (December, 2009): 445-465.

[89] Michael St A. Miller, "Eschatology and Ecclesiology: Reflections Inspired by Revelation 21:22," *Encounter* 64/2 (December, 2003): 109-138.

[90] Jan A du Rand, "The New Jerusalem as Pinnacle of Salvation: Text (Rev 21:1-22:5) and Intertext," *Neotestamentica* 38/2 (2004): 275-302.

[91] David J. MacLeod, "The Sixth 'Last Thing': The Last Judgment and the End of the World (Rev 20:11-15)," *Bibliotheca Sacra* 157/627 (December, 2000): 315-330.

reveals that salvation remains central to God's Mission. Those whose names are found in the book, those redeemed by the Lamb, are spared from the second death, highlighting the Missional urgency to proclaim the gospel so that all peoples might be included in God's eternal Kingdom.[92]

Following this scene of judgment, Revelation transitions to a vision of the new creation, the ultimate hope of the Church.[93] Revelation 21:1-4 declares: *Then I saw a new heaven and a new earth...And I saw the holy city, the new Jerusalem, coming down out of heaven from God...And I heard a loud voice from the throne saying, 'See, the home of God is among mortals. He will dwell with them; they will be his peoples, and God himself will be with them.'* This imagery demonstrates that the final goal of Mission is not the abandonment of the world but its renewal. The descent of the New Jerusalem signifies God's intention to dwell eternally with humanity, fulfilling the covenantal promise that God will be their God and they God's people. The new creation represents the full realization of the *Missio Dei*, where redeemed humanity lives in restored fellowship with God.[94] In verses 6-7, this eschatological hope is described in personal and relational terms: *To the thirsty I will give water as a gift from the spring of the water of life... Those who conquer will inherit these things, and I will be their God and they will be my children* (Revelation 21:6-7). The offering of the water of life and the promise of divine inheritance point to the fulfilment of all that Christian Mission seeks salvation, reconciliation, and eternal communion with God. At the same time, Revelation 21:8 issues a warning concerning those who reject God's truth, emphasizing the eternal consequences of rejecting the gospel.

Conclusion

The General Epistles and the Book of Revelation provides rich perspectives on the Mission of God, contributing significantly to the broader biblical understanding of the Church's calling in the world. While these texts often address suffering communities and emerging challenges in the post-apostolic era, they do not retreat from the call to Mission. Instead, they reaffirm it with depth and urgency. These writings are not isolated exhortations but are deeply integrated with the broader narrative of Scripture, from the call of Israel to be a light to the nations (Isaiah 49:6), to

---

[92] Alexandra Pârvan, "Revelation 20:12--15: Augustine on the 'Book of Life,' and the Conflicting Picture of Predestination in De Civitate Dei 20,14--15," *Zeitschrift Für Antikes Christentum* 21/3 (December, 2017): 472-495.

[93] John E. Stanley, "The New Creation as a People and City in Revelation 21:1-22:5: An Alternative to Despair," *The Asbury Theological Journal* 60/2 (December, 2005): 25-38.

[94] Dean E. Flemming, "Revelation and the *Missio Dei*: Toward a Missional Reading of the Apocalypse," *Journal of Theological Interpretation* 6/2 (December, 2012): 161-177.

Jesus' commissioning of His disciples (Matthew 28:18-20), and to the final vision of redeemed nations worshiping God (Revelation 7:9). The General Epistles and Revelation extend and reinforce this narrative by showing how the early Christian communities were called to embody the Mission of God amid real-world trials and transitions. They remind us that Mission is not limited to evangelism alone but includes the full life of the Church, its suffering, ethics, love, truthfulness, worship, and hope in God's final restoration. Ultimately, the General Epistles and Revelation call the Church to remain rooted in the truth of the gospel and to shine as a faithful witness to the world. They urge believers not only to proclaim the good news but to embody it in every aspect of life until Christ returns and God's redemptive purposes are fully realized in the "New Creation."

18

Missio Dei
A Holistic Perspective on God's Mission

The term *Missio Dei*, Latin for "the Mission of God," has become a foundational concept in Christian Mission since the mid-twentieth century. Unlike older views that placed the church at the centre of Mission (*Missio Ecclesia*), *Missio Dei* asserts that Mission originates in the being and nature of the Triune God, and that the church is called to participate in this divine purpose rather than to initiate it. As David Bosch summarized: "Mission is not primarily an activity of the church, but an attribute of God. God is a Missionary God." Over time, scholars and theologians have broadened this understanding by emphasizing that *Missio Dei* incorporates not only evangelistic outreach but also social justice, ecological care, reconciliation, and cultural engagement, reflecting God's holistic concern for creation. This more expansive understanding is often referred to as Holistic Mission, which integrates word and deed, Gospel proclamation and social transformation. Today, *Missio Dei* serves as a Missiological framework that shapes both the identity of the church and the role of individuals. It calls Christians not just to proclaim a message, but to engage in God's ongoing work of renewing all things spiritually, socially, and environmentally. In this vision, Mission becomes the church's privileged participation in the Mission of God, rather than the church's own.

Biblical Foundations of *Missio Dei*

The theme of *Missio Dei* is deeply rooted in the Bible. It emphasizes that Mission begins not with the church, but with the Triune God. As Christopher Wright and others argue, the entire biblical narrative can be read through the lens of a Missionary God whose actions span creation, redemption, and renewal, revealing God's nature and purpose for the world. The Old

Testament already presents God as one who calls individuals like Abraham, Moses, and Isaiah to participate in His sending purposes (Genesis 12; Exodus 3; Isaiah 6), demonstrating a consistent pattern of divine initiative even before the New Testament era. In the New Testament, this Mission motif is fully revealed in Jesus Christ and continues through the Church by the power of the Holy Spirit. The Gospels and Mission narratives portray Jesus as sent by God, the Spirit sent by God and Jesus (John 14-16), and the Church sent into the world (Matthew 28; Acts). This affirms that the Church's Mission is not self-generated but grounded in the sending activity of God. The dominant Missional hermeneutic of contemporary theology maintains that Scripture must be interpreted with the understanding that all divine action flows from a Missionary God, an essential foundation for *Missio Dei*.

Missio Dei in the Old Testament

The Old Testament reveals that God has always been a Missionary God. From the beginning of creation, God's activity shows a desire to bring life, order, and blessing to the world. In Genesis 1-2, God creates humanity in God's image and gives them the responsibility to care for creation. This sets a pattern of stewardship and involvement in God's purposes. God's covenant with Abraham in Genesis 12 is especially significant for the theme of Mission. Here, God promises to bless Abraham and, through him, bless "all the nations of the earth." This covenant is not only a promise to one family or people but a Mission-focused commitment to the entire world. Israel is chosen not just for its own sake but to become a channel of God's blessing to others. The prophets continue this theme by declaring that Israel is to be a "light to the nations," and they envision a future where God's name is worshiped globally. In this way, the Old Testament shows that Mission is not a New Testament invention, rather, it is deeply rooted in God's purposes from the very beginning.

The Creation as Missio Dei

The creation narration in Genesis offers an important foundation for understanding *Missio Dei*. The first act of *Missio Dei* in the Bible begins with creation, where God brings order out of chaos. It describes as: *the earth was complete chaos, and darkness covered the face of the deep* (Genesis 1:2). This image reflects a state of disorder and emptiness.[1] However, God's Spirit was present: *while a wind from God swept over the face of the waters* (Genesis 1:2), preparing to bring structure and life. God's creative word

[1] Richard Neville, "Differentiation in Genesis 1: An Exegetical Creation *ex nihilo*," *Journal of Biblical Literature* 130/2 (Summer, 2011): 209-226.

follows, bringing light, form, and purpose to the formless void.[2] This shows that the Mission of God is not only about making the world but also about restoring order, peace, and purpose. Creation is thus the beginning of God's Missional activity, where God acts to transform chaos into a place where life can flourish. This opening theme continues throughout the Scripture, where God's Mission repeatedly confronts and overcomes chaos with order, justice, and beauty.

Then in Genesis 2:15, God places the first human in the garden *to till it and keep it.* This act is not just about agriculture or survival, rather, it shows that humanity is entrusted with responsibility for God's creation. This is often called the "creation mandate," and it implies that caring for the earth is part of God's Mission.[3] The *Missio Dei*, therefore, includes the natural world. Stewardship of the environment, responsible use of resources, and protection of life are all ways in which humanity participates in God's purposes. The ecological aspect of Mission reminds us that salvation and restoration are not limited to human souls but extend to all of creation.[4] This broader understanding challenges the Church to see environmental care as part of its calling under the *Missio Dei.*

The Abrahamic Covenant and Global Blessing as Missio Dei

The covenant God made with Abraham in Genesis 12:1-3 is one of the clearest expressions of God's global Mission in the Old Testament. God calls Abraham to leave his homeland and promises to make his descendants into a great nation. But the promise does not stop there. God also says: *and in you all the families of the earth shall be blessed* (Genesis 12:3). This shows that Israel's purpose was not only to enjoy God's blessing but also to share it with others.[5] Thus, the Abrahamic covenant provides the foundation for the rest of the Bible's Mission narrative. The Apostle Paul refers back to this covenant when explaining that the Gospel fulfils God's promise to bless the nations (Galatians 3:8). The idea of blessing "all nations" reflects the heart of *Missio Dei*: God's intention to restore and redeem the entire world through

---

[2] P. A. Nordell, "The Old Testament Doctrine of the Spirit of God," *The Old Testament Student* 4/10 (June, 1885): 433-444.

[3] Joel S. Gillespie, "The Creation Mandate," *Faith and Practice* 1 (December, 1995): 12-19.

[4] Cha-yong Ku, "*Imago Dei, Dominium Terrae, Missio Dei*: A Missiological-Theological Study on the Creation of Humanity in Genesis," *Mission Theology* 43 (January, 2016): 9-36.

[5] Jobymon Skaria, "Reading the Promises to Abraham in Genesis 12:1-3 through the Post-Exilic Deuteronomic Eyes," *Vidyajyoti Journal of Theological Reflection* 81/9 (December, 2017): 663-678.

God's chosen people.[6] This covenant is a foundation for understanding the Mission of both Israel and the Church in God's redemptive plan.

Israel's Vocation as Missio Dei: A Light to the Nations

In the Old Testament, Israel is not only a recipient of God's grace but also a people with a Mission. God calls Israel to be *a priestly kingdom and a holy nation* (Exodus 19:6). This means that Israel was meant to represent God to the world, showing God's justice, mercy, and holiness.[7] The prophet Isaiah repeatedly describes Israel as "a light to the nations" (Isaiah 42:6; 49:6), a people through whom God's salvation would reach the ends of the earth. This role as a witness to the nations is central to the identity of Israel in the Old Testament. However, the prophetic writings also show that Israel often failed in this vocation, turning inward or neglecting the poor and oppressed.[8] Still, the calling remained: to live in such a way that the world would come to know and worship the one true God. This vocation directly anticipates the role of the Church in the New Testament, which continues the call to be a witness to all nations under the *Missio Dei*.

Prophetic Vision and the Hope for All Nations as Missio Dei

The Old Testament prophets expand the vision of God's Mission by pointing beyond Israel to a time when all nations will know and worship God. Prophets like Isaiah, Micah, and Malachi speak of justice, righteousness, and global worship. For example, Isaiah 42:4 speaks of establishing justice on earth, and Malachi 1:11 envisions God's name being great *from the rising of the sun to its setting*.[9] These prophetic passages reveal that God's concern is not limited to one people or place but includes all humanity. They also highlight the social dimensions of Mission, caring for the poor, defending the oppressed, and promoting righteousness are essential parts of God's will for His people. This prophetic hope points forward to the New Testament, where Jesus' ministry to the poor, sick, and marginalized fulfils

---

[6] Jacob Bullock, "Promises to Abraham and Their Relation to Gentiles in the Church: A Study of Galatians, Chapter 3," *Journal of Biblical Theology* 6/1 (January, 2023): 99-110.

[7] Michael Ufok Udoekpo, "An Analysis of the Ministry of the Royal Priesthood in Exodus 19:6 and Its Theological Expansion in 1 Peter 2:5, 9-10," *Journal of Biblical Theology* 6/2 (January, 2023): 127-147.

[8] Michael F. Bird, "'A Light to the Nations' (Isaiah 42:6 and 49:6): Inter-Textuality and Mission Theology in the Early Church," *The Reformed Theological Review* 65/3 (December, 2006): 122-131.

[9] James Swetnam, "Malachi 1:11: An Interpretation," *The Catholic Biblical Quarterly* 31/2 (December, 1969): 200-209.

the vision of Isaiah 61:1-2.[10] The prophets teach that true Mission involves both proclaiming God's truth and embodying His justice in the world.

Missio Dei in the New Testament

The New Testament builds on the Old Testament theme of God's Mission by revealing it fully in the life and ministry of Jesus Christ. In the New Testament, *Missio Dei* becomes even clearer as God sends Jesus into the world to bring salvation and restoration to all people. Jesus' ministry, death, and resurrection mark the beginning of a new era in God's redemptive plan. After His resurrection, Jesus sends His disciples to continue Jesus' Mission, empowered by the Holy Spirit. The book of Acts and the letters of Paul show how this Mission spreads across cultures and nations, fulfilling God's promise to bless all the families of the earth. The New Testament emphasizes that the Church is not the origin of Mission, but rather a participant in the ongoing Mission of God. This understanding is also affirmed by modern ecumenical reflections, which highlight that the Church's calling is rooted in God's desire to heal and restore all creation.

Jesus Christ as the Fulfilment of Missio Dei

The New Testament presents *Missio Dei* as fully revealed in the life, death, and resurrection of Jesus Christ, and continued through the Church by the power of the Holy Spirit. The Gospels repeatedly emphasize that Jesus was sent by God to fulfil God's redemptive plan. John 3:16 declares that *for God so loved the world that he gave his only Son*, and in John 20:21, the risen Jesus affirms, *As the Father has sent me, so I send you*. This declaration shows that the Church's Mission is directly linked to Jesus' own Mission from God.[11] In Luke 4:18-19, Jesus announces His purpose using the words of Isaiah: "to bring good news to the poor, freedom to the oppressed, and healing to the broken."[12] Thus, Jesus' earthly ministry demonstrates that God's Mission includes both spiritual salvation and social restoration.

The Great Commission as Missio Dei

After His resurrection, Jesus commissions His disciples to continue this Mission. In Matthew 28:18-20, known as the Great Commission, Jesus

---

[10] Bradley C. Gregory, "The Postexilic Exile in Third Isaiah: Isaiah 61:1-3 in Light of Second Temple Hermeneutics," *Journal of Biblical Literature* 126/3 (December, 2007): 475-496.

[11] John Paul II, "Messianic Preaching of Jesus Christ and the Fulfilment of the Kingdom of God," *La Documentation Catholique* 84 (December, 1987): 422-423.

[12] Mary Jerome Obiorah and Favour Chukwuemeka Uroko. "'The Spirit of the Lord God Is upon Me' (Is 61:1): The Use of Isaiah 61:1-2 in Luke 4:18-19," *HTS Theological Studies* 74/1 (January, 2018): 1-6.

instructs his disciples to go and make disciples of all nations. This global scope reflects the fulfilment of God's earlier promise to Abraham to bless all nations through his descendants.[13] The book of Acts then shows how the Holy Spirit empowers the early Church to become witnesses "to the ends of the earth" (Acts 1:8). Through the Spirit's work, the Church expands across cultural and ethnic boundaries, showing that God's Mission includes the unity and inclusion of diverse peoples.[14]

Paul's Missionary Work as Participation in Missio Dei

The Apostle Paul also connects his Missionary work to God's larger redemptive story. He teaches that Jesus' death and resurrection mark the beginning of a new creation (II Corinthians 5:17) and that salvation by grace through faith fulfils God's promise to Abraham (Galatians 3:8). Paul understands himself as sent by God to preach the gospel to the Gentiles, showing that his Mission is not personal ambition but participation in God's eternal plan to reconcile the world to Godself.[15] In this way, the New Testament frames the Church not as the originator of Mission, but as God's agent, continuing the work begun in Christ.

Classical Foundations of *Missio Dei*

The concept of *Missio Dei* is often seen as a modern development in Christian theology. However, its roots go back to the early and medieval Church, where key thinkers explored the idea of God as a sending God. Long before the term *Missio Dei* was used, thinkers like Augustine, Thomas Aquinas, and Karl Barth described how God sends Jesus and the Holy Spirit into the world. Their teachings showed that Mission is not just something the Church does, but something that begins with God. Their insights, the idea of Mission in connection with the Trinity, laid a strong foundation for the modern understanding that Mission belongs to God, and the Church is called to participate in what God is already doing in the world.

Augustine and the Trinitarian Origin of Mission

Augustine, one of the most influential thinkers in the early Church, provided a foundational understanding of Mission within the context of the Trinity. In his work *De Trinitate* (On the Trinity), Augustine described how the concept of "sending" (*Missio*) originally referred to the inner life of God. He

---

[13] Scott. Geminn, "Staying within the Story: Understanding the Great Commission According to Matthew's Gospel," *Lutheran Mission Matters* 32/1 (December, 2024): 89-97.

[14] Chris Burnett, "The Missionary's Guide to the Great Commission: An Exegetical Analysis," *The Master's Seminary Journal* 36/1 (December, 2024): 45-63.

[15] Jason Hentschel, "Thomas Aquinas, 2 Corinthians 5, and the Christian Hope for Life after Death," *Journal of Theological Interpretation* 8/1 (December, 2014): 63-80.

explained that God sends Jesus into the world through the incarnation, and God also sends the Holy Spirit to live within believers.[16] These "sendings" reveal the eternal relationships within the Trinity: Jesus is eternally begotten by God, and the Holy Spirit proceeds from God and, according to Augustine, also from the Son. Thus, for Augustine, Mission is not merely an outward action of the Church but a reflection of the inner life and love of God.[17] Therefore, Mission begins with God's own being and becomes visible in the world through the sending of the Son and the Spirit.

Thomas Aquinas and the Divine Missions

Thomas Aquinas, a medieval Catholic theologian, built on Augustine's Trinitarian theology by further developing the idea of "divine Missions." In his major theological work *Summa Theologica*, Aquinas explained that the sending of the Jesus and the Holy Spirit into the world is deeply connected to their eternal origin within the Trinity.[18] Jesus is sent by God to become human and redeem the world, and this Mission reflects Jesus' eternal relationship as the one begotten by God. Likewise, the Spirit is sent to live in believers, which reflects the Spirit's procession from both God and Jesus. For Aquinas, these divine Missions are not only about salvation but also about showing who God is.[19] Mission, therefore, is a natural expression of God's desire to restore human beings and bring them into fellowship with Godself. This makes Mission both deeply theological and rooted in God's eternal love.

Karl Barth and the Recovery of God-Centred Mission

Karl Barth, a leading Reformed theologian of the twentieth century, played a key role in shaping the idea of *Missio Dei*. In his 1932 lecture "Theology and Mission," Barth emphasized that Mission is first and foremost the activity of God.[20] He argued that God is the one who acts: God sends Jesus, God and Jesus send the Holy Spirit, and through the Spirit, the Church is sent into the world. For Barth, Mission is not primarily about the Church's efforts or

---

[16] Michel R. Barnes, "Augustine in Contemporary Trinitarian Theology," *Theological Studies* 56/2 (December, 1995): 237-250.

[17] Poitras, Edward W. "St. Augustine and the *Missio Dei*: A Reflection on Mission at the Close of the Twentieth Century," *Mission Studies* 16/2 (1999): 29-30.

[18] Torey J. S. Teer, "'As the Father Has Sent Me, Even so I Am Sending You': The Divine Missions and the Mission of the Church," *Journal of the Evangelical Theological Society* 63/3 (December, 2020): 535-558.

[19] Eugene Richard Schlesinger, "A Trinitarian Basis for a 'Theological Ecology' in Light of *Laudato Si'*," *Theological Studies* 79/2 (December, 2018): 339-355.

[20] Lindsay G. Robertson, "*Missio Dei*: Karl Barth and the Mission of the Church," *Hill Road* 9/2 (December, 2006): 3-19.

obedience but about joining what God is already doing in the world.[21] He criticized Mission approaches that placed too much focus on human activity and instead called the Church to recognize that Mission flows from God's very nature. In this view, the Church does not own or initiate Mission but participates in the sending movement of the Triune God.[22] Thus, Barth's understanding of Mission helps to move Mission thinking away from a Church-centred model to a God-centred one.

Modern Understanding of *Missio Dei*

In the middle of the 20th century, Christian thinkers experienced a major shift in how they understood Mission. Instead of seeing Mission as primarily the task of the Church, they began to recognize it as starting with God. This transformation became stronger at the International Missionary Council's 1952 conference in Willingen, Germany. Here, leaders from various Christian traditions emphasized that Mission belongs first to the Triune God, and the Church is invited to join God's work rather than initiate it itself. The key person in making this concept popular was the German Missiologist Karl Hartenstein, who coined the term *Missio Dei* in the early 1930s and helped to clarify it after the Willingen conference. He distinguished *Missio Dei*, God's Mission, from *Missio Ecclesiae*, the Church's own Mission, stating that Mission is a divine act, not merely a Church program. This Missiological shift has deeply influenced contemporary Mission thinking, helping Christians understand that Mission flows from who God is rather than from what the Church does.

The 1952 Willingen Conference and Recovering God as the Source of Mission

The idea that Mission belongs first to God, not to the Church, became a central theme in modern Missiology and was clearly expressed at the International Missionary Conference held in Willingen, Germany, in 1952.[23] At that time, the world was recovering from the devastation of two world wars, and Mission work was being questioned due to its close ties with colonialism. Many leaders began to ask whether Mission should continue and what its true purpose was.[24] In response, the Willingen Conference

---

[21] Veli-Matti Kärkkäinen, "The Ecumenical Potential of Pneumatology," *Gregorianum* 80/1 (1999): 121-145.

[22] Lindsay G. Robertson, "*Missio Dei*: Karl Barth and the Mission of the Church…

[23] Chung-Hyun Baik, "A Critical Analysis of the Concept of *Missio Dei*: Suggestions for a Trinitarian Understanding," *Neue Zeitschrift Für Systematische Theologie Und Religionsphilosophie* 63/3 (Deceber, 2021): 329-340.

[24] Jonas Sello Thinane, "*Missio Dei* through Complexity Theory: Complexity to Total Salvation," *In Die Skriflig* 56/1 (January, 2022): 1-8.

emphasized that Mission is not simply a program of the Church or a result of human obedience. Instead, it is the work of the Triune God, who sends the Church into the world.[25] Although the term *Missio Dei* was not directly used in the final statements, the idea was clearly present: Mission begins with God and the Church is invited to participate in it.

Karl Hartenstein and the Shift from Missio Ecclesiae to Missio Dei

Karl Hartenstein, a German Missiologist, played a key role in developing and clarifying this concept. Drawing on the understanding of Karl Barth, Hartenstein introduced the term *Missio Dei* to describe the divine origin of Mission.[26] He distinguished it from *Missio Ecclesiae*, which refers to the Church's own Mission efforts. Hartenstein argues that Mission must not be understood as something the Church owns or controls. Instead, it is God's ongoing work in the world, and the Church exists to serve that Mission. In his report following the Willingen Conference, he explained that the sending of the Son and the Spirit by the Father is the foundation for the Church's own sending.[27] His ideas helped to shift the focus of Missiology from Church-centred approaches to a God-centred understanding. This Missiological correction laid the foundation for much of contemporary Mission thought, where the Church is seen as a servant and instrument of God's greater Mission in the world. From then, *Missio Dei* has become increasingly important in the field of Missiology and in understanding the Mission of the church.

From Trinitarian Roots to a Holistic Understanding of *Missio Dei*

After the 1952 Willingen Conference, Missiology shifted decisively: Mission came to be understood as derived from the very nature of God and rooted in the Trinity. The final statement of the conference affirmed, "The Missionary movement of which we are a part has its source in the Triune God Himself," indicating that Mission flows directly from the Trinity, not from ecclesial structures or human programs.[28] Missiologists emphasized that Mission should be situated within the context of the doctrine of the Trinity rather than solely within ecclesiology or soteriology. This shift reframed the Church's role: Mission became less about organizational outreach and more about participation in God's own sending activity. The

---

[25] Theo Sundermeier, "*Missio Dei* Today: On the Identity of Christian Mission," *International Review of Mission* 92/367 (December, 2003): 560-578.

[26] Jürgen Schuster, "Karl Hartenstein," *Mission Studies* 19/1 (2002): 53-79.

[27] Tormod Engelsviken, "*Mission Dei*: The Understanding and Misunderstanding of a Theological Concept in European Churches and Missiology," *International Review of Mission* (October, 2003): 481-497.

[28] Chung-Hyun Baik, "A Critical Analysis of the Concept of *Missio Dei*...

Trinitarian basis ensured that Mission was recognized as God's dynamic initiative, rather than merely an initiative of the church.

However, in the decades that followed, scholars began to expand and critique this framework. While affirming the importance of its Trinitarian roots, they argued that Mission also includes other dimensions that extend beyond traditional theological categories.[29] These include biblical themes such as creation care, justice, and covenant, as well as contextual concerns like liberation from oppression, interreligious dialogue, and cultural engagement. Such perspectives broaden the scope of *Missio Dei* to include not only the Church's spiritual witness but also its responsibility for social transformation and ecological stewardship.[30] As a result, the modern understanding of *Missio Dei* has evolved into a more holistic and inclusive vision, reflecting the multifaceted nature of God's work in the world.

Theological Interpretations Beyond the Trinitarian Model

While the concept of *Missio Dei* is often rooted in the Trinitarian model, theologians have expanded this understanding by exploring other dimensions. These alternative perspectives do not reject the Trinitarian foundation but aim to deepen and widen the Church's vision of God's Mission in the world. By engaging with biblical, historical, and contextual themes, these interpretations show that *Missio Dei* involves more than divine relationships within the Godhead. They emphasize God's commitment to covenant, justice, and creation. Covenantal theology highlights God's eternal purpose through God's promises to humanity. Liberation theology draws attention to God's Mission as the deliverance of the oppressed and the transformation of unjust systems. Ecological theology emphasizes the care of creation as central to God's redemptive plan.

Missio Dei and the Covenant Framework

In reformed and covenantal theology, *Missio Dei* is often understood through the lens of God's eternal covenants. This approach connects the *Missio Dei* to God's unchanging purpose throughout history.[31] Louis Berkhof explains that the relationships within the Trinity serve as a model for God's historical covenants with humanity. This includes what some theologians call the "covenant of redemption," an eternal agreement within the Trinity in which the God sends the Jesus for the salvation of the world, and the Jesus willingly fulfills this purpose.[32] David Bosch also noted that

---

[29] Jonas Sello Thinane, "*Missio Dei* through Complexity Theory…

[30] Chung-Hyun Baik, "A Critical Analysis of the Concept of *Missio Dei*…

[31] J. S. Thinane, "The Presbyterii Fidelium Representative of God's-Human Covenant in *Missio Dei*," *Pharos Journal of Theology* 105/5 (December, 2024): 1-14.

[32] Louis Berkhof, *Systematic Theology* (Grand Rapids: Eerdmans, 1938), 271-278.

after the Willingen Conference, theologians increasingly placed Mission in the context of the Trinity and connected it to the Church's calling. This fits with Reformed theology, where Mission is not a new idea but part of God's unified plan from the beginning.[33] John Murray, another Reformed thinker, describes the Abrahamic covenant as the central path through which God's redemptive plan unfolds, pointing forward to Christ and the Church.[34] In this view, *Missio Dei* is deeply rooted in God's faithfulness and long-standing promise to bless all nations through the chosen people.

Liberation Theology and Missio Dei as Justice

Liberation theology presents *Missio Dei* as God's active involvement in setting people free from oppression and injustice. This view is especially strong in Latin American, Black, and other marginalized theological traditions. Key theologians like René Padilla and Samuel Escobar argue that true Mission must combine both evangelism and social action. They describe these two aspects as "like the two wings of a bird," neither can be ignored. They introduced the term *misión integral* (integral Mission) to describe a holistic approach where preaching the Gospel includes transforming unjust systems.[35] Theologians such as Gustavo Gutiérrez draw from passages like Luke 4:18-19 and the Exodus story to emphasize that God's Mission includes spiritual, emotional, and social liberation.[36] In this perspective, *Missio Dei* means joining God in the struggle for justice, peace, and reconciliation, especially among the poor, the excluded, and the exploited. The Church is not simply called to preach the good news but to live it out in practical ways that address poverty, racism, violence, and inequality. This view helps recover the Gospel's relevance in places where suffering and injustice are part of daily life.

Creation-Centered Theology and Ecological Mission

An ecological or creation-centred theology expands *Missio Dei* to include the entire natural world. According to Genesis 1-2, God created the world and declared it "very good," giving humanity the responsibility to care for it (Genesis 2:15). This means that stewardship of the earth is not a secondary

---

[33] David J. Bosch, *Transforming Mission: Paradigm Shifts in Theology of Mission* (Maryknoll: Orbis, 1991), 389-393.

[34] John Murray, *The Covenant of Grace* (London: Tyndale Press, 1954), 19-30.

[35] C. René Padilla, "Integral Mission and Its Historical Development," in *Mission as Transformation: Learning from Catalysts*, edited by Vinay Samuel and Chris Sugden (Oxford: Regnum, 1999), 63-73.; Samuel Escobar, "Evangelism and Man's Search for Freedom, Justice, and Fulfilment," in *Let the Earth Hear His Voice*, edited by J. D. Douglas (Minneapolis: World Wide Publications, 1975), 303-322.

[36] Gustavo Gutiérrez, *The Power of the Poor in History* (Maryknoll: Orbis, 1983), 35-47.

issue but part of God's Mission.[37] Modern ecological theology argues that the environmental crisis is not only scientific or political, it is also a spiritual and moral problem. In such a framework, humans are called to live as faithful stewards, not exploiters of God's creation. African theologian Harvey Kwiyani illustrates this through the concept of *umunthu* (similar to *ubuntu*), a worldview found in Malawian culture that emphasizes living in harmony with God, people, ancestors, and nature.[38] Within this framework, *Missio Dei* includes healing broken relationships between humanity and the environment. Many evangelical Mission groups now emphasize "creation care" as part of their calling, integrating climate action and sustainability with the Gospel message. Romans 8:19-21 speaks of creation "groaning" for redemption, showing that God's Mission is not limited to saving souls but includes restoring all creation. This creation-focused view enriches the Church's understanding of *Missio Dei* by reminding believers that the Gospel is good news for the whole cosmos.

Western Theological Contributions and Historical Context

The development of *Missio Dei* in Western theology must be understood within its broader historical and cultural context. During the 18th and 19th centuries, Christian Mission was often closely tied to colonial expansion. Many Missionaries worked with good intentions, yet Mission was frequently framed as a Church-driven effort to convert non-Christians while also spreading Western cultural norms. As a result, critics argued that Mission in this era often appeared as "Western culture in a box," reducing the Gospel to a tool of imperialism. In response to this problematic history, the 20th century saw major Missional shifts in the West. Key movements including the rise of ecumenical dialogue, the Second Vatican Council in the Catholic Church, the Lausanne Evangelical Congress, and the global growth of Pentecostalism challenged earlier models and helped reframe Mission as *Missio Dei*. These developments played a crucial role in the rediscovery and reformulation of *Missio Dei* as the foundational idea that Mission originates in the heart of the Triune God, and the Church is called to participate in that Mission with humility, justice, and global awareness.

Early Ecumenical Shifts: From Church-Centered to God-Centered Mission

In the early 20th century, Western Missiology began to shift away from church-dominated approaches that had been closely tied to colonial

[37] Glenn E. Schaefer, "The *Missio Dei*: The Man's 'Hidden' Restoration of Humankind's Co-Regency over All Creation," *Lutheran Theological Review* 13 (January, 2001): 42-55.

[38] Harvey C. Kwiyani, *Multicultural Kingdom: Ethnic Diversity, Mission, and the Church* (London: SCM Press, 2020), 45-52.

expansion. One major turning point was the 1910 Edinburgh Missionary Conference, which marked the beginning of global cooperation in Mission among Protestant churches. Over time, theologians moved from a church-centric understanding of Mission to a God-centered one. This shift became vibrant after the 1952 Willingen Conference, where Mission was redefined as beginning with God, not the Church. Karl Hartenstein reported that the delegates had "rediscovered that Mission depends first and foremost on God's own activity."[39] Influential thinkers like Karl Barth and David Bosch built on this insight, with Bosch later summarizing that Mission "was understood as being derived from the very nature of God."[40] The World Council of Churches (WCC) further shaped this ecumenical view in its assemblies, expanding Mission to include not only evangelism but also justice, reconciliation, and healing of cultures.[41] These developments laid the groundwork for *Missio Dei* as a guiding theological vision in global Mission.

Roman Catholic Renewal and Vatican II

In the Roman Catholic Church, a major theological renewal occurred during the Second Vatican Council (1962-1965). The Council's document *Ad Gentes* declared that the Church is "Missionary by its very nature," emphasizing that Mission is not optional but central to the Church's identity. This marked a significant shift from earlier understandings of Mission as primarily about converting non-Christians. Following Vatican II, Pope John Paul II in *Redemptoris Missio* (1990) reaffirmed the Church's global Missionary calling and called all Catholics to participate in evangelization. Pope Francis deepened this emphasis by linking Mission to justice, ecological responsibility, and care for the poor. His encyclicals *Evangelii Gaudium* and *Laudato Si'* stress that preaching the Gospel must go hand in hand with serving the marginalized and protecting creation. In this way, the Catholic understanding of *Missio Dei* expanded to include a more integrated approach to Mission, one that reflects God's concern for the whole person and the whole world.

Evangelical Contributions: The Lausanne Movement and Missio Dei

Evangelical theology also contributed significantly to the development of *Missio Dei*, especially through the Lausanne Movement. The first Lausanne Congress in 1974 brought together evangelical leaders from around the

[39] David J. Bosch, *Transforming Mission*..., 389-393.

[40] David J. Bosch, *Transforming Mission*..., 390

[41] Stephen B. Bevans and Roger P. Schroeder, *Constants in Context: A Theology of Mission for Today* (Maryknoll: Orbis Books, 2004), 287-294.

world.[42] Latin American theologians René Padilla and Samuel Escobar played a crucial role by challenging the narrow focus on evangelism alone. They introduced the concept of *misión integral* (Integral Mission), arguing that evangelism and social action are inseparable.[43] Their influence led the Lausanne movement to officially adopt a more integrated vision of Mission. Later documents, such as the Cape Town Commitment (2010), reaffirmed this view by urging Christians to confront economic, racial, and ecological injustice as part of their Gospel witness.[44] This broadened perspective helped to reshape evangelical Mission thinking to align more closely with *Missio Dei*, emphasizing that proclaiming Christ also involves working for transformation and justice in society.

Pentecostal and Charismatic Perspectives on the Missio Dei

Pentecostal and Charismatic churches, especially those in the Global South, have also enriched the understanding of *Missio Dei* by emphasizing the role of the Holy Spirit in Mission. Unlike traditional Western Mission models that often relied on structure and doctrine, Pentecostalism stresses a Spirit-empowered witness that crosses cultural and geographic boundaries.[45] Pentecostal Mission is marked by spiritual vitality, healing, and transformation, often rooted in personal encounters with God. These churches see the Spirit not only as the source of evangelistic power but also as the one who leads believers into new communities and unreached areas. They often focus on holistic transformation that includes deliverance, social upliftment, and reconciliation.

Western Theological Renewal and the Maturing of Missio Dei

Through these various Western theological channels, ecumenical, Catholic, evangelical, and Pentecostal thinking, *Missio Dei* has developed from a theological idea into a comprehensive Mission paradigm. Each movement contributed to correcting earlier problems such as church triumphalism, colonialism, and a narrow focus on conversion.[46] In their place, a more

[42] Knud Jørgensen, "Inspiration and Challenges from Cape Town and Edinburgh to Church and Mission," *Transformation* 29/4 (October, 2012): 293-303.

[43] Sherron K. George, "Constructing Latin American Missiology," *International Bulletin of Mission Research* 40/1 (December, 2016): 30-41.

[44] Sherron K. George, "Constructing Latin American Missiology…

[45] Amos Yong, "Pentecost as Facet of the Church-in-Mission or Culmination of the *Missio Dei*?: A Pentecostal Renewing of Bosch's (Reformed) Mission Theology," *Missionalia* 47/2 (December, 2019): 151-164.

[46] Darren Cronshaw, "*Missio Dei* Is *Missio Trinitas*: Theological and Biblical Foundations for Inter-Congregational Collaboration in Mission and Formation," *SEDOS Bulletin* 55/3-4 (December, 2023): 6-18.

holistic, Spirit-led, justice-oriented, and God-centred vision has emerged. This shift influenced many Christian bodies, such as the Anglican Communion, which adopted the Five Marks of Mission, integrating evangelism, teaching, service, justice, and environmental care.[47] Ultimately, these developments reflect Western theology's attempt to realign Mission with the sending love of God, showing that Mission belongs to God first, and the Church is called to participate in it with humility and purpose.

Non-Western Perspectives on Mission

In the Majority World, particularly Africa, Asia, and Latin America, Christianity has grown rapidly and developed in unique cultural, social, and historical contexts. Unlike traditional Western approaches to Mission, which have often focused on doctrinal teaching and church structures, non-Western theologies of Mission are shaped by local struggles, communal values, and the everyday realities of people's lives. These regions have experienced colonialism, poverty, political oppression, and social inequality, and their theological reflections on *Missio Dei* often respond directly to these experiences. As a result, churches in the Global South offer fresh and contextually rich insights into the nature of God's Mission. In these perspectives, *Missio Dei* is not only about proclaiming the Gospel but also about community development, justice for the oppressed, liberation from social systems, and care for creation.

African Perspectives of Missio Dei: Ubuntu, Community, and Creation in Mission

African theologians bring a rich, community-centred understanding to *Missio Dei* by drawing from cultural values such as *Ubuntu* or *Umunthu*, which emphasize human interconnectedness, solidarity, and harmony with God, people, and creation.[48] In this context, Mission is not just about preaching the Gospel but about living in relational wholeness. African churches often combine evangelism with social outreach, such as education, healthcare, and conflict resolution. The ethic of generosity expressed through hospitality, caring for widows, orphans, and the poor is viewed as an essential expression of Christian Mission.[49] Moreover, ancestral reconciliation (through healing and forgiveness rituals) reflects how Mission connects the spiritual and communal dimensions of life. As some theologians from Malawi argue, an

[47] Chul Ho Yun, "*Missio Dei Trinitatis* and *Missio Ecclesiae*: A Public Theological Perspective," International Review of Mission 107/1 (December, 2018): 225-239.

[48] Jonas Sello Thinane, "*Missio Hominum* Guided by an Understanding of *Ubuntu* for *Missio Dei*: Nico Smith's Discovery," *HTS Theological Studies* 77/4 (January, 2021): 1-7.

[49] Johannes Jacobus Knoetze, "Perspectives on Family and Youth Ministry Embedded in the *Missio Dei*: An African Perspective," *In Die Skriflig* 49/1 (January, 2015): 1-9.

umunthu-based understanding of *Missio Dei* leads to identifying with the marginalized and caring for the environment.[50] African Independent and Pentecostal churches also emphasize God's active presence in daily life, making Mission a dynamic force for community development, healing, and ecological responsibility.

Asian Perspectives of Missio Dei: Mission as Liberation and Contextual Justice

In Asia, Missiology often arises from experiences of suffering, social injustice, and marginalization. One key example is Minjung theology in Korea, which developed during times of military dictatorship. "Minjung" refers to the oppressed masses, and theologians describe Jesus as the "Minjung Messiah" who stands in solidarity with the suffering.[51] For Minjung theology, *Missio Dei* is God's ongoing work of liberation, freeing people from unjust systems.[52] Similarly, in India, Dalit theology centres on God's Mission to lift up the untouchables and challenge the deeply rooted caste system. Drawing on Jesus' ministry among lepers, outcasts, and the poor, Dalit theologians interpret Mission as social transformation and human dignity.[53] Asian theological voices emphasize that Mission must be shaped by local struggles and cultural narratives, not imported models. Some Asian-American theologians even suggest that Mission should begin in "liminal spaces" the in-between realities of migrants and minorities, where the Gospel can be understood from the perspective of the marginalized.[54] This makes Mission not just proclamation, but participation in God's justice in the context of real-life oppression.

---

[50] Aaron Takalani Muswubi, "Reflection on Glocal Worship in Missiology in the Context of the Marginalised, yet Never Silenced, Black African Worship Music from *Missio Dei* Perspective" *Missionalia* 45/1 (December, 2017): 5-28.

[51] Hi Heon Kim, "Minjung Messiah and Process Panentheism," *Process Studies* 37/1 (December, 2008): 73-91.

[52] Byungohk Lee, "Toward a Korean Missional Church: A Dialogue between Missional Theology and Minjung Theology," Chongshin Theological Review 44/3 (December, 2012): 273-294.

[53] Matouš Holeka, "Reading the Bible in Various Streams of Liberation Theology: Latin American Theology, South African Black Theology and Indian Dalit Theology," *Communio Viatorum* 56/2 (December, 2014): 169-196.

[54] Sang Hyun Lee, "Claiming Our Liminal Spaces," *The Princeton Seminary Bulletin* 27/3 (December, 2006): 193-195.; Benjamin H. Kim, "Liminality and the *Missio Dei*: An Asian American Theology of Mission," *Asian American Theological Forum* 11/1-2 (December, 2024): 13-26.

Latin American Perspectives of Missio Dei: Integral Mission and Social Transformation

Latin American theologians have contributed deeply to *Missio Dei* through the concept of 'Integral Mission,' which emphasizes the inseparability of evangelism and social action. Starting from key conferences in Medellín (1968) and Puebla (1979), church leaders and theologians insisted that preaching the Gospel must be matched by living it out in society.[55] Samuel Escobar explained that the Spanish word integral (meaning whole or complete) reflects the idea that Mission needs two wings, such as, 'word and deed' to truly fly. In practice, many Latin American churches engage in church planting alongside literacy programs, micro-credit systems, and healthcare initiatives. These activities are seen not as separate from Mission but as part of God's redemptive work.[56] The writings of Latin American theologians like José Míguez Bonino and Leonardo Boff have also emphasized cosmic reconciliation, seeing Christ as reconciling all things, spiritual, social, and ecological (Colossians 1:20).[57] This broader view connects *Missio Dei* with the transformation of both people and the systems they live in.

Decolonial Interpretations of *Missio Dei*

The concept of *Missio Dei* emerged in part as a theological critique of the colonial-era model of Christian Mission, which too often served imperial plans rather than the gospel's liberating power. In the eighteenth and nineteenth centuries, European empires commonly equated the advance of Christianity with the expansion of Western culture and political control. Mission stations frequently functioned as extensions of colonial authority, imposing European languages, educational systems, and church structures on Indigenous peoples. Yet even within this context, pioneering Missionaries such as Bartholomeus Ziegenbalg, William Carey, and David Livingstone resisted and at times suffered under their own governments and their sponsors, revealing the tension between the Spirit's work and imperial interests. A decolonial interpretation of *Missio Dei* uses this history to critique how Mission has sometimes fostered dependency rather than empowerment and to reorient the Church toward a truly God-governed, Spirit-led Mission among all peoples.

---

[55] Knud Jørgensen, "Inspiration and Challenges from Cape Town…, 293-303.

[56] Sherron K. George, "Constructing Latin American Missiology…, 30-41.

[57] Paul Davies and Johannes Reimer, "Faith Seeking Effectiveness: Missiological Insights from the Hermeneutics of José Míguez Bonino," *Missionalia* 43/3 (December, 2015): 306-322.; Carlos Raúl Sosa Siliezar, "The Use of the New Testament in Latin American Ecclesiologies: Critique and Dialogue between the Proposals of Leonardo Boff and René Padilla," *Journal of Latin American Theology* 16/1 (December, 2021): 19-64.

One of the earliest and most striking examples is Bartholomeus Ziegenbalg, the first protestant Missionary sent by the Danish king to Tranquebar, Tamil Nadu, in 1706. Ziegenbalg quickly learned Tamil, translated the New Testament, and founded schools. But his efforts to respect local culture clashed with colonial officials who wanted a monopoly on trade and control of the local population. Danish authorities accused him of undermining their revenue and even sent him to prison for months. Despite this, Ziegenbalg insisted that Mission must serve Christ and the local community, not the interests of empire.

A similar tension raised a century later with William Carey, the British Missionary, who is known as the "father of modern Missions." Carey arrived in Serampore, India, in 1793 under the patronage of the East India Company, which officially forbade its employees from evangelizing. Carey's work among Bengali speakers, translating scriptures, founding a college, and campaigning against social evils like *sati* (widow burning), provoked hostility from Company officials. He and his colleagues were often denied legal protection and viewed with suspicion as threatening British commercial interests. Only when the Danish government granted him land in Serampore did Carey secure a legal base for his ministry separate from British colonial structures.

David Livingstone in nineteenth-century Africa refused to partner his medical and evangelistic work with the British government's expansionist agenda. He insisted that trade routes and Mission stations be established only with the consent of African leaders. Even some Catholic Missionaries in the Belgian Congo spoke out against forced labour and exploitation under King Leopold II. In each case, Missionaries found themselves in disagreement with the very powers that claimed to bring "civilization" alongside the gospel.

These examples exemplify the need of a decolonial reading of *Missio Dei* today. It reminds the Church that Mission at its best resists all forms of domination and seeks the empowerment of local communities. Rather than repeating colonial patterns, where Mission creates dependency and reinforces foreign power. But, a decolonial *Missio Dei* calls the Church to stand in solidarity with the oppressed, to honour indigenous cultures, and to work for their flourishing on their own terms. It demands that Mission be understood as God's that critiques empire, transforms cultures from within, and empowers every people to bear witness to Christ.

Missio Dei and Contextual Empowerment

Bartholomeus Ziegenbalg's Mission in India models a *Missio Dei* that begins with deep engagement in local culture. Upon arrival in Tranquebar in 1706, Ziegenbalg committed himself to learning Tamil, translating the New Testament, and establishing schools that used the local language and teaching methods. Rather than imposing Danish forms of worship or Western educational styles, he empowered local Christians to shape liturgy, hymnody, and theological reflection in Tamil. This approach directly challenged the colonial assumption that the Gospel must travel in European cultural garb, instead, it demonstrated that the Spirit of God works authentically through every culture's own expressions and wisdom. This Contextual Empowerment model of *Missio Dei* affirms that God's redemptive work precedes and transcends any human culture. The Holy Spirit indwells every people group (Acts 2) and equips them to witness within their own context. In this way, the *Missio Dei* becomes a collaborative journey, where empowerment flows from the Spirit's work in diverse communities, fostering a truly global and contextualized Church.

Missio Dei and Legal Autonomy

William Carey's life and ministry in Serampore highlights another side of a decolonial *Missio Dei* as securing institutional autonomy from colonial powers. As an employee of the East India Company, Carey faced bans on evangelism. Undiscouraged, he negotiated with Danish authorities to establish the Serampore Mission as a legally separate entity. This independence allowed Carey and his colleagues to translate Scripture, run schools, and preach the Gospel without fear of arrest or corporate interference. Their model explains how Mission, rooted in the *Missio Dei*, must sometimes divorce itself from political or economic structures that distort its purpose. The Legal Autonomy model of *Missio Dei* claims that authentic Mission bodies maintain the freedom to follow the Spirit's leading without allegiance to secular interests. The Church's first loyalty is to protect the integrity of the Gospel and enable Mission to serve the marginalized rather than reinforce systems of power, hierarchy and nepotism which are the manifestations of colonialism, thus opposes *Missio Dei*.

Missio Dei and Prophetic Solidarity

David Livingstone's work in 18th century Africa exemplifies a Prophetic Solidarity within the *Missio Dei* that refuses to align the Gospel with colonial exploitation. As a medical Missionary, Livingstone insisted on African consent for the placement of Mission stations and opposed the forced labour practices of British colonialists. He understood that the Spirit-empowered Mission must stand with the oppressed, not with the oppressor. His example challenges Missions today to adopt solidarity, advocating for justice and human dignity even when it puts them at odds with their own governments or sponsors. Such an understanding of *Missio Dei* stresses that the Holy Spirit equips the Church to be God's prophetic voice in the world. Mission is not merely about church planting but about witnessing to God's justice, peace, and mercy among all peoples and to identify with the poor, contest systems of injustice, and work for societal transformation. Thus, *Missio Dei* is participating in the Spirit's Mission of reconciling creation to itself and to the Creator (II Corinthians 5:18-19).

Missio Dei and Holistic Partnership

The Holistic Partnership model of *Missio Dei* envisions Mission as an integrated, Spirit-led collaboration across cultures, legal frameworks, and socioeconomic contexts. In this model, local and global churches work together in equal partnership, sharing theological reflection, resources, and leadership. Indigenous Missions contribute their culturally-shaped insights while Mission agencies provide strategic support, all under the guidance of the Holy Spirit. This reciprocal relationship reflects the Trinitarian nature of *Missio Dei*, wherein God, Jesus and Holy Spirit work in partnership with the Church. Thus, Holistic Partnership affirms that the *Missio Dei* is by definition shared and multidimensional. The Spirit forms a diverse yet unified body of Christ (I Corinthians 12:12-13), mobilizing gifts for service, advocacy, and worship that address spiritual and material needs. By honouring local leadership, maintaining structural autonomy, and standing in prophetic solidarity, the Church lives out a decolonial witness. This comprehensive approach ensures that Mission is not an export of Western methods but a global movement shaped by the Spirit's activity in every culture, all for the glory of God and the flourishing of humanity.

Contemporary Practical Applications of *Missio Dei*

In today's world, the concept of *Missio Dei* need to take new expressions as churches respond to complex global challenges. Rather than limiting Mission to traditional activities such as evangelism or church planting, it is the high time to understand God's Mission as including the pursuit of justice, peace, ecological sustainability, and holistic human flourishing. This broader view reflects a shift from Mission as a Church-centred task to Mission as participation in God's redemptive work in all areas of life. Such an understanding of *Missio Dei* is Scriptural and guided by the Holy Spirit, since *Missio Dei* is engaging in ministries that serve both spiritual and practical needs. From environmental stewardship and community wellbeing to reconciliation efforts and advocacy for the marginalized, these demonstrate that *Missio Dei* is active wherever the Church joins in restoring lives, communities, and creation.

Justice and Peacebuilding as Expressions of Missio Dei

In today's world, it is important to understand justice as an essential part of God's Mission. It no longer sees Mission only as preaching or church planting, but also as actively working to address poverty, inequality, and systemic oppression. Mission engages in ministries such as education, healthcare, human rights advocacy, and fighting human trafficking. These efforts reflect the belief that God's reign is about restoring life, dignity, and justice for all people. The World Council of Churches' document Together Towards Life (2012) speaks of "life with a capital L," referring to the abundant life Jesus promised (John 10:10). This includes not only spiritual renewal but also social and economic wellbeing, that makes Mission "Holistic."

Reconciliation as the Heart of Missio Dei

Another key expression of *Missio Dei* today is its characteristics of reconciliation. Based on Scriptures like *through him God was pleased to reconcile to himself all things, whether on earth or in heaven* (Colossians 1:19-20) and *in Christ God was reconciling the world to himself* (II Corinthians 5:18-19), *Missio Dei* believe that God's Mission includes restoring broken relationships between individuals, communities, even nations, including the creation. A statement from the World Council of Churches explains that the Holy Spirit leads a ministry of reconciliation, made possible through Christ and now entrusted to the Church. In response, many churches engage in community mediation, interfaith dialogue, and healing ministries. Such dimensions of Mission help people forgive, rebuild trust, and live together in peace. Reconciliation work shows that *Missio Dei* is not just about proclamation, it is about restoring wholeness in human relationships, which mirrors God's desire to reconcile all things to Godself.

Creation Care and Environmental Mission as the Core of Missio Dei

As concern for the environment grows globally, it is important now to see care for creation as a direct expression of *Missio Dei*. Biblical mandate to stewardship in Genesis 2, strengthens Mission in joining the effort to protect the planet. Thus, environmental Mission is no longer considered separate from evangelism. Catholic Church is strongly founded in 'creation care' mandate of Mission. Through Pope Francis's encyclical *Laudato Si'*, have strongly affirmed that evangelization and ecological responsibility must go together. Similarly, Protestant and Anglican churches promote initiatives like "Green Churches," where congregations reduce waste, plant community gardens, or teach about climate change. These initiatives are seen as participating with God in Mission to restore the harmony of creation. Through environmental stewardship, the Church bears witness to a God who cares for the earth and calls humanity to live responsibly within it. Thus, *Missio Dei* is the Church participating in God's Holistic Mission.

Conclusion

The concept of *Missio Dei* offers a powerful and unifying vision for the Church's identity and purpose. Biblically, Mission begins in creation, continues through God's covenants with Israel, is fulfilled in the life, death, and resurrection of Christ, and extends through the Church into the world. From Genesis to Revelation, Scripture shows a God who sends, restores, and redeems. Missiologically, this is not limited to a Trinitarian framework alone, rather, it also includes covenantal, social, and cosmic dimensions. It reflects God's deep concern for justice, healing, and the flourishing of all creation. Contributions from both Western and non-Western theologians have enriched the understanding of *Missio Dei*. Thinkers like Karl Barth and David Bosch emphasized that Mission begins with God, not the Church. Latin American and African theologians have helped us see the importance of community, solidarity with the poor, and the integration of word and action. Asian theologians have highlighted Mission's role in liberation and contextual engagement. Most importantly, decolonial voices have reminded the global Church to confront past injustices and to develop Mission models that are truly inclusive and rooted in mutual respect. Ultimately, *Missio Dei* calls the Church to participate in God's holistic work, to reconcile all things (Acts 3:21; Colossians 1:20), to proclaim the Gospel in word and deed, and to reflect God's love in every context.

19

Holistic Mission
A Biblical and Contextual Vision of Mission in a Broken World

Holistic Mission represents a growing recognition within global Christianity that the Gospel is not limited to the salvation of souls, but extends to the transformation of all areas of life. Defined as the integration of evangelism and social action, Holistic Mission embraces both the vertical relationship with God and the horizontal commitment to justice, peace, and the flourishing of the whole creation. Rooted in Isaiah 61 and Luke 4:18-21, Holistic Mission reflects the ministry of Jesus, who proclaimed good news to the poor, healing for the broken-hearted, and liberty for the oppressed. This understanding of Mission moves beyond narrow categories of spiritual outreach to include concerns such as poverty, inequality, ecological crisis, and human dignity. Grounded in *Missio Dei*, Holistic Mission invites the Church to participate in God's redemptive activity across all spheres of life. It calls Mission to responds to the concrete realities of human suffering and brokenness, and it finds particular relevance in contextual theology, which emphasizes that Mission must be shaped by local histories, cultures, and struggles. Thus, Holistic Mission expands the meaning of Mission to include the transformation of unjust structures and the healing of relationships between people, God, and creation.

Biblical Foundations of Holistic Mission

The foundation for Holistic Mission is deeply rooted in Scripture. Both the Old and New Testaments present a vision of God's Mission that includes not only spiritual restoration but also social, economic, and physical renewal. The Bible portrays a God who is deeply concerned about justice, healing, and liberation. Holistic Mission is, therefore, not a new innovation but a faithful expression of the biblical narrative. The Old Testament prophets emphasized God's concern for the oppressed and broken-hearted, while the New Testament reveals how Jesus personified and fulfilled this Mission. Together, both the Old and New Testaments offer a strong biblical command for a Mission that unites evangelism with social action, showing that the Gospel addresses every aspect of human life.

Old Testament Foundation

The Old Testament provides a strong foundation for Holistic Mission by showing that God is deeply concerned about all areas of human life such as spiritual, social, emotional, and physical.[1] A central passage is Isaiah 61:1-3, where the prophet declares that the Spirit of the Lord has anointed him to preach good news to the poor, bind up the broken-hearted, proclaim freedom for the captives, and release for the prisoners. This text reflects God's Mission of healing, restoration and liberation. It includes a message of hope for those who mourn, promising *a garland instead of ashes* and *the oil of gladness instead of mourning* (Isaiah 61:3).[2] These images point to a comprehensive transformation of lives and communities, not just spiritual forgiveness but restoration of dignity and well-being.

This vision is found in other books of the Old Testament as well. For example, in Deuteronomy presents God as one who: *who executes justice for the orphan and the widow, and who loves the strangers, providing them food and clothing. You shall also love the stranger, for you were strangers in the land of Egypt* (Deuteronomy 10:17-19). The Israelites are commanded to reflect this concern by showing love and justice to the marginalized. Similarly, Micah 6:8 sums up God's expectation: *to do justice and to love kindness and to walk humbly with your God*. These instances make it clear that God's covenant people are called not only to worship God but also to demonstrate compassion and justice in society, thus Holistic Mission is a contextual Mission perspective.[3]

The concept of *shalom*, often translated as "peace," also supports Holistic Mission. In the Hebrew Bible, *shalom* is more than the absence of

---

[1] Deborah Ajulu, "Development as Holistic Mission," in *Holistic Mission: God's Plan for God's People*, edited by Brian Woolnough and Wonsuk Ma (Oxford: Regnum Books International, 2010), 166.

[2] Brian Woolnough and Wonsuk Ma, "Preface and Acknowledgements," in *Holistic Mission: God's Plan for God's People*, edited by Brian Woolnough and Wonsuk Ma (Oxford: Regnum Books International, 2010), xi.

[3] Samuel Jayakumar, "The Work of God as Holistic Mission: An Asian Perspective," in *Holistic Mission: God's Plan for God's People*, edited by Brian Woolnough and Wonsuk Ma (Oxford: Regnum Books International, 2010), 90-93.

conflict, rather, it means wholeness, harmony, and well-being in relationships with God, others, and creation (Jeremiah 29:7). Holistic Mission, therefore, seeks to restore such kind of *shalom* in broken communities.[4] Thus, God's Mission in the Old Testament is about restoring what sin has damaged, such as, relationships, communities, and even the land receives restoration in the Year of Jubilee (Leviticus 25).

New Testament Fulfilment

The New Testament shows how Jesus Christ fulfils the Holistic Mission of God revealed in the Old Testament. Jesus reads from Isaiah 61 and applies it directly to His own Mission: *The Spirit of the Lord is upon me, because he has anointed me to bring good news to the poor. He has sent me to proclaim release to the captives and recovery of sight to the blind, to set free those who are oppressed, to proclaim the year of the Lord's favour* (Luke 4:18-19).[5] This makes clear that, Jesus' ministry was not limited to preaching about eternal life, rather, it included healing the sick (Mark 1:34), feeding the hungry (Mark 6:30-44), forgiving sins (Mark 2:1-12), and restoring outcasts to society (Luke 5:12-13; John 4). Thus, Jesus brought hope and dignity to those marginalized by religion, illness, or poverty.

The teachings of Jesus also affirm a holistic view of Mission. In Matthew 25:31-46, Jesus describes the final judgment, where those who fed the hungry, clothed the naked, and visited the sick are commended. He says, "Whatever you did for one of the least of these brothers and sisters of mine, you did for me." This passage teaches that faithfulness to God includes caring for people's physical and social needs.[6] After resurrection, Jesus gave the Great Commission in Matthew 28:18-20, commanding the followers to "make disciples of all nations," which involves teaching them to obey everything Jesus taught including teachings on justice, mercy, and love.[7] The book of Acts records how the early Church continued this Mission: they preached the Gospel and also shared their possessions so that: *There was not a needy person among them* (Acts 4:34).

The Apostle Paul also presents a vision of Holistic Mission. In Romans 8:18-23, he describes creation itself as groaning for redemption, showing that

---

[4] Chris Sugden, "Mission as Transformation: Its Journey Among Evangelicals Since Lausanne 1," in *Holistic Mission: God's Plan for God's People*, edited by Brian Woolnough and Wonsuk Ma (Oxford: Regnum Books International, 2010), 32.

[5] Brian Woolnough and Wonsuk Ma, "Preface and Acknowledgements…, xi.

[6] Benedict Viviano, "Choosing Sides: Matthew 25:31-46," *The Bible Today* 58/1 (December, 2020): 30-37.

[7] Mary Hinkle Shore, "Preaching Mission: Call and Promise in Matthew 28:16-20," *Word & World* 26/3 (December, 2006): 322-328.

salvation in Christ includes the renewal of the whole world.[8] In Colossians 1:19-20, Paul says that through Jesus, God is reconciling "all things" to Himself "whether on earth or in heaven." This includes not only individuals but relationships, communities, and even creation itself. Therefore, the New Testament confirms and expands the Old Testament vision of a God who heals, restores, and sends His people into the world to reflect His justice, compassion, and truth. Thus, Holistic Mission was central to the life and purpose of the Church because it flows from the Mission of Jesus Himself.

Missio Dei and Holistic Mission

The concept of *Missio Dei*, the Mission of God, forms a theoretical foundation for Holistic Mission.[9] *Missio Dei* emphasizes that Mission originates in the very nature of God, not merely as a task assigned to the Church, but as God's ongoing work to redeem and restore all of creation. This understanding shifts the focus from human-centred Mission methods to participation in God's own redemptive activity. Key biblical texts support this broader vision. In Colossians 1:19-20, Paul declares that: *God was pleased to dwell, and through Christ God was pleased to reconcile to Himself all things, whether on earth or in heaven.* This highlights that God's Mission is not limited to saving souls, but includes the reconciliation of the entire cosmos, relationships, communities, and the created world.[10] Likewise, Romans 8:18-23 portrays creation as "groaning" under the weight of sin and waiting eagerly for redemption. Here, Paul speaks of a future where not only humanity but all of creation will be set free from its bondage to decay.[11] These texts reveal that *Missio Dei* is deeply holistic in scope, involving spiritual, social, and ecological restoration.

Building on this, African theologian Deborah Ajulu asserts that Holistic Mission is equivalent to *Missio Dei.* She argues that the two are inseparable because the Mission of God is concerned with the total well-being of individuals and societies.[12] From this perspective, proclaiming the Gospel must go hand in hand with actions that bring healing, justice, and transformation in every dimension of life. Whether addressing systemic

---

[8] Cherryl Hunt, David G. Horrell and Christopher Southgate, "An Environmental Mantra? Ecological Interest in Romans 8:19-23 and a Modest Proposal for its Narrative Interpretation," *The Journal of Theological Studies* 59/2 (2008): 546-579.

[9] Deborah Ajulu, "Development as Holistic Mission…, 166.

[10] Teresa Okure, "'In Him All Things Hold Together': A Missiological Reading of Colossians 1:15-20," *International Review of Mission* 91/360 (December, 2002): 62-72.

[11] Cherryl Hunt, David G. Horrell and Christopher Southgate, "An Environmental Mantra? Ecological Interest in Romans 8:19-23 and a Modest Proposal for its Narrative Interpretation," *The Journal of Theological Studies* 59/2 (2008): 546-579.

[12] Deborah Ajulu, "Development as Holistic Mission…

poverty, environmental destruction, or broken relationships, Holistic Mission reflects God's intention to renew all things in Christ. Therefore, understanding Holistic Mission through the lens of *Missio Dei* helps the Church to see its role not just as a messenger of salvation, but as a participant in God's comprehensive plan to make all things new (Revelation 21:5).[13] This theological link provides both the mandate and the model for a Mission that is faithful to Scripture and responsive to the needs of a hurting world.

Theological Perspectives on Holistic Mission

The concept of Holistic Mission has been shaped not only by biblical insights but also by various theological reflections from different contexts around the world. Theologians have interpreted Holistic Mission in ways that speak to their communities' specific needs, drawing attention to issues such as poverty, caste discrimination, and African ecclesiology. These perspectives reveal that Holistic Mission is not simply as approach but a dynamic expression of *Missio Dei* that responds to brokenness in different forms, whether spiritual, social, or relational. This can be understood from the perspectives of Tulo Raistrick, who interprets poverty as a result of broken relationships; Samuel Jayakumar, who highlights Holistic Mission in the Indian Dalit context; and Deborah Ajulu, who grounds Holistic Mission in the theological concept of *Missio Dei* within African Christianity.

Tulo Raistrick: Poverty and Broken Relationships

Tulo Raistrick, a Christian development thinker, proposes a relational understanding of poverty that connects deeply with Holistic Mission. He argues that poverty is not only a lack of resources, but primarily the result of broken relationships with God, with oneself, with others, and with creation. When these relationships are damaged, people experience not only economic hardship but also spiritual emptiness, social isolation, and ecological harm. For Raistrick, this brokenness is the true root of poverty. He believes that Holistic Mission must seek to restore these relationships so that people can flourish in every area of life. The local church, in his view, is central to this healing process. As a visible body of Christ, the church is called to be a place of reconciliation, healing, and transformation, restoring human dignity, promoting justice, and encouraging care for creation.[14] This

[13] Candida R. Moss and Liane M. Feldman. "The New Jerusalem: Wealth, Ancient Building Projects and Revelation 21-22," *New Testament Studies* 66/3 (January, 2020): 351-366.

[14] Tulo Raistrick, "The Local Church: Transforming Community," in *Holistic Mission: God's Plan for God's People*, edited by Brian Woolnough and Wonsuk Ma (Oxford: Regnum Books International, 2010), 138.

view emphasizes that Mission is not just about preaching but also about rebuilding communities through love and compassion.

Samuel Jayakumar: Dornakal Mission as a Holistic Mission Model

Samuel Jayakumar provides an important case study of Holistic Mission from South India, focusing on the Dornakal Mission among the Dalit communities. In the caste-based Indian context, Dalits have been historically oppressed, denied dignity, and treated as outcasts. Jayakumar argues that Holistic Mission in Asia must address this deep social injustice. The Dornakal Mission, founded and established by Bishop V. S. Azariah in the early 20th century, combined evangelism with social transformation. It promoted Dalit empowerment through education, community development, and theological training, helping them recover a sense of identity and worth. Jayakumar sees this Mission as an example of how Asian contextual theology can drive holistic ministry. The Mission did not separate Gospel proclamation from practical action, rather, it saw them as parts of one divine calling.[15] This case shows that Holistic Mission must engage local cultures and struggles, confronting unjust systems while proclaiming the liberating message of Christ.

Deborah Ajulu: Holistic Mission as Missio Dei

Deborah Ajulu, an African theologian, sets a theological framework that connects Holistic Mission directly with *Missio Dei*, the Mission of God. She argues that Holistic Mission is not simply a strategy or program of the Church, but an expression of God's own work to restore creation. According to Ajulu, this understanding helps to shift the focus from church-centred Mission to God-centred Mission. She believes that Holistic Mission reflects God's intention to bring about transformation in every part of life such as spiritual, social, political, and ecological. This theological grounding has significant implications for African churches, which often serve in contexts marked by poverty, political instability, and broken community life. Ajulu urges the African Church to become a living agent of God's holistic work, addressing not just personal salvation but also justice, peace, and development.[16] Her approach affirms that when the Church joins in *Missio Dei*, it reflects the full scope of God's redemptive love for the world.

---

[15] Samuel Jayakumar, "The Work of God as Holistic Mission: An Asian Perspective," in *Holistic Mission: God's Plan for God's People*, edited by Brian Woolnough and Wonsuk Ma (Oxford: Regnum Books International, 2010), 90-93.

[16] Deborah Ajulu, "Development as Holistic Mission," in *Holistic Mission…*, 166.

Contextual and Social Dimensions

Holistic Mission becomes most meaningful when it engages with the real-life struggles of people in specific contexts, particularly in situations marked by poverty, inequality, and historical injustice. Missiologists and theologians from the Global South such as Samuel Escobar (Mission must respond to both personal salvation and social transformation), René Padilla (gospel must address structural sins such as, poverty, exploitation, and political oppression), A. P. Nirmal (salvation cannot be separated from social liberation and justice for marginalized communities), and C. S. Song (Mission must engage with the real-life struggles of people in Asia, including issues of colonialism, suffering, and poverty) have emphasized that Mission must respond not only to individual spiritual needs but also to structural and systemic realities like poverty, caste, gender injustice, and political oppression. In contexts where communities face deprivation and marginalization, Holistic Mission serves as both a message of hope and a strategy for transformation. In such a context it is important to highlights two important voices: Nicta Lubaale, who insists that in deprived contexts Holistic Mission is not optional but essential, and Esther Mombo, who critiques colonial models of Mission and calls for a shift in both the geography and language of Mission practice.

Holistic Mission in Deprived Contexts: Nicta Lubaale's Perspective

Nicta Lubaale, a theologian and church leader from Africa, strongly argues that in social contexts of deprivation, Holistic Mission is not just one approach among many, but it is essential. In societies marked by economic poverty, political instability, and cultural marginalization, separating spiritual proclamation from social action creates an incomplete witness. According to Lubaale, there is no line between preaching the Gospel and pursuing justice; both are expressions of God's Mission. For him, churches that focus only on individual salvation miss the broader call to participate in God's healing of broken societies. Holistic Mission in this view includes feeding the hungry, educating the illiterate, healing the sick, and challenging unjust systems, alongside proclaiming Christ. Lubaale sees the church as a powerful agent of transformation when it embodies this full Gospel.[17] His perspective urges the Church to integrate faith and action, showing that God's love is both proclaimed and demonstrated in concrete ways, especially among those who are most vulnerable.

---

[17] Nicta Lubaale, "The Emerging Church in Africa and Holistic Mission: Challenges and Opportunities," in *Holistic Mission: God's Plan for God's People*, edited by Brian Woolnough and Wonsuk Ma (Oxford: Regnum Books International, 2010), 84-86.

Postcolonial Critique of Holistic Mission: Esther Mombo's Perspective

Esther Mombo, a Kenyan theologian, puts forth a critical postcolonial analysis of traditional Mission models, especially those shaped by a geographic North-to-South dynamic, where Mission flowed from Western nations to the rest of the world. She critiques how such models often assumed Western superiority, presenting Mission as something "done to others" rather than with them. This approach, she argues, contributed to dependency, cultural domination, and the marginalization of local voices. Mombo challenges the language of Mission itself, which frequently reflected colonial attitudes by focusing on numbers of conversions, Mission stations, and church buildings. She calls for a relational and mutual understanding of Mission, one in which local churches are empowered to shape their own theology and practice. For Mombo, Holistic Mission becomes a corrective to these colonial patterns by emphasizing partnership, mutual respect, and context-specific action. It involves listening to local needs, affirming local leadership, and valuing indigenous knowledge and spirituality.[18] Her vision is of a Mission that no longer exports Western ideals but engages in true dialogue and shared transformation.

Holistic Mission and Contemporary Challenges

In today's world, the Church faces complex social, cultural, and environmental challenges that demand a deeper and broader understanding of Mission. Issues like poverty, inequality, ecological crisis, and public debates over the role of faith in justice have raised important questions about the relevance of traditional Mission practices. Holistic Mission offers a fresh approach by insisting that evangelism and social engagement must go hand in hand. Rooted in *Missio Dei*, this approach helps the Church respond to contemporary concerns in ways that reflect the full Gospel, addressing both spiritual and structural brokenness.

Evangelism and Social Justice in Tension?

One of the most debated topics in modern Mission is the perceived division between evangelism and social action, often framed as a choice between the "Gospel" and the "social Gospel." Some Christian traditions have treated them as separate priorities, with one focused on saving souls and the other on improving society. However, Holistic Mission, grounded in the concept of *Missio Dei*, rejects this division. It affirms that God's Mission includes both the spiritual transformation of individuals and the healing of unjust systems. Jesus Himself modelled this in Jesus' ministry, as seen in Luke

---

[18] Esther Mombo, "From Fourfold Mission to Holistic Mission: Towards Edinburgh 2010," in *Holistic Mission: God's Plan for God's People*, edited by Brian Woolnough and Wonsuk Ma (Oxford: Regnum Books International, 2010), 43-46.

4:18-19, where preaching good news to the poor is combined with freeing the oppressed and healing the broken.[19] Holistic Mission thus calls the Church to proclaim Christ while also working for justice, reflecting the truth that God's kingdom brings renewal to every part of life. When evangelism and social justice are united, Mission becomes a powerful force for both eternal hope and present change.

Gender, Race, and Class in Mission

Holistic Mission also confronts power-based inequalities, especially those rooted in gender, race, and class. These injustices often manifest as structural sin, deep systems of discrimination that oppress individuals and communities.[20] In many situations, women, ethnic minorities, and the economically poor continue to suffer from exclusion, violence, and lack of opportunity.[21] But Holistic Mission insists that true Christian witness must address these issues, not just as political concerns but as part of the Church's call to embody God's justice. The Mission of Jesus included standing with the marginalized, uplifting the outcast, and confronting unjust religious and political systems (Luke 7:36-50; John 4:1-26).[22] In this milieu, Mission must manifest as *Missio Dei* by empowering women, affirming racial justice, and dismantling systems that benefit the few at the expense of the many. In doing so, the Church reflects the heart of a God who brings down the proud and lifts up the lowly: *He has brought down the powerful from their thrones and lifted up the lowly; he has filled the hungry with good things and sent the rich away empty* (Luke 1:52-53).

Ecological Dimensions of Mission

In recent years, there has been growing awareness that care for creation is an essential part of God's Mission. The ecological crisis, climate change, environmental degradation, and species extinction threatens not only nature but also human life, especially for the poor who depend on the land and

---

[19] Walter F. Kedjierski, "Papal Contributions to the Development of the Church's Missionary Spirit: From *Ad Gentes* to *Evangelii Gaudium*," *Logos: A Journal of Catholic Thought and Culture* 23/1 (2020): 92-95.

[20] Aruna Gnanadason, "We Have Spoken So Long O God: When Will We Be Heard? Theological Reflections on Overcoming Violence against Women," *Theology & Sexuality* 13/1 (2006): 9.

[21] Evangeline Anderson Rajkumar, "Practicing Gender Justice as a Faith Mandate in India," *Studies in World Christianity* 13/1 (2007): 33-34.

[22] Hyunju Bae, "The Depths of Christ's Love: Revisiting the Encounter between Jesus and the Woman in Luke 7:36-50," *The Ecumenical Review* 74/2 (December, 2022): 295-312.

water for survival.[23] The Bible shows that creation matters to God. In Genesis 2:15, God placed humanity in the garden *to till it and keep it*, assigning us the role of stewards. In Romans 8:19-21, Paul describes creation groaning for liberation, waiting for redemption along with humanity.[24] These passages affirm that God's redemptive plan includes the renewal of the natural world, not just human souls. Holistic Mission embraces ecological stewardship as part of witnessing to the Gospel. This includes promoting sustainable agriculture, protecting forests and rivers, reducing pollution, and supporting climate justice initiatives.[25] Thus, when the Church cares for creation, it participates in God's desire to reconcile all things, humans and nature, through Christ (Colossians 1:20).

Toward a Shared Sacred Space for Holistic Mission

The idea of Shared Sacred Places for Holistic Mission reflects a growing awareness that Mission is not only about proclamation or service, but also about creating spaces, both physical and relational, where God's presence, justice, and healing can be experienced together. In a world marked by fragmentation, injustice, and exclusion, the Church is called to model a new kind of community that embodies God's inclusive and transforming love. The phrase "Shared Sacred Places for Holistic Mission" suggests a vision of Mission that is grounded in community, inclusivity, and transformation.[26] Such a space is not limited to a church building, but includes homes, streets, schools, hospitals, anywhere people gather to encounter God and one another in truth and love. These shared spaces are sacred because they are where God is present, and shared because they are open to all, especially the marginalized. This affirms that Mission is not about one group "doing something" to another, but about mutual participation in God's work. Justice is central to this vision: a sacred space must also be a safe space, where people are treated with dignity, and where power is not used to exclude or dominate. Contextual witness means that these spaces reflect local cultures, struggles, and hopes, making God's love visible in ways people can understand and trust. The Church, then, is not just a preaching institution,

---

[23] David M. Rhoads, "A Beloved Earth Community: Christian Mission in an Ecological Age," *Currents in Theology and Mission* 43/2 (April, 2016): 1-10.

[24] Calvin DeWitt, "Ecology and Ethics: Relation of Religious Belief to Ecological Practice in the Biblical Tradition," *Biodiversity and Conservation* 4 (1995): 840-844.

[25] Lynn White Jr., "The Historical Roots of Our Ecological Crisis," in *This Sacred Earth: Religion, Nature, Environment*, edited by Roger S. Gottlieb (New York: Routledge, 2004), 209.

[26] Vinod S. Sailus, *Borderless Spirituality: An Intercultural Inquiry into the Appropriation of Faiths in South Indian Religious Context* (Bangalore: Omega Book World, 2023), 11-14.

but a community of presence living among people, listening, serving, and inviting transformation through relationship.[27] Therefore, shared sacred spaces become signs of that restoration, places where God's grace, truth, and justice come together in everyday life.

Conclusion

This study has explored the concept of Holistic Mission by tracing its biblical, theological, contextual, and practical dimensions. It began by showing that the foundation of Mission lies in the very nature of God, *Missio Dei*, and is evident throughout the biblical narrative. In the Old Testament, God's concern for justice, healing, and restoration is expressed through covenants and prophetic visions (Isaiah 61:1-3). In the New Testament, Jesus embodies this Mission in His life, death, and resurrection (Luke 4:18-21), inviting the Church to continue it in both word and deed. Mission, then, is not only about saving souls but also about restoring broken relationships, with God, self, others, and creation (Colossians 1:20; Romans 8:18-23). Tulo Raistrick, Samuel Jayakumar, and Deborah Ajulu have emphasized that Holistic Mission involves addressing poverty, injustice, and exclusion in context. Their perspectives reveal that Holistic Mission is not a secondary concern but the very heart of *Missio Dei*. In light of these foundations, the phrase Shared Sacred Places for Holistic Mission offers a meaningful and integrative expression of what this Mission looks like in practice. It suggests that Mission happens wherever the Church becomes a presence of grace, justice, and healing. These sacred spaces, whether physical or relational, are where the Gospel is both proclaimed and lived out. They are inclusive, contextually rooted, and centred on restoring what sin and systems have broken. The Church, then, is not merely a sending institution but a community of presence, called to embody God's reconciling love in the world. Thus, Holistic Mission is not about choosing between evangelism and social action, but about living out the full Gospel in every dimension of life.

[27] Vinod S. Sailus, *Borderless Spirituality…*

20

The Holy Spirit and the Church's Mission
A Pneumatological Foundation for Christian Mission

Pneumatology, the study of the Holy Spirit's person and work, is essential for understanding the Church's Mission in the world. The Holy Spirit is not a distant or passive presence but the active agent in God's Mission (*Missio Dei*), working to renew creation and empower the people of God. In Mission, it is the Spirit who sends, equips, and sustains the Church to proclaim and embody the gospel of Christ. Through the Spirit, believers receive boldness to witness, wisdom to engage diverse cultures, and power to live out the values of the Kingdom of God. The Church's Mission, therefore, is deeply dependent on the Spirit's presence and activity. Without the Spirit, Mission becomes a human effort; with the Spirit, it becomes a divine partnership. Pneumatology thus provides the framework to understand how the Spirit enables the Church to faithfully participate in God's redemptive work in the world.

Biblical Foundations of Pneumatology and Mission

The biblical foundations of pneumatology and Mission reveal that the Holy Spirit has always been actively involved in God's redemptive work from creation to the birth and expansion of the Church. In the Old Testament, the Spirit of God appears as the divine breath of life (Genesis 1:2), the power behind prophetic calling (Isaiah 61:1; Joel 2:28-29), and the agent of inner renewal and national restoration (Ezekiel 36:26-27). This same Spirit is central in the Mission of Jesus, who was conceived, baptized, and led by the Spirit, and who proclaimed the good news in the power of the Spirit as the fulfilment of Isaiah's prophecy (Luke 3:21-22; 4:1, 18-21). After Jesus' resurrection, the Spirit is poured out on the early Church at

Pentecost (Acts 2), marking the beginning of a global Mission empowered by divine presence. Throughout Acts, the Spirit continues to guide and send Missionaries, opening new frontiers for the gospel (Acts 8, 10, 13, 16). These biblical witnesses show that the Holy Spirit is not merely a background character but the main driving force behind God's Mission across all ages.

The Spirit in the Old Testament Mission Narrative

The Old Testament lays a strong theological foundation for understanding the role of the Holy Spirit in God's Mission. From the beginning of creation to the prophetic movements and the promise of renewal, the Spirit appears not as a distant force but as the active presence of God working to bring life, order, freedom, and transformation.[1] These early manifestations of the Spirit reveal that Mission is not a New Testament innovation, but rather rooted in God's ongoing intention to redeem and renew the world through His Spirit.

The first mention of the Spirit appears in the creation narrative, where the Spirit of God is portrayed as the divine power that brings order out of chaos. Genesis declares that: *the earth was complete chaos, and darkness covered the face of the deep, while a wind from God swept over the face of the waters* (Genesis 1:2). The phrase "wind from God" or "Spirit of God" indicates the dynamic and life-giving presence of the Spirit that prepares the world for God's creative word. This sets the tone for understanding the Spirit as the initiator of life and the one who breathes divine purpose into creation.[2] The Spirit's presence at creation reveals that God's Mission begins with forming a world capable of sustaining life, beauty, and relationship, a foundational act of divine generosity that prefigures the Spirit's ongoing Mission throughout Scripture.

The Spirit's Missional role continues as Spirit empowers individuals to speak and act on God's behalf, particularly the prophets of Israel. The prophetic tradition in the Old Testament is deeply tied to the Spirit's enabling presence. Isaiah speaks of being anointed by the Spirit to carry out a Mission of justice and restoration: *The spirit of the Lord God is upon me because the Lord has anointed me; he has sent me to bring good news to the oppressed, to bind up the broken-hearted, to proclaim liberty to the captives and release to the prisoners* (Isaiah 61:1). This highlights that the Spirit equips individuals for a Mission of compassion and liberation, particularly toward

---

[1] YunGab Choi, "The Role of the Spirit of God in the Old Testament: With Special Reference to the Kingdom of God," *ACTS Theological Journal* 41 (January, 2019): 89-139.

[2] Rinse Herman Reeling Brouwer, "The Work of the Spirit in Creation: According to Barth's Exegesis of the First Chapters of Genesis," *Zeitschrift Für Dialektische Theologie* 34/1 (December, 2018): 118-140.

the marginalized and suffering.[3] Joel expands this vision with a promise that in the last days, the Spirit will be poured out on all people: *Then afterward I will pour out my spirit on all flesh; your sons and your daughters shall prophesy, your old men shall dream dreams, and your young men shall see visions* (Joel 2:28). This democratization of the Spirit signifies a shift toward a more inclusive Mission, where every generation and social group is invited to participate in God's redemptive purposes.[4] These texts show that the Spirit's work in Mission is not limited to religious elites but is available to all whom God calls.

The Old Testament also presents the Spirit as the agent of deep spiritual renewal and inner transformation. This aspect of the Spirit's Mission is especially evident in the prophetic vision of Ezekiel, who looks forward to a time when God's people will be restored not only politically but also spiritually. In Ezekiel God promises as: *A new heart I will give you, and a new spirit I will put within you, and I will remove from your body the heart of stone and give you a heart of flesh. I will put my spirit within you and make you follow my statutes and be careful to observe my ordinances* (Ezekiel 36:26-27). This prophecy anticipates a Mission of internal renewal that only the Spirit can accomplish, changing the human heart, restoring obedience, and drawing people into covenant relationship with God. This inner transformation is essential to the larger Missional goal of forming a community that reflects God's holiness, justice, and mercy to the nations. The Spirit's role in this process reveals that true Mission involves both the renewal of individuals and the reformation of communities.[5] Thus, the Old Testament presents the Spirit as the Creator who gives life, the Empowerer who sends prophets, and the Renewer who transforms hearts.

The Spirit in the Mission of Jesus

The Mission of Jesus is deeply rooted in the presence and power of the Holy Spirit. From the beginning of Jesus' public ministry, Jesus is portrayed as the one anointed and led by the Spirit, fulfilling Old Testament expectations and inaugurating the kingdom of God. The Gospels, especially Luke's account, emphasize that Jesus' life and Mission were not carried out in His own human strength alone but were completely dependent on the guidance

---

[3] Mary Jerome Obiorah and Favour Chukwuemeka Uroko, "'The Spirit of the Lord God Is upon Me' (Is 61:1): The Use of Isaiah 61:1-2 in Luke 4:18-19," *HTS Theological Studies* 74/1 (January, 2018): 1-6.

[4] Norberto Saracco, "I Will Pour out My Spirit on All People: A Pastoral Reading of Joel 2:28-30 from Latin America," *Calvin Theological Journal* 46/2 (December, 2011): 268-277.

[5] Pieter de. Vries, "The Relationship between the Glory of *YHWH* and the Spirit of *YHWH* in Ezekiel 33-48," *Old Testament Essays* 28/2 (January, 2015): 326-350.

and empowerment of the Holy Spirit.[6] This connection between the Spirit and Jesus' Mission is foundational for understanding the role of the Spirit in the Church's Mission as a continuation of Jesus' Spirit-empowered work in the world.

Jesus' public ministry begins with His baptism, a moment marked by the clear manifestation of the Holy Spirit. Luke writes: *Now when all the people were baptized and when Jesus also had been baptized and was praying, the heaven was opened, and the Holy Spirit descended upon him in bodily form like a dove. And a voice came from heaven, "You are my Son, the Beloved; with you I am well pleased"* (Luke 3:21-22). This event affirms both Jesus' divine identity and His anointing for Mission through the Spirit. Immediately after this, Luke notes: *Jesus, full of the Holy Spirit, returned from the Jordan and was led by the Spirit in the wilderness* (Luke 4:1), showing that Jesus' entire ministry flows from the Spirit's leading. The pivotal moment comes when Jesus reads from the scroll of Isaiah in the synagogue, declaring the purpose of His Mission in the power of the Spirit: *The Spirit of the Lord is upon me, because he has anointed me to bring good news to the poor. He has sent me to proclaim release to the captives and recovery of sight to the blind, to set free those who are oppressed, to proclaim the year of the Lord's favour* (Luke 4:18-19).[7] This quoted from Isaiah 61 becomes Jesus' own Mission statement, rooted in the Spirit's anointing and aimed at healing, liberation, and hope.

By publicly proclaiming this Isaiah passage, Jesus reveals that His Mission is a Spirit-driven fulfilment of prophetic promise. After reading the text, Jesus boldly announces: *Today this scripture has been fulfilled in your hearing* (Luke 4:21). This declaration confirms that the long-awaited age of the Spirit and the reign of God had arrived in Him. The good news to the poor, the healing of the broken, and the freedom of the oppressed are not future possibilities but present realities in the person and ministry of Jesus.[8] Through the power of the Holy Spirit, Jesus confronts evil, restores the marginalized, and announces the arrival of God's Kingdom on earth. His miracles, teachings, and acts of compassion are not merely signs of divine power but manifestations of the Spirit's active presence in human history. In this way, Jesus' Mission becomes the model and foundation for the Church's Mission, which must likewise be empowered and directed by the Holy Spirit. Just as Jesus depended on the Spirit for every aspect of His ministry, so must

---

[6] Jacques Matthey, "Luke 4:16-30, The Spirit's Mission Manifesto, Jesus' Hermeneutics," *SEDOS Bulletin* 32/6 (December, 2000): 187-191.

[7] Mary Jerome Obiorah and Favour Chukwuemeka Uroko, "'The Spirit of the Lord God…

[8] Robert W. Canoy, "Turning the Table: Luke's Inclusive Invitation to Communion," *Review & Expositor* 116/3 (December, 2019): 305-319.

the Church today rely on the Spirit to continue His redemptive work in the world.

The Spirit in Acts and the Early Church

The Book of Acts offers the most detailed biblical account of the Holy Spirit's role in the expansion of the early Church. It presents the Spirit not only as the divine power behind the birth of the Church but also as the continuing guide, teacher, and Missionary planner who directs the Church's engagement with the world. Acts begins where the Gospel of Luke ends, with the risen Christ promising the Holy Spirit to His disciples as the essential source of empowerment for Mission.[9] The Spirit is not an optional influence but the very means by which the Church participates in the Mission of God. Through the Spirit, the early believers are transformed from a fearful and uncertain group into a bold and dynamic community sent to the ends of the earth.

The pivotal moment in Acts is the day of Pentecost, when the promised Spirit is poured out on the gathered believers in Jerusalem. Jesus had told His disciples: *But you will receive power when the Holy Spirit has come upon you, and you will be my witnesses in Jerusalem, in all Judea and Samaria, and to the ends of the earth* (Acts 1:8). This verse outlines both the geographical scope and the spiritual power of the Church's Mission.[10] The fulfilment of this promise occurs in Acts 2, where we read: *When the day of Pentecost had come, they were all together in one place. And suddenly from heaven there came a sound like the rush of a violent wind, and it filled the entire house where they were sitting. Divided tongues, as of fire, appeared among them, and a tongue rested on each of them. All of them were filled with the Holy Spirit and began to speak in other languages, as the Spirit gave them ability* (Acts 2:1-4). This event marks the beginning of the Church's Mission, demonstrating that the Spirit enables believers to communicate the gospel across linguistic and cultural barriers.[11] Peter interprets the event in light of Joel's prophecy, affirming that this outpouring of the Spirit is the sign that the last days have begun and that God's saving Mission is now reaching all people.

Beyond Pentecost, the Spirit continues to guide the Church's Missionary movement in specific and strategic ways. Throughout Acts, the apostles and other believers are repeatedly directed by the Spirit in their preaching,

---

[9] Mark P. Surburg, "The Holy Spirit and Baptism in the Book of Acts," *Concordia Theological Quarterly* 88/1 (December, 2024): 27-54.

[10] Huber L. Drumwright Jr. "Holy Spirit in the Book of Acts," *Southwestern Journal of Theology* 17/1 (December, 1974): 3-17.

[11] Stephen S. Smalley, "Spirit, Kingdom and Prayer in Luke-Acts," *Novum Testamentum* 15/1 (1973): 59-71.

travels, and decision-making.[12] For example, when Philip is sent to the Ethiopian eunuch, "the Spirit said to Philip, 'Go over to this chariot and join it'" (Acts 8:29), resulting in the gospel reaching a new region.[13] In the case of Peter's visit to Cornelius, the Spirit both initiates the encounter and confirms God's inclusion of Gentiles: *While Peter was still thinking about the vision, the Spirit said to him, "Look, three men are searching for you. Now get up, go down, and go with them without hesitation, for I have sent them."* (Acts 10:19-20). Later, in the sending of Paul and Barnabas, the Spirit plays a decisive role: *While they were worshiping the Lord and fasting, the Holy Spirit said, "Set apart for me Barnabas and Saul for the work to which I have called them"* (Acts 13:2). Similarly, Paul's travels are directed by the Spirit: *They went through the region of Phrygia and Galatia, having been forbidden by the Holy Spirit to speak the word in Asia* (Acts 16:6). These instances reveal that the Spirit is not merely a source of inspiration but the active leader in the Church's Mission, opening doors, breaking boundaries, and ensuring that the gospel advances according to God's plan.

Thus, the Book of Acts demonstrates that the Holy Spirit is the origin, power, and guide of the early Church's Mission. From Pentecost to the Missionary journeys, the Spirit is consistently portrayed as the one who enables, speaks, sends, and confirms. This dynamic role of the Spirit underscores the truth that Christian Mission is not human-led but Spirit-driven, and that faithful participation in God's Mission requires deep dependence on the ongoing presence and direction of the Holy Spirit.

Theological Themes Linking Mission and Pneumatology

The relationship between Mission and pneumatology is deeply rooted in the understanding that the Holy Spirit is the active agent of God's redemptive work in the world. The Spirit does not merely support the Church's Mission but is essential to its origin, direction, and effectiveness. As part of the *Missio Dei*, the Holy Spirit continues the sending movement of God and Jesus by empowering, guiding, and sustaining the Church in its witness. This connection gives rise to several key theological themes that shape how the Church understands and practices Mission. First, the Spirit is revealed as the divine agent of the *Missio Dei*, drawing the Church into participation in God's Mission through Trinitarian sending (John 20:21-22). Second, the Spirit empowers believers with boldness, speech, and spiritual gifts, equipping them to bear faithful and powerful witness to Christ

---

[12] Helen Bergin, "Searching out the Holy Spirit via Earth's Elements," *New Blackfriars* 83/973 (2002): 136-147.

[13] Thinandavha Derrick Mashau, "Rethinking the Use of Disruptive Pop-up Encounters for Transformation: A Missional Reading of Acts 8:26-40," *Missiology* 50/2 (December, 2022): 184-195.

(Acts 4:31; I Corinthians 2:4; 12-14). Third, the Spirit enables cultural translation by breaking down linguistic and ethnic barriers and guiding the contextualization of the gospel across diverse settings (Acts 2; Acts 10).

The Spirit and the Missio Dei

A central theological theme in the relationship between Mission and pneumatology is the role of the Holy Spirit in the *Missio Dei*. The term *Missio Dei* refers to the understanding that Mission is not primarily the Church's initiative but God's own activity in the world, carried out through the sending of the Son and the Spirit. In this framework, the Holy Spirit is not only the power behind Mission but its primary agent, actively carrying forward God's redemptive purposes in creation, history, and human lives.[14] The Spirit works within and beyond the boundaries of the Church, preparing hearts, opening doors, convicting of truth, and drawing people toward Christ. This view shifts the focus of Mission from institutional expansion to participation in the dynamic and ongoing work of the Triune God.

Jesus Himself articulated this Trinitarian pattern of sending in the Gospel of John: *Jesus said to them again, "Peace be with you. As the Father has sent me, so I send you." When he had said this, he breathed on them and said to them, "Receive the Holy Spirit"* (John 20:21-22). This passage reveals that Mission flows from God, through Jesus, and is continued through the Spirit. The disciples are not merely given a task; they are drawn into the very life and Mission of God.[15] The act of Jesus breathing on His disciples recalls the creation narrative in Genesis 2:7, where God breathes life into the human being, suggesting that this new Mission is also a work of new creation through the Spirit. It is the Spirit who animates the Church and equips it to serve as the living body of Christ in the world.[16] Therefore, understanding the Holy Spirit as the agent of the *Missio Dei* emphasizes that Christian Mission is not only empowered by the Spirit but fundamentally shaped and guided by the presence of the Spirit. Thus, the Spirit's role in Mission is not occasional or peripheral, rather, it is essential, constant, and sovereign.

Empowerment for Witness

Another key theme that connects Mission and pneumatology is the Holy Spirit's role in empowering believers for witness. In the New Testament, especially in the Book of Acts and the Pauline letters, the Spirit is described

---

[14] David Ian Starling, "'Life Because of Righteousness': The Spirit, the Church, and the *Missio Dei* in Romans," *Mission Studies* 33/3 (December, 2016): 376-390.

[15] Craig S. Keener, "Sent like Jesus: Johannine Missiology (John 20:21-22)," *Asian Journal of Pentecostal Studies* 12/1 (December, 2009): 21-45.

[16] Tom Scheuring, "The Baptism in the Holy Spirit Equips Us to Serve Others," *New Covenant* 20 (December, 1991): 12-13.

as the one who enables the Church to speak, act, and live in ways that reveal the truth and power of the gospel. Christian witness is not merely a task of communicating information; it involves bold proclamation, spiritual authority, and the manifestation of God's presence in both word and deed. The Spirit equips ordinary believers with the courage, wisdom, and supernatural gifts necessary to make Christ known in a world that often resists the gospel.[17] Without the Spirit, Mission becomes human-centred and weak; with the Spirit, it becomes a powerful expression of divine truth and grace.

In the early Church, the Holy Spirit is repeatedly shown as the one who grants courage and speech in the face of opposition. After the apostles prayed for strength during persecution, Luke records: *When they had prayed, the place in which they were gathered together was shaken, and they were all filled with the Holy Spirit and spoke the word of God with boldness* (Acts 4:31). This boldness is a direct result of the Spirit's presence and is essential for faithful witness.[18] Similarly, the apostle Paul writes about his own preaching: *My speech and my proclamation were made not with persuasive words of wisdom but with a demonstration of the Spirit and of power* (I Corinthians 2:4). This shows that Christian Mission does not rely on persuasive rhetoric or human skill, but on the Spirit's power to convince hearts and reveal truth.[19] The Spirit enables believers to speak in ways that are both courageous and spiritually effective, especially when the message of the cross challenges the values of the world.

The Spirit also empowers the Church through the distribution of charismatic gifts that build up the body of Christ and serve the Mission of God. Paul explains in his letter to the Corinthians that these gifts are diverse and are given for the common good: *Now there are varieties of gifts but the same Spirit, and there are varieties of services but the same Lord, and there are varieties of activities, but it is the same God who activates all of them in everyone. To each is given the manifestation of the Spirit for the common good* (I Corinthians 12:4-7). These gifts such as healing, prophecy, tongues, teaching, and discernment are not private spiritual experiences, but tools for Mission.[20] They make the gospel visible and tangible, especially in cross-

---

[17] David C. Cramer, "'It Has Seemed Good to the Holy Spirit and to Us': From Biblicist Arguments to Pneumatological Witness," *Direction* 50/1 (December, 2021): 14-27.

[18] Jimmy Myers, "The Politics of God: Christian Encounters with Empire in Acts 4-5," *Journal of Theological Interpretation* 17/2 (December, 2023): 201-219.

[19] Jake Eggertsen, "The Virtuous Preacher and Subversive Rhetoric: An Exploration of 1 Corinthians 2:4 and Its Implications for Preaching Today," *The Global Anglican* 137/2 (December, 2023): 140-153.

[20] José Lead Pastor González, "Open to the Spirit: Covenant Dialogue with Charismatic Movements," *The Covenant Quarterly* 79/1 (December, 2021): 19-33.

cultural and frontier contexts. Paul later emphasizes that these gifts must be exercised in love and order (I Corinthians 13-14), showing that the Spirit's empowerment is both powerful and purposeful. The presence of these gifts in the early Church reflects the Spirit's desire to equip all believers, not just a few leaders, for active participation in God's Mission.

The Spirit and Cultural Translation

A vital theological theme in connecting Mission and pneumatology is the Holy Spirit's role in enabling the gospel to cross cultural, linguistic, and social boundaries. From the earliest days of the Church, the Spirit has served as the divine bridge that makes cultural translation possible, helping the gospel to be understood in diverse contexts without being bound to one language or culture.[21] This active movement is not merely an approach of human adaptation but a work of the Spirit who ensures that the good news of Jesus Christ speaks to all peoples in ways that are faithful to the message and meaningful within specific cultures. Thus, the Spirit enables the Church to carry out its Mission in ways that are both universally true and locally relevant.

The Day of Pentecost provides the clearest example of the Spirit facilitating cultural and linguistic translation. In Acts 2, the Holy Spirit descends on the disciples and empowers them to speak in the languages of the gathered nations. The text records: *All of them were filled with the Holy Spirit and began to speak in other languages, as the Spirit gave them ability. Now there were devout Jews from every people under heaven living in Jerusalem. And at this sound the crowd gathered and was bewildered, because each one heard them speaking in the native language of each* (Acts 2:4-6). This event indicates that the gospel is not restricted to one culture or people, but is meant for all nations. Later, in Acts 10, the Spirit again facilitates cultural crossing when Peter is led to the house of Cornelius, a Gentile.[22] *While Peter was still speaking, the Holy Spirit fell upon all who heard the word* (Acts 10:44), showing that the Spirit works even beyond the boundaries of Jewish tradition. These incidents demonstrate that the Spirit is not limited by human divisions but actively moves the Church outward, affirming the dignity of every language and culture as a place where God's grace can be received.

In the ongoing Mission of the Church, the Spirit continues to lead in contextualization, the faithful translation of the gospel into new cultural settings. Contextualization is not about changing the essence of the gospel

---

[21] Georgii Petrovich Fedotov, "The Work of the Holy Spirit in Nature, Human Life and Culture," *Sourozh* 24 (December, 1986): 6-17.

[22] Matthew Barrett, "'I Will Pour out My Spirit on All Flesh': Are Acts 2 and 10 Proof-Texts for Inclusivism?," *Detroit Baptist Seminary Journal* 17 (January, 2012): 79-98.

but about expressing it in ways that resonate within different worldviews and social realities.[23] This requires spiritual discernment and cultural sensitivity, both of which are guided by the Holy Spirit. The Spirit helps the Church to avoid both cultural imperialism and theological compromise, enabling it to be both rooted in Christ and relevant to the world. The Holy Spirit consistently leads the Church in translating the gospel into diverse cultural settings.[24] In Acts 1:8, Jesus declares that the Spirit will empower the disciples to be his witnesses *in Jerusalem, in all Judea and Samaria, and to the ends of the earth*, marking a global, cross-cultural Mission. The Spirit directs Philip to the Ethiopian eunuch in Acts 8:29-38, leading to the gospel's expansion into Africa through an outsider reading Isaiah. In Acts 10:19-20, the Spirit instructs Peter to go to Cornelius, challenging Jewish boundaries and affirming that *God shows no partiality* (Acts 10:34). The Spirit commissions the first Missionary journey in Acts 13:2-4, sending Barnabas and Saul beyond their cultural borders. In Acts 15:28, during the Jerusalem Council, the Church discerns with the Spirit not to impose the law on Gentile believers, reflecting adaptive Mission. Paul's speech at the Areopagus (Acts 17:22-31) exemplify contextual proclamation, as he quotes Greek poets and speaks of the "unknown god" to present Christ within Athenian philosophy. In I Corinthians 9:19-23, Paul, led by the Spirit, becomes "all things to all people" for the sake of the gospel. Finally, Galatians 3:28 reveals the Spirit's work in forming a new humanity "in Christ Jesus," transcending ethnic, social, and gender boundaries. These passages affirm that the Holy Spirit actively guides the Church in faithfully contextualizing the gospel across cultures.

Practical Implications for the Church's Mission

The Holy Spirit plays a vital role in shaping how the Church carries out its Mission in the world. The New Testament shows that the Spirit is not just a source of personal strength but is deeply involved in guiding, forming, and empowering the Church for faithful witness. The Church's Mission is not something it does on its own, but something it shares in through the leading and power of the Spirit. This means that the Church must always depend on the Spirit, not only for direction, but also for strength, wisdom, and unity. In every part of Mission, whether in preaching, service, or daily witness, the Spirit helps the Church respond faithfully to God's call and the needs of the world.

---

[23] Andrew M. Lord, "The Holy Spirit and Contextualization," *Asian Journal of Pentecostal Studies* 4/2 (December, 2001): 201-213.

[24] Michael Downey, "Luminous Traces: The Inbreaking Spirit amid Cultural Fragmentation," *Review for Religious* 58 (January, 1999): 118-136.

Discernment and Guidance

One of the most important practical implications of pneumatology for the Church's Mission is the role of the Holy Spirit in providing discernment and guidance. In the book of Acts, the Spirit is portrayed not simply as a source of personal inspiration, but as the one who leads and directs the Mission of the Church in concrete ways.[25] In Acts 13:2-4, the early Church in Antioch receives a clear directive from the Holy Spirit during a time of communal worship and fasting:[26] *While they were worshiping the Lord and fasting, the Holy Spirit said, 'Set apart for me Barnabas and Saul for the work to which I have called them.' Then after fasting and praying they laid their hands on them and sent them off. So, being sent out by the Holy Spirit, they went down to Seleucia; and from there they sailed to Cyprus* (Acts 13:2-4). This passage highlights that Missionary initiative was not merely a human decision or administrative plan, but a Spirit-initiated and Spirit-guided act of obedience.

In practical terms, this means that the Church must continually seek the guidance of the Holy Spirit in its Mission, through prayer, communal discernment, attentiveness to Scripture, and openness to the Spirit's voice. Discernment involves not just choosing the right approaches, but aligning the Church's vision and priorities with God's ongoing work in the world.[27] This calls for spiritual attentiveness rather than reliance on purely technical or managerial solutions. Spirit-led Mission also implies flexibility and readiness to respond to unexpected opportunities or changes in direction, just as Paul and his companions were redirected by the Spirit from Asia to Macedonia (Acts 16:6-10).[28] Therefore, true Mission is not static but dynamic, shaped by the Spirit's initiative and the Church's willingness to listen and obey. This makes discernment a crucial discipline in the life of any Missional community.

---

[25] Anthony Egan, "Conscience, Spirit, Discernment: The Holy Spirit, the Spiritual Exercises and the Formation of Moral Conscience," *Journal of Theology for Southern Africa* 138 (December, 2010): 57-70.

[26] Erwin Ochsenmeier, "Antioch as a Church Planting Community: Revisiting Barnabas and Paul's Departure in Acts 13:1-4," *Neotestamentica* 56/2 (December, 2022): 317-336.

[27] Robert Allen Sorensen, "Paul's Vision of 'a Certain Macedonian' in Troas: How Might Luke's Original Audience Have Heard the Narration of Acts 16:9?," *Logia* 21/2 (December, 2012): 11-14.

[28] Matteo Crimella, "The Vision of the Macedonian: Acts 16:6-10," *Revue Biblique* 121/3 (January, 2014): 392-403.

Formation and Empowerment

The Holy Spirit not only guides the Church in Mission but also forms and empowers believers for effective service in the world. Throughout the New Testament, the Spirit is consistently portrayed as the one who equips disciples with the character, wisdom, and power needed to fulfil their calling. This formation begins with inward transformation, as the Spirit renews hearts and shapes believers into the likeness of Christ.[29] According to Galatians 5:22-23, the fruit of the Spirit: *love, joy, peace, patience, kindness, generosity, faithfulness, gentleness, and self-control* provides the moral and spiritual foundation necessary for a life of witness and service (Galatians 5:22-23). In this way, spiritual formation is not optional for Mission; it is essential, as those who represent Christ must also reflect His character.

In addition to inner formation, the Holy Spirit empowers the Church with spiritual gifts for building up the community and serving the world.[30] As Paul explains, *To each is given the manifestation of the Spirit for the common good* (I Corinthians 12:7), and he lists a wide variety of gifts including wisdom, healing, prophecy, and discernment (I Corinthians 12:8-10). These gifts are not given for personal status but for the sake of the Church's Mission. They enable ordinary believers to participate actively in ministry, making the Church a Spirit-filled body rather than a passive institution.[31] The empowering work of the Spirit also grants boldness for witness, as seen in Acts: *When they had prayed, the place in which they were gathered together was shaken; and they were all filled with the Holy Spirit and spoke the word of God with boldness* (Acts 4:31). Therefore, the Mission of the Church depends not on human ability but on the Spirit's power to form disciples and equip them for faithful and fruitful service in every context.

Unity and Diversity in the Spirit

A crucial implication of pneumatology for the Church's Mission is the Spirit's role in fostering both unity and diversity within the body of Christ. The Holy Spirit unites believers from different backgrounds into one community while also distributing diverse gifts and roles to serve the Mission of God.[32] In I Corinthians 12, Paul emphasizes that although there

---

[29] Brian Allen DeVries, "Divine Empowerment: The Holy Spirit and Church Revitalisation," *In Die Skriflig* 49/1 (January, 2015): 1-8.

[30] Elizabeth Reichert, "Aquinas and the Gifts: Contemporary Contributions to the Place of the Gifts of the Holy Spirit in the Christian Moral Life," *Annales Theologici* 36/1 (January, 2022): 203-230.

[31] Thomas A. Jackson, "Concerning Spirtual Gifts: A Study of I Corinthians 12," *Faith and Mission* 7/1 (January, 1989): 61-69.

[32] H. L. Murre-Van den Berg, "Bible Study: I Corinthians 12: Mission Relationships and Partnership: New Models of Partnership?," *International Review of Mission* 91/363 (December, 2002): 583-588.

are *varieties of gifts, but the same Spirit*, and *varieties of services, but the same Lord*, all these are *activated by one and the same Spirit, who allots to each one individually just as the Spirit chooses* (I Corinthians 12:4-6, 11). This balance of unity and diversity is essential to the Church's life and witness. The Spirit does not erase cultural, ethnic, or personal differences, but integrates them into a harmonious whole for the sake of Mission.

This dynamic is also evident in the Pentecost event, where people from many nations hear the gospel in their own languages through the power of the Spirit (Acts 2:4-11). The Spirit's work at Pentecost affirms that the gospel transcends cultural and linguistic barriers without demanding uniformity.[33] In the same way, the early Church experienced a Spirit-led expansion of its community across ethnic lines, as seen in Acts 10, when the Holy Spirit falls on Gentiles in the house of Cornelius, showing that God's Mission includes all peoples.[34] Such moments demonstrate that the Spirit creates a new humanity marked by reconciliation and mutual service, which becomes a powerful witness to the world. Thus, the unity of the Church is not based on institutional conformity but on shared life in the Spirit, while its diversity reflects the creativity and inclusiveness of God's Mission. Therefore, embracing both unity and diversity in the Spirit is essential for a healthy and faithful participation in the *Missio Dei*.

Intercultural and Prophetic Mission

The Holy Spirit empowers the Church for a Mission that is both intercultural and prophetic, enabling it to cross boundaries and speak truth in diverse contexts. From its beginning at Pentecost, the Church has been a Spirit-filled, multicultural community. In Acts 2:4-11, the Spirit enables the apostles to speak in many languages, allowing people from various nations to hear the gospel in their own tongues.[35] This moment reveals that the Mission of God is not bound to one culture or language but is meant for all peoples. The Spirit continues to enable the Church to engage in contextual Mission, helping it to translate the gospel meaningfully into new cultural settings without compromising its core message.

In addition to its intercultural dimension, Mission empowered by the Spirit is also prophetic. The Holy Spirit enables the Church to challenge injustice, proclaim God's truth, and stand in solidarity with the poor and

---

[33] Jason S. Wendel, "Are Luke's Community Summaries in Acts 2 and 4 a Cultural Appeal?," *Journal for the Study of the New Testament* 46/4 (December, 2024): 607-629.

[34] Abraham Friesen, "Acts 10: The Baptism of Cornelius as Interpreted by Thomas Müntzer and Felix Manz," *The Mennonite Quarterly Review* 64/1 (December, 1990): 5-22.

[35] J. G. Davies, "Pentecost and Glossolalia," *The Journal of Theological Studies* 3/2 (1952): 228-231.

marginalized.[36] In Luke 4:18-19, Jesus declares the Spirit's anointing upon Him *to bring good news to the poor... to proclaim release to the captives and recovery of sight to the blind, to let the oppressed go free, to proclaim the year of the Lord's favour* (Luke 4:18-19). This Mission becomes the model for the Church, which is called to be a prophetic presence in society. Thus, the Spirit equips believers with courage, wisdom, and the gifts necessary to address systemic sin, speak truth to power, and embody God's justice and peace in the world.[37] Intercultural and prophetic Mission, therefore, are not optional tasks but essential expressions of life in the Spirit. They reflect the Spirit's work in creating a Church that is both globally inclusive and deeply engaged in the moral and spiritual renewal of society.

Conclusion

The Holy Spirit plays an essential and irreplaceable role in the Mission of God. From creation to the early Church, and from the biblical witness to contemporary expressions of global Christianity, the Spirit is the primary agent who empowers, guides, and sustains the Church's participation in the *Missio Dei*. Pneumatology, when rightly understood, is not a secondary doctrine but a foundational lens through which the Church must understand its Mission. The Spirit was active in the Old Testament as the breath of life, the power behind prophetic witness, and the source of renewal and restoration. In the life and ministry of Jesus, the Spirit anointed, empowered, and directed Jesus in fulfilling God's redemptive purposes. In the Acts of the Apostles and throughout Church history, the Spirit has continued to form communities, send Missionaries, and shape the Church into a people that reflects the diversity and unity of God's Kingdom. Thus, the Church today is called to embody a Mission that is Spirit-led, discerning, and empowered. It must rely not merely on human plans or institutional strength, but on the Spirit's guidance for direction, formation, contextual engagement, and prophetic witness. The global Church, especially in an age marked by cultural plurality, social fragmentation, and spiritual hunger, must listen afresh to what the Spirit is saying. Only by walking in step with the Spirit can the Church faithfully and fruitfully proclaim the gospel in word and deed. As Jesus said to His disciples, *Receive the Holy Spirit* (John 20:22), this remains the ongoing invitation for the Church to live and serve as a Spirit-filled witness to the ends of the earth.

---

[36] Benjamin D. Crace, "Prophetic Mediums: Channeling the Holy Spirit(S)," *Journal of Pentecostal Theology* 33/2 (December, 2024): 276-295.

[37] Patrick Yankyera, "An Examination of the Role of the Holy Spirit in the Ministry of Jesus in Luke 4:18-19 with an Emphasis on Pentecostal and Charismatic Churches in Ghana," *Pentecostalism, Charismaticism and Neo-Prophetic Movements Journal* 4/2 (December, 2024): 13-24.

21

Towards a Transformative Soteriological Missiology Contextualizing Salvation and Mission in a Pluralistic and Changing World

Soteriology is the study of salvation, and Missiology is the study of the Church's Mission in the world. When these two areas are brought together, they form what is called Soteriological Missiology, an approach that explores the meaning of salvation within the context of Mission. Salvation is one of the deepest concerns of humanity across all cultures and religions. People have always searched for healing, wholeness, and hope, whether in this life or beyond. In the Christian faith, this desire is closely connected to God's saving work through Jesus Christ and the Church's calling to share that salvation with the world. In today's pluralistic and rapidly changing world, traditional views of salvation are being re-examined. Mission is no longer understood as merely converting individuals to Christianity but as participating in God's wider work of healing, justice, peace, and reconciliation. Therefore, Soteriological Missiology seeks to understand how the Christian message of salvation can be faithfully and meaningfully expressed in different cultural, social, and religious contexts. This argues that Soteriological Missiology must be both contextual and practical by taking seriously the biblical vision of salvation, the uniqueness of Christ, and the real human issues faced in our world today.

Biblical Foundations for Soteriological Missiology

Soteriological Missiology finds its foundation in the biblical narrative of salvation, which comprehends personal, communal, spiritual, and physical dimensions. In the Old Testament, salvation is expressed through themes like *shalom* (peace), deliverance from oppression, and the restoration of right relationships. In the Gospels, Jesus enacts a soteriology through healing, liberation, and radical inclusion, showing that salvation is not only about forgiveness but also about entering a new way of life within God's Kingdom. Paul further develops this vision by emphasizing justification by faith, reconciliation, and the transformation of believers into a new creation through the Spirit. All of this is framed within an eschatological prospect, where salvation is both a present reality and a future hope, as the Church awaits the full renewal of all creation.

Old Testament Visions of Holistic Salvation

The Old Testament offers a deeply holistic and integrated understanding of salvation, rooted not only in individual spiritual renewal but also in the restoration of community, justice, land, and creation. Central to this vision is the Hebrew concept of *shalom*, which incorporates peace, well-being, completeness, and harmony in all relationships such as divine, human, and ecological. Salvation in the Old Testament is not abstract or merely future-oriented, rather, it is tangible and immediate, expressing God's ongoing commitment to the flourishing of his people and creation.[1] It reflects a covenantal theology in which God's saving acts are deeply intertwined with the call to justice, faithfulness, and communal restoration.

The word *shalom* appears repeatedly as a sign of God's desired condition for God's people. It represents more than the absence of war, rather, it is the presence of righteousness, stability, and divine favour.[2] In Leviticus God promises Israel: *And I will grant peace in the land, and you shall lie down, and no one shall make you afraid; I will remove dangerous animals from the land, and no sword shall go through your land* (Leviticus 26:6). Here, peace includes security, ecological harmony, and freedom from fear. Similarly, Psalm 85 speaks poetically of the unity of divine attributes in salvation: *Steadfast love and faithfulness will meet; righteousness and peace will kiss each other* (Psalm 85:10). This imagery shows that salvation, in God's vision, brings moral, relational, and spiritual integrity.

Deliverance is another core dimension of Old Testament salvation. The Exodus narrative serves as the foundational model of salvation in Israel's collective memory. God's liberation of the Israelites from Egyptian bondage is not only a historical event but a paradigm for understanding divine salvation

---

[1] Joel R. Beeke and Devon Rossman, "The Mission of God and the Old Testament: Tracing God's Redemptive Plan of Salvation," *Puritan Reformed Journal* 15/1 (December, 2023): 153-167.

[2] R. W. L. Moberly, "Salvation in the Old Testament," *Journal of Theological Interpretation* 15/2 (December, 2021): 189-202.

throughout Scripture.[3] As Exodus records: *Say therefore to the Israelites, 'I am the Lord, and I will free you from the burdens of the Egyptians and deliver you from slavery to them. I will redeem you with an outstretched arm and with mighty acts of judgment* (Exodus 6:6). This act of redemption highlights God's concern for the oppressed and God's power to intervene in human history to bring justice and freedom. Later prophets invoke this motif to inspire hope in times of exile and oppression.[4] For example, Isaiah declares: *Do not fear, for I have redeemed you; I have called you by name, you are mine* (Isaiah 43:1), reaffirming God's personal and covenantal relationship with God's people.

Restoration as a community, both spiritual and material, is another central theme in Old Testament soteriology. After the periods of judgment, sin, or exile, God promises to renew the covenant and restore his people. This includes healing the land, rebuilding ruined cities, and renewing the people's joy and dignity.[5] In Ezekiel God says: *I will take you from the nations, and gather you from all the countries, and bring you into your own land. I will sprinkle clean water upon you, and you shall be clean from all your uncleannesses...A new heart I will give you, and a new spirit I will put within you* (Ezekiel 36:24-26). Here, salvation involves cleansing, inner transformation, and the reestablishment of life in the promised land, that transforms a community as a whole. Similarly, Joel speaks of God's restorative generosity: *I will repay you for the years that the swarming locust has eaten... You shall eat in plenty and be satisfied, and praise the name of the Lord your God...* (Joel 2:25-26). God's salvation extends to economic restoration and communal joy as well.

Missiologically, the Old Testament visualizes salvation as God's dynamic, faithful action to bring God's people into fullness of life in every area such as moral, spiritual, social, and ecological. It is covenantal, in that it is grounded in God's promises and Israel's response. It is communal, focused not on isolated individuals but on the people of God as a whole.[6] It is also prophetic, calling for repentance and justice as prerequisites for renewal. In Micah the prophetic call to live out salvation is made clear: *He has told you, O mortal, what is good; and what does the Lord require of you but to do justice, and to love kindness, and to walk humbly with your God?* (Micah 6:8).

---

[3] John H. Stek, "Salvation, Justice and Liberation in the Old Testament," *Calvin Theological Journal* 13/2 (December, 1978): 133-165.

[4] John H. Stek, "Salvation, Justice and Liberation in the Old Testament…

[5] Claus Westermann, "Salvation and Healing in the Community: The Old Testament Understanding," International Review of Mission 61/241 (December, 1972): 9-19.

[6] Walter C. Kaiser Jr. "Salvation in the Old Testament: With Special Emphasis on the Object and Content of Personal Belief," *Jian Dao* 2 (December, 1994): 1-18.

Thus, it is clear that the Old Testament portrays salvation as a comprehensive vision of life in right relationship with God, others, and creation. It includes deliverance from external oppression, internal renewal of the heart, and the restoration of peace and justice in all areas of life. This holistic vision lays the foundation for understanding Jesus' Mission in the New Testament and continues to shape Christian Missiology today.

Jesus' Mission and Soteriology

The Mission of Jesus in the Gospels presents a holistic vision of salvation that incorporates healing, liberation, and inclusion. Jesus' soteriology is not limited to the forgiveness of sins or the promise of heaven but includes the full restoration of human life physically, socially, spiritually, and relationally.[7] At the beginning of public ministry, Jesus declares His Mission using the words of the prophet Isaiah: *The Spirit of the Lord is upon me, because he has anointed me to bring good news to the poor. He has sent me to proclaim release to the captives and recovery of sight to the blind, to let the oppressed go free, to proclaim the year of the Lord's favour* (Luke 4:18-19). This manifesto outlines a Mission plan where salvation involves tangible acts of liberation and healing. Jesus heals the sick, restores sight to the blind, raises the dead, and delivers people from demonic oppression, thus demonstrating that salvation touches every aspect of broken human existence.[8] For example, when healing a paralytic, Jesus says, *Friend, your sins are forgiven you* (Luke 5:20), linking physical healing with spiritual restoration.

Liberation in Jesus' Mission includes release from sin, but also deliverance from economic, social, and spiritual bondage. Jesus' interactions with the marginalized such as lepers, tax collectors, women, and Gentiles show that salvation breaks down barriers and restores dignity. In John, Jesus proclaims that: *So, if the Son makes you free, you will be free indeed* (John 8:36), indicating the deep liberation that comes through union with Jesus. Moreover, Jesus challenges oppressive systems and religious legalism that excluded people from experiencing God's grace.[9] Jesus' radical inclusion of outsiders is evident when Jesus dines with sinners and tax collectors (Matthew 9:10-13) and when Jesus engages in life-giving conversation with the Samaritan woman, offering her "living water" (John 4:10). The healing of the bleeding woman also exemplifies this inclusive salvation: *Daughter,*

---

[7] Kwong-pui Chan, "The Role of Jesus in Salvation: The Confucian Soteriology of Wu Leichuan," *Hill Road* 8/1 (December, 2005): 79-93.

[8] Richard F. Zehnle, "Salvific Character of Jesus' Death in Lucan Soteriology," *Theological Studies* 30/3 (December, 1969): 420-444.

[9] Milan Kostresevic, "What Did Jesus Write on the Ground?: Exegetical Analysis of John 8: 6-8," *Nicholai Studies* 1/1 (January, 2021): 17-52.

your faith has made you well; go in peace, and be healed of your disease (Mark 5:34). Here, Jesus restores not only her health but also her status in society.

Jesus' soteriology is thus best described as Missional and restorative. It brings wholeness to individuals and communities and extends God's Kingdom to the marginalized and forgotten. This comprehensive vision of salvation sets the pattern for the Church's ongoing Mission as to proclaim good news, heal the broken, and embody God's inclusive love.[10] Jesus' life and ministry show that salvation is not just about going to heaven after death but about experiencing the transforming power of God in the present. Jesus' declaration that: *I came that they may have life, and have it abundantly* (John 10:10) thus, summarizes the heart of Jesus' saving Mission is a call to abundant, whole, and restored life here and now.

Pauline Mission and Eschatology

The Apostle Paul presents a vision of salvation that is deeply Missional, grounded in the redemptive work of Christ, and oriented toward personal transformation and cosmic renewal. One of the central themes in Paul's understanding of salvation is justification by faith, which affirms that human beings are made right with God, not through works or law, but by trusting in Jesus Christ.[11] Paul writes, *Therefore, since we are justified by faith, we have peace with God through our Lord Jesus Christ* (Romans 5:1). Justification is not merely a legal declaration; it is the beginning of a reconciled relationship with God that transforms the believer's identity and standing. This new relationship also brings reconciliation, restoring broken relationships between humanity and God, and among people.[12] Paul powerfully states that: *All this is from God, who reconciled us to himself through Christ, and has given us the ministry of reconciliation* (II Corinthians 5:18). This makes salvation inherently Missional, as believers are not only recipients of reconciliation but also agents who carry that message into the world.

In Paul's understanding, salvation is not limited to the forgiveness of individual sins, but involves becoming a new creation through the power of the Holy Spirit. This transformation affects every aspect of life, turning

[10] Pintor Marihot Sitanggang, "Towards and Inclusive and Contextual Church: A Proposal," *Encounter* 83/1 (December, 2023): 27-40.

[11] Rollin G. Grams, "Contextualisation, Intertextuality, and Paul's Soteriology," *Transformation* 23/1 (2006): 3-16.

[12] Presian R. Burroughs, "Wesley's Representation of Salvation in 'The Scripture Way of Salvation': A Pauline Assessment," *Wesleyan Theological Journal* 51/1 (December, 2016): 203-208.

believers into participants in God's redemptive work.[13] As Paul declares: *So if anyone is in Christ, there is a new creation: everything old has passed away; see, everything has become new!* (II Corinthians 5:17). This newness extends beyond personal renewal to include the restoration of creation itself, as seen in Romans: *The creation itself will be set free from its bondage to decay and will obtain the freedom of the glory of the children of God* (Romans 8:21). Paul's eschatological vision, his understanding of the "already and not yet" dimension of salvation also shapes his Missiology. Salvation is already experienced in the present through faith, but its fullness is yet to come in the final renewal of all things.[14] As Paul writes: *For in hope we were saved. Now hope that is seen is not hope. For who hopes for what is seen?* (Romans 8:24).

Therefore, Paul's soteriology provides a comprehensive framework that unites personal faith, communal responsibility, and cosmic restoration. His understanding calls the Church to a Mission rooted in God's reconciling love, active in the world through Christ, and moving toward the final transformation of all creation. Justification, reconciliation, and new creation are not only theological truths but Missional imperatives for the people of God.

The Eschatological Horizon of Salvation: Already and Not Yet

The New Testament teaches that salvation exists within an eschatological horizon, meaning it is both a present reality and a future hope. The "already" dimension affirms that through Christ's saving work, believers now receive salvation as a gift of grace, gaining new life and identity by faith (Ephesians 2:8; John 5:24).[15] At the same time, the "not yet" reminds us that the fullness of salvation is still to come, as creation and humanity await final redemption and the renewal of all things when Christ returns (Romans 8:22-23; Revelation 21:4). This tension calls Christians to live with both urgency and hope, participating in God's Mission by embodying justice, mercy, healing, and reconciliation while looking forward to the ultimate fulfilment of God's kingdom (Philippians 3:20). In this way, the "already and not yet" vision of salvation provides present transformation and future assurance, shaping the Church's life and witness in the world.

---

[13] Peter Frick, "The Means and Mode of Salvation: A Hermeneutical Proposal for Clarifying Pauline Soteriology," *Horizons in Biblical Theology* 29/2 (December, 2007): 203-222.

[14] Cara Pfeiffer, "Healing and the Holy Spirit: A Manifestation of the 'Already, but Not yet' Kingdom of God," Vision 13/1 (December, 2012): 48-55.

[15] Robert A. Kelly, "Preservation and Salvation: The Significance of Eschatology for the Mission of the Church," Consensus 14/1 (December, 1988): 49-63.

Historical Foundations of Soteriological Missiology

The awareness of salvation has always been at the centre of the Christian Mission. From the early Church to the modern era, Christians have been concerned with how people are saved and how the message of salvation should be shared with the world. This connection between salvation (soteriology) and Mission (Missiology) has developed over time in response to changing theological, cultural, and global situations. In the past, salvation was often seen as something available only through the Church. Later, it was closely tied to saving individuals from hell through personal conversion and life affirming.[16] However, as the world changed, especially after the early 20th century, Christian thinkers and Missionaries began to understand salvation in broader terms, reaching not just individual souls, but also communities, societies, and even creation itself.

Classical Christian View

In early Christianity, salvation was understood in an ecclesiocentric way, expressed in the phrase *Extra Ecclesiam Nulla Salus* (outside the Church there is no salvation).[17] Church Fathers like Cyprian taught that the Church was the ark of salvation, and participation in its life and sacraments was necessary for God's grace, since Christ had established the Church as His body (Acts 4:12; John 14:6). In the Patristic period, Eastern theologians emphasized salvation as *theosis*, sharing in the divine nature (II Peter 1:4), while the Western tradition, especially Augustine, highlighted deliverance from sin through God's grace mediated by the Church.[18] The medieval Church reinforced this view by stressing baptism, Eucharist, and penance as means of salvation, seeing the Church as the mediator of grace.[19] As Ephesians explains, Christ loved and sanctified the Church to present it holy and without blemish (Ephesians 5:25-27). Thus, classical Christian thought saw salvation not only as personal faith in Christ but as belonging to the visible, sacramental, and hierarchical Church.

---

[16] Christina Manohar, "The Spirit in Mission", in *Foundations for Mission*, edited by Emma Wild-Wood and Peniel Rajkumar (Oxford: Regnum Books International, 2013), 145.

[17] Matthew J. Ramage, "*Extra Ecclesiam Nulla Salus* and the Substance of Catholic Doctrine: Towards a Realization of Benedict XVI's 'Hermeneutic of Reform,'" *Nova et Vetera* 14/1 (December, 2016): 295-330.

[18] Anna Marie Aagaard, "'My Eyes Have Seen Your Salvation': On Likeness to God and Deification in Patristic Theology," *Religion & Theology* 17/3-4 (December, 2010): 302-328.

[19] Jeremy Cohen, "The Mystery of Israel's Salvation: Romans 11:25-26 in Patristic and Medieval Exegesis," *Harvard Theological Review* 98/3 (December, 2005): 247-281.

19th to Early 20th Century Missiology

In the 19th to early 20th century, Christian Mission was shaped by a soteriology that focused mainly on saving souls from eternal damnation through personal faith in Jesus Christ. Salvation was seen in individualistic and spiritual terms, centred on conversion, repentance, and assurance of eternal life in heaven (John 3:16; Mark 16:16; Acts 2:38; Romans 10:13).[20] Missionaries preached urgently, believing that proclaiming the gospel to all nations would hasten Christ's return (Matthew 24:14), making Mission both a rescue from hell and a preparation for the second coming.[21] While this era produced great zeal and helped spread Christianity worldwide, it was limited by its narrow focus on the afterlife, often neglecting themes of justice, reconciliation, and community transformation, and at times became entangled with colonialism and Western cultural imposition.

Shift in the Post-1910 Era

The post-1910 era brought a major shift in the theology of Mission, moving from the narrow belief of *extra ecclesiam nulla salus* (outside the Church no salvation) to a broader vision of *extra mundum nulla salus* (outside the world no salvation).[22] This new understanding recognized that God's saving work is not limited to the institutional Church but embraces the whole world, calling the Church to participate in God's redemptive activity in every part of life and creation. Influenced by the 1910 Edinburgh Missionary Conference, Mission came to be seen not only as calling individuals to faith but also as addressing the world's brokenness through healing, reconciliation, justice, and peace (II Corinthians 5:19; Luke 4:18-19; Romans 8:21).[23] Salvation was understood as both personal and cosmic, spiritual and social, focusing not on escaping the world but on transforming it in Christ. The Church's role was to be a sign of God's Kingdom by proclaiming the gospel and demonstrating it through action, joining in God's purposes for the renewal of all creation.

---

[20] Donald A. Carson, "Kingdom, Ethics, and Individual Salvation," *Themelios* 38/2 (December, 2013): 197-201.

[21] Samson Uytanlet, "Motivations for Mission: Revisiting the Evangelical Interpretations of Matthew 24:14," *Evangelical Missions Quarterly* 57/1 (January, 2021): 4-6.

[22] Wouter Biesbrouck, "*Extra Ecclesiam Nulla Salus, Sed Extra Mundum Nulla Damnatio*: Reappropriating Christ's Descent into Hell for Theology of Religions," *Louvain Studies* 37/2-3 (January, 2013): 107-132.

[23] Stephen B. Bevans, "Revisiting Mission at Vatican II: Theology and Practice for Today's Missionary Church," *Theological Studies* 74 (2013): 275-278.

Key Thinkers and Their Contributions

The development of Soteriological Missiology has been deeply shaped by the work of key theologians and Missiologists who have helped the Church understand salvation in new and meaningful ways. They have responded to the changing needs of the world and the growing diversity of cultures, religions, and human experiences. Through their writings and insights, they have challenged narrow views of salvation and offered broader, more compassionate, and more contextual understandings of how God's saving work is shared through Mission. In this context it is important to discuss the contributions of three such scholars: David Bosch, Stephen Bevans, Alan Tippett and M. M. Thomas. Each of them brings a unique perspective to the relationship between salvation and Mission.

David Bosch

David Bosch, one of the most influential Missiologists of the 20th century, placed salvation at the very centre of Mission, seeing it as the "throbbing heart of Missiology" because it speaks to humanity's deepest needs for meaning, hope, and reconciliation with God. In Transforming Mission, he argued that Mission is not about expanding the Church or spreading doctrine but about participating in God's work of life, healing, and reconciliation (I Timothy 2:3-4).[24] Bosch stressed the balance between God's initiative in salvation, which is purely by grace (Ephesians 2:8-9), and human participation through justice, compassion, and proclamation. For him, Mission is a dialogue between God, who offers salvation in Christ, and a broken world longing for redemption, making Mission a partnership in God's liberating work (II Corinthians 6:1). In this way, Bosch expanded the understanding of salvation from individual souls to the transformation of communities, societies, and even creation itself, calling the Church to embody God's saving love in every dimension of life.[25]

Stephen Bevans

Stephen Bevans, a leading contemporary Missiologist, presents salvation as a deeply contextual and inclusive reality that must be understood within specific cultural, social, and religious settings. For him, salvation is not a fixed formula but the discovery of what it means to be truly human in each context, affirming human dignity and uniqueness (Psalms 139:14).[26] It is about transformation into a new humanity in Christ, living as people who

---

[24] David Jacobus Bosch, *Transforming Mission: Paradigm Shifts in Theology of Mission…*, 402.

[25] David Jacobus Bosch, *Transforming Mission: Paradigm Shifts in Theology of Mission…*, 402-409.

[26] Stephen B. Bevans, "Revisiting Mission at Vatican II…, 277.

are free, loving, and whole (II Corinthians 5:17). Salvation, Bevans argues, is experienced not only personally but also communally, through worship, hospitality, service, and shared life that reflects the Kingdom of God (Acts 2:46-47). His vision extends beyond the Church to embrace the whole creation and people of other religions, affirming that God's reconciling work in Christ reaches all (Colossians 1:19-20). Without denying Christ's uniqueness, Bevans encourages a humble, dialogical Mission that listens and learns from others, making salvation visible in love, justice, and community.[27] In this way, he offers a human-centred, relational, and cosmic understanding of salvation as God's transforming work in history and creation.

Alan Tippett

Alan Tippett, a pioneer in Missiological anthropology, shaped Soteriological Missiology by stressing that Mission must begin with cultural sensitivity and a deep understanding of the people being reached. He argued that salvation cannot be communicated meaningfully if foreign ideas or practices are imposed, but must be expressed in ways that resonate with local cultures, much like Paul's approach of becoming "all things to all people" (I Corinthians 9:22).[28] Tippett warned against paternalism and ethnocentrism, noting how colonial attitudes often distorted the gospel and harmed the dignity of those evangelized. Instead, he called for a humble, respectful, and dialogical Mission that honours local values and worldviews. He also emphasized that Mission must be rooted in real human conditions such as poverty, injustice, sickness, and cultural identity, while remaining faithful to the truth of the gospel. Drawing on biblical foundations like Philippians 2:3-4 and Micah 6:8, Tippett envisioned Mission as a lived expression of justice, mercy, humility, and compassion, allowing the gospel to take root authentically within every cultural context.[29]

Madathilparampil Mammen Thomas

The Indian theologian M. M. Thomas developed the idea of salvation as humanization to respond to the social, political, and religious challenges of modern India. He argued that salvation in Christ is not only about personal forgiveness or spiritual rescue but about restoring the fullness of human dignity, freedom, and life in history.[30] For Thomas, the incarnation shows that in Jesus God reveals true humanity, and to be saved is to become truly

---

[27] Stephen B. Bevans, "Revisiting Mission at Vatican II…, 277.

[28] Alan R. Tippett, *Introduction to Missiology* (Pasadena: William Carey Library, 1987), 152-157.

[29] Alan R. Tippett, *Introduction to Missiology*…, 152-157.

[30] M. M. Thomas, *Salvation and Humanization* (Madras: CLS, 1971), 52-60.

human, living in love, service, and justice. Drawing on biblical themes like the *Imago Dei* (Genesis 1:26-27), abundant life (John 10:10), and the renewal of creation (II Corinthians 5:17; Colossians 1:20), he connected salvation with the transformation of society.[31] He saw the Church's Mission as joining God's work of humanization, which includes social reform, interreligious dialogue, justice, peace, and cultural renewal, while affirming both the uniqueness of Christ and God's universal saving action.[32] Thus, the Church must embody the gospel by standing with the oppressed, confronting dehumanizing systems, and becoming a sign of the new humanity in Christ. In this way, Thomas presents a holistic vision of salvation that unites personal transformation with social responsibility and points toward the ultimate fulfilment of humanity in Christ.

Conclusion

Soteriology, the doctrine of salvation, remains at the very heart of Christian Missiology. Throughout history, the Church's Mission has been shaped by how it understands and proclaims the meaning of salvation. While earlier models often focused narrowly on individual conversion or institutional belonging, the development of soteriological Missiology calls for a broader, deeper, and more dynamic understanding of salvation that speaks to the full reality of human life and the needs of the world today. Salvation is not only about the soul's destiny after death but also about healing, reconciliation, justice, and transformation in the here and now. In today's pluralistic, interconnected, and rapidly changing world, the Church is challenged to articulate a vision of salvation that is both faithful to the gospel and sensitive to cultural, social, and global contexts. This includes engaging in respectful dialogue with other religions, addressing systems of oppression, listening to marginalized voices, and responding to new questions raised by technology and global crises. Soteriology must therefore be inclusive, contextual, and participatory, grounded in Scripture and lived out in action.

[31] M. M. Thomas, *Revolution in India and Christian Humanism* (New Delhi: Forum for Christian Concern for People's Struggle, 1978), 2.

[32] K. C. Abraham, "Explorations into Spirituality and Humanization: The Revolutionary Thought of M. M. Thomas," in *A Light to the Nations: The Indian Presence in the Ecumenical Movement in the 20th Century*, edited by Jesudas M. Athyal (Geneva: WCC Publications, 2016), 108.

22

Mission in the Roman Catholic Tradition From Ecclesial Expansion to Trinitarian Witness

The Roman Catholic Church has a long and influential tradition in the thinking and practice of Christian Mission. For many centuries, Catholic Mission was closely linked to the expansion of the institutional Church, with an emphasis on preaching the gospel, administering the sacraments, and bringing people into communion with the "See of Rome." Mission was often carried out by religious orders such as the Jesuits, Franciscans, and Dominicans, particularly during the age of European colonization. In this period, Mission was frequently associated with European culture, authority, and political power, sometimes leading to a lack of sensitivity to local traditions. The First Vatican Council (1869-1870) played an important role in shaping the Catholic approach to Mission during the modern era. Although it did not directly address Mission, it strongly emphasized the central authority of the Pope and the doctrinal unity of the Church, including the definition of 'papal infallibility.' This contributed to a more centralized and institutional model of Mission, where Missionary efforts were coordinated by Rome and focused on defending the faith in an increasingly secular world. The result was a model that valued unity and orthodoxy, but often lacked openness to dialogue or cultural adaptation. A major turning point came with the Second Vatican Council (1962-1965), which offered a renewed and broader understanding of Mission. In its decree *Ad Gentes*, the Council taught that Mission flows from the very nature of the Church, which is rooted in the Mission of the Triune God. Vatican II emphasized that Mission is not only about bringing people into the Church, but also about witnessing to Christ through service, dialogue, justice, and respect for all cultures and peoples. It encouraged the Church to listen, learn, and engage with the modern world in a spirit of humility and love.

The Historical Development of the Catholic Understanding of Mission

Before the Second Vatican Council (1962-1965), the Roman Catholic Church largely operated with a Christendom model of Mission, shaped by centuries of Western European dominance in theology, politics, and culture. Mission was often understood as a task of expanding the institutional Church, converting non-Christians, and bringing them into sacramental and doctrinal conformity with Roman Catholic structures. The theology of Mission emphasized baptism, sacramental life, and obedience to ecclesiastical authority. Evangelization was closely linked with civilization and colonization, particularly during the age of European expansion (16th to 19th centuries). In many cases, the spread of the gospel was intertwined with European languages, customs, and education systems, which often led to cultural dominance rather than authentic inculturation. This institutional model saw Mission as the Church's work to bring individuals into the one true Church, with the Latin Rite and Roman authority at the centre. The laity had a limited role, and Mission was primarily carried out by ordained clergy and religious orders. Dialogue with other Christian denominations or non-Christian religions was rare or discouraged. The aim was conversion and incorporation into the Roman Catholic Church, rather than mutual engagement or contextual adaptation.

The Role of Vatican I: Centralization and Doctrinal Assurance

The First Vatican Council (1869-1870) reinforced this traditional, centralized view of Mission. Although the council did not issue specific documents on Mission, its key theological affirmations had a lasting impact. The doctrine of papal infallibility and the emphasis on papal primacy gave Rome a strong central authority over global Mission efforts.[1] Missionary orders and bishops reported to the Congregation for the Propagation of the Faith (*Propaganda Fide*), reflecting the Council's focus on maintaining doctrinal purity and institutional control.[2] In the context of growing secularism and rationalism, Vatican I aimed to defend the Church's teaching authority and the divine origin of revelation. This gave Missionaries confidence in proclaiming the Catholic faith as the absolute and unchanging truth. However, this also led to a one-way model of Mission, where the Church was seen as the only teacher

---

[1] Suan Sonna, "Roman and Catholic: A Biblical and Historical Defense of Vatican I Papal Theology in Response to Jerry Walls," *Heythrop Journal* 64/1 (January, 2023): 120-134.

[2] Camillus Nimalan Johnpillai, "Journey of Propaganda Fide (400 Years): Mission Then and Now," *SEDOS Bulletin* 54/9-10 (June, 2022): 5-16.

and others were simply recipients.[3] There was little room for dialogue, cultural adaptation, or mutual learning. While Vatican I helped preserve the unity and orthodoxy of the Catholic faith during a time of upheaval, it also unintentionally limited the scope of Mission to structural expansion and theological defence. This approach lacked attention to the complexities of culture, pluralism, and the modern world. It would take the renewal of Vatican II to correct and reframe the Church's understanding of Mission in a more holistic, dialogical, and inclusive direction.

Vatican II and the Renewal of Catholic Mission Theology

The Second Vatican Council (1962-1965) marked a major turning point in the Catholic Church's theology and practice of Mission. With its decree *Ad Gentes* (1965), the Council affirmed that the Missionary nature of the Church flows directly from the Trinity, not just from papal authority or institutional expansion.[4] Mission was now understood as participation in the Mission of God (*Missio Dei*), the sending of Jesus and the Holy Spirit into the world, and the Church's call to share in that divine movement of love, reconciliation, and renewal. Rather than focusing solely on conversion and church membership, Vatican II emphasized that Mission involves witness, dialogue, service, and solidarity.[5] The Council affirmed the importance of local cultures and languages, encouraging inculturation, the expression of the gospel in forms meaningful to each people and culture.[6] It also emphasized the role of the whole people of God in Mission, not only priests and religious. Lay people, families, and even local churches were recognized as essential agents of evangelization in their everyday contexts. Vatican II also opened the Church to ecumenical and interfaith dialogue, recognizing that elements of truth and grace can be found outside the visible boundaries of the Catholic Church.[7] This marked a major departure from earlier exclusivist attitudes. The goal of Mission was no longer just to "convert" others into Catholicism, but to cooperate with all people of goodwill in building God's Kingdom on earth, especially through justice, peace, and human dignity.

---

[3] Massimo Faggioli, "Vatican I, the New Papacy, and the Crisis of Catholic Globalization," *Newman Studies Journal* 17/2 (April, 2020): 5-21.

[4] Mat Schramm, "Catholic Charismatics and Ecumenical Translation after Vatican II," *Journal of Ecumenical Studies* 59/3 (December, 2024): 352-370.

[5] Massimo Faggioli, "The Liturgical Reform and the 'Political' Message of Vatican II in the Age of a Privatized and Libertarian Culture," *Worship* 90/1 (January, 2016): 10-27.

[6] Mark R. Francis, "Liturgy and Inculturation since Vatican II: Where Are We? What Have We Learned?," *Worship* 91 (January, 2017): 24-42.

[7] John Daniel Dadosky, "Interreligious Friendship as Method for Interfaith Relations: Vatican II and Beyond," *Journal of Ecumenical Studies* 60/1 (Winter, 2025): 5-22.

Ecclesial Documents and Their Role in Shaping the Catholic Understanding of Mission

The official teachings of the Catholic Church have played a vital role in shaping its understanding of Mission over time. These teachings provide both a clear theological foundation and practical direction for how the Church responds to the changing needs of the world. In the modern era, the Church has recognized that Mission is not just one of its activities, but an essential part of its identity, flowing from the love of the Triune God. This understanding has led to a deeper and more dynamic vision of Mission, one that goes beyond traditional views centred only on conversion. Instead, the Church started emphasizing evangelization as a joyful witness to the gospel, expressed through personal faith, social action, cultural dialogue, and care for the whole of creation. This broader view of Mission also affirms the role of all the faithful such as, clergy, religious, and laity alike in carrying out the Church's Mission in everyday life. Together, these teachings have helped the Catholic Church grow into a more holistic, inclusive, and context-sensitive approach to Mission, rooted in the life and message of Jesus Christ.

Papal Encyclicals and Missionary Orders Before Vatican II

Before the Second Vatican Council, the Catholic Church's understanding of Mission gradually developed through important councils, papal teachings, and the work of Missionary orders. Although the theology of Mission was not yet fully formed, the Church began to move away from older patterns tied to colonial power and toward a more spiritual and global approach. Doctrinal decisions, especially about the authority of the Pope and the identity of the Church, provided the foundation for a more unified and organized Mission strategy. At the same time, Popes and church leaders started to emphasize the importance of local leadership, cultural respect, and ethical engagement in Mission work. These developments encouraged the training of indigenous clergy, the involvement of laypeople, and a deeper concern for justice and human dignity. Together, they prepared the way for a renewed theology of Mission that would emerge more clearly in the teachings of Vatican II.

The Council of Trent and the Foundations of Post-Reformation Catholic Mission

The Council of Trent (1545-1563) played an important role in shaping the Catholic Church's understanding of Mission, even though it did not produce a direct Missionary document. The Council was a response to the Protestant Reformation, aiming to clarify Catholic doctrine and reform Church practices.[8] This effort to strengthen the Church from within led to a period known as the Counter-Reformation, which had a strong Missionary impact. The Council affirmed the importance of the sacraments, church tradition, and the authority of the Pope, teachings that Missionaries would later carry to different parts of the world. It also inspired the founding and expansion of Missionary religious orders, such as the Jesuits, who played a key role in spreading the gospel in Asia, Africa, and the Americas. The Missionaries not only preached but also built schools, studied languages, and engaged with local cultures.[9] Although the Council of Trent did not define Mission theologically as Vatican II later would, it provided a doctrinal foundation and spiritual renewal that fuelled Catholic Missionary activity for centuries.

Propaganda Fide: Centralizing Catholic Mission under the Holy See

One of the most important developments in Catholic Mission before Vatican I was the creation of the Congregation for the Propagation of the Faith, commonly known as *Propaganda Fide*, established in 1622 by Pope Gregory XV. This Vatican office was designed to organize and coordinate the Church's global Missionary efforts, especially in non-Christian regions.[10] Until then, much of Catholic Mission was linked to European colonial powers, who often controlled where and how Missionaries worked. *Propaganda Fide* shifted authority away from colonial governments and placed it directly under the Holy See, allowing the Church to take a more independent and spiritual approach to Mission.[11] It supported the training of Missionaries, the translation of Christian texts into local languages, and the promotion of indigenous clergy. This move helped the Church to build a more universal and unified Missionary strategy and became a central institution for shaping Catholic Mission until the modern era.

Vatican I and the Doctrinal Foundations of Catholic Mission

The First Vatican Council (1869-1870), though not focused directly on Mission, played an important role in shaping the theological foundations of Catholic Missionary work. Its key document, *Pastor Aeternus* (1870), issued under Pope Pius IX, defined the primacy and infallibility of the Pope in matters of faith and doctrine.[12] This teaching strengthened the

---

[8] Robert L. Fastiggi, "The Contributions of the Council of Trent to the Catholic Reformation," *Perichoresis* 18/6 (December, 2020): 3-20.

[9] Robert L. Fastiggi, "The Contributions of the Council of Trent…

[10] Camillus Nimalan Johnpillai, "Journey of Propaganda Fide…

[11] Bernardo Cervellera, "Propaganda Fide and Mission as Communication," *The Hong Kong Journal of Catholic Studies* 14 (December, 2023): 143-158.

[12] Christian D. Washburn, "*Pastor Aeternus*, Robert Bellarmine, and the Possibility of a Heretical Pope," Theological Studies 85/2 (January, 2024): 309-316.

idea of a universal Church under central papal leadership, which had clear implications for Mission. By affirming the Pope's supreme authority, the Council helped justify a centralized approach to global evangelization, often carried out through religious orders and Missionary congregations under the direction of the Vatican.[13] Although Vatican I did not present a direct theology of Mission, it provided the doctrinal clarity and institutional structure that supported the Catholic Church's global Missionary expansion in the 19th and early 20th centuries.

Maximum Illud: A Turning Point Toward Ethical and Global Catholic Mission

In 1919, Pope Benedict XV issued *Maximum Illud*, a groundbreaking encyclical often considered the first modern Mission document of the Catholic Church. Written in the aftermath of World War I and colonial expansion, it marked a turning point in Catholic Mission thinking.[14] The Pope strongly urged Missionaries to separate the gospel from colonialism and nationalism, warning that using Mission as a tool of empire could damage both the Church's witness and the dignity of local peoples. He called for greater respect for indigenous cultures and emphasized the importance of training local clergy to lead their own churches.[15] This encyclical shifted the Church's focus away from a Eurocentric view of Mission and laid the groundwork for a more ethical, inclusive, and globally responsible approach.[16] Its principles would later influence the renewed vision of Mission at Vatican II.

Rerum Ecclesiae: Building Local Churches and Expanding the Role of Mission

Pope Pius XI expanded the vision of Catholic Mission with his 1926 encyclical Rerum Ecclesiae, which reaffirmed and built upon the teachings of *Maximum Illud*.[17] He called for an increased urgency in global Mission

---

[13] John Stayne, "The Charism of Infallibility: Re-Receiving Pastor Aeternus' Teaching on Papal Infallibility in Light of *Iuvenescit Ecclesia*'s Teaching on Charismatic Gifts," *Ecclesiology* 19/1 (December, 2023): 70-92.

[14] Therese D'Orsa, "A Missionary Impulse Capable of Transforming Everything," The Australasian Catholic Record 97/3 (January, 2020), 259-274.

[15] Jianmin Zhao, "Missio Ad Gentes in the Chinese Context: From Maximum Illud to the Provisional Agreement," *Prajñā Vihāra* 26/1 (January-June, 2025): 51-64.

[16] Prudence De Letter, "A Pontifical Vista of Forty Years," *Worldmission* 12 (1961): 20-23.

[17] James Kroeger, "Papal Mission Wisdom: Five Mission Encyclicals 1919-1959," in *A Century of Catholic Mission Roman Catholic Missiology 1910 to the Present*, edited by Stephen B. Bevans (Oxford: Regnum Books International, 2013), 93-95.

work, especially in regions still heavily dependent on foreign Missionaries. The document emphasized the need to train local priests and catechists, and to develop self-governing churches with local leadership, what he called "native hierarchies."[18] Pope Pius XI also acknowledged the important role of women in Mission, particularly in education and healthcare ministries. His call for fully inculturated local churches was a major step toward empowering non-Western communities and reducing dependency on European structures.[19] This vision of autonomous churches later became a central theme in *Ad Gentes* at Vatican II.

Evangelii Praecones: Maturity, Justice, and Respect in Missionary Growth

In *Evangelii Praecones* (1951), Pope Pius XII addressed the rapid expansion of Catholic Missions in the first half of the 20th century. While celebrating the growth of the Church worldwide, he also warned of the continuing danger of cultural domination and foreign dependence in Missionary work.[20] He emphasized that true Mission must lead to mature, self-sustaining churches, rooted in their own cultures and values.[21] The document encouraged Missionaries to respect local traditions and to see education, healthcare, and social justice not as secondary concerns but as essential to evangelization. Significantly, *Evangelii Praecones* recognized the growing importance of lay involvement in Mission, marking a shift from a purely clerical enterprise to a broader participation of all the faithful.[22] It helped move the Church toward a more inclusive and just Mission strategy.

Fidei Donum: A New Model of Shared Mission Across the Global Church

Pope Pius XII continued to expand the Church's Mission vision in *Fidei Donum* (1957), an apostolic letter that introduced a new and practical model of inter-church cooperation. Recognizing the fast growth of churches in Africa and other Mission territories, the Pope encouraged bishops in more established regions, especially in Europe, to send diocesan priests to support

---

[18] Robert Culhane, "The Primary Purpose of the Foreign Missions," *The Irish Ecclesiastical Record* 73 (1950): 390-395.

[19] Angelyn Dries, "The 1925 Vatican Mission Exposition and the Interface between Catholic Mission Theory and World Religions," *International Bulletin of Mission Research* 40/2 (2016): 120-123.

[20] Mark R. Francis, "Another Look at the Constitution on the Sacred Liturgy and the Substantial Unity of the Roman Rite," *Worship* 88/3 (May, 2014): 240-245.

[21] James Kroeger, "Papal Mission Wisdom: Five Mission Encyclicals 1919-1959..., 97.; Fulton J. Sheen, "A Commentary on *Evangelii Praecones*," *World Mission* 2 (1951): 6-8.

[22] John J. Considine, "*Evangelii Praecones*," *The Homiletic and Pastoral Review* 5 (1952): 420-422.

these emerging communities.[23] This marked a significant shift by involving not just Missionary orders but also diocesan clergy and entire dioceses in the Mission effort. *Fidei Donum* reflected a vision of the Church as a global family where all parts support one another, anticipating the idea of mutual Mission later emphasized at Vatican II.[24] The document also opened the door for greater lay involvement, showing that Mission is the responsibility of the whole Church, not just a select few.

Papal Encyclicals and Missionary Orders During and After Vatican II

Since the time of the Second Vatican Council, the Catholic Church has deepened and expanded its understanding of Mission through a series of official teachings and reflections. These teachings have helped the Church respond to the changing needs of the world and offered new ways of thinking about how to share the gospel. Moving beyond older views that focused mainly on conversion or church expansion, the modern Church now sees Mission as something much broader and richer. It includes caring for creation, promoting peace and justice, renewing cultures, and reaching out to those who feel distant from the Church. These Church documents emphasize that Mission is not just the work of priests or Missionaries, but the responsibility of all baptized believers. They also show that true Mission comes from love, joy, and a deep relationship with God, expressed in both word and action. Together, these teachings offer a fresh and compassionate vision of what it means to be a Missionary Church in the modern world.

Ad Gentes: Affirming Mission as the Heart of the Church's Identity

The Decree on the Missionary Activity of the Church, *Ad Gentes*, issued by the Second Vatican Council in 1965, is the first official Catholic document fully dedicated to the theology of Mission. It marked a turning point by declaring that the Church is Missionary by its very nature, participating in the Mission of the Triune God.[25] The document moved the Church beyond a colonial or institutional model of Mission and emphasized the need to plant and grow local churches, respecting the unique cultures and traditions of each people. *Ad Gentes* highlighted the importance of inculturation, dialogue, and the active involvement of all members of the Church, not just priests and Missionaries.[26] It introduced a vision of Mission that was

[23] Francis Anekwe Oborji, "Missiology in an African Context: Toward a New Language," *Missiology: An International Review* XXXI/3 (July, 2003): 325-230.

[24] James Kroeger, "Papal Mission Wisdom: Five Mission Encyclicals 1919-1959..., 98.

[25] William Richey Hogg, "Vatican II's *Ad Gentes*: A Twenty-Year Retrospective," *International Bulletin of Missionary Research* 9/4 (October, 1985): 140-146.

[26] Stephen B. Bevans, "Mission at the Second Vatican Council: 1962-1965," in *A Century of Catholic Mission Roman Catholic Missiology 1910 to the Present*, edited by

relational, people-centred, and rooted in love, setting the tone for all future Catholic teaching on Mission.

Evangelii Nuntiandi: Evangelization as Renewal of Culture and Society

Issued by Pope Paul VI in 1975, *Evangelii Nuntiandi* (On Evangelization in the Modern World) is considered one of the most influential documents on Catholic evangelization in the 20th century.[27] In it, Pope Paul VI affirmed that the purpose of the Church is to evangelize all areas of human life, not only through preaching but also through the witness of life, service, and justice. The document described evangelization as a dynamic process that involves the renewal of individuals, societies, and cultures.[28] It laid the foundation for the idea of the "new evangelization," urging the Church to reach out not only to non-believers but also to those who had become distant from the faith. *Evangelii Nuntiandi* encouraged a Church that listens to the world, adapts to cultural changes, and speaks the gospel in ways that are both faithful and relevant.[29]

Redemptoris Missio: Reawakening Mission through the Call to New Evangelization

In 1990, Pope John Paul II issued *Redemptoris Missio* (The Mission of the Redeemer), renewing the Church's call to evangelize with boldness and joy.[30] The document emphasized two key directions in Mission: the ongoing need for "Mission *ad gentes*", preaching the gospel to those who have never heard it, and the importance of the "new evangelization" for those in traditionally Christian societies who have lost a living sense of faith.[31] Pope John Paul II highlighted that Mission belongs to all baptized Christians, not only Missionaries or clergy. He also stressed the importance of dialogue with cultures and other religions, as well as the connection between Mission

---

Stephen B. Bevans (Oxford: Regnum Books International, 2013), 110.

[27] Samuel Escobar, "Together towards Life: Mission and Evangelism in Changing Landscapes," *International Bulletin of Missionary Research* 38/4 (October, 2014): 193.

[28] James A. Scherer, *Gospel, Church and Kingdom: Comparative Studies in World Mission Theology* (Minneapolis: Augsburg Publishing House, 1987), 40.

[29] Roger P. Schroeder, "Catholic Teaching on Mission after Vatican II: 1975-2007," in *A Century of Catholic Mission Roman Catholic Missiology 1910 to the Present*, edited by Stephen B. Bevans (Oxford: Regnum Books International, 2013), 114-115.

[30] John Paul II, "Encyclical Letter *Redemptoris Missio*: On the Permanent Validity of the Church's Missionary Mandate (Excerpts)," *International Bulletin of Missionary Research* 15/2 (April, 1991): 50.

[31] *Redemptoris Missio*, 55-57.; Gerard V. Hall, "Prophetic Dialogue: A Foundational Category for Practical Theology," *International Journal of Practical Theology* 14/1 (2010): 44.

and human development.[32] *Redemptoris Missio* affirmed that proclaiming Christ is the greatest act of love, and it called the Church to be both faithful to tradition and responsive to the needs of a changing world.

Deus Caritas Est: Love as the Soul of the Church's Missionary Witness

Deus Caritas Est (God Is Love) was the first encyclical of Pope Benedict XVI, released in 2005. While not a typical Mission document, it has great Missiological value because it centres the Church's Mission on the love of God revealed in Jesus Christ.[33] Pope Benedict emphasized that the Church's three essential tasks such as, preaching the Word, celebrating the sacraments, and practicing charity are all part of its Mission.[34] The document taught that Christian love, especially shown through acts of mercy and justice, is a powerful form of evangelization. Benedict also warned against separating spiritual and social dimensions of Mission, insisting they belong together.[35] *Deus Caritas Est* shaped the Church's Mission by reminding Catholics that love, lived in truth and action, is the heart of evangelization.

Verbum Domini: Proclaiming the Word of God at the Centre of Mission

In 2010, Pope Benedict XVI published *Verbum Domini* (The Word of the Lord), a post-synodal apostolic exhortation on the role of Sacred Scripture in the life and Mission of the Church. The document emphasized that the Word of God is central to evangelization, guiding both the Church's teaching and its personal witness.[36] Pope Benedict called for greater biblical literacy among clergy and laity, so that Mission is rooted in the living Word. He encouraged preaching, catechesis, and personal study of Scripture as key elements of the Church's outreach.[37] *Verbum Domini* also affirmed the importance of Scripture in interreligious dialogue and ecumenism, showing how the Bible connects with the hearts of believers and seekers alike.[38] This

---

[32] Roger P. Schroeder, "Catholic Teaching on Mission after Vatican II: 1975-2007," in *A Century of Catholic Mission Roman Catholic Missiology 1910 to the Present*, edited by Stephen B. Bevans (Oxford: Regnum Books International, 2013), 110-115.

[33] Daniel Zoumaya, "The Social Teaching in Benedict XVI's *Deus Caritas Est*," *The Catholic Social Science Review* 28 (December, 2023): 133-143.

[34] Geoffrey Wainwright, "Reflections on Pope Benedict XVI's First Encyclical, *Deus Caritas Est*," *Pro Ecclesia* 15/3 (Summer, 2006): 263-266.

[35] Thomas Gerard Weinandy, "*Deus Caritas Est*: Defining the Christian Understanding of Love," *Pro Ecclesia* 15/3 (Summer, 2006): 259-262.

[36] Janusz Królikowski, "Theology of the Word of God in the Apostolic Exhortation *Verbum Domini* by Benedict XVI," *Wrocławski Przegląd Teologiczny* 31/2 (January, 2023): 61-84.

[37] John Deehan, "Formed by the Word," *The Tablet* 264/8874 (December, 2010): 15.

[38] Beatrice Oiry and Bada Silas, "From *Verbum Domini* to the Sunday of the Word of God," *One in Christ* 55/1 (December, 2021): 116-119.

document strengthened the spiritual foundation of Catholic Mission and deepened its connection to the revealed Word of God.

Evangelii Gaudium: A Joyful and Inclusive Call to Missionary Discipleship

Evangelii Gaudium (The Joy of the Gospel), released in 2013 by Pope Francis, is considered his Missionary vision for the Church in the 21st century. The document calls for a "Missionary conversion" of the entire Church, encouraging every baptized person to become a "Missionary disciple." Pope Francis emphasized that evangelization must be marked by joy, mercy, and compassion, not by pressure or fear. He challenged the Church to go out to the "existential peripheries" to the poor, the forgotten, and those alienated from religion. *Evangelii Gaudium* also called for pastoral reform so that all church structures support evangelization. It urges the Church to speak with simplicity, to listen more, and to trust in the Holy Spirit's work in people's lives. The document reaffirms Mission as the joyful and loving witness of the gospel in a wounded world.

Laudato Si': Ecological Conversion as a New Frontier of Mission

Laudato Si' (Praise Be to You), published by Pope Francis in 2015, is a groundbreaking encyclical that connects care for the environment with the Church's Mission in the world. Francis introduced the concept of "integral ecology", which sees the environmental crisis, economic injustice, and social inequality as deeply connected. He called the Church and all humanity to repent for ecological sins, care for creation, and defend the rights of the poor and vulnerable. From a Missiological perspective, *Laudato Si'* expands the meaning of Mission to include responsibility for the Earth, urging Christians to see ecological action as a form of gospel witness. This document repositions Catholic Mission within the context of global sustainability, intergenerational justice, and love for all creatures.

Fratelli Tutti: Fraternity, Dialogue, and Peace as the Mission of the Church in the World

In 2020, Pope Francis issued *Fratelli Tutti* (All Brothers), an encyclical on fraternity and social friendship. While not directly about Mission in the traditional sense, it strongly shapes the Church's Mission by focusing on building peace, overcoming divisions, and promoting global solidarity.[39] Pope Francis draws on the parable of the Good Samaritan to describe a universal Mission of love, crossing boundaries of nationality, race, and religion. He encourages a Church that promotes dialogue, forgiveness,

---

[39] Martín Carbajo Núñez, "The Lord Gave Me Brothers and Sisters: Francis of Assisi, Inspirer of the Encyclical *Fratelli Tutti*," *Carthaginensia* 39/75 (December, 2023): 69-91.

and inclusive communities.[40] *Fratelli Tutti* challenges the Church to live out its Mission by confronting social injustices, rejecting violence, and becoming a sign of unity in a fragmented world.[41] It presents Mission not just as preaching, but as a lived witness to human dignity and universal brotherhood.

Conclusion

The development of Catholic Mission before Vatican II was shaped by a series of important events, teachings, and institutional changes that laid the groundwork for the Church's renewed understanding of Mission in the modern world. The Council of Trent strengthened Catholic identity and inspired Missionary orders like the Jesuits, who carried the gospel across cultures through education and service. The establishment of *Propaganda Fide* centralized Mission efforts under the Holy See, reducing colonial influence and giving the Church more control over its global outreach. Vatican I, while not focused directly on Mission, provided key theological support by affirming the Pope's authority, which helped unify the Church's Missionary strategy. In the early 20th century, a new series of papal documents began to reshape Mission thinking. These writings emphasized respect for local cultures, the need for indigenous leadership, and the importance of separating Mission from colonialism. They also encouraged greater participation by laypeople and diocesan clergy, moving Mission beyond religious orders. Altogether, these developments reflect a growing awareness that Catholic Mission must move beyond mere ecclesial expansion. Rooted in the love and sending nature of the Triune God, Mission is now seen as a call to communion, justice, and respectful witness to Christ in every culture. These early reforms set the stage for the Trinitarian theology of Mission that would fully emerge at Vatican II.

---

40 Suzanne Mulligan, "'Builders of a New Social Bond': Reflections on *Fratelli Tutti*," *The Furrow* 71/12 (December, 2020), 647-653.

41 Prakash Louis, "*Fratelli Tutti*: A Call to Collective Consciousness, Collective Action and Common Good," *Vidyajyoti Journal of Theological Reflection* 84/1 (November, 2020): 842-856.

23

Orthodox Perspectives on Christian Mission Ecclesial, Liturgical, and Trinitarian Foundations for Mission in a Pluralistic World

The Orthodox understanding of Mission emerges from a deeply theological and ecclesial vision that distinguishes it significantly from many Western Missiological paradigms. Rather than viewing Mission primarily as a functional activity or a programmatic response to religious obligation, the Orthodox tradition perceives Mission as a natural extension of the Church's very being. In this context, Mission is not an optional task but an essential expression of the Church's identity, rooted in her participation in the divine life of the Holy Trinity. This perspective shifts the focus from approaches of expansion or institutional success to the lived communion of the faithful with God and with one another, manifesting the Kingdom of God within the world. In contrast to certain Western traditions where Mission has often been shaped by colonial impulses, evangelical activism, or denominational agendas, Orthodox Missiology emphasizes continuity with the apostolic faith, the role of the Holy Spirit, and the Eucharistic nature of the Church. It seeks to integrate worship, witness, and service as inseparable elements of Christian life. Orthodox Mission is deeply shaped by theological convictions such as the Trinitarian foundation of all Christian activity, the pneumatological empowerment of the Church, and an eschatological vision of creation's renewal. These elements ground the Church's Missionary vocation in a broader cosmic and spiritual framework rather than limiting it to human-centred plans or isolated acts of charity. Moreover, the Orthodox Church upholds the significance of local and contextual engagement through what has been termed the "Church of Nations," embodying the Gospel within specific cultures and communities. Concepts like "liturgy after the liturgy" demonstrate that Orthodox Mission is not confined to preaching but extends from the altar into the world, calling believers to serve the poor, advocate for justice, and witness to God's presence in the midst of daily life. In contemporary contexts, this vision has found expression in responses to pluralism, interreligious dialogue, and postcolonial critiques, affirming Mission as both incarnational and intercultural.

The Ecclesiological Foundation of Orthodox Mission

In Orthodox theology, Mission is not something the Church simply does, rather, it is something the Church is. The Church is seen as the Body of Christ, called to reflect the life and love of the Triune God in the world. Therefore, the Church itself becomes the primary space where Mission is lived and expressed.[1] This understanding means that Mission is not an external program or project but arises from the very nature and identity of the Church. The Church exists to be a living sign of God's Kingdom, and its Mission flows from its life of worship, communion, and participation in divine grace.[2] As such, the Church is not merely an instrument for Mission, but, it is the embodiment of Mission through its existence, its sacraments, and its communal life.

The Orthodox tradition does not separate Mission from the internal life of the Church. Rather, Mission is the natural result of ecclesial communion, the fellowship of believers united with Christ and one another. This communion is expressed most fully in the Eucharist, where the faithful are united in Christ and then sent into the world as witnesses of God's love. Mission, then, is the outward movement of the Church's inner unity. It is not a specialized task done by a few individuals but the shared calling of the entire ecclesial body. The strength and authenticity of Mission depend on the depth of this communion.[3] When the Church lives in true unity, love, and holiness, it becomes a powerful witness to the world, drawing others into that same fellowship with God.

Orthodox Mission is rooted in what is often called "living theology", a theology that is not abstract or theoretical, but embodied in the worship, life, and witness of the Church. In this view, theology is not just a set of ideas or doctrines to be taught but a living experience of God that shapes the

---

[1] Petros Vassiliadis, "Theological Foundations of Mission: An Orthodox Perspective," in *Orthodox Perspectives on Mission* edited by Petros Vassiliadis (Oxford: Regnum Books International, 2013), 180-190.

[2] N. A. Nissiotis, "Interpreting Orthodoxy: The Communication of Some Eastern Orthodox Theological Categories to Students of Western Church Traditions," *The Ecumenical Review* 14/1 (October, 1961): 10-26.

[3] Petros Vassiliadis, "Introductory Remarks," in *Orthodox Perspectives on Mission* edited by Petros Vassiliadis (Oxford: Regnum Books International, 2013), 1-4.

life of the community.[4] This living theology guides all aspects of Mission, ensuring that it remains faithful to the Gospel and centred on Christ. It also prevents Mission from becoming ideological or purely social in focus, reminding the Church that her witness must always flow from spiritual depth and theological integrity.[5] Thus, Orthodox Mission is not just about activity or outreach, rather, it is about sharing the divine life that the Church herself experiences through prayer, worship, and sacramental communion.

Theological Pillars of Orthodox Missiology

The Orthodox understanding of Mission is deeply rooted in theology. It is not based on strategies, programs, or institutional goals, but on the very nature of God and God's relationship with the world. Orthodox Missiology, thus, begins with the conviction that Mission must reflect the mystery of the Triune God and flow from the life of the Church that participates in this divine communion. Mission is not a human-made duty, but a sharing in God's love, God's purpose, and God's saving work in creation. These include the Trinitarian foundation, where Mission is understood as participation in the life of the Triune God, the pneumatological dimension, which highlights the Holy Spirit as the power and guide behind all Missionary activity, the eschatological perspective, which sees Mission as a sign of the coming Kingdom of God; and the cosmic dimension, which views salvation as a renewal of all creation, not just individual souls.

Trinitarian Foundation: Mission as Participation in the Life of the Triune God

Orthodox Mission begins with the understanding that God is a Trinity. The Triune God is a communion of love, and Christian Mission is a participation in that divine life.[6] From this perspective, Mission is not a human invention but originates in God's own being and action. God sends Jesus into the world, and Jesus, in turn, sends the Holy Spirit and the Church. This Trinitarian model shapes how Orthodox Christians view Mission, not as a task driven by human initiative, but as an extension of the love and purpose of the Trinity. Mission, therefore, is not only about proclaiming the Gospel but about drawing people into the communion of love that exists eternally within God.

---

[4] John A. McGuckin, "Eschaton and Kerygma: The Future of the Past in the Present Kairos: The Concept of Living Tradition in Orthodox Theology," *St Vladimir's Theological Quarterly* 42/3-4 (December, 1998): 225-271.

[5] Anastasios Yannoulatos, "Orthodox Mission: Past, Present, Future," in *Orthodox Perspectives on Mission* edited by Petros Vassiliadis (Oxford: Regnum Books International, 2013), 10-15.

[6] Petros Vassiliadis, "Introductory Remarks," in *Orthodox Perspectives on Mission*..., 7.

Pneumatological Dimension: The Holy Spirit as Agent and Source of Mission

The Orthodox Church emphasizes the role of the Holy Spirit as the active agent of Mission. It is the Spirit who empowers, guides, and sustains the Church in its Missionary work.[7] The Spirit does not act independently of Christ but makes present the saving work of Christ in the world. In Orthodox theology, the Spirit is not simply a helper but the source of new life and transformation. Without the Holy Spirit, the Church's Mission would be empty and powerless.[8] Therefore, Mission is always carried out in dependence on the Spirit's presence and leading.[9] This means that prayer, discernment, and spiritual readiness are essential for faithful Mission, as they open the Church to the renewing and sending power of the Spirit.

Eschatological Perspective: Mission Pointing Towards the Kingdom of God

Orthodox Mission is deeply shaped by an eschatological vision, that is a view of the future fulfilment of God's plan. The Church does not see Mission as just solving present-day problems but as preparing the world for the coming of God's Kingdom. Every act of Mission is a sign pointing toward the new creation promised by Christ. This eschatological hope gives Mission its meaning and urgency, but also its humility. The Church does not build the Kingdom by its own strength, rather, it lives as a foretaste of what is to come. In this way, Mission becomes a witness to the final restoration of all things, calling people to repent, believe, and live in the light of eternity.

Cosmic Dimension: The Holistic and Creation-oriented view of Salvation

Orthodox Mission includes not only the salvation of individual souls but the transformation of the entire creation. This cosmic vision is grounded in the belief that Christ came to redeem all that God has made humanity, society, and the natural world. The Orthodox Church sees salvation as the healing and renewal of the whole cosmos, not just a spiritual escape from the world. This understanding leads to a holistic Mission that embraces care for the environment, concern for justice, and the sanctification of everyday life. The Church is called to be a sign of God's presence in the world and a means of restoring harmony in all areas of life. Thus, Orthodox Mission is cosmic in scope, affirming that God's love embraces all of creation.

---

[7] Petros Vassiliadis, "Reconciliation as a Pneumatological Mission Paradigm: Some Preliminary Reflections by an Orthodox," *International Review of Mission* 94/372 (January, 2005): 30-42.

[8] Benjamin D. Crace, "Towards a Global Pneumatological Awareness: A Comparative Account and Assessment of the Charismata in the Coptic Orthodox Church," *Journal of Pentecostal Theology* 30/1 (December, 2021): 123-144.

[9] N. A. Nissiotis, "Interpreting Orthodoxy: The communication…, 26.

"Liturgy After the Liturgy": The Liturgical Basis of Mission

One of the most distinctive contributions of Orthodox Missiology is the concept of "liturgy after the liturgy."[10] This phrase expresses the idea that Christian Mission begins in the worship of the Church, especially the Eucharist, and then continues in the life of the faithful as they are sent into the world.[11] In the Orthodox tradition, liturgy is not just a spiritual experience for the believer but a participation in the Kingdom of God. Through the liturgy, the Church encounters the risen Christ, is nourished by His presence, and is united in communion with one another.[12] However, this sacred gathering does not end at the church door. The faithful are sent forth to live out what they have received, bringing God's love, peace, and justice into society.[13] The phrase "liturgy after the liturgy" first gained prominence in the context of Orthodox contributions to the ecumenical movement in the 1970s, especially through theologians like Ion Bria. It became a way of explaining how Orthodox Mission is not separated from worship, but is its natural continuation.[14] Mission, in this sense, is not an optional activity, but the unfolding of the Church's liturgical life into the world. It affirms that worship and witness are two sides of the same reality: both are responses to God's saving action in Christ.

Historical Emergence and Theological Implications of the Concept

The idea of "liturgy after the liturgy" developed within the Orthodox Church during the 1970s, especially in ecumenical dialogues about how worship and Mission are connected.[15] Orthodox theologians, such as Ion Bria, introduced this phrase to express that the Divine Liturgy does not end when the congregation leaves the church building.[16] Instead, the liturgy continues in daily life as believers live out their faith through service, justice, and love in

---

[10] Georges Khodr, "Christianity in a Pluralistic World: The Economy of the Holy Spirit," *The Ecumenical Review* 23 (1971): 118-128.

[11] Athanasios N Papathanasiou, "Tradition as Impulse for Renewal and Witness: Introducing Orthodox Missiology in the IRM," in *Orthodox Perspectives on Mission* edited by Petros Vassiliadis (Oxford: Regnum Books International, 2013), 164.

[12] Ion Bria, "The Liturgy after the Liturgy," in *Orthodox Perspectives on Mission* edited by Petros Vassiliadis (Oxford: Regnum Books International, 2013), 46.

[13] Emmanuel Clapsis, "The Eucharist as Missionary Event in a Suffering World," in *Orthodox Perspectives on Mission* edited by Petros Vassiliadis (Oxford: Regnum Books International, 2013), 61.

[14] Anastasios Yannoulatos, *Mission in Christ's Way: An Orthodox Understanding of Mission* (Brookline: Holy Cross Orthodox Press, 2010), 25.

[15] Ion Bria, "The Liturgy after the Liturgy," in *Orthodox Perspectives on Mission...*, 47.

[16] Anastasios Yannoulatos, *Mission in Christ's Way...*, 25.

the world. This concept came as a response to the tendency in some churches to separate liturgy (worship) from Mission (outreach), and it emphasized that Orthodox Mission naturally flows from worship.[17] Missiologically, it means that worship is not an escape from the world but a source of power to return to the world with Christ's presence.

Eucharist as the Sending Moment for Mission

In Orthodox worship, the Eucharist is the central and most sacred act. During the Divine Liturgy, the Church gathers as the Body of Christ, offers thanksgiving, and partakes in the real presence of Christ through bread and wine.[18] However, the Eucharist is not only a personal spiritual experience. It is also a moment of being sent. At the end of the liturgy, the priest dismisses the people with words like "Let us go forth in peace," which means the faithful are being sent into the world as witnesses. This sending is not just symbolic, but it carries real responsibility. Those who have received Christ in the Eucharist are now called to be His hands and feet in the world.[19] The Eucharist becomes a source of Mission, reminding the Church that it is not gathered for itself alone but for the life of the world.

The Unity of Worship and Witness: Liturgy Transforming into Service

The Orthodox vision of Mission emphasizes that worship and witness are not two separate parts of Christian life. Instead, they are deeply united. Worship transforms the believer and the community, so that they become witnesses of God's love and justice in the world.[20] This means that prayer must lead to action, and contemplation must lead to compassion. If the Church celebrates the liturgy but ignores the cries of the poor, the hungry, or the oppressed, then the worship becomes empty. Orthodox theologians like Emmanuel Clapsis have warned that liturgy without social concern becomes ritualism, while Mission without worship becomes ideology.[21] In the concept of "liturgy after the liturgy," the Church is reminded that every liturgical celebration should overflow into acts of mercy, peace-making, and healing, extending God's presence beyond the altar to the streets, homes, and communities of the world.

---

[17] Ion Bria, "The Liturgy after the Liturgy," in *Orthodox Perspectives on Mission…*, 51.

[18] Emmanuel Clapsis, "The Eucharist as Missionary Event in a Suffering World…, 62.

[19] Anastasios Yannoulatos, *Mission in Christ's Way: An Orthodox Understanding of Mission…*, 30-37.

[20] Geevarghese Mar Osthatios, "Divine Sharing: Shape of Mission for the Future," *International Review of Mission* 76/301 (January, 1987): 16-20.

[21] Emmanuel Clapsis, "The Eucharist as Missionary Event in a Suffering World…, 62.

Reflections from the WCC Melbourne Conference (1980): "Eucharist as Pilgrim Bread"

The significance of this concept was further recognized at the World Council of Churches' Conference on World Mission and Evangelism in Melbourne in 1980. In its report, the conference spoke of the Eucharist as "pilgrim bread," highlighting that the Eucharist is not only spiritual nourishment but also strength for the journey of Mission.[22] Just as bread strengthens the body, so too the Eucharist gives the Church spiritual power for its Mission in a broken world. This image of "pilgrim bread" fits closely with the Orthodox understanding that Mission is not a journey away from worship, but a continuation of worship into the world.[23] The Eucharist strengthens the Church to be a community of hope, love, and service on the move, carrying the presence of Christ wherever there is suffering, injustice, or need.

The Local and Contextual Nature of Orthodox Mission

Orthodox Mission is not only rooted in theology and worship, but also deeply attentive to culture and context. From its earliest history, the Orthodox Church has recognized the importance of making the Gospel meaningful within the specific cultural settings of each community. Rather than promoting a common model of Mission, Orthodoxy emphasizes the incarnation of the Church in every local context.[24] This means that the Church must take on the language, customs, and concerns of the people it serves, just as Christ took on human nature to dwell among us. Theologians such as Ion Bria and Radu Ionita highlights the importance of inculturation, the risks of cultural essentialism, and the need for an intercultural approach to Mission today.[25] These perspectives help the Church understand that culture is not a barrier to Mission, but a pathway through which the Gospel can be faithfully expressed and lived. Orthodox Mission, therefore, is not about imposing uniform traditions, but about allowing the Gospel to take root and bear fruit within the diverse cultural soils of the world.

---

[22] Arthur Frederick Glasser, "Liberation Is in, the Unreached out in Melbourne View of the Kingdom: The WCC Commission on World Mission and Evangelism," *Christianity Today* 24/12 (June, 1980): 48.

[23] David J. Bosch, "The Melbourne Conference: Between Guilt and Hope," *International Review of Mission* 69/276-277 (October-January, 1981): 512-518.

[24] Viorel Ionita, "One Gospel and Diverse Cultures: Towards an Intercultural Mutuality," *International Review of Mission* 86/340-341 (January-April 1997): 53-56.

[25] Ion Bria, "The Liturgy after the Liturgy," in *Orthodox Perspectives on Mission…*, 51.

One of the key voices in Orthodox Missiology, Ion Bria, introduced the idea of the "Church of Nations." This concept highlights the importance of planting and developing the Church within each specific culture and community.[26] For Bria, true Mission does not impose foreign customs or languages but allows the Church to take root in the life, traditions, and expressions of each people group. Just as the early Church used the Greek language and local customs to proclaim the Gospel, modern Orthodox Mission should encourage the Gospel to be expressed in the local language and cultural forms of every nation.[27] This approach values diversity and sees each culture as a unique space where Christ can be made known. Mission, in this view, is not about creating uniformity but about allowing the Church to be fully present and alive in different cultural settings.

The Orthodox Church understands Mission as an incarnational process, meaning that just as Christ took on human flesh and entered into a specific culture, so too the Church must enter into the life of every people and place.[28] This means that the Church is not simply transplanted from one place to another with the same forms and structures. Instead, it must be born anew in each culture, speaking the language of the people, respecting their values, and engaging their struggles. This is not a compromise of faith but a faithful expression of the Gospel that becomes truly meaningful to the people it seeks to serve.[29] In this way, Mission becomes an act of deep respect and love for each culture, seeking to transform it from within rather than dominate it from the outside. The Church becomes a living presence of Christ that shares in the joys and sufferings of the local people.

Social and Ethical Dimensions of Mission

The Orthodox Church understands Mission not only as proclaiming the Gospel but also as engaging in acts of justice, compassion, and social responsibility. Mission must involve service to the poor, the oppressed, the sick, and the marginalized, those whom Christ Himself identified with throughout His ministry (Matthew 25:31-46).[30] From an Orthodox perspective, salvation is not limited to personal spiritual transformation but includes the renewal of human relationships and the healing of broken communities. Orthodox theologian Emmanuel Clapsis strongly argues

---

[26] Doru Marcu, "Contemporary Critical Reflections on Ion Bria's Vision for Ecumenical Dialogue," *Religions* 15/3 (March, 2024): 1-9.

[27] Doru Marcu, "Contemporary Critical Reflections on Ion Bria's Vision…, 1-9.

[28] Ion Bria, "The Liturgy after the Liturgy," in *Orthodox Perspectives on Mission…*, 51.

[29] Emmanuel Clapsis, "The Eucharist as Missionary Event in a Suffering World…, 62.

[30] Stanley S. Harakas, "European Multiformity and Dimensions of Orthodox Christian Social Ethics," *The Greek Orthodox Theological Review* 54/1-4, (Spring-Winter 2009): 97-113.

that the Church cannot separate worship from justice.[31] For him, "liturgy without justice is ritualism", meaning that worship becomes empty and even hypocritical if it ignores the suffering of others. At the same time, "Mission without worship becomes ideology," a political or social movement that may lose its spiritual foundation and divine purpose.[32] Therefore, true Orthodox Mission integrates both spiritual communion with God and active love toward one's neighbour. The Eucharist, which is central to Orthodox life, sends believers into the world not only as witnesses of faith but also as agents of love, peace, and justice. In this way, the Church becomes a sign of God's Kingdom by embodying Christ's compassion and standing in solidarity with those who are forgotten, excluded, or mistreated by society.[33] Social Mission is not optional, rather, it is the natural fruit of authentic worship and the practical expression of the Gospel in public life.

Orthodox Contributions to *Missio Dei* and Ecumenism

The Orthodox Church has made significant contributions to the understanding of Christian Mission, especially through its role in shaping the theology of *Missio Dei*, the idea that Mission begins with God, not the Church.[34] Orthodox theologian Petros Vassiliadis has been a key voice in highlighting that Mission is not a human project, but a divine activity in which the Church is invited to participate.[35] According to this view, the Church does not "own" the Mission; rather, it cooperates with what God is already doing in the world through the power of the Holy Spirit. This deeply Trinitarian understanding of Mission is also emphasized by Archbishop Anastasios Yannoulatos, who insists that Orthodox Mission must be centred on the witness to the living Triune God. For him, Mission is not about increasing numbers or spreading influence, but about revealing the love and communion of the Trinity to all people.[36] This approach stands in contrast to past models of Mission that were sometimes tied to

---

[31] Christopher J. Helali, "The Pluralistic Horizon: Orthodox Theology in the Age of Human Rights," *International Journal of Orthodox Theology* 4/3 (December, 2013): 25-30.

[32] Emmanuel Clapsis, "The Eucharist as Missionary Event in a Suffering World…, 62.

[33] Stylianos Ch. Tsompanidis, "'Liturgy after the Liturgy': The Conciliar Process for Justice, Peace and Integrity of Creation (JPIC) from the Perspective of Orthodox Theology," *The Ecumenical Review* 76/4 (October, 2024): 413-435

[34] Cristian-Sebastian. Sonea, "*Missio Dei*: The Contemporary Missionary Paradigm and Its Reception in the Eastern Orthodox Missionary Theology," *Review of Ecumenical Studies* 9/1 (April, 2017): 70-91.

[35] Petros Vassiliadis, "Theological Foundations of Mission: An Orthodox Perspective…, 180-190.

[36] Anastasios Yannoulatos, *Mission in Christ's Way: An Orthodox Understanding of Mission…*, 30-37.

colonialism or institutional expansion. Instead of dominating or controlling others, Orthodox Mission focuses on humility, repentance, and unity. It seeks to restore broken relationships between people, with creation, and with God. Through its liturgical life, theological depth, and commitment to reconciliation, the Orthodox Church offers a distinctive and much-needed voice in the global ecumenical movement. It reminds the wider Christian world that Mission must always reflect the love, humility, and unity of the God who sends.

Mission in a Pluralistic and Postcolonial World

In today's world, marked by religious diversity and the painful legacy of colonialism, the Orthodox Church offers a fresh and critical voice on how Mission should be carried out with respect and love. Theologian Njoroge critiques earlier models of Mission that were tied to colonial control, cultural superiority, and religious domination. These past approaches often confused the Gospel with Western values and ignored the dignity and richness of other cultures and religions.[37] In contrast, Orthodox Mission emphasizes humility, mutual respect, and deep listening. A leading theologian in this area is Metropolitan Geevarghese Mar Ostathios, who argued that Mission in a multi-religious context like India must be grounded in the incarnation of love. He taught that true Mission is not about converting others through power or persuasion, but about sharing God's love and holiness in ways that honour the truths found in other religions while remaining faithful to the Gospel. He proposed a Mission model built on both conviction and compassion, holding truth and tolerance together.[38] Building on this, Orthodox voices like Ionita have stressed the importance of intercultural Mission, where cultures are seen not as fixed or isolated, but as constantly interacting and influencing one another. This intercultural approach moves beyond traditional inculturation by encouraging cultural dialogue and mutual transformation. It views Mission not as a one-way process of teaching, but as a shared journey where both the Church and the culture grow in deeper understanding.[39] In a pluralistic and postcolonial age, the Orthodox Church calls for Mission that is not about superiority or expansion, but about

---

[37] Kosmas John Ngige Njoroge, "Missiological Context of the Eastern Orthodox Churches in Africa," *International Review of Mission* 106/2 (December, 2017): 356-368.

[38] Geevarghese Mar Osthatios, "Divine Sharing: Shape of Mission for the Future…, 16-20.

[39] Viorel Ionita, "One Gospel and Diverse Cultures: Towards an Intercultural Mutuality…, 53-56.

serving, listening, and witnessing to the love of God in Christ with humility and openness.[40]

Sacramental and Personal Dimensions of Mission

In the Orthodox tradition, Mission is deeply rooted in the sacramental and personal life of the believer. According to Archbishop Anastasios, the life of a Missionary is not simply a role or task but a continuation of the earthly ministry of Jesus Christ. This means that every Christian who participates in the life of Christ is also called to participate in His Mission to the world. Central to this calling is the Eucharist, which in Orthodox theology is not only the celebration of communion with God but also the moment of being sent into the world. The Eucharist nourishes the faithful with Christ's body and blood, and in doing so, it empowers them to become His living presence in the world.[41] Thus, Mission is not separate from worship; rather, the Eucharistic life shapes the identity and purpose of every Christian. The sacraments of the Church, particularly Baptism, Chrismation, and the Eucharist, are seen as the means of sanctification, making a person holy and equipping them to live out their Mission.[42] They are not private religious experiences but communal and dynamic actions that connect the believer to the ongoing Mission of the Church. In this way, Orthodox Mission flows from a deep inner transformation and communion with God, which then naturally leads to a life of witness, service, and love in the world.[43] The sacraments, therefore, are not only signs of God's grace but also the source of strength, direction, and unity for all Missionary efforts.

Conclusion

The Orthodox understanding of Mission is deeply shaped by its ecclesial, liturgical, trinitarian, and intercultural identity. Orthodox Mission is not viewed as a separate or external activity but as a natural extension of the life of the Church, flowing from the communion of believers in Christ. It is rooted in the Trinitarian life of God, and the Church is sent into the world to witness to this divine love. The liturgy, especially the Eucharist, is not only the centre of worship but also the starting point of Mission, what is received

---

[40] Kosmas John Ngige Njoroge, "Incarnation as a Mode of Orthodox Mission: Intercultural Orthodox Mission-Imposing Culture and Inculturation," in *Orthodox Perspectives on Mission* edited by Petros Vassiliadis (Oxford: Regnum Books International, 2013), 244.

[41] Anastasios Yannoulatos, *Mission in Christ's Way: An Orthodox Understanding of Mission...*, 30-37.

[42] Geevarghese Mar Osthatios, "Divine Sharing: Shape of Mission for the Future," *International Review of Mission* 76/301 (January, 1987): 16-20.

[43] Kosmas John Ngige Njoroge, "Incarnation as a Mode of Orthodox Mission..., 243.

in communion is shared in service, leading to the idea of a "liturgy after the liturgy." Orthodox Mission is also local and intercultural, seeking to embody the Gospel in diverse cultural contexts while maintaining the unity of faith. This approach avoids cultural domination and instead encourages mutual respect and dialogue. In the modern world, the Orthodox Church is called to engage with pluralistic societies, ecological concerns, interfaith realities, and social injustices, offering a Mission that is both faithful to tradition and responsive to contemporary needs. Its contribution to the wider Christian understanding of *Missio Dei* and ecumenical dialogue reminds the global Church of the importance of worship, community, and repentance in all Missionary activity.

24

Christian Mission in the Ecumenical Tradition Towards a Unified Witness in a Pluralistic World

The Ecumenical Tradition in Christianity refers to the movement and theological approach that seeks unity among different Christian churches and denominations. It aims to overcome divisions through dialogue, cooperation, and shared witness, based on a common faith in Jesus Christ. Rooted in the prayer of Jesus "that they may all be one" (John 17:21), the ecumenical tradition encourages mutual respect, theological understanding, and joint action in Mission and service. Thus, ecumenism seeks to overcome divisions among Christian churches and to promote unity in Mission and witness. In the ecumenical tradition, Mission is neither purely a denominational activity nor a private spirituality. Rather, it is founded in shared Christian traditions, theological reflection, social ethics, and structured cooperation.

Foundations Shaping Ecumenical Mission Thinking and Practice

The ecumenical approach to Christian Mission is grounded in the belief that the Church's unity is essential for its faithful witness in the world. Over the time, churches have come to recognize that their divisions hinder the effectiveness of the gospel and weaken their moral voice in society.[1] In response, the ecumenical movement has developed through a variety of theological, ethical, cultural, and practical influences. James R. Kelly identifies five major sources that have shaped this movement in modern times: the symbolic vision of unity in Christ, theological reflection on church division and communion, ethical concern for justice and public credibility, the effects of pluralistic culture, and the need for administrative

[1] John W. Crossin, "Developments in Ecumenism: What Catechists Need to Know," *International Journal of Evangelization and Catechetics* 4/1 (Winter, 2023): 31-43.

cooperation.[2] These foundations provide multidimensional understanding of why ecumenism matters for Mission and how it continues to influence both church thinking and practice today.

Symbolic Structure: Universal Solidarity in Christ

One major source of ecumenical Mission thinking is the symbolic structure of Christian faith, especially the biblical vision of unity in Christ.[3] Passages like *There is neither Jew nor Greek, slave nor free, male nor female, for you are all one in Christ Jesus* (Galatians 3:28), inspire the belief that all human beings are called into a shared identity in Christ. This deep truth forms a powerful story of universal solidarity, where social, racial, and doctrinal barriers are meant to be overcome. In the ecumenical tradition, this symbolic vision motivates churches to move beyond separation and work together as one body in Mission.[4] It challenges Christians to embody the unity they proclaim, not only spiritually but also visibly in the world.

Theological Reflection on Church Unity

Theology also plays a key role in shaping ecumenical Mission. For centuries, different traditions understood unity in different ways. Catholics emphasized authority and institutional continuity, while Protestants valued freedom and conscience.[5] These differences caused long-standing divisions. However, after the Second Vatican Council, the Catholic Church took a major step by recognizing Protestant communities as "ecclesial bodies" through which grace is present. At the same time, many Protestants began to see church division not just as a historical fact to tolerate, but as a serious moral and spiritual failure. This shift in theological reflection has helped both sides rethink unity, not as uniformity, but as communion in diversity.[6] It has opened the door to serious dialogue and cooperation in Mission.

Social, Ethical and the Moral Justice

Another important source of ecumenical Mission is the ethical concern for justice in society. As churches around the world faced poverty, war, racism,

---

[2] James R. Kelly, "Spirals Not Cycles: Towards an Analytic Approach to the Sources and Stages of Ecumenism," *Review of Religious Research* 32/1 (September, 1990): 5-15.

[3] Dana L. Robert, "One Christ-Many Witnesses: Visions of Mission and Unity, Edinburgh and Beyond," *Transformation* 33/4 (October, 2016): 270-281.

[4] George Lindbeck and Georges Lindbeck, "Two Kinds of Ecumenism: Unitive and Interdenominational," *Gregorianum* 70/4 (1989): 647-660.

[5] Douglas Pratt, "Interreligious Dialogue: A Case Study Approach in Respect to the Vatican and the World Council of Churches," in World Christianity: Methodological Considerations, edited by Martha Frederiks and Dorottya Nagy (London: Brill, 2021), 179-203.

[6] Douglas Pratt, "Interreligious Dialogue: A Case Study Approach…

and inequality, many leaders began to see that division among Christians weakened their witness.[7] Denominational rivalry in the Mission field often appeared as confusion or even competition to non-Christians. This created a moral scandal that hurt the credibility of the gospel. As a result, both Protestant and Catholic leaders started to work together on social issues like poverty relief, human rights, and peacebuilding.[8] The realization that the Mission of the church must include justice and mercy helped push the ecumenical movement from theological discussion to practical cooperation on the ground.

Modern Pluralism and Folk Ecumenism

In today's pluralistic and secular societies, many ordinary Christians have developed a kind of "folk ecumenism" an everyday tolerance and mutual respect across denominational lines. People often attend events in different churches, marry across traditions, and share in community service without much concern for doctrinal boundaries.[9] This grassroots openness reflects the reality that Christians live and serve side by side, regardless of theological differences. However, while folk ecumenism promotes peaceful coexistence, it does not automatically lead to formal unity or deep cooperation. Without theological reflection and institutional support, it risks becoming a polite indifference.[10] Still, this everyday tolerance creates space for deeper ecumenical engagement when the churches choose to act on it.

Administrative Rationality and Institutional Cooperation

The practical demands of church life have also driven ecumenical Mission. As churches seek to serve communities efficiently, they often realize that sharing resources, coordinating ministries, and recognizing each other's work are necessary.[11] This leads to the formation of ecumenical councils, joint commissions, and cooperative projects, such as the World Council of Churches (WCC), which began in 1948. These structures support common worship, theological dialogue, and social action. Administrative rationality is not just about efficiency, it is about recognizing the need for visible

---

[7] Mary R. Sawyer, "Black Ecumenical Movements: Proponents of Social Change," *Review of Religious Research* 30/2 (December, 1988): 151-161.

[8] Mary R. Sawyer, "Black Ecumenical Movements…

[9] Andrew Pratt, "'Out of One, Many-Within One, Many': Religious Pluralism and Christian Ecumenism in the United States," *Perspectives in Religious Studies* 42/2 (Summer, 2015): 143-157.

[10] Andrew Pratt, "'Out of One, Many-Within One, Many…

[11] George Oliver Lillegard, "Modern Ecumenism and Cooperation in Externals," Quartalschrift 56/4 (October, 1959): 233-250.

structures of unity that support Mission in real and sustainable ways.[12] It reflects the understanding that ecumenism must be organized, not only inspired, to make lasting impact in the world.

Key Moments in Ecumenical Mission Practice

The ecumenical movement seeks to overcome divisions among Christian churches and to restore unity in faith, Mission, and witness. While theological dialogue and spiritual fellowship have been important, the ecumenical tradition also values visible expressions of unity, where churches work together in concrete, structured ways. Throughout the 20th century, several historic events have shaped the thinking and practice of visible ecumenism. These include the 1910 Edinburgh Missionary Conference, the formation of the Church of South India in 1947, the establishment of the World Council of Churches in 1948, and the Second Vatican Council of the Roman Catholic Church from 1962 to 1965. Each of these events marked a significant step toward Christian unity, showing how churches can cooperate in Mission, worship, and service while honouring their differences.

Pietism and the Evangelical Awakenings as Early Models of Ecumenism

Although Pietism and the Evangelical Awakenings were not organized ecumenical movements, they acted as important early models by encouraging unity across denominational positions. Pietism, which began in 17th century, focused on personal faith, Bible study, and holy living rather than theological controversy or church structure. Leaders like Philipp Jakob Spener and August Hermann Francke promoted fellowship among all true believers, regardless of church affiliation.[13] Similarly, the Evangelical Awakenings of the 18th century led by personalities such as John Wesley, George Whitefield, and Jonathan Edwards stressed conversion, revival, and a personal relationship with Christ.[14] These revivals attracted large crowds from various denominations, creating a spirit of unity around the gospel. Although doctrinal differences remained, the emphasis on shared experience of grace, Mission, and moral transformation laid a foundation for later ecumenical cooperation. In this way, Pietism and the Awakenings prepared the way for more structured efforts toward unity, such as the 1910 Edinburgh Missionary Conference.

---

[12] Jean Metropolitan Zizioulas, "The Existential Dimension of Ecumenism," *L'Osservatore Romano* 2401 (June, 2015): 7-8.

[13] Donald F. Durnbaugh, "New Understandings of Anabaptism and Pietism," *Brethren Life and Thought* 63/2 (Fall-Winter, 2019): 3-14.

[14] D. Bruce Hindmarsh, "The 'Toronto Blessing' and the Protestant Evangelical Awakening of the Eighteenth Century Compared," *Crux* 31/4 (December, 1995): 3-13.

The Evangelical Alliance (1846) as a Model of Early Ecumenism

The formation of the Evangelical Alliance in 1846 was a major step toward visible unity among Protestant Christians in the 19th century.[15] Established in London, it brought together leaders from various denominations including Anglican, Methodist, Baptist, Presbyterian, and Reformed traditions, who shared a common commitment to core evangelical beliefs such as the authority of the Bible, the centrality of Christ, and the need for personal conversion. Although the Alliance did not seek to merge churches or resolve all theological differences, it created a platform for cooperation, fellowship, and joint action. The Alliance focused on promoting religious freedom, social reform, prayer, and moral renewal, especially in response to the challenges of modern society.[16] By uniting Christians around shared convictions while respecting denominational diversity, the Evangelical Alliance became an early model of how doctrinal unity and visible cooperation could coexist. Its emphasis on spiritual fellowship and public witness anticipated the goals of later ecumenical movements in the 20th century.

World Missionary Conference Edinburgh 1910

The 1910 Edinburgh Missionary Conference is often seen as the beginning of the modern ecumenical movement. It brought together over 1,200 Protestant Mission leaders from different denominations to discuss how to work together more effectively in global Mission.[17] Although it did not include Roman Catholics or Orthodox Christians, it was a major step toward visible unity among Protestants. The key idea that emerged was that Christian divisions weakened Mission work, especially in non-Christian regions. The conference encouraged cooperation instead of competition and helped leaders see the importance of unity in spreading the gospel.[18] This historic event laid the theological and organizational foundation for future ecumenical developments.

The Formation of the Church of South India (CSI)

The formation of the Church of South India in 1947 was one of the first and most powerful examples of visible Christian unity. It was a historic union of Anglican, Methodist, Congregational, Presbyterian, and Reformed

[15] Lane Scruggs, "Evangelicalism and Ecumenism: The World Evangelical Alliance and Church Unity," *Fides et Historia* 49/1 (Winter-Spring, 2017): 85-103.

[16] Lane Scruggs, "Evangelicalism and Ecumenism...

[17] H. Edward Pruitt, "The Effects of Theological Convergence: Ecumenism from Edinburgh to Lausanne," *Journal for Baptist Theology & Ministry* 10/2 (Fall, 2013): 46-69.

[18] H. Edward Pruitt, "The Effects of Theological Convergence...

churches.[19] These churches agreed to become one body, sharing leadership, sacraments, and Mission, while respecting their different traditions. Unlike earlier efforts that focused only on dialogue or joint action, the CSI became a fully united church, showing that true unity is possible even among churches with different structures and beliefs.[20] It also showed how ecumenism could take root in non-Western contexts and shape Mission and ministry in newly independent nations like India.

The World Council of Churches (WCC)

The World Council of Churches, formally established in 1948, is one of the most important global instruments for visible ecumenism.[21] It brings together hundreds of Protestant, Anglican, and Orthodox churches from all over the world. Its goal is to promote unity, theological dialogue, and common action among churches. Through various commissions such as Faith and Order and Mission and Evangelism, the WCC encourages churches to work together in worship, social justice, peacebuilding, and Mission. Although the Roman Catholic Church is not a full member, it cooperates closely with the WCC in many areas.[22] The WCC has made ecumenism more structured, global, and inclusive, supporting visible signs of unity through shared Mission and witness.

Second Vatican Council

The Second Vatican Council (1962-1965) was a turning point in the Roman Catholic Church's approach to ecumenism. For centuries, the Catholic Church had viewed other Christian communities mainly as heretical or separated.[23] Vatican II changed this by recognizing Protestants and Orthodox as "separated brethren" and acknowledging the presence of grace and truth in their churches.[24] The Council encouraged dialogue, mutual respect, and cooperation in Mission and social issues. It led to the creation of official Catholic-Protestant dialogues and closer involvement with ecumenical

---

[19] Andrew C. Stout, "A Presbyterian Bishop: Lesslie Newbigin and Reformed Ecumenism," *Pro Ecclesia* 26/3 (Summer, 2017): 278-296.

[20] Andrew C. Stout, "A Presbyterian Bishop: Lesslie Newbigin…

[21] Hieromonk Patapios and Chrysostomos Metr of Etna, "Ecumenism Marches on: The World Council of Churches: A Visible Expression of the Una Sancta?," *Orthodox Tradition* 13/3-4 (January, 1996): 4-10.

[22] Lukas Vischer, "Roman Catholic Ecumenism and the World Council of Churches," *The Ecumenical Review* 16/4 (July, 1964): 378-394.

[23] Joseph P. Chinnici, "Ecumenism, Civil Rights, and the Second Vatican Council: The American Experience," *U.S. Catholic Historian* 30/3 (Summer, 2012): 21-49.

[24] Luc Forestier, "What Does Catholicity Mean?: Ecumenism, Synodality and Cultures According to Pope Francis," *One in Christ* 54/2 (December, 2020): 199-217.

bodies like the WCC. Vatican II made visible ecumenism more inclusive by bringing the Catholic Church into the heart of the modern ecumenical movement.[25]

Unity as a Journey: The Process Model of Ecumenical Mission

Modern ecumenical thinking no longer sees Christian unity as something that must be achieved all at once through structural merger. Instead, many churches and theologians understand unity as a gradual and relational process, shaped by time, trust, and mutual growth. This approach is known as the process model of ecumenism, which emphasizes ongoing engagement rather than immediate institutional union.[26] It reflects the view that unity must be lived and practiced before it can be fully formalized. The model includes three main components: reception, where churches learn from one another; internal reform, where each tradition deepens its own faith and structures; and spiral growth, where periods of dialogue are followed by consolidation and practical cooperation.[27]

Reception: Learning from One Another Across Traditions

One important part of the ecumenical process is reception, where churches receive spiritual gifts, insights, and practices from one another. Rather than seeing other denominations as rivals or threats, ecumenism encourages Christians to recognize what the Holy Spirit is doing in other traditions.[28] For example, the Roman Catholic Church has renewed its focus on Scripture, inspired in part by Protestant emphasis on Bible study and preaching. Likewise, many Protestant churches have rediscovered the value of liturgy, sacraments, and historical continuity by engaging with Orthodox and Catholic traditions.[29] Reception requires humility and discernment. It does not mean uncritical acceptance, but a willingness to learn and grow through the richness of the wider Christian family. This mutual exchange strengthens each church's witness and draws them closer in understanding and practice.

---

[25] Nikos A. Nissiotis, "Ecclesiology and Ecumenism of the Second Session of the Vatican Council II," *The Greek Orthodox Theological Review* 10/1 (Summer, 1964): 15-36.

[26] William Henn, "At the Heart of '*Unitatis Redintegratio*' Unity in Diversity," *Gregorianum* 88/2 (2007): 329-351.

[27] Conrad L. Kanagy, "Social Action, Evangelism, and Ecumenism: The Impact of Community, Theological, and Church Structural Variables," *Review of Religious Research* 34/1 (September, 1992): 34-50.

[28] Keith W. Clements, "What Is Distinctive about Christian Ecumenism and Why Does It Matter?," *Current Dialogue* 56 (December, 2014): 15-21.

[29] Stanley S. Harakas, "What Orthodox Christian Ethics Can Offer Ecumenism," *Journal of Ecumenical Studies* 45/3 (Summer, 2010): 376-384.

Internal Reform: Preparing for Unity through Spiritual Renewal

True unity cannot be achieved only through dialogue or agreements between leaders, rather, it also requires internal reform within each church. As churches open themselves to ecumenical insights, they must also examine and deepen their own life, especially in areas such as spirituality, worship, governance, and community life.[30] This process is not about losing identity but about becoming more faithful to one's own calling in Christ. When churches reform from within, they become stronger partners in the journey toward unity. In doing so, some churches may renew their prayer life or improve their leadership structures to be more transparent and inclusive. Others may recover forgotten traditions or make space for diverse voices.[31] Thus, internal reform helps churches grow in maturity and readiness for deeper relationships with others, making visible unity not only possible but meaningful.

Spiral Growth: Deepening Unity through Cycles of Dialogue and Practice

Ecumenical unity does not happen all at once. Instead, it follows a pattern of spiral growth, where churches go through alternating periods of intense dialogue and practical consolidation. In one phase, churches may engage in theological discussions, issue joint statements, or explore common beliefs. In the next phase, they may step back to reflect, apply what they have learned, and grow in mutual trust.[32] Over time, these cycles build a deeper foundation for unity without demanding total agreement or uniformity. This spiral model respects the complexity of church traditions and allows space for gradual change. It also avoids the unrealistic goal of immediate structural union. Instead, unity is seen as a growing relationship, where cooperation deepens step by step, and each stage brings the churches closer to the fullness of communion.

Mission Models in the Ecumenical Tradition

The ecumenical movement has brought with it a renewed understanding of Christian Mission, one that reflects the call to unity, justice, and shared witness in a divided world. Instead of competing with one another, churches are encouraged to engage in Mission together, embodying the gospel through cooperation, mutual learning, and common action. This vision of Mission is closely linked to the process model of ecumenism, which understands unity as a journey rather than an immediate goal. In this journey, different models

[30] Maxwell E. Johnson, "Ecumenism and the Study of Liturgy: What Shall We Do Now?," *Liturgical Ministry* 20/1 (Winter, 2011): 13-21.

[31] John Robert Nelson, "Explorations and Responses: What Hope for Ecumenism?," *Journal of Ecumenical Studies* 8/4 (Fall, 1971): 913-920.

[32] Douglas Pratt, "Interreligious Dialogue: A Case Study Approach…

of Mission have emerged, offering practical and theological expressions of how churches can serve together while honouring their differences.

Mission as Common Witness: Proclaiming the Gospel Together

The foundation of ecumenical Mission is the commitment to common witness. This model urges churches to present a united voice in proclaiming the gospel, contributing in public service, and addressing social issues. When Christians work together in areas such as evangelism, education, health care, or humanitarian aid, they demonstrate the love and truth of Christ in practical and visible ways.[33] It also helps avoid the confusion and division that arise when churches act independently or even in competition. Common witness shows that the Church's Mission is not about institutional success, but about pointing to the one Lord and Savior as it affirms in Jesus' prayer in John 17:21, that all his followers may be one so that the world may believe.

Mission as Dialogue: Building Relationships Through Listening and Understanding

The ecumenical tradition sees dialogue, both among Christian denominations and with people of other faiths, as an essential form of Mission. Unlike traditional models that focused only on preaching or conversion, the model of dialogue highlights the importance of mutual listening, respectful engagement, and spiritual encounter.[34] Through ecumenical dialogue, churches discover areas of theological agreement, clarify misunderstandings, and build trust. In interfaith settings, dialogue allows Christians to stand together on issues of justice, peace, and human dignity, while remaining faithful to their identity.[35] Rather than compromising truth, Mission as dialogue reflects the humility of Christ and opens the door for mutual transformation through relationship and shared concern.

Mission as Justice and Peace: Responding to Human Suffering

Another key model in the ecumenical movement is Mission as justice and peace.[36] This approach insists that preaching the gospel must be accompanied by action for social transformation. Inspired by Luke 4:18 and

---

[33] Dana L. Robert, "Witness and Unity in 21st Century World Christianity," *Transformation* 30/4 (October, 2013): 243-256.

[34] Gabriella Fallacara, "Ecumenism: Dialogue and Encounter," *Catholic International* 11/4 (November, 2000): 381-382.

[35] Paul Ladouceur, "Christian Ecumenism and Interreligious Dialogue: Convergences and Divergences," *Journal of Ecumenical Studies* 55/2 (Spring, 2020): 167-189

[36] Pope Francis, "An Ecumenism of Suffering," *L'Osservatore Romano* 2345 (May, 2014): 3.

Micah 6:8, it calls the Church to stand with the poor, resist oppression, and speak out against injustice. Whether through advocacy for human rights, support for refugees, or engagement in peacemaking, ecumenical Mission involves working together for a more just and compassionate world.[37] It also recognizes that injustice is often rooted in systems and structures, requiring united effort to challenge and reform them. In this model, the Mission of God (*Missio Dei*) is not limited to saving souls, but includes the healing of communities and nations.

Mission as Unity in Diversity: Honouring Difference While Seeking Communion

The ecumenical vision does not aim to erase denominational differences but to celebrate and integrate them within a shared Mission.[38] The model of Mission as unity in diversity encourages churches to honour their own traditions, cultures, and theological emphases, while cooperating in love and service. Unity is seen not as uniformity, but as communion in diversity, like the many parts of one body: *For just as the body is one and has many members, and all the members of the body, though many, are one body, so it is with Christ* (I Corinthians 12). Each tradition brings unique gifts. Some emphasize prophetic witness, others sacramental life, others charismatic spirituality or social action. Together, 'Mission as Unity in Diversity' enrich the whole church's Mission.[39] This model promotes humility, mutual respect, and the belief that diversity can reflect the fullness of God's grace when guided by the Spirit of unity.

Mission as Reconciliation: Healing Divisions and Building Peace

Mission as reconciliation is a powerful response to both church divisions and global conflict. It focuses on repairing broken relationships between denominations, ethnic groups, or nations. Historically, many Christian traditions have been separated because of its structures, teachings, controversies and even violence.[40] Ecumenical Mission seeks to heal these wounds through repentance, forgiveness, and shared discipleship. This Mission also addresses broader social divisions caused by racism, war, or injustice. As it is mentioned: *All this is from God, who reconciled us to*

---

[37] Dominik Morawski, "Suffering and Ecumenism," *Inside the Vatican* 7 (December, 1999): 19.

[38] William Henn, "At the Heart of '*Unitatis Redintegratio*' Unity in Diversity," *Gregorianum* 88/2 (2007): 329-351.

[39] David M. Chapman, "Ecumenism and the Visible Unity of the Church: 'Organic Union' or 'Reconciled Diversity'?," *Ecclesiology* 11/3 (December, 2015): 350-369.

[40] Jeffrey Gros, "The Gospel and Reconciliation: Reaping the Harvest of Ecumenism," *Emmanuel* 105 (January-February, 1999): 4-12.

himself through Christ and has given us the ministry of reconciliation; that is, in Christ God was reconciling the world to himself, not counting their trespasses against them, and entrusting the message of reconciliation to us. So we are ambassadors for Christ, since God is making his appeal through us; we entreat you on behalf of Christ: be reconciled to God (II Corinthians 5:18-20), the Church is called to be a "ministry of reconciliation," acting as Christ's ambassadors in a broken world.

Mission as Creation Care: Stewarding the Earth Together

In recent years, creation care has emerged as a vital area of ecumenical Mission. Environmental crises such as climate change, deforestation, and pollution demand urgent action. Churches across traditions now recognize that caring for the Earth is a biblical responsibility and a spiritual act of worship. Mission as creation care involves collaborative environmental advocacy, ecological education, and practical efforts such as tree planting, reducing carbon footprints, and supporting climate justice.[41] Working together in this area not only serves the world's needs but also strengthens unity among Christians through shared responsibility. It affirms that the gospel is not only about saving souls but also about renewing all of creation under Christ: *For the creation waits with eager longing for the revealing of the children of God...in hope that the creation itself will be set free from its enslavement to decay and will obtain the freedom of the glory of the children of God. We know that the whole creation has been groaning together as it suffers together the pains of labour* (Romans 8:19-22).

Mission as Mutual Learning: Growing Through Spiritual Exchange

The model of mutual learning is rooted in the belief that each Christian tradition has something valuable to offer and something to learn. This involves a process called reception, where churches receive the spiritual gifts and theological insights of others with openness and discernment. For example, Catholics have been renewed by Protestant insights into Scripture and lay participation, while Protestants have been enriched by Catholic and Orthodox traditions of liturgy, sacraments, and monastic spirituality.[42] Such mutual learnings deepen theological understanding, fosters humility, and creates space for spiritual ecumenism, a form of unity grounded in shared discipleship rather than formal agreement. It transforms Mission into a two-way journey of discovery and growth.

---

[41] Anthony J. Kelly, "The Ecumenism of Ecology," *Australian Journal of Theology* 22/3 (December, 2015): 193-205.

[42] Paul D. Murray, "Receptive Ecumenism and Ecclesial Learning Receiving Gifts for Our Needs," *Louvain Studies* 33/1-2 (Spring-Summer, 2008): 30-45.

Conclusion

A central strength of the ecumenical movement is its commitment to reciprocal learning. Thus, the ecumenical tradition understands Christian Mission not as the task of one church or denomination, but as a shared journey of faith, rooted in the common calling of all Christians to bear witness to the gospel of Jesus Christ. This spiritual journey is grounded in the divine stories of the Church and its foundational truth such as the unity of all people in Christ, the reconciliation of the world to God, and the vision of a new creation. These spiritual stories shape not only theology but also inspire a Mission that is inclusive, compassionate, and collaborative. Churches learn from one another's spiritual practices, theological insights, and historical experiences, leading to a richer and more faithful expression of the gospel. This mutual exchange deepens understanding and encourages internal renewal. It helps churches become more open, humble, and prepared for unity in both Mission and identity. Thus, the ecumenical tradition offers a powerful and hopeful vision that despite differences, the churches of Christ can walk together, serve together, and speak with one voice. By continuing this journey with patience, faith, and shared purpose, the ecumenical Mission can become a true sign of the unity for which Christ prayed and the world still longs.

25

Mission in the Evangelical Tradition Theological Foundations, Mission Methodologies, and Holistic Engagement

Mission in the Evangelical tradition is rooted in a strong trust in Jesus Christ's true divinity, His miraculous virgin birth, and His death as a perfect sacrifice for sin. Evangelicals also hold firmly to the Bible as the accurate and authoritative word of God and stress the need for each person to experience a real, personal faith in Christ. Together, these beliefs form the theological foundation that sees God as the one who sends the church into the world. Building on this foundation, Evangelical Mission uses three main methods: 'presence' calls believers to live among people in a way that shows Christ's love through actions and relationships, 'dialogue' invites sincere listening and respectful conversation, helping Missionaries understand local cultures before sharing the gospel and 'proclamation' that clearly explaining the good news of Jesus and inviting people into a restored relationship with God. Over the years, gatherings like the 1966 Berlin Congress and the 1974 Lausanne Congress have helped Evangelicals refine and spread these approaches around the globe. In recent decades, Evangelical Mission has grown more holistic, recognizing that sharing the gospel also includes addressing real-life needs such as poverty, health care, and justice.

Defining Evangelical Missiology

Evangelical Missiology is the study and practice of Christian Mission grounded in the core theological convictions of Evangelicalism. It is shaped by a commitment to biblical truth, personal faith in Christ, and the belief that the Church is sent by God to share the gospel with all people.[1] Evangelical Missiology emphasizes both the message and method of Mission, focusing on proclaiming the good news of Jesus Christ and fostering local churches among new believers. It combines faithful theology with practical strategies that are sensitive to cultural contexts and social realities.[2] As a result, it seeks not only to lead individuals to salvation but also to bring lasting transformation through Holistic Mission rooted in God's purposes for the world.

Core Convictions: Deity of Christ, Virgin Birth, Substitutionary Atonement

At the heart of Evangelical Missiology is the firm belief in the unique identity and saving work of Jesus Christ. Evangelicals affirm that Jesus is fully God and fully human, the eternal Son of God who entered history through the virgin birth. This miracle points to his divine origin and sinless nature, which are essential for his role as Savior.[3] Evangelicals also uphold the doctrine of substitutionary atonement, which teaches that Jesus died on the cross in the place of sinners, bearing the punishment they deserved so they could be forgiven and reconciled to God. These truths are not only central to Evangelical theology but also form the core message of Evangelical Mission.[4] Mission, therefore, is not simply a call to ethical living or religious experience, but a proclamation of what God has done through Christ to redeem a lost world.

Authority and Accuracy of Scripture

Another significant view of Evangelical Missiology is a high view of Scripture. Evangelicals believe that the Bible is the inspired, inerrant, and trustworthy word of God. It is the final authority in all matters of faith, doctrine, and practice. This conviction gives Evangelical Mission a clear foundation for its message and methods. Scripture is not only the source of the gospel but also the guide for how to live and share that gospel in the world. In Mission contexts, this means that Missionaries rely on Scripture for understanding God's will, for shaping their preaching and teaching, and

---

[1] Harold Netland, "Evangelical Missiology and Theology of Religions: An Agenda for the Future," *International Journal of Frontier Missiology* 29/1 (January-March, 2012): 5-12.

[2] Harold Netland, "Evangelical Missiology and Theology of Religions…

[3] David M. Gustafson, "Evangelical Convictions in Response to Liberal Theology: The Bible Institute and Academy of the Norwegian-Danish Evangelical Free Church, 1910-1949," *Trinity Journal* 40/1 (Spring, 2019): 37-63.

[4] Olivia Jayne Schultz, "Navigating Evangelical Affect: Convictions, Promises, and Dissonance in Adolescent Adherence to Purity Teachings," *Theology & Sexuality* 29/2-3 (March, 2023): 148-163.

for confronting spiritual error or injustice.[5] Because Evangelicals believe the Bible is accurate and relevant across all cultures and times, they also give more importance to Bible translation, literacy, and teaching as key parts of Mission work.

Personal Conversion and Spirit-Empowered Relationship with God

Evangelical Missiology also emphasizes the need for personal conversion and a living relationship with God through the Holy Spirit. Conversion is understood as a conscious, individual response to the gospel, marked by repentance, faith in Christ, and a transformed life. Evangelicals believe that salvation is not inherited or received through rituals alone, but comes through a personal decision to follow Jesus.[6] This emphasis on personal faith shapes the way Evangelicals carry out Mission, focusing on helping individuals hear the gospel clearly and respond in faith. Along with this, Evangelicals affirm that true Christian life is empowered by the Holy Spirit, who dwells in believers and enables them to grow, witness, and serve.[7] Thus, Mission is not merely a human effort, but a Spirit-led movement that calls people into a dynamic and growing relationship with God.

Historical Development of the Post World Wat II Evangelical Mission Movement

The Evangelical Mission movement after World War II emerged as a global response to both theological decline in mainline churches and a renewed desire to fulfil the Great Commission. It was shaped by a strong commitment to biblical truth, the urgency of evangelism, and a concern for worldwide gospel proclamation. As secularism and liberal theology gained influence, Evangelicals sought to clarify and reclaim the Missionary task of the Church. This historical development, marked by key gatherings, Mission partnerships, and theological statements, evolved from a focus on individual salvation to comprehend Mission methods, social engagement, and cross-cultural awareness, becoming one of the most influential forces in modern Christian Mission.

---

[5] Michael D. Williams, "Theology as Witness: Reading Scripture in a New Era of Evangelical Thought Part I Christopher Wright, The Mission of God," *Presbyterion* 36/2 (Fall, 2010): 71-85.

[6] J. Duane Beals, "The Knowledge Which Comes by Faith: A Look at the Evangelical Conversion and Worldview," *Reflections* 7/1-2 (Spring-Fall, 2003): 118-126.

[7] M. J. van den Toren-Liefting, "Spirit-Empowered Migrants in the Anthropocene: The Defining Role of the Spirit in the Entanglements of Charismatic Evangelical Churches, Latin American Migration and the Spanish Public Sphere," *Scriptura* 121/1 (January, 2022): 1-13.

Roots in Mid-20th Century American and Western Evangelicalism

The foundations of the modern Evangelical Mission movement were laid in the mid-20th century, especially in North America and Western Europe. In response to the theological liberalism of the early 20th century, Evangelicals began to stress a return to core gospel truths and personal faith in Christ. Important personalities like Billy Graham and Carl F. H. Henry helped in shaping a new generation of Evangelicals who valued both biblical faithfulness and cultural engagement. Institutions such as Christianity Today and the Billy Graham Evangelistic Association (BGEA) played major roles in promoting global evangelism. During this time, the movement also began to distance itself from fundamentalism by emphasizing cooperation, intellectual rigor, and global Mission.[8] This created a productive context for renewed Missionary activity that combined strong theology with deliberate outreach.

The 1966 World Congress on Evangelism: "One Race, One Gospel, One Task"

A major turning point came with the World Congress on Evangelism held in Berlin in 1966. Organized by Christianity Today and the BGEA, the congress responded to the growing influence of the World Council of Churches (WCC), which many Evangelicals felt had shifted away from evangelistic priorities. The Berlin Congress gathered Evangelical leaders from around the world to reaffirm the centrality of gospel proclamation. Under the theme "One Race, One Gospel, One Task," the congress emphasized the unity of humanity, the uniqueness of the gospel, and the shared responsibility of the Church in Mission. It marked a strong public commitment to evangelism and helped to form a global network of Evangelical Mission thinking and practice.[9] The success of the Berlin Congress laid the foundation for future international Evangelical cooperation in Mission.

Lausanne I: From "Evangelism" to "Evangelization"

The First International Congress on World Evangelization held in Lausanne, Switzerland in 1974 marked a defining moment in modern Evangelical Mission history. Under the leadership of Billy Graham and the theological guidance of John Stott, the congress brought together over 2,400 Evangelical leaders from across the globe to reflect on the Church's global Missionary task. One of the most significant contributions of Lausanne I was the shift

[8] Kevin E. Lawson, "Evangelical Christian Education in the Mid-20th Century: Cooperation in Parachurch Ministries," *Christian Education Journal* 1/1 (Fall, 2003): 73-77.

[9] Robert D. Preus, "Reflections on the World Congress on Evangelism Held at Berlin, Germany, Oct 26-Nov 4, 1966," *Concordia Theological Monthly* 38/3 (March, 1967): 185-188.

in emphasis from "evangelism" that understood narrowly as the verbal proclamation of the gospel, to "evangelization", which embraced a more comprehensive view of Mission. This broader approach recognized the need to reach not only individuals but entire cultures and social structures with the transforming message of the gospel.[10] The Missiological significance of Lausanne I lies in its strong affirmation of both proclamation and social responsibility. The Lausanne Covenant, the congress's theological statement, clearly stated that "evangelism and sociopolitical involvement are both part of our Christian duty." This was a groundbreaking moment for Evangelical Mission, as it formally integrated social action such as addressing poverty, injustice, and human suffering into the Church's Mission mandate, without compromising the central task of preaching Christ. Lausanne I also emphasized the role of the whole Church, including the growing Church in the Global South, in the task of global evangelization.[11] It set the foundation for a globally conscious, theologically balanced, and contextually relevant Evangelical Missiology that continues to shape Mission efforts.

Growth of the Lausanne Committee and Subsequent Congresses

Following Lausanne I, the formation of the Lausanne Committee for World Evangelization in 1976 aimed to carry forward the vision of global Mission cooperation. The Committee facilitated networking, theological reflection, and strategic planning among Evangelical leaders and Mission agencies. It provided a platform for Evangelicals worldwide to address emerging Missiological challenges and adapt Mission methods to changing global contexts. Two major international congresses such as Lausanne II in Manila (1989) and Lausanne III in Cape Town (2010) built upon and expanded the original Lausanne vision.

Lausanne II in Manila (1989) focused on the implementation of Lausanne I's vision, highlighting the importance of contextualization, the rise of non-Western Mission leadership, and the role of local churches in global evangelization. It stressed that Mission should be shaped by local cultures while remaining faithful to the gospel, which encouraged deeper reflection on cultural sensitivity and indigenous expressions of faith.[12] Lausanne III in Cape Town (2010) addressed new global realities, including post-modernism, religious pluralism, urbanization, and digital culture. The resulting Cape Town Commitment called for a holistic approach to Mission

---

[10] Valdir R. Steuernagel, "Social Concern and Evangelization: Our Journey since Lausanne I," *Transformation* 7/1 (1990): 12-16.

[11] Chris Sugden, "Theological Developments since Lausanne I," *Transformation* 7/1 (1990): 9-12.

[12] N.A. "WORLD BULLETIN BOARD: Evangelicals at WCC Conference Send Letter to Lausanne II," *Transformation* 6/4 (1989): 1-18.

that affirms the Lordship of Christ over all areas of life. It emphasized reconciliation with God, one another, and creation, pointing to the Mission of God as comprehensive in scope. One of the most important Missiological contributions of Cape Town was its strong stand against relativism, its call for integrity in Mission, and its affirmation of the Trinitarian basis of Mission.[13]

Theological Foundations of Evangelical Missiology

The practice of Mission in the Evangelical tradition is firmly rooted in theological convictions drawn from Scripture and shaped by the historic Christian faith. These foundations are not simply background doctrines but essential truths that guide and empower the Church's participation in God's Mission. Evangelical Missiology views Mission as more than a human project, rather, as the outworking of God's redemptive plan for the world. Understanding this Mission theologically ensures that the Church engages in it with humility, faithfulness, and a clear sense of identity and purpose. Three core theological themes such as: *Missio Dei*, Christology and the atonement, and the biblical mandate for Mission form the pillars of Evangelical thinking and practice in global outreach.

Missio Dei: God's Initiative and the Trinity in Mission

The concept of *Missio Dei*, (the Mission of God), has become a central theological framework in Evangelical Missiology. It emphasizes that Mission originates with God, not with the Church. God is a Missionary God who sends Jesus and the Spirit into the world to redeem and restore creation. The Mission, therefore, is not primarily an activity of the Church, but a participation in the ongoing work of the triune God: God, Jesus, and Holy Spirit. God sends Jesus (John 3:16), Jesus sends the Holy Spirit (John 14:26), and the risen Christ sends the Church into the world (John 20:21). This Trinitarian understanding of Mission gives depth and direction to Evangelical engagement, reminding believers that they are not the source of Mission but co-workers in God's sovereign plan.[14] It also shapes the Church's posture, emphasizing dependence on God's initiative, unity within the global body of Christ, and the holistic scope of redemption that includes both individuals and societies.

---

[13] Rose Dowsett, "Reflections on a Century: Edinburgh 1910, Edinburgh 2010, and Lausanne III," *Scottish Bulletin of Evangelical Theology* 30/1 (Spring, 2012): 66-77.

[14] Harold Godfrey, "An Evangelical Understanding of The *Missio Dei* as Inclusion of Social Justice: A Critical Theological Reflection," *Pharos Journal of Theology* 100 (December, 2019), 1-10.

Christology and Atonement as Missional Centre

In Evangelical Missiology, the person and work of Jesus Christ stand at the very centre of Mission. Evangelicals affirm the full divinity and humanity of Christ and understand Jesus' death on the cross as a substitutionary atonement, where Jesus bore the penalty of sin on behalf of humanity. This belief grounds the urgency and content of Mission: the world is lost without Christ, and salvation comes only through Jesus' redemptive work.[15] The gospel message proclaimed in Evangelical Mission is therefore centred on the life, death, and resurrection of Jesus as Paul declares: *Christ died for our sins according to the Scriptures...he was buried...and he was raised on the third day* (I Corinthians 15:3-4). Christ's victory over sin and death becomes the foundation for calling people into reconciliation with God.[16] From a Missiological standpoint, this focus gives Evangelical Mission both clarity and boldness, while also offering a message of hope that addresses the deepest needs of humanity.

Biblical Mandate and Hermeneutics for Mission

Evangelical Missiology is deeply committed to the authority of Scripture as the foundation for Mission. Evangelicals see the Bible not only as a source of doctrine but also as a Missional text, one that tells the story of God's redemptive purpose from Genesis to Revelation. Key passages such as the Great Commission (Matthew 28:18-20), the sending of the seventy (Luke 10:1-12), and the vision of all nations worshiping God (Revelation 7:9-10) form the biblical mandate for Mission in Evangelical Missiology.[17] However, Evangelical Mission is not limited to isolated texts. It is shaped by a broader hermeneutical approach that sees the entire biblical narrative as centred on God's desire to bless the nations through his covenant people (Genesis 12:1-3) and ultimately through Christ. This "Mission hermeneutic" reads Scripture with a view to God's sending activity and the Church's role in it. The result is a theology that motivates obedience, shapes priorities, and equips the Church to engage the world with both faithfulness and relevance.[18] It calls the Church to proclaim, live, and embody the gospel in every context, guided by the Word of God.

---

[15] J. Denny Weaver and Gerald J. Mast, "Anabaptist Christology, Racial Reconciliation, and Postconservative Evangelical Theology," *Direction* 41/1 (Spring, 2012): 125-138.

[16] J. Denny Weaver and Gerald J. Mast, "Anabaptist Christology…

[17] Amos Yong, "The Mandate of Asian American Evangelical Theology," *Evangelical Review of Theology* 39/3 (July, 2015): 204-217.

[18] Moanungsang, "Biblical Mandate and Emerging Theology: Integral Spirituality: A Transformative Practice," *REFLEXUS* 10/15 (2016): 149-165.

Missional Methodologies in the Lausanne Framework

The Lausanne Movement has played a major role in shaping Evangelical Mission by offering a balanced and biblically grounded vision of how the gospel should be shared across cultures and contexts. One of its most important contributions has been the development of three complementary Mission methods: presence, dialogue, and proclamation. These approaches were formally recognized in the Lausanne Covenant (1974) and further expanded in later congresses, especially Cape Town 2010. Rather than separating social engagement from spiritual witness, the Lausanne framework emphasizes that these elements must work together to reflect the full message of the gospel. Each methodology highlights a distinct way in which the Church can embody and communicate Christ's love to the world.

Presence: Incarnational Living and Witness through Deeds

Presence, as understood in the Lausanne framework, refers to the Church's physical and relational presence among people, especially in places of need and suffering. It draws inspiration from the incarnation of Jesus Christ, who took on human flesh and lived among humanity (John 1:14). In this sense, Christian Mission begins not with speaking, but with being, by living among others in humility, love, and service. This approach emphasizes deeds over words, where the character and lifestyle of believers become a visible testimony to the gospel. In Missiological terms, presence is a form of incarnational Mission, where Missionaries and local Christians seek to reflect God's compassion and holiness in everyday life. Whether through acts of mercy, social service, or simply sharing life in community, presence allows others to see the gospel in action.[19] It prepares the ground for deeper conversation and invites others to ask questions about the source of Christian hope and love.

Dialogue: Listening, Contextual Understanding, and Respectful Engagement

Dialogue, in the Lausanne tradition, involves respectful and open communication with people of other beliefs and cultures. It is not a method of compromise but of deep listening, sincere engagement, and seeking understanding. Lausanne III, Cape Town 2010, emphasized that in a world of increasing religious pluralism and postmodern scepticism, dialogue is an essential path for building trust and breaking down misunderstandings. Following the example of the Apostle Paul in Acts 17, where he engaged both Jews and Gentiles with sensitivity to their worldviews, Evangelical

[19] Denis Mawunyo Adufuli, "The Nexus Between German Pietism and the Mission, Theology, and Spirituality of the Evangelical Presbyterian Church, Ghana," *Transformation* 40/4 (October, 2023): 304-316.

Mission seeks to listen first and speak second.[20] Dialogue enables Missionaries to understand the social, cultural, and religious contexts of those they serve. From a Missiological perspective, dialogue opens the door for contextualization, where the gospel is communicated in ways that are faithful to Scripture yet meaningful within local settings. It also reflects the humility of Christ and respects the dignity of others. Lausanne understands dialogue as a stepping stone toward effective witness, not an end in itself.[21] When carried out with integrity, it creates space for honest questions and genuine encounters with the gospel, fostering bridges between worldviews while maintaining the uniqueness of Christ.

Proclamation: Gospel Communication and Call to Reconciliation

Proclamation remains at the heart of Evangelical Mission. For the Lausanne Movement, proclamation refers to the clear and faithful communication of the good news of Jesus Christ, based on Jesus' life, death, and resurrection. It involves calling people to repentance, faith, and reconciliation with God, and is based on the belief that salvation comes only through Christ. Lausanne leaders have consistently affirmed that while social action and dialogue are essential, they cannot replace the explicit preaching of the gospel.[22] As the Cape Town Commitment declared, "We cannot separate what God has joined together: the proclamation of the gospel and the demonstration of the gospel." The Missiological significance of proclamation lies in its power to bring people into a personal and saving relationship with God. It is not merely a transfer of information but a divine invitation to transformation. In a world filled with competing truth claims and spiritual confusion, Lausanne affirms the need to boldly proclaim Jesus as the way, the truth, and the life (John 14:6). This proclamation must be clear, culturally sensitive, and Spirit-led, aiming not to win arguments but to invite people into the story of God's redeeming love.[23] When combined with presence and dialogue, proclamation reflects the full scope of Mission, speaking with both truth and grace to a world in need of salvation.

---

[20] Walter Sawatsky, "Orthodox-Evangelical Protestant Dialogue on Mission-Challenges and Shifting Options," *Acta Missiologiae* 1 (2008): 11-31.

[21] Walter Sawatsky, "Slavic Evangelicals in Mission within the Commonwealth of Independent States: Inter-Church Mission Dialogue-Orthodox, Catholic, Protestant and Evangelical," *Transformation* 21/3 (July, 2004): 195-204.

[22] Felix Körner, "Mission-Dialogue-Proclamation: Redefining Evangelization in Christian-Muslim Interaction," *Zeitschrift Für Missionswissenschaft Und Religionswissenschaft* 106/1-4 (January, 2022): 223-231.

[23] Edward T. Wright, "Thus Sayeth the Matthean Lord: Exploring the Intersection of the Quest for the Historical Jesus and the Proclamation of the Biblical Jesus," *The Asbury Journal* 74/1 (Spring, 2019): 108-130.

Holistic Mission: Integrating Social Action and Evangelism

In recent decades, Evangelical Missiology has increasingly embraced the concept of Holistic Mission, a model that brings together the proclamation of the gospel and the practice of social responsibility. This integrated approach arises from the recognition that the message of salvation in Jesus Christ addresses not only the soul but also the full scope of human life, including physical needs, social structures, and cultural realities. The life and ministry of Jesus serve as the clearest example of this integration, as Jesus preached the kingdom of God while also healing the sick, feeding the hungry, and defending the oppressed. Evangelical Missiology now strongly affirm that evangelism and social action are not separate tasks but united expressions of the same gospel. This understanding of Mission has been deepened by global Evangelical gatherings such as the Lausanne Congresses and articulated further through voices like Catharine Padilla, who emphasized the theological and practical commitments required for genuine holistic engagement. As Evangelicals move beyond a narrow focus on individual salvation, they are increasingly concerned with how the gospel can bring transformation to both individuals and communities, addressing issues such as poverty, injustice, health care, and education. Holistic Mission thus reflects the Missional nature of God (*Missio Dei*), who seeks to redeem not only people but also the systems and relationships within which they live.

Defining Holistic Mission: Inseparable Gospel and Social Engagement

Holistic Mission is the belief that the Christian gospel speaks to every part of human life: spiritual, physical, social, and emotional. It rejects the traditional idea that evangelism and social action are separate or competing priorities. Instead, both are seen as essential expressions of the same gospel, following the example of Jesus, who preached the Kingdom of God while healing the sick, feeding the hungry, and welcoming the outcast. This approach reflects the incarnation, God becoming human, in Christ to bring full salvation to the whole person. Holistic Mission thus, calls the Church to care for people's eternal needs without ignoring present suffering, injustice, or loss of dignity. Evangelism without compassion becomes irrelevant, and social work without the gospel lacks eternal hope.[24] True Holistic Mission keeps Christ at the centre while working for righteousness, peace, and wholeness in a broken world.

---

[24] Won-Seop Bae, "The Emergence and Discussion of Holistic Mission: Explore Changing Views among Evangelical Protestants around Lausanne Movement on the Relationship between Evangelism and Social Concern (1966-2010)," *Theology and Practice* 90 (December, 2024): 331-355.

Six Characteristics of Holistic Mission

There are six key commitments that shape Evangelical Holistic Mission. First is commitment to Jesus Christ as Lord of all creation, affirming Jesus' reign over every part of life. Second is commitment to one another, building unity and care within the Christian community. Third is commitment to the world as the object of God's love, approaching it with compassion and a desire for transformation. Fourth is the priesthood of all believers, meaning every Christian shares responsibility for Mission, not only pastors or Missionaries. Fifth is leadership through service, following Christ's example of humility. Sixth is flexibility in church structures, adapting forms and methods to different cultural and social contexts.[25] Together, these principles challenge the false divide between evangelism and social responsibility, presenting a biblically grounded, context-sensitive vision of Mission that addresses the whole person in the whole world.

Practical Phases: Assessment, Planning, Implementation, Evaluation

Holistic Mission needs careful methods, not just good intentions. Four practical phases guide this process. 'Assessment' means understanding the local context, listening to communities, learning their needs, and respecting cultural realities. 'Planning' takes these insights and turns them into clear, gospel-shaped goals with realistic strategies. 'Implementation' is putting the plan into action with teamwork, cultural sensitivity, and a servant's heart, whether in evangelism, healthcare, education, or justice work. 'Evaluation' then measures impact, not only in numbers but in transformed lives, restored communities, and deeper faith.[26] This cycle ensures that Mission remains thoughtful, responsive to the Holy Spirit, and effective in addressing rcal needs while staying faithful to the message of Christ.

Conclusion

Evangelical Mission is rooted in strong theological convictions such as the deity of Christ, the authority of Scripture, and the call to personal conversion, all of which are shaped by the belief that Mission flows from God's own redemptive work, *Missio Dei*. Historically, the post-World War II Evangelical movement, especially through the Lausanne gatherings, has helped redefine Mission from mere evangelism to a broader understanding of evangelization that includes proclamation, presence, and dialogue. The Lausanne framework also emphasized the integration of social responsibility with gospel witness, leading to a vision of Holistic Mission that addresses

[25] C. René Padilla, "Integral Mission," in *The Local Church, Agent of Transformation: An Ecclesiology for Integral Mission* (Oxford: Regnum Books, 2010), 57-72.

[26] David G. R. Keller, "Affirming Mission-Centered Strategy in Planning the Future of Theological Education," *Sewanee Theological Review* 53/3 (December, 2010): 301-315.

both spiritual and social needs. Theologically, the evangelical tradition upholds the centrality of Christ's atonement, the guidance of the Holy Spirit, and the biblical mandate for global Mission. Methodologically, it promotes contextualized approaches, through cross-cultural sensitivity, cultural engagement, and the empowerment of indigenous leaders that allow the gospel to take root authentically in diverse settings. Contemporary models of Mission now include discipleship, socio-political action, worldview transformation, and renewed emphasis on justice, mercy, and advocacy. Today, the Holistic nature of Mission today is seen in how it responds to global realities like poverty, inequality, and the search for dignity and hope. Ultimately, Evangelical Mission is a call to faithful witness to proclaim Christ, serve with humility, and embody the gospel in word and deed for the transformation of all nations.

26

Pentecostal Missiology in a Pluralistic World Towards a Holistic Legacy of Mission from Azusa Street to the Ends of the Earth

In Pentecostal studies, "Mission" refers not only to the formal sending of Missionaries but to the broader work of God's Spirit moving believers outward in word and deed. This scope comprehends evangelistic proclamation, church planting, social action, and interreligious engagement. Pentecostal Mission thus includes the proclamation of the gospel, the empowering presence of the Holy Spirit in communities, and acts of compassion and justice that bear witness to God's kingdom. By defining Mission in this way, we recognize that Pentecostal outreach is both spiritual and practical, public and personal. Missiologically, Pentecostal Mission highlights lived experience and Spirit-led praxis over purely doctrinal formulations. Rather than starting with abstract theological systems, Pentecostal Mission begin with the testimonies, worship practices, and community initiatives that believers themselves describe as Spirit-empowered Mission. This experiential approach argues that Pentecostal Mission emerges from a dynamic interplay of three central factors: spiritual experience, eschatological urgency, and social engagement. Together, these form a Holistic Missiology that is simultaneously Spirit-driven, future-oriented, and socially committed.

Historical and Theological Roots

The Pentecostal movement came from streams of Christian renewal and different cultural settings. Its early pioneers built on the Wesleyan-Holiness focus on deep heart conversion and sanctification, which soon found dramatic expression in the interracial revival at Azusa Street in 1906.

Over time, Pentecostalism received ecumenical encouragement from the wider Charismatic Renewal and even from Roman Catholic and Eastern Orthodox mystical traditions, as twentieth-century theologians saw that the Holy Spirit works beyond denominational boundaries. At the same time, the unique worship, music, and prophetic courage gave Pentecostalism a strong community spirit and a concern for justice that have remained central to its identity. Together, these historical influences and theological insights shaped a movement that sees Mission as both a Spirit-empowered calling and a lived practice rooted in Scripture, energized by encounters with God, and expressed through vibrant community life.

Origins in the Holiness Movement

In the late nineteenth century, many Protestant churches in North America and Britain experienced a wave of spiritual renewal known as the Wesleyan-Holiness Movement. Leaders such as Phoebe Palmer, Charles Finney, and A. B. Simpson taught that after conversion believers could receive a "second blessing" or "entire sanctification," in which the Holy Spirit would cleanse the heart from inward sin and empower them for holy living.[1] These revival gatherings emphasized constant prayer, heartfelt confession, and testimony, and often produced visible life-changing results among participants. The movement's key conviction was that Christians need not struggle continually against the power of sin but could walk in victory through an immediate work of grace.[2] This teaching of Spirit-empowered holiness laid vital groundwork for Pentecostalism, which would later claim that sanctification is not only transformative but often accompanied by spiritual gifts.

Wesleyan-Holiness Emphasis on Sanctification

A central biblical foundation for the Holiness emphasis is drawn from Acts that says: *All of them were filled with the Holy Spirit and began to speak in other languages, as the Spirit gave them ability* (Acts 2:4), and from Paul's warning in I Thessalonians: Do not quench the Spirit (I Thessalonians 5:19). Early Pentecostal pioneers read these texts as promises that God still grants a powerful, heart-cleansing encounter with the Spirit. They believed this encounter not only set believers free from moral failure but also enabled

[1] Jay Riley Case, "And Ever the Twain Shall Meet: The Holiness Missionary Movement and the Birth of World Pentecostalism, 1870-1920," *Religion and American Culture* 16/2 (Summer, 2006): 125-159.

[2] Randall J. Stephens, "The Convergence of Populism, Religion, and the Holiness-Pentecostal Movements: A Review of the Historical Literature," *Fides et Historia* 32/1 (Winter-Spring, 2000): 51-64.

them to live with Christ-like love and boldness.[3] In practice, this meant that personal devotion, group prayer, and the expectation of tangible Spirit baptism became hallmarks of emerging Pentecostal gatherings, a clear extension of Wesleyan-Holiness teaching, but with extra emphasis on visible manifestations of the Spirit.

The Catalytic Role of the 1906 Azusa Street Outpouring

In April 1906, a racially mixed fellowship meeting at 312 Azusa Street in Los Angeles drew international attention when participants experienced speaking in tongues, prophetic words, and powerful healing. Led by William J. Seymour, an African American preacher trained in the Holiness tradition, the Azusa meetings broke social norms by welcoming all races and classes to worship together. Eyewitnesses reported spontaneous singing, trembling under the Spirit's power, and an atmosphere of radical equality. News of this revival spread through newsletters and testimonies, seeding similar gatherings across the United States and abroad.[4] The Azusa Street Revival thus became the definitive spark that transformed small Holiness groups into a global Pentecostal movement, characterized by its emphasis on Spirit baptism accompanied by "fruits" and "gifts" of the Spirit.

Ecumenical and Charismatic Streams

Over the twentieth century, the free movement of the Spirit found expression beyond Pentecostal denominations in what came to be known as the Charismatic Renewal. Beginning in the 1960s, members of mainline Protestant, Anglican, and Roman Catholic churches reported experiences of Spirit baptism that included speaking in tongues, prophecy, and healing. This ecumenical wave affirmed that the spiritual gifts are not confined to any single tradition and encouraged cooperation across historic church boundaries. Pentecostals both influenced and learned from these streams, sharing liturgical innovations such as laying on of hands and theological insights about the Spirit's normative work in the Church today.[5] As a result, Pentecostalism gained broader recognition and engaged more deeply in conversations with other Christian bodies about Mission, doctrine, and worship.

---

[3] Jean Stockard, Susie Cunningham Stanley and Benton Johnson, "Moving from Sect to Church: Variations in Views Regarding Sanctification among Wesleyan/Holiness Clergy," *Review of Religious Research* 43/1 (September, 2001): 70-92.

[4] Allan Heaton Anderson, "The Azusa Street Revival and the Emergence of Pentecostal Missions in the Early Twentieth Century," *Transformation* 23/2 (April, 2006): 107-118.

[5] Gerald W. King, "Streams of Convergence: The Pentecostal-Fundamentalist Response to Modernism," *PentecoStudies* 7/2 (December, 2008): 64-84.

Impact of Vatican II's Ad Gentes

In 1965, the Second Vatican Council issued *Ad Gentes*, a decree on the Church's Missionary activity. It boldly stated, "The pilgrim Church is Missionary by her very nature, since it is from the Mission of the Son and the Mission of the Holy Spirit that she draws her origin" (*Ad Gentes* 2). Pentecostal scholars and leaders welcomed this affirmation because it echoed their own conviction that Mission is intrinsic to the Church's identity. By highlighting the Missionary work of the Holy Spirit alongside Jesus, *Ad Gentes* provided a theological bridge for dialogue between Pentecostals and Roman Catholics.[6] This shared language of Spirit-driven Mission opened doors for collaborative evangelism projects, joint social initiatives, and mutual respect in theological forums.

African American Spirituality

African American church life, born out of the trauma of slavery and later segregation, gave Pentecostalism much of its musical, prophetic, and communal soul. Spirituals, gospel hymns, and call-and-response singing created worship spaces where the body and emotions were fully engaged in praising God. From this heritage came the understanding that music and movement themselves convey theological truths about freedom, hope, and divine presence. Prophetic utterances, spoken in the power of the Spirit, offered words of comfort, correction, and vision for the future, reinforcing the belief that God speaks directly to God's people today.[7] The communal solidarity forged in those churches showed that Mission is not an individual effort, but a shared journey of support, accountability, and social uplift.

Rhythmic Praise, Prophetic Utterance, and Communal Solidarity

The rhythmic heartbeats of drums and vibrant choir music in African American Pentecostal churches embody a theology of the body that invites full participation including clapping, dancing, and raising hands in worship. This physical expressiveness affirms that salvation and sanctification touch every dimension of human life: body, mind, and spirit. Prophetic utterance, often arising in the midst of worship, functions as a dynamic feedback loop between the Spirit and the community, guiding decisions and encouraging believers. These practices create strong social bonds, since worshipers experience vulnerability and empowerment together. In turn, this communal solidarity enriched Mission understanding that: a group that prays, sings,

---

[6] Richard H. Bliese, "Speaking in Tongues and the Mission of God *Ad Gentes*," *Journal of Pentecostal Theology* 20/1 (December, 2011): 38-47.

[7] Wolfgang Vondey, "The Making of a Black Liturgy: Pentecostal Worship and Spirituality from African Slave Narratives to American Cityscapes," *Black Theology* 10/2 (August, 2012): 147-168.

and discerns together is better equipped to serve, advocate, and bear witness in the complex, pluralistic contexts of the modern world.[8]

Foundations of Pentecostal Missiology

Pentecostal Missiology rests upon a distinct theological vision in which the Holy Spirit occupies the primary role in sending, empowering, and guiding the church's outreach. Rather than viewing Mission as originating primarily from human initiative or institutional strategy, Pentecostals locate Mission's source in the Spirit's ongoing activity in the world. This pneumatological emphasis shapes how Pentecostals read Scripture, pray for direction, and organize their Missionary efforts. At the same time, Pentecostal Mission is marked by an eschatological urgency that flows from the conviction that Christ's return is near. The tension of the kingdom "already" breaking in and "not yet" fully realized drives believers to combine fervent proclamation with compassionate service. Thus, Pentecostal Missiology integrates a high view of biblical authority with expectations of contemporary prophetic insight, ensuring that Mission remains both rooted in apostolic witness and open to fresh, Spirit-led guidance.

Pneumatology as Missionary Principle

Pentecostal Missiology begins with the theological conviction that the Holy Spirit is the primary agent of Mission. Rather than viewing Mission as primarily a church program or human initiative, Pentecostal scholars argue that every act of outreach flows from the Spirit's presence and power. This pneumatological orientation means Mission planning begins with prayerful dependence on the Spirit's guidance, often expressed through communal worship, laying on of hands, and expectancy for spiritual gifts.[9] In Missiological terms, Pentecostal Mission locates the source, authority, and efficacy of Mission in the Spirit's ongoing activity, thereby distinguishing it from approaches that prioritize ecclesial structures or strategic models alone.

"Mission of the Spirit" as Originating Source

Scripture itself grounds Pentecostal Mission in the Spirit's sending. Jesus promises: *the Advocate, the Holy Spirit, whom the Father will send in my name, will teach you everything, and remind you of all that I have said to you* (John 14:26). After his resurrection, he breathes on the disciples and

---

[8] Frederick L. Ware, "Neo-Pentecostal Spirituality and Theology of Creativity in the Work of Barbara A. Holmes," *Pneuma* 35/1 (December, 2013): 75-86.

[9] Abraham Adebanjo Okunade, Janet Oluwoye, and Elisha Olabamiji, "Ecumenical Perspectives on Pentecostal Pneumatology," *Journal of Biblical Theology* 6/4 (October-November, 2023): 202-216.

says, *Receive the Holy Spirit* (John 20:22), pointing to a commission for ministry. Pentecostal Missiology thus read these texts as foundational: Mission does not originate with human resolve but with the Spirit's divine initiative.[10] Hence, Missiological reflection begins with discerning how the Spirit functions as both sender and enabler of the church's witness.

Veli-Matti Kärkkäinen on Spirit-Derived Missionary Impulse

Pentecostal ecumenical theologian Veli-Matti Kärkkäinen synthesizes classical pneumatology with contemporary Missiology by asserting that the church's Missionary nature derives entirely from the Spirit's sending. Drawing on the Second Vatican Council's *Ad Gentes*, Kärkkäinen writes that "the pilgrim church is Missionary by her very nature," since it is birthed in the Mission of the Spirit as well as of the Son. In his view, Missiology must therefore move beyond programmatic approaches and instead cultivate practices such as corporate discernment and prophetic dialogue that allow the Spirit's impulses to shape Missionary identity, methods, and praxis.[11]

Eschatological Fervour

A second cornerstone of Pentecostal Missiology is eschatology, the study of last things. Pentecostals maintain that Christ's return is imminent, creating an urgent imperative for Mission. This eschatological vision is not merely theoretical but deeply practical. The expectation of Christ's appearing motivates believers to pursue accelerated evangelism, prayer for revival, and holiness of life.[12] In Missiology discourse, this Eschatological Fervour generates a sense of "*kairos*" (God's appointed time), wherein Mission actions are evaluated by their ability to hasten the kingdom, prepare the church, and awaken the world to God's reign.

"The Kingdom Now, but Not Yet" and Urgency of Proclamation

Pentecostal eschatology embraces the "already and not yet" tension of the Kingdom of God. Jesus' inaugural proclamation: *The time is fulfilled, and the kingdom of God has come near; repent, and believe in the good news* (Mark 1:15) serves as the Missiological authorization for this urgency. From the perspective of Pentecostal Missiology, this passage is read as both descriptive and prescriptive: the kingdom has broken into history through

---

[10] Scott D. Seay, "The Spirit Poured Out on All Flesh: Stone-Campbell Missions and the Emergence of Global Pentecostalism," *Encounter* 79/3 (December, 2019): 1-22.

[11] Veli-Matti Kärkkäinen, "The Pentecostal Understanding of Mission," in *Pentecostal Mission and Global Christianity*, edited by Wonsuk Ma, Veli-Matti Kärkkäinen and J. Kwabena Asamoah-Gyadu (Oxford: Regnum Books International, 2014), 26-27.

[12] Huibert Zegwaart, "Apocalyptic Eschatology and Pentecostalism: The Relevance of John's Millennium for Today," *Pneuma* 10/1 (Spring, 1988): 3-25.

Christ's life, death, and resurrection, yet awaits consummation at Christ's return.[13] Mission, therefore, necessitates both present transformation through Spirit-filled communities and active invitation for others to enter the kingdom before its final establishment.

Emphasis on "Indigenous Church" within an End-Time Framework

Pentecostal eschatology extended into a model by advocating for the development of 'indigenous churches' in every context. The 'indigenous churches' is a movement that, within the end-time framework, genuine Mission must foster self-governing, self-supporting, and self-propagating congregations that reflect local cultures under the Spirit's leading. This emphasis challenges dependency on foreign leadership and promotes contextual theology, whereby the universal gospel is expressed through diverse cultural idioms.[14] This proposals remain influential in academic discussions in developing Mission methods and ecclesiology, particularly in African, Asian, and Latin American contexts.

Scripture-Centred Yet Experiential

While Pentecostalism is often associated with charismatic experience, it simultaneously upholds a high view of Scripture as the normative authority for faith and practice. Pentecostal hermeneutics therefore integrate rigorous biblical study with expectancy for Spirit-led insight during worship and Mission.[15] Missiologically, this creates a dynamic hermeneutical circle: exegesis informs experience, and experiential revelations prompt fresh engagement with the biblical text. Consequently, Pentecostal Missiology resists divergence of doctrine and experience, instead modelling a unified approach where Scripture and Spirit mutually illumine Missionary understanding.

High View of Prophetic Witness

Finally, Pentecostal Missiology balances reverence for the apostolic witness with openness to contemporary prophecy. Believers affirm that the Bible is "God-breathed" (II Timothy 3:16) while also expecting God to speak through dreams, visions, and prophetic utterances. This dual posture is Missiologically significant because it prevents Mission from fossilizing into

---

[13] Amos Yong, "Proclamation in/of the Spirit: Toward a Pneumatological Theology of Preaching. The Spirit and Proclamation: A Pneumatological Theology of Preaching (Continued) III," *The Living Pulpit* 24/2 (Summer, 2015): 34-38.

[14] Allan Heaton Anderson, "Pentecostalism in East Asia: Indigenous Oriental Christianity?," *Svensk Missionstidskrift* 87/3 (December, 1999): 319-340.

[15] Scott A. Ellington, "Pentecostalism and the Authority of Scripture," *Journal of Pentecostal Theology* 4/9 (October, 1996): 16-38.

rigid programs. Rather, Missionary methods remain adaptable, as leaders continually test emerging prophecy against scriptural norms.[16] The result is a living theology of Mission that is both anchored in historical revelation and sensitive to the Spirit's fresh movements in ever-changing contexts.

Holistic Mission: Evangelism and Social Concern

While evangelism is often at the forefront of Pentecostal Mission, there is growing recognition that the gospel must address not only spiritual needs but also the physical, emotional, and social well-being of individuals and communities. This holistic approach has become increasingly visible in what came to be known as "progressive Pentecostalism,"[17] which incorporates health care, education, economic development, and justice initiatives into Missionary work. Rooted in the example of Jesus who preached and healed, Pentecostals today are embracing a more integrated Mission that reflects the full scope of the Kingdom of God.[18] This dual emphasis on soul and society challenges older dichotomies between spiritual salvation and social action, revealing a mature and biblically grounded Missiological framework.

Conclusion

The Pentecostal view of Mission combines spiritual vitality, firm theological conviction, and active engagement with the world. Emerging from the Holiness Movement and the Azusa Street Revival, it places the empowering presence of the Holy Spirit at the centre of the church's Missionary calling, motivating believers to proclaim the gospel with urgency, compassion, and boldness in every cultural context. Rooted in a pneumatology that sees the Spirit as both the initiator and sustainer of Mission, Pentecostal Missiology carries a strong expectation of Christ's soon return, which fuels evangelistic zeal while also calling believers to address physical, emotional, and social needs in the present. This eschatological vision is not stagnant but mobilizing, inspiring participation in God's redemptive work here and now. Holding a high view of Scripture alongside a strong experiential faith, Pentecostals trust in both the authority of the written Word and the present guidance of the Spirit. Missiologically, the movement is marked by flexibility, pragmatism, and a holistic vision, adapting strategies to different contexts and emphasizing relational, experiential witness. Altogether,

---

[16] Marius Nel, "Prophetic Witness in Weakness: A Response to Prof Robert Vosloo from a Pentecostal Perspective," *In Die Skriflig* 53/4 (January, 2019): 1-7.

[17] Bryant L. Myers, "Progressive Pentecostalism, Development, and Christian Development NGOs: A Challenge and an Opportunity," *International Bulletin of Missionary Research* 39/3 (July, 2015): 115-120.

[18] Donald E. Miller, "Progressive Pentecostals: The New Face of Christian Social Engagement," *Journal for the Scientific Study of Religion* 46/4 (December, 2007): 435-445.

Pentecostal Missiology stands as a dynamic model that is deeply spiritual, thoroughly biblical, and practically engaged, arising from lived experience, communal worship, and the Spirit's active presence, offering the global church a vibrant and relevant way to bear witness to the good news "to the ends of the earth" (Acts 1:8).

27

Contextual and Methodological Issues in Christian Mission and Evangelism

The Mission of the Church has always been carried out within specific cultural, social, and historical contexts. For this reason, both context and methodology play a vital role in shaping an effective Christian Mission. Context refers to the real-life situations, traditions, languages, and worldviews of the people among whom the Gospel is shared. Methodology refers to the practical approaches and strategies used in communicating and living out that Gospel. Without careful attention to context, the Mission can become disconnected from the lives of people. Without sound methodology, the message may fail to reach hearts and minds in a meaningful way. In Christian theology, Mission refers to God's redemptive work in the world, carried out through the Church, to make Christ known and to invite people into the kingdom of God (Matthew 28:18-20; Acts 1:8). It is rooted in the belief that God sends His people to witness to the Good News in both word and action. Evangelism, as a part of Mission, focuses more specifically on proclaiming the Gospel message and calling individuals to personal faith in Jesus Christ (Romans 10:14-15). While evangelism is often about direct communication of the Good News, Mission is broader, including acts of service, justice, and love that embody the Gospel in every sphere of life.

Biblical and Theological Foundations for Mission and Evangelism

Christian Mission and evangelism are not human inventions but are deeply rooted in the Bible and in the theological understanding of God's work in the world. The Scriptures reveal God as the One who sends, calling God's people to be witnesses of God's love, justice, and salvation. From the call of Abraham to bless all nations (Genesis 12:1-3) to Jesus' command to make disciples of all nations (Matthew 28:18-20), the Bible presents Mission as central to God's plan. Theology helps the Church understand and carry out this Mission by interpreting who God is (*Missio Dei*), who Christ is (Christology), the role of the Holy Spirit (pneumatology), and the purpose of the Church (ecclesiology). Thue, the biblical witness and theological reflection provide the vision, motivation, and direction for the Church's work in proclaiming the Gospel and living it out in word and action.

Scriptural Basis for Mission and Evangelism

The Mission of the Church is firmly rooted in the teachings of Scripture.[1] One of the clearest expressions is found in Jesus' Great Commission: *Go therefore and make disciples of all nations, baptizing them in the name of the Father and of the Son and of the Holy Spirit, and teaching them to obey everything that I have commanded you* (Matthew 28:19-20). Here, Mission is understood as both going out to others and helping them grow in faith and obedience to Christ. Similarly, in Acts 1:8, Jesus tells His disciples: *You will receive power when the Holy Spirit has come upon you; and you will be my witnesses in Jerusalem, in all Judea and Samaria, and to the ends of the earth.* These passages reveal that Mission is not merely a human initiative but a divine command empowered by the Spirit. Evangelism, as the verbal proclamation of the Good News, is therefore an essential expression of this biblical mandate.

Theological Motivations for Mission

Christian Mission is grounded in the nature and purpose of God, often described by the term *Missio Dei*, the "Mission of God."[2] This means that Mission begins in God's own desire to redeem and restore creation (John 3:16-17). Christology, the study of the person and work of Jesus Christ, shapes Mission by presenting Jesus as the model Missionary who *came to seek out and to save the lost* (Luke 19:10).[3] Pneumatology, the doctrine of the Holy Spirit, reminds us that Mission is Spirit-led, as the early Church was empowered at Pentecost to speak in ways that reached diverse peoples (Acts 2:1-11).[4] Ecclesiology, the study of the Church, emphasizes that the community of believers is both the instrument and witness of God's Mission

---

[1] Taito Almar Kantonen, "The Scriptural and Theological Basis of Evangelism and Stewardship," *Lutheran Quarterly* 3/3 (August, 1951): 271-277.

[2] M. A. Kruger, "God-Centered Evangelism," *Missionalia* 4/2 (1976): 88.

[3] Justin S. Ukpong, "Christian Mission and the Recreation of the Earth in Power and Faith: A Biblical-Christological Perspective," *Mission Studies* 9/2 (December, 1992): 134-147.

[4] Christoffer H. Grundmann, "Reconciliation and the New Identity in Christ: Pneumatological Perspectives of Christian Mission in Its Third Millennium," *International Review of Mission* 97/386-387 (July-October, 2008): 255-272.

(I Peter 2:9).[5] These theological dimensions together give Mission its divine authority, Christ-centred focus, Spirit-empowered vitality, and communal expression.

Holistic Mission

Biblical Mission is holistic, involving the whole person and the whole community. It includes evangelism, proclaiming the Gospel so people may believe (Romans 10:14-15) and discipleship, which helps believers grow in maturity and obedience to Christ's teachings (Matthew 28:20). It also embraces the call to justice, defending the oppressed and caring for the poor as an expression of God's Kingdom values (Micah 6:8; Luke 4:18-19). Reconciliation is another essential aspect, as the Gospel seeks to restore broken relationships between people and God, and between human communities (II Corinthians 5:18-19).[6] In this way, Mission is not only about converting individuals but also about transforming societies so that they reflect the peace, justice, and love of God.[7] These biblical and theological foundations for Mission and evangelism can be seen in the life of the Christian church throughout history.

Historical Perspectives on Mission and Evangelism

The methods used in Christian Mission have developed over the centuries in response to cultural, political, and theological changes. From the earliest days of the Church, believers sought practical ways to communicate the Gospel and embody it in their communities. These methods have included direct proclamation, acts of compassion, educational work, and social reform. While some approaches have produced lasting fruit, others have raised questions about cultural sensitivity, justice, and the true nature of Gospel witness.

Early Church Models

The earliest models of Christian Mission are found in the book of Acts and the writings of the early Church Fathers. In Acts, the apostles engaged in both public preaching and personal witness. For example, Peter proclaimed to the crowd at Pentecost: *Repent, and be baptized every one of you in the*

---

[5] Marie Joseph Le Guillou, "Mission as an Ecclesiological Theme," *Concilium* 3/2 (March, 1966): 43-67.

[6] Chris Sugden, "Mission as Transformation: Its Journey Among Evangelicals Since Lausanne 1," in *Holistic Mission: God's Plan for God's People*, edited by Brian Woolnough and Wonsuk Ma (Oxford: Regnum Books International, 2010), 32.

[7] Catharine R F Padilla, "Holistic Mission," in *Dictionary of Mission Theology: Evangelical Foundations* edited by John Corrie (Nottingham: InterVarsity Press, 2007), 161-162.

name of Jesus Christ so that your sins may be forgiven (Acts 2:38), leading to the growth of the early Christian community.[8] The apostle Paul used flexible strategies such as preaching in synagogues, engaging in discussions in public spaces, and building relationships in homes (Acts 17:16-34; 20:20).[9] The early Church Fathers, such as Justin Martyr and Irenaeus, defended the faith through reasoned arguments and demonstrated Christian love through acts of mercy. These early models reveal that Mission was both Spirit-led and adaptable, responding to the needs and understanding of different audiences.

Medieval and Colonial Missions: Gains and Pitfalls

During the medieval period, Mission work expanded alongside the growth of monastic movements and the influence of the institutional Church. Monks such as Patrick in Ireland[10] and Boniface in Germany[11] combined preaching with community building, education, and care for the poor. However, during the colonial era, Mission was often linked with political and economic expansion, leading to both opportunities and serious challenges. While many heard the Gospel and received education, the close association between Mission and colonial power sometimes led to cultural suppression and exploitation.[12] This tension calls to mind the warning of Jesus: *What will it profit them if they gain the whole world but forfeit their life?* (Mark 8:36). The medieval and colonial experiences remind the Church that methods must serve the Gospel rather than political or economic agendas.

Modern Mission Movements: From "Sending" to Partnership

In the 18th and 19th centuries, modern Mission movements emerged, often through Mission societies such as the London Missionary Society and the American Board of Commissioners for Foreign Missions. These movements focused heavily on "sending" Missionaries from Europe and North America to other parts of the world. This approach brought significant benefits, such as Bible translation, schools, and hospitals. However, in the 20th century,

---

[8] Paul R. House, "Models of Biblical Evangelism," *The Southern Baptist Journal of Theology* 1 (Winter,1997): 2-3.

[9] Ralph E. Knudsen, "Evangelism in New Testament Terms," *Review & Expositor* 45/3 (July, 1948): 291-300.

[10] Michael Gibbons, "Croagh Patrick: The Glorious Climb of Ireland's Holy Mountain," *Road to Emmaus* 12/2 (Spring, 2011): 3-41.

[11] John Foster, "Boniface of Crediton, Apostle of Germany, 716," *The Expository Times* 102/5 (February, 1991): 140.

[12] Lisa Blake, "'Civilizing' the Village: Protestant Missionary Writings and the Civilizing Mission in Colonial South India," *ARC: The Journal of the School of Religious Studies* 42 (January, 2014): 71-92.

there was a growing recognition that Mission should be a partnership rather than a one-way effort. Churches in Africa, Asia, and Latin America began to contribute actively to global Mission, reflecting Paul's teaching that: *the body does not consist of one member but of many* (I Corinthians 12:14).[13] This shift has encouraged mutual respect, shared leadership, and the recognition that every church, regardless of location, has both the responsibility and the ability to participate in God's Mission.

Shifts in Methodology: From Proclamation to Contextual Engagement

Over time, Mission methodology has shifted from focusing almost exclusively on verbal proclamation to embracing contextual engagement. This means that while preaching the Gospel remains central, Missionaries increasingly seek to understand and respect the local culture, language, and worldview. This approach is exhibited in Paul's ministry at Athens, where he began with the religious beliefs of his audience before introducing the Gospel (Acts 17:22-23). In today's world, contextual engagement often includes community development, advocacy for justice, interfaith dialogue, and environmental care. This mirrors the example of Jesus, who proclaimed the kingdom of God not only through words but also through acts of healing, compassion, and inclusion (Luke 4:18-19).[14] Such an approach recognizes that the Gospel must be lived as well as spoken, and that Mission is most effective when it grows out of genuine relationships and shared life.

Contextual Challenges in Contemporary Mission

The Mission of the Church today takes place in a world that is rapidly changing and increasingly complex. Global communication, migration, political shifts, and environmental challenges all shape how the Gospel is heard and lived out. Christian Mission must therefore be sensitive to diverse contexts while remaining faithful to the biblical message. These challenges include engaging with people of other faiths, responding to secular and postmodern worldviews, ministering in multicultural and digital spaces, and addressing urgent social and ecological crises. Each challenge calls for thoughtful theological reflection and creative Missional practice.

Religious Pluralism and Interfaith Relations

In many parts of the world, Christians live alongside people of different religious traditions. The New Testament acknowledges this reality; Paul in Athens recognized the people's religious devotion before introducing the

---

13 Kirsteen Kim, "Mission's Changing Landscape: Global Flows and Christian Movements," *International Review of Mission* 100/2 (November, 2011): 244-267.

14 Robert J. Priest, "The Value of Anthropology for Missiological Engagements with Context: The Case of Witch Accusations," *Missiology* 43/1 (January, 2015): 27-42.

Gospel (Acts 17:22-23). Theologically, Christians believe that salvation is found in Christ alone: *I am the way, and the truth, and the life* (John 14:6), yet they are also called to love their neighbours and respect their dignity (Mark 12:31). This balance has led to different approaches: some emphasize proclamation of the Gospel as the only means of salvation, while others stress openness to learn from and work with people of other faiths in addressing common concerns.[15] A key challenge is balancing respectful dialogue with the biblical mandate to proclaim Christ. Dialogue can build trust, break down prejudice, and create space for honest discussion, reflecting Peter's call to give an account for hope *with gentleness and reverence* (I Peter 3:15). At the same time, proclamation remains central to Mission, as seen in Paul's bold witness before diverse audiences (Acts 26:22-23). The tension between these two approaches requires discernment so that engagement with other faiths is neither forced nor silent about the Gospel.[16]

Postmodernity and Secularism

In many societies, especially in the West, the influence of Christianity has declined, and people often view faith as a private or irrelevant matter. This post-Christian setting reflects aspects of the early Church's environment, where the Gospel was introduced to people with little or no biblical background. Paul's reminder that: *faith comes from what is heard, and what is heard comes through the word of Christ* (Romans 10:17) challenges the Church to find fresh ways to communicate the message in culturally relevant terms without compromising its truth. In a postmodern worldview, absolute truth claims are often questioned, and personal experience is valued more than doctrinal statements.[17] This creates an opportunity for the Church to present the Gospel as a compelling story rather than simply a set of propositions. Jesus Himself often used parables, inviting people into a narrative that challenged and transformed their worldview (Luke 15:11-32). Reframing the Gospel means highlighting how God's story intersects with personal and communal stories, making it both credible and meaningful in today's culture.

Urbanization and Globalization

Urban centres today are marked by cultural diversity, constant movement, and strong digital connectivity. This reflects aspects of the first-century

[15] Robert Preston Sellers, "Interfaith Relations and the Christian Discipline: Living with Others in the Way of Jesus," *Review & Expositor* 114/1 (December, 2017): 34-42.

[16] S. M. Haas, "The Analysis of Norms in Statements on Interfaith Relations," *Studies in Interreligious Dialogue* 20/1 (December, 2010): 5-23.

[17] J. Andrew Kirk, "Following Modernity and Postmodernity: A Missiological Investigation," *Mission Studies* 17/1-2 (December, 2000): 217-239.

world, where cities like Corinth and Ephesus were hubs for trade, ideas, and cultural exchange. Paul adapted his Mission to these dynamic contexts, working as a tentmaker, engaging in public debate, and forming diverse church communities (Acts 18:1-4; 19:8-10). In the 21st century, Mission in urban and globalized contexts requires intercultural sensitivity, the ability to minister among people on the move, and the use of digital platforms to connect and disciple.[18] The Gospel can now cross borders instantly, but this also calls for wise and responsible use of technology in Mission.

Poverty, Injustice, and Ecological Crisis

The Gospel is not only about personal salvation but also about God's justice and care for creation. Jesus' Mission included good news for the poor, release for the oppressed, and restoration for all of God's creation (Luke 4:18-19). Mission today must address systemic poverty, human trafficking, racial injustice, and the environmental damage threatening the earth.[19] The biblical vision of Mission integrates evangelism and social action. The prophet Micah summarizes this call: *to do justice, and to love kindness, and to walk humbly with your God* (Micah 6:8). Liberation theology emphasizes God's concern for the oppressed, while integral Mission, affirmed by movements like the Lausanne Covenant, sees proclamation and service as inseparable. Caring for creation is also part of discipleship, since the earth belongs to God (Psalm 24:1).[20] This holistic approach reflects the kingdom values of righteousness, peace, and stewardship.

Methodological Issues in Evangelism

Evangelism is the heart of the Church's Mission, but the way it is carried out must reflect the cultural context, biblical truth, and the changing realities of society. Methodology matters because it shapes how people hear and respond to the Gospel. Effective evangelism today requires a balance between faithfulness to Scripture and sensitivity to the people we serve. This includes speaking the Gospel in local languages and cultural forms, integrating word and deed in a holistic way, equipping disciples for leadership, and using technology wisely. Each of these methodological issues plays a vital role in ensuring that evangelism is both faithful to the message of Christ and relevant to the world we live in.

---

[18] Minh Ha. Nguyen, "Globalization, Urbanization, Migration, and Rethinking the People Groups Concept," *Evangelical Missions Quarterly* 56/4 (October-December, 2020): 32-35.

[19] Nelus Niemandt, "Ecodomy in Mission: The Ecological Crisis in the Light of Recent Ecumenical Statements," *Verbum et Ecclesia* 36/3 (January, 2015).

[20] David M. Rhoads, "A Beloved Earth Community: Christian Mission in an Ecological Age," *Currents in Theology and Mission* 43/2 (April, 2016): 9-10.

Inculturation and Contextualization

Inculturation (the process of expressing and living out the gospel within the life and values of a local culture) and contextualization (the adaptation of the gospel message and ministry methods to a specific cultural context without compromising biblical truth) aim to present the Gospel in ways that make sense within a local culture.[21] This approach follows the example of the apostle Paul, who adapted his language and references depending on his audience, saying: *I have become all things to all people, that I might by all means save some* (I Corinthians 9:22). By using local stories, art forms, and symbols, the Gospel becomes accessible and meaningful without losing its core message.[22] While contextualization seeks to communicate the Gospel in culturally relevant ways, it must also guard against syncretism, blending Christian faith with beliefs that contradict the truth of the Gospel.[23] Jesus prayed that His disciples would be "in the world" but not "of the world" (John 17:14-15). The challenge is to affirm what is good and true in a culture while helping people to express their faith in Christ in ways that remain faithful to Scripture.

Holistic and Transformational Approaches

Biblical evangelism is more than speaking about Jesus, it is also living in ways that demonstrate His love. Jesus' ministry combined teaching with acts of healing, feeding, and compassion (Matthew 9:35). Evangelism as word, deed, and presence means proclaiming the Good News, serving practical needs, and being a consistent witness in everyday life. Holistic Mission recognizes that spiritual transformation is linked to social and physical well-being. Meeting needs through education, healthcare, and development projects reflects Jesus' concern for the whole person (Luke 4:18-19).[24] Such ministries open doors for the Gospel while also embodying its message of God's kingdom breaking into the world.

Discipleship and Church Planting Models

Effective evangelism does not end with conversion but continues through discipleship, helping believers grow in faith and obedience to Christ. Paul told Timothy: *what you have heard from me through many witnesses entrust to faithful people who will be able to teach others as well* (II Timothy 2:2).

[21] Paul M. Collins, *Christian Inculturation in India* (Routledge: New York, 2016), 28.

[22] Cyril Veliath, "Thomas Stephens: A Human Monument of Inculturation in India," *Bulletin of the Faculty of Foreign Studies of Sophia University* 46 (2011): 152-157.

[23] Stephen B. Bevans, *Models of Contextual Theology* (New York: Orbis Books, 2002), 3-7.

[24] Paul Walter Mueller, "Transformational Mission Work-A Definition," *Missio Apostolica* 22/2 (November, 2014): 319-341.

Training local leaders ensures that churches are sustainable and culturally rooted. Many growing churches today use small group or house church models, similar to the early believers who met "in the temple and…at home" (Acts 2:46). These models allow for personal relationships, accountability, and the rapid multiplication of disciples.[25] In real contexts, such movements spread the Gospel more effectively than large, centralized institutions.

Use of Technology and Media

The digital age has opened new opportunities for evangelism. Through these new opportunities like social media, the Gospel can reach people far beyond physical church buildings. Paul used the fastest communication of his day, letters, to strengthen and guide churches (Colossians 4:16), and the Church today can use digital tools for similar purposes. While technology offers many advantages, it also poses challenges. The digital age can lack the depth of face-to-face fellowship, and digital content can easily be lost in the flood of information. Hebrews 10:24-25 urges believers not to neglect meeting together.[26] Therefore, digital ministry must be combined with personal relationships and local community engagement to nurture genuine discipleship.

Missiological Models and Frameworks

Over time, Christian Mission has been shaped by different models and frameworks, each reflecting theological convictions, cultural realities, and historical circumstances. Classical Mission paradigms often emphasized sending Missionaries from established churches to other parts of the world, while contemporary approaches focus more on partnership, contextual relevance, and mutual learning. Movements such as the World Missionary Conference 1910, Vatican II (1962 to 1965), Lausanne (1974), the writings of Lesslie Newbigin, insider movements, and regional contextual theologies have influenced how the Church understands and practices Mission. These frameworks help the Church remain faithful to the Gospel while responding creatively to the challenges and opportunities of a globalized world.

Classical vs. Contemporary Mission Paradigms

Classical Mission models, prominent from the 18th to mid-20th centuries, often saw Mission as a one-way activity that Missionaries were sent from the "Christian" West to the "non-Christian" world. This was grounded in

---

[25] Derek Seipp, "Which Should Come First--Discipleship or Church Planting?," *Evangelical Missions Quarterly* 45/2 (April, 2009): 142-143.

[26] Nathan Hedt, "Missional Spirituality among Digital Natives: Technology, Spirituality and Mission in an Age of Social Media," *Lutheran Theological Journal* 47/3 (December, 2013): 187-202.

texts like Matthew 28:19-20, where Jesus commands: *Go therefore and make disciples of all nations*. While these approaches resulted in significant evangelistic growth, Bible translation, and church planting, they sometimes assumed that the sending culture's forms of Christianity were superior to local expressions. Contemporary Mission paradigms, shaped by gatherings like the World Missionary Conference 1910, Vatican II (1962 to 1965), the Lausanne Movement (1974) and the thought of Lesslie Newbigin emphasize the Gospel's engagement with culture, the importance of the local church as the primary witness, and the Mission of the whole people of God. Newbigin argued for a "Missionary encounter" with culture, where the Gospel both affirms and challenges local worldviews (Acts 17:22-31). Contemporary models encourage humility, dialogue, and the recognition that Mission happens in every direction, not just from one part of the world to another.

Insider Movements and Contextual Theologies

Insider movements refer to groups of people who follow Jesus while remaining culturally embedded in their original communities, often retaining certain cultural or religious forms. This approach reflects Paul's principle: *Let each of you remain in the condition in which you were called* (I Corinthians 7:20), as long as these practices do not contradict the Gospel. Such movements aim to reduce unnecessary cultural barriers to accepting Christ.[27] Contextual theologies developed in African, Asian, and Latin American contexts interpret the Gospel through the lens of local history, culture, and struggles. African theologies highlight community and reconciliation, on the other hand, Asian theologies engage with religious pluralism and interdependence, and Latin American theologies, influenced by liberation theology, emphasize God's preferential concern for the poor (Luke 4:18-19). These theologies affirm that the Gospel speaks with equal power in every culture and that theology must be rooted in local realities while remaining faithful to Scripture.

From "Mission To" to "Mission With"

The shift from "Mission to" to "Mission with" reflects a move away from one-directional Mission towards a mutual partnership between churches in different parts of the world. This aligns with Paul's vision of the body of Christ, *where the members of the body that seem to be weaker are indispensable* (I Corinthians 12:22). Every church, regardless of size or location, has gifts to contribute to the global Mission of God. Reciprocity means that Mission is a two-way exchange of resources, ideas,

[27] David Garrison, "Church Planting Movements vs Insider Movements: Missiological Realities vs Mythological Speculations," *International Journal of Frontier Missions* 21/4 (October-December, 2004): 151-154.

and encouragement.[28] Churches in the Global South and North now send Missionaries to each other, share leadership, and collaborate in addressing global issues such as poverty, migration, and climate change. This approach reflects the spirit of partnership seen in the early Church, where believers shared generously to meet one another's needs (Acts 4:32-35).[29] It emphasizes humility, interdependence, and the belief that God's Mission is carried forward most faithfully when the whole body of Christ works together.

Conclusion

Christian Mission and evangelism are rooted in the biblical narrative and shaped by theological convictions that affirm God's initiative in the *Missio Dei*. From the Great Commission (Matthew 28:18-20) to the Spirit's empowerment at Pentecost (Acts 1:8), Scripture presents Mission as both the proclamation of the Gospel and the embodiment of God's Kingdom in the world. Theology provides the framework for understanding this calling, centred on Christ, empowered by the Spirit, and carried out through the Church as God's chosen instrument. Historically, Mission methods have evolved in response to changing contexts. The early Church combined bold proclamation with compassionate service, the medieval period saw both faithful witness and unhealthy links with political power, and the modern era brought new sending structures along with greater global partnership. Today, Mission faces complex contextual challenges: religious pluralism, secularism, urbanization, globalization, poverty, injustice, and ecological crises. These realities require careful discernment, cultural sensitivity, and creative approaches that remain faithful to the Gospel. Methodologically, effective evangelism must balance contextualization with faithfulness to Scripture, integrate word and deed in holistic ministry, prioritize discipleship and local leadership, and wisely use digital tools for communication and community. But, in every era, the heart of Mission remains unchanged: to bear witness to Jesus Christ in the power of the Spirit for the glory of God and the transformation of the world. The task is urgent, the contexts are varied, and the challenges are real. But the promise of Christ still stands: *And remember, I am with you always, to the end of the age* (Matthew 28:20).

---

[28] Anton Knuth, "Who Is the Subject of Mission?: The Need to Decolonize Mission From the Perspective of 'the Margins,'" *Transformation* 37/2 (April, 2020): 131-139.

[29] A. Wati Longchar, "Collective Resistance as Prophetic Witness: Mission from the Margin's Perspective," *International Review of Mission* 105/2 (November, 2016): 280-292.

28

Mission, Conversion, and Context Biblical, Theological, and Missiological Perspectives from the Indian Context

The concept "conversion" is understood as both a spiritual and a social transformation. In its theological sense, conversion is a work of God that brings a person from sin to new life in Christ. It involves repentance from past ways, faith in Jesus as Lord and Saviour, and the beginning of a renewed life empowered by the Holy Spirit (Acts 3:19; II Corinthians 5:17). Conversion in its very sense, is not only an inward change of heart but also an outward change in relationships, values, and community belonging. However, in the Indian context, the term conversion has become deeply controversial and politically sensitive. It is often misunderstood as a purely social or legal act of changing religious affiliation, and at times it is portrayed as a threat to cultural or national identity. This has led to legal restrictions, social tensions, and accusations against Christian Mission work, making the topic highly charged in public discourse. Therefore, it is important to examine the issue of conversion in two main dimensions. First, it needs to clarify its theological meaning in light of Scripture, showing it as a spiritual transformation rooted in God's saving work. Second, it needs to identify the socio-political challenges faced by Christian Mission in the Indian context. By doing so, it will outline a contextual methodology that engages faithfully with the biblical vision of conversion while addressing the realities of the contemporary Indian situation.

Biblical Models of Mission and Conversion

The Bible offers many examples that show how God works through Mission to bring people to conversion. These stories reveal that conversion is not a uniform experience but can take many forms like public or private, sudden or gradual, individual or communal. They also show that God is the primary agent in conversion, working through the Holy Spirit, the witness of believers, the proclamation of the Word, and the circumstances of life.[1] Together, these models demonstrate that Mission is both the clear communication of the gospel and the loving presence of God's people in diverse contexts.

Models of Mission and Conversion in the Old Testament

In the Old Testament, the story of Nineveh in Jonah 3 explains a public and communal conversion. The prophet Jonah, though initially reluctant, proclaimed God's message of judgment, and the entire city, from the king to the common people believed, fasted, and turned from their evil ways. This mass repentance was sudden yet genuine, showing that God can transform entire communities through a single prophetic message.[2] The account of Naaman the Syrian in II Kings 5 demonstrates a personal and gradual conversion. Initially sceptical, Naaman was eventually healed of leprosy after obeying Elisha's simple instruction to wash in the Jordan. His healing led him to acknowledge the God of Israel as the only true God.[3] This conversion came through both the miraculous work of God and the faithful witness of a servant girl, revealing God's Mission to people outside Israel.

In the same way, Ruth the Moabite (Ruth 1:16-17) shows relational and covenantal conversion. Her decision to follow Naomi's God was not the result of a dramatic miracle or public sermon, but of personal relationship, loyalty, and lived witness. Her journey was gradual, leading her to become part of God's redemptive plan in Israel's history.[4] Similarly, Rahab of Jericho (Joshua 2) illustrates a private yet decisive conversion. Having heard of God's mighty acts, Rahab chose to align herself with Israel's God by protecting the spies, risking her life in the process.[5] Her faith was expressed in action and led to her inclusion in the covenant community.

[1] Christopher J. H. Wright, "Implications of Conversion in the Old Testament and the New," *International Bulletin of Missionary Research* 28/1 (January, 2004): 14-19.

[2] Grazia Papola, "A Biblical Story of Conversion: The Book of Jonah," *The Person and the Challenges* 6/2 (December, 2016): 153-174.

[3] Emmanuel O. Nwaoru, "The Story of Naaman (2 Kings 5:1-19): Implications for Mission Today," *Svensk Missionstidskrift* 96/1 (December, 2008): 27-41.

[4] Jonathan A. Thambyrajah, "Israelite or Moabite?: Ethnicity in the Book of Ruth," *Journal for the Study of the Old Testament* 46/1 (September, 2021): 44-63.

[5] Donald John Wiseman, "Rahab of Jericho," *Tyndale House Bulletin* 14 (June, 1964): 8-11.

Models of Mission and Conversion in the New Testament

In the New Testament, conversion is shown through many real-life stories where people encounter God and experience complete transformation. On the day of Pentecost (Acts 2:37-41), Peter preached about the death and resurrection of Jesus, and the hearers were repenting, being baptised, and receiving the Holy Spirit. About three thousand joined the community that day.[6] Similarly, Saul of Tarsus (Acts 9:1-19), once a fierce persecutor of Christians, was confronted by the risen Christ on the road to Damascus. Blinded, humbled, and healed through Ananias' ministry, he became the Apostle Paul, a great Missionary to the Gentiles. Both accounts show that conversion is a Spirit-led turning to Christ, often initiated by God's sovereign action, and marked by repentance, baptism, and a new way of life.[7]

Other stories show how God works across cultures and boundaries. Cornelius, a Roman centurion (Acts 10:1-48), received a vision from God and sent for Peter, who also had a vision that challenged his prejudices. When Peter preached, the Holy Spirit came upon Cornelius' household, and they were baptised, showing that the gospel is for all people.[8] In Philippi, Paul and Silas (Acts 16:25-34) prayed and sang hymns in prison until an earthquake broke their chains. Their compassion towards the jailor led to his question, "What must I do to be saved?" That night, he and his family were baptised.[9] These examples highlight that conversion can happen in surprising situations, breaking social and ethnic barriers through acts of love and faithful witness.

Personal encounters with God also play a key role in conversion. The Ethiopian eunuch (Acts 8:26-40) was reading Isaiah without understanding it until Philip, led by the Spirit, explained how it pointed to Jesus, leading the eunuch to request baptism.[10] The Samaritan woman at the well (John 4:1-42) met Jesus in a personal conversation where He revealed her life story and

---

[6] Jerry Horner, "The Credibility and the Eschatology of Peter's Speech at Pentecost," *Pneuma* 2/1 (Spring, 1980): 22-31.

[7] Johnny B. Awwad, "From Saul to Paul: The Conversion of Paul the Apostle," *Theological Review* 32/1 (April, 2011): 3-14.

[8] Richard P. McBrien, "When Peter Met Cornelius, History Changed," *National Catholic Reporter* 38/13 (February, 2002): 16.

[9] Abraham Smith, "Incarceration on Trial: The Imprisonment of Paul and Silas in Acts 16," *Journal of Biblical Literature* 140/4 (December, 2021): 797-817.

[10] Fred L. Horton and Jeffrey A. Blakely, "'Behold, Water!': Tell El-Hesi and the Baptism of the Ethiopian Eunuch (Acts 8:26-40)," *Revue Biblique* 107/1 (January, 2000): 56-71.

offered "living water." She believed and led her whole community to Him.[11] Zacchaeus (Luke 19:1-10), a corrupt tax collector, responded to Jesus' invitation with repentance, restitution, and generosity.[12] These narratives show that genuine conversion often begins with a personal encounter, deep conviction, and the willingness to change one's life in response to Jesus.

Some conversions affected entire communities. Lydia in Philippi (Acts 16:11-15) believed when the Lord "opened her heart," and her whole household was baptised, with her hospitality becoming a sign of her new faith.[13] The Thessalonian believers (I Thessalonians 1:8-10) turned "to God from idols" to serve Him and became examples to others through their public witness and steadfast hope.[14] These models reveal that conversion is not only an individual matter but can spread through households and entire communities, producing faith, service, and transformation that inspire others to follow Christ.

Conversion and Resistance in the Indian Context

In the Indian context, Christian conversion is not only a theological matter but also a deeply connected to social issue. Thomas Menamparampil observes that conversion necessarily implies change, and change often meets resistance, especially when it affects long-standing traditions and social structures.[15] In many Indian communities, religious identity is closely tied to family honour, caste networks, and cultural heritage. Any shift in religious affiliation can therefore be perceived as a disruption of social cohesion, prompting defensive reactions.

Religious and cultural institutions in India frequently respond with caution or hostility toward Christian Mission, viewing it as a potential threat to the existing social order. These reactions are not merely theological disagreements but are often rooted in a desire to preserve cultural continuity and collective identity. Public debates and legal restrictions on conversion reflect this defensive posture, aiming to limit what is seen as destabilising influence. Sebastian Kim notes that conversion in India is often interpreted through the lens of history, particularly the colonial period. For many, the

---

[11] Peter J. Scaer, "Jesus and the Woman at the Well: Where Mission Meets Worship," *Concordia Theological Quarterly* 67/1 (January, 2003): 3-18.

[12] Richard C. White, "A Good Word for Zacchaeus: Exegetical Comment on Luke 19:1-10," *Lexington Theological Quarterly* 14/4 (October, 1979): 89-96.

[13] Luba Lukova and David Philippart, "Lydia, Leader of the Church at Philippi," *Environment & Art Letter* 15/2 (April, 2002): 32.

[14] Nijay K. Gupta, "The Thessalonian Believers, Formerly 'Pagans' or 'God-Fearers'?: Challenging a Stubborn Consensus," Neotestamentica 52/1 (December, 2018): 91-113.

[15] Thomas Menamparanpil, "Conversion: The Cultural Dimension," *Mission Today* 10 (2008): 1-6.

spread of Christianity is associated with Western domination, political motives, and cultural displacement.[16] This historical memory fuels suspicion, leading some to view Christian Mission as an extension of foreign power rather than an expression of local faith.

As a result, there remains a widespread perception that the Church is a tool for external influence and social disruption. Accusations of unethical or forced conversions though frequently unsubstantiated are used to discredit Christian witness. In such an environment, Mission work is often met with scrutiny, legal challenges, and social opposition.[17] Understanding this resistance is essential for developing a contextual and sensitive approach to Mission in India, one that remains faithful to the gospel while addressing historical grievances and cultural concerns.

In recent decades, political and ideological movements in India have intensified resistance to Christian Mission and conversion. Ashok Singhal, a prominent leader of the *Vishva Hindu Parishad* (VHP), once criticised the awarding of the Nobel Prize in Economics to Amartya Sen, suggesting it reflected a Western agenda to undermine Hinduism. Such remarks reveal a broader suspicion that Christianity, along with other minority religions, is part of an international conspiracy to weaken India's cultural and religious identity.[18]

One significant expression of this suspicion is the *Ghar Wapsi* (homecoming) movement, a reconversion campaign led by Hindu nationalist groups. This initiative seeks to bring people who have embraced other faiths, particularly Christianity and Islam, back into the Hindu fold.[19] Advocates of *Ghar Wapsi* present it as a restoration of original cultural identity, but many Christians see it as a form of coercion, embedded within a wider Hindutva project to assert Hindu dominance in public life. For Christian communities, such reconversion programs are not isolated efforts but part of a larger political

---

[16] Sebastian C. H. Kim, *In Search of Identity: Debates on Religious Conversions in India* (New Delhi: Oxford University Press, 2003), 5, 188.

[17] Paul G. Hiebert, "Missiological Issues in the Encounter with Emerging Hinduism," *Missiology an International Review* XXVIII/1 (January, 2000): 47-54.

[18] Gauri Viswanathan, "Literacy in the Eye of the Conversion Storm," in *The Invention of Religion: Rethinking Belief in Politics and History*, edited by Derek R. Peterson and Darren R. Walhof (New Brunswick, New Jersey & London: Rutgers University Press, 2002), 190.

[19] Sebastian Kim, "Religious Freedom, Minorities and the Concept of Religion: Critical Issues in Legislation on Conversion in India," in *Religious Freedom and Conversion in India: Papers from 4th SAIACS Academic Consultation*, edited by Aruthuckal Varughese John, Atola Longkumer and Nigel Ajay Kumar (Bengaluru: SAIACS Press, 2017), 28.

agenda to suppress the presence and growth of religious minorities.[20] This aligns with the *Hindutva* vision of India as a Hindu nation, where minority faiths exist only under restrictive conditions. The ideological emphasis on cultural homogeneity often sidelines the constitutional guarantee of religious freedom.

Conversion to Christianity in India is frequently linked with aspirations for social mobility, justice, and liberation from caste-based oppression. In many Dalit and tribal communities, embracing the Christian faith offers dignity, equality, and access to education and healthcare. However, these liberating aspects of conversion also make it a perceived threat to dominant caste structures and political powers that benefit from the status quo.[21] Consequently, political resistance to conversion is not merely about theology but about preserving entrenched systems of power and social hierarchy.

Methodological Considerations for Mission in Contexts of Opposition

In contexts where Christian Mission encounters strong social and political resistance, a thoughtful and sensitive methodology is essential. One key principle is contextualization, which involves presenting the gospel in ways that connect meaningfully with Indian cultural values, traditions, and ways of thinking, without diluting or altering the central message of Scripture.[22] This approach follows the example of the Apostle Paul, who adapted his communication to different audiences while remaining faithful to the gospel (I Corinthians 9:22-23). In the Indian context, this means engaging respectfully with local customs, languages, and worldviews, and showing how the message of Christ speaks to the deepest spiritual and social needs of the community.

Equally important is the emphasis on freedom of conscience. Mission work must affirm the God-given dignity of each person to choose their faith freely, whether that choice is for or against Christianity.[23] As Joshua declared to the Israelites, *choose this day whom you will serve* (Joshua 24:15), so too Christian witness must respect the individual's right to make an unpressured decision.

---

[20] Packiam T. Samuel, "The Rhetoric of Hindutva," *The Bulletin of the Henry Martin Institute of Islamic Studies* 12/3&4 (July-December, 1993): 13-14.

[21] Dorothy Yoder Nyce, "Faithful and Pluralistic: Engagement Among People of Living Faiths," *Crosscurrents* (2003): 210-214.

[22] K. C. Abraham, "The Mission and Ministry of the Church in the Present-Day Indian Context…, 29.; Victor Raj, "Missiology of Recontextualization," *Lutheran Mission Matters* 25/1 (2017): 9.

[23] Sharada Sugirtharajah, "Hinduism and Feminism: Some Concerns," *Journal of Feminist Studies in Religion* 18/2 (2002): 100.

True conversion is a matter of inner conviction through the work of the Holy Spirit, not the result of coercion, material inducement, or social pressure. Evangelism should therefore focus on clear proclamation of the gospel, prayerful dependence on God's Spirit, and the demonstration of Christ's love in action.[24] In contexts of poverty or marginalization, it is especially important to avoid the appearance of manipulation or exploitation. Practical service such as education, healthcare, or social development should be offered unconditionally, without attaching it to religious obligation.

By combining cultural sensitivity, respect for personal freedom, and a commitment to authentic, Spirit-led witness, Christian Mission can maintain integrity and credibility even in environments of strong opposition. Such an approach not only honours the biblical vision of Mission but also builds trust, encourages honest dialogue, and reflects the character of Christ in a complex and often hostile setting.

Mission Models in the Context of Christian Mission and the Issue of Conversion

Christian Mission in the context of conversion must be understood as both a spiritual calling and a practical engagement with complex social realities. The biblical vision of Mission calls believers to proclaim the good news of Jesus Christ, inviting people into repentance, faith, and new life through the power of the Holy Spirit. Yet, in the Indian context, conversion is a contested and politicized issue, often linked with questions of cultural identity, historical memory, and social change. Effective Mission therefore requires a variety of approaches, or "models," that remain faithful to Scripture while engaging meaningfully and respectfully with the surrounding context. The following seven models present complementary ways in which Christian Mission can be pursued in situations where conversion is viewed with suspicion or resistance.

Theological Transformation Model

'Theological Transformation Model' views conversion primarily as a work of God, grounded in biblical teaching and centred on the transformation of the whole person.[25] In Acts 2:37-41, the crowd at Pentecost responds to Peter's message with repentance, baptism, and the reception of the Holy Spirit. Similarly, Saul's encounter with the risen Christ in Acts 9 shows that conversion is not simply adopting a new religion, but a complete

---

[24] John Aloisi, "The Paraclete's Ministry of Conviction: Another Look at John 16:8-11," *Journal of the Evangelical Theological Society* 47/1 (March, 2004): 55-69.

[25] Benjamin Akano, "Imperatives for Sustaining Transformation Dynamics in Theological Education in a Post-Pandemic Era," *Trinity Journal of Church and Theology* 21/3 (September, 2023): 34-57.

reorientation of life, values, and Mission. This model emphasises that true conversion is initiated by the Holy Spirit, involves a personal response of faith, and results in a new creation in Christ (II Corinthians 5:17). Mission in this model focuses on clear proclamation of the gospel, prayer, and the nurturing of new believers through ongoing discipleship.

Contextual Sensitivity Model

In contexts where cultural traditions are deeply valued, Mission must communicate the gospel in ways that echo with local worldviews and practices without compromising biblical truth.[26] The Apostle Paul's approach in I Corinthians 9:22-23 becoming "all things to all people" so that some may be saved, offers a scriptural foundation for this model. In India, this may involve using familiar cultural symbols, storytelling, music, or festivals to convey Christian truth in meaningful ways. By showing respect for local customs, language, and identity, this model builds trust and reduces unnecessary offence, helping the gospel to be heard as good news rather than a foreign imposition.

Freedom of Conscience Model

This model upholds the principle that faith in Christ must be freely chosen.[27] It resists any form of coercion, manipulation, or inducement in evangelism, in line with Joshua's challenge to *choose this day whom you will serve* (Joshua 24:15). In a context where conversion is often accused of being forced or purchased, the Freedom of Conscience Model insists that Mission must safeguard the dignity and agency of each person. In the present-day context, Mission should focus on presenting the truth of the gospel clearly and lovingly, allowing individuals to respond under the conviction of the Holy Spirit.

Holistic Witness Model

The Holistic Witness Model integrates the verbal proclamation of the gospel with tangible acts of love and service.[28] Following the example of Jesus, who preached the Kingdom of God and healed the sick (Luke 4:18-19), Mission in this model addresses the spiritual, physical, and social needs of individuals and communities. In India, this may include education, healthcare, and empowerment programs for marginalised groups, offered

---

[26] Dan Sheffield, "Assessing Intercultural Sensitivity in Mission Candidates and Personnel," *Evangelical Missions Quarterly* 43/1 (January, 2007): 22-28.

[27] Rex J. Ahdar, "Is Freedom of Conscience Superior to Freedom of Religion?," *Oxford Journal of Law and Religion* 7/1 (February, 2018): 124-142.

[28] Arthur Dück, "Holistic Witness in Religiously Diverse Societies," *Direction* 41/2 (Fall, 2012): 267-276.

unconditionally and without hidden agendas. Such actions not only validate the compassion of Christ but also make the gospel credible by showing its transformative power in real life.

Prophetic Challenge Model

Conversion in many parts of India is linked to liberation from oppressive social systems, especially caste discrimination.[29] The Prophetic Challenge Model recognises that the gospel is inherently a call to justice and equality, as reflected in Galatians 3:28, which declares that in Christ there is *no longer Jew or Greek...slave or free...male and female*. Mission in this model not only proclaims personal salvation but also confronts unjust structures that deny dignity to Dalits, tribal groups, and other marginalised communities. By offering an alternative community where all are equal before God, this model challenges the dominance of entrenched caste and class hierarchies.

Reconciliation and Dialogue Model

Because conversion in India is often misunderstood as a rejection of cultural heritage or an act of betrayal, Mission also requires dialogue and bridge-building.[30] The Reconciliation and Dialogue Model seeks to address historical wounds, such as the association of Christianity with colonialism, by engaging respectfully with leaders and members of other faiths. Inspired by Paul's appeal in Romans 12:18 to "live peaceably with all," this model promotes open conversations that clarify misconceptions, build trust, and create space for mutual understanding. It sees dialogue not as a compromise of the gospel, but as an opportunity for honest witness and the breaking down of barriers to faith.

Perseverance under Opposition Model

In contexts marked by political hostility, such as the *Hindutva*-driven *Ghar Wapsi* campaigns, Mission often requires patient endurance.[31] This model takes encouragement from Jesus' words in Matthew that: *the one who endures to the end will be saved* (Matthew 10:22). It recognises that opposition, whether through legal restrictions, public suspicion, or social pressure, cannot be avoided, but it can be met with humility, wisdom, and steadfast faith. Mission in this model continues to proclaim Christ without

---

[29] John J. Bp Fitzpatrick, "The Challenge of Being Prophetic and Pastoral," *America* 166 (April, 1992): 294-296.

[30] Ross Oliver Langmead, "Transformed Relationships: Reconciliation as the Central Model for Mission," *Mission Studies* 25/1 (December, 2008): 5-20.

[31] Dirk G. Van der Merwe, "Perseverance through Suffering: A Spirituality for Mission," *Missionalia* 33/2 (August, 2005): 329-354.

retaliation, responding to hostility with love and prayer, and trusting that God's purposes will prevail despite human resistance.

Constitutional Awareness Model: Freedom of Religion in India

The Indian Constitution, under Article 25, guarantees every person the freedom of conscience and the right to profess, practise, and propagate religion, provided it respects public order, morality, and health.[32] This protection affirms that conversion must be a voluntary act of personal conviction, free from coercion or manipulation. In a diverse, multi-religious society, such legal provisions align with biblical examples where God's Mission honours human freedom while inviting people into faith. For Christian Mission in India, this means practising humility, transparency, and respect for individual dignity, offering the gospel as an invitation rather than an imposition. By integrating biblical principles with constitutional rights, the Church can witness faithfully while contributing to justice, human dignity, and peaceful coexistence in a pluralistic nation.

Conclusion

The biblical models of conversion show that turning to Christ is both a deeply personal transformation and a community-shaping event. From Pentecost to the household conversions in Acts, Scripture reveals that the gospel works through the Spirit, the faithful witness of believers, and God's initiative to bring people into a new relationship with Him. However, Mission and conversion are never carried out in a social vacuum. In hostile environments, Christians often face ethical dilemmas, especially when the message of Christ challenges entrenched power structures, cultural traditions, or political interests. In such contexts, humility, transparency, and authenticity are essential to maintain the integrity of the Mission. Faithful Mission also requires the Church to uphold justice, dignity, and human rights as part of its witness. Conversion is not only about changing religious affiliation but also about embodying the Kingdom values of love, fairness, and reconciliation. In pluralistic societies, including India, the Church's witness must include respectful inter-religious dialogue, showing the truth of the gospel not merely in words but in actions that affirm the value of every person. Such an approach builds bridges rather than barriers, even when theological convictions remain firm.

In the Indian context, conversion is inseparably linked to complex questions of identity, power, caste, and freedom. These realities demand that Christian Mission be both wise and courageous, holding firmly to the gospel while navigating resistance with patience and grace. The Church must avoid

[32] Viju Wilson, "Freedom of Religion, Communal Politics, and Religious Minorities in India," *Journal of Asian Evangelical Theology* 23/1 (March, 2019): 37-56.

triumphalism or coercion, instead demonstrating that true conversion is a voluntary, Spirit-led transformation that honours human dignity. Ultimately, Christian Mission must be defined by a commitment to justice, contextual sensitivity, and genuine spiritual renewal. The goal is not simply to increase numbers but to see lives and communities transformed by Christ. By following the biblical models and engaging ethically in contemporary contexts, the Church can remain faithful to its calling, proclaiming the gospel of Jesus Christ in a way that is both truthful and life-giving for all.

29

Mission to the Margins and with the Margins Reimagining Christian Mission in Solidarity with the Oppressed

In the context of Christian Mission, "the margin" refers to individuals and communities who live on the peripheries of society socially, economically, politically, culturally, or religiously marginalized. These include the poor, oppressed, casteless, displaced, refugees, tribal groups, women, persons with disabilities, religious minorities, and others who are excluded from structures of power and dignity. From a theoretical perspective, Mission to the margins means reaching out to those whom society ignores or rejects, while Mission with the margins involves empowering them to become active agents of God's Mission. The Mission of Jesus Christ is deeply rooted in His identification with the poor, the sick, and the outcast: *to bring good news to the poor…to let the oppressed go free* (Luke 4:18-19), and throughout His life Jesus showed solidarity with tax collectors, sinners, lepers, and foreigners, saying: *Those who are well have no need of a physician, but those who are sick…I have come to call not the righteous but sinners* (Matthew 9:12-13). For much of history, Christian Mission has often been directed "to" the margins, doing things for the poor from a position of distance or authority. In recent decades, however, there has been a shift toward Mission "with" the margins, walking alongside the oppressed as equal partners in God's work. This approach reflects Paul's vision that: *the members of the body that seem to be weaker are indispensable* (I Corinthians 12:22) and calls the Church to recognize that God is already at work among the marginalized. In this way, the poor and oppressed are not passive recipients but active participants and co-creators in the Kingdom of God, embodying the very centre of Jesus' transforming Mission.

Biblical and Theological Foundations

The Bible consistently reveals God's concern for those on the margins of society. From the exposition of God's nature, role of the Law and the Prophets in the Old Testament to the ministry of Jesus and the Mission of the early Church, Scripture shows that God's saving work often begins with the poor, the excluded, and the oppressed. This priority is not accidental, rather, it flows from God's character as a God of justice, mercy, and compassion. In Christian theology, this has been understood as part of the *Missio Dei*, God's Mission to redeem and renew all creation, beginning with those most in need. These biblical and theological foundations challenge the Church to align itself with God's preferential care for the marginalized.

Old Testament Concerns

From the beginning of Israel's story, the God of the covenant is revealed as one who hears the cries of the oppressed.[1] In the Book of Exodus, God says: *I have observed the misery of my people who are in Egypt; I have heard their cry on account of their taskmasters* (Exodus 3:7), and God's acts decisively to deliver them. This same compassionate character is reflected in God's covenant law. The Book of Deuteronomy declares that God *executes justice for the orphan and the widow, and...loves the strangers, providing them food and clothing* (Deuteronomy 10:18, NRSV), and commands Israel to do the same (Deuteronomy 10:19). Centuries later, the prophetic voice of the Book of Isaiah calls God's people back to this standard: *Learn to do good; seek justice, rescue the oppressed, defend the orphan, plead for the widow* (Isaiah 1:17). These passages reveal that care for the marginalized is not an optional act of charity but a central expression of covenant faithfulness, flowing from the very nature of the God who sees, hears, and responds to human suffering.

Jesus and the Margins

Jesus' ministry was marked by His intentional presence among those who were excluded and stigmatized in society.[2] When a man covered with leprosy approached Him: *Jesus stretched out His hand, touched him, and said, 'I do choose. Be made clean!'* (Luke 5:13). By touching the untouchable, Jesus broke social and religious barriers, embodying God's compassion in action. In Jericho, He restored dignity to Bartimaeus, a blind beggar, by asking him directly what he wanted and granting his request for healing (Mark 10:46-52). These encounters reveal that Jesus did not merely preach to the

---

[1] Benjamin Bixler, "Trauma, Revenge, and Cycles of Violence in the Exodus Story," *The Conrad Grebel Review* 40/1 (Winter, 2022): 59-77.

[2] Paul Hertig, "The Multi-Ethnic Journeys of Jesus in Matthew: Margin-Center Dynamics," *Missiology* 26/1 (January, 1998): 23-35.

marginalized, rather, He lived among them, restored their humanity, and invited them into the fullness of God's Kingdom.

The Kingdom of God as Reversal of Worldly Hierarchies

In the teachings of Jesus, the Kingdom of God turns human power structures upside down.[3] In the Beatitudes, Jesus declares: *Blessed are you who are poor, for yours is the Kingdom of God* (Luke 6:20), while warning the rich and self-satisfied of coming judgment (Luke 6:24-26). Paul echoes this when he reminds the Corinthians that: *God chose what is low and despised in the world...so that no one might boast in the presence of God* (I Corinthians 1:28-29). In God's reign, greatness is measured not by status or wealth but by humility, service, and solidarity with the least. This reversal challenges the Church to resist patterns of privilege and to stand alongside those who are often overlooked.

The Missio Dei as a Movement toward the Margins

The *Missio Dei*, God's Mission in the world, naturally moves toward the margins, because God's justice seeks to lift up the oppressed and heal what is broken.[4] In Scripture, this movement is seen in God's liberating work for Israel in Egypt, in the prophets' call for justice, and in Jesus' announcement of *good news to the poor...release to the captives...and freedom for the oppressed* (Luke 4:18). The Church, as a participant in God's Mission, is called not simply to serve the marginalized from a distance, but to join in their struggles for liberation and transformation. This is not only an act of obedience but a sign of the Kingdom, where justice and mercy embrace, and where the last are brought to the centre of God's purposes.

Understanding the Margins Today

In today's world, the "margins" are not merely a metaphor but a lived reality for millions. These are individuals and communities excluded from social, economic, political, and religious life because of poverty, discrimination, or systemic injustice. While their contexts differ, they share a common experience of being pushed to the edges of society, often voiceless in decision-making and vulnerable to exploitation. The biblical call to justice and compassion demands that the Church recognize these groups not as objects of charity but as partners in God's Mission. Understanding who the

---

[3] J. M. Na, "Echoes of the Kingdom: Tracing the Influences of Second Temple Literature on Paul's Strategic Use of the Phrase 'Kingdom of God' in 1 Corinthians," *Novum Testamentum* 67/1 (December, 2025): 39-57.

[4] Philip L. Wickeri, "Mission from the Margins: The *Missio Dei* in the Crisis of World Christianity," *International Review of Mission* 93/369 (April, 2004): 182-198.

margins are today is essential for shaping a Mission that is faithful to the gospel and relevant to contemporary realities.

Economically Poor and Landlessness

Economic poverty and landlessness remain among the most visible signs of marginalization. Without secure access to resources, millions are trapped in cycles of deprivation, unable to meet basic needs for food, shelter, and education.[5] According to Gnana Robinson now the level of poverty in the country is extremely high that many in the country eat inedible things like rat meat, mango kernels, grass and some even eat mud and drink water.[6] Scripture affirms God's special concern for the poor: *Those who oppress the poor insult their Maker, but those who are kind to the needy honour Him* (Proverbs 14:31). In societies where land ownership determines livelihood and dignity, dispossession results in deep social exclusion. A biblical Mission to the economically poor and landless must go beyond relief efforts, seeking structural change that restores their right to live with dignity and security.

Dalits and Tribals in South Asia

In South Asia, Dalits and tribal communities experience centuries-old patterns of exclusion and oppression rooted in caste hierarchies and economic exploitation. Dalits, once labelled "untouchable," face systemic discrimination in education, employment, and social participation, while many tribal communities are dispossessed from their ancestral lands. The biblical witness of God's justice stands in sharp contrast to such dehumanization. Just as God delivered Israel from slavery in Egypt (Exodus 3:7-8), the Church is called to stand with Dalits and tribals in their struggles for equality, land rights, and cultural dignity, affirming that all are created in the *Imago Dei*, the image of God.

Refugees, Migrants, and Displaced Peoples

Forced migration due to war, persecution, climate change, or economic hardship is one of the defining humanitarian crises of our time. Refugees and migrants often live in precarious conditions, facing hostility and legal uncertainty. The Bible reminds God's people: *You shall also love the stranger, for you were strangers in the land of Egypt* (Deuteronomy 10:19). This identification with the displaced is central to the Christian Mission,

---

[5] Kavita Iyengar and Sujatha Viswanathan, eds., *Understanding Poverty in India* (Asian Development Bank, 2011), 15.

[6] Gnana Robinson, "Dealing with Poverty in India," in *Mission with the Marginalized*, edited by Samuel W. Meshack (Tiruvalla: Christava Sahitya Samithi, 2007), 347.

calling for hospitality, advocacy for fair policies, and practical support that restores hope and human dignity to those far from home.[7]

Religious Minorities and Persecuted Communities

Religious minorities frequently face harassment, social exclusion, and even violence because of their faith. In some contexts, they are denied equal rights, restricted in worship, or targeted for conversion to the majority religion. Jesus warned His followers: *If they persecuted me, they will persecute you* (John 15:20), reminding the Church to expect and address such suffering. The Mission of God includes protecting the freedom of belief and ensuring that all people can live without fear.[8] Solidarity with persecuted communities is not only a matter of religious freedom but a witness to the inclusive love of God.

Women, Children, and People with Disabilities

Women, children, and people with disabilities often experience compounded forms of marginalization due to gender discrimination, age, and physical or cognitive differences.[9] The Gospels show Jesus breaking such barriers by welcoming children (Mark 10:14), restoring women's dignity (Luke 8:48), and healing those with physical impairments (Luke 13:12). A Mission that reflects Jesus' example must confront patriarchal systems, protect the rights of children, and ensure accessibility and inclusion for people with disabilities, affirming that all are equally valued in God's Kingdom.

Those Suffering from Systemic Violence, Caste, and Patriarchy

Many forms of marginalization are rooted in deeply entrenched systems of violence, caste oppression, and patriarchal domination. These systems perpetuate inequality through laws, customs, and social attitudes that normalize injustice.[10] The prophets denounced such structures, declaring: *Woe to those who make unjust laws…to deprive the poor of their rights* (Isaiah 10:1-2). In the light of the gospel, the Church cannot be neutral but must actively work to dismantle these systems through advocacy, education,

---

[7] Vince Henry M. Salles, "The Biblical Foundations of the Marian Title Solace of Migrants and Its Potential for Pastoral Encounter with Migrants, Refugees, and Internally Displaced Persons," *Landas* 36/1 (December, 2024): 73-95.

[8] Herbert Hoefer, "Why Are Christians Persecuted in India: Roots, Reasons, Responses," *Missio Apostolica* 7/2 (November, 1999): 77-86.

[9] Mark Arnold, "Mission with Children and Young People with Additional Needs and Their Families," *Anvil* 38/1 (December, 2022): 20-23.

[10] Evangeline Anderson Rajkumar, "Practicing Gender Justice as a Faith Mandate in India," *Studies in World Christianity* 13/1 (2007): 33-34.

and public witness, partnering with those who resist oppression in pursuit of God's justice.

Mission to the Margins: Historical and Contemporary Approaches

The Church's Mission to the margins has taken many forms throughout history, shaped by cultural contexts, theological convictions, and social realities. While some approaches have brought genuine transformation and empowerment, others have unintentionally reinforced inequality through paternalism or colonial attitudes. The biblical vision of Mission calls for presence, solidarity, and justice, where the good news is embodied in word and deed. Examining historical and contemporary models helps us discern practices that align with the example of Jesus, who proclaimed: *The Spirit of the Lord is upon me…to bring good news to the poor* (Luke 4:18), and challenges us to reimagine Mission as partnership with the marginalized in God's redemptive work.

Historical Mission among the Poor: Education, Healthcare, and Relief

From the early Church to modern Missionary movements, ministries among the poor have often centred on education, healthcare, and relief work.[11] Schools and literacy programs opened opportunities for the disadvantaged, while hospitals and clinics addressed urgent health needs. Relief efforts during famines, wars, and natural disasters embodied the compassion of Christ, reflecting His call, *I was hungry and you gave me food, I was thirsty and you gave me something to drink* (Matthew 25:35). While these initiatives have been life-giving, they also remind us that true Mission must combine immediate aid with long-term strategies that address the root causes of poverty.

Liberation Theologies and Contextual Theologies that Prioritize the Oppressed

In the twentieth century, liberation theologies in Latin America, black theology in the United States, Dalit theology in South Asia, and other contextual approaches redefined Mission as God's preferential option for the poor and oppressed.[12] Portraying examples from passages such as *He has brought down the powerful from their thrones, and lifted up the lowly* (Luke 1:52), these theologies insist that the gospel is inseparable from the struggle for justice. They challenge the Church to read Scripture from the

---

[11] Tina Holland, "How Education Will Influence Mission Identity," *Health Progress* 98/5 (September-October, 2017): 25-29.

[12] Manohar Chandra Prasad, "Dalit Theology: Methodological Issues in a Contextual Theology of Liberation," *The Asia Journal of Theology* 23/1 (April, 2009): 166-175.

perspective of the marginalized and to engage in social transformation as an expression of faithfulness to Christ.

Holistic Mission: Addressing Physical, Emotional, and Spiritual Needs

Holistic Mission integrates proclamation of the gospel with tangible acts of compassion, recognizing that people's needs are not only spiritual but also physical, emotional, and social. Jesus healed the sick, fed the hungry, forgave sins, and restored relationships, offering a model for Mission that addresses the whole person.[13] As James reminds us: *If a brother or sister is naked and lacks daily food, and one of you says to them, 'Go in peace; keep warm and eat your fill,' and yet you do not supply their bodily needs, what is the good of that?* (James 2:15-16). This approach resists dualism and embodies the kingdom of God in both word and action.

Critique of Top-down, Paternalistic, and Colonial Mission Models

Not all Mission to the margins has been liberating. In many historical cases, Mission was shaped by top-down structures that treated the poor as passive recipients rather than active participants. Colonial Mission models often intertwined evangelism with cultural domination, imposing foreign customs and undermining local identities.[14] Such approaches contradict the example of Jesus, who humbled Himself (Philippians 2:5-7) and empowered His followers to minister in their own contexts. Contemporary Mission must learn from these failures, fostering mutual respect, local leadership, and partnership rather than dependency, so that the gospel can be truly good news for all.

Mission With the Margins: Empowerment and Solidarity

Christian Mission, when shaped by the example of Jesus, moves beyond acts of charity toward genuine partnership with the marginalized. It recognizes that the poor, the excluded, and the oppressed are not merely passive recipients of help but active participants in God's redemptive work. The biblical vision affirms that all members of the body of Christ are gifted and called to share in God's Mission, regardless of social or economic status. This approach challenges traditional "top-down" Mission models and seeks instead to build communities where mutual respect, shared leadership, and solidarity are central. In such a vision, Mission "with" the margins becomes

---

[13] Samuel Jayakumar, "The Work of God as Holistic Mission: An Asian Perspective," in *Holistic Mission: God's Plan for God's People*, edited by Brian Woolnough and Wonsuk Ma (Oxford: Regnum Books International, 2010), 90-93.

[14] Jon Miller, "Class Collaboration for the Sake of Religion: Elite Control and Social Mobility in a Nineteenth-Century Colonial Mission," *Journal for the Scientific Study of Religion* 29/1 (March, 1990): 35-53.

a space for empowerment, transformation, and the witness of God's Kingdom.

Recognizing the Marginalized as Subjects, Not Objects, of Mission

A central shift in contemporary Mission thinking is to see marginalized communities as agents of their own transformation rather than passive beneficiaries of outside aid. This perspective is grounded in the way Jesus engaged with people in the Gospels, speaking to them, listening to their stories, and affirming their dignity (John 4:7-26). When the marginalized are treated as full subjects of Mission, they are empowered to bring their own gifts, insights, and faith to the life of the Church.[15] This challenges power imbalances and resists paternalistic models of Mission, making space for the marginalized to define their needs and shape the forms of ministry that serve them best.

Mutuality and Participation: Being Co-workers in God's Mission

The Apostle Paul describes believers as *God's servants, working together* (I Corinthians 3:9). Mission with the margins is rooted in this principle of mutuality, where all participants are co-workers, not divided into "givers" and "receivers." This means creating opportunities for shared decision-making, mutual learning, and joint action in God's work. By embracing mutuality, the Church acknowledges that the Spirit speaks through every member of the community, especially those whose voices have been historically silenced.[16] Such partnership reflects the Trinitarian nature of God's Mission, which is inherently relational and inclusive.

Grassroots Leadership Development and Theological Formation

Empowering marginalized communities requires intentional investment in grassroots leadership and theological training that is contextually relevant. This mirrors the way Jesus trained His disciples, not in the halls of political power, but among fishermen, tax collectors, and ordinary people (Mark 3:13-15). When leadership arises from within marginal contexts, it ensures that ministry is deeply rooted in local realities and responsive to the needs of the people.[17] Contextual theological formation also equips leaders to

---

[15] Patrick McCloskey, "Recognizing God in Marginalized People," *Saint Anthony Messenger* 118/1 (June, 2010): 5.

[16] Amy M.RSM Hoey, "'Co-Workers in the Vineyard of the Lord': A Third and Complementary Document on Church Ministers," *Seminary Journal* 12/1 (Spring, 2006): 71-75.

[17] Bala Kiran Kumar Hrudayaraj, "Grassroots Activism and Representational Politics as Integral to Evangelization a Christian Response," *Asian Horizons* 18/3 (September, 2024): 481-501.

interpret Scripture in ways that speak directly to their struggles and hopes, enabling the gospel to be lived out authentically in their communities.

Churches of the Poor: Ecclesial Communities Rooted in Marginal Contexts

The vision of "churches of the poor" embodies the idea that the Church should not only serve the poor but also emerge from among them. In Latin America, for example, Base Ecclesial Communities have become spaces where faith is nurtured in the midst of poverty, and where the gospel is read in the light of daily struggles for justice.[18] Such communities embody Acts 2:44-47, where believers "had all things in common" and ensured that no one was in need. Rooted in local contexts, these churches become signs of God's Kingdom, demonstrating that the poor are not outsiders to Mission but its primary witnesses and bearers.

Methodological Reflections

Mission with the margins requires methods that are shaped by both the gospel and the lived realities of marginalized communities. Such methods must resist imposing external cultural forms and instead seek to express the good news in ways that are authentic to local contexts. They should foster participation, mutual learning, and empowerment, while also enabling the Church to speak prophetically against injustice. By drawing on narrative, testimony, and practical engagement, these approaches make Mission holistic, integrating proclamation, service, and advocacy.

Contextualization: Letting the Gospel Speak in the Language of the Marginalized

Contextualization means communicating and embodying the gospel in forms that are meaningful within a particular cultural, social, and linguistic context. This follows the pattern of the incarnation, where *the Word became flesh and lived among us* (John 1:14). For the marginalized, this involves allowing their symbols, music, art, and cultural expressions to shape how the gospel is proclaimed and lived out. Contextualization affirms that God's truth can be expressed in multiple cultural forms, and that Mission is not about importing a foreign style of faith but about discovering how Christ is already present and active in the life of the community.[19]

---

[18] Vhumani Magezi, "Making Community Development at Grassroots Reality: Church-Driven Development Approach in Zimbabwe's Context of Severe Poverty," *In Die Skriflig* 51/1 (January, 2017): 1-12.

[19] Nelus Niemandt, "Mission as Breaking down Walls, Opening Gates and Empowering Traders: From Contextualisation to Deep Contextualisation," *HTS Theological Studies* 73/1 (January, 2017): 1-6.

Participatory Mission Models: Listening, Accompanying, Empowering

Participatory Mission seeks to break the hierarchy between "Mission giver" and "Mission receiver" by creating space for active collaboration. This involves listening to the voices of the marginalized, walking alongside them in their struggles, and supporting them in shaping their own future. Jesus modelled this approach when He walked with His disciples on the road to Emmaus, listening to their grief before revealing Himself to them (Luke 24:13-35).[20] Such participation transforms Mission into a journey of shared discipleship, where all learn from one another and are equally responsible for the work of God's Kingdom.

Public Theology from the Margins: Addressing Injustice Through Prophetic Voice

Public theology from the margins calls the Church to speak into the public sphere with the authority of lived experience. The biblical prophets, such as Amos and Micah, denounced injustice and proclaimed God's concern for the poor and oppressed (Amos 5:24; Micah 6:8). When the marginalized speak for themselves in theological and public discourse, they expose systems of oppression and call society to repentance and transformation.[21] This prophetic witness is essential for Mission, ensuring that the gospel challenges not only personal sin but also structural evil.

Use of Narrative and Testimony: Recovering Lived Experiences as Theological Sources

The stories of the marginalized are powerful sources of theology. Just as the psalmists poured out their laments and praises, shaping Israel's worship (Psalm 34:6; Psalm 40:1-3), so the testimonies of those at the margins reveal God's presence in the midst of suffering and hope. Recovering and sharing these narratives allows the Church to see theology not as abstract doctrine but as the living witness of God's work in real lives.[22] Testimony humanizes Mission, making it relational and deeply connected to the everyday realities of faith.

---

[20] Will Sohns, "The Antioch Model for Faithful Participation in Christ's Mission," *Lutheran Mission Matters* 27/1 (May, 2019): 107-117.

[21] Felix Wilfred, "Public Theology in Service of Liberation," *Vidyajyoti Journal of Theological Reflection* 83/7 (July, 2019): 485-504.

[22] John Smith, "CWM: Re-Writing the Drama of Mission: A European Testimony," *International Review of Mission* 76/304 (October, 1987): 493-497.

Integration of Advocacy, Development, and Pastoral Care in Missional Praxis

Holistic Mission at the margins must weave together advocacy for justice, development for sustainable living, and pastoral care for spiritual and emotional well-being. Jesus' ministry embodied this integration. He healed the sick, fed the hungry, challenged oppressive leaders, and comforted the broken-hearted (Matthew 9:35-36). Advocacy addresses the systemic causes of poverty and exclusion. Development equips communities with skills and resources for a better future, and pastoral care nurtures faith and hope in the midst of struggle.[23] Together, these elements reflect the fullness of God's Mission in Christ.

Case Studies and Global Examples

Across the globe, Christian Mission with the margins has taken diverse forms shaped by local histories, struggles, and theological insights. These case studies reveal that Mission is never one-size-fits-all but is deeply contextual, drawing from the lived realities of communities who read the gospel through the lens of their own experiences of oppression and hope. They also demonstrate that theology from the margins is not merely for the marginalized but is a gift to the whole Church, offering new understandings of God's justice, compassion, and Kingdom. The following examples illustrate how different communities have embodied Mission in solidarity with the oppressed.

Dalit Theology and Mission in India

Dalit theology emerges from the experience of caste-based oppression in India, identifying with the God who sides with the "least of these" (Matthew 25:40). Rooted in the Exodus story and Jesus' ministry among the marginalized, Dalit theologians present Christ as the "Dalit God" who suffers with His people and redeems them. Mission in this context involves challenging caste discrimination, advocating for social equality, and empowering Dalit communities through education, leadership development, and cultural affirmation.[24] It transforms the Church into a space of dignity and resistance, breaking barriers that exclude.

Black Liberation Theology and the Civil Rights Struggle in the U.S.

Black Liberation Theology, articulated by figures such as James Cone, arose during the African American struggle for equality in the mid-20th

[23] Bradley A. Binau, "Pastoral Theology for the Missional Church: From Pastoral Care to the Care of Souls," *Trinity Seminary Review* 34/1 (Winter-Spring, 2014): 1128.

[24] Chakali Chandra Sekhar, "In Search of a Touchable Body: Christian Mission and Dalit Conversions," *Religions* 10/1 (December, 2019): 1-14.

century. Drawing on the biblical witness of God delivering Israel from slavery (Exodus 3:7-8) and the liberating Mission of Jesus (Luke 4:18-19), it proclaims that God identifies with the oppressed and calls for justice. Mission shaped by this theology engages in dismantling racism, advocating for civil rights, and building communities where Black identity is affirmed.[25] Churches became centres for organizing, worship, and prophetic action in the face of systemic injustice.

Latin American Liberation Theology and the Poor in Slums

In Latin America, Liberation Theology emerged from the harsh realities of poverty and political oppression, especially in urban slums and rural areas. Inspired by the Magnificat's vision of the lowly being lifted up (Luke 1:52-53) and Jesus' Kingdom teaching, theologians like Gustavo Gutiérrez emphasized the "preferential option for the poor." Base Ecclesial Communities became small, participatory gatherings where Scripture was read in light of daily struggles, leading to both spiritual renewal and social action.[26] Mission here is holistic, seeking to transform both hearts and unjust structures.

Refugee Ministry in Europe and the Middle East

The refugee crises of recent decades caused by war, persecution, and economic collapse have called the Church to respond with hospitality and advocacy. In light of God's command to "love the stranger" (Deuteronomy 10:19) and Jesus' own refugee experience as a child in Egypt (Matthew 2:13-15), refugee ministry provides shelter, legal assistance, language education, trauma counselling, and integration support. In both Europe and the Middle East, churches and Christian agencies have offered safe spaces where refugees find dignity, community, and a witness to Christ's compassion.[27]

Feminist and Eco-Feminist Theological Responses in Mission

Feminist and eco-feminist theologies address the intersection of gender, creation care, and justice. They affirm that Mission must confront patriarchy, gender-based violence, and environmental degradation. Grounded in the biblical vision that men and women are equally created in God's

---

[25] Wilson Muoha Maina, "Black Lives Matter (Blm): A Perspective from Liberation," *Journal for the Study of Religion & Ideologies* 22/64 (Spring, 2023): 20-33.

[26] Nicolás Panotto, "Decolonizing the Triune God: Contributions from Latin American Liberation Theologies," *International Review of Mission* 113/2 (November, 2024): 280-296.

[27] Jamie N. Sanchez, Dzubinski, M. Leanne and Jacqueline Parke, "Ministry Amidst the Refugee Crisis in Europe: Understanding Missionary-Refugee Relationships," *Transformation* 38/4 (October, 2021): 344-358.

image (Genesis 1:27) and in the call to steward the earth (Genesis 2:15), these approaches promote inclusive leadership, safe spaces for women, and ecological sustainability. Eco-feminist Mission recognizes that the exploitation of women and the environment are interconnected, and calls for holistic transformation that nurtures both human dignity and the earth's wellbeing.[28]

Challenges and Critiques

While Mission with the margins offers a transformative vision for the Church's calling, it is not without challenges and necessary critiques. Engaging deeply with marginalized communities requires careful theological reflection, humility, and awareness of the risks and tensions that can arise. These challenges remind the Church that faithfulness in Mission involves ongoing discernment, repentance, and a willingness to be corrected.

Risk of Romanticizing Poverty or Marginality

There is a temptation to idealize poverty or the experience of marginality, treating it as inherently virtuous. While Scripture calls the Church to side with the poor (Proverbs 31:8-9) and affirms God's special concern for them (Luke 6:20), it does not glorify suffering itself. Poverty is a condition to be overcome, not a permanent state to be preserved. Romanticizing marginality can lead to shallow engagement, overlooking the structural injustices that create and perpetuate it, and failing to work toward liberation.

Resistance from Institutional Churches and Power Structures

Prophetic Mission with the margins often meets resistance from established ecclesial and political powers. Just as Jesus faced opposition from religious leaders who feared the disruption of the status quo (Mark 11:18), advocates for justice today may encounter suspicion, exclusion, or suppression. Institutional churches may resist reorienting resources or priorities toward marginalized communities, preferring familiar patterns of ministry. Such resistance requires patient dialogue, courageous witness, and the willingness to bear the cost of discipleship.

The Complexity of Intersectionality (Class, Caste, Gender, Ethnicity)

Marginality is not a single, uniform experience but is shaped by overlapping systems of oppression, such as class, caste, gender, and ethnicity. The Church's Mission must acknowledge this complexity, recognizing that liberation in one area does not automatically resolve other forms of

[28] Sophie Chirongoma, "Karanga-Shona Rural Women's Agency in Dressing Mother Earth: A Contribution towards an Indigenous Eco-Feminist Theology," *Journal of Theology for Southern Africa* 142 (March, 2012): 120-144.

injustice. As Paul wrote, in Christ: *there is no longer Jew or Greek...slave or free...male and female* (Galatians 3:28), yet this unity must be lived out in ways that address the particular and intersecting realities people face. Intersectionality calls for nuanced, multi-layered Mission strategies.

Maintaining Theological Orthodoxy While Affirming Radical Contextual Mission

Radical contextual Mission seeks to express the gospel in ways that are faithful to local cultures and struggles, but it must also remain rooted in the core truths of the Christian faith. The challenge is to avoid both cultural imperialism, which imposes one theological framework on all contexts, and theological relativism, which neglects the biblical witness. As Paul urged Timothy, the Church must *guard the good treasure entrusted to you* (II Timothy 1:14) while also allowing the Spirit to speak afresh through local realities. This balance requires deep biblical study, communal discernment, and openness to the global body of Christ.

Conclusion

Mission to and with the margins reflects the very heart of the gospel, for in Jesus Christ we encounter God's decisive identification with the poor, the oppressed, and the excluded (Luke 4:18-19). Throughout His ministry, Jesus did not simply reach out to those on the margins; He lived among them, shared meals with them, and restored their dignity in the face of social rejection (Matthew 9:10-13). The Church, as the body of Christ, is therefore called to be a community that is both from and for the poor, not merely offering charity but embodying solidarity, mutuality, and justice. This requires a shift from paternalistic Mission "to" the marginalized toward a participatory Mission "with" them, recognizing their God-given agency and gifts. True Missional transformation begins at the periphery, for it is often in the forgotten and despised places that God's Spirit brings forth new visions of hope, justice, and reconciliation. The Church must resist the temptation to romanticize poverty or to treat the margins as a "Mission field" for institutional growth, rather, it must receive the margins as a theological and spiritual locus from which the gospel continually calls the centre to repentance and renewal. Thus, today walking with the marginalized is not an optional ministry for select believers, rather, it is an essential dimension of Christian discipleship and a non-negotiable expression of the *Missio Dei.*

30

New Creation and New Humanity in Christian Mission
Missiological Foundations for Eschatological Hope and Social Transformation

Christian Mission finds its deepest meaning when understood as participation in God's work of renewing all creation and reconciling humanity. The biblical vision of "new creation" speaks of the eschatological renewal of the whole cosmos through Jesus Christ, as expressed in II Corinthians 5:17, *So if anyone is in Christ, there is a new creation: everything old has passed away; see, everything has become new* and fulfilled in Revelation 21:1-5, where God declares, *See, I am making all things new*. This renewal is not limited to individual spiritual transformation but extends to the restoration of relationships, societies, and the created world under God's reign. Closely connected is the idea of "new humanity" in Ephesians 2:15, where Christ is said to have created "one new humanity" by reconciling divided peoples, breaking down walls of hostility, first between Jew and Gentile, and by extension, across all human divisions of ethnicity, caste, class, and gender. This places Mission within the hope of creation's liberation from bondage and its ultimate renewal. In this light, Christian Mission is not merely about saving souls for heaven but about anticipating and embodying God's future in the present, rather, a future where creation is restored, communities are reconciled, and humanity flourishes as one. This holistic and eschatological vision calls the Church to engage in the transformation of relationships, the pursuit of justice, the healing of creation, and the building of communities that reflect the reconciling love of Christ.

Biblical and Theological Foundations

The vision of new creation and new humanity is deeply rooted in the biblical records, where God's Mission is portrayed as the restoration of all things in Christ. This vision is not abstract or distant, rather, it shapes the very identity and practice of the Church's Mission today. From the apostolic proclamation to the final visions in Revelation, the Scriptures present a consistent theme: God is reconciling the world, renewing creation, and forming a unified people through Jesus Christ. The biblical foundation calls Christians to live as a foretaste of this coming reality, participating in God's work of reconciliation, justice, and renewal for the whole creation.

New Creation in Christ

Paul's bold proclamation in II Corinthians: *So if anyone is in Christ, there is a new creation: everything old has passed away; see, everything has become new* (II Corinthians 5:17) points to a radical transformation brought by union with Christ. This new creation is both personal and cosmic. It means the old ways of living shaped by sin, fear, and injustice are replaced with the life of Christ, marked by love, justice, and reconciliation. In Mission, the Church becomes a community where this renewal is visible in restored relationships, acts of mercy, and structures of justice.[1] It is not simply about telling people the message but demonstrating through our life together that God is already at work making all things new.

New Humanity in Christ

In Ephesians, Paul writes that Christ *is our peace; in his flesh he has made both groups into one and has broken down the dividing wall, that is, the hostility between us* (Ephesians 2:14-16). The "both groups" originally referred to Jews and Gentiles, two communities separated by deep religious and cultural barriers. In Christ, these barriers are destroyed, and a "new humanity" is created, one reconciled body united in love and worship of God. In today's world, this message speaks powerfully against racism, caste discrimination, gender inequality, and all forms of division.[2] Mission is, therefore, not only preaching Christ but also actively creating communities where these walls no longer exist, where people of every background share in the same dignity and belonging in Christ.

---

[1] Jerry L. Sumney, "'In Christ There Is a New Creation': Apocalypticism in Paul," *Perspectives in Religious Studies* 40/1 (Spring, 2013): 35-48.

[2] Molly Truman Marshall, "The Fullness of Incarnation: God's New Humanity in the Body of Christ," *Review & Expositor* 93/2 (Spring, 1996): 187-201.

Creation Groaning for Redemption

Paul's teaching in Romans 8:19-22 broadens the scope of Mission to the whole created order. He writes that: *the creation waits with eager longing for the revealing of the children of God* and that *the whole creation has been groaning in labour pains until now.* This means that God's redemptive plan is not only for humanity but for all creation, which suffers under the effects of human sin, pollution, exploitation, and environmental destruction. Mission, therefore, includes ecological responsibility as a witness to God's care for the earth.[3] When the Church plants trees, reduces waste, protects water, or stands with communities harmed by environmental injustice, it is participating in God's promise that creation itself will be *set free from its bondage to decay* (Romans 8:21).

The Vision of New Heavens and New Earth

In Revelation 21-22, the final vision of Scripture reveals the completion of God's Mission: *Then I saw a new heaven and a new earth* (Revelation 21:1) and See, *I am making all things new* (Revelation 21:5). This is not the destruction of the old creation but its transformation into the dwelling place of God with humanity. The picture of the New Jerusalem, where there is no more death, mourning, or pain, and where the tree of life brings healing to the nations (Revelation 22:2), gives Mission its ultimate direction.[4] Mission is not simply reacting to present needs but moving toward God's promised future, embodying even now signs of that renewed world such as communities of peace, economic justice, racial reconciliation, and joyful worship.[5] This eschatological vision fills Mission with hope and perseverance, knowing that our labour is part of God's unstoppable plan to make all things new.

Christological and Pneumatological Perspectives

The Mission of God is revealed most fully in the person of Jesus Christ and carried forward by the power of the Holy Spirit. A Christ-centred Mission affirms that Jesus is not only the Savior of individuals but also the Lord of all creation, inaugurating a new humanity that reflects God's original intention for the world. A Spirit-led Mission recognizes that the work of redemption is ongoing, transforming lives, reconciling communities, and renewing the whole cosmos. Together, Christology and Pneumatology shape

---

[3] James W. Thompson, "The Groaning and Redemption of Creation: Does Paul Speak to the Environmental Crisis?'," *Restoration Quarterly* 66/3 (December, 2024): 170-183.

[4] Kwame Bediako, "The Ultimate Vision: New Heaven and New Earth: Bible Study on Revelation 21:1-4," *Mission Studies* 5/2 (December, 1988): 32-38.

[5] Mark Vernon, "Visions of a New Heaven and a New Earth," *The Tablet* 266/8958 (August, 2012): 4-5.

the Church's understanding of Mission as a participation in the life of the Triune God, who creates, redeems, and renews all things.

Christ as the Firstborn of All Creation and the Beginning of the New Humanity

In Colossians, Paul presents a majestic vision of Christ: *He is the image of the invisible God, the firstborn of all creation; for in him all things in heaven and on earth were created* (Colossians 1:15-20). Christ is not only the source of creation but also its goal, the one in whom "all things hold together."[6] Through his death and resurrection, Christ becomes the beginning of the new humanity, a reconciled community in which God's image is restored. This means that Mission is not an optional program of the Church but the very outworking of Christ's cosmic lordship.[7] When the Church proclaims Christ, it announces the renewal of all creation and invites all people into the reconciled humanity God is forming in him.

The Role of the Holy Spirit in Sanctification, Reconciliation, and Cosmic Renewal

The Holy Spirit, poured out at Pentecost, is the continuing presence of Christ in the world. The Spirit sanctifies believers, shaping them into the likeness of Christ; reconciles broken relationships by healing divisions and fostering unity; and renews the entire cosmos by working toward the liberation of all creation from the effects of sin. The Spirit's work is not confined to the walls of the Church but moves in the world, preparing hearts, stirring movements for justice, and sustaining hope in times of suffering.[8] The Spirit is both the gift and the guide of Mission, empowering the Church to live in holiness, practice radical reconciliation, and join God's work of restoration in the world.

Mission as Assistance with the Spirit in Justice and Healing

Since Mission is God's work, the Church's role is one of assistance with the Holy Spirit. This means discerning where the Spirit is already at work and joining in. Jesus' ministry, empowered by the Spirit, brought healing to the sick, freedom to the oppressed, and good news to the poor (Luke 4:18-19). The same Spirit calls the Church to embody these works today, caring for the wounded, confronting systems of injustice, and fostering peace among

---

[6] Steven M. Baugh, "Firstborn Over All," *Kerux* 1/3 (December, 1986): 28-34.

[7] Kerry S. Robichaux, "Christ the Firstborn," *Affirmation & Critique* 2 (December, 1997): 30-38.

[8] Wibowo Moses, "The Role of the Holy Spirit for Church Believers in the Hermeneutic Context between Biblical Authority, Illumination and Interpretation," *Pharos Journal of Theology* 103/2 (December, 2022): 1-9.

divided peoples.[9] Mission is therefore not a human-centred enterprise but a Spirit-led partnership that seeks to manifest God's kingdom through acts of compassion, advocacy for justice, and the pursuit of reconciliation across all divisions.

Missional Implications of the New Creation

The biblical vision of the new creation is not simply a future hope that awaits the consummation of God's Kingdom; it is a present reality breaking into the world through the Mission of God's people. In Christ, the Church is summoned to live as a foretaste of the restored world God is bringing into being a world where harmony, justice, and peace will be fully realized (Revelation 21:1-5). This eschatological perspective widens the scope of Mission beyond the personal and spiritual sphere to encompass the renewal of every dimension of life: spiritual, relational, social, and ecological. In this sense, Mission becomes a participation in God's cosmic project of making "all things new" (Revelation 21:5), bearing witness through both word and deed to the kingdom's present inbreaking and its promised fulfilment.

Restoring Broken Relationships with God, with Others, and with Creation

The fall disrupted the original shalom of creation, severing humanity's communion with God, distorting human relationships, and alienating the natural world from its Creator. The Mission of the Church, grounded in Christ's reconciling work, seeks to address all three dimensions of this fracture. Evangelism and worship restore the God-human relationship by calling people back into covenant fellowship with their Maker (II Corinthians 5:18-20).[10] Community-building, mutual forgiveness, and peace-making restore human relationships, embodying Jesus' teaching on reconciliation (Matthew 5:23-24). Creation care, whether through environmental stewardship, sustainable practices, or prophetic advocacy reflects God's original mandate to "till and keep" the earth (Genesis 2:15) and anticipates the renewal of the entire created order (Romans 8:19-21).[11] By engaging all three relational dimensions, the Church participates holistically in God's Mission of restoration.

---

[9] Nancy McGrath-Whitman, "The Healing Flames (Healing with the Assistance of the Heavens)," *The Journal of Religion and Psychical Research* 21/3 (July, 1998): 160-165.

[10] Jo Ann Davidson, "Creator, Creation, and Church: Restoring Ecology to Theology," *Andrews University Seminary Studies* 45/1 (Spring, 2007): 101-122.

[11] Katrina Moss, "Restoring the Place of Creation and Creativity as Tools in Mission," *Anvil* 34/3 (December, 2018): 33-37.

Embracing Justice, Peace, and Reconciliation as Essential to Gospel Witness

The gospel is not a disembodied spiritual message, rather, it is the good news of God's reign, which brings justice, peace, and reconciliation to the whole creation. The prophets repeatedly emphasised that true worship is inseparable from justice: *What does the LORD require of you but to do justice, and to love kindness, and to walk humbly with your God?* (Micah 6:8). Jesus' own ministry revealed the inseparability of proclamation and social transformation, as He healed the sick, restored the outcast, and proclaimed good news to the poor (Luke 4:18-19). The Church's Mission therefore includes confronting structures of oppression, advocating for the vulnerable, and fostering peace in divided communities.[12] Justice, peace, and reconciliation are not secondary "attachments" to evangelism, but they are intrinsic to the gospel's truth and necessary for its credibility in the public sphere.

Evangelism and Discipleship as Part of God's Renewing Work in Persons and Communities

Evangelism is the announcement that God's new creation has begun in Jesus Christ and that all are invited to enter it through repentance and faith. Discipleship is the process by which individuals and communities are formed to live within this new reality. The two are inseparable: evangelism without discipleship risks shallow conversions, while discipleship without evangelism becomes insular and self-focused. In the New Testament, evangelism leads to transformed lives, and discipleship shapes those lives into Christlike maturity (Matthew 28:19-20; Colossians 1:28). This transformation affects personal ethics, family relationships, vocational integrity, and social engagement, such that the renewed life of believers becomes a witness to the reality of God's Kingdom.[13] In this way, the Church's teaching and pastoral care become instruments of God's ongoing creative work in the world.

Church as the Foretaste of the New Creation

The Church is not simply a messenger of the new creation, rather, it is itself a sign and instrument of it. In its worship, fellowship, and Mission, the Church embodies God's future in the present. Its unity in diversity mirrors the reconciled humanity of the Kingdom (Ephesians 4:4-6), its sacramental life points to the marriage supper of the Lamb (Revelation 19:9), and its

[12] Milton Mejía, "Violence, Justice, and Peace in Colombia: Evangelical Fundamentalisms and New Paths to Reconciliation," *Journal of Latin American Theology* 19/1 (December, 2024): 91-118.

[13] Vitalii Stankevych, "Renewing Discipleship in Today's Evangelical Community as a Return to the New Testament Ideal," *Theological Reflections* 24 (December, 2020): 141-154.

acts of service display the love that will characterise the new creation. The Church, as "first fruits" of the Kingdom (James 1:18), is called to model the values of God's restored world in concrete ways, through hospitality to the stranger, care for the vulnerable, and solidarity with the oppressed.[14] When the Church lives in this manner, it becomes a beacon of hope in a fragmented world, inviting others to taste and see the goodness of the Lord.

New Humanity and Reconciliation

In Christ, God is forming a new humanity that transcends every barrier of ethnicity, class, caste, and gender. This new humanity is not an abstract theological idea but a lived reality in the body of Christ, where the reconciled community becomes both the fruit and the instrument of God's Mission. The divisions that fragment society, whether maintained by prejudice, economic inequality, or systemic injustice are dismantled in Christ's body, making the Church an alternative social reality that anticipates the unity of the Kingdom. The ministry of reconciliation is thus central to the Church's vocation, requiring both the proclamation of God's reconciling work and the embodiment of that reconciliation in relationships, practices, and structures.

Ethnic, Racial, and Caste Divisions Abolished in Christ

The apostle Paul's declaration in Galatians: *There is no longer Jew or Greek, there is no longer slave or free, there is no longer male and female; for all of you are one in Christ Jesus* (Galatians 3:28) is a revolutionary vision of social identity. In Christ, the hierarchies of privilege and exclusion are dismantled, and all stand on equal footing before God.[15] Colossians 3:11 reinforces this by declaring that "Christ is all and in all." This theological truth has Missional implications: the Church must challenge cultural norms and systems that perpetuate inequality, whether based on ethnicity, race, caste, or gender.[16] The Mission of God cannot be fulfilled while barriers of hostility remain intact, for the gospel itself proclaims a reconciled humanity as part of the new creation.

Church as an Alternative Community of Equality, Inclusion, and Hospitality

The Church is called to be a living demonstration of God's reconciled world, a counter-cultural community where equality, inclusion, and hospitality are

---

[14] J. Duncan M. Derrett, "New Creation: Qumran, Paul, the Church, and Jesus," *Revue de Qumran* 13/1-4 (October, 1988): 597-608.

[15] Paul B. Decock, "Galatians 3:28: Working towards Unity in Christ-Respecting Diversity," *Proceedings of the Congress of the Panafrican Association of Catholic Exegetes* 19 (January, 2021): 427-448.

[16] Mark J. Keown, "The Vision for Intercultural Church in Ephesians 2 and Colossians 3," *Lexington Theological Quarterly* 521-4 (December 31, 2022): 15-35.

not ideals but daily practices. This includes welcoming the marginalised, valuing the contributions of all members, and ensuring that leadership and decision-making reflect the diversity of the body. The Eucharistic table symbolises this reality, where believers of every background share one bread and one cup (I Corinthians 10:16-17). Such hospitality extends beyond liturgy into daily life, where the Church opens its homes, resources, and hearts to strangers.[17] By embodying this radical inclusivity, the Church not only proclaims the gospel but also enacts it in ways that the surrounding world can see and experience.

Mission as Bridge-Building across Divisions

In a world fractured by prejudice, hostility, and systemic oppression, Mission is fundamentally about bridge-building. This involves moving toward those on the other side of social, cultural, or ideological divides, creating spaces for dialogue, and cultivating mutual understanding. The Church is called to embody the ministry of Christ, "who is our peace" and "has broken down the dividing wall" (Ephesians 2:14). This peace-making Mission is not passive but proactive, requiring intentional efforts to dismantle barriers, mediate conflicts, and promote reconciliation at both interpersonal and societal levels.[18] Such bridge-building is itself a sign of the kingdom, pointing to the day when all nations will walk together in God's light (Isaiah 2:2-4).

Participation in Movements for Social Healing and Public Justice

Reconciliation in Christ extends into the public sphere, calling the Church to participate in efforts that address the wounds of society. This may involve advocacy for the oppressed, participation in interfaith or intercultural peace initiatives, or involvement in community development projects that restore dignity and opportunity.[19] The prophetic tradition demonstrates that God's concern for justice is not limited to the covenant community but extends to the nations (Amos 5:24; Isaiah 58:6-12).[20] Therefore, the Church's public witness must include active engagement in movements that seek systemic change, promote restorative justice, and foster healing in divided societies. By joining such efforts, the Church not only speaks about reconciliation but

[17] Judith Woodall, "The Pentecostal Church: Hospitality and Disability Inclusion. Becoming an Inclusive Christian Community by Welcoming Mutual Vulnerability," *Journal of the European Pentecostal Theological Association* 36/2 (September, 2016): 131-144.

[18] Clark H. Pinnock, "Building the Bridge from Academic Theology to Christian Mission," *Themelios* 9/3 (April, 1984): 3-6.

[19] Donald Paul ullins, "The Healing Community: A Catholic Social Justice Critique of Modern Health Care," *The Linacre Quarterly* 81/2 (May, 2014): 172-181.

[20] Valerie Miles-Tribble, "Restorative Justice as a Public Theology Imperative," *Review & Expositor* 114/3 (December, 2017): 366-379.

also enacts it in ways that contribute to the common good and anticipate the peace of the new creation.[21]

Challenges in Mission toward New Creation

The pursuit of Mission in light of the biblical vision of new creation faces several significant challenges in both theology and practice. One recurring issue is the fragmentation of Mission between evangelism and social action, as if proclaiming the gospel and addressing social, economic, or ecological issues were separate and competing priorities. This false dichotomy weakens the holistic witness of the Church and undermines the biblical mandate to love both God and neighbour (Matt. 22:37-40). Another obstacle is the ecclesial resistance to addressing structural and systemic dimensions of injustice. Many churches hesitate to confront political, economic, or cultural systems that perpetuate inequality, preferring a focus on individual morality over societal transformation. There is also the risk of secularizing the eschatological hope, reducing the new creation to a human-made utopia rather than the sovereign work of God's grace. Such a reduction can result in Mission being shaped more by political ideologies than by the gospel. Furthermore, the biblical vision of the Kingdom of God involves the "already/not-yet" tension, God's reign has been inaugurated through Christ, yet it awaits full consummation at His return. Holding these two realities in balance is difficult: emphasising the "already" can lead to unrealistic expectations of perfect justice now, while overemphasising the "not-yet" can lead to passivity and disengagement from pressing issues in the present. The challenge, therefore, is to engage in Mission with urgency and hope, without losing sight of the ultimate fulfilment that lies in God's hands.

Conclusion

Christian Mission, at its heart, is eschatological. It looks forward to the consummation of God's purposes in the renewal of all creation. The Church is called not only to anticipate this reality but also to embody it here and now as a community of hope. This means living as a foretaste of the new creation and new humanity, where reconciliation, justice, peace, and creation care are not merely ideals but daily practices. The vision of the gospel, as expressed in passages like II Corinthians 5:17 and Ephesians 2:15, demands a Mission that is holistic and transformative, rooted in Christ's reconciling work on the cross and empowered by the Spirit's renewing presence. In a world marked by deep divisions, persistent violence, ecological degradation, and systemic oppression, the Church's Mission is to proclaim and practice God's renewing power both in word and deed. This is not an optional dimension of

[21] Felix Wilfred, "Transforming Our Cities: Public Role of Faith and Theology," *Concilium* 1 (January, 2019): 45-57.

Christian life but the very essence of faithfulness to the gospel. To participate in God's Mission toward new creation is to witness to the reality that, in Christ, the old has passed away and the new has come. It is to live and serve in such a way that communities, relationships, and even the natural world are drawn into the hope and wholeness of God's Kingdom. In this way, the Church becomes not only a messenger of the new creation but also a sign of it, pointing beyond itself to the day when God will make all things new (Revelation 21:5).

31

Mission in Multi-Faith and Multicultural Contexts A Journey Through Theological Challenges and Practical Witness

In today's globalized world, societies are increasingly manifested by religious diversity and cultural change. Mission in such multi-faith and multicultural contexts involves the Church's active engagement in sharing the gospel, serving people, and bearing witness to Jesus Christ amid these complex realities. This scenario requires Missionaries to be deeply aware of different religions, customs, languages, and ways of understanding the world. Mission in this context faces the challenge of balancing two important tasks: faithfully proclaiming the uniqueness of Christ and engaging respectfully in dialogue with people of other faiths. The Church must avoid a triumphal or superior attitude, while remaining committed to the gospel's truth. As Peter instructs, as believers are called to: *always be ready to make your defence to anyone who demands from you an accounting for the hope that is in you; yet do it with gentleness and reverence* (I Peter 3:15-16). Likewise, in Acts 17:22-31, the Apostle Paul models respectful engagement by acknowledging the Athenians' religious beliefs before proclaiming the gospel. Thus, Missionary work in multi-faith and multicultural contexts is more than just preaching; it involves building relationships, promoting peace, and showing Christ's love across religious and cultural divides.

Biblical and Theological Foundations

Missionary work in multi-faith and multicultural contexts finds its deepest roots in the Bible and Christian theology. The way Jesus and the early apostles engaged with people outside their own religious community offers important lessons for today's Missions. The Bible teaches not only the uniqueness of Christ but also the universal nature of God's salvation plan. These foundations help Missionaries to proclaim the gospel faithfully while showing respect for diverse religious and cultural backgrounds, which is especially important in today's multi-faith world.

Multi-Faith and Multicultural Engagement in the Old Testament

The Old Testament reveals that God's Mission has always incorporated people from diverse nations and cultures.[1] From the beginning, God's covenant with Abraham carried a universal purpose: *in you all the families of the earth shall be blessed* (Genesis 12:3), showing that Israel's calling was never solely for itself but for the benefit of all peoples. The Book of Jonah portrays God's compassion for Nineveh, a foreign and hostile city, as God sends God's prophet to call them to repentance and spares them when they respond (Jonah 3:10). Similarly, the story of Naaman, the Aramean military commander healed by the prophet Elisha (II Kings 5:14-15), demonstrates that God's saving power reaches beyond the borders of Israel.[2] These accounts affirm that God's concern is not limited by ethnic, cultural, or religious boundaries, and they lay the theological groundwork for engaging in Mission within multi-faith and multicultural contexts.

Jesus and the Samaritans, Gentiles, and Outsiders

Jesus' ministry often challenged social and religious boundaries by reaching out to those considered outsiders or enemies by many in his own community. The story of Jesus and the Samaritan woman in John 4 is a powerful example. Samaritans were despised by many Jews, yet Jesus crosses cultural and religious lines to speak with her, offering "living water" that symbolizes eternal life (John 4:10-14). This encounter shows Jesus' willingness to engage openly and respectfully, breaking down barriers of ethnicity, gender, and religion.[3] Similarly, in Matthew 15:21-28, Jesus meets a Canaanite woman, a Gentile, who boldly asks for healing for her daughter. Jesus initially seems hesitant, yet he praises her great faith and grants her request. This incident reveals Jesus' Mission extends beyond Israel and

---

[1] Solomon Sule-Saa, "The Emergence of World Christianity: The Fruit of God's Use of Ethnicity in His Mission," *Journal of African Christian Thought* 27/1 (June, 2024): 14-21.

[2] Shelley Trebesch, "A Theology for Transcending Culture in Leadership: The Mission of God in Conversation with the Cultural Dimension of Power Distance," *Journal of Religious Leadership* 12/1 (Spring, 2013): 35-61.

[3] Aynos Masotcha Moyo, "The Gospel and Common Humanity: Jesus' Tolerant Attitude towards the Samaritans in the Gospel of Luke," *Africa Theological Journal* 24/2 (December, 2001): 91-97.

highlights his openness to those from different backgrounds.[4] These stories teach Missionaries today to approach people of other faiths with respect, empathy, and readiness to share Christ's love without prejudice.

Paul's Cross-Cultural Mission: Acts 17 as a Model for Contextual Proclamation

Paul's speech at the Areopagus in Athens (Acts 17:22-31) offers a valuable model for Mission in pluralistic settings. Athens was a city full of idols and various religious ideas. Instead of outright rejecting their beliefs, Paul begins by affirming their religiosity and referring to an altar "to an unknown god" (Acts 17:23). He uses this as a starting point to introduce the one true God who created all people and nations.[5] Paul's approach shows sensitivity to his audience's worldview, using familiar ideas to explain the gospel clearly and respectfully. This method demonstrates the importance of understanding the cultural and religious context when sharing the message of Christ.[6] Missionaries today can learn from Paul's example to engage thoughtfully, build bridges, and avoid alienating those they seek to reach.

Theological Affirmations: Christ as the Only Way

Christian theology clearly teaches that Jesus Christ is the unique and exclusive way to God. Jesus himself said: *I am the way, and the truth, and the life. No one comes to the Father except through me* (John 14:6). This claim sets Christianity apart from other religions and defines the core message of Christian Mission.[7] The early church affirmed this truth when Peter declared in Acts that: *there is salvation in no one else, for there is no other name under heaven given among mortals by which we must be saved* (Acts 4:12). While this exclusivity challenges Missionaries to remain faithful to the gospel's core, it also demands humility and love in how they communicate.[8] Faithful proclamation does not mean disrespect or condemnation, but a sincere witness to the truth of Christ as Savior for all humanity.

---

[4] Kara J Lyons-Pardue, "A Syrophoenician Becomes a Canaanite: Jesus Exegetes the Canaanite Woman in Matthew," *Journal of Theological Interpretation* 13/2 (December, 2019): 235-250.

[5] Reuben E. Duniya, "Paul's Attitude at Athens (Acts 17:16-34): Spiritual Mapping or Cultural Naiveté," *Pneuma* 41/2 (December, 2019): 236-254.

[6] Karl Olav Sandnes, "Paul's Areogagus Speech (Acts 17:16-34): Some Hermeneutical Challenges for Mission," *Theology & Life* 37 (December, 2014): 59-82.

[7] M. Thomas Thangaraj, "Jesus the Christ: The Only Way to God and to Human Flourishing," *Journal of Ecumenical Studies* 52/1 (December, 2017): 44-49.

[8] Karl Müller, "Is Christ the Only Way to Salvation: A Study Conference in Sankt Augustin," *Mission Studies* 7/2 (December, 1990): 234-237.

Universality of the Gospel and the Dignity of All Peoples

The gospel message is intended for every person and culture without exception. God's promise to Abraham included a blessing for *all the families of the earth* (Genesis 12:3), which points to the global scope of God's redemptive plan.[9] The book of Revelation envisions a future where people *from every nation, from all tribes and peoples and languages* stand before God's throne, worshiping together (Revelation 7:9). This biblical vision affirms the dignity and worth of all peoples and encourages Missionaries to embrace cultural diversity as part of God's plan.[10] The gospel transcends cultural boundaries while honouring the uniqueness of each culture, inviting all people into a loving relationship with God.

Understanding Multi-Faith Contexts

Today's world is marked by the coexistence of many religions and cultures in close proximity. Missionary work in such contexts requires more than just knowing the gospel, it demands understanding the beliefs, values, and customs of other faith traditions. This understanding promotes respect and helps Missionaries avoid misunderstandings that can hinder the message of Christ. Being informed about different religions also enables Missionaries to engage in meaningful and loving dialogue, showing Christ's love in ways that are relevant and sensitive.

Major World Religions and Indigenous Traditions

Multi-faith contexts include religions such as Christianity, Islam, Hinduism, Buddhism, Judaism, and various indigenous spiritual traditions. Each has its own rich history, sacred texts, rituals, and beliefs about God, the world, and human purpose. For example, Islam emphasizes submission to Allah and the teachings of the Prophet Muhammad; Hinduism includes diverse beliefs about gods, *karma*, and reincarnation; Buddhism focuses on the path to enlightenment through ethical living and meditation.[11] Indigenous traditions often connect spirituality closely with nature and community life. In this milieu, it is important to understand these religions to communicate respectfully and clearly, avoiding simple stereotypes or misunderstandings.[12]

---

[9] Heinrich Fries, "The Gospel of Jesus Christ and Universality of Faith, from an Ecumenical Viewpoint," *Universitas* 24/4 (December, 1982): 231-237.

[10] Catherine Clark Kroeger, "Melchizedek and the Universality of the Gospel: The Application of an Allegory," *Priscilla Papers* 17/2 (December, 2003): 3-5.

[11] Maximilian Becker, "Exploring the Concept of Evil through the Lens of Major World Religions," *European Journal for Philosophy of Religion* 16-2 (January, 2024): 1-17.

[12] Seth Schermerhorn, "Comparison and the Academic Study of Indigenous Religious Traditions," *Method & Theory in the Study of Religion* 32/4-5 (December, 2020): 464-474.

Knowledge about these faiths helps Missionaries find common ground and address specific spiritual questions in culturally appropriate ways.

Respect for Religious Beliefs and Practices

Religious beliefs and practices are deeply personal and often form the core of people's identity. Thus, Missionaries should approach others with genuine respect and sensitivity toward what is sacred in their faith. This respect does not mean compromising the gospel but recognizing the value in others' spiritual experiences and honouring their dignity as human beings created in God's image. The Bible commands believers to love their neighbours (Mark 12:31), which includes respecting people of different faiths.[13] When Missionaries show respect, they create opportunities for dialogue and trust, which can open hearts to the gospel message.

Importance of Religious Literacy in Mission

Religious literacy refers to the knowledge and understanding of the beliefs, values, histories, and practices of various religions. This literacy is crucial for Missionaries to communicate the gospel effectively and sensitively. Without it, Missionaries risk offending or alienating their audience, or failing to answer important questions. Religious literacy helps Missionaries to identify points of connection and difference, to address misconceptions, and to engage in informed dialogue.[14] It also demonstrates humility and respect, showing that the Missionary values the person they are speaking to, not just their conversion.

Shared Moral Values and Spirituality

Despite theological differences, many religions share similar moral values such as honesty, compassion, justice, and care for the poor. They also express spiritual longings for meaning, peace, healing, and connection with the divine. Recognizing these shared values and needs can help Missionaries to build bridges with people of other faiths. It shows that the gospel meets universal human needs and desires.[15] By addressing these common concerns, Missionaries can present Christ not only as the unique Savior but also as the one who truly understands and fulfils the deepest hopes of the human heart.

---

[13] Hans Gustafson, "Religious Diversity, Secularization, and Indifference," *The Journal of Interreligious Studies* 43 (December, 2024): 109-114.

[14] Ken Lokensgard, "Religious Literacy, the First Amendment, and Public Education," *The Council of Societies for the Study of Religion Bulletin* 38/2 (April, 2009): 41-45.

[15] Sanjoy Mukherjee, and Sumona Ghosh, "Enhancing Effectiveness of Values and Ethics Education through Spirituality," *Journal of Management, Spirituality & Religion* 19/3 (May, 2022): 275-301.

Cross-Cultural Sensitivity and Contextualization

Mission in diverse cultural settings requires careful sensitivity and a deep understanding of how the gospel can be expressed meaningfully in different cultural contexts. This process, often called contextualization or inculturation, involves adapting the message of Christ without changing its truth. It respects local customs, languages, and symbols, allowing the gospel to take root and flourish in every culture without domination or distortion.

Need for Inculturation and Contextual Theology

Inculturation refers to the process by which the gospel is communicated and embodied within the cultural forms of a particular people. It is essential because faith cannot be separated from the cultural context in which it is lived. Contextual theology arises from reflecting on Scripture and Christian tradition in light of a specific culture's worldview, history, and challenges. This approach ensures that Christianity is not seen as a foreign import but as a faith that truly speaks to people's lives and experiences. Without inculturation, the gospel risks being misunderstood or rejected as irrelevant.[16] Because contextual theologies in Africa, Asia, and Latin America have developed by reflecting their cultures' values, struggles, and hopes, they have enriched through global Christianity.

Paul's Principle of Becoming "All Things to All People"

Paul's statement to Corinthians reflects the attitude of contextualization in Mission. Paul writes: *I have become all things to all people, that I might by all means save some* (I Corinthians 9:19-23). He adapts his behaviour, speech, and approach depending on his audience such as Jews, Greeks, or others, while remaining faithful to the gospel message. This flexibility shows that Missionaries must enter into the cultural world of those they seek to reach, respecting their customs and language, to communicate the gospel effectively.[17] However, this approach is balanced by the need to hold firmly to the core truths of Christianity without compromise.

Avoiding Cultural Imperialism and Ethnocentrism

One significant danger in cross-cultural Mission is cultural imperialism, where Missionaries impose their own culture, customs, or ways of worship on others. Ethnocentrism is the belief that one's own culture is superior to others. Both attitudes can hinder the gospel and cause unnecessary offense or rejection. True Mission respects the cultural identity of others, recognizing

---

[16] Ignatius Hirudayam, "Christian Awareness of the Need of Inculturation," *Journal of Dharma* 5/4 (October-December, 1980): 352-365.

[17] John G. Lodge, "All Things to All: Paul's Pastoral Strategy," *Chicago Studies* 24 (November, 1985): 291-306.

that the gospel transcends culture but does not erase it. The Apostle Paul himself did not force Gentile believers to become Jews but welcomed them as they were, emphasizing unity in Christ rather than uniformity in culture (Acts 15).[18] This affirms that, Missionaries today are called to serve humbly, allowing local churches to express their faith authentically within their culture.

Role of Native Language, Symbols, and Practices in Communicating the Gospel

Language is more than words, because, it carries meaning, emotion, and identity. Using the local language in Mission shows respect and helps the gospel message connect deeply with people's hearts. Similarly, local symbols and cultural practices can communicate spiritual truths in powerful ways. In the present-day context, many churches around the world have incorporated indigenous music, art, and rituals that resonate with their culture while expressing Christian faith.[19] This contextual use of language and symbols helps avoid misunderstandings and shows that Christianity is not a foreign religion but one that embraces and transforms culture for God's glory.

Interfaith Dialogue and Christian Witness

In multi-faith contexts, dialogue between Christians and people of other religions is a vital part of Mission. Dialogue is not about compromising the gospel but about bearing witness to Christ through listening, humility, and service. It builds relationships, deepens understanding, and opens opportunities for sharing the good news in ways that honour both truth and respect.

Dialogue as Witness Through Listening, Humility, and Service

Christian dialogue with other faiths is first and foremost an act of witness, showing the love of Christ through respectful listening and genuine humility. It means valuing the other person as God's creation and being willing to learn from them without weakening the gospel message.[20] Jesus reflected this attitude by engaging with people from different backgrounds with

---

[18] Russell T. McCutcheon, "Taming Ethnocentrism and Trans-Cultural Understandings," *Method & Theory in the Study of Religion* 12/1-4 (December, 2000): 294-306.

[19] Nelus Niemandt, "Mission as Breaking down Walls, Opening Gates and Empowering Traders: From Contextualisation to Deep Contextualisation," *HTS Theological Studies* 73/1 (January, 2017): 1-6.

[20] Donna Geernaert, "Conversation and Conversion: Dialogue as Witness," *Touchstone* 40/2 (June, 2022): 16-25.

compassion and openness (John 4; Luke 7:36-50). Dialogue also requires patience and a servant heart, reflecting the command to love one's neighbour (Mark 12:31). Thus, it is not giving up on truth but living it authentically and respectfully in relationship.

Dialogue as Mutual Understanding

Dialogue in the Christian Mission begins with mutual understanding. It is not only about speaking but also about listening carefully to others with respect. Mutual understanding in dialogue reflects the truth that all people are created in the image of God and deserve respect.[21] It allows Christians to show the humility of Christ, who welcomed people from every background. Paul reminds the Philippians: *Let each of you look not to your own interests, but to the interests of others* (Philippians 2:4). This means Christians are called to engage with people of different faiths and cultures in humility and openness, seeking to understand their perspectives. Such dialogue reflects the love of Christ, who reached out to people with compassion and patience.

Dialogue as Shared Action

Dialogue is not complete if it stays only at the level of words; it must also lead to shared action for the good of all. Shared action in dialogue expresses the biblical call to love our neighbour in practical ways. It shows that faith is not only spoken but lived out together in acts of justice and mercy.[22] James teaches: *What good is it, my brothers and sisters, if you say you have faith but do not have works?* (James 2:14). In the same way, dialogue should inspire Christians and others to work together for justice, peace, and care for creation. Through shared action, dialogue becomes a living expression of God's Kingdom values in society, showing faith through deeds of service and cooperation.

Dialogue as Common Witness

Dialogue also becomes a form of common witness when Christians join with others to testify to truth, love, and hope in the world. Common witness in dialogue reveals the unity of God's Mission in a divided world. It allows Christians to point beyond themselves to the reconciling work of Christ.[23]

[21] Lucas Tha Ling Sum, "Dialogue as a Path for Mutual Understanding and Peace between Christianity and Buddhism," *SEDOS Bulletin* 47/11-12 (November-December, 2015): 236-243.

[22] Karen E. Allen, Celia Castellano and Sophia Pessagno. "Using Dialogue to Contextualize Culture, Ecosystem Services, and Cultural Ecosystem Services," *Ecology & Society* 26/2 (June, 2021): 1-16.

[23] Günther Gassmann, "Lutherans and Catholics in the Homeland of the Reformation: From Bitter Battles to Dialogue and Common Witness," *Seminary Ridge Review* 14/2 (Spring, 2012): 12-25.

Jesus prayed for his followers: *that they may all be one...so that the world may believe that you have sent me* (John 17:21). When Christians engage in dialogue and stand together with people of goodwill, they give a visible witness to unity and reconciliation. Such witness does not erase differences but highlights a shared commitment to values that reflect God's Mission in the world.

Dialogue as Revealing Christ in Unexpected Ways

Christians believe the Holy Spirit continues to work in the world in surprising and sometimes hidden ways.[24] Jesus said: *When the Spirit of truth comes, he will guide you into all the truth* (John 16:13). The Spirit can prepare hearts, reveal Christ's presence, and open doors for the gospel even where Missionaries least expect it. Recognizing the Spirit's work encourages Missionaries to remain humble and open, trusting God to bring growth and understanding beyond human efforts.[25] It also reminds Christians that Mission is ultimately God's work.

Incarnational Dialogue

Effective evangelism in multi-faith contexts is relational and incarnational and focuses on living out the gospel through relationships and demonstrating Christ's love in everyday life. Instead of aggressive debates or confrontations, evangelism involves patient listening, caring service, and honest conversations.[26] This approach reflects Jesus' incarnation, God becoming human and entering human culture with humility and love. When Christians embody Christ's character, their witness becomes powerful and attractive, allowing others to see the gospel's truth in action rather than just hear it in words.

Practical Approaches to Mission in Multi-Faith Contexts

Missionary work in multi-faith contexts involves more than simply preaching or teaching. It requires a holistic approach that embodies the love and compassion of Christ in tangible ways. By engaging with people from diverse religious backgrounds, Missionaries must build meaningful relationships, offer practical help, and communicate the gospel through

---

[24] James M. Dawsey, "The Unexpected Christ: The Lucan Image," *The Expository Times* 98/10 (July, 1987): 296-300.

[25] Lambert Leijssen, "'When the Spirit of Truth Comes, He Will Guide You into All the Truth...' (John 16:13): Sacraments: God's Revelation in Word and Spirit," *Questions Liturgiques* 94/1-2 (January, 2013): 7-26.

[26] Alon Goshen-Gottstein, "Judaisms and Incarnational Theologies: Mapping out the Parameters of Dialogue," *Journal of Ecumenical Studies* 39/3-4 (Summer-Fall, 2002): 219-247.

actions that reflect Jesus' life and teachings. This approach allows the gospel to be seen and experienced as well as heard, helping to overcome barriers created by cultural and religious differences.

Mission as Building Relationships

Hospitality is a vital expression of Christian love and an effective way to build bridges across religious boundaries. Offering hospitality means welcoming others into one's home or community with generosity, kindness, and openness, creating a safe space where dialogue and friendship can flourish.[27] In the Bible, hospitality is consistently praised as a virtue (Romans 12:13; Hebrews 13:2), and Jesus himself welcomed and ate with people from many backgrounds, including sinners and outsiders (Luke 19:1-10). By patiently living alongside people of other faiths, Missionaries demonstrate God's love in practical and personal ways. Presence, simply being with others, sharing in their joys and struggles, breaks down stereotypes and builds trust, which is essential for any meaningful gospel witness.

Mission as Shared Service and Peacebuilding

Serving communities through practical initiatives such as education, healthcare, disaster relief, and peacebuilding offers concrete evidence of the gospel's transformative power. These actions meet urgent human needs and reflect Christ's compassion for the whole person. Education helps people gain knowledge and skills, healthcare addresses physical suffering, disaster relief provides immediate aid in crises, and peacebuilding fosters reconciliation in divided societies.[28] These service efforts often require collaboration with people from multiple faiths, creating opportunities for respectful partnership and mutual understanding. They reveal the gospel as a message not only of spiritual salvation but also of holistic healing and justice, aligning with Jesus' Mission *to proclaim good news to the poor* and *to set the oppressed free* (Luke 4:18).

Mission as Storytelling and Testimony: Non-Confrontational Evangelism

Storytelling and personal testimony provide a gentle and authentic means of evangelism that respects others' beliefs and invites reflection rather

[27] Ken Chitwood, "Building Bridges: Toward Constructing a Christian Foundation for Inter-Religious Relationships in the Shift from Religious Privilege to Spiritual Plurality," *Missio Apostolica* 22/2 (November, 2014): 225-246.

[28] Max O. Stephenson Jr, "Considering the Relationships among Social Conflict, Social Imaginaries, Resilience, and Community-Based Organization Leadership," *Ecology & Society* 16/1 (March, 2011): 1-11.

than confrontation.[29] Jesus used parables, stories rooted in everyday life, to reveal spiritual truths in ways that listeners could relate to and ponder (Matthew 13). Likewise, when Missionaries share how God has worked in their own lives, they offer living examples of faith that touch hearts more deeply than abstract arguments. Testimony invites curiosity and opens space for questions, enabling a natural and relational sharing of the gospel. It avoids the pitfalls of aggressive debate and instead fosters a respectful atmosphere where faith can be explored freely and meaningfully.[30]

Mission as Community Development: Bridge for Gospel Witness

Community development work such as improving local infrastructure, supporting sustainable agriculture, or enhancing economic opportunities addresses long-term needs and contributes to the well-being of entire communities.[31] When Missionaries participate in such development, they demonstrate the gospel's relevance to everyday life and social flourishing. This approach shows that Christian faith is not only about personal salvation but also about restoring communities and promoting human dignity. Development projects build goodwill, establish ongoing relationships, and provide a natural context for sharing the gospel in a way that respects cultural identity and local priorities.[32] This practical engagement reflects God's justice and care for the marginalized, reflect the Kingdom of God on earth.

Conclusion

Engaging in Mission within diverse religious and cultural settings requires more than enthusiasm or strategy, but it calls for deep spiritual discernment to understand God's guidance in complex environments. At the same time, theological clarity is essential to faithfully communicate the gospel's core truths without compromise. This combination ensures that Mission remains both respectful and authentic, overcoming tensions between conviction and openness with wisdom and grace. Mission involves embodying and proclaiming the gospel with both confidence in its truth and compassion for all people. Conviction drives Missionaries to bear faithful witness to Jesus Christ as the way, truth, and life (John 14:6), while compassion moves them

[29] Katharine Bp. Jefferts Schori, "Creation and the Effective Word: Holy Storytelling, Creation, and God's Mission," *Anglican Theological Review* 99/3 (Summer, 2017): 519-529.

[30] Debie Thomas, "The Truth about Testimonies," *The Christian Century* 137/5 (February, 2020): 35.

[31] Kasebwe T. L. Kabongo, "Leadership Development for Missions in Poor Urban Communities," HTS *Theological Studies* 75/1 (January, 2019): 1-8.

[32] Matt Brain, "No One Gets Left behind: The Local Church as the Bridge between Gospel and Culture," *St Mark's Review* 217 (August, 2011): 30-42.

to serve, listen, and walk alongside others in their spiritual journeys. These two qualities, conviction and compassion, work together to create a Mission that is both bold and loving, inviting people into the transforming power of Christ's love without coercion or judgment. While conversion remains a vital aspect of Mission, the broader and deeper goal is the transformation of relationships, communities, and societies through Christ's love. Mission seeks to restore broken human connections, promote justice and peace, and cultivate environments where the gospel's values can flourish. This transformational vision aligns with John's declaration: *And the Word became flesh and lived among us, and we have seen his glory* (John 1:14).